A survey of

HISTORIC PARKS & GARDENS IN WORCESTERSHIRE

CONTENTS

LIST OF PLATES

Colour

Black & White

ABBREVIATIONS

BoE	Buildings of England; Worcestershire, A. Brooks and N. Pevsner, 2007
c.	circa/century
CL	Country Life
CRO	County Records Office – now WAAS
EH	English Heritage
ff.	following from
HE	Historic England
HER	Historic Environment Record
HWGT	Hereford and Worcester Gardens Trust
NT	National Trust
OS	Ordnance Survey Maps
op. cit.	sources quoted
p./pp.	page/pages
NE	Natural England
SMR	Sites & Monuments Record – now HER in Worcestershire
VCH	Victoria County History, Vols. 3 & 4, 1913, 1924
WAAS	Worcestershire Archive & Archaeology Service
WCC	Worcestershire County Council
WCM	Worcester City Monuments
WSM	Worcestershire Sites & Monuments

ACKNOWLEDGEMENTS

This book, when first commissioned by the Hereford and Worcester Gardens Trust in 1996 was encouraged by Jeffrey Haworth, Ginnie Scott and John Comins. My thanks went then to Paul Stamper and David Whitehead for opening some of the mysteries of garden history to me. Jeffrey Haworth gave me the opportunity to work on the Croome Court archive which was made possible by John Henderson and Jill Tovey. Robin Whittaker and the staff of the County Record Office at Nunnery Wood and St. Helen's, provided essential help and guidance for the 1st edition. Adrian Gregson, Victoria Bryant and the staff of the Worcester Archive and Archaeology Service at the Hive have facilitated a search for relevant information in hundreds of documents of various sizes - principally maps, plans and sale particulars – towards this *Survey*.

I am indebted to Jane Patton and her team for the essential comments on the status quo arising from site visits made over recent years and I am similarly indebted for some technical information as well as the majority of the picture Illustrations. Jane Patton's contribution in these areas is disguised under the word "compiling"!

Among the historians who have shared their research into a number of sites, as indicated in the text are: Stephen Price, David Whitehead, Jane Bradney, Michael Cousins, Pat Hughes, Catherine Gordon, John Harcup, Peter Walker, Richard Webb and Stuart Davies. Others who have shared their expert knowledge on individual sites are: Katherine Alker, Mary Anton, John Comins, Adrian and Matthew Darby, Karen Davidson, Caroline and Martin Davis, Stuart Denyer, James Dinn, James Edgar, David Everett, Nigel Goodman, Margaret Goodrich, Joe Hawkins, Sandy Haynes, Caroline and Anthony Hornyold, David and Sarah Houle, Roger Leake, Alec Mackie, Peter Norbury, Sheena Payne-Lunn, Chris Penney, Jo Roche, Pete and Sue Savery, Martin Schoelles, John Shew, Virginia Wagstaff, John Yorke and Vincent Yorke.

The site entries do not acknowledge the many owners who have welcomed *Survey* visitors and my apologies for acknowledging them only in a general way and not individually. Working on 230 individual sites, is my only excuse for forgetting anyone who has made a valued contribution.

Some family archives are accessible through deposit at the Hive and therefore acknowledged through references. Three other archives besides Shropshire Archives and Gloucestershire Archives have been used at first or second hand, and my thanks go otherwise to Henry Berkeley and the Spetchley Archive, the Trustees of the Sandys Estate, Mrs Jayne Cadbury, Sir Andrew Winnington Bart. Perhaps the most significant impact on Worcestershire's historic landscape has been made by active conservation projects based upon Reports commissioned by owners which have been shared with the Survey: the Abberley Hall Foundation; Viscount Cobham, Hagley Hall; the National Trust, Hanbury Hall and Croome Court; the Hartlebury Castle Building Preservation Trust.

Richard Lockett

Editorial thanks goes to the many Hereford & Worcester Gardens Trust volunteers who have helped in a myriad of ways. Special thanks to Virginia Hopkinson who spent many hours looking up the postcodes and checking OS grid references; Pauline Gardiner who cheerfully undertook the tedious task of trawling through the photographic archive at The Hive and Jane Bradney who heroically visited all the sites in the Malvern Hills District and shared much of her own research.

In the early days Mary Worsfold at Bromsgrove District Council helped draw up the list of potential sites in her area; staff at Worcestershire County Council let me borrow their maps and later, John France, the Senior Archival Photographer at The Hive did a superb job of photographing the maps and archive images, particularly the wrinkled, vellum Doharty plans. Lastly, our thanks goes to the helpful staff of other collections who helped to facilitate the use of their images.

Jane Patton

SUBSCRIBERS

Mr. & Mrs. David & Gay **Adam**
Katherine **Alker**
Mr. & Mrs. Philip & Ann **Amphlett**
Mr. & Mrs. Chris & June **Aston**
Mrs. Deborah **Barber**
Mr. Mark **Birchley**
Prof. & Mrs. Peter & Deirdre **Brook**
Mr. & Mrs. **Chenevix-Trench**
Lord **Cobham**
Mr. John **Comins**
Mr. Michael **Cousins**
Mr. Adrian **Darby**
Mr. & Mrs. John & Sue **Del Mar**
Mr. & Mrs. Bill & Christina **Denny**
Mr. David **Fletcher**
Mr. James **Fletcher**
Dr. & Mrs. Derek & Maria **Foxton**
Mrs. Pauline **Gardiner**
Dr. Catherine **Gordon**
Mr. John **Gregory**
Mrs. Carol **Hallett**
Mr. & Mrs. Frank & Maggi **Harriss**
Mr. Jeffrey **Haworth**
Mrs. Antony **Hornyold**
Mr. Philip **Jones**
Mrs. Deanna **Jones**
Mr. & Mrs. Andrew and Anne **Langton**
Rebecca **Lashley**
Mr. Malcolm **Meikle**
Mr. Chris **Milton**
Mrs. Elizabeth **Owen**
Earl of **Plymouth**
Kevin & Elizabeth **Rolf**
Mr. & Mrs. Andrew & Annabel **Sanders**
Mr. & Mrs. George & Penny **Shetliffe**
Mr. & Mrs. Roger & Judy **Smith**
Mr. & Mrs. Guy & Wendy **Spollen**
Mrs. Ann **Stallard**
Mrs. Lesley **Tanner**
Elizabeth **Taylor**
Mr. Alan **Taylor**
Mrs. Christine **Tebbett**
Mr. & Mrs. Tony & Linda **Tidmarsh**
Mr. Peter **Walker**
Mr. Tom **Wall**
Mr. & Mrs. Richard & Marigold **Webb**
Mr. Robin **Whittaker**
Mr. David **Whitehead**
Mr. John **Yorke**

FOREWORD

Hewell Grange, the pivoted stone slab door to the Quarry Garden. Photograph circa 1902, courtesy of Country Life.

The Hereford and Worcester Gardens Trust was founded twenty-eight years ago, prompted by the need to protect and secure a future for 'Capability' Brown's Croome Park, then threatened by redevelopment for golf. English Heritage policy at the time was to support such investment in damaged parks, even those Grade One on its Register of Historic Parks and Gardens (Only Croome and Hagley enjoy this distinction in Worcestershire).

Our early priority was to publish data not only to interest and inform our Members, but especially to help Planners and Conservation Officers when faced with proposals affecting historic parks and gardens in our two counties. Within a decade we had published glossaries for each county. David Whitehead's on Herefordshire (2001) was highly detailed and based on archive research and knowledge of what survives on the ground. The earlier edition of the present book was archive-based almost exclusively. Now much more information is available, greatly expanded by the Internet and from visits.

Richard Lockett highlights major sites where attempts have been made to repair and reinstate past glories. This is an opportunity to thank the stalwarts who have stuck with these projects and made them excellent, Neil Cook at Hanbury and Katherine Alker at Croome, both Head Gardeners in the traditional sense (though the National Trust doesn't call them that). At Hagley, Joe Hawkins is Lord Cobham's Head of Landscape, a worthy title for a researcher and vigorous practitioner on site. Very soon the public will have access to the riches of the mid-18th Hagley park, more akin to what Warre Bampfylde was doing at Hestercombe, with many distinct scenes rather than the sweeping, continuously flowing landscapes of Brown and his followers.

At Witley Court, government action by taking it into Guardianship put a stop to it being a source of Architectural Salvage. Consolidation of the ruined house has been followed by conservation of the extensive remnants of the Nesfield formal garden, culminating in the repair and recommissioning of the great fountain with its exciting 30 metre high principal jet. Also, on a much smaller scale, it has been rewarding to glimpse Cofton Hall and its setting from the train, as they were resuscitated from a squalid state.

A continuing advisory committee at Hewell Grange has helped the Home Office understand the setting of the magnificent Grade One Victorian mansion and the important ruin of its predecessor around which Repton staged the best-surviving and most extensive of his Worcestershire landscapes. Our first Secretary, Ginny Scott, fund-raised to repair Repton's island and the iron footbridge connecting it to the lawn of the old house. Repton's superb Red Book informed the project.

Recently Jane Patton and David Whitehead worked very hard to persuade Historic England to include Ombersley on its highly selective Register of Historic Parks and Gardens. It deserved to have been on the Register from the start as a major, virtually undamaged, Regency landscape by John Webb dubbed "The Northern Repton" (who was responsible for much of the celebrated parks at Shugborough and far-off Lowther). Fortunately the house is to continue in private

Foreword continued

occupation and not be altered and extended for institutional use as had once been contemplated and which could have had worrying implications for the setting.

It is perhaps surprising that more medium-scale houses have not been built on old sites, thus promoting care of remnant gardens and surroundings, where tired groups of Victorian ornamental trees languish unloved. The submitted drawings for a new house on the site of Ham Court, near Upton, did not prepare us for the result with its suave Palladian interior opening onto the immaculately planted sunken garden there.

We have been keen to encourage the current construction of a 3-storey Viewing Tower in an old walled garden at a low-lying house near Pershore, which will permit glimpses of Bredon Hill and the Malverns. Quinlan Terry is the Architect.

This is in the same vein as the 6th Lord Coventry's Panorama Tower, on high land outside his park at Croome, designed by James Wyatt, the most fashionable Architect of his day at the height of his powers. A visit to the Panorama Tower is especially rewarding now that it is exquisitely repaired by the National Trust. At ground level, each intercolumniation frames a beautiful view. From the viewing platform upstairs one surveys the landscape for many miles around. The landscape can never have looked better, with its grazed fields and tree-grouping a tribute to neighbouring farmers and landowners and the absence of ugly buildings or other intrusions a tribute to Planners and Conservation Officers.

A quarter of a century ago it could not have been envisaged that the clock would be wound back by the National Trust at Croome or that the slumbering Hagley landscape would be immaculately repaired by its private owner.

This book owes much to owners and gardeners, to many Gardens Trust volunteers and especially to the two tireless experts who have brought it to fruition. Landscape Architect Jane Patton is organising editor and has visited almost all the sites described. Art Historian Richard Lockett, who knows more about Worcestershire's historic parks and gardens than anyone else, has written the text. They are volunteers on a magnificent scale, for which we are immensely grateful.

Jeffrey Haworth
Chairman of the Hereford and Worcester Gardens Trust

June 2019

A survey of HISTORIC PARKS & GARDENS IN WORCESTERSHIRE

INTRODUCTION

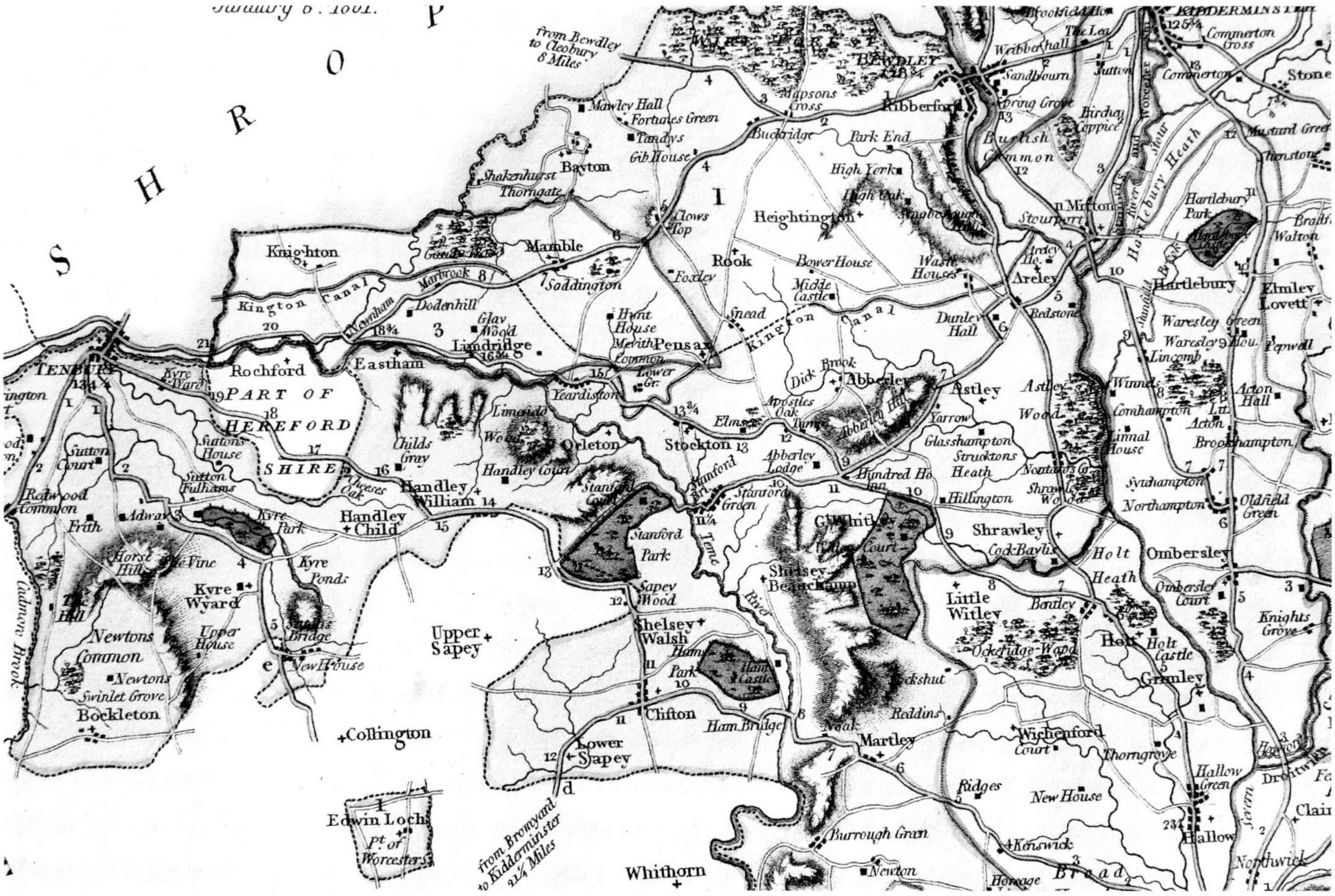

Christopher Smith, *New Map of the Co. of Worcester,* 1804, detail.

In 1997 when the first edition of this *Survey* was published, my brief was to identify historic parks and gardens from published, printed sources although I did not ignore additional information from manuscripts met along the way. The documents were then held at the Worcester County Record Office, Nunnery Wood and at St. Helen's Church, Worcester. Bulk Accession catalogue references were then given as CRO but here are referenced also as WAAS for these archives curated by the Worcestershire Archives and Archaeology Service at The Hive, Worcester. The Croome Court archive, now moved there was then curated at the Estate Office where I studied it for Camilla Beresford's *Landscape Study* (op. cit.), commissioned by the National Trust towards the restoration of 'Capability' Brown's landscape; this was my introduction to garden history. Because the 6th Earl of Coventry never threw away any bill, everything survives to document the organisation of the house staff and the ground staff (divided into their several departments), the contractors employed on piece work to improve the infrastructure of an agricultural estate and the nurseries which supplied trees, shrubs and plants to the Nursery, Shrubberies and Kitchen Gardens. Horticultural Invoices for Croome multiplied from the 1740s and became international with imports from North America in the 1750s and from the Far East in the 1770s. Arthur Young ranked Croome second only to Kew as a botanical show piece in 1801 (op. cit.). William Dean, the head gardener published a catalogue – *Hortus Croomensis* - in 1824 confirming this status (op. cit.).

The objective of the HWGT *Survey* was to identify the historic parks and gardens worthy of care in the context of Planning Development. At the time there were only 15 Registered Parks and Gardens in Worcestershire and English Heritage's interest in adding to the List languished until recently when recognition was given to Gheluvelt Park, opened with

Introduction continued

homes for Ist World War veterans in 1922 (2015), and to Ombersley Court as redeveloped by John Webb of Lichfield after 1810 for the Marchioness of Downshire (2017). Ombersley Court shares with Croome Court the distinction of having a single architect for both mansion and landscape.

Although the number of sites in the *Survey* has reduced from 283 to 230, there is still an imbalance between entries virtually unchanged and some 70 sites about which much more can be said due to research, not all yet published, e.g. for Abberley Hall, Hewell Grange, Pull Court, Hagley Hall, Ombersley Court, Hadzor Hall and Stanford Court. This new research has been shared most generously by authors, by those who commissioned the research and by the owners and custodians of the properties concerned. The fullest analysis of some parks and gardens now exists in the form of the conservation reports generated to secure Heritage Lottery and other grants essential for major conservation projects. In 1997 there was no interpretative survey of the County's parks and gardens but this yawning gap has been filled by Timothy Mowl in his *Historic Gardens of Worcestershire*, 2006, which provides for the first time an overview of the County's parks and gardens and places them within a national context. The present book does not have the same ambition and is otherwise constricted by a cut-off date of 1940 for "historic" and therefore favours the 18th and 19th centuries as against the 20th century. Post-2nd World War developments are mentioned only if they relate to sites with an earlier, published history. The 20th century demands its own book.

The Appendix for Walled Gardens has removed a few sites from the main text and provides a check-list for this significant corner of garden history. The Index of Personal Names identifies some individuals central to this *Survey*, i.e. surveyors, landscape architects and garden designers at least between 1700 and 1850; "map maker" indicates authors of printed maps and "surveyor" of manuscript surveys, sometimes with a date to indicate period of activity. In the first half of the 18th century the Dougharty family were the leading surveyors in the County. John Dougharty senior had established a school of mathematics in Bewdley in 1709 (covering pure and applied mathematics, measuring, book keeping, navigation and astronomy). He published the first of several editions of his *Mathematical Digests* in 1751. His Worcester career progressed from becoming a lay clerk at the Cathedral in 1716 and also Inspector of Works and Keeper of Stores, i.e. surveyor for building works such as re-roofing. He otherwise acted as librarian and choirmaster! In 1720 he transferred his school in the High Street to the Edgar Tower which he leased and in which he had a library of 800 books and a "hall" room fitted out with furniture, china cabinets, pictures and busts of Roman Emperors. Having pupils from leading county families no doubt promoted the family's surveying business. Father and both sons contributed to the major project, the '*Book of Maps*' made for Bowater Vernon of Hanbury Hall in 1731-2 (Manors of Hanbury and Shrawley). Other clients besides the Dean and Chapter, included Lord Foley (Great Malvern, Holt), Lord Coventry (Feckenham) and Lord Sandys (Ombersley). John Doharty junior made the majority of the maps referred to here, often on a scale of 20 ins. to the mile, at a charge increasing over the years from 3d to 6d per acre. He produced the first larger-scale map of the City of Worcester in 1741 and another of Kidderminster in 1753. The Doughartys developed two pleasure gardens in Worcester, one on the west bank of the Severn on Holywell Hill, Henwick Lodge which was advertised in 1746 as having a cold bath, terraced gardens, a sundial and ornamental pyramids, and the other (**Plate 19**), at Diglis beside the Castle Mound (Gaol), which had a bowling green, banquetting house and riding school (Smith, ops. cit.).

The *Survey* considers some other amenities which anticipated the public parks of the 19th century. Malvern Spa offered a wide range of amusements to its specialised (medical) tourist trade, e.g. hotels (some with gardens), tea-rooms and a library in addition to the facilities for drinking the waters and, from mid-century, for suffering cold bath treatments (hydrotherapy). Guide books covered the principal walks to be enjoyed on the Hills (Princess Victoria opened a new one in 1831) and recommended excursions to picturesque houses in the hinterland such as Birtsmorton Court and Madresfield Court. The Clent Hills provided more popular entertainment such as tea rooms and donkey rides; the setting up of shooting booths along the perimeter of the Commons circa 1880 provoked neighbours such as John Amphlett of Clent House to put up fences regarded by the Conservators as incursions; a court case followed that went on for nearly 40 years.

This boundary dispute between private grounds and commons was a latter-day example of the ancient tension around Royal forests and deer parks. Even before deer parks had disappeared or changed into landscape parks, the distinction between a hunting ground and a mixed, agricultural resource was blurred. Stuart Davies's researches into Bewdley Park/Tickenhill Park during the earlier-17th century show how difficult it was for owners to maintain their privileged

Introduction continued

space with park pales and gates against the towns people of Bewdley for whom the only boundary of interest was the one between the deer and their own gardens. The agricultural resources of wood (browse wood for heating and timber building) and grazing for cattle and pigs as well as deer, could be over exploited by both the lessees (local gentry) as well as the towns people. Wood was needed to maintain the park pale and the Palace itself which was needed occasionally for Royal use in Tudor times; the last royal visit to Bewdley-Tickenhill was made by Charles 1 in 1644 (Davies, op. cit.). Hostility to deer parks was expressed particularly during the English Civil War after which many were not revived.

Each great woodland has its own story. Eymore Park (Wood): "The *Parco de Eymore* on the east bank of the Severn, just west of Kidderminster (SO 7779) is first recorded in a charter of 1298 and was acquired by the Priory (of Worcester) c. 1312 ... It was one of the principal sources of timber for the cathedral until at least the 18th century as well as a hunting ground" (Fearn & Simpson op. cit.). Its history as managed woodland, following rules laid down by Henry VIII after his seizure of church lands, can be traced in surveys made for Elizabeth I in 1579 and 1592 (concerned with Royal revenues and shipbuilding) and for Parliament in 1649-50 to raise money. The compartmentalising of the Eymore woods into "sales, falls or coppices", one coppice to be felled each year, is found on a map made for the Dean and Chapter of Worcester in 1756. Such management of historic woodland did not survive industrial exploitation from the late-18th century before the Cathedral lost more of its landed estates to the Church Commissioners in 1861. The Eymore Wood landscape was further changed by the building of the Severn Valley Railway and the making of the Trimpley Reservoir. Traditional planting has been replaced in recent times by nurseries of exotic species of fir, pine and larch (Fearn and Simpson, op. cit.).

My overall impression gained from comparing maps with the landscape today, is that the fundamentals have changed remarkably little over a long period of time, i. e. that woods and watercourses, field boundaries and field names have retained their shape and identification and the main constituents of the landscape can be followed from map to map until we reach the larger-scale OS maps of a century or more ago. There is usually continuity from the 18th century when manuscript maps become available. Parks in particular have a long life and are at their most assertive circa 1900 when the 6 inch scale OS maps, the base document used here, indicate them as defined by their owners. A century and a half later we have returned to official listing and to numbers equivalent to the parks identified on 18th century maps!

The *Survey* relies on printed maps beginning with Christopher Saxton's *Wigorniensis : Comitatus Sabrinae,* first published in 1577, which was incorporated in 1586 into his Atlas of County Maps. Hand-colouring, when applied to the prints, helps to emphasise hills and rivers, towns and villages, forest and parks. Saxton identifies (his spelling): Kyre; Sutton pk; Maumble; Tycknel; Aberley; Hallow; Blackmore pk; Battenhall pk; Wadborow; Strensham; Feckenham; Alchurche; Beley. Worcestershire was priviledged to be selected by Ralph Sheldon for one of his tapestry maps, the one in the Bodleian Library, Oxford, which has been dated to the 1590s is signed by Richard Hyckes (Hickes) and measures approximately 13ft x 11 ft but is based upon Saxton's printed map, not much larger than a sheet of A3 paper (Humphreys, op. cit.). Sheldon's woollen tapestries enlarge on the proprietor-entrepreneur's interests and feature houses, churches and bridges such as that over the Severn at Worcester; the beacons at Lickey and Broadway are flamboyant. Sheldon's deer park pales are robust and the parks are otherwise labelled: WADBOROW; BATNOL PA; BEOLEY; FECKNAM PARKE; WHITELEY PAR; ROCHFORD PARS; STRENSHAM; KYRE; BLACKMORE PA. The tapestry's most impressive addition to the printed map are the two surviving borders which are filled with Elizabethan, Renaissance imagery, flower vases and arbours, and verses to express the character of the County:

Hear hills doe lift ther head aloft, from whence sweet springs doo flowe
Whose moistur good doth fertile make the valets couchte belowe.
Hear goodly orchards planted are in fruite, which doe abounde
Thin ey wold make thin hart reioice to see so pleasant grounde.
(Turner, op. cit.).

After Saxton (and Speed's 1610 edition with Worcester city plan), little if any new information is provided by the numerous, small-scale maps published between 1610 and Isaac Taylor's map of 1772, Christopher Smith's of 1804 and Christopher Greenwood's of 1822, which are on a larger scale and resulted from new surveying. Taylor's county map of 1772, surveyed at one inch to the mile, used shading or hatching to describe hills and gives a stronger impression

Introduction continued

of relief. He included large farms as well as mansions and churches and introduces industries: windmills, paper mills, glass houses (glass manufactories), forges (the first iron works). Taylor specifies fenced deer parks at Pull Court or Bushley, Croome Court, Westwood Court, Ham Castle, Elmley Castle, Hewell Grange, Witley Court, Stanford Court (and Northwick Park then in the County). Other parks not shown as deer parks, are Blackmore Park, Hartlebury Park, (Overbury), The Park (Feckenham), Brine Park (north of Droitwich), Bordesley Old Park, and Hagley Park.

Christopher Smith (1804) retained Taylor's conventions for hills and parks, conventions which continued to be enhanced by hand colouring into the 20th century. Christopher Greenwood's 1822 county map was a grander effort and has been greeted by Harley (op. cit.) as "the climax of the 18th century tradition". This map was dedicated to the Nobility, Gentry and Clergy of the County and had a separate published Index - *Worcestershire Delineated* – naming 78 occupants (many of them tenants) "and their different Parks, Lawns, Pleasure Grounds, Lakes or Sheets of Water, and other ornaments." Little is said about these amenities in the Index but the map itself sometimes details the internal lay-out of parks, artificial lakes, lawns, tree-lined avenues etc. Greenwood was interested in land use, e.g. woods, heaths and commons but doesn't feature orchards and urban gardens, i.e. the emerging market garden industry. Harley says that Greenwood would not have had access to the OS surveys at 2 inch scale and that only the principal triangulation points for Worcestershire were available to him; Greenwood had to construct his own network of minor triangles using a theodolite with telescopic sights (Harley, op. cit.).

The Ordnance Survey initiated by the Royal Engineers in the 1790s, was soon dominated by the military needs of the Napoleonic Wars but nonetheless transformed the surveying business (Hewitt, op. cit.). Southern England benefited first but the surveying of Worcestershire at 2 inches to the mile was underway by 1811 (Harley, op. cit.) The 2 inch OS is useful for parks but was still too small to identify interesting grounds or gardens. The OS one inch to the mile published between 1828 and 1835 can be scrutinised for parks although the similarity of conventions for woods and parks is limiting and of course, parks were identified by their owners. Later editions have better identification for parks to compensate for their diminishing presence amongst roads, canals and railways. The 1876 edition of the 1831 OS one inch (Worcs. SW No. 54) was printed by electrotype.

Before the circa 1880s first edition OS 6 inch maps, manuscript surveys at greater scale are the only resource for gardens. However, manuscript surveys can be summary when describing gardens, being focussed on ownership, acreages and rental value. Site specific information is even more difficult to gather from town maps even from the best such as George Young's 1779 or Valentine Green's 1795 or Charles Crisp's 1832 maps covering Worcester. A combination of factors, the small-scale of printed maps, the lack of other printed documentation and a low survival rate on the ground has frustrated efforts to construct a history for potential urban candidates for the *Survey*.

Many major sites suffered a break in continuity of ownership at the Protestant Reformation when monasteries, granges and estates fell into secular hands, often those of existing tenants, who had different requirements for their grounds, gardens and other amenities. Discussion must be speculative about moated gardens, e.g. at Alvechurch Palace and Hartlebury Castle (both belonging to the Bishops of Worcester) or Grafton Manor (Talbot family) or Huddington (Winter family) or Harvington (Pakington and Throckmorton families) or Madresfield (Lygon family). Published information about 16th century gardens is sparse, the 1535 inventory for Huddington says nothing about the gardens, the 1554 survey for the Duke of Northumberland at Hartlebury makes no mention of gardens within the moat or within the castle itself; John Blaye's gardening at Grafton Manor documented in 1569, may be the origin of the terraces there.

Most tantalising of all is Tickenhill Palace, a major residence of the Mortimers which passed to the House of York and then to the Tudors. Prince Arthur was married to Catherine of Aragon by proxy there in 1499 and was resident there on and off between 1493 and 1502. For Princess Mary (Mary I) at Tickenhill in 1525, instructions were given that she should "at Seasons convenient to use moderate exercise on taking open air in the gardens sweet and wholesome places and walks which may confer on her health." In 1582 Sir Henry Sidney made repairs, brought in a water supply and set up "a fair fountain made with limestone and lead" decorated with the Royal Arms.

Many gardens no doubt lived on relatively unchanged into the 17th century, the English Civil War being a watershed for new fashions arriving from the Continent after the Stuart Restoration. Judge Nicholas Lechmere developed his gardens at Severn End in the 1650s in a conservative spirit; his terraced garden with study pavilion survives to represent

Introduction continued

undocumented contemporary terraced gardens at Grafton Manor or Holt Castle. Other sites to bear in mind for such gardens are Ham Castle (Ham Castle Farm), Ribbesford House, Westwood House and Woollas Hall. The moated gardens of Madresfield Court which enjoyed several campaigns in the 19th century and, through Thomas Mawson, in the early-20th century, can evoke lost parterres and yew hedges as once existed in many 16th and 17th century, Worcestershire gardens.

John Evelyn comes into the Worcestershire story through his friendship with Robert Berkeley of Spetchley Park; in 1683 Evelyn's diary noted Berkeley as a young man "very curious in gardening". David Smith (op. cit.) has amplified this note from their surviving correspondence between 1684 and 1693. Evelyn developed his own gardens at Says Court, Kent after his return from France in 1652 having also spent time in Italy and Holland during the Commonwealth. His *Sylva; or a Discourse on Forest Trees* was presented to the newly founded Royal Society in 1664 and Berkeley will have been flattered to be mentioned in Evelyn's *Kalendarium Hortense* in 1691. Berkeley listed his plantings at Spetchley for Evelyn: cypress, ilex, holly, laurel, yew, juniper, pine, pyrocanthus, rosemary, orange and lemon trees and reported on their relative survival after a hard winter. He wrote to Evelyn: "I have some cedars to set out but am loath to expose them till I know yours have endured the winter". Cedars remain a prominent feature of the Spetchley landscape. In 1685 Evelyn shared his latest information on Dutch greenhouses "which at small changes in the fabric secures their curiosities without stove or fire during the severest seasons." In 1693 Berkeley was building a conservatory "something in imitation of yours but with this addition, having each side of it wings" (David Smith, op. cit.). Evidently, Spetchley Park was at the forefront of gardening practice at this moment.

There are no pictures for Spetchley Park but there are of Westwood Park as developed before and after the English Civil War. The famous bird's eye engraving in Jan Kip and Leonard Knyff's *Britannia Illustrata*, 1714, (their only Worcestershire selection) makes Westwood look somewhat old fashioned besides the other up-to-date great houses. The engraving shows the gardens immediately around the house stretching into the park, itself surrounded by a thick fringe of plantations cut through with avenues radiating out from the centre. The arrangement of the gardens reflects the eccentric plan of the house and might be interpreted on each side as: lawns/bowling green between gatehouse and front door; formal garden with terrace between pavilions and a formal walled garden with gateway into an orchard extending into the park; tilt yard between house and stables; flower and other gardens with lesser status within walls on the 4th side. The principal feature of the Westwood gardens are the pavilions, 4 in the engraving and 2 surviving.

George Hickes, a former Dean of Worcester, in his Anglo-Saxon *Dictionary* published in 1694, shared his experience of the Westwood grounds through a Latin dedication to his patron, Sir John Pakington: "There are porches, vestibules, columns, gardens, walks covered and open, straight and winding, all contributing to learned thought; there are groves, woods, shrubberies, meadows, fields, lawns, pastures, nor is there anything there that is not restful and pleasing." (Treadway Nash was the first historian to quote this dedication in Vol. 1 of his *History*, 1781, op. cit.).

Westwood enjoyed a revival of taste for Jacobethan architecture that was characteristic of the early Victorian period, a revival which extended to gardens. Westwood was chosen for one of the plates in Joseph Nash's *Mansions of England in the Olden Time* published in 1839. Westwood may even have been a leader in this fashion since Edward Frances Burney painted a watercolour, circa 1800, representing house and gatehouse with figures in 17th century costume returning from the hunt; the house traditionally began life as a hunting lodge.

By the mid-18th century, there are guide books and private correspondence to provide a rich, contemporary critique of contemporary developments; Hagley Hall was one of the most highly promoted venues with literary associations both with Alexander Pope and James Thomson. Thomson composed part of his poem the *Seasons* at Hagley in 1743/4. William Shenstone's The Leasowes was sometimes "puffed" alongside Hagley (1765) despite being on a much more modest scale, a comparison which could be to its detriment. Thomas Jefferson, future President of the United States, commented sniffily in a *Memorandum* written in 1784: "it is not even an ornamental farm, it is only a grazing farm with a path round it, here and there a seat of board, rarely anything better. Architecture has contributed nothing, the obelisk is of brick. Shenstone has but £300 a year and ruined himself by what he did." Apparently, Hagley Hall was still fashionable in 1819 when Dugdale published *The New Traveller* which suggests a tour of the grounds moving from stand to stand or station to station as recommended by William Gilpin in his *Tour of the Wye* in 1771. Dugdale conducts you step by step: "walk winding to the right, from which there is a view of the Clee-Hill: this leads into a grove, when a view of the tower breaks in, to the seat of contemplation. Hence you arrive at a rotunda of the Ionic order; from which you look down across water and a lawn to a Palladian-Bridge", and so on (Dugdale, op.cit.).

Hagley Hall is one of a trilogy of houses that give Worcestershire a national status in 18th-century landscape gardening. Hanbury Hall and Croome Court exhibit the planned relationship between a mansion and its setting, i.e. the immediate grounds and further landscape. It is now possible to appreciate what George London was offering to his client at Hanbury because the National Trust has realised his designs for the second time. From the formality of Hanbury, one can move to the classical landscape - nature with architectural ornament carrying literary associations understood by the educated visitor, particularly if briefed by a contemporary guide or guide book. Lord Lyttelton developed Hagley with a coterie of friends versed in contemporary fashion together with professional advice from James 'Athenian' Stuart. Lord Coventry at Croome attempted to manage nature on a greater scale with eye-catchers spread over a larger canvas and worked through professional hands, those of Lancelot Brown, Robert Adam and James Wyatt. Croome with its shrubberies and nurseries and further botanical interests has a more commercial feel about it. Hagley remained a more private, personal, even poetic experience to be shared with Virgil and James Thomson.

Nash features several of Worcestershire's grander houses in their landscape setting in his two volume *Collections for the History of Worcestershire* published in 1781-2. Several engraved illustrations stress the importance of the River Severn as the location for mansions either set above the river as The Rhydd, Holt Castle and Winterdyne or, less precipitously near its banks as at Arley Castle or Hallow Park or, just nearby as at Ham Court, Pull Court, Severn End and Ribbesford. Nash sometimes supplies the missing centre piece, e.g. lost mansions at Ham Court, Strensham Court and Glasshampton. (For some of these see Reid, op. cit.: Clent House, Elmley Castle, (old) Hewell Grange, Perdiswell Hall, Wick House).

Mansions and their grounds are not Nash's principal interest as an antiquarian. Characteristically, he treats the Hereford Beacon as a building in elevation and section rather than as a part of the landscape of the Malvern Hills. Nash built himself a new mansion, Bevere House, with a small park next door to his inherited, manor house but does not comment otherwise on it except to place a vignette illustration at the front of his first volume. Two of Nash's plates of town and country are especially informative for us; one, a gentleman taking tea in the Porto Bello Gardens contemplating the City and Cathedral of Worcester across Pitchcroft and the River Severn, and the other, the owners of Stanford Court or their guests viewing house, landscape and eye-catcher church across the lake with pleasure boat. Nash writes: "Stanford Court ... is situated in a very extensive park (with) ... delightful prospects (and) ... fine groves of oak (and) ... two large pieces of water, made by Sir Edward Winnington ... a cedar of Libanus, planted only 28 years ago, that is more than 3 yards round". Francis Ingram, Sir Edward's brother-in-law, explains in a memorandum written in 1795, the context for his own developments at nearby Tickenhill Palace. "In the year 1776 Sir Edward Winnington on the marriage of their son (who had inherited Stanford Court) came to be resident at Winterdyne"; "from the consideration that Sir Edward Winnington was preparing to build near me on the Rocks of Winterdyne where he soon erected a very elegant villa which he adorned with delightful walks and pleasure grounds and told me he intended it as the place of residence for my sister Lady Winnington after his death".

The 19th century opens with Humphry Repton active at Hewell Grange and John Webb at Ombersley Court (both in 1810-12). David Whitehead and Jane Bradney (op. cit.), in their recent assessment of Repton's activity at Hewell Grange, have demonstrated the extent to which proposals presented in his Red Book (1812) as criticisms of Brown's, were taken up by Lord Plymouth. Mid-19th, and late-19th century developments associated with Bodley and Garner's newly-sited mansion (1884-1891), further changed park and grounds as left by Brown and Repton. Other landscape designers, including Edward Milner, took Hewell further into the 20th century. The late-19th century gardens survive only in outline but are recorded in Bedford Lemere's photographs and in contemporary coverage by *Country Life* (1902, 1913, **Plate 34**).

A short client's brief exists for Ombersley Court expressed in a letter to John Webb from the Marchioness of Downshire in 1819. She required the new "entrance into the Park from the Worcester Side, where the Lodge shod (sic) be, to commence at Bourne's Dingle carried as Mr. Webb may judge best to secure the distant views of Malvern & the Surrounding Country ... Respecting the Kitchen Garden & Hot Houses I am decidedly of opinion that the upper Garden may be done away with & laid into Pasture. The new Kitchen Garden giving a sufficient supply for myself and family. I wish likewise to lessen the Hot Houses & save the expense of building a Green House by having only two houses for

Introduction continued

Pines, & the other turned into a Green House. The Houses are at present much more for shew than for profit. I wish the Walls no longer to be heated" (Martin Davis). This cost sensitive advice is difficult to reconcile with the surviving, early-19th century glasshouse, an imposing cast-iron structure with a single slope, lean-to roof, set against a large, arcaded, brick structure designed for heating.

Another early-19th century property, Hadzor Hall, can be viewed in its hay-day in 1901 through *Country Life*. There is an earlier glimpse of it given in sale particulars of 1823 when prospective owners were invited to take in the "exceedingly beautiful views, grounds disposed in the best possible order, a kitchen garden ... lawns, shrubberies leading imperceptibly to the romantic and beautiful plantations abounding with shady walks, extended drives and vistas in almost every direction ... this incomparable retreat has been assimilated to Paradise". Sale particulars could be enhanced by illustration such as the charming lithographs made by Thomas Underwood of Birmingham to promote the sale of Sion Hill House in 1836. Similar lithographs were made for the sale of Abberley Hall in 1845 and Crown East in 1853. Photography took over from lithography in the last quarter of the 19th century to help market the escalation of property sales that took place before, during and immediately after the Ist World War. Today, colour photographs reign supreme and sale brochures often give the best coverage for gardens as well as for houses.

Arley Castle is the outstanding Worcestershire property from the first half of the 19th century. The grounds were developed by a noted botanist, the 2nd Earl of Mountnorris, in the 1830s and his plantings as further developed by 1907 merited their own catalogue, the *Hortus Arleyiensis*. The arboretum received a 2 acre addition in 2001. For a less concentrated collection of specimen trees one might turn to Kyre Park for the early-18th century and to St. James's, West Malvern for an early-20th century candidate. Arley Castle benefitted from the interest of several successive Directors of Kew Gardens including Sir Joseph and Sir William Hooker. The castle itself, built in 1844, has been demolished (Reid, op. cit.) leaving some substantial picturesque remains to benefit the modern house, while the castellated entrance to the walled garden retains something of the architectural atmosphere. The walled garden is dominated by formal elements in contrast to the picturesque Naboth's vineyard, a wooded, miniature valley with icehouse, watercourses, bridges and falls which once also featured a rustic building for picnics (Nigel Goodman, *The Gardens of Arley*, 2003, 2007).

There were a few significant landscape architects active in the county in the mid-19th century: Alexander Roos worked at Hadzor Hall and Blackmore Park and the more famous William Andrews Nesfield at Witley Court and Pull Court. From later in the century, there are Pulhamite Gardens at Abberley Hall, Impney Park (Chateau Impney), Madresfield and Davenham House, Malvern.

Worcestershire's 19th century achievements have been obscured by losses from fire, demolition, unsympathetic development and, but not always, limited access following from a change of use. Education has taken over Abberley Hall, Crown East, The Rhydd and St. James's, West Malvern, Hewell Grange is an HM Prison, Burcot Grange, Sion Hill House and Winterdyne are residential care homes, Brockencote, and Impney Park are hotels. Madresfield should be singled out as unchanged in use and as a survival of mansion and contents in its immediate, moated grounds and with its further park landscape, all dating from different 19th and early-20th century moments. Chateau Impney (Impney Park) on the other hand (John Corbett's French Renaissance Chateau built between 1869 and 1875 by Auguste Tronquois) is the creation of a single campaign. Chateau Impney has suffered losses, particularly its water features but can be appreciated in its complete state from John Hughes's recent book (op. cit.).

Witley Court, the county's most ambitious 19th century creation, survives as a magnificent ruin. The gardens, to rival any of their time in England, will require an enormous effort to regain even if restoration is limited to the hard landscape. Historic England has begun by restoring the *Perseus and Andromeda* fountain (by James and William Forsyth to the designs of William Andrews Nesfield) which required the most advanced, hydraulic works. Waterworks were the spectacular centre pieces of the Witley parterre gardens, a drama which Lord Dudley occasionally shared with the public. Something beyond *son-et-lumière* may be needed to replicate Lord Dudley's hospitality. A similar approach is needed to evoke the seasonally, changing plantings created by an army of gardeners. By this time, the gardening press had replaced tour guide literature and could review new gardens almost on creation. The *Gardener's Chronicle* characterised the restlessness of Witley in 1873 where Mr. Westland "sometimes whips out the *box* altogether and carpet beds the entire space to the tune of 20,000 plants of *alternatheras, golden feathers, echeverias, semper vivreus* ... And then *Box* again is replaced."

Introduction continued

Samuel Daukes was employed at both Abberley Hall and Witley Court around 1845/6. Abberley, like Witley, continued to develope further in the 1870s and 1880s. At Abberley, James Lamb of Manchester redecorated the principal ground floor rooms and James Pulham added to the water garden. The major missing element from the 1880s is the glass house which ran from the main entrance on the north side around the east (water garden) front. The saloon's full-height windows provided access to the glass house fernery on the east side. To quote the *Journal of Horticulture* in 1887: Abberley Hall possessed "one of the most beautiful glass houses in the country ... a magnificent marble fountain occupies the centre, the fernery adjoining a delightful retreat. The Ferns are planted amongst boulders and sight and sound of trickling water amongst the latter render it still more enjoyable." (Glass Houses are a lost element to a number of Worcestershire houses.) The Abberley Clock Tower, designed by J. P. St. Aubyn, and built in 1883/4, must be the eye-catcher of all eye-catchers, at least for Worcestershire.

A few garden designers of national importance, who began their careers before 1900, were active to a minor degree in the County. Ellen Willmott has been described as the greatest plantswoman of her day to whom even Gertrude Jekyll deferred; both women were highly influential writers on gardens. Willmott's best-known book, *The Genus Rosa* was published in 1910. She helped develope the gardens at Spetchley Park with her sister Rose Berkeley from 1891 making this the most important Worcestershire garden of its period. The Willmott-Berkeley garden of circa 1900 has been described as an ornamental botanic garden, to give it the briefest possible description. Much less substantial are Mowl's "disorderly trio" (op. cit.): Field House, Clent with the Japanese Garden by Gertrude Jekyll; Holland House, Cropthorne a somewhat damaged garden by Sir Edwin Lutyens; Holt Castle developed by Mrs Pepys Cockerell. Gertrude Jekyll's work at Hanley Court, which has proved ephemeral, is memorable for the compliment she paid to her client Mrs Newport when writing from Munstead Wood in August 1906: "It is a great satisfaction to me to hear of the success of the planting ... I only wish all my clients would trust the plans I give and follow them exactly, as you have done."

Richard Lockett,
Worcester,
August 2019.

R. Lockett, *A Survey of Historic Parks and Gardens in Worcestershire,* 1997.
C. Beresford, *Croome Court: Historical Landscape Survey*, 1996, National Trust (unpub.).
Arthur Young, *Annals of Architecture*, 1801.
William Dean, *An Account of Croome d'Abitot: Hortus Croomensis and Observations of the Propagation of Exotics*, 1824.
B. S. Smith, "The Dougharty Family of Worcester; Estate Surveyors and Mapmakers", *Worcester Historical Soc.*, NS, 5, Miscellany II, 1967.
B. S. Smith, "The Dougharty Family, Eighteenth-Century Mapmakers", *Worcester Archaeol. Soc., Trans.*, 3rd Series, Vol. 15, 1996.
S. Davies, *"There having beene a greate wynde"*: trees, deer and conflict in Bewdley Park in the 17th century, 2017 (unpub.).
K. Fearn & G. Simpson, "Worcester Cathedral as a Source of Forest and Woodland History", *Archaeology at Worcester Cathedral*, 7th Annual Symposium, 1997.
J. Humphreys, "Sheldon Tapestry Maps", *Birmingham and Midland Archaeol. Soc.,* Vol. 43, 1917, p. 5.
H. Turner, *No Mean Prospect: Ralph Sheldon's Tapestry Maps,* 2010.
J. B. Harley, "Christopher Greenwood County Map-Maker and his Worcestershire Map of 1822", *Worcs. Historical Soc. Journal,* 1962.
C. & J. Greenwood, *Worcestershire Delineated*, 1822.
M. Hewitt, *Map of a Nation: A Biography of the Ordnance Survey*, 2011.
D. J. Smith, *John Evelyn's Influence on Spetchley garden's and pleasure grounds,* 2103, unpub.
T. R. Nash, *Collections for the History of Worcestershire*, 2. Vols., 1781-2.
J. Dugdale, *The New and Complete British Traveller*, 1819.
P. Reid, Burke's & Savills *Guide to Country Houses, Vol. II, Herefordshire, Shropshire, Warwickshire, Worcestershire*, 1980.
D. Whitehead & J. Bradney, *'In the Enemy's Quarters': Humphry Repton in the West Midlands*, 2018.
R. Woodward, *Hortus Arleyiensis*, 1907.
N. Goodman, *The Gardens of Arley*, 2003, 2007
J. R. Hodges, *Chateau Impney*, 2009.
T. Mowl, *Historic Gardens of Worcestershire,* 2012.

EDITORIAL NOTES

The first edition of this *Survey* was gamely produced by Richard Lockett without the help of digital aids or modern computers. When the Hereford and Worcester Gardens Trust decided that it needed to be updated, technology had moved on and it was apparent that, as editor, I could also act as graphic designer and put his text together with images to create the final book. I had already edited David Whitehead's survey for Herefordshire and HWGT agreed that the new Worcestershire survey should be produced as a companion volume so that the two books would visually relate to one another.

Chateau Impney, photograph taken circa 1900. Courtesy of R. Spollen.

Richard had based his archive research on the 1905 6 inch OS maps because they clearly mark many, but not all, of the landscape parks. However, I decided to use the first edition 6 inch OS maps of the 1880s for most entries as, being older, they were likely to capture more of the historic features. The cartography of these maps is also superb: for example, individual freestanding trees are accurately plotted and, in those days before the Forestry Commission, woodland that had a conifer symbol was likely to be ornamental. However, these maps do not always indicate parkland, so I have shaded the areas of historic parks and gardens in order to easily locate them. Usually, they tally with the 1905 maps but occasionally land had been taken out of parkland, as at Blakeshall Hall, or, less often, put into parkland, as at Caldewell, by 1905. In these cases, and also where the 1905 maps ignore parks and gardens, I have added shading to the first edition maps to show the extent of the park and garden in the 1880s. In some cases, such as Middle Hill, the designed landscape encompassed the general landscape, there being no recognisable park and therefore is unshaded. In other cases such as Farncombe Abbey, the extent of the designed landscape is not clear from research and I have therefore also left it unshaded. In some instances the extent of the park is not obvious but could be deduced from place names, informed scrutiny of the maps and other archive research. In these cases, such as Bewdley Park, the park has been shaded and a note has been added to explain that this has been deduced.

We have been fortunate to have had access to a great number of images from a variety of sources. The Worcestershire Archive and Archaeology Service has been particularly helpful in allowing us to use the images from their archives. Where we have been able to trace the copyright owner, they have been contacted and credited. However, there are a few old photographs where we have been unable to attribute copyright. Please contact us if you notice an unattributed photograph that you believe is yours.

The original *Survey* did not have the benefit of site visits and we have therefore visited every site in the book in order to give an informed contemporary comment. An occasional modern photograph has been included, especially where it would be informative but generally, because many sites are private residences, we have not used modern photographs. Where modern photographs have been used, the permission of the owner has been given.

Amongst the 230 sites described in this book there are 17 historic parks and gardens that are currently Registered by Historic England. Only those important parks and gardens that Historic England considers to be sufficiently special to merit national or international recognition are included in the Register of Historic Parks and Gardens. The various types of designed landscape included on the Register are treated by Historic England in four thematically arranged selection guides:

Editorial notes continued

- **Rural Landscapes** deals with parks and gardens around mainly private houses, and notably landscaped parks around country houses
- **Urban Landscapes** deals with town squares and walks, and also the municipal parks which are such a feature of England's towns and cities
- **Landscapes of Remembrance** treats burial grounds, cemeteries and crematoria gardens
- **Institutional Landscapes** discusses the designed settings of institutions such as schools and universities.

Each guide gives a brief overview of:
- The types of designed landscape covered in the guide
- Current understanding, both of their history and development
- In some cases, how many examples are known.

The second half of each document sets out the over-arching registration criteria, before moving on to offer guidance relevant to the particular assets themselves. A select bibliography gives suggestions for further reading.

All sites included on the Register of Historic Parks and Gardens must hold a level of importance defined as 'special historic' interest in a national context. Nine general criteria have been defined, five relating to date and rarity, and four to other considerations.

Date and rarity: the older a designed landscape is, and the fewer the surviving examples of its kind, the more likely it is to have special interest. Likely to be designated are:
- sites formed before 1750 where at least a proportion of the original layout is still in evidence
- sites laid out between 1750 and 1820 where enough of the layout survives to reflect the original design
- sites laid out between 1820 and 1880 which are of importance and survive relatively intact
- sites with a main phase of development post-1880 which are of special interest and importance, the degree of required special interest rising as the site becomes closer in time
- particularly careful selection is required for sites from the period after 1945. Sites of less than 30 years old are normally registered only if they are of outstanding quality and under threat.

Further considerations: these may influence selection, and may exceptionally be sufficient by themselves to merit designation. In each case there is an expectation that at least a significant proportion of the main elements of the designed landscape layout survives.
- Sites which were influential in the development of taste, whether through reputation or reference in literature
- Sites which are early or representative examples of a style of layout or a type of site, or the work of a designer (amateur or professional) of national importance
- Sites having an association with significant persons
- Sites with a strong group value with other heritage assets.

The many unregistered historic parks and gardens in Worcestershire that are of special local interest are distinguished by additional specific criteria employed by the Hereford and Worcester Gardens Trust. These are:
- Parks must be older than, or present on the 1905 6in. OS maps. This ensures that the sites are over a century old
- Gardens must be notable examples, which, although they may be of more recent origin (but pre-second world war), must be of local importance
- Urban and suburban public parks and gardens are included when they reflect developments in a particular historical era or show continuous development over time.

Jane Patton,
Spetchley,
August 2019.

Abberley Hall and Park

Parish: Abberley

HER Ref: WSM28918/WSM34848.
Grid Ref: SO 745 665.
Postcode: WR6 6DD.
O.S. 6" Map No: 20NE/SE.
Date of Map: 1884, with extent of park & gardens shaded as H. E. Register.

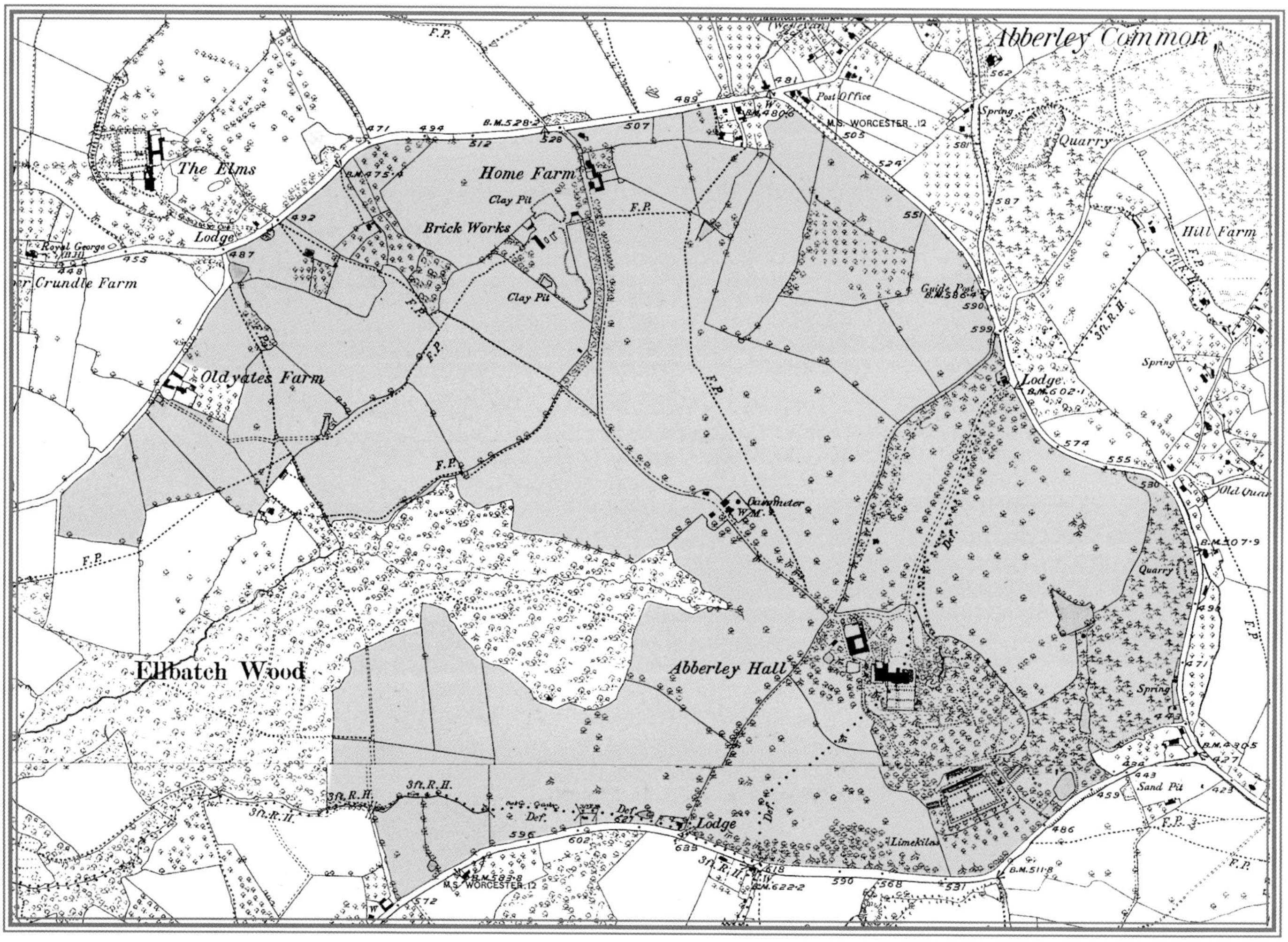

Included within Historic England's Register of Historic Parks and Gardens of special historic interest in England.

ABBERLEY HALL

Abberley Hall, formerly called Lodge, has been a school since 1916. The House, garden features, stables, coach house, clock tower, 4 lodges and associated walls etc. are on the Heritage Register. The existing Hall incorporates an earlier-18th century building and, as illustrated by Treadway Nash, (1, 1781, p. 5), was approached by a broad drive between an avenue of trees. Addison's Walk, presumed to be from circa 1700, lay "between two rows of tall, pollarded horse chestnuts in the shrubberies of the Hall" (Moilliet, 1905); Addison's Walk today is identified with a short avenue of yews and beeches just below the east terrace and Pulhamite rocks. Abberley's possible association with "Sir Roger de Coverley" derives from William Walsh's friendship with the author, Joseph Addison.

Current conservation work on the existing grounds (supported by an NE grant, the Country Houses Association and the Abberley Foundation) suggests that more is owed to the 18th century and to the Bromley family than was previously thought, for example the icehouse with its splendid brick vaulting now revealed and restored. (There are 3 lime kilns sited near to the mansion). Abberley was included in a list of principal

..........continued from previous page

Postcard image, 1938.

Clock tower and Pulham garden, 1887. *Journal of Horticulture.*

county seats circa 1800 although maps indicate the house rather than any grounds. An 1814 guide (*Beauties*, p. 289) describes Abberley Lodge as "a quiet retreat of modern elegance, a pleasant summer residence". Some details of the grounds at this date can be deduced from the 1828 OS 1 inch.

The House and its landscape backdrop is recorded by a lithograph in the 1836 sale particulars (CRO,4600/(ii)) when the mansion and garden is credited with 5 acres, the pleasure grounds with 7, the plantations with 35 and the park lands in hand with 192. The kitchen garden (surviving walls) was already established with its splayed walls and fountain to the south of the house. The kitchen garden in fact is recorded by the OS two inch 1813 survey for the 1828 OS one inch. A parish map of circa 1841 (CRO, 974/2) shows serpentine drives through plantations to the south and west of the property.

Abberley Hall and its grounds today were developed in 3 phases during the 19th century, the first following the acquisition of the estate from the Bromleys in 1844 by Jean Louis Moilliet, a Swiss who had established a successful Bank in Birmingham. He employed Samuel Daukes to build him a new mansion largely destroyed by fire in 1845 but immediately rebuilt to the first designs. An account of the fire refers to "a high tower" (CRO 372/1), presumably the Belvedere tower (now without its upper story) set at the elbow of an L-shaped plan. A second phase (including the Stable block) was undertaken by Joseph Jones who acquired the estate in 1867. A third phase was carried out by Jones's cousin, John Joseph Jones in the 1880s including the dramatic bell tower designed by J. P. St. Aubyn raised in 1883-4 to his cousin's memory. The elaborate North and South Gates and Lodges belong to this latter phase (BoE, pp. 100-102).

J. J. Jones also added a large Conservatory on the corner of the north and east fronts with access via full height windows on the east side. This was reviewed by the *Journal of Horticulture and Cottage Gardener* on October 13th 1887 as "one of the most beautiful glass houses in the country ... a magnificent marble fountain occupies the centre. The fernery adjoining (making) a delightful retreat. The Ferns are planted amongst boulders, and sight and sound of trickling water amongst the latter render it still more enjoyable." The *Worcester Herald* for 28th July 1883 detailed that "in the centre, masses of travertine form a cavity surrounding a basin of translucent water into which droppings from the roof continuously fall ... visitors (as on a guided tour) next descended the terraces which form the gardens, in which water is curiously confined by slabs of stone ... much as Mr. Jones has done, he contemplates doing much more to this paradisiacal retreat." (Askew Nelson pp. 31 & 35 & 37).

The gardens adjoining the mansion today closely reflect the 1880s but also owe much to earlier moments. By 1845 the garden of this Italianate house already had terraces (3 descending terraces on the south side) (Askew Nelson, fig.1) with the principal ladder of steps on the east side of the terraces rather than, as later, centred on the south front's colonnaded loggia (post 1867). The 1867 Sale particulars then describe more generally "broad gravelled walks; lawns, interspersed with flower beds" (CRO, 4600/160 ii). At that time, the pleasure grounds (14 acres)

..........continued from previous page

Lithograph by T. Underwood circa 1850.

contained a spring, fountain, rockery and alcoves and a "valley of rocks" (old quarry) on the east side close to the road boundary. Emma Sophia Moilliet, granddaughter of J. L. Moilliet) recalled this "Cousins Bower" as "a lovely winding valley with steep sides, mostly covered with shrubs and trees and winding paths – now and then coming upon a rustic seat ... Fir trees grew so well at Abberley and father (James) had planted many plantations especially of larches, his favourite tree." (Askew Nelson, p. 29).

The *JHCG* in 1887 credited some of the latest improvements to the new Head Gardener, Arthur Young, e.g. the fruit trees planted in the Kitchen Garden (1½ acres). Woodland was cleared to plant shrubs: "Several specimens of *Leycesteria formosa* and *Salisburia adiantifolia* have also been planted."

This article also featured the Pulhamite Garden, in all essentials surviving today: "Stone boulders skilfully arranged in a semblance of nature round a central pool ... above this is a series of small caves." These support the terrace replacing a plain wall as shown by Underwood's lithograph of circa 1845. Claude Hitching notes that Abberley is not included in a booklet published by James Pulham circa 1877 and therefore proposes a date between 1877 and 1887 (Pulham Legacy Website). The fullest and illustrated account of the Pulhamite gardens at Abberley are in the *HWGT* Newsletter (op. cit).

The kitchen garden, 3 lodges (south, north-west, north-east) and another lodge building on the north- west drive towards the Home Farm, all survive. The south drive has an avenue of mature limes and the north drive a younger lime avenue for part of its length; the principal drives are also footpaths.

The principal drive was planted in the mid-19th century with horse chestnuts which were replaced 25 years ago with sweet chestnuts. "The Drive follows the standard fashion of the Victorians, a Lodge, some special trees, (Deodar cedars, copper beech), a winding approach through the formally planted chestnuts backing onto woodland, the contrived *percée* with its distant views then leading the visitor past the vista to the clock tower into more prestigious trees, so eventually opening after beds of Rhododendrons to the Grand Entrance." (Askew Nelson).

Sited towards the north-east part of the Grounds is the model farm in construction in 1887.

There are 2 ponds within the park, Green Pond and the Inkport; the former has a small bridge, the latter has a dam on one side and dates from circa 1887.

St. Aubyn's Clock Tower of 1883-5 is the *ne plus ultra* of garden buildings and is a County landmark. Being built on higher ground, it dominates the mansion and reverses the role of garden buildings as eye-catchers. It is a gigantic gazebo (50 metres high) providing spectacular views in all directions either from the very top or from 2 stages lower

..........continued from previous page

Abberley Hall, late 19th century photograph with glasshouse, now demolished. Jo Roche Collection.

down, from a parlour with fireplace, window seats, tiled decoration and stained glass, a highly successful Victorian imagining of a medieval moment.

ABBERLEY PARK

A deer park is recorded on the earliest printed maps: Saxton 1577 and Sheldon's tapestry map developed from it; Speed 1610; Blome 1693; Morden 1695. The park continues to be represented on maps throughout the 18th century, located between Stockton and Abberley Hill (to the east of Abberley Hall). The deer park presumably descended from that documented circa 1280, 1322, 1349 (VCH, 4, p. 220) with references to the park keepers. Askew Nelson suggests that the medieval deer park lay to the west of Abberley Hall (p. 18). Leland in the 16th century says that there was once a castle at Abberley; Habington in the 17th century describes a Lodge surrounded by a park on a mighty hill.

The Registered (Landscape) Park "is bounded in the east by the A443 from Ludlow to Worcester ... The B4203 runs along the southern boundary of the park. The pleasure grounds and park around the Hall are bounded to the west by the drive north from Elbatch Lodge and its continuation; the wider parkland to the west is defined by field edges. The area here Registered is circa 50Ha" (Askew Nelson). Within this is an area of circa 15 hectares with mature parkland trees. The *Parkland Plan* contains a detailed analysis of the planting and specimen trees by Bede Howell: "Remnant Scots pines, known to be in excess of two centuries old show that much of the site which is now woodland must at some time have been planted ... varying tree cover of mixed conifer and broadleaved trees ... clearly shown on the Ist (1883) and 2nd Edition Ordnance Survey (1905), chiefly beech with some areas of oak, nursed by European larch ... The parkland and areas closer to the Hall show a scattering of ancient or old native trees – oak, ash and yew, with some evidence of younger trees ... The Victorian Garden ... keeping up with the fashion and assembling a fine pinetum ... some of these trees may have been bought as fairly large pot-grown specimens ... typically spiralling roots ...".

A major restoration of the grounds has been undertaken since 2013 under the Askew Nelson *Parkland Plan.*

Revd. J. L. Moilliet, *Abberley Manor, Worcestershire,* 1905.

Askew Nelson Ltd, *Abberley Hall Parkland Plan,* 2013.

J. Patton, "Abberley Hall and AGM"; J. Patton and J. Roche, "The History"; J. Patton, "Pulham Rock Gardens", *HWGT, Newsletter,* 45, Summer 2015.

Jo Roche, *Abberley Hall and Clock Tower,* n.d.

A. Brooks & N. Pevsner, *Worcestershire,* 2007 (BoE).

Beauties of England and Wales, Vol. XV, 1814.

Victoria County History, Vol. 4, 1924 (VCH).

"Abberley Hall", *Journal of Horticulture and Cottage Gardener,* 18. 10. 1887.

HE *Register of Parks & Gardens,* 1998.

Abberton Hall

Parish: Abberton

HER Ref: WSM29038.

Grid Ref: SO 995 534. Postcode: WR10 2NR.

O.S. 6" Map No: 35NW/SW.

Date of Map: 1884, with deduced extent of park & gardens shaded (not shaded on 1905 OS).

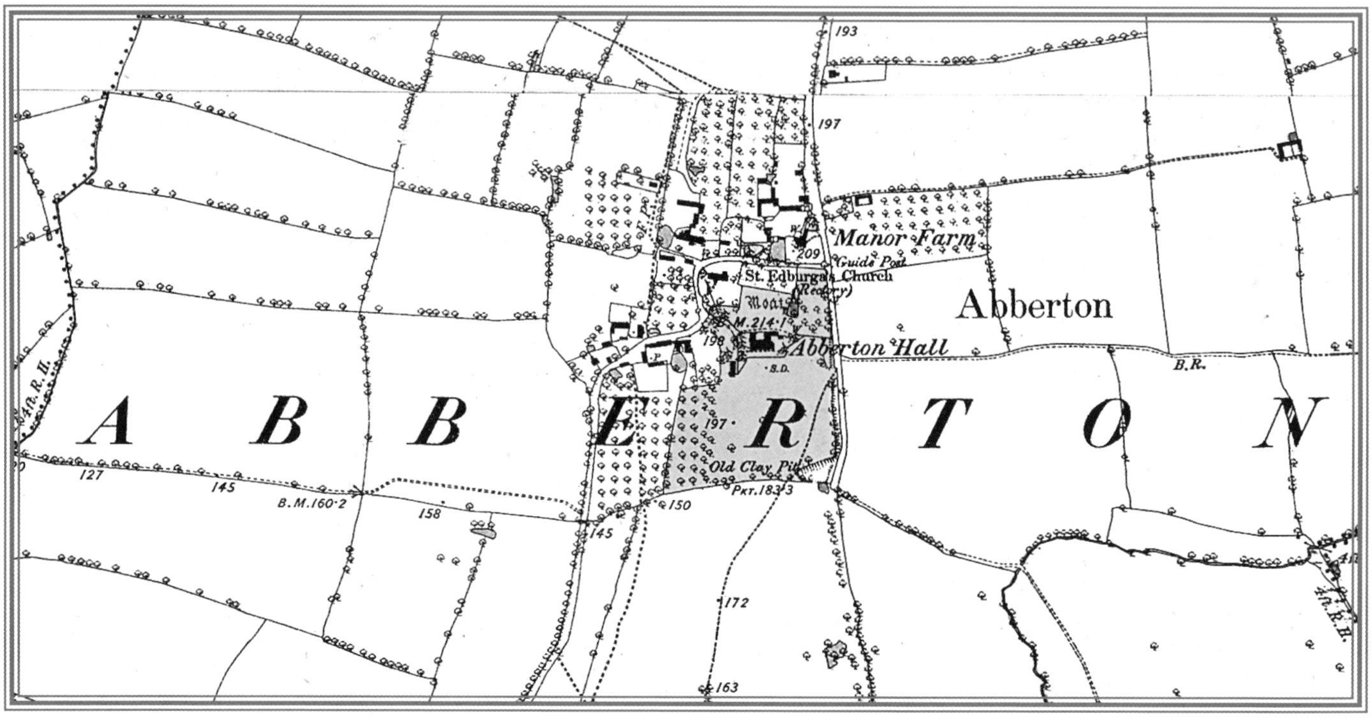

The Hall is a 17th century house rebuilt in the mid-19th century (BoE, p. 103). Although it is not shown with a park on the 1884 OS, the VCH in 1924 (4, p. 2 with illus. p. 4) described Abberton as standing high in a fine park. Grounds are shown on earlier OS maps, e.g. 1828 OS one inch and 1852. The drive avenue on these maps becomes less prominent later. The 1925 Sale particulars offered 26 acres of well-shrubbed and beautifully timbered pleasure grounds ... rosary with pergola ... flagged terrace walk ... finely grown umbrella-shaped Portugal laurel (WAAS, 5044/9)

About 1937, a garden loggia was decorated with frescoes by Benjamin Gibbon, creating an extremely unusual if not unique garden building for the County.

The house and its immaculate gardens still dominates the small village of Abberton.

Abberton Hall. Postcard image.

A. Brooks & N. Pevsner, *Worcestershire,* 2007 (BoE).

Beauties of England and Wales, Vol. XV, 1814.

Victoria County History, Vol. 4, 1924 (VCH).

Alvechurch Palace

Parish: Alvechurch

HER Ref: WSM01232/01829.

Grid Ref: SP 030 729.

Postcode: B48 7SR.

O.S. 6" Map No: 16NE/SE.

Date of Maps: 1883.

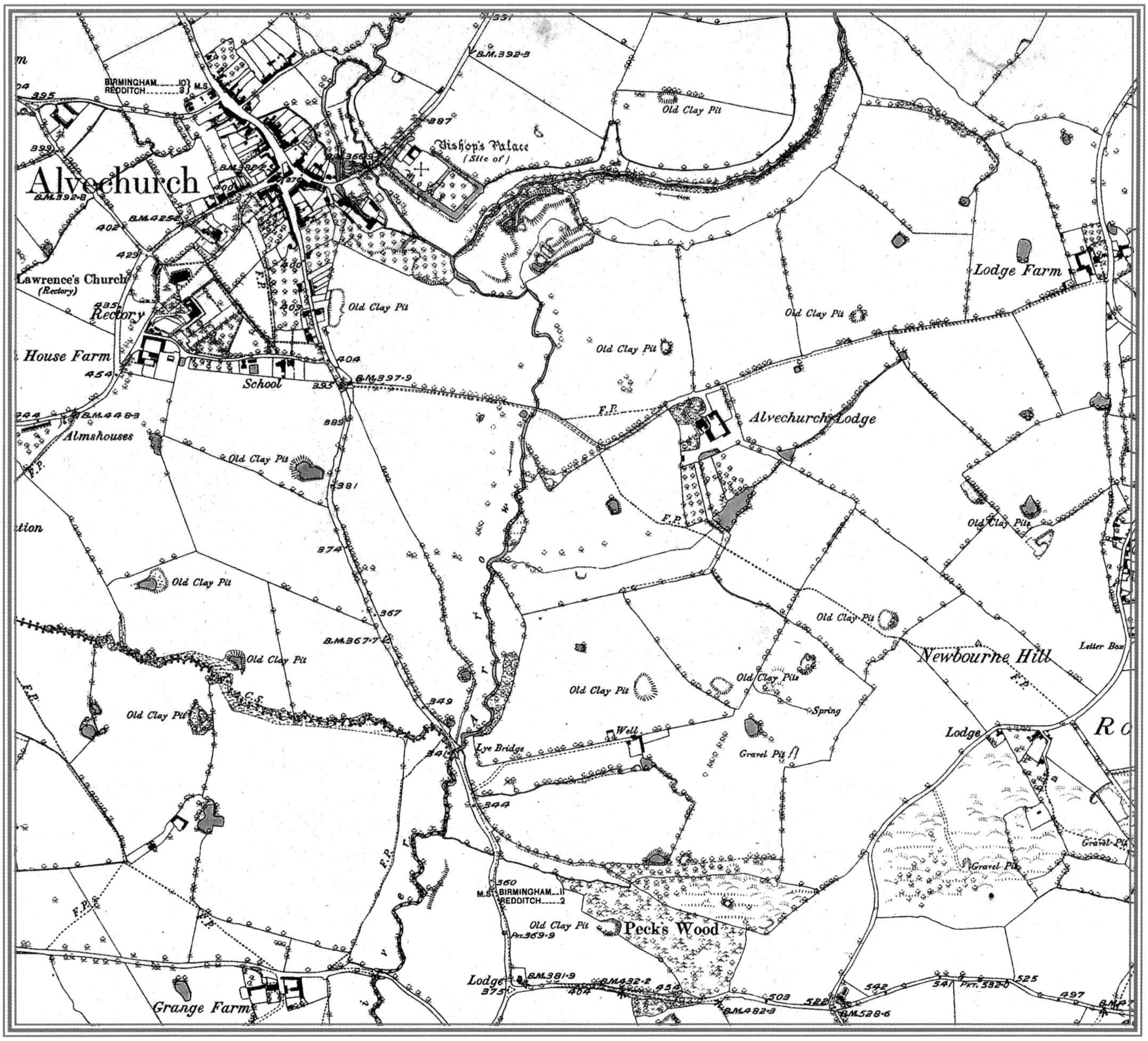

A double moat and fishponds (earthworks) on the other side of the River Arrow mark the site of the medieval Bishop's Palace (Moat House), a major residence of the Bishops of Worcester associated with a deer park. Double moats, particularly when excavation reveals no evidence of buildings, may indicate that the manor, in this case palace, had a garden within the moated precinct. A Map of 1701 shows orchards within the moats (CRO 4437/1). Within the context of medieval gardens, Thacker makes a positive statement that "the Bishop's Palace is known to

..........continued from previous page

have had a 2 acre garden with double moats."

There is documentary evidence for the park in the 12th, 13th, 14th and 16th centuries (HER and VCH, 3, p. 252). Bishop Giffard extended the park in the 13th century. A very detailed description of the livestock that the park could sustain as well as deer, i.e. its value, is given in an assessment of 1299. This also notes fisheries (besides the Palace moat and mill pond) based upon 2 other ponds (Bond, p. 208).

John Leland remarked on a half-timbered building and a park in Henry VIII's reign and a park is marked on Saxton's 1577 county map. It was sold off during the Commonwealth period but regained by the Bishop at the Restoration and is shown by Blome (1673), Morden (1695) and on 18th century maps from 1701. Nash records that the house had recently been demolished and the park converted into farms (1, 1781, p. 25). A 1739 map by John Doharty jun. shows the deer fence still in place but the ground within divided into fields (CRO 5317).

Aston, (p. 113) gives the area of the deer park as bounded by the Radford road along the north side, the B 4120 (now A441) on the west, the Holloway across the south and Rowney Green Lane along the east. A ditch or bank can be traced along most of this boundary (Letter from A. Hoghton and the Rowney Green Historical Records Group to English Heritage, 1994). This area is supported by the HER recording of boundary and field name evidence around Peck Wood. The south-west point of this park is at SO 036 711.

The A441 has sliced its way north/south between the Palace and Alvechurch Lodge Farm and the M40 overhangs the northern boundary of the deer park.

The 1739 Doharty map defines a smaller area, approximately the north half, with a north boundary at Radford road and the footpath (as in the Pathfinder OS 1993 map) linking the B4120 and Rowney Green Lane at Rowney Lodge Farm. The south-west point of this smaller park is at SO 030 728, however, no trace remains of the park today.

The Rectory, (SO 026 723) described by the BoE (p. 109) as an 18th century H plan masking some 15th century work adjoining the Church and Glebe, is depicted by Doharty in 1739 with substantial farm buildings and the Rectory itself with lawns bordered by paths. These arrangements are confused in the 1883 OS and reversed in the OS 1905 with High House Farm for the Rectory.

C. J. Bond, *The Red Book of Worcester*, Vol. 2, Worcs. Hist. Soc., 1937.

M. Aston, *Interpreting the Landscape,* 1985. Re excavations and plans.

T. Mowl, *Historic Gardens of Worcestershiure,* 2006, p. 23-4.

S. Lainsberg, *The Medieval Garden,* British Museum, 1998, pp. 67-8. [plan]

C. Thacker, *The Genius of Gardening,* 1994, p. 35.

A. Brooks & N. Pevsner, *Worcestershire,* 2007 (BoE).

Victoria County History, Vol. 3, 1913 (VCH).

T. R. Nash, *Collections for the History of Worcestershire,* Vol. I, 1781.

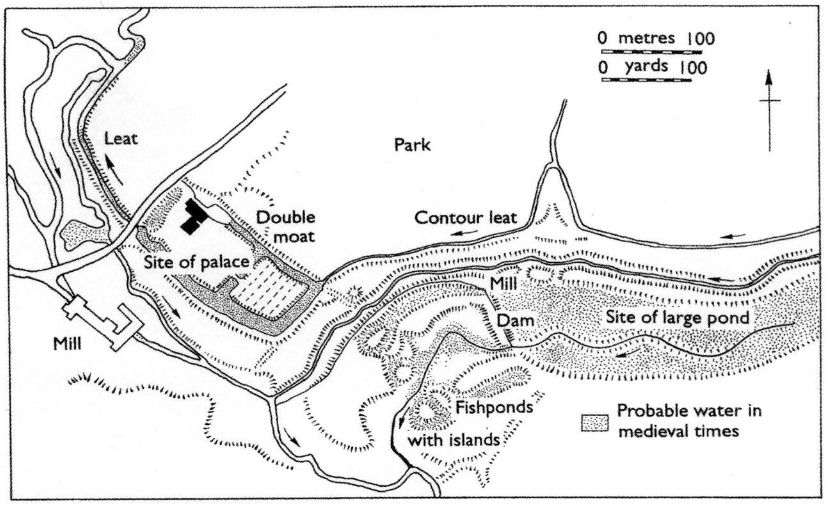

The double-moated palace is perched high on the valley side, and fed by an inlet and outlet channel. A large mill pond once existed, with fishponds at its dam. each with an island. Orchards or kitchen gardens could have been laid out within the moated areas.

S. Lainsberg, *The Medieval Garden,* British Museum, 1998, p.67-8 (plan).

Areley Hall

Parish: Stourport-on-Severn

HER Ref: WSM29039.

Grid Ref: SO 801 707. Postcode: DY13 0AR.

O.S. 6" Map No: 14SW.

Date of Map: 1888, with extent of park & gardens shaded as 1880s OS.

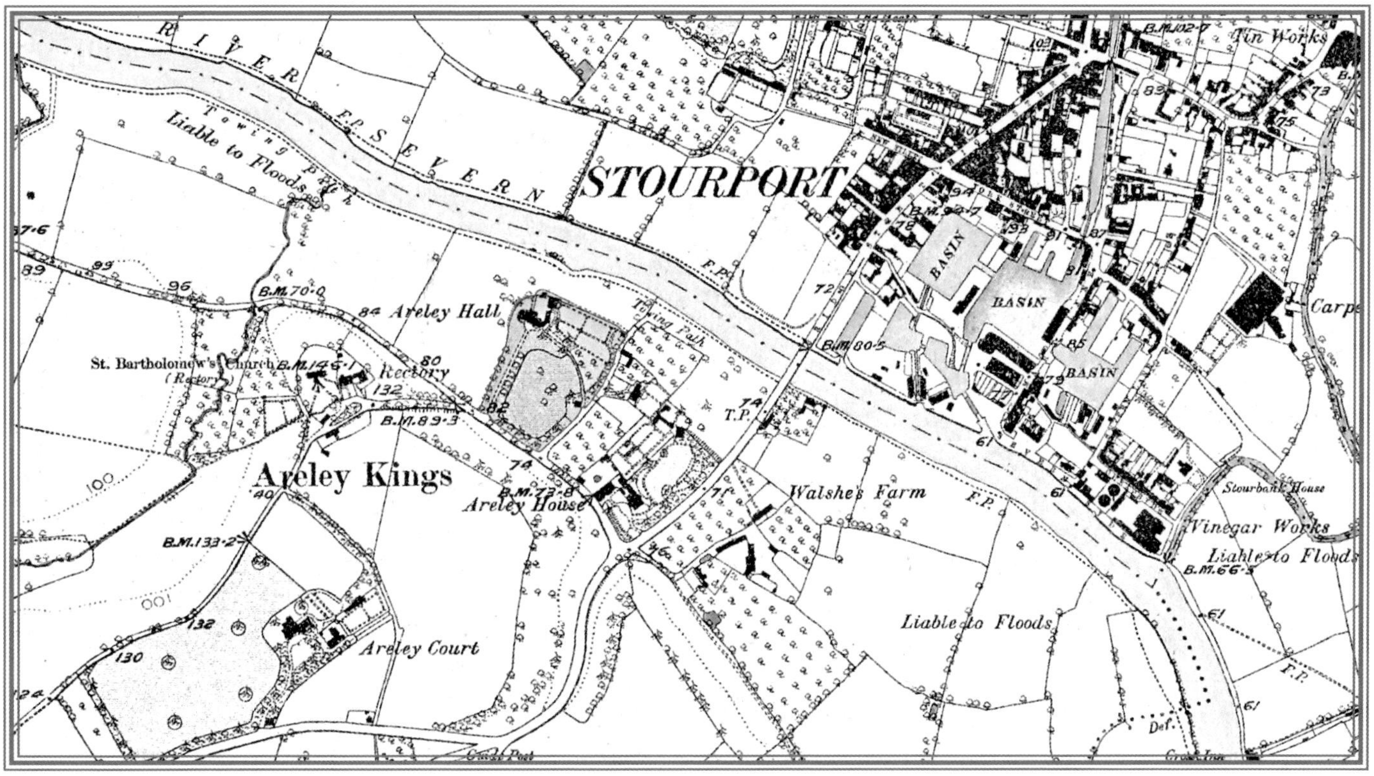

This was the manor house of Areley Kings (VCH, 4, p. 228) "said to be of 1605" (BoE, p. 111). It is listed amongst county seats circa 1800 (*Traveller*) and 1814 (*Beauties*) and in 1837 (*Directory*). Alterations were made to the house in 1828 when the OS 1 inch shows grounds. The 1882 6 inch shows a very small park (smaller than that of the neighbouring Areley Court), grounds, and kitchen garden Areley Hall remains substantially unchanged, although its lodge is now a private residence. The lime avenue still strides across the small park to the front entrance and the riverside gardens are intact.

Victoria County History, Vol. 4, 1924 (VCH).
Beauties of England and Wales, Vol. XV, 1814.
Bentley's *Guide & Directory of Worcester,* 1837.
J. Dugdale, *The New British Traveller,* 1819.

Areley Rectory

Parish: Stourport-on-Severn

HER Ref: WSM12801.
Grid Ref: SO 802 710.
Postcode: DY13 0TB.
O.S. 6" Map No: 14SW.
Date of Map: 1888.

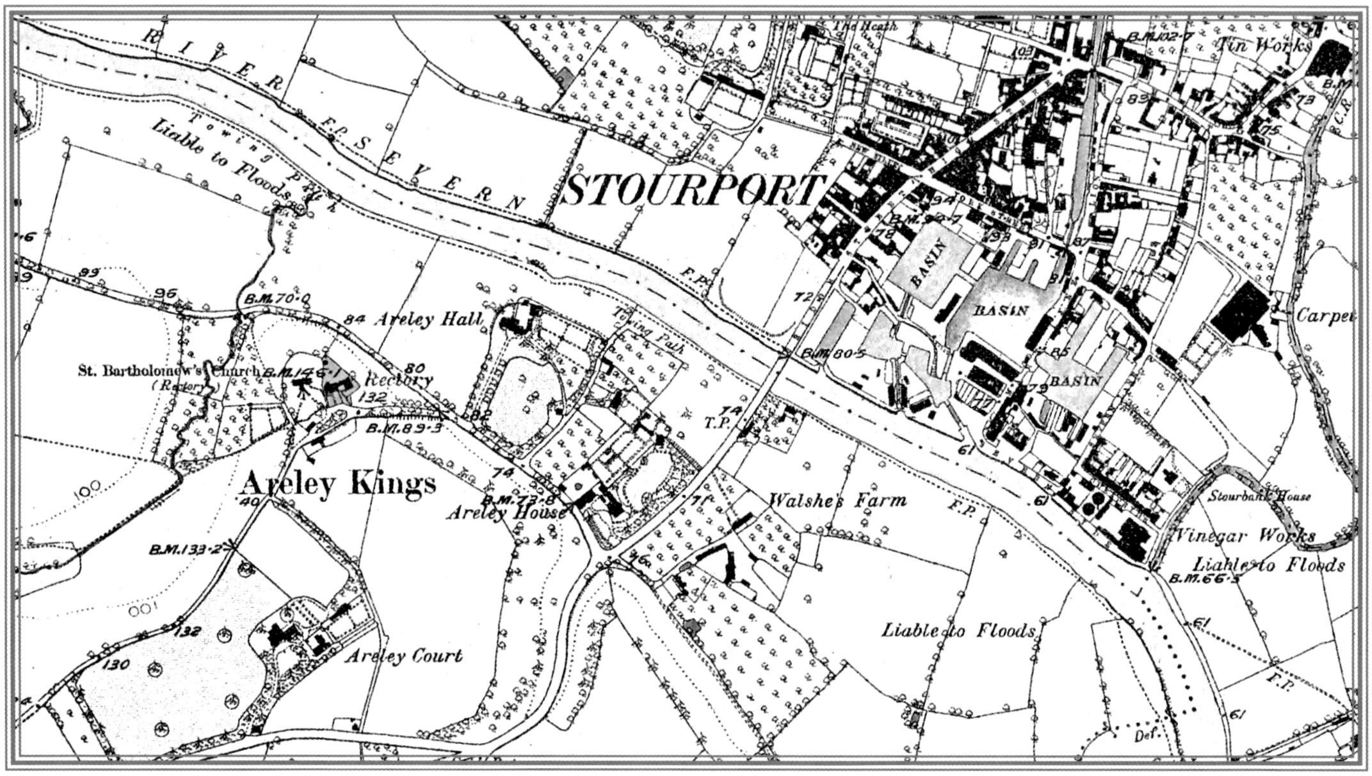

The Rectory, a building of the 17th and 18th centuries, is included here for its two-storied summer-house or gazebo built in 1728 by the Revd. Richard Vernon overlooking the churchyard and the chancel of the church. The garden buildings included a Chinoiserie fence and a concave viewing seat facing Stourport and overlooking the river.
Tree growth now obscures views from the Rectory garden, the gazebo and the seat facing the River Severn, Stourport and the canal basin.

T. Mowl, *Historic Gardens of Worcestershire*, 2006, pp. 81-2, fig. 39.

The Summer-house at Areley Rectory, 2019. Photo, R. Lockett.

Arley House/Castle

Parish: Upper Arley

HER Ref: WSM34849/WSM34850.

Grid Ref: SO 763 806.

Postcode: DY12 1SQ.

O.S. 6" Map No: 7NE.

Date of Map: 1883 with extent of park & gardens shaded as H. E. Register.

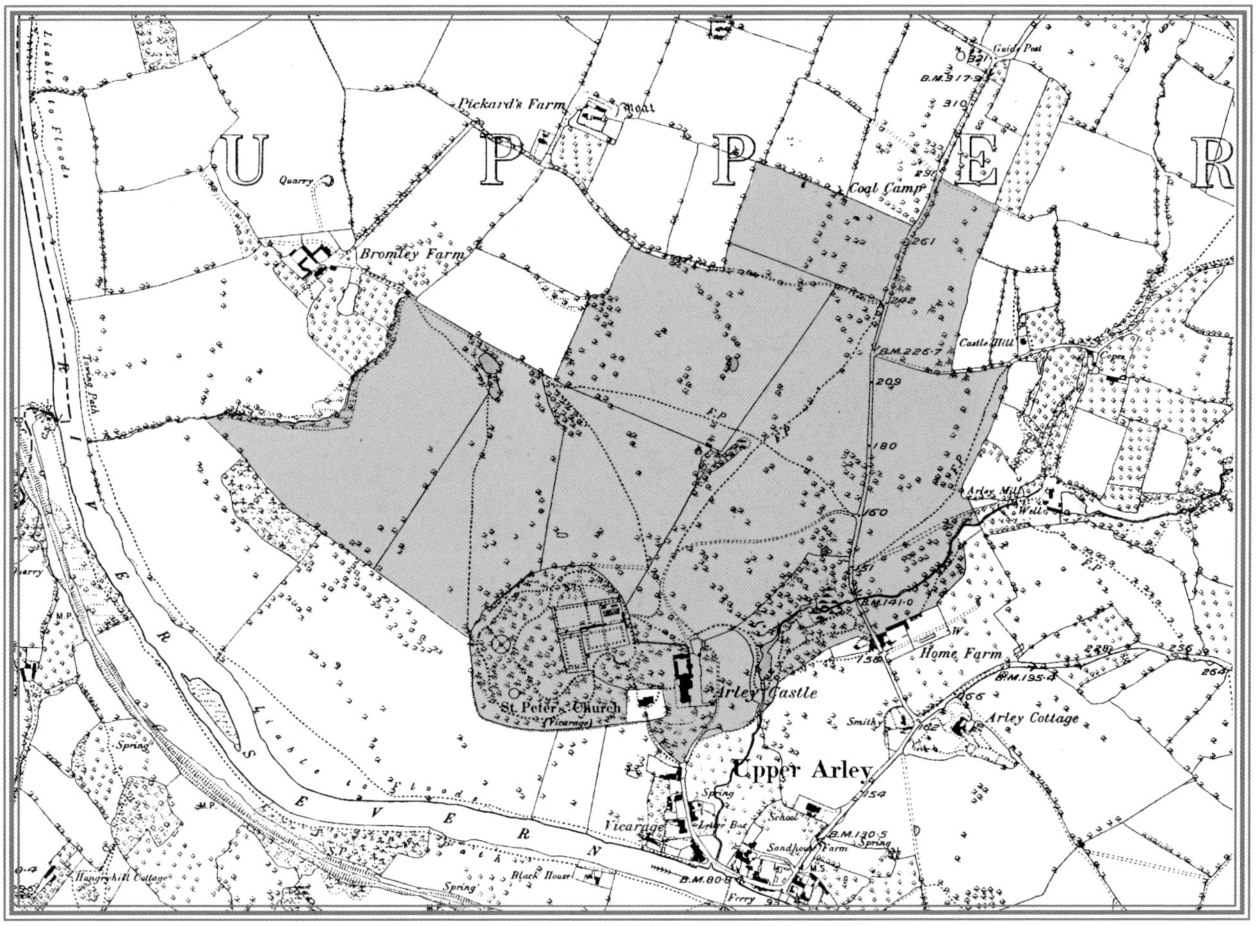

Included within Historic England's Register of Historic Parks and Gardens of special historic interest in England.

The present house, built in 1967-8, replaced the neo-gothic Castle built for the 2nd Earl of Mountnorris (1770-1844) by Richard Varden, a local Worcester architect, in 1843-4; this was demolished in 1962.

The Varden Castle incorporated an Elizabethan house much modified in the earlier-19th century. Greenwood in 1822 referred to a "handsome, modern mansion". Mountnorris inherited Arley in 1783 from his mother whose family, the Lyttletons, had made Arley their principal residence after their house at Frankley was badly damaged in the English Civil War. It seems likely that work was done to Arley after the Stuart Restoration and before the Lyttletons moved to Hagley Hall. An 1824 watercolour painting illustrates a relatively plain south-west elevation and earlier features (mullion windows) and the appearance of part of the pre-1844 mansion. Nash (1781) illustrates the earlier mansion.

The outlines of the park and gardens are shown in the OS 1882/3 6 inch and by Bartholomew (1906).

The fullest extent of the landscape park to the north, north-west and north-east of the Castle is marked on the 1905 OS. The park was enlarged by the 2nd Earl of Mountnorris (1770-1844) to 86 acres.

The appreciation of the landscape park as a picturesque creation now requires some imagination as only the Barbican survives of the central feature with its castellated silhouette and it is the pleasure grounds rather than the Park that now dominate. Interestingly, Lord Mountnorris started to rebuild his mansion 50 years after he began to exploit his considerable knowledge of trees and plants; he had become a Fellow of the Linnean Society and of the

..........continued from previous page

Royal Society in 1796.

Also pre Varden, is an estate map dated 1838 (CRO 2412/7). This shows two distinct areas of managed landscape or grounds, the larger one fenced off from fields (park) and containing the Church, the Hall and the Walled Garden and a second fenced area providing the water element to the landscape park known as Naboth's Vineyard. Both parts of the pleasure grounds have carefully arranged walks or drives and other designed features outside the formal flower and kitchen walled gardens. Mountnorris had begun his redevelopment of Arley by 1801 and made "a variety of considerable plantations". In 1809 he published a 3 volume book on his *Travels* to Africa and India via Abyssinia and the Cape ("the richest field for botany I ever met with")." His four and a half years of travel gave him a taste for exotic and tropical plants and shrubs and these he set about cultivating in the gardens and green houses at Arley" (Goodman, 2003).

The principal area of grounds as described in 1838, is roughly oval in shape with the Walled garden more or less at its centre. A castellated gateway is missing (as shown in a mid-19th century watercolour) which was built after Mountnorris's death in 1844 completing a single, picturesque composition. A third or a quarter of the area of the walled garden is given over to a lawn, perhaps a bowling green. An equivalent area is given over to formal compartments with paths and a rectangular basin of water similar to the Italian garden today. There are extensive hot houses, melon pits etc. Outside the flower and kitchen gardens, serpentine paths go about the wooded grounds and discover two circular groves, one of which has the water feature as fountain on the 1929 OS. The Arboretum, in which the walled garden is situated, amounts to 15 acres.

Naboth's Vineyard (7 acres) has the water: two larger pieces separated by picturesque falls and two bridges. The name of this discrete part of the landscape park refers to the manner in which Mountnorris acquired the site, from a widow who occupied one of village houses; according to the Revd. Mayer, there was also a flour mill. An ice house is sited at one end of this miniature valley. A special feature of the valley was a thatched cottage (i.e. picturesquely rustic) which had an elaborately furnished interior/Elizabethan dining room used for banqueting. The latter was illustrated in *The Mirror* in 1840: "This charming valley is a perfect fairy land and presents as exquisite a specimen of ornamental gardening as ever I met with" (Whitehead). The water at the top end of the valley has some small islands and a stone bridge across to one of them. Walks round the wooded slopes make the most of this relatively small part of the pleasure grounds. The hard landscape included the entrance via a narrow stone passage and under an arch. Although separated from the Castle and the Arboretum by an interval of park, Naboth's Vineyard does in fact house 111 out of the 424 specimen trees listed in the *Hortus Arleyensis* of 1907 so that it was not exempted from Lord Mountnorris's plantings. "The collection of trees complements those of the Arley Arboretum" (Goodman, 2003). The Woodward family have made considerable efforts to reclaim some of the lost features of this early-19th century garden and its restoration is being completed by the R. D. Turner Charitable Trust. Roger Turner acquired the Arley Estate (1600 acres) in 1959 and gave it to the Trust in 1999.

It would be foolish to try to condense Nigel Goodman's comprehensive account of Mountnorris's planting both of exotic plants and of imported specimen trees: "Almost all the trees he planted in the arboretum were rare and non-indigenous." J. C. Loudun in 1838 featured Mountnorris's personal, botanical achievements including "several splendid varieties (of Tree Peony) far excelling those imported from China".

The estate was sold in 1852 together with Mountnorris's various collections of art and his collection of shells which was of national significance. The loss of a considerable botanical library which was housed in the walled gardens next to the Head Gardener's House, must also be regretted. Goodman concentrates on three Robert Woodwards from whose botanical knowledge and enthusiasm Arley profited. The family was consistently assisted by Directors of Kew Gardens beginning with Sir William Hooker, who was a relation and the father of the better-known Sir Joseph Hooker. The Arley Arboretum consisting of 424 specimen trees was catalogued in 1907 – *Hortus Arleyensis* – among them two *sorbus domestica* planted in the early-19th century from seedlings taken from a specimen discovered in the Wyre Forest in 1677 and destroyed by a vagrant in 1862.

Goodman (2007) brings the story up to date by mentioning the post 1959 contributions of Roger Turner to the Walled Garden, turning what was called the Flower Garden into an Italian Garden "planted on 2 sides with pleached lime ... creating a Classical formal garden of great beauty and tranquility". A new inventory of the Arboretum was made in 1991 before it was expanded by an additional 3 acres in 2001.

Plate 21, photograph of Arley Castle
Plate 22, 1838 Estate Map

R. Woodward, *Hortus Arleyensis,* 1907.
Revd. H. R. Mayer, *Annals of Arley*, 1914.
D. Jacques, *Georgian Gardens*, 1983.
D. Whitehead, "A Valley Elysium at Upper Arley", *HWGT Newsletter*, 15, Summer 2000.
N. Goodman, "Arley Arboretum and Naboth's Vineyard", *HWGT, Newsletter*, 33, Summer 2009.
N. Goodman, *The Gardens of Arley*, 2003, 2007.
T. R. Nash, *Collections for the History of Worcestershire,* Vol I, 1781.
HE *Register of Parks & Gardens,* 1997.

Astley Hall

Parish: Astley & Dunley

HER Ref: WSM28804.

Grid Ref: SO 799 678. Postcode: DY13 0RW.

O.S. 6" Map No: 21NW.

Date of Map: 1885, with extent of park & gardens shaded as 1880s OS.

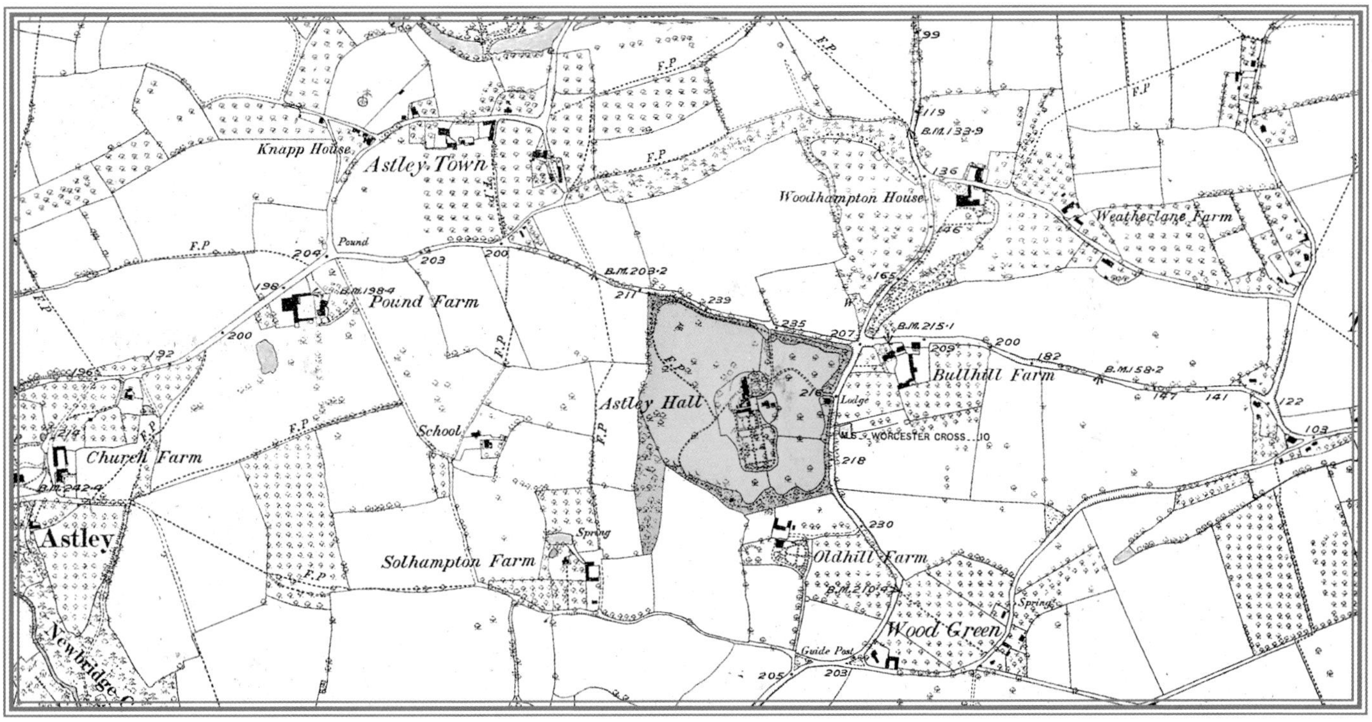

The 1885 OS 6 inch shows a small park, roughly a square with the house in the centre, with lodge, formal garden and kitchen garden. The formal garden was appropriate to a neo "Elizabethan to Jacobean" house (Pevsner, p. 73). Reid (p. 192) illustrates the House of circa 1838 with early-20th century additions made by Stanley, 1st Earl Baldwin, (three times Prime Minister) and some shaped yews in the garden. A sale plan of 1846 shows that there had been no departure from a park of 20 acres with fringe planting with conifers (and a summer house within the south fringe). There was also a croquet lawn, walled garden and Lodge (now extended) circa 1838. A drive made a circuit around the perimeter of the park.

The Hall, now a residential care home, retains park-like grounds with the perimeter woodland belt and many parkland trees, particularly to the north and west. Fragments of the original formal garden survive. The Lodge is now extended and the walled garden, in separate ownership put down to horse paddocks.

Stanley Baldwin at Astley Hall circa 1930.

N. Pevsner, *Worcestershire,* 1968

P. Reid, *Burke's & Savills Guide to Country Houses,* Vol 2, 1980

Astley Rectory

Parish: Astley & Dunley

HER Ref: WSM28806.

Grid Ref: SO 786 675.

Postcode: DY13 0RJ.

O.S. 6" Map No: 21NW.

Date of Map: 1885, with extent of gardens shaded as 1880s OS.

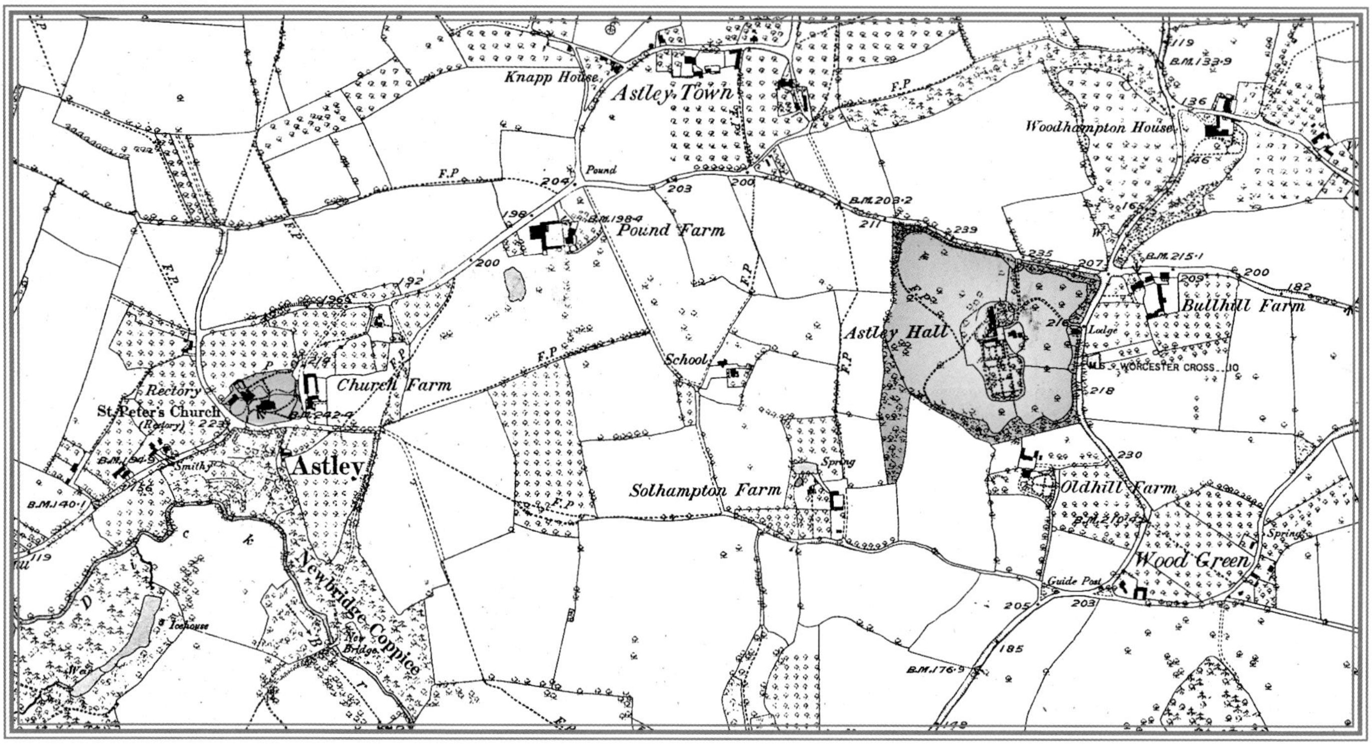

The Revd. W. H. Havergal, father of Frances, another notable hymn writer, was Rector from 1820-1842. He created an arboretum of over 30 acres on the glebe land; cedars, walnuts, weeping beeches, giant redwood and silver fir are singled out by Conley. There is now a wood south of the Rectory and the Church with mature trees including fir which may represent this arboretum. A Scots Pine in the nearby churchyard is said to have been planted in 1863. Surviving brick walls suggest the original walled garden.

S. A. Conley, *Notes on the History of Astley*, 1987.

Avonbank

Parish: Wick

HER Ref: WSM28801.

Grid Ref: SO 957 448. Postcode: WR10 3JP.

O.S. 6" Map No: 41SE.

Date of Map: 1884, with extent of park & gardens shaded as 1905 OS.

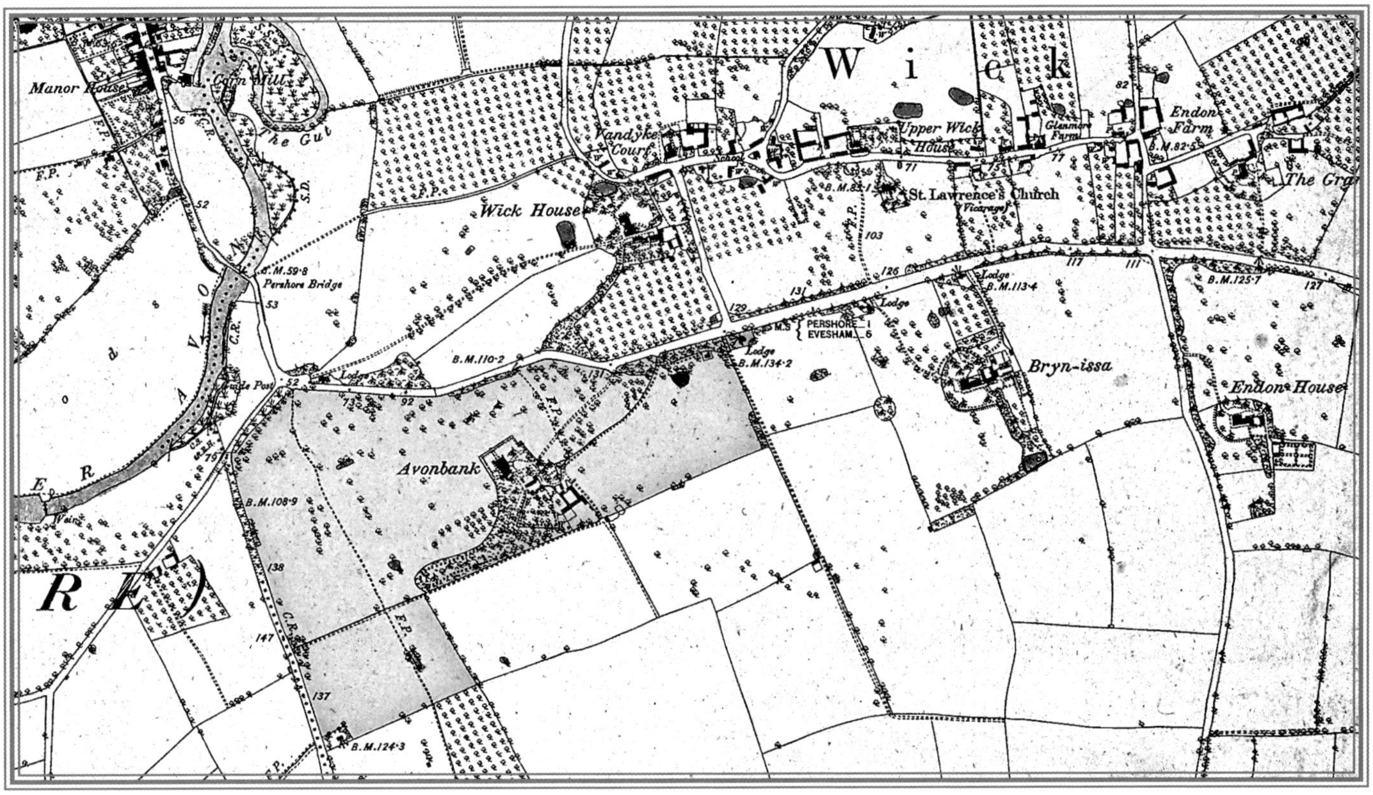

Avonbank, first built in 1805, now the Pershore College of Horticulture, was known in 1822 as Grove House (Greenwood). Its park and grounds were taken out of the park of Wick House at about this time, the land retaining its park etc. on the north side of the Pershore/ Evesham road. A circa 1820 *Map and Survey of the Estate belonging to Thomas Hudson Esq.,* (CRO 5240/14) shows Avon Bank as amounting to 192 acres with a pool in the north-east corner close to the London Road and 5 plantations also along this road. There is a shrubbery and garden south of the house, and land called Paddock north and west of the house is marked as park (House with Paddock = 37 acres). The grounds were developed during the 19th century and continue to develop, e.g. with an arboretum established in the 1950s (Marriott's Bank - Sidwell, p. 79/80). The park is defined on the 1884 OS 6 inch, then directly adjoining the small park of Lower Hill/Bryn Issa on its east side. Endon Hall beside Bryn Issa had a small park on the 1905 OS.

Photo, courtesy of M. Meikle.

R. Sidwell, *West Midlands Gardens,* 1981.
C. & J. Greenwood, *Worcestershire Delineated,* 1822.

Barbers Farm

Parish: Martley

HER Ref: WSM60006.

Grid Ref: SO 760 600. Postcode: WR6 6QA.

O.S. 6" Map No: 27NE/SE.

Date of Map: 1884, with deduced extent of park & gardens shaded (not shaded on 1905 OS).

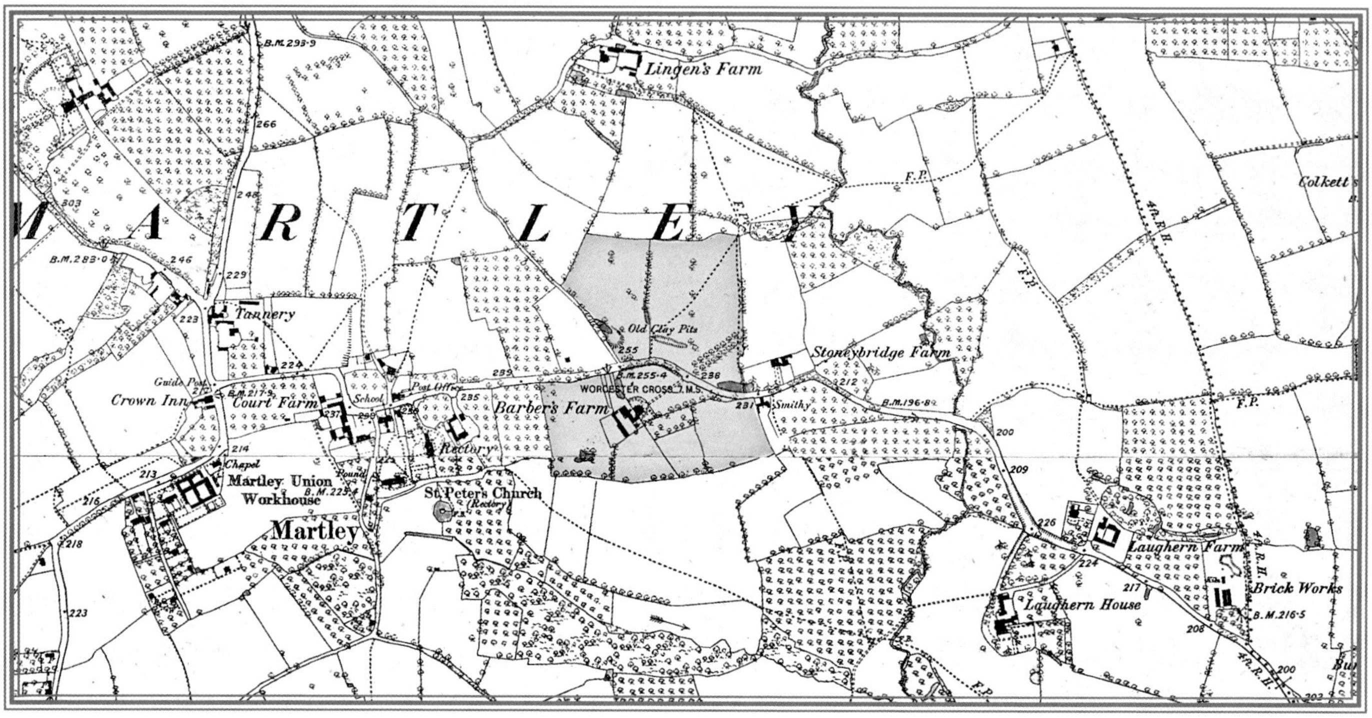

Barbers was the Dower House to the Nash property, the Noak. The house can be found on a 1730 estate map of Cockshoot Farm (WAAS, 6134/44). The original road access with surviving piers is of circa 1800. The gardens today are of the 1930s and 1960s; only one wall of the walled garden is original (circa 1800). The Listed garden pavilion was the gardener's bothy. The thatched stone building by the pool is relatively recent (Richard Webb). There is no trace of the avenue to the northern side of the lane as shown on the 1884 6 inch OS map.

Baughton Hill, The Ridings and The Tower

Parish: Hill Croome

HER Ref: WSM29034/29041/31229.

Grid Ref: SO 892 417, The Ridings: SO 890 418, The Tower.

Postcode: WR8 9DG.

O.S. 6" Map No: 48NW/48SW.

Date of Map: 1888.

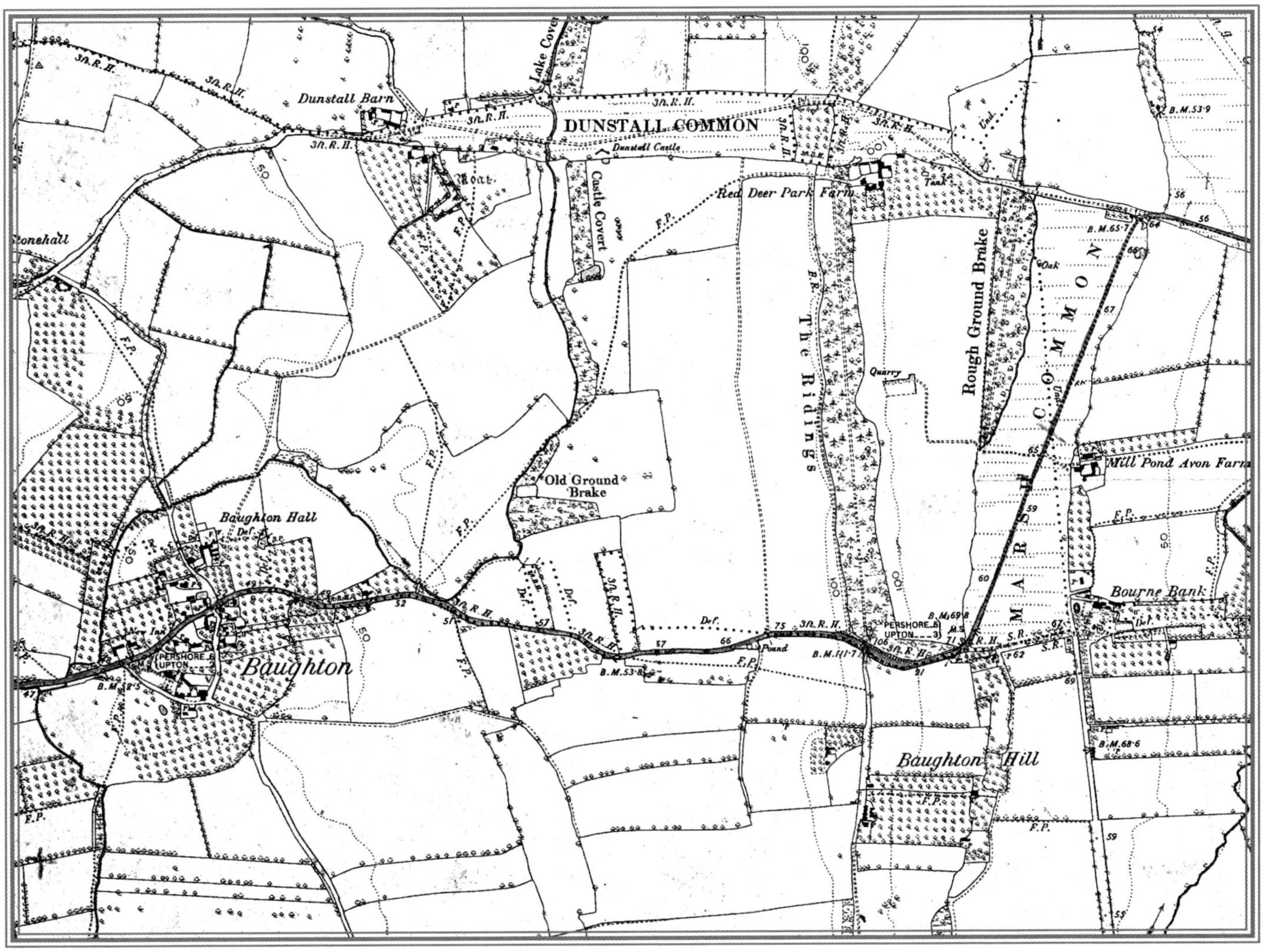

THE RIDINGS

A narrow strip of wood, sometimes delineated as an avenue, is shown on late-18th century maps and later; this links Baughton Hill and Red Deer Farm. This is shown as an avenue for half its length turning into a strip of woodland on the 1905 OS 6 inch. This was within the south section of the Croome Red Deer Park; the 1838 tithe apportionment for Earl's Croome describe the Ridings as a plantation in hand. This narrow plantation is now used as cover for pheasants. The arrow straight walk through the trees emerges to give good views of the Malvern Hills to the west.

THE TOWER

The octagonal Tower (cottage) of circa 1800 (architect unidentified) was no doubt built as an eye-catcher for Croome Court. The window tracery is gothick. The Tower gives spectacular views towards the Malvern Hills. It was set at the south end of the south section of the Croome Red Deer Park but after this section was no longer part of the park. The tower is visible from an approach road and from the M5. There is no historic garden associated with the Tower.

Beaucastle

Parish: Bewdley

HER Ref: WSM28987.
Grid Ref: SO 765 749.
Postcode: DY12 2QS.
O.S. 6" Map No: 13NE.
Date of Map: 1885.

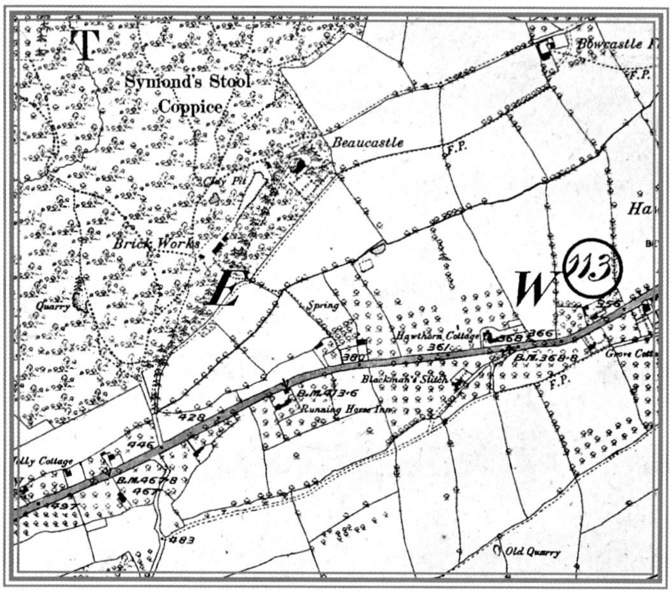

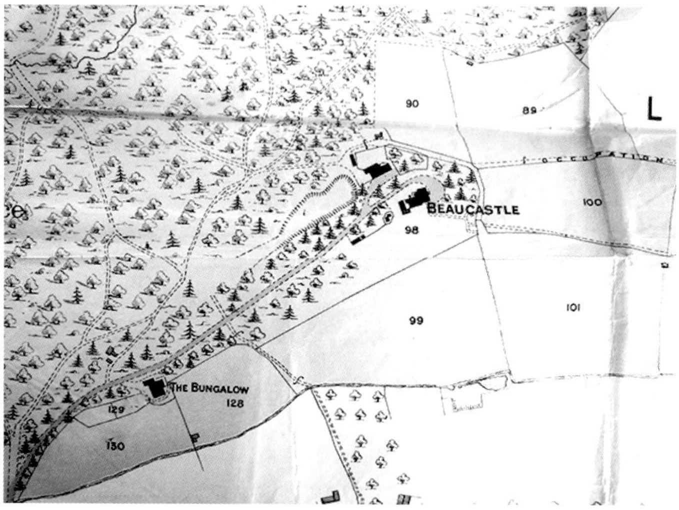

Plan of Beaucastle from sales particulars, 1925. © WAAS 5723.

The gardens of Beaucastle begin with the building of a "Ruskinian" house by William Doubleday for George Baker, "a personal friend and admirer of John Ruskin" in 1877 for a "residential and sporting estate" (Churchill op. cit.). There were earlier claypits and a brick works near the site. The Venetian Gothic style was adopted for a relatively small site surrounded by plantations. The original gardens were small but were developed further as recorded by sales particulars of 1925 (CRO 5723) and 1949 (CRO 5240/5) by which time they included "charmingly planted ornamental gardens (south and east) and a wide gravelled terrace above lawns and beds (east) with a small spinney in the south east corner of the garden". There were rustic archways, a rustic bridge and a rustic pergola and a "picturesque lake" of 1/2 an acre. The gardens have been extended since 1950 to 10 acres (4 ha) and now include a chain of pools (Sidwell, pp. 24-27).
In 2016 the house and immaculate gardens were protected by imposing gates and surrounded by the beech woodland of Wyre Forest.

The towered frontage, sales particulars, 1925. © WAAS 5723.

R. Sidwell, *West Midlands Gardens*, 1981.
Country Life, 26. 8. 2009, P. Churchill, "Ruskin's Venetian Fantasy".

Beckford Hall

Parish: Beckford

HER Ref: WSM28944.
Grid Ref: SO 977 359.
Postcode: GL20 7AD.
O.S. 6" Map No: 56SW.
Date of Map: 1891.

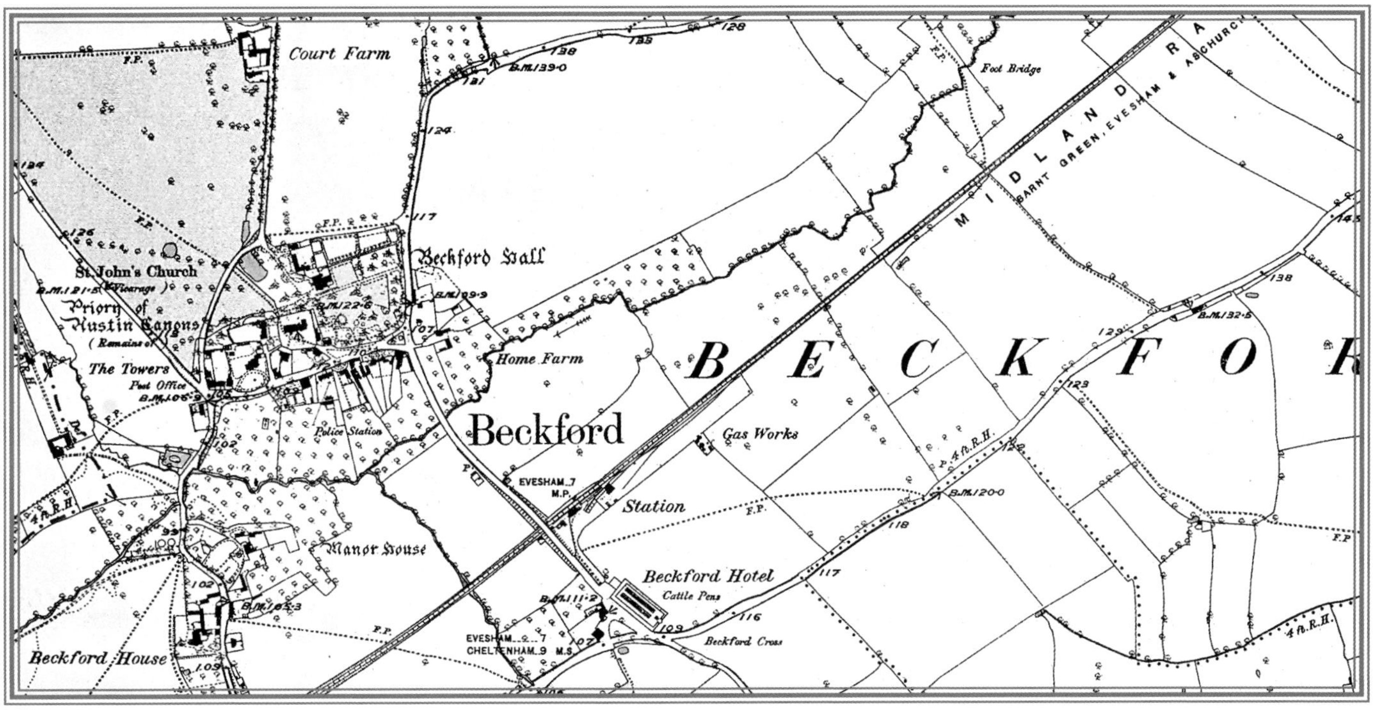

Before the Reformation, the house belonged to Augustinian Canons and parts of the house go back to the 12th century. After the Protestant Reformation the property was owned by the Wakeman family (1586-1836). Their mid-17th century house was added to in 1858 and 1884 (including a Chapel). The Salesian Fathers who came to Beckford in 1936 added a cemetery.
For a view of the garden front see Reid (p. 193). There are gates, piers and walls of the 18th and 19th centuries and an avenue of box trees which are thought to be considerably more ancient. There is an arboretum of mature trees south of the house. Other garden features include a well (restored 1870) with well head, a bothy with tiled floor and a large pond. Since 1976, houses have been built within the walled garden.

P. Reid, *Burke's & Savills Guide to Country Houses*, Vol 2, 1980.

Beckford Hall, 1974. Courtesy of Newsquest.

Bell Hall

Parish: Belbroughton

HER Ref: WSM06613.

Grid Ref: SO 934 770. Postcode: DY9 9UL.

O.S. 6" Map No: 9SE.

Date of Map: 1938, with extent of park & gardens shaded as 1905 OS.

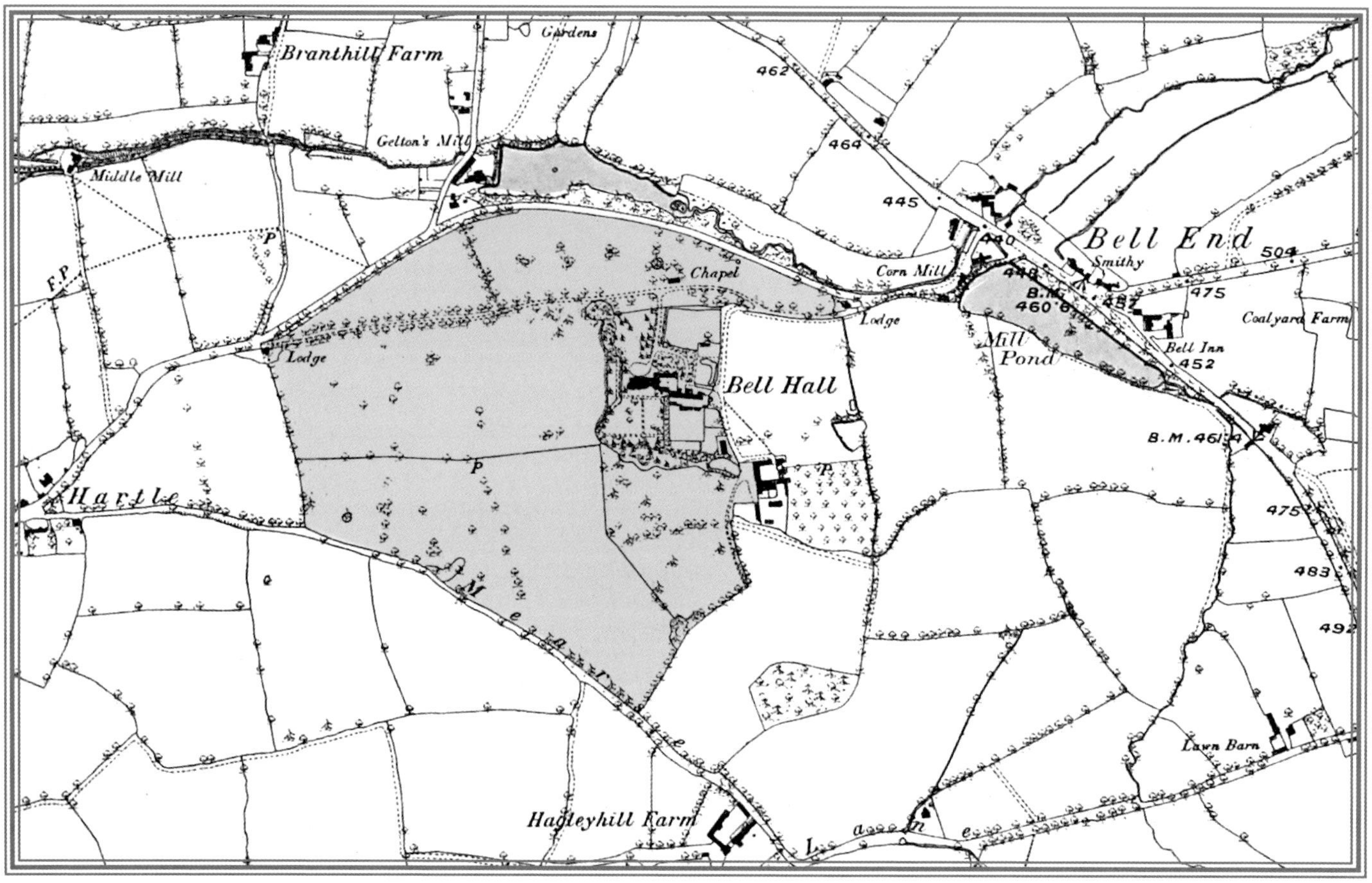

The property is noticed by Greenwood (1822) and Paterson (1829) and some grounds are shown on the 1852 OS one inch. An 1836 plan of the estate (CRO 4423/7) shows the mansion as let with 20 acres out of a total estate of 933 acres. The lawn and pleasure ground in 1836 were only an acre. A 5 acre field called "Coneygree" implies an early warren on the site. Early-20th century photographs show an upper and lower lawn, partly walled and connected with steps. The 1882 OS 6 inch shows the furthest extent of the property with park, 2 lodges, boat house, walled kitchen garden and the 12th century chapel in the garden.

In 2013 the property was still in private ownership with the chapel, parkland and gardens intact and well maintained and still stocked with fine mature trees.

C. & J. Greenwood, *Worcestershire Delineated*, 1822.

Paterson's Roads, 1829.

Bell's Castle

Parish: Kemerton

HER Ref: WSM28989.
Grid Ref: SO 953 383.
Postcode: GL20 7JW.
O.S. 6" Map No:48SE.
Date of Map: 1883.

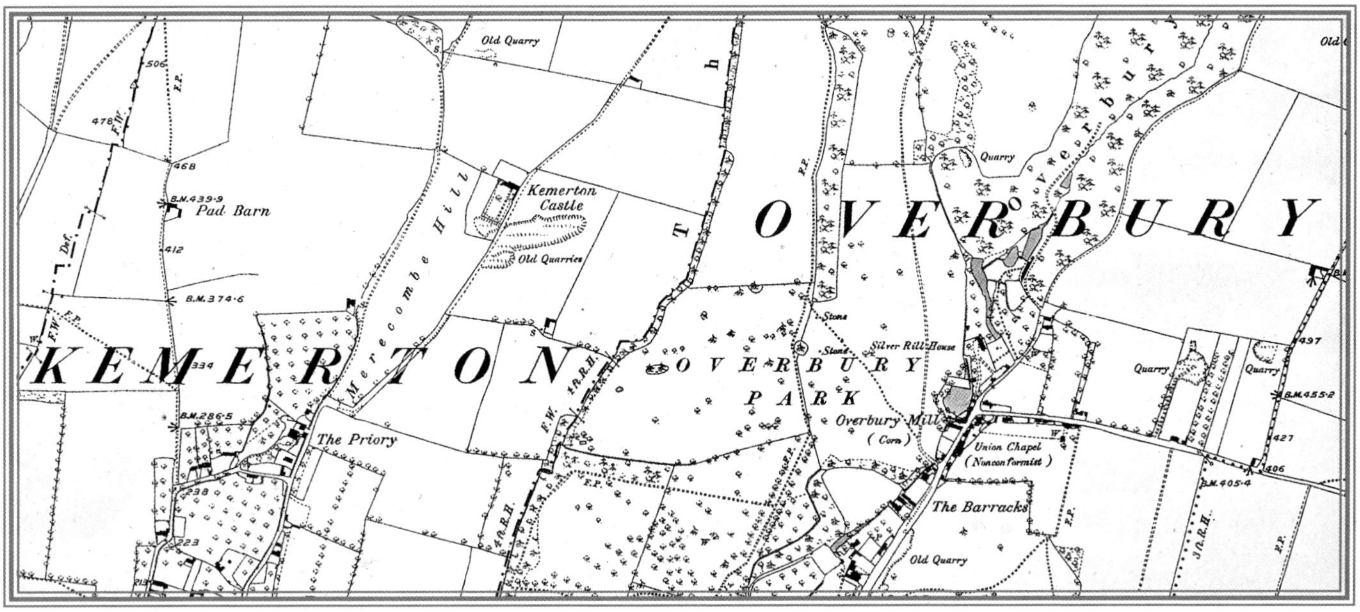

The look-out tower dates from the 17th century and was developed in the neo-gothic style between 1825 and 1838 by Admiral Bell. Ernest Newton extended and altered the Castle in the early 20th century at which time further work was done by Herbert Baker. The garden, within a retaining wall, has 3 terraces with castellated walls descending south down the hill, one containing "a wealth of garden statuary (from Venice) and "a semi-circular Doric Garden House" (Mowl pp. 157-158). The lowest terrace contains a swimming pool. Mowl describes the gardens and their atmosphere in detail. Sidwell described substantial herbaceous gardens in the kitchen garden (Sidwell pp. 27/8).
The property is shown as Kemerton Castle on the 6in. OS map (above).

Bell's Castle, 1910. Postcard image, Antona.

T. Mowl, *Historic Gardens of Worcestershire,* 2006.
R. Sidwell, *West Midlands Gardens,* 1981.

Bentley Manor and Bentley Pauncefoot Park

Parish: Bentley Pauncefoot

HER Ref: WSM03051/28916.

Grid Ref: SO 999 654. Postcode: B97 5TD.

O.S. 6" Map No: 23SW.

Date of Map: 1884, with extent of park & gardens shaded as 1905 OS.

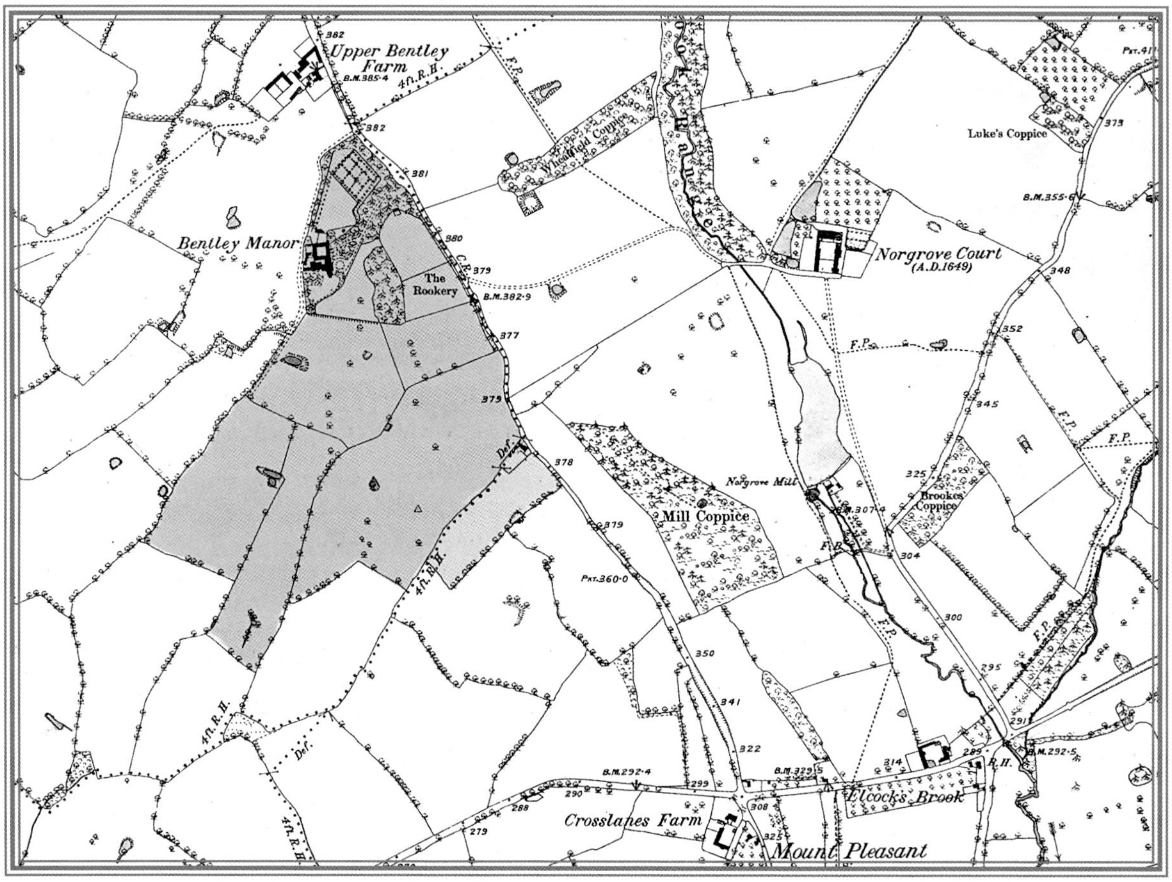

The HER lists a post-medieval park as Bentley Pauncefoot Park and as "The Parks", the name given to most of the area shaded as the park with Bentley Manor on the 1905 OS 6 inch.

Cary, in 1805, marks Bentley as a residence.

By the beginning of the 21st century the house had been demolished and the site of the gardens overgrown. No trace of the park is discernible from the ground but aerial photographs show it as partially intact and degraded with no surviving parkland trees.

Bentley Manor being demolished, May 1950. WAAS, Bentley Pauncefoot/9.

Beoley Hall and Park

Parish: Beoley

HER Ref: WSM 03346/28807/41573. Grid Ref: SP 064 703.

Postcode: B98 9AL. O.S. 6" Map No: 17SW, 23NE, 24NW.

Date of all Maps: 1884, with extent of park & gardens shaded as 1905 OS.

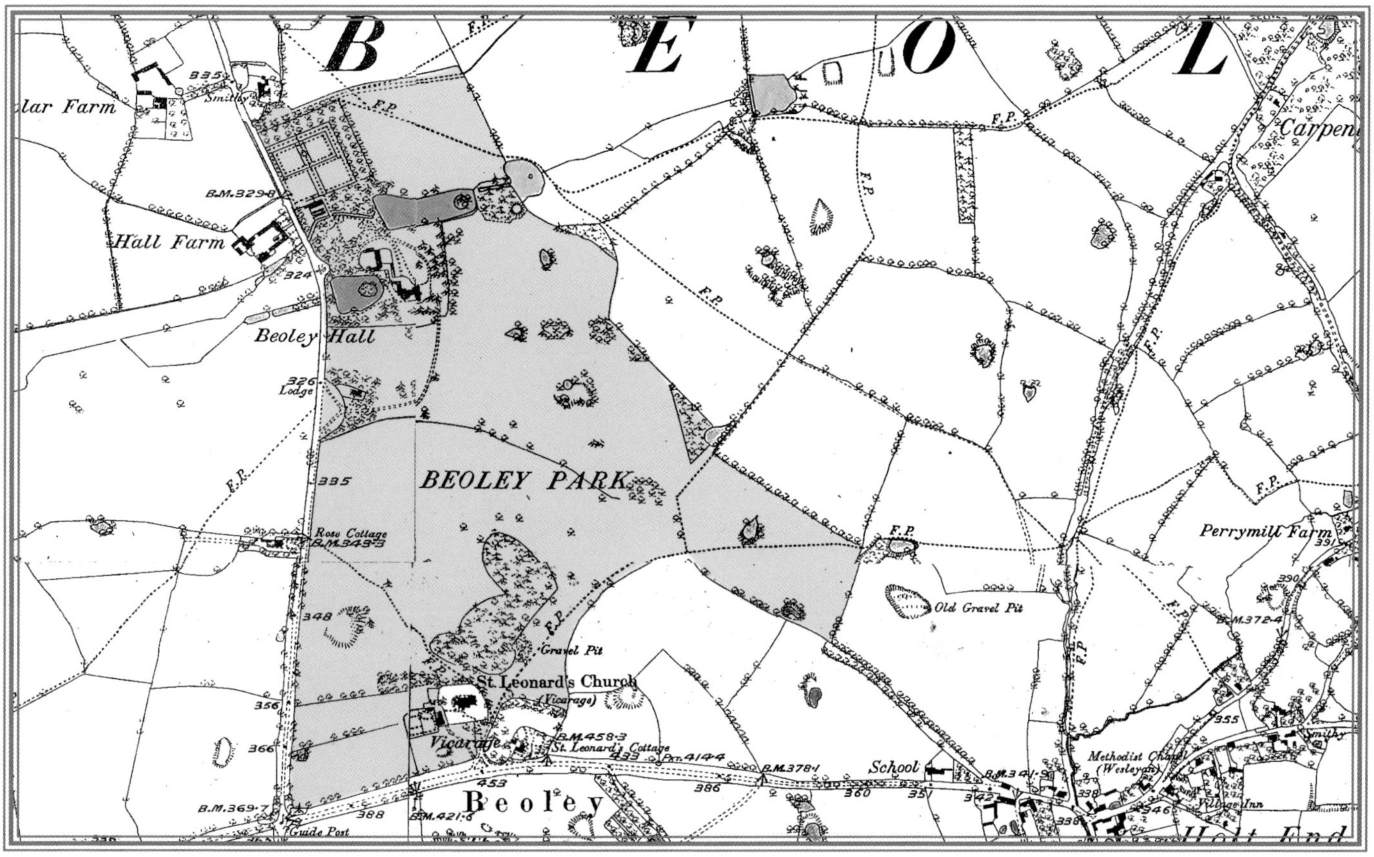

Thomas Habington circa 1600 noted the remains of a castle, perhaps the mount earthwork across the road immediately south of Beoley Church. The deer park originated in the mid-13th century and by the early-14th century there is reference to 2 parks, old and new. Two distinct parks are mentioned again in the mid-17th century as Lodge Park and Red Deer Park. The former is presumably the one dis-parked in 1788, as Red Deer Park was then conveyed with the manor (VCH, 4, 1924, p. 15). A fenced deer park is shown by Saxton in 1577 and by Sheldon's tapestry map of the 1590s (Oxford Bodleian Library). The HER records a holloway and a field name - Great Doe Bank from the circa 1840 tithe award which should be associated with the park. The HER locates this in the area of Hob Hill to the north of Beoley Hall whereas the latter's park lay entirely to the south of the house. A park some distance from Beoley Hall is shown by Cary in 1805. "Bosley Park" as belonging to Lord Foley is shown by John Doharty jun. in 1739 as north-east of Alvechurch Park (CRO 5317).

John Sanders considerably enlarged Beoley Hall in 1791 and this is shown on a map of 1805. Grounds rather than a park are indicated on the 1815 survey for the first OS one inch but the 1840 Tithe map shows a park. The park is shown on the 1905 OS 6 inch. Sales in 1886 and 1895 refer to the finely timbered park, charming pleasure grounds (10 acres), ornamental lake etc. The park trees are described as oak, elm, beech, chestnut. Park and pleasure grounds amounted to 223 acres out of a total for the estate of 1095 acres in 1895 (CRO 4788/4 and 8189/9). By 1919 (CRO 11,697/2) the Park had been reduced to 82 acres. There are several pieces of water, a lodge south of the house and a large walled kitchen garden north of the house shown on an 1886 Sale Plan (CRO 8189/9).

Beoley Hall is situated beside Icknield Street. The Hall is now in multiple ownership with the grounds around the house subdivided and well maintained. Many original features survive. Most of the park is under permanent pasture and woodland with some fine surviving parkland trees.

Victoria County History, 1924, Vol. 4, (VCH).

Besford Court

Parish: Defford cum Besford

HER Ref: WSM29014.

Grid Ref: SO 915 452. Postcode: WR8 9LZ.

O.S. 6" Map No: 41SW.

Date of Map: 1891, with deduced extent of gardens shaded (not shaded on 1905 OS).

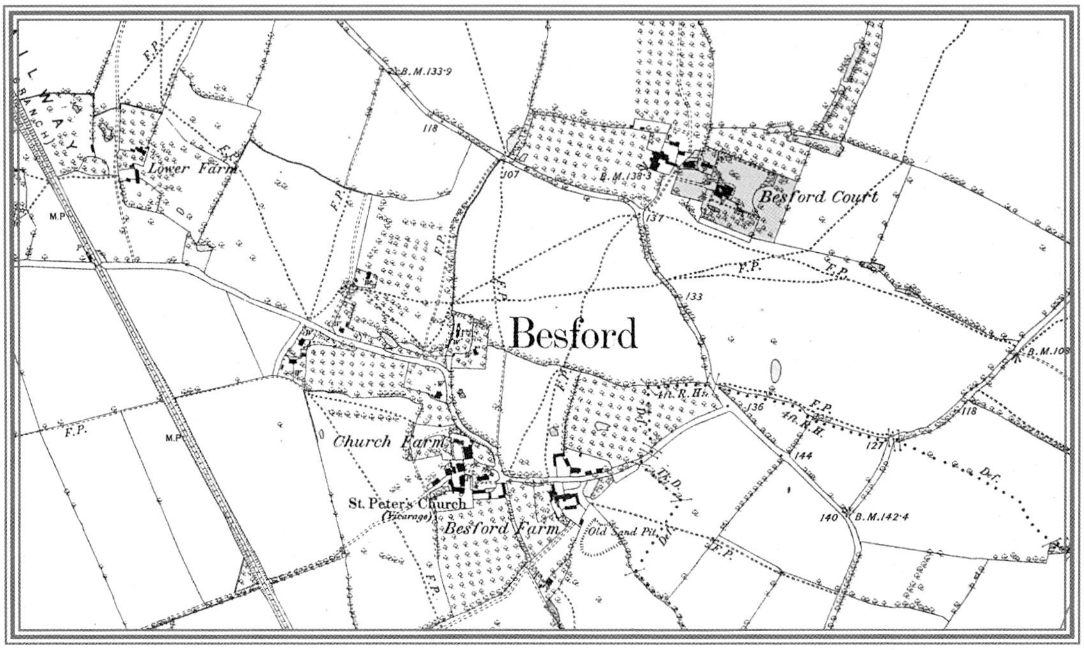

The Listing includes walls and gate piers which have been dated to the 16th and 18th centuries. Nash says that there was a large demesne and park at Besford circa 1300 (Vol. 1, 1781, p. 76) but a medieval park is not otherwise documented.

Isaac Taylor (1772) shows a prominent avenue running north from the Court as do Cary (1805) and the 1811 survey for the first OS one inch but these map conventions may imply plantations/woodland rather than any formal avenue. Niven in 1873 mentions "an avenue of yew which crosses the approach to the house."

Neither the first or second editions of the OS 6 inch give Besford a park and the garden improvements lauded in the 1914 sale particulars, when the gardens with a plantation amounted to 11 acres, must have been very recent: terraces, lawns, flower parterres, tennis courts, ornamental fishponds and superb specimen trees "aid the Horticulturalist to complete the general scheme already commenced" (CRO 5240/6). The house of circa 1600 was remodelled in Tudor style in 1912 and is featured by Aslet. Besford Court was a Special School from 1917 to 1996 and has since been converted to housing with some enabling development in the grounds (BoE, p. 138). Very little besides a large walled garden, partially redeveloped, survives from 20th century development except a rebuilt section of a crinkle-crankle wall presumably inspired by that at Besford Church Farmhouse. Conifers are most prominent in planting close to the main mansion.

C. Aslet, *The Last Country Houses,* 1982.
A. Brooks & N. Pevsner, *Worcestershire,* 2007 (BoE).
T. R. Nash, *Collections for the History of Worcestershire,* Vol I, 1781.
W. Niven, *Illustrations of Old Worcestershire Houses,* 1873.

Besford Court, 1933. WAAS, Besford/1870.

Bevere House

Parish: North Claines

HER Ref: WSM29046.

Grid Ref: SO 840 594. Postcode: WR3 7RG.

James Ross, vignette from T. R. Nash, *Collections for the History of Worcestershire,* Vol.1, 1781.

An earlier house is recorded on John Doharty junior's map of the Dean and Chapter's lands in Claines (**Plate 5**) made in 1751 (CRO 5403/10) (Whitehead, op. cit., fig. 2.). This shows a substantial house with a wide avenue of trees linking it with Bevere Green having a forecourt with a low wall surround with a convex exit towards the avenue. The Revd. Dr. Treadway Nash (1724-1811), who inherited Bevere Manor, acquired Bevere House which he developed between 1766 and 1770, employing Anthony Keck as his architect who also worked for his brother-in-law, John Martin at Ham Court. Keck was also the architect appointed for the new Royal Infirmary in Worcester with which Nash was closely involved. Nash put Bevere House on the title page of Vol. 1 of his *Collections for the History of Worcestershire* (1781) and replaced this with another, the House hiding among trees and behind a large Bevere Elm, on the title page of a later edition (1799).

It is not straightforward to distinguish the respective grounds of Manor and House on maps nor to decide if the landscape as divided between the Manor and the House was redesigned as a unit. It is not documented that Keck designed the landscape with pool and bridge that went with the House and Whitehead has discovered evidence for Nash's own activity, e.g. establishing a kitchen garden/ flower garden to the north of the house and employing a gardener for 15 guineas a year in the 1790s. Nash's principal intervention in 1766 was to create a terrace view over the Severn, a walk going north from the mansion and then curling back south along and above the river bank. This snake-like path is illustrated from a circa 1830 map (Whitehead op. cit., fig. 6). The *Beauties of England and Wales* (1814, p. 163) noting that the house was for sale following Dr. Nash's death, describes "shrubbery, walks and terrace, which are a mile in circuit, a landscape rich in wood, water, and picturesque scenery. Mowl (op. cit., p 84) gives an overview: "Though slight and absorbed within minutes, Bevere [House] is, like Hewell and Kyre, in the great English mainstream of the professional, Brownian, Picturesque ...".

Cooke, circa 1800 refers to the waterworks, a reservoir with a canon on top! Auctioned again in 1834, House, Gardens, Paddocks etc. are given as a little over 3 acres, the Lawn in front of the house (pasture) as 22 acres and the Terrace next the Severn (i.e. a detached area regarded as part of the gardens) 2 acres and Shrubbery, Pools and Plantation listed separately at 3 acres. The extensive Lawn, Beautifully Timbered, belted by a Shrubbery planted with Firs, Holly, and other Forest Trees with a pleasant Carriage Drive through the same to the principal entrance, "A neat Porter's House Lodge at the Entrance Gate from Bevere Green". Also available was a cottage for a Gardener or Farming Assistant (i.e. agricultural labourer). Both the Garden and Paddock or Orchard have walls to the west and north and the garden is furnished with pumps for hard and soft water. The plan with the 1834 auction particulars was by R.T. Jackson, Surveyor.

The extent of the park according to the 1883 OS was defined to the west by the lane separating the grounds of Manor and House running north from Bevere Green and extended north and east of the mansion into a large field with straight boundaries. The 1930 OS shows the park as occupying the same area extending south-east of the fish ponds to Bevere Lane; Bevere Green.is also shaded as park.

G. A. Cooke, *A Topographical and Statistical Description of the Co. of Worcester,* circa 1800.

T. Mowl, *Historic Gardens of Worcestershire,* 2006.

D. Whitehead, "Patron and Architect; the Revd. Treadway Russell Nash, Bevere and the Career of Anthony Keck", *Trans. of Worcestershire Archeological Soc.,* 3rd Series, 24, 2014, p. 225 ff.

Beauties of England and Wales, Vol. XV, 1814.

T. R. Nash, *Collections for the History of Worcestershire,* Vol I, 1781.

Bevere Manor

Parish: North Claines

HER Ref: WSM28877.
Grid Ref: SO 840 594.
Postcode: WR3 7RG.
O.S. 6" Map No: 28SE.
Date of Map: 1886.

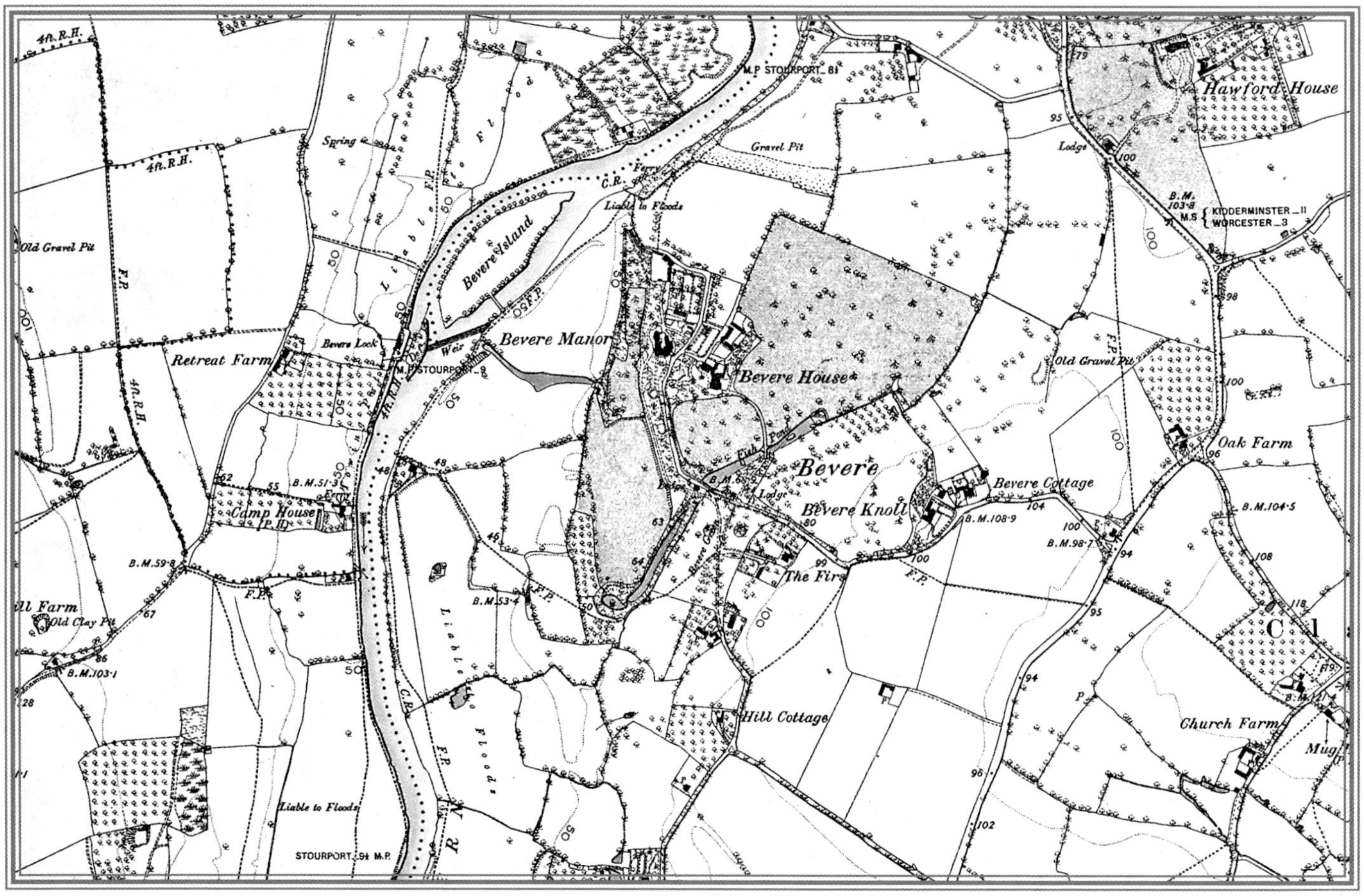

John Doharty junior's 1751 map (CRO 5403/10) shows the Dean and Chapter's lands in Claines as leased separately between Bevere Manor and Bevere House, with the road from Bevere Green running between them and on towards the river bank; Bevere Isle was leased with the Manor House. Doharty's map (**Plate 5**) includes a miniature illustration of the Manor House as an E shaped building without the central bar with an entrance forecourt with oval lawn leading to the lane and the Green. The house had a facade towards the river with a large formal garden laid out on that side with beds of asymmetric pattern. The other landscape feature is a line of trees running north towards the river which becomes a fenced road or drive with a line of trees on its east side and a plantation along the river bank on the west. This drive linked the house with lands, also let with the Manor, which extended to the Salwarpe.

A 1798 map of a Farm of 64 acres let to William Bromley included a park area of 11 acres with the Manor then called Bevere Hill, the name given to a large, 10 acre field south-east of the manor house on an early-19th century map by James Webb (CRO 385/80). The latter gives 1a. (acre) 1p. (perch) to the Garden and 1a. 5p. to the house and its other buildings and meadow names (except for Bevere Hill) to the adjoining fields.

Plans of 1840 (CRO 438/13) show that the property attached to the Manor House had become restricted to land to the west and south. A walled kitchen garden adjoins the house on the north side with small pleasure grounds (10 acres) immediately round the house and spreading south in a narrow strip to the lodge and then in a strip along the west side of the Green with two pools. This linear pleasure ground was connected by a drive. These arrangements survived in sales particulars of 1896 and 1937 (**Plate 12**), (CRO 5240/5 & 6).

Bewdley Park

Parish: Bewdley

HER Ref: WSM28986. Grid Ref: SO 766 737.
Postcode: DY12 2UD. O.S. 6" Map No: 13NE, 14NW.
Date of Map: 1885, 1883, with shaded extent of park deduced from text.

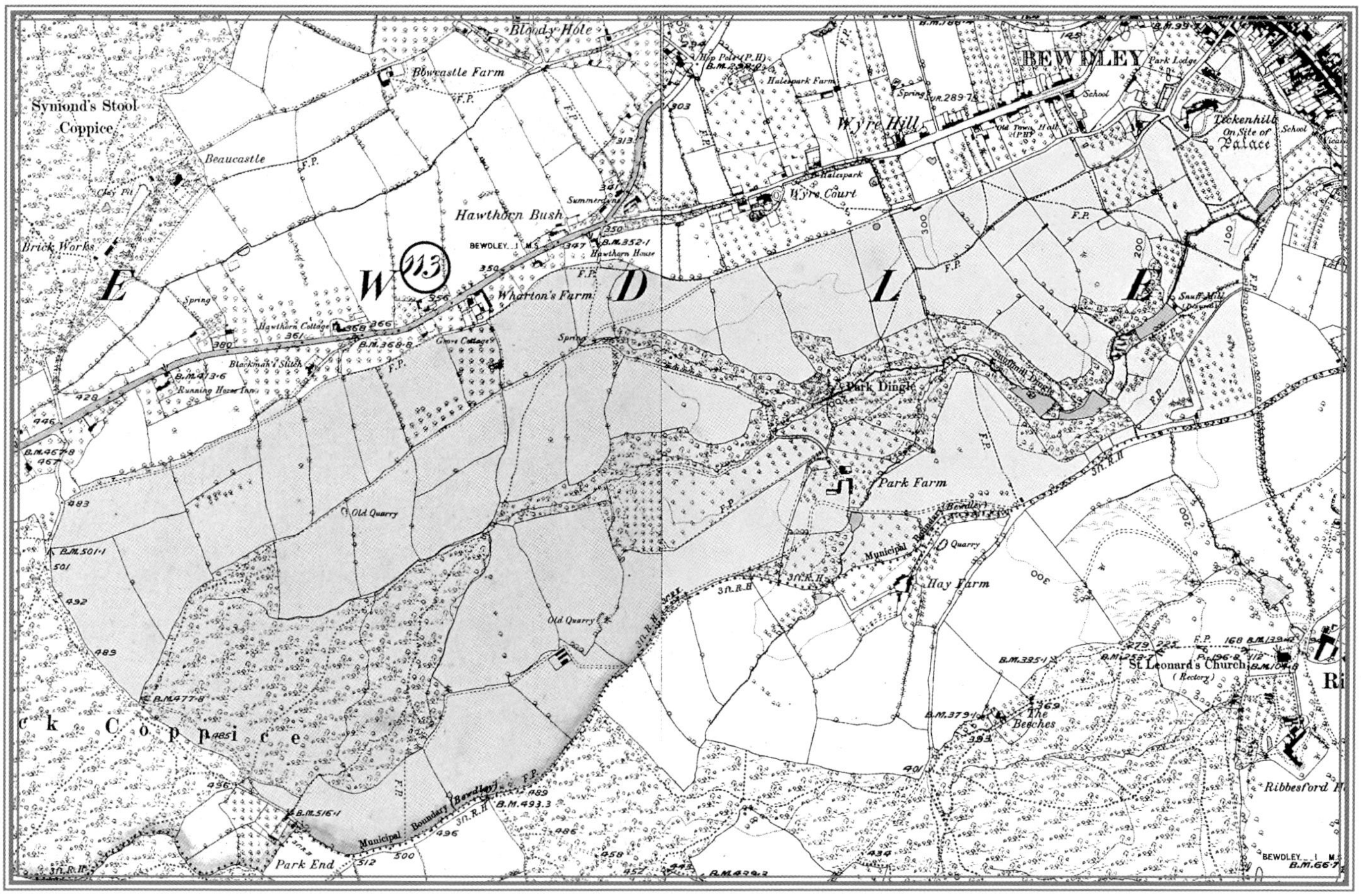

A park at Bewdley is first documented in 1301 as belonging to the Mortimers and there is reference to "one park" and "a certain park" 3 years later. In 1336 there are references to "a capital messuage situated in the park" and "a great park containing 600 acres of great oaks". The VCH interpreted some of these references as indicating 2 parks, one at Bewdley and the other at Tickenhill and therefore the first edition of the *Survey* suggested that a larger park belonged to Bewdley and the smaller to Tickenhill. A "Chase of Wyre" (Forest)" is documented in 1381 out of which any deer park would have been taken. Following recent research by Dr. Stuart Davies (Correspondence, 2017), only one park at Tickenhill is proposed in this edition of the *Survey* and after 1424 only one park is in fact documented. Christopher Saxton's 1577 map has "Tychnell" in the centre of a conventional, fenced deer park alongside BEWDELEY between park and river. This location and identification (with a variety of spellings) is repeated on later printed maps dependent on Saxton, such as John Speed (1610), Jan Janson (1624), Richard Blome (1673) and Emanuel Bowen (1773).

A survey in 1612 estimated the park at 600 acres, half of which was heath land; there were 3,500 old trees and 100 deer. In 1623 the walls and pales were said to be in ruins and there were no deer (Lea, op. cit.). The park was leased with the manor from the early-17th century until it was sold off in lots in 1872 (VCH, pp. 311-312) but the 1885 OS map still shades the park as an identifiable whole. "After the granting of a charter to the town in 1472, the manor is generally called 'Bewdley' and the park 'Bewdley Park' (Davies, Correspondence, 2017). Davies has described the competing interest of the Crown as landlord, the lessees of the manor and park and the citizens of Bewdley Town for all of whom the park was an economic resource. The history of the park is otherwise discussed here under Tickenhill Park and Palace.

Revd. E. Lea, "Notes on the History of the Wyre Forest", *Worcestershire Naturalists Club*, 1923.

Victoria County History, 1924, Vol. 4, (VCH).

S. Davies, *"There having beene then a greate wynde"*: trees, deer and conflict in Bewdley Park in the 17th century. (unpublished, 2017).

The Birches

Parish: Hagley

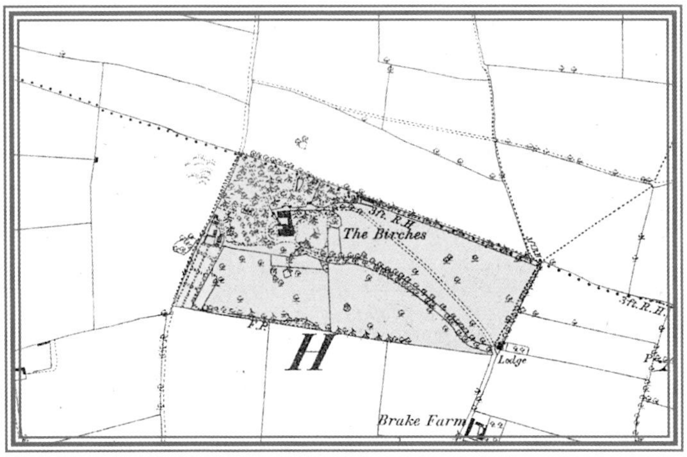

HER Ref: WSM28862.

Grid Ref: SO 896 810.

Postcode: DY8 2XN.

O.S. 6" Map No. 9NW.

Date of Map: 1887, with extent of park & gardens shaded as 1880s OS.

BoE p. 340: "A large villa of circa 1839" is shown with a Park and a Lodge on the OS map in 1887. In 2014 the property was still in private ownership. Part of the park was under arable cultivation and the remainder planted up to extend the garden.

A. Brooks & N. Pevsner, *Worcestershire,* 2007 (BoE).

Birlingham (Old) Rectory

Parish: Birlingham

HER Ref: WSM03639.

Grid Ref: SO 932 431.

Postcode: WR10 3AB.

O.S. 25" Map No. 48-3.

Date of Map: 1904, with extent of gardens shaded, (info. from J. Comins).

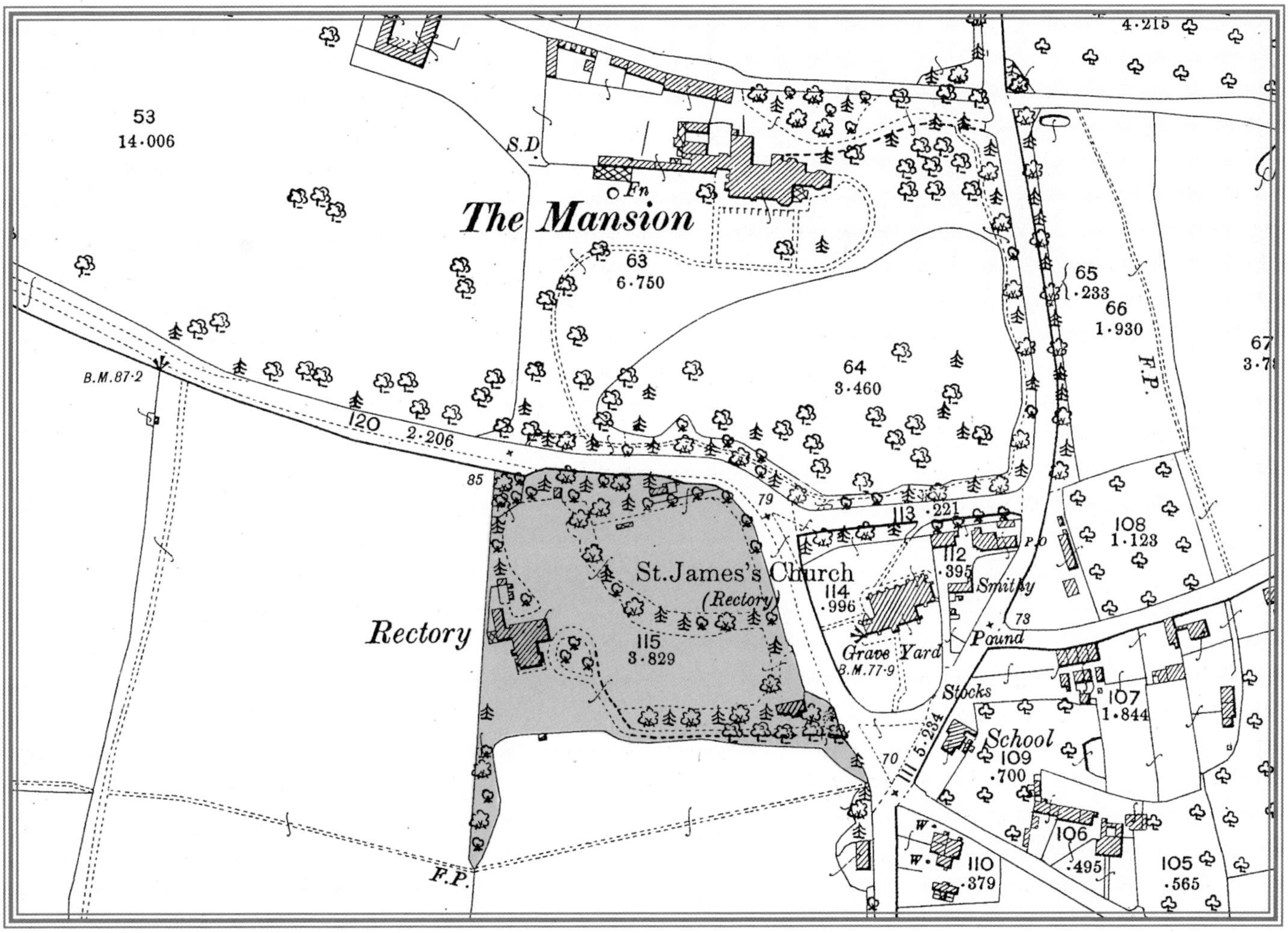

The house of 1774 was enlarged post 1829 by the Revd. R. E. Landor, brother of the poet Walter Savage Landor. The Rectory had already been noticed by Paterson in 1829 as occupied by the Revd. A. Lucas. Landor redeveloped the small grounds with a chapel (1830s) and a freestanding sandstone column with barley stick spirals. He also developed 4 acres of kitchen garden with green houses looked after by two gardeners. Landor's later developments included stone basins one of which was topped by a Repton basket. The Rectory was approached by an avenue of lime trees underplanted with cyclamen and aconites. A nut walk led down to a small pool overlooked by a gazebo. W. S. Landor describing his brother's life style in 1841 alluded to the garden:

"He has neither horse nor servants of the male sex, except a couple of gardeners - one for his melons etc. ... to keep in perfect order about 4 acres of lawn before the house." (John Comins). Landor died in 1870 to be succeeded by his niece's husband and the church was rebuilt by Benjamin Ferrey with funds he bequeathed. The lime avenue was felled in the 1970s but "Over the last thirty years over 50 specimen trees have been planted and the garden extended to the south." (Patton, p. 15).

T. Mowl, *Historic Gardens of Worcestershire*, 2006, p. 107.

J. Patton, "AGM at Birlingham", *HWGT, Newsletter*, 33, Summer 2009.

Birtsmorton Court

Parish: Berrow

HER Ref: WSM07609.

Grid Ref: SO 801 355. Postcode: WR13 6JS.

O.S. 6" Map No: 54NW/SW.

Date of Map: 1884, with deduced extent of park & gardens shaded (not shaded on 1905 OS).

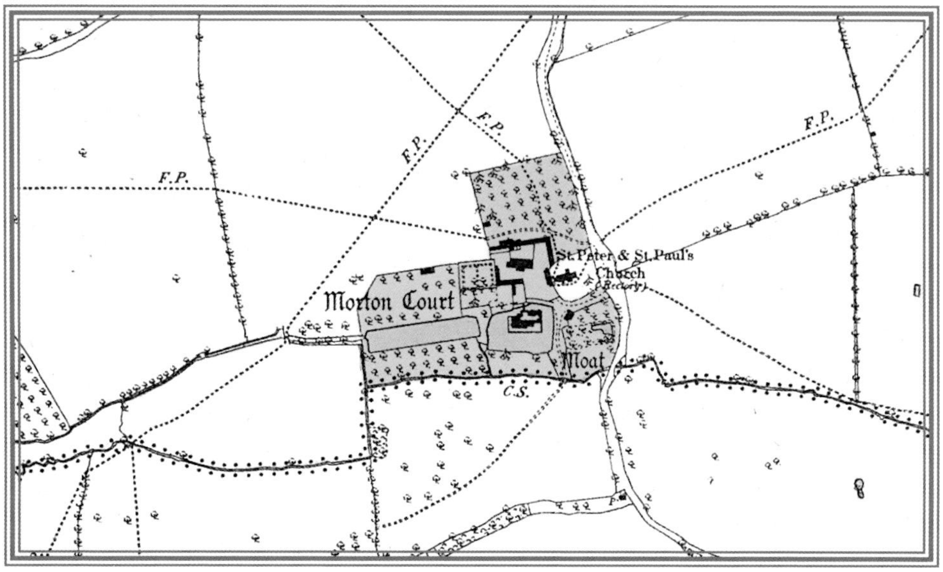

The present house dates back to the 13th century with significant contributions from the 15th, 16th and 20th centuries. Nash (1781) notices Birtsmorton when owned by the Earl of Bellamont as "very antient, moated round". The moated manor house no doubt had a garden but nothing perhaps older than the 19th century exists today. The Westminster Pool (rectangular) is associated by legend with the Abbey and the ancient yew similarly with Cardinal Wolsey. Sidwell (pp. 30-31) says of the topiary garden that it "has the ring of the 19th century." The *VCH* in 1902 mentions Birtsmorton as the residence of Joseph Padfield.

Mowl (p. 167) features the contribution of the present owners and their garden designers: "that image of whimsical poetry which Veronica Adams and Mike Roberts have devised." In 1975 "the walled garden was completely empty, apart from the yew hedges and topiary put in some 200 years ago … at the heart of the walled garden (is) the white garden … planned to celebrate the Millenium designed by Veronica Cross" (*Country Life*).

Plate 20, fountain in garden

V. Bourne, *Country Life,* 16. 6. 2012.
Victoria County History, Vol. 2, 1902.
T. Mowl, *Historic Gardens of Worcestershire,* 2006, p. 167.
R. Sidwell, *West Midlands Gardens,* 1986.
T. R. Nash, *Collections for the History of Worcestershire,* Vol I, 1781.

Postcard image circa 1900. Tilley & Son, Ledbury.

The same view 100 years later. Photo, R. Lockett.

Blackmore Park

Parish: Hanley Castle

HER Ref: WSM05773. Grid Ref: SO 799 434.
Postcode: WR8 0EF. O.S. 6" Map No: 47NW, 40SW.
Date of Maps: both 1885, with extent of park & gardens shaded as 1905 OS.

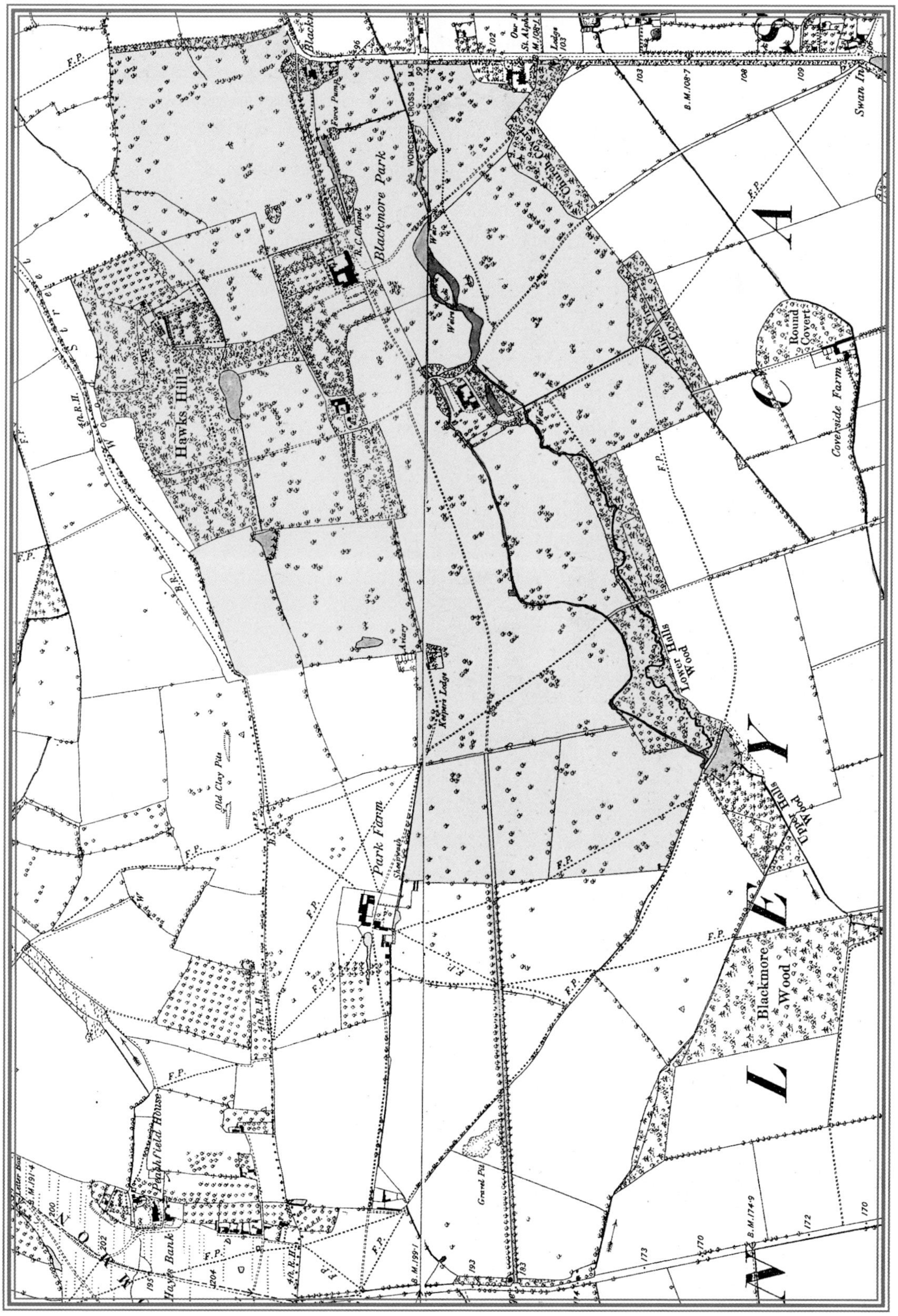

..........continued from previous page

A house with a park of 40 acres existed at Blackmore in 1280 (Smith op. cit.) and a deer park had definitely been established out of Malvern Chase, the Royal Forest, by circa 1345. This was granted in the time of Henry VIII to John Hornyold but was further granted to Lord Clinton in 1545 (VCH). It was purchased from Nicholas Bacon for £1150 in 1548 when the house was rebuilt (Smith) and by the end of the 16th century the Park had grown to 300 acres. After the disafforestation of Malvern Chase in 1632, Blackmore Park grew further to 700 acres (1638). Blackmore proved a good source of timber planking for the rebuilding of the Navy by Samuel Pepys and the Naval Commissioners for the Dutch Wars. The deer park is shown on Saxton (1577) and the Sheldon tapestry (1590s; Oxford Bodleian Library) and on maps down to and including E. & T. Bowen in 1778. The Blackmore Estate continued to grow in the 18th century and particularly under the enclosure act of 1797.

More information about the Park timber is remembered by present members of the Hornyold family who developed the park from the mid-16th century until a sale of most of the estate, including 3,000 acres of parkland in 1919. "Blackmore Park was disparked after the Battle of Worcester (1651), £5,000 of timber being cut down. Then in the 1820s, Thomas Charles Hornyold (1790-1859) cut down £14,000 worth of timber. His great nephew Charles Gandolfi-Hornyold started replanting the park in 1867; he planted mostly limes, horse chestnuts, elms and sycamores. When his son sold the property in 1919 and 1925, trees were felled again" (Anthony Hornyold). The house was demolished in 1925. A hospital was sited within the north-east corner of the park during the 2nd World War.

The 1930 OS 6 inch shows the park as then surviving around the mansion site with the exception of the north-west quartile and the layout of gardens and rides into plantations to the north around Blackmore House.

Little or nothing is known of the house acquired by John Hornyold in the mid-16th century and redeveloped by him although the "modern and elegant structure" noticed by the Revd. Barrett in 1796 contained priest holes. Blackmore Park as a mansion is marked on Isaac Taylor's map of 1772 and was a significant residence in Tunnicliff's *New Map of Worcestershire*, 1788. Nash (Vol. 1, 1781, f. p. 559) illustrates the mansion with a garden behind a low wall with a trellis gate leading into a park with some avenue planting. A watercolour view of the House and its immediate surroundings in the 1840s is illus. by Hodgetts. By the early-19th century, its formal gardens were out of fashion being "laid down by square and rule" (*Beauties*, 1814, p. 331).

The Revd. J. Barrett's *Description of Malvern*, 1796 reviews: "a modern and elegant finished structure ... prospects not very extensive ... adjacent grounds ... large quantity of fine elm, planted uniformly in rows ... does not afford that picturesque appearance as groups of trees detached at various distances. In the neighbourhood are several large pieces of water." Several avenues are marked on the 1812 survey for the first OS one inch. A park is shown on Greenwood's 1822 county map. Hurle (op. cit.) illustrates Taylor and Greenwood side by side.

Charles Gandolfi-Hornyold (1846-1906), recorded surviving parts of the garden belonging to the mansion built in 1861 which, after a fire in 1880, was replaced by the same architect, David Brandon in 1881-3. "In front of the house was a small lawn in which stood the cedar and cork oak etc. The shrubbery wood touched the east side, and the yew trees were alone spared when it was done away with, as it hid the view from the deer park. The old flower garden which is little changed joined the said shrubbery and was bounded south by a sunk fence in which there were a number of large snakes – I have killed many there." Anthony Hornyold confirms that the cork oak and yews remain together with one wall of the Kitchen Garden.

The family has discovered that "The flower garden in front of the house was designed by Mr. Alexander Roos, a Dutch architect. The rest of the garden was set out by Mrs Hornyold (née Charlotte Langdale) after many alterations." Roos (1776-1836) is known principally as an architect rather than a landscape designer and made a Pompeian Room at Hadzor Hall for J. H. Galton sometime after he came to England in 1835. He designed a parterre garden for Brockhampton Park, Bromyard in 1865 and he designed the Cathays Park development for the Butes in Cardiff (Caroline Hornyold).

The grounds are described and illustrated with photographs in the 1919 Sale particulars (CRO 5240/2a), e.g. the sunk, formal garden and terrace walk, two rustic summer houses with urns and geometric beds and a fountain surviving partially today. Modern development now impinges on the park area but the walled garden and parts of the formal flower garden still survive.

Michael Hodgetts, *Blackmore Park: 1596-1846-1996,* 1996.
Pamela Hurle, *Hanley Castle, the Heart of Malvern Chase,* 1978.
Hornyold, *Family Papers.*
Victoria County History, Vol. 4, 1924.
Beauties of England and Wales, Vol. XV, 1814.
B. S. Smith, *A History of Malvern,* 1964.
T. R. Nash, *Collections for the History of Worcestershire,* Vol I, 1781.
F. & M. Collins, *Blackmore Park in World War Two,* 2008.

Blakeshall Hall

Parish: Wolverley and Cookley

HER Ref: WSM28808.

Grid Ref: SO 829 814. Postcode: DY11 5XP.

O.S. 6" Map No: 8NE.

Date of Map: 1882, with extent of park & gardens shaded as 1905 OS.

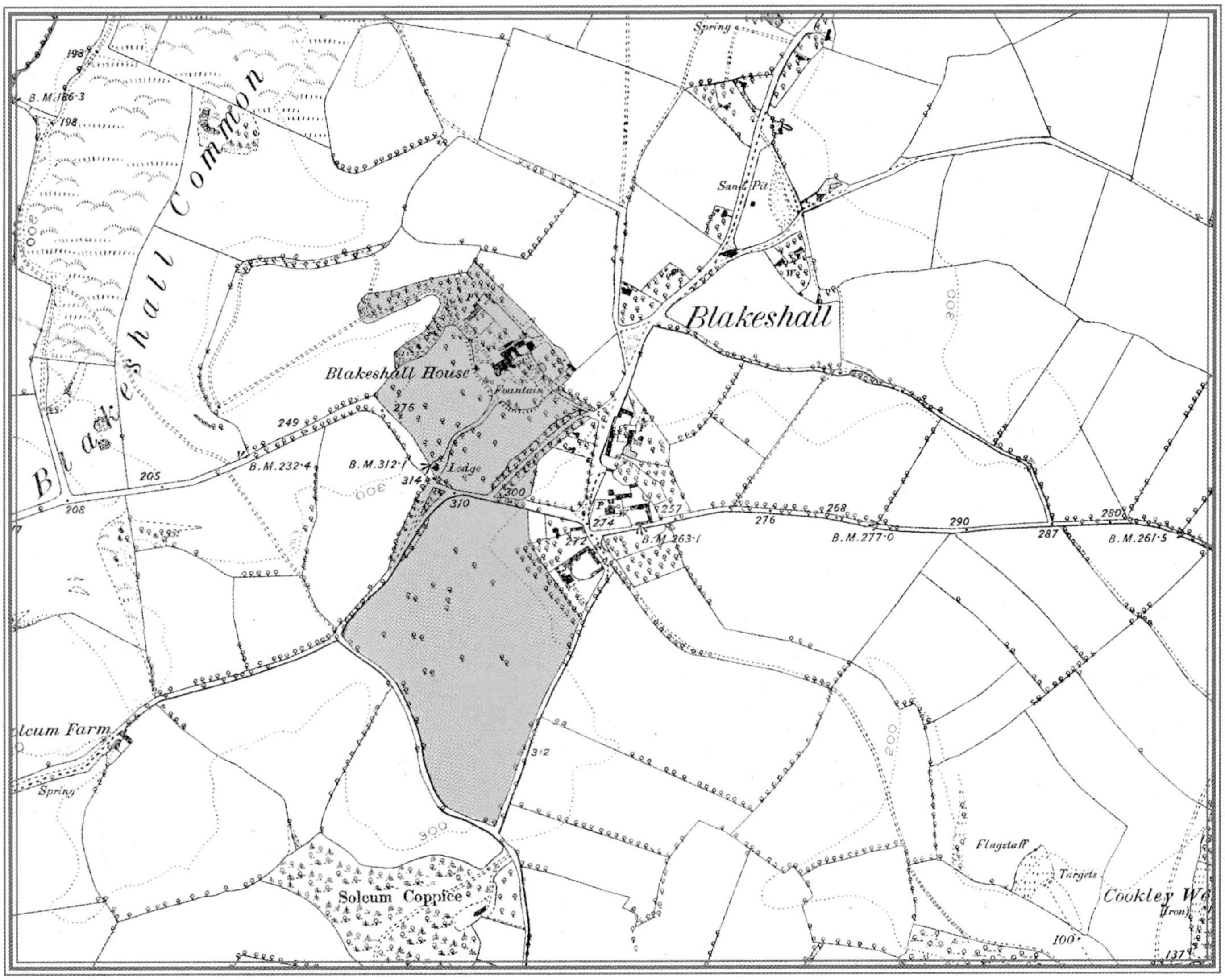

A map dated 1778 (CRO 1289) shows small grounds "about ye house" and an area separated from the house as "Park" then under separate ownership or tenancy. The BoE (p. 667) describes a small country house built for William Hancock, 1845 ... on a wooded knoll in the grounds with a brick obelisk erected circa 1850 as a memorial to the Presbyterian divine Richard Baxter (1615-1691). A circular icehouse survives from the 18th century grounds. A small park, with lodge and garden with fountain, is recorded by the 1905 OS 6 inch edition (IX, NW).

At the time of writing these are still intact, although the parkland has few trees. The fountain has been filled with soil and planted. The double walled garden is in excellent condition and newly planted with a formal layout.

A. Brooks & N. Pevsner, *Worcestershire,* 2007 (BoE).

Bockleton Court/Study Centre

Parish: Stoke Bliss, Kyre & Bockleton

HER Ref: WSM28811. Grid Ref: SO 587 622. Postcode: WR15 8PR. O.S. 6" Map No: 25NE, 26NW.

Date of Maps: both 1884, with extent of park & gardens shaded as 1905 O).

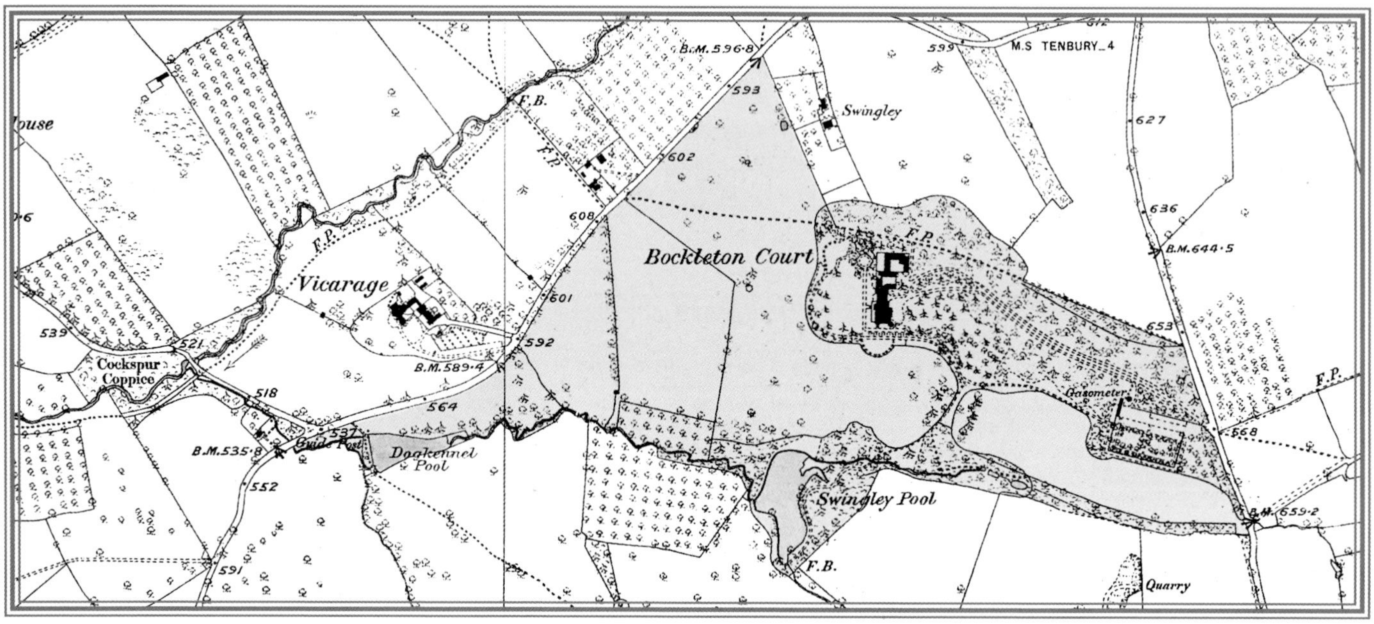

The original Bockleton Court, now Bockleton Farm, is situated next to the church and is presumably the residence indicated on Cary's 1805 map. A new Court (now known as Bockleton Study Centre) was built on a green field site after the acquisition of the property by Mrs Prescott from the Millers who had in turn acquired the estate from the Baldwyns of Kyre circa 1775 (C. Pritchard, CRO 8901/7). The landlord living in the old Bockleton Court kept a record of his tree planting from 1805 to 1826 (CRO 8901/4). The Planting Memoranda includes native woodland and orchard trees as well as many different ornamental conifer and evergreen species. Stock was bought in from various nurserymen and developed in a nursery at Bockleton. Miller's planting was not of a landscape park but was scattered about the farms into which the estate was divided. However, terms related to creating landscape effects are also used by him, e.g. clumps, belts, plantations. Some of his planting was round old Bockleton Court (SO 592 606), e.g. "planted avenue to Bockleton Church ... planted the oak grove at the head of the new pool also the two clumps at the end adjoining the dog-kennel ... destroyed the old garden in front of the house, and made it a lawn." The principal historical interest in the landscape today must relate to this burst of early-19th century planting.

The elaborate neo-Jacobean house built after 1865 had a large kitchen garden sited next to the lodge which the same architect, Henry Curzon added in the 1880s. Curzon had travelled with W. E. Nesfield on the Continent early in his career (Hancox, Cox and Whiting, op. cit.). The main feature of the grounds was Swingley pool which predated the Victorian house. The 1905 sale particulars document the contribution to the pleasure grounds (35 acres) "laid out under the supervision of the well-known landscape gardener E. Milner Esq., of Sydenham" (Edward Milner, 1819-1884) which included "Broad Gravelled Terraced Walks, a Circular bowling green and "extensive lawns admirably adapted for Lawn Tennis, Cricket, Crocquet and other purposes, having parterres of flowers at the boundaries, beyond which there are sequestered Winding Walks". All of this however was inexpensive to keep up! The estate nursery in 1905 extended to 144 acres. The walled kitchen garden sited near the Lodge contained glasshouses for grapes, peaches, nectarines and salad vegetables and there was a productive orchard of plum, cherry, apples and pear trees.

Hancox et al. add that specimen trees and shrubs were intermixed with traditional trees while, close to the house dahlias, geraniums, lobelias, sweet peas and fuchsias were mixed in to the formal beds. Rockeries and a sunken garden with a waterfall were planned but the garden was not realised. According to the BoE, there are only slight remains of the formal gardens. However, a visit in 2015 found the Milner terrace and pleasure grounds largely intact, although much degraded. The walled garden next to the Lodge is now grassed over but the walls still survive in reasonable condition.

A. Brooks & N. Pevsner, *Worcestershire* 2007 (BoE).
Hancox, Cox and Whiting, *Bockleton Court*, 1986.
C. Pritchard, *Changes in the Agricultural Geography of the Parishes of Bockleton.....* n. d.

Bockleton Vicarage/Cockshutt Hall

Parish: Stoke Bliss, Kyre & Bockleton

HER Ref: WSM67915. Grid Ref: SO 582 622.

Postcode: WR15 8PR. O.S. 6" Map No: 25NE, 26NW.

Date of Maps: both 1884, with extent of park & gardens shaded as 1905 OS.

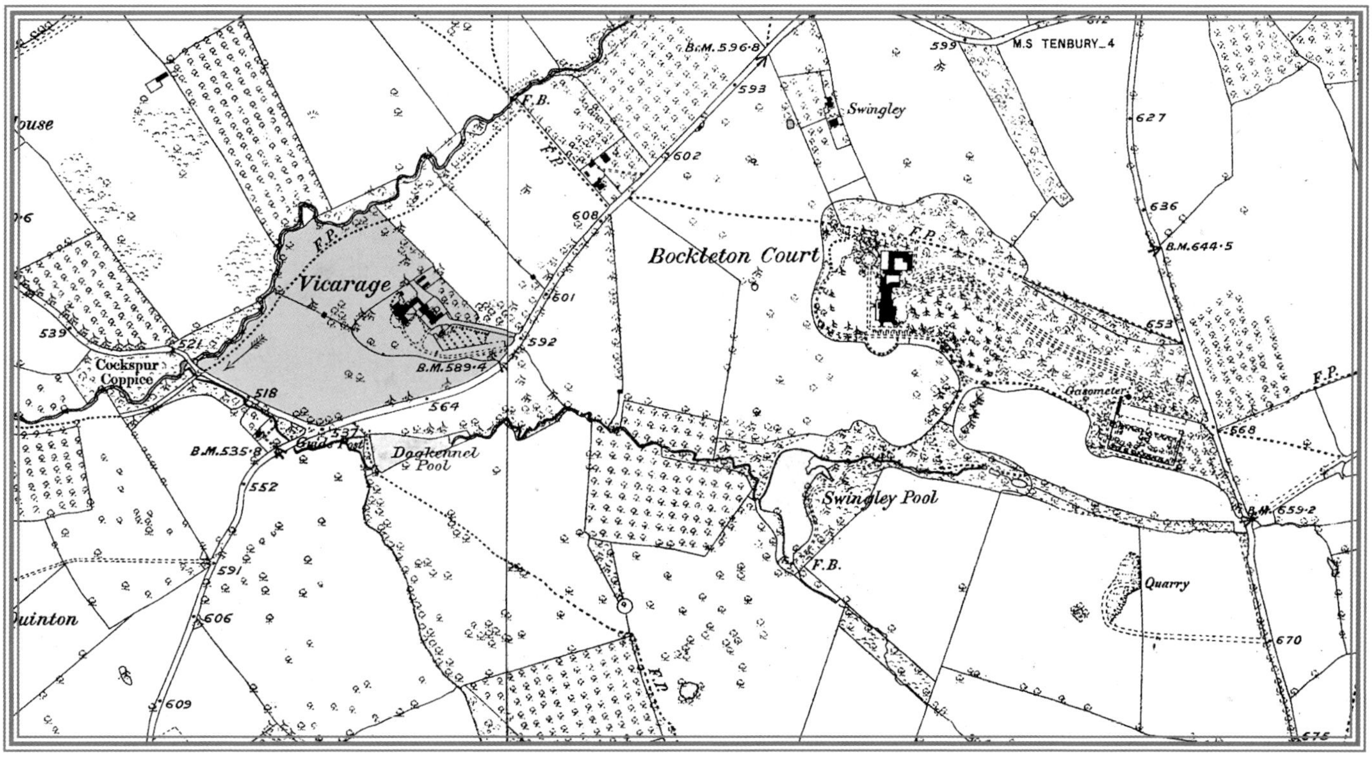

The BoE describes the Vicarage as mostly 1842 (p. 160). The 1883 OS 6 inch records the Vicarage, (then Cockspur and now Cockshutt Hall) with a small park. In the early-19th century the Vicar was the Revd. T. E. Miller who inherited the manor of Bockleton from an uncle who had purchased the property from a Baldwyn of Kyre (C. Pritchard, CRO 8901/7). This small park is in effect an extension of the park of Bockleton Court. In 1865 the Parsonage House was described as standing in "well-timbered park-like grounds" of 45 acres (CRO 8901/4).

The dry-stone ha-ha still marks out two sides of the pleasure grounds to the north and west of the house. The surviving mature conifers convey a parkland character that connects to that of the adjacent Bockleton Court which is now the Bockleton Study Centre.

A. Brooks & N. Pevsner, *Worcestershire,* 2007 (BoE).

C. Pritchard, *Changes in the Agricultural Geography of the Parishes of Bockleton.....* n. d.

Bordesley Hall and Park

Parish: Alvechurch

HER Ref: WSM28813/28815
Grid Ref: SP 040 710
O.S. 6" Map No. 16SE

Postcode: B48 7QQ
Date of Map: 1905

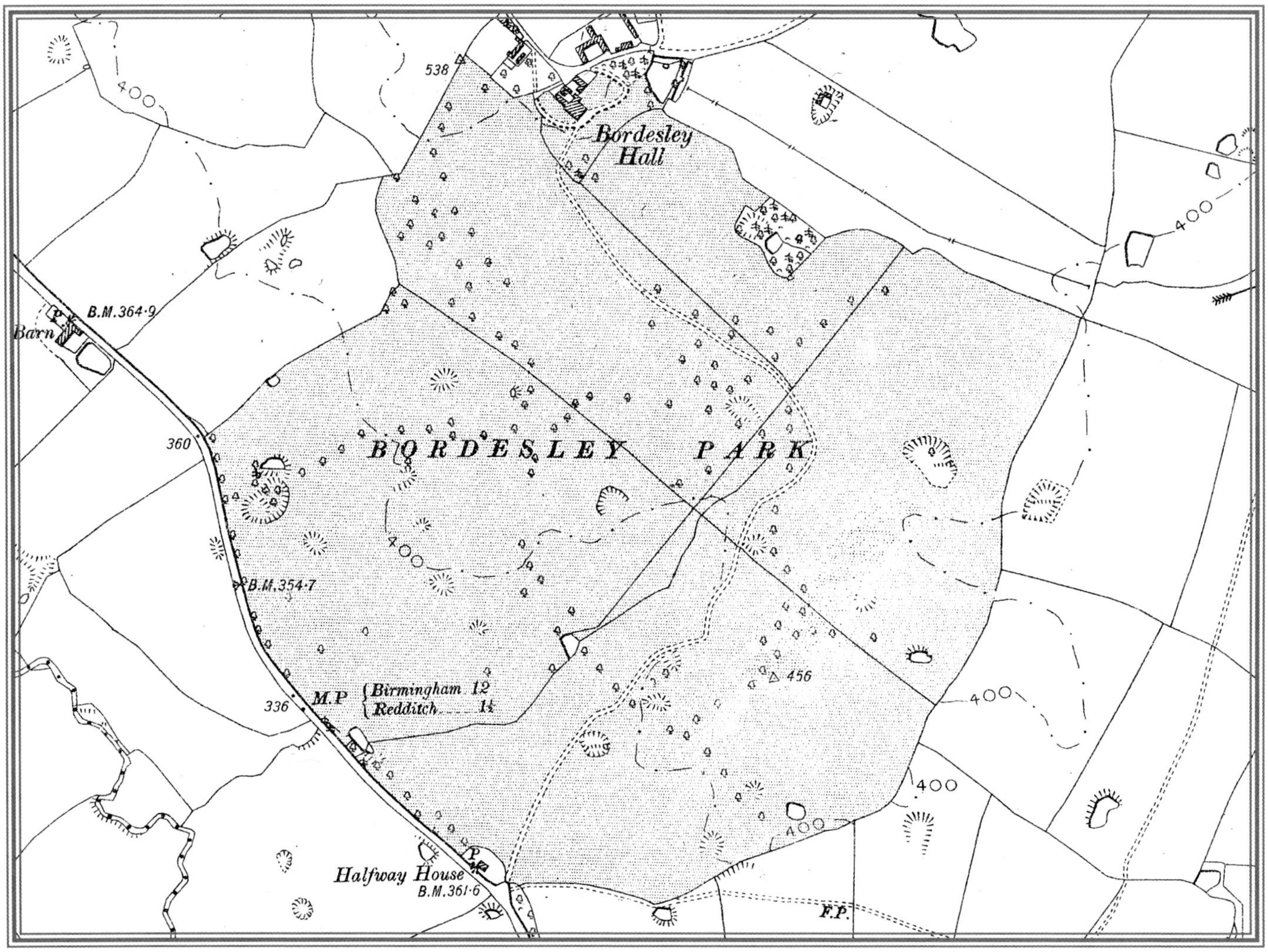

The earliest reference to a Park is connected with the Reformation; the *Valor Ecclesiasticus* commissioned by Henry VIII refers to Bordesley Park Farm (Nash, 1, 1781, p. 27). This was, presumably, a deer park belonging to Bordesley Abbey but not otherwise documented.

Lord Windsor obtained a licence to impark 1,000 acres in Bordesley and Tardebigge in 1561. Taylor's 1772 map has "Bordesley Old Park" as a name only. Nash (2, 1782, p. 404) notes that Bordesley Park had been sold some time ago to Lord Foley. Foley had acquired the estate by 1704, the date of a survey of the Manor which does not indicate any park. The VCH (3, 1913, p. 225) says that the park belonged to the Taylors of Moseley by around 1750.

The relationship of the landscape park of Bordesley Hall with the earlier deer park is not established; Isaac Taylor (1772) marks "Bordesley Old Park" and 18th and 19th century maps often confuse Bordesley with Beoley Park to the east. The 3 inch 1835 map by J. & C. Walker is among the most precise and shows the park lying to the east of the A451 with Lower Park Farm due east. The 1905 OS 6 inch definition of the park is essentially the same, ending to the south at Halfway House but excluding parkland towards the north-east. In 1840 Bentley described the neat and tastefully situated mansion as "surrounded by its delightful, extensive, and well-wooded park" (p. 49). In 1913 the park enclosed 200 acres (VCH, 3, p. 225). A 1933 sale describes the pleasure grounds with: "ornamental lawn in front of the house ... v. fine cedar ... 2 tennis lawns ... a pretty rose garden ... a charming pergola and pool ... walled kitchen garden ... excellent modern Green House by Messengers."

The parkland, it has to be said, is no longer recognisable.

Victoria County History, 1913, Vol. 3, (VCH).

T. R. Nash, *Collections for the History of Worcestershire,* Vol I & II, 1781/2.

Bradford House

Parish: Belbroughton

HER Ref: WSM29033/57758.

Grid Ref: SO 921 763.

Postcode: DY9 0DP.

O.S. 6" Map No. 9SE.

Date of Map: 1938.

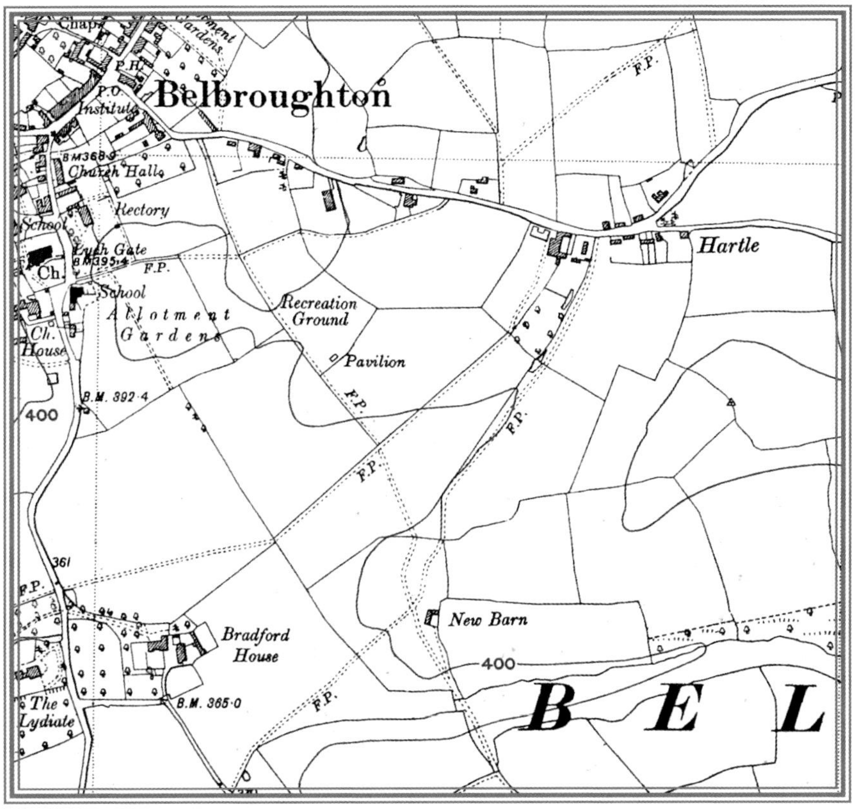

The House dates from the late-17th century and has a later-18th century wing and stable block (BoE, p. 131). The 1812 survey for the inaugural OS one inch shows a small park north and south of a moated site. The house and adjoining walls are listed and the latter are dated by the listing as 17th to 20th centuries.

The house and grounds are now in multiple ownership and well maintained. The parkland has been subdivided with hedges and is mainly down to grass. No parkland trees survive.

A. Brooks & N. Pevsner, *Worcestershire,* 2007 (BoE).

Bredon Manor

Parish: Bredon, Bredon's Norton & Westmancote

HER Ref: WSM28964.
Grid Ref: SO 919 370.
Postcode: GL20 7FG.
O.S. 6" Map No: 55NW.
Date of Map: 1884.

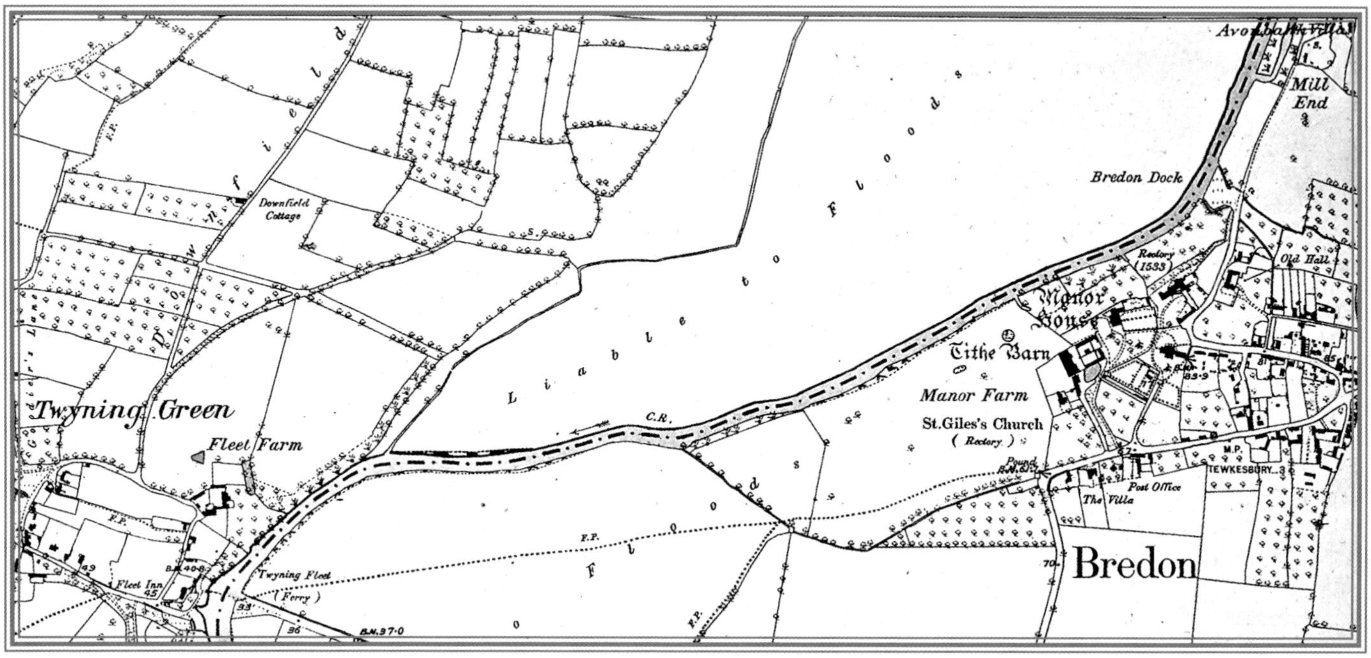

The house is described by the BoE as 18th century set in ample grounds with walled gardens. The Lodge is circa 1830. The neighbouring, 14th century tithe barn is famous. In 1907 the grounds were described as most attractive … with fine ornamental timber. Later-20th century gardens were designed by Russell Page (Whitehead).

A. Brooks & N. Pevsner, *Worcestershire,* 2007 (BoE).
D. Whitehead, "Bredon Manor", *HWGT Newsletter,* 11, Summer 1998.

Bredon Tower

Parish: Kemerton

HER Ref: WSM28963.
Grid Ref: SO 956 401.
Postcode: WR10 3DN.
O.S. 6" Map No: 55NW.
Date of Map: 1883.

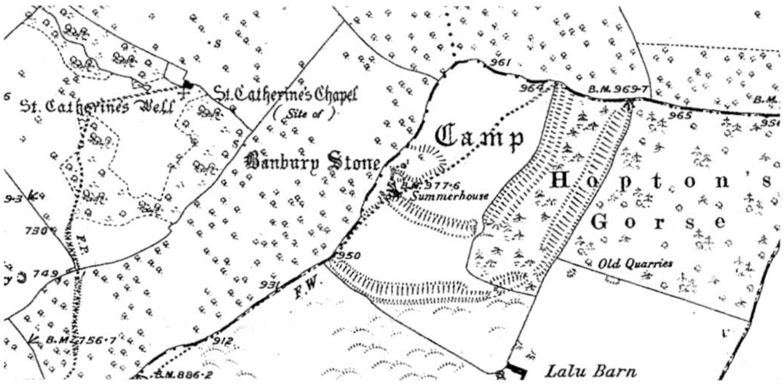

Bredon Tower (circa 1765, BoE, p. 168), was also known as Parsons's Folly after Mr. John Parsons of Kemerton (Lower) Court and is included here as a park and landscape feature (gazebo) although it stands, isolated from any park. It is set within the Iron Age hill fort on St. Catherine's Hill. It is labelled "Summerhouse" on the 1883 and 1905 OS.

A. Brooks & N. Pevsner, *Worcestershire,* 2007 (BoE).

Bredons Norton Manor House

Parish: Bredon, Bredon's Norton & Westmancote

HER Ref: WSM04635.
Grid Ref: SP 930 390.
Postcode: GL20 7EZ.
O.S. 6" Map No: 48SE.
Date of Map: 1887.

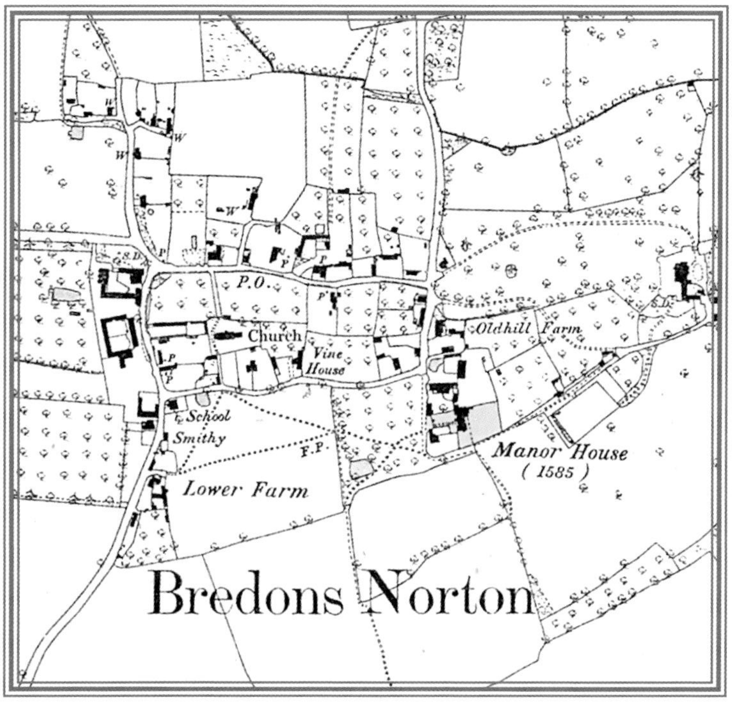

The Manor House is included here for its entrance forecourt which connects house and Grounds: "The forecourt remains much as it was laid out at the end of the 16th century, with its elaborate gateway (1585) and plain enclosing walls, with buildings at the north and south angles." (VCH, 3, 1913, p. 280). The latter have been rebuilt or replaced since 1913. The house was probably built by Thomas and Margaret Copley who, with George Hornyold purchased the manor in 1577. Mrs Victoria Martin (see Norton Park) began to restore the house circa 1906 and put it to use as a training centre for women in agriculture (International Agricultural Club and School of Intensive Petite Culture).

Mrs. Martin, the first woman to speak in the US Congress and a champion of women's rights in the USA, was attracted to Bredon's Norton as representing the "England of Folk song and tradition" (Barrett, op. cit.). Barrett describes the entrance courtyard as in 1925: "the stone archway almost hidden in a mantle of crimson American pillar roses, the grassy forecourt, with its surrounding walls covered with masses of various rambling roses ... in the centre a nearly upright hollow old poplar tree with a chair inside with a stone seat around it and close by a sun-dial dated 1659." The property survived as a country club until 1957 (Leatherbarrow, op. cit.) and is now a private residence.

T. Mowl, *Historic Gardens of Worcestershire,* 2006, p. 32.
Canon J. S. Leatherbarrow, "A Worcestershire Enigma: Bredon's Norton Manor", *Trans.,Worcs., Archaeol. Soc.*, 3rd Series, 3, 1970-2, pp. 93-104.
Victoria County History, Vol. 3, 1913.
R. M. Barrett, *The Manor House, Bredon's Norton, Tewkesbury,* 1925, reprinted from *The British American.*

Bretforton Manor House

Parish: Bretforton

HER Ref: WSM02859.
Grid Ref: SP 092 439.
Postcode: WR11 7JH.
O.S. 6" Map No: 50NW.
Date of Map: 1884.

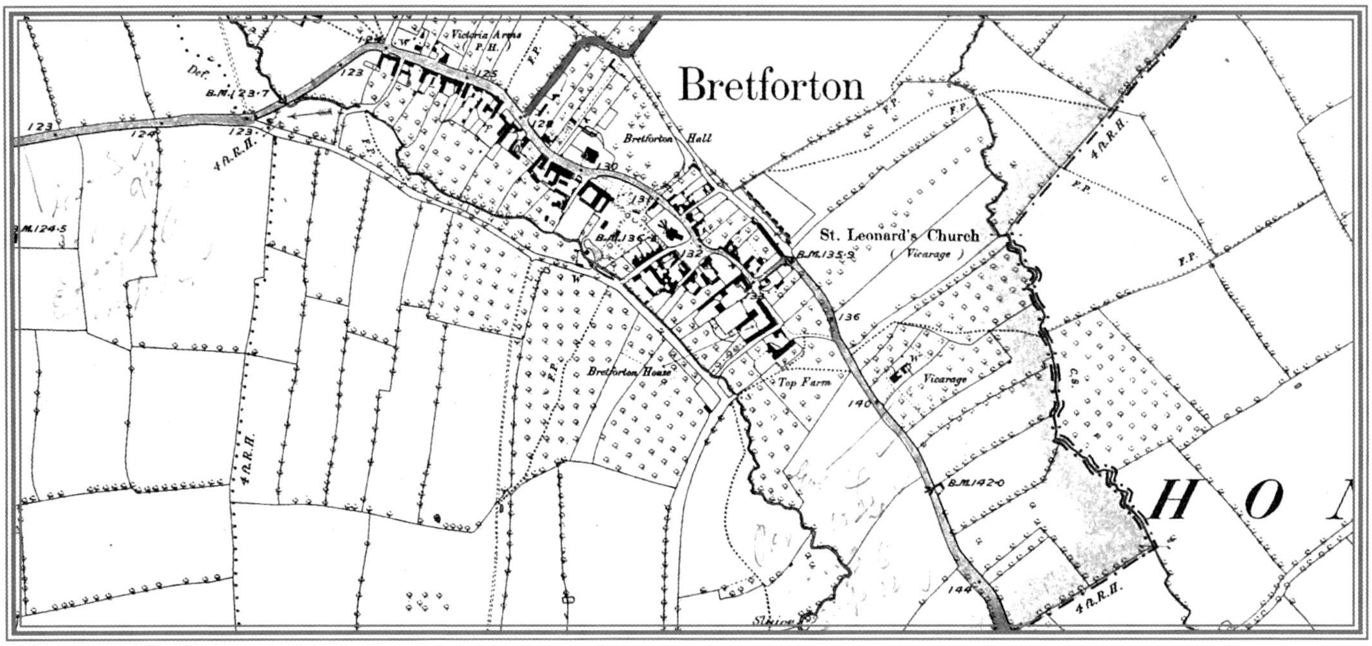

The Manor House dates from the early-17th to the late-19th century. There is evidence for its gardens during the 18th and 19th centuries. A Survey dated 1764 and 1780 shows a fenced garden with 4 beds or squares (CRO 4352/13). The site is noted for its 18th century summer-house but should also be remarked for a set of agricultural buildings: a cider house, dovecote, apiary, and village stocks. A plan of circa 1800 (CRO 4352/18) has two fields labelled Far Park and Home Park.

In the later-19th century Bretforton was developed as a nursery for fruit trees documented by a manuscript called a *Catalogue of Fruit Trees and where Growing* (CRO 7775/27), 1875, containing some loose pages dated 1894/5. There is a manuscript list of 74 apple varieties in alphabetical order from Alfriston to Yorkshire Beauty. "In January 1871, I (James Ashwin) planted 39 Pear Trees on each side of the brook dividing Home and Far Park, viz. 19 on the north side and 20 on the south side... from Jas Dickson & Sons, Chester and from Joseph Jones of Badsey." The Shinnell Orchard housed 49 varieties of Pear and 50 varieties of Plum. 9 orchards are noted as "Orchard planted recently". The gardens are still in good order but there is little orcharding left.

Bricklehampton Hall

Parish: Elmley Castle, Bricklehampton & Netherton

HER Ref: WSM29043. Grid Ref: SO 978 422.

Postcode: WR10 3HQ.

O.S. 6" Map No: 49NW.

Date of Map: 1884, with extent of park & gardens shaded as 1880s OS.

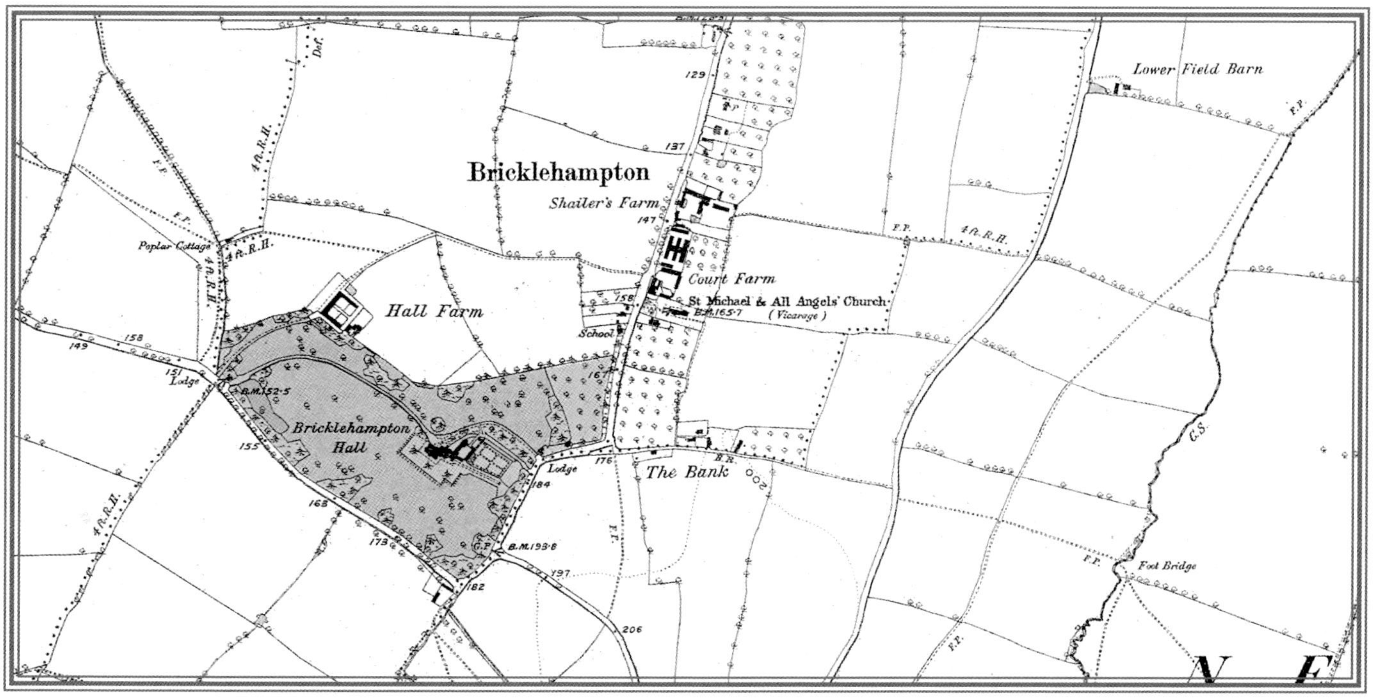

Samuel Daukes's house of Bath stone was built in 1848 with two Lodges. Additions were made to the House in 1868 (illus. Reid, p. 195). A modern house has been built in the south-east corner of the grounds.

A plan of 1787 shows that the site was occupied previously by homesteads and old enclosures. There is an 1818 survey of land that later became part of the Bricklehampton Estate which records the number of different trees, no doubt for valuation purposes: oak, ash, elm, lime, sycamore, apple, pear, oak pollard, ash pollard, withy, that pre-dated the mid-19th century development. The details of the pleasure ground and small park (only 34 acres) as recorded in 1861 (CRO 3744/1) are exactly the same in the 1883 OS 6 inch, i.e. some fringe planting round the pleasure ground which contained two pools and a large, walled kitchen garden near the house; a summer-house is at the end of the "Long Walk". There was some fringe planting also at the south-east boundary of the park which was divided into fields. The kitchen garden walls (possibly early-19th century) are decorated with recessed gothic arches but their render is now in poor condition. There are two lodges at present in separate ownership.

Bricklehampton Hall is now a residential care home. The park and much of the gardens are still intact with some fine parkland trees. The gardens are well cared for.

P. Reid, *Burke's and Savills Guide to Country Houses,* Vol. 2 1980.

Brinton Park, Kidderminster

Parish: Kidderminster

HER Ref: WSM22985.

Grid Ref: SO 825 759. Postcode: DY11 7BB.

O.S. 6" Map No. 8SE, 14NE. Date of Maps: 1903.

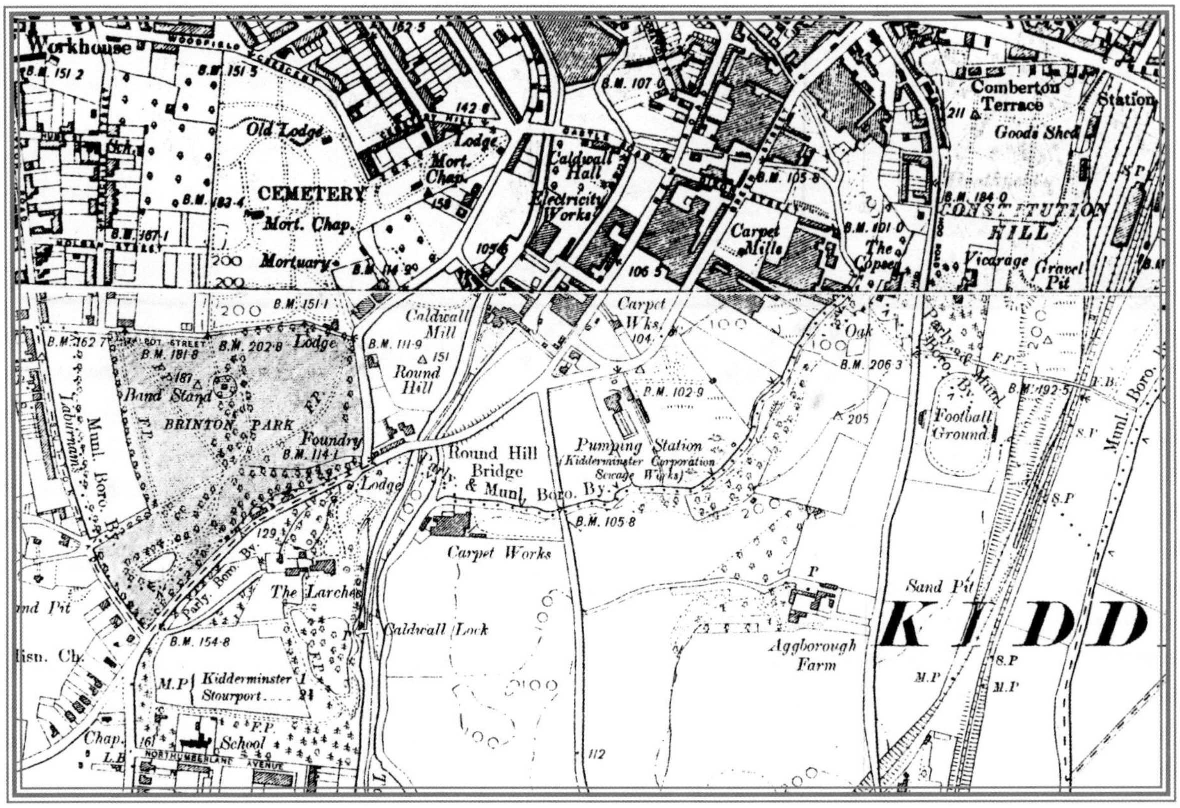

The park was given to Kidderminster in 1887 by John Brinton. It is an exceptionally large park to be established so late in a town centre; it had a lodge, pool, and bandstand and gardener's house. The drinking fountain in memory of Richard Eve is Listed. The large open central space and perimeter plantings gives this urban park the feel of a landscape park. It contains a fine collection of mature trees e.g. horse chestnut, beech, sweet chestnut, lime, plane, holly, yew, monkey puzzle, acacia, cedar, and varieties of fir and pine. The original green houses sited in the south-west corner of the park have been replaced. The park has the cemetery as a landscape neighbour on the north side and this also has Victorian lodges.

Photograph taken 1997, R. Lockett.

Brinton Park circa 1930. Photo, courtesy of F. Frith & Co..

The Broadway Sites

Located in the south-east corner of the County on the road from Evesham to Stow on the Wold, Broadway occupies an inlet into the Cotswolds. "A glance at the map shows how Worcestershire has plundered Broadway from Gloucestershire, no doubt because it was a possession of Pershore Abbey from at least the late 10C" (BoE, p. 176). The Cotswold Way passes through it and the Roman or pre-Roman Buckle Street lies to the east. Several *Survey* sites are neighbours of Broadway Village itself and relate to it, e.g. Broadway Tower; Farncombe Abbey and the Fish Inn; Middle Hill.

Broadway is an exception within this *Survey* which is devoted to parks and gardens being regarded by county guide books as a picturesque village rather than anything else. "It has been frivolously suggested that all good Americans, when they die go to Paris. They are very much alive every summer at Broadway, Worcestershire, and it is a certain success with Transatlantic visitors. Nothing could be less like New York's Great White Way than this long, wide street with its borders of shaven turf as well as footpaths, its shady trees everywhere, its gracious stone houses in all the subtle range of grey and gold tints, the stone glinting delicately when the sunshine picks out traces of quartz … Nowhere else, even in Worcestershire, are there such impeccably neat, as well as picturesque, gardens, such stone gate posts with great stone balls on top (Noake, p. 44)". This appreciation was published in 1949.

The individual houses are noticed in this *Survey* in a rather arbitrary manner. Alan Brooks records garden walls and garden buildings belonging to several other Broadway houses (op. cit. pp. 175-188) and otherwise has most to say in respect of gardens for Russell House. Lees-Milne in 1969, besides Austin House, only refers to "The Abbot's Grange [on the Green], secluded by a grey wall and thick yew hedge (op. cit.)". Court Farm and Abbot's Grange are the two properties singled out in another guidebook, published in 1974 (Neville Havins, p. 48). Court Farm, Farnham House and Russell House are the houses with gardens particularly associated with the American invasion in the last years of the 19th century and with such celebrities as Henry James and John Singer Sargent. Broadway has been appreciated for its apparently unchanged appearance but this in fact masks bold, arts and crafts associated architecture and decoration as well as garden design around 1900. Gordon Russell's father bought the Lygon Arms in the late-19th century from which the Russell workshops developed.

J. Lees-Milne, *Worcestershire, Shell Guide*, 1969.

V. Noake, *Worcestershire*, 1949.

P. J. Neville Havins, *A Portrait of Worcestershire*, 1974.

A. Brooks & N. Pevsner, *Worcestershire*, 2007 (BoE).

Victoria County History, 1924, Vol. 4, (VCH).

C. Gordon, *Gazetteer of Arts and Crafts Architecture in the Cotswold Region*, Cheltenham Art Gallery, 1992.

Marion Mako, "The Broadway Gardens of Alfred Parsons", *HWGT, Newsletter*, 30,Winter, 2007/8.

Catherine Gordon, Correspondance, 2015.

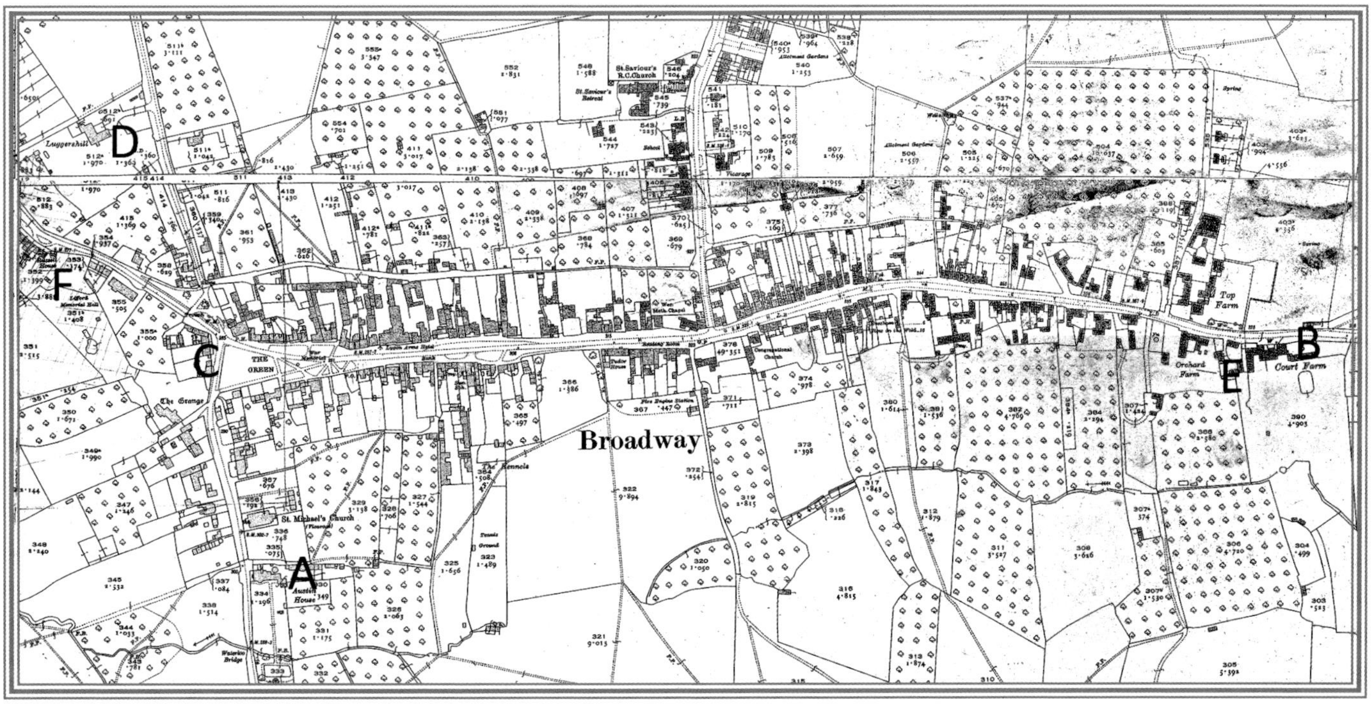

(A) Broadway, Austin House

HER Ref: WSM28955

Postcode: WR12 7AB

The 18th century gate piers and garden walls of this circa 1700 house are Listed. In addition to "a large and productive kitchen garden", the 48 acres sold in 1876 boasted a "pleasure garden with ornamental water stocked with trout... a never failing stream and fine ornamental trees" (CRO 6088/110). The BoE refers to the alterations carried out by Guy Dawber in 1898 which included a new garden lay out (op. cit. p. 180). Lees-Milne mentions "Within the long garden wall a pile of rugged yews."

J. Lees-Milne, *Worcestershire, Shell Guide,* 1969.
A. Brooks & N. Pevsner, *Worcestershire,* 2007 (BoE).

Austin House, 1905. Postcard image, J. Jacques Junr.

Broadway, The Court

HER Ref: WSM29031.

Postcode: WR12 7JS.

The Court retains the 16th century gatehouse from Broadway Court, demolished in 1773 which had two gardens in 1573 (VCH, 4, 1924, p. 36). It is not established whether or not these lay within the moated site to the north. Weaver describes The Court House, Broadway as in origin no more than the gatehouse to the estate of Middle Hill (op cit. pp. 126-130). The house was substantially enlarged by E. Guy Dawber in partnership with Whitwell in 1898 for Edgar Flower. The west garden was laid out with yew hedging and a gazebo in its north-west corner.

C. Gordon, *Cotswold Arts and Crafts Architecture,* 2009, pp. 138-40.
Sir L. Weaver, *Small Country Houses; Their Repair and Enlargement,* 1914.
Victoria County History, 1924, Vol. 4, (VCH).

Court House, 1904. Postcard image, J. Jacques Junr.

(B) Broadway, Court Farm

HER Ref: WSM01840.

Postcode: WR12 7AW.

Court Farm (17th century) was linked on its garden front via a music room with Bell Farm (14th century) by A. N. Prentice for Antonio de Novarro and his wife Mary Anderson, an American actress. The garden of 7 acres/2.8 ha was developed after 1896 by Alfred Parsons (Mowl, p. 127, Gordon, p. 10). Mako explains that the gardens were developed in two phases, the first north of Court Farm with yew hedges and topiary birds, rose garden, tennis court, viewing platform and paths leading to the wild garden, and the second phase, after the acquisition of Bell Farm, with "a swimming pool fed by a Holy Well spring and above it a bank covered in daffodils" ... "Beyond the bank, Parsons developed "a wide herbaceous border flanked on one side by a rose pergola and the other by a formal line of lime-trees"(op. cit. p. 6 quoting from Mary Anderson, *A Few More Memories,* 1936.). ".

Noake (op. cit.) gives the fullest of descriptions with a stress on the patron's personal impact:

"It was a very spacious garden, reaching to the foot of the Cotswold slopes, and even the paths were paved with stone. Lead figures of children played with fishes and dolphins, and a figure of St. Francis of Assisi presided over the bird bath, to welcome his "little sisters" to whom he used to preach. A Della Robbia Madonna looked down from a Wedgwood blue plaque, and Mme. de Novarro's passion for blue found expression in whole borders of flowers in every shades of it – gentians, delphiniums, larkspurs, cornflowers, and many more exotic. There was a furnished garden-house, with a bust of Shakespeare smiling benignly - Mary Anderson was famous for her playing of his great ladies. There is still a fountain whose basin is lined with blue mosaic, and a big square pool, for punting and swimming lined with blue tiles. At the end of the garden a stream runs through a "wild garden", artfully careless in its beauty, and an unexpected Calvary among the trees reminded visitors of their hostess's deep feeling for her religion."

A fine yew hedge forms the boundary with the adjoining churchyard of Broadway Church, which itself has a group of clipped yews at this point. In 1981 Sidwell considered this as "perhaps the least altered of 19th century gardens in the area" (pp. 40-42). Mako confirms that 35 years later "it retains all the key features within its layout and therefore a sense of how it looked and was used".

Court Farm c.1939. Postcard image, Packer's studio.

Court Farm 1939. Valentine's postcard image.

Rose garden at Court Farm, designed by Alfred Parsons, circa 1900. Postcard image.

R. Sidwell, *West Midlands Gardens,* 1981.
C. Gordon, *Gazetteer of Arts and Crafts Architecture in the Cotswold Region,* Cheltenham Art Gallery, 1992.
T. Mowl, *Historic Gardens of Worcestershire,* 2006.
M. Mako, "The Broadway Gardens of Alfred Parsons", *HWGT, Newsletter,* 30, Winter 2007/8, pp. 5-8.
V. Noake, *Worcestershire,* 1949, Ch. VII, Some Cotswold Villages.

(C) Broadway, Farnham House

HER Ref: WSM01307.

Postcode: WR12 7AE.

The house is of circa 1660 and was rented in 1885 by the Americans E. A. Abbey and F. Millet who invited the painter J. S. Sargent to stay in 1885. "They were joined by Henry James, Edmund Gosse, Alfred Parsons, the Shakespeare actress Mary Anderson and others" (Alfrey, p. 160). Quite a house party! Sargent's famous painting – *Carnation, Lily, Lily, Rose* is set at Farnham (Mowl, p. 124) and was completed at Russell House, Broadway (Mako, op. cit.).

N. Alfrey, *The Art of the Garden,* Tate Gallery Exhibition, 2004.
T. Mowl, *Historic Gardens in Worcestershire,* 2006.
M. Mako, "The Broadway Gardens of Alfred Parsons", *HWGT Newsletter,* 30, Winter 2007/8.

Broadway, Fish Inn

HER Ref: WSM10933.

Postcode: WR12 7LD.

The Fish Inn was built in 1771 as a summer-house for Farncombe Abbey. The Revd. Stebbing Shaw in 1778 said: "Sir John Cotterel, Knt, has lately erected, on the side of this hill, a castle-looking place, fronting the vale", "a small house of entertainment, the Fish, on Broadway-hill, where we spent an hour in glorious contemplation, from the room built like a summer-house, for this purpose." Lord Torrington, on tour in 1781 held it to be "the most extraordinary gaze-about house in the world". *Beauties* in 1814 elaborated that the Fish Public-house was "an ornament to the scenery being built in the antique style." Although in Gloucestershire, it is included here as part of Cotterell's landscape with Farncombe Abbey.

The Fish Inn circa 1951. Photo, courtesy of Birmingham Post.

Revd. Stebbing Shaw, *History and Antiquities of Staffordshire,* Vol. 1, 1798.
Beauties of England and Wales, Vol XV, 1814.
C. Bruyn Andrews (ed.), *The Torringtons Diaries: Tour to the West, 1781*, 1954.

(D) Broadway, Luggers Hall

HER Ref: WSM48266.

Postcode: WR12 7BT.

Luggers Hill was built in the years between 1903 and 1911 by A. N. Prentice for Alfred Parsons, the artist and garden designer featured by Mowl in his *Historic Gardens of Worcestershire*, Ch. 9, "Alfred the Uncertain and the American Invasion of Broadway". Mowl illustrates the "long castellated yew hedge" with the suggestion that it might have been inspired by Rous Lench. "Luggers Hall has recently been restored to its original design as a classic early-20th century revivalist garden – lots of formality and plenty of hedges – but there is still the wide sweep of lands, across which there is a distant view of Broadway Tower. This scene was painted by Alfred Parsons in late spring with pink blossom of the cherries and beds full of colour co-ordinated tulip" (Whitehead, op. cit.). Mako (pp. 8-9) distinguishes between the original garden of 5 acres characterised by period features such as "rose gardens with sundials and battlemented yew hedges, a nut walk, walled vegetable gardens on either side" and 3 garden buildings, stone pergola, circular gazebo with Buddhist reliefs and a summer-house, removed in the 1980s. The summer-house is recorded in one of Parsons's own paintings (1912) and was inspired by a visit to Japan in 1892. Mako concludes: "Kay and Red Haslem have expertly restored and rejuvenated this garden with several classical touches of their own."

T. Mowl, *Historic Gardens of Worcestershire*, 2006.
N. Alfrey, *The Art of the Garden*, Tate Gallery, 2004.
D. Whitehead, "Some garden visits", *HWGT, Newsletter* 13, Summer 1999, p. 3 with plan.
M. Mako, "The Broadway Gardens of Alfred Parsons", *HWGT Newsletter*, 30, Winter 2007/8.

(E) Broadway, Orchard Farm

HER Ref: WSM10898.

Postcode: WR12 7AW.

Weaver gives a chapter in his book on smaller country houses to Orchard House as first built around 1620, conservatively developed a century later and remodelled for Lady Maud Bowes-Lyon by A. N. Prentice circa 1905. Weaver summarised: "Mr. Prentice is to be congratulated on the skill with which he has evolved order out of decay, and given a new lease of life to a very characteristic piece of Cotswold building." With 8 photographs, a ground plan and a bird's eye view, Weaver provides a relatively full idea of the gardens and their integration with the house. He comments on an old outbuilding converted into a summer-house and the paved courtyard that was created between the music room and the new kitchen wing: "Much of the garden space is to the north-west of the house, and it is delightfully divided up by stone walls into little pleasaunces, each with its own character." Fifty years later all this was summarised by Hunt (p. 299): "Seven acres of gardens, in general formally laid out, with topiary. Water garden. Orchards. Bulbs naturalised in grass." Hunt only notices four other Worcestershire gardens in his national survey!

140 *Small Country Houses: Their Repair and Enlargement.*

205.—BIRD'S-EYE VIEW.

Birds eye view from Weaver, *Small Country Houses*.

P. Hunt, *Shell Garden Book*, 1964, p. 299.
Sir L. Weaver, *Small Country Houses; their Repair and Enlargement*, 1914. Ch. XXIV, The Orchard Farm, Broadway.
Catherine Gordon. Correspondence, 2015.

(F) Broadway, Russell House

HER Ref: WSM28956.

Postcode: WR12 7BU.

The listing notices 18th century gate, rusticated piers, flanking walls, Gothick gazebo, icehouse, castellated garden pavilion (Belvedere). *Country Life* in 1911 (XXIX, p. 54) recorded with photographs recent alterations and extensions to the garden: "The Flowery Way" between Abbot's Grange and Russell House planted with perennials - chrysanthemums, phlox, godecias - backed by a wall (100 yards) supporting fruit trees. "The garden incidents that they found have been greatly added to by Mr. and Mrs. Millet. The old garden has been laid out in grass paths and herbaceous borders retaining squares for tidier vegetables." A central alley led to a semi-circular loggia. The additional meadow then acquired was used for tennis and croquet lawns set behind a hedge. Alfrey gives a view of the central alley and loggia in a photo of 1911. Alfrey believes that Alfred Parson's painting - *Orange, Lilies, Broadway,* - showing a lawn path fringed with clipped yews and some white doves was of the garden of Russell House that he was making from 1886 (p. 169). Mowl also attributes another of Parsons's paintings - *China Roses, Broadway* (1890) - to Russell House. Mako adds that - *Carnation, Lily, Lily, Rose,* begun at Farnham House, was finished at Russell House, Parsons' first garden commission in Broadway. Mowl's general comment is that it is the hard landscape from Parsons's gardens that survive while the plantings vanish: "What remains at Russell House is a tastefully subdued ghost of Parsons's original vision" (op. cit. p. 129).

N. Alfrey, *The Art of the Garden,* Tate Gallery (Exhibition), 2004, pp. 220-1.
T. Mowl. *Historic Gardens of Worcestershire,* 2006. Ch. 9 passim.
M. Mako, "The Broadway Gardens of Alfred Parsons", *HWGT Newsletter,* 30. Winter 2007/8.

Broadway Tower

HER Ref: WSM01293.

Postcode: WR12 7LB.

Broadway Tower, set on Beacon Hill, is included in the *Survey* as a garden or landscape building, a viewing platform for the landscape which included Croome 15 miles away. It was erected 1797-9 by the 6th Earl of Coventry close to his brother's house at Springhill, to celebrate Admiral Duncan's 1797 naval victory at the Battle of Camperdown; carpentry and plumbing work was still going on in 1804. Lord Coventry's architect was James Wyatt (plan and elevation by Wyatt illus. by Gordon, *Coventrys of Croome,* p. 131). The name of the "Saxon Tower" reflects the 18th century confusion between Anglo-Saxon and Norman architectural styles. Broadway Tower, set within the Springhill Plantations, was built as a retreat from the hospitality of Croome Court of which its owner said "It has always been an Inn and always must remain so." The Tower was acquired by Sir Thomas Phillips in 1824 to house his famous library (see Middle Hill) and was used to house his private printing press until 1862.
It was repaired and re-decorated in 1867 (Gordon, p.11). The Tower is now within Broadway Countryside Park.

Photo 1958, courtesy of Evesham Journal

C. Gordon, *Gazetteer of Arts and Crafts Architecture in the Cotswold Region,* Cheltenham Art Gallery, 1992.
C. Gordon, *The Coventrys of Croome,* 2000.

Brockencote Hall

Parish: Chaddesley Corbett

HER Ref: WSM28978.

Grid Ref: SO 888 732. Postcode: DY10 4PY.

O.S. 6" Map No: 15NW.

Date of Map: 1883, with extent of park & gardens shaded as 1905 OS.

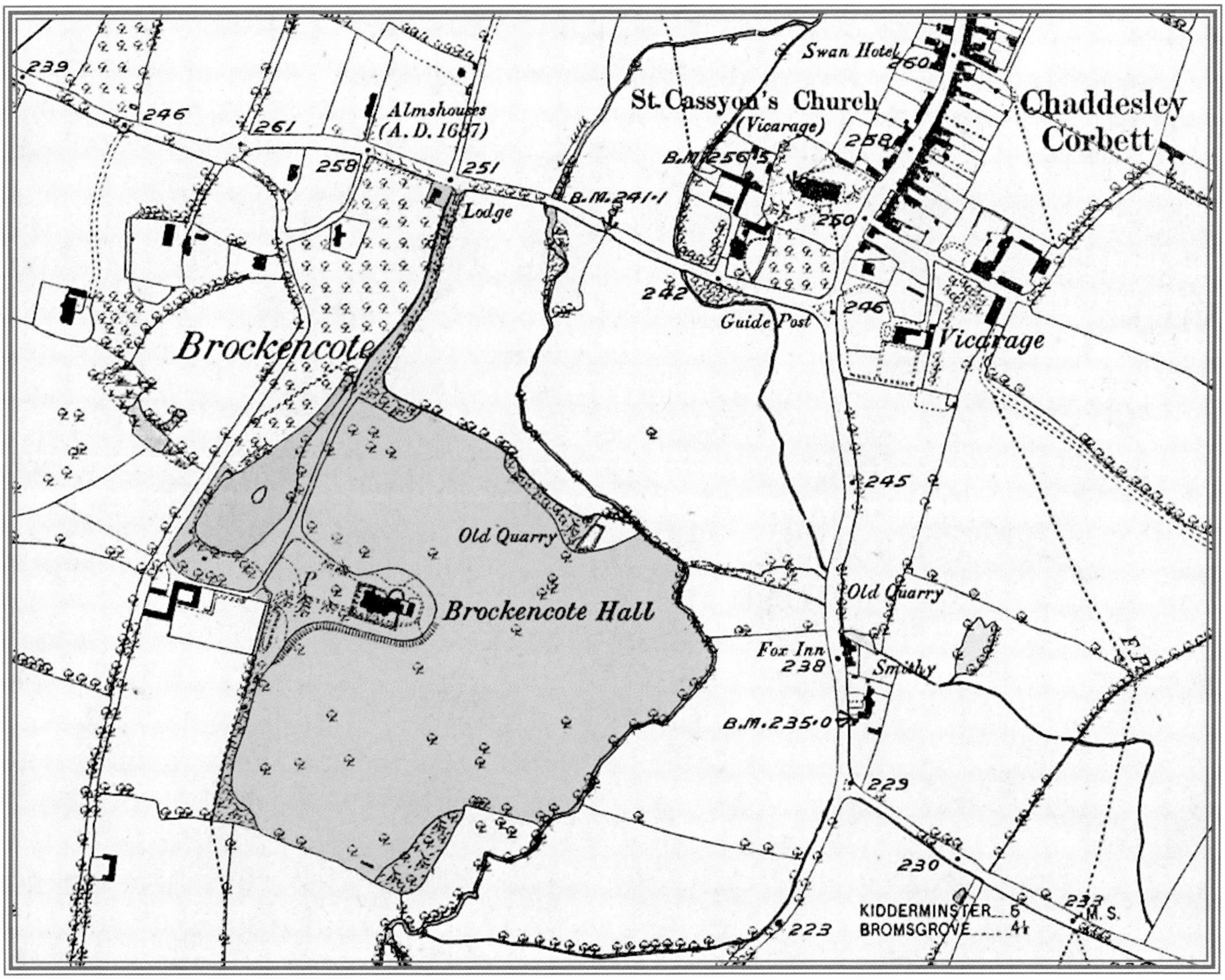

No substantial house or grounds are shown on a manuscript map of 1744/5 of the Throckmorton estate in Chaddesley Corbett (CRO 844) and significant grounds are first shown in the 1815 survey for the first OS one inch. The grounds are categorised as park in the first OS 6 inch of 1882 which also shows a boathouse and Lodge. The Doverdale Brook forms an eastern boundary to the park. The house was sold in 1914 with 55 acres (CRO 3762) as built circa 1882 in the "French Chateau style". The property offered a model farm, walled garden, a range of glass houses and, in another garden, a 17th century dovecote and watercress bed (to the right of the entrance drive). Photographs with the 1914 particulars show a small lean-to glass house designed in-between two projecting bays of the house which is set on a terrace with a steep bank and steps down to a low stone wall and ha-ha, all looking to the park.

Brockencote Hall is now a hotel. The parkland is intact and well stocked with trees but the gardens have been simplified. The boathouse still survives. The walled garden now provides garden space for the adjacent converted barns; the walls are intact.

Brookfield Hall

Parish: Belbroughton

HER Ref: WSM28957.

Grid Ref: SO 913 771.

Postcode: DY9 0DL.

O.S. 6" Map No. 9SW.

Date of Map: 1885, with extent of park & gardens shaded as 1880s OS.

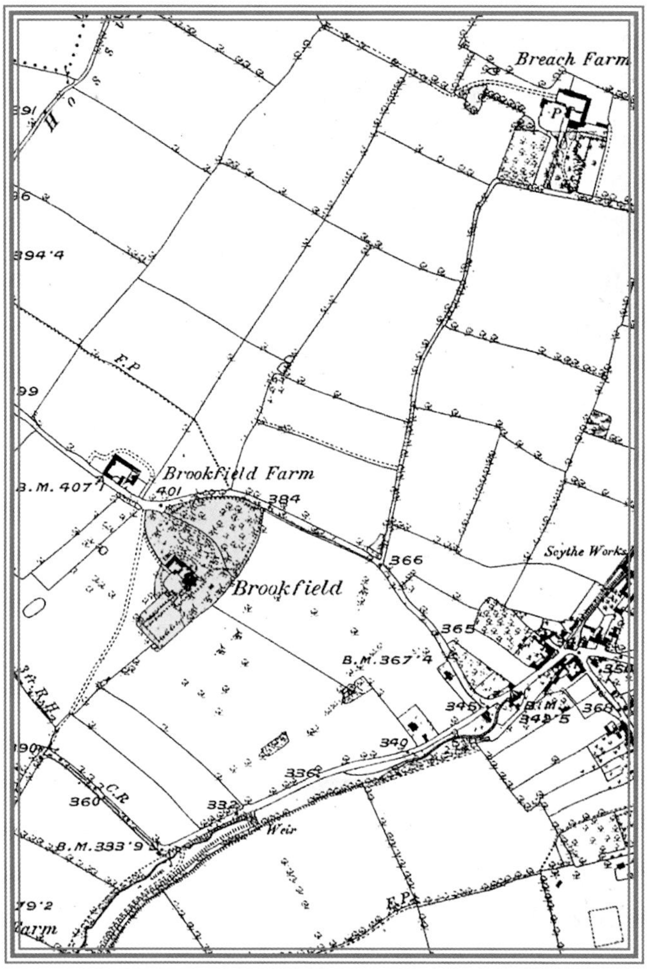

Brookfield Hall, 1973. WAAS, Belbroughton 49763.

The grounds were first noticed by the *Beauties* in 1814 and by maps from the 1830s, e.g. OS 1831.
A small park is shown on the 1882 OS 6 inch. The Orangery has now been converted into a dwelling with an associated walled garden. There are some fine garden trees, an arboretum and some intact parkland.

Beauties of England and Wales, Vol XV, 1814.

Broome House

Parish: Broome

HER Ref: WSM28943.

Grid Ref: SO 902 784. Postcode: DY9 0HB.

O.S. 6" Map No: 9SW.

Date of Map: 1887, with deduced extent of park & gardens shaded (not shaded on 1905 OS).

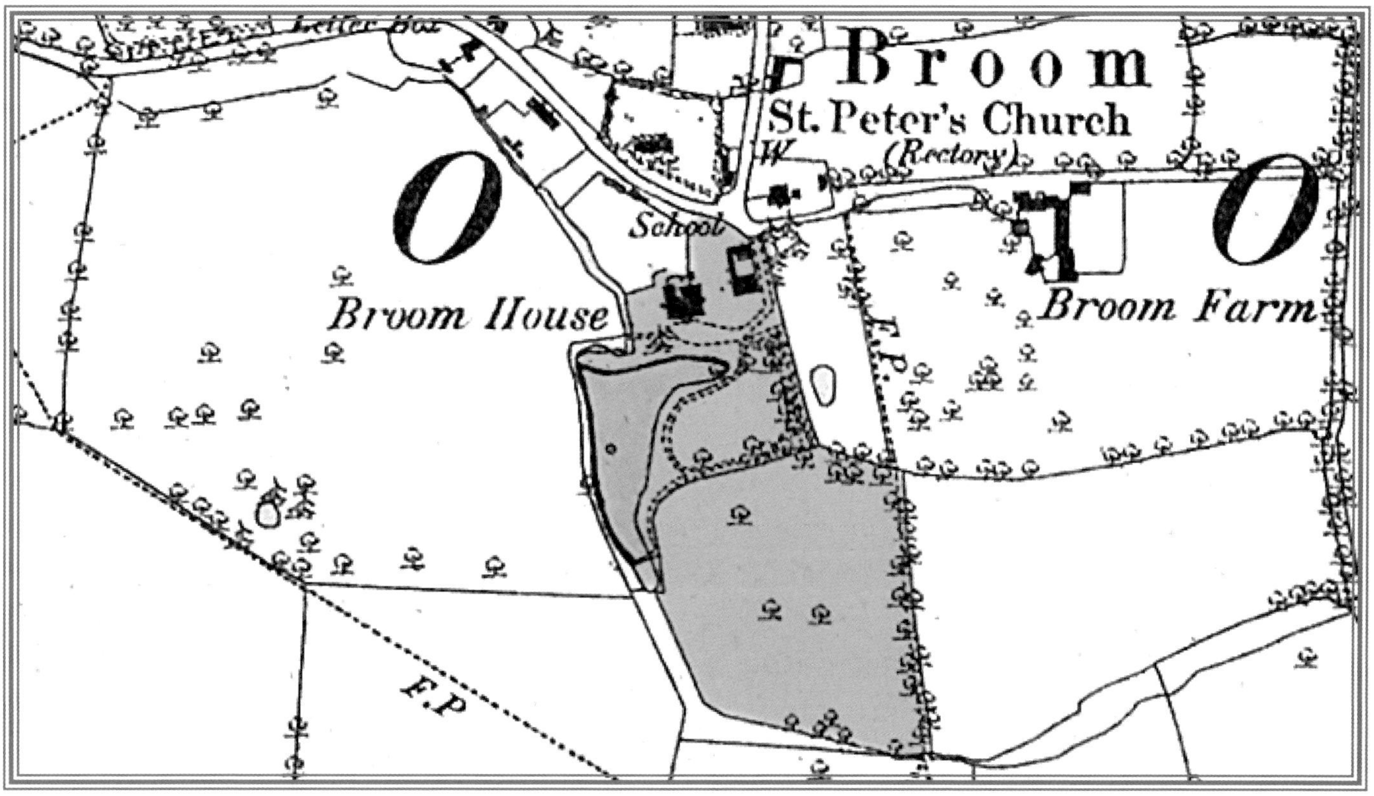

A recent sale that included 8 acres of beautifully tended grounds has the origin for the property as a hunting lodge owned by the Lytteltons (*Country Life*); Hagley is only 2 miles distant. The house is 18th century and later and is attributed to W. and D. Hiorn by Gomme. Mowl comments on its "wild Gothick detail" (p. 84). The OS 6 inch in 1905 does not give Broome a park but the VCH in 1913 remarks on it standing in "beautifully kept grounds" (3, p. 33). Mowl goes much further "if any small layout in the County can be held up as an example of Worcestershire's Picturesque garden-park then this is it." (op. cit. p. 84). Mowl emphasises the variety of evergreens including a Wellingtonia. The water, a small lake, a stream and other pools and two bridges all contribute to the atmosphere of the garden. There is a walled kitchen garden to compliment the Picturesque.

Photo 1970, courtesy of Kidderminster Shuttle.

A. Gomme, *Architectural Outsiders,* 1985.
T. Mowl, *Historic Gardens of Worcestershire,* 2006.
Country Life, 26. 8. 2009.
Victoria County History, 1913, Vol. 3, (VCH).

Bushley Park

Parish: Bushley

HER Ref: WSM28960.

Grid Ref: SO 873 341.

Postcode: GL20 6HP.

O.S. 6" Map No: 54SE, 55SW.

Date of Maps: both 1884, with shaded extent of park & gardens deduced from text.

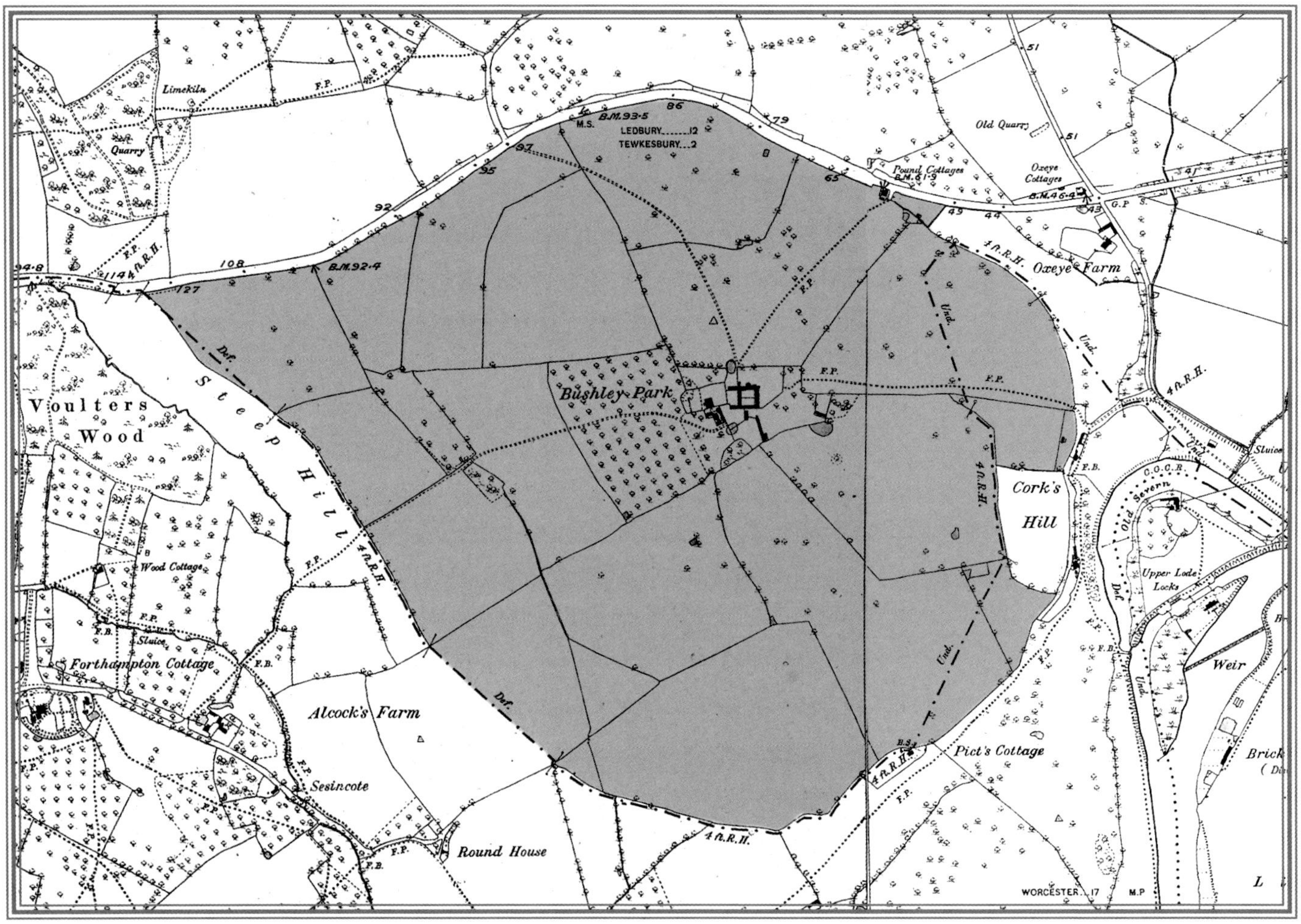

The deer park extended to 210 acres in 1545; it is not mentioned as such after the 18th century (VCH, 4, 1924, p. 46) although Isaac Taylor shows a fenced park as late as 1772. Pull Court was sometimes confused in Guide books with Bushley Park e.g. the *Traveller* circa 1800 has Bushley Park as a principal seat and omits Pull Court which was developed by the Dowdeswells as a park in preference.

Bushley Park however survives as a place name on the OS Pathfinder map; a footpath runs through the centre of the park area. A map of 1811 based upon maps of 1792, otherwise covering the Pull Court estate, has Bushley Park Farm in the centre of a park-like area with a Park Hill Field immediately south of the farmhouse. The road/track from Bushley to Upper Lode called Park Lane is a likely park boundary from north to east. The southern part of this track is now only a footpath. Bushley Park as suggested in 1792 is located some way south of Bushley Green.

The land is now a mix of arable and dairy grazing with no remaining parkland character.

Victoria County History, Vol. IV, 1924.

J. Dugdale, *The New British Traveller,* 1819.

Caldewell

Parish: Drakes Broughton & Wadborough

HER Ref: WSM28853/28939. Grid Ref: SO 913 486.

Postcode: WR7 4RL.

O.S. 6" Map No: 41NW.

Date of Map: 1884, with extent of park & gardens shaded as 1880s OS.

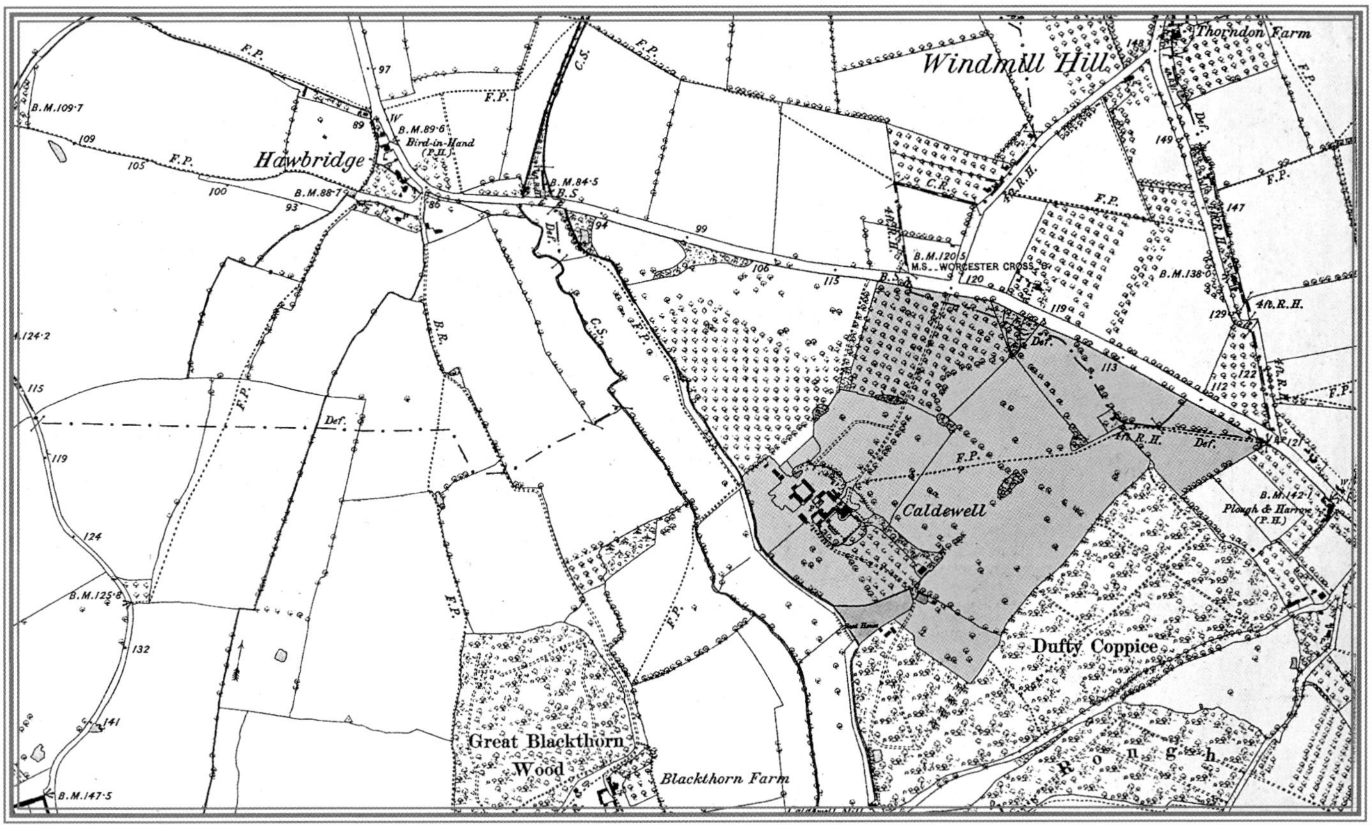

The house dates from the early-19th century and has a Lodge dated 1888 at the end of a long drive.

The 1905 OS shows the park and lodge extending along the Pershore - Worcester road and, immediately south-east of the house, a thin strip of fish pond extending south to the Caldwell Mill. When sold in 1920 (CRO 5240/2a) with 166 acres, the park of 30 acres was described as a "fine old timbered park". "The front lawns are divided from the park by a sunk fence and are planted with ornamental cedar, evergreen, oak and other forest trees and shrubs". The kitchen gardens included conservatory, fernery, vinery and peach house, all of which have been lost. The present owners have restored the gardens and are returning the park to its original character. Many of the fine parkland trees survive between the house and the A44.

Castle Bourne

Parish: Belbroughton

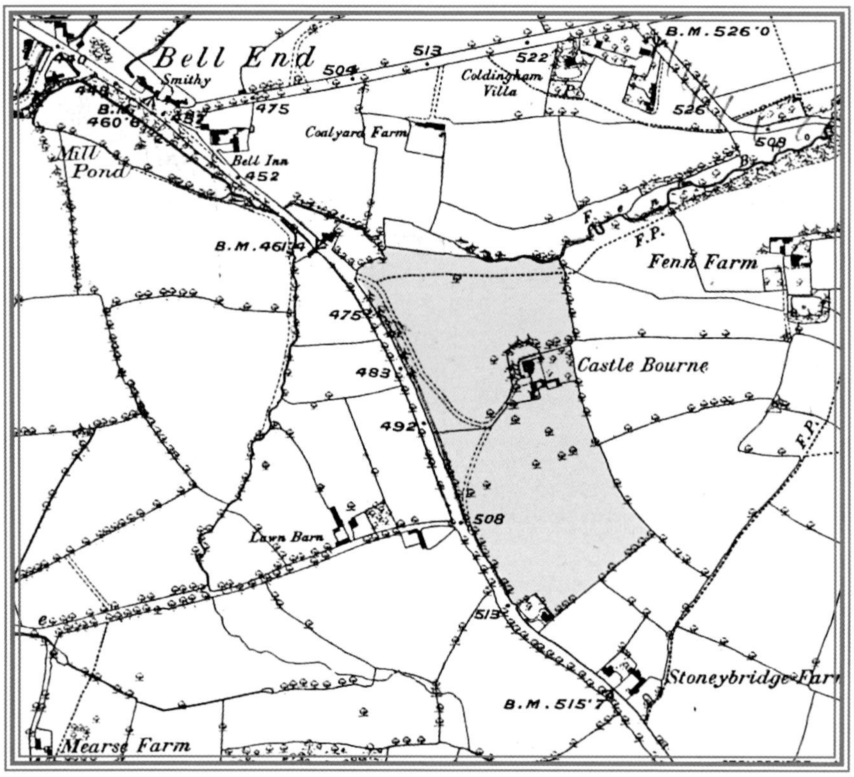

HER Ref: WSM28954.

Grid Ref: SO 944 769.

Postcode: DY9 9XX .

O.S. 6" Map No. 9SE.

Date of Map: 1884, with deduced extent of park & gardens shaded (not shaded on 1905 OS).

There is an 18th century, castle folly (see Clent Grove) and wall joining a mid-19th century house. Mowl calls this landscape "a home-grown, towered Picturesque" (pp. 82-3). The 1882 OS 6 inch shows a small park from which a few trees survive.

T. Mowl, *Historic Gardens of Worcestershire,* 2006, pp. 82-3.

Chaddesley Corbett Park

Parish: Chaddesley Corbett

HER Ref: WSM10308.

Grid Ref: SO 896 736.

Postcode: unidentified.

O.S. 6" Map No: 15NW.

Date of Map: 1883.

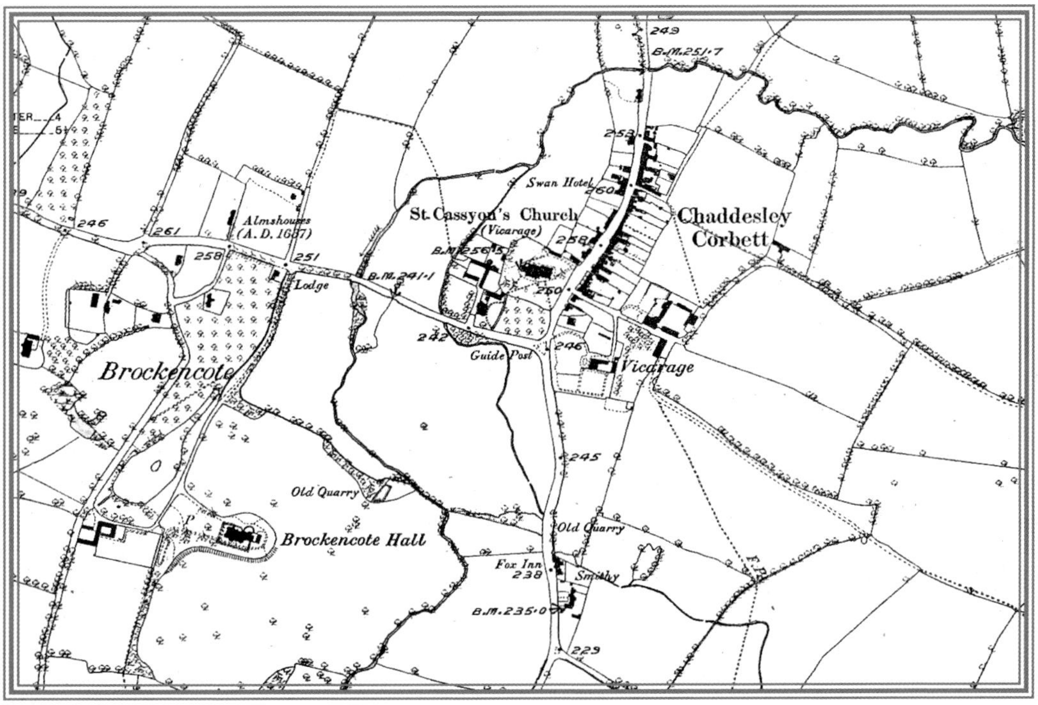

The HER has identified the medieval deer park as documented in the 14th century when, in the ownership of the Beauchamp family, it was sold to John Pakington in the 15th century; repairs were made to the Deer House in 1417. A 1754 valuation of the Throckmorton Estate (CRO 4000/298) has several park names attached to fields to an area north-east of SO 887 736 (SMR) which is close to Brockencote Hall and also close to Lodge Farm and Fold Farm situated either side of the village street. The relevant field names are located to the west of the street north and south of the village: Pirkell Park; Potter's Park; Long Park; Middle Park; Upper Park; Dyall Park; Yew Tree Park; Watch Oak Park. Dyall Park was part of Lady Yate's property in the 17th century (see Harvington Hall). The suggested location of the medieval park is well defined on the OS Pathfinder 953 as north and south of the Mustow Green to Chaddesley Corbett road with Dobes Lane as a west boundary to the south and its continuation as a footpath towards Bluntington to the north-east. The garden of the house called Dial Park has been open occasionally in recent years as part of the National Gardens Scheme. The parkland is now open farmland but retains some parkland quality with mature trees and long vistas.

Chadwich Manor

Parish: Bromsgrove

HER Ref: WSM06610.

Grid Ref: SO 973 760.

Postcode: B61 0QG.

O.S. 6" Map No. 16NW, 10SW.

Date of both Maps: 1883.

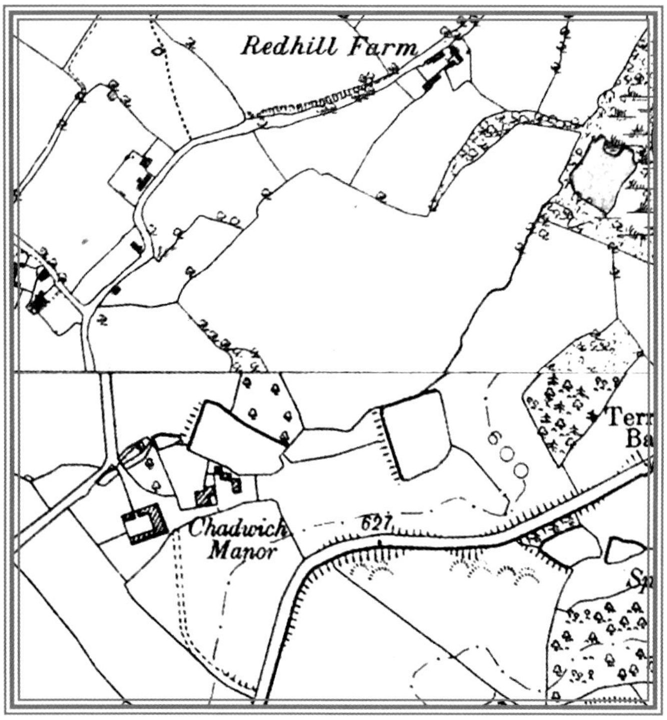

Pevsner (p. 257) dates the present farmhouse to the late 17th century. A substantial manor house is illustrated in miniature in a 1764 map (CRO 4370/43 iii) of Manor and Farm. A 1787 plan (CRO 5119/35) shows the house with a fenced garden. Chadwich is on Cary's 1805 map as a residence. Sale particulars of 1836 (CRO 5119/35) give the area covered by mansion house, yards and court garden (1) as 2.2 acres with the great pool adjoining and the whole property as 591 acres.

On the 1906 Bartholomew map the park lies between Redhill Lane (north-west) and the A38 (south-east side); Manor Farm today is bounded by the M5 to the west with the line of fishponds hard up against the A38. The Holy Well (chalybeate Spring) is sited slightly closer to Rubery to the north-east of the site. The National Trust now manages the gardens and a substantially intact park landscape.

N. Pevsner, *Worcestershire,* 1968

Chambers Court

Parish: Longdon, Queenhill & Holdfast

HER Ref: WSM08777. Grid Ref: SO 844 355.

Postcode: GL20 6AS.

O.S. 6" Map No: 54NE/SE.

Date of Map: 1884, with extent of park & gardens shaded as 1905 OS.

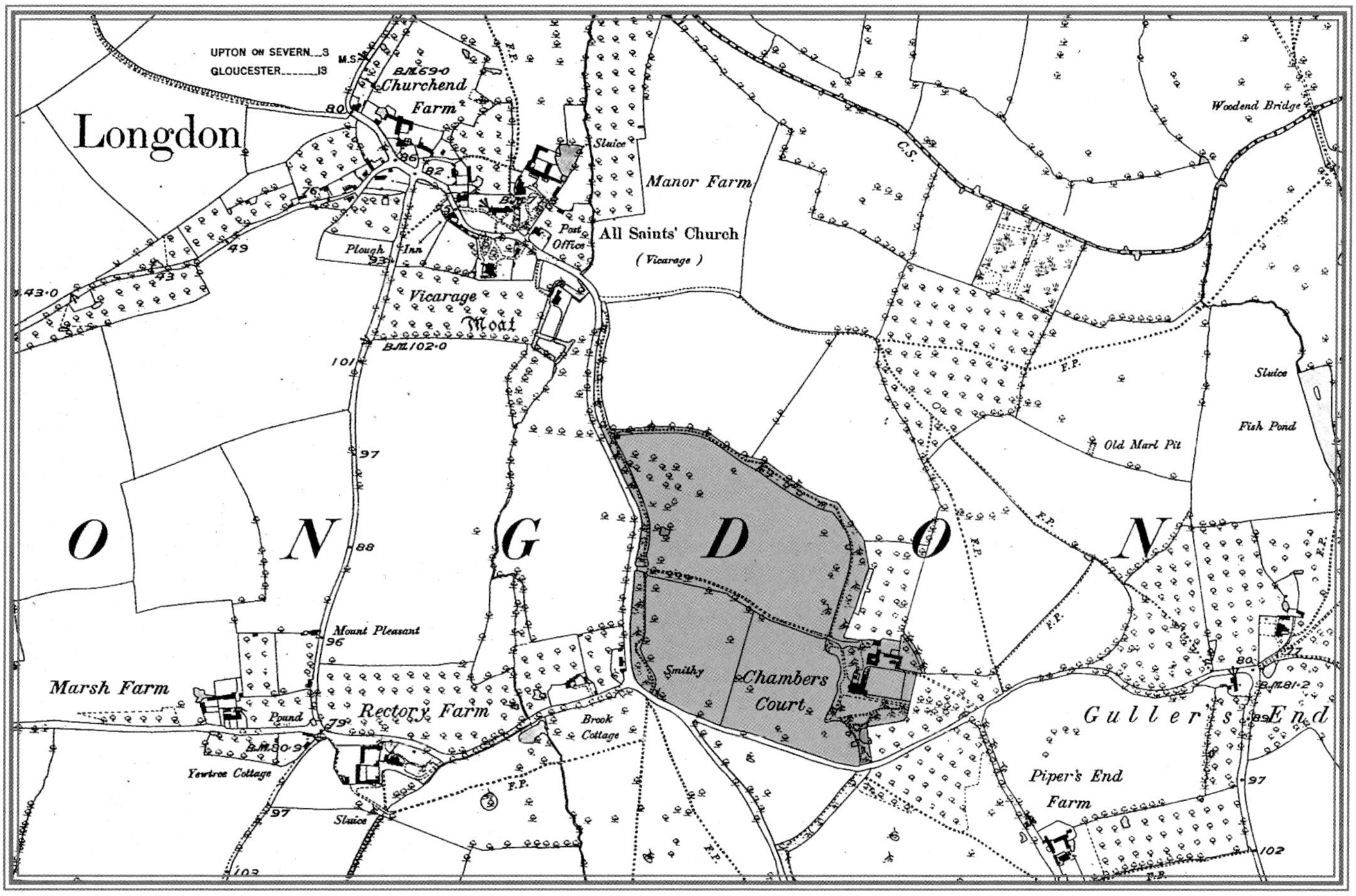

The 1882 OS 6 inch shows a park exactly defined by the corner between the B4211 and the M50.
The house accompanying this small park is circa 1850 around an 18th century core. The stone conservatory is remarked by BoE (p. 437).
In 2016 much of the park, walled garden and conservatory remain unchanged.

A. Brooks & N. Pevsner, *Worcestershire,* 2007 (BoE).

Cleeve Prior Manor House

Parish: Cleeve Prior

HER Ref: WSM21264.
Grid Ref: SP 089 494.
Postcode: WR11 5LQ.
O.S. 6" Map No: 43NW.
Date of Map: 1884.

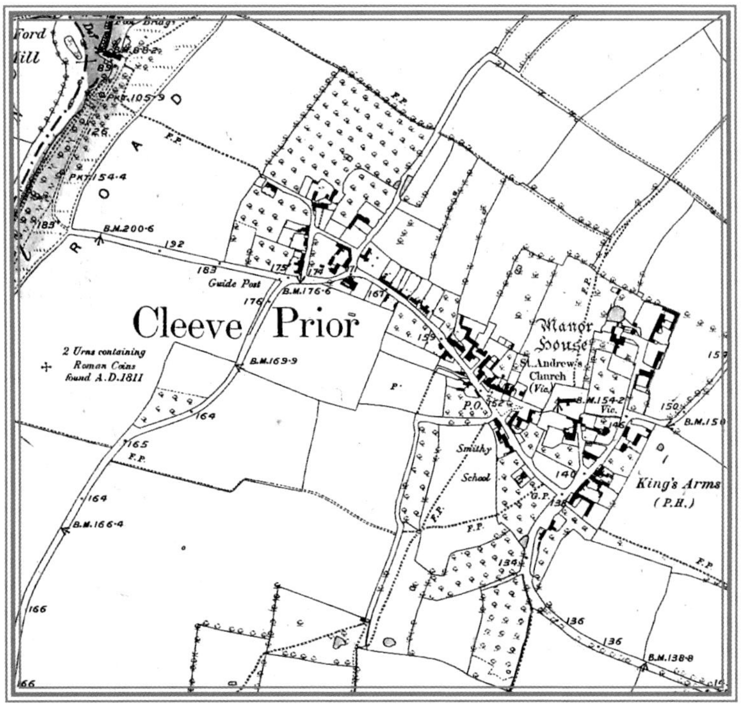

Both images from G. Jekyll & C. Hussey, *Garden Ornament,* 1914/1927.

The house is late-16th century with substantial 18th century alterations. The outbuildings include an 18th century summer-house. The 16 topiared (probably 17th century) yew trees are said to represent the 12 Apostles and the 4 Evangelists, "a masterpiece of garden handicraft" (*Country Life*, VII, 1900, p. 656 & p. 736, with illus.). The listing: "The yew walk runs east from the Manor for 30 metres to the entry gate and steps, and is formed of a double row of clipped yews ... Lawn to either side, with fine herbaceous borders" (HE Register 1986).
Mowl (p. 130 with illus.) quotes the reverential response of Sir Arthur Quiller-Couch and the artist-designer Alfred Parsons who visited Cleeve Prior while canoeing on the Avon circa 1892. Their experience is well-captured by Tyndale's watercolour published in 1909. Jekyll & Hussey's 1914/1927 book on garden ornament has illustrations under two headings: Gates and Topiary Work. Gates, plate 38 is described as "Wooden gate of excellent design at Cleeve Prior Manor, Worcestershire. Painted white, it shows up well against the background of yews". Topiary Work, plate 11 is described as "The great clipped yews called the Twelve Apostles... Another example of a design, originally trim, swollen with the years into the most curious shapes".

A Plan by John Snape of 1772 shows a single row of yews across the front of the Manor and a double line of yews across a field (Well Close), i.e. in a T formation. A path parallel with the house connected it with the Church yard. A formal garden with two beds was laid out at this end of the house, separated from an orchard by another row of trees (probably yews). Very substantial farm buildings lay around the other two sides. Robert Settiplace, Esq. was the lessee of 375 acres and of the relevant grounds of the "Manor House, Barns, Orchard, Garden" by the Dean and Chapter of Worcester as Lords of the Manor (CRO 1691).
The yew walk has changed very little over the last century.

G. Elgood & G. Jekyll, *Some English Gardens,* 1905, p. 70.
C. Holme, *Gardens of England in Midland and Eastern Cities,* 1908, pl. 36.
T. C. Tyndale and A. G. Bradley, *Worcestershire Watercolours,* 1909.
T. Mowl, *Historic Gardens of Worcestershiure,* 2006.
G. Jekyll & C. Hussey, *Garden Ornament,* 1914/1927.
Country Life, VII, 1900 p. 656 & 736.
HE *Register of Parks & Gardens,* 1986.
(no longer on HE Register).

The Clent Sites

The Parishes of Lower Clent and Clent extend north-south along the west side of Hagley Park and the Clent Hills. A number of properties had small parks attached to them according to the early editions of the OS 6 inch and are included in the *Survey*. Field House, Clent House, Clent Grove and Broom House are the properties in Clent that *Paterson's Roads* chose to point out in 1829. Clent Grove with a folly castle in its grounds and Clent House adjoin each other beside Clent Hills Common and close to Adam's Hill. Clent Hall lies immediately south of Clent Church. Clent Grange is further south and south of Holy Cross. Field House, the youngest of these properties is situated west of Clent Grove and Clent House. In landscape terms they are all later developments to Clent Hills Common and Walcot Hill Common now combined within the Clent Hills Country Park. The latter became a popular place for recreation from the earlier-19th century with disagreeable implications for some of their grander neighbours described here.

Clent Field House

Parish: Clent

HER Ref: WSM29007.

Grid Ref: SO 911 795.

Postcode: DY9 0HN.

O.S. 6" Map No. 9NW/SW.

Date of Map: 1887, with extent of park & gardens shaded as 1880s OS.

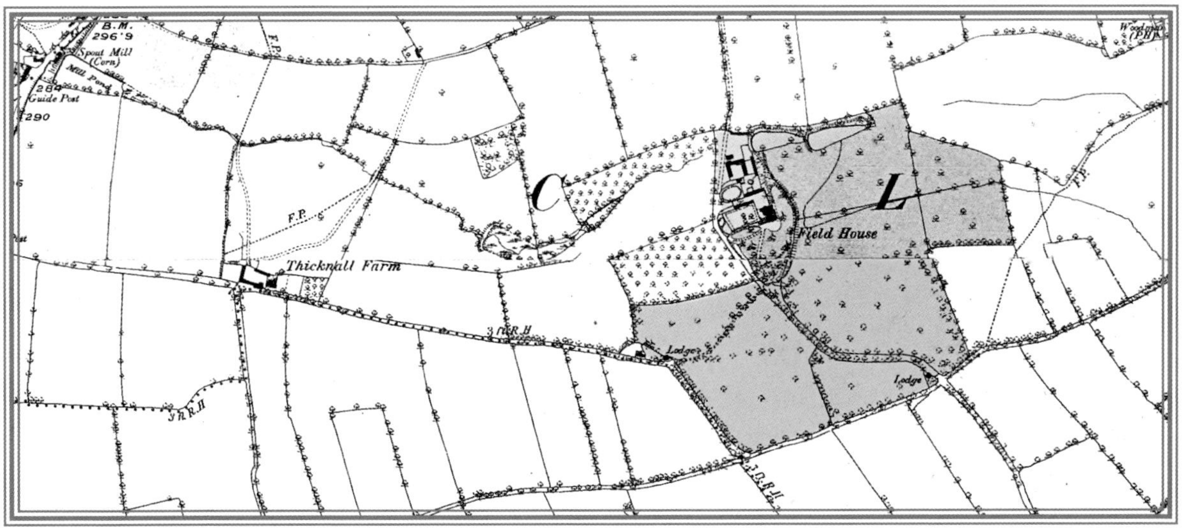

Field House, now a Residential Home, is still shown with a small park on the 1967 OS. It is situated between West Hagley and Holy Cross in Lower Clent with Broome Lane as its south boundary and the A491 to the east. The house is principally of circa 1750 and 1921 (ballroom, 1929) with an 18th century Orangery now converted into a house (Mowl, fig. 72). Field House has grounds on printed maps from 1822 (Greenwood) and already claims a park on the 1816 survey for the first OS one inch as well as on the first OS 6 inch, 1883. There were 3 pools on the property and two lodges (1870), with avenues along the drives; some of the planting along the south drive survives. 19th century maps show an embankment running round the east side of the house and farm buildings to the start of the drive to the south-east lodge. The line of pools is the distinctive feature of this landscape and are labelled Fish Ponds on the 1904 6 inch.

Gertrude Jekyll designed a Japanese Water Garden here in 1914 which is still substantially intact. Lewis illustrates the 19th century stone Conservatory and some topiary work in the garden (surviving). Mowl describes this garden as "enjoyably quirky" (pp. 149-51 & fig. 72). The parkland is now under arable crops.

K. Lewis, *Clent Remembered*, 1988.

T. Mowl, *Historic Gardens of Worcestershire,* 2006.

A. Brooks & N. Pevsner, *Worcestershire,* 2007, (BoE).

Clent Grove

Parish: Clent

HER Ref: WSM28854.

Grid Ref: SO 923 799.

Postcode: DY9 9PB.

O.S. 6" Map No. 9NE.

Date of Map: 1884, with extent of park & gardens shaded as 1905 OS.

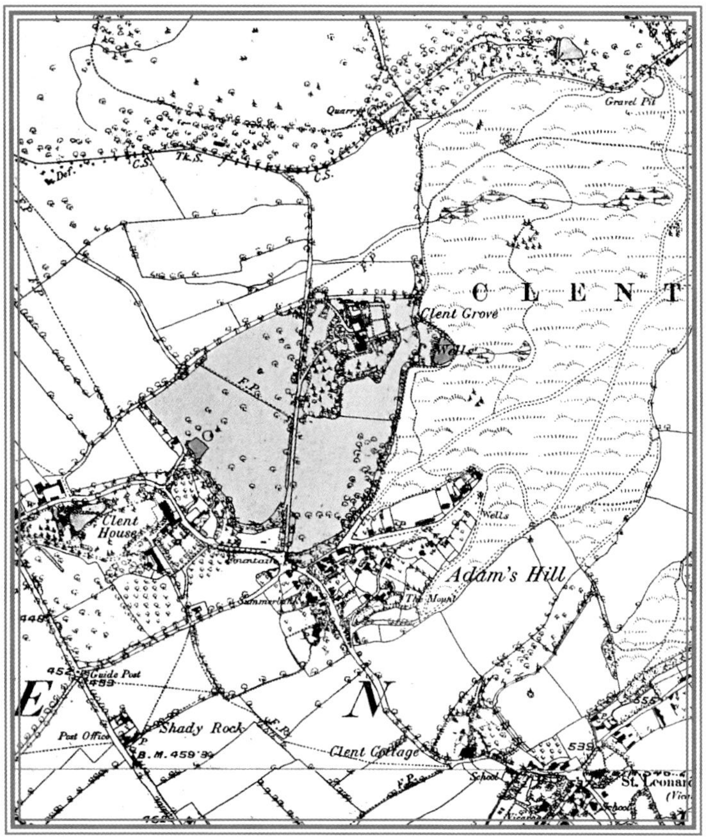

The castle folly at Clent Grove, 2014. Photo, J. Patton.

Clent Grove is noticed by Paterson's Roads in 1829 (p. 155) when it belonged to the Misses Liell; John Liell Franklin sold the property in 1871. Clent Grove was rebuilt circa 1863 in a sub-Italianate style (BoE, p. 232). An early-19th century plan of the estate (WAAS 1947/2) shows most of the landscape features found in a plan of 1871 (WAAS 1947/1) and on the first edition of the OS 6 inch surveyed in 1881/2.

The small park then had a lodge, two pools, one at each end of the property and the late 18th century "castle". In 1871 house and garden occupied 2 acres, the upper park 11 acres, the plantation and castle 1 acre and the Middle and Lower Parks 4 and 9 acres respectively. One walled kitchen garden was attached to the lodge and another to the Home Farm. A drive linked the house to the north pool, plantation and castle.

A watercolour of circa 1800 shows the house behind a large lawn with a large urn (Lewis). The east boundary of the small park is now the west boundary of the Clent Hills Country Park.

Today, much of the parkland survives with veteran trees, as does one walled garden and the castle folly.

An outline plan of circa 1773 (WAAS 866/15) documents as planned a "Castle", "New Pool", "Garden", "Hall" and "Malt House". Clent Castle on Adam's Hill, is composed of two linked, round towers with gothick windows which the BoE compares to the folly at Castle Bourne. Its interior decoration had gone by 1974 (Jones, p. 340). The building of the Castle (Grade II) is attributed to Thomas Liell who may have acquired the Gate House and redeveloped and renamed it Clent Grove which was then redeveloped in its turn (Liell Franklin). It is now Sunfield residential school.

T. Mowl, *Historic Gardens of Worcestershire*, 2006.
B. Jones, *Follies and Grottoes*, 1974.
K. Lewis, *Clent Remembered*, 1988.
A. Brooks & N. Pevsner, *Worcestershire*, 2007 (BoE).
Paterson's Roads, 1829.

Clent Hall

Parish: Clent

HER Ref: WSM28953.

Grid Ref: SO 929 792.

Postcode: DY9 9PL.

O.S. 6" Map No. 9NE/SE.

Date of Map: 1884, with extent of park & gardens shaded as 1880s OS.

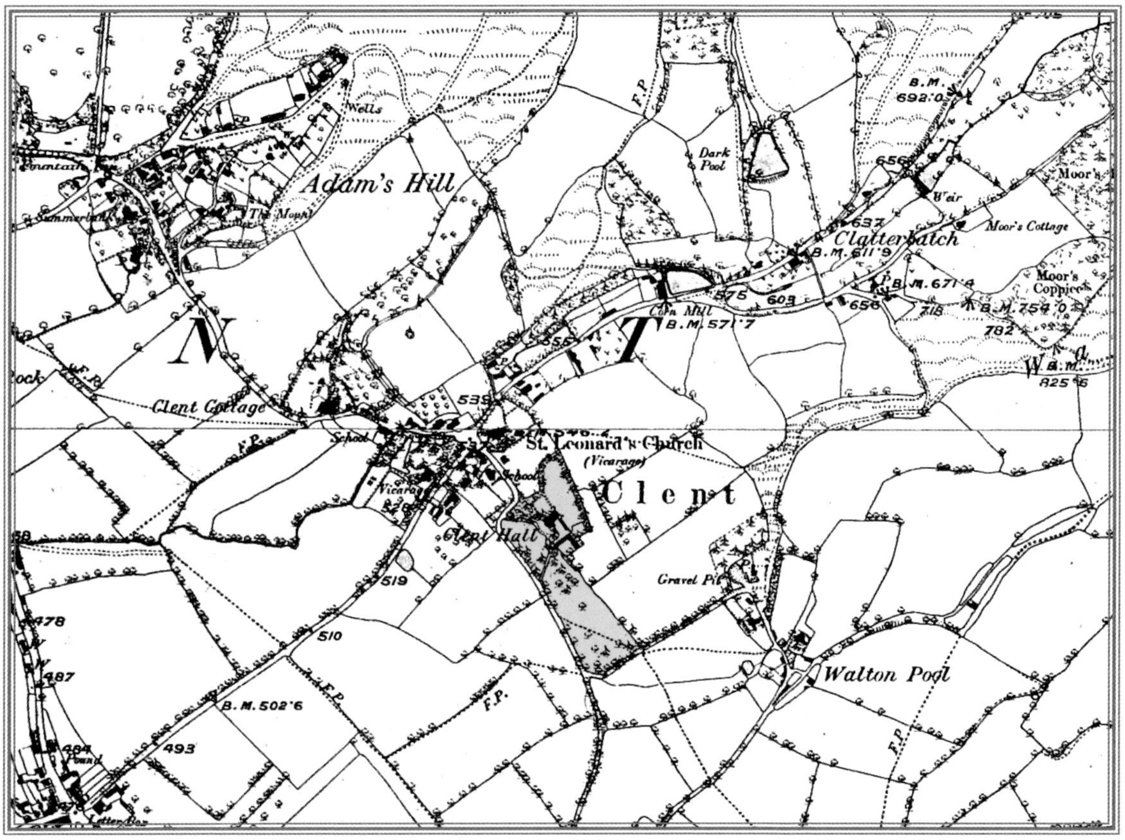

The house is late-17th to 19th century and Grade II Listed. A view in Lewis only shows a small lawn with modest pieces of topiary and 2 terraces leading down to the lawn from the house. The Listing notes that the garden was laid out circa 1875 by Sir Joseph Hooker, Director of Kew Gardens. Little is shown on a sale plan of 1863 when part of the ground was being offered for sale for villas. Sidwell details a small semi-formal water garden and rock garden and the addition in 1903-1925 of a pets' cemetery (pp. 37-8).

In 2013 the original Hooker layout was still substantially intact and the garden well maintained.

R. Sidwell, *West Midlands Gardens,* 1981.
K. Lewis, *Clent Remembered,* 1988.
A. Brooks & N. Pevsner, *Worcestershire,* 2007 (BoE).

Clent Hills Country Park

Parish: Clent

HER Ref: WSM28952.

Grid Ref: SO 923 806.

Postcode: DY9 9LG.

O.S. 6" Map No. 9NE/SE.

Date of Map: 1884.

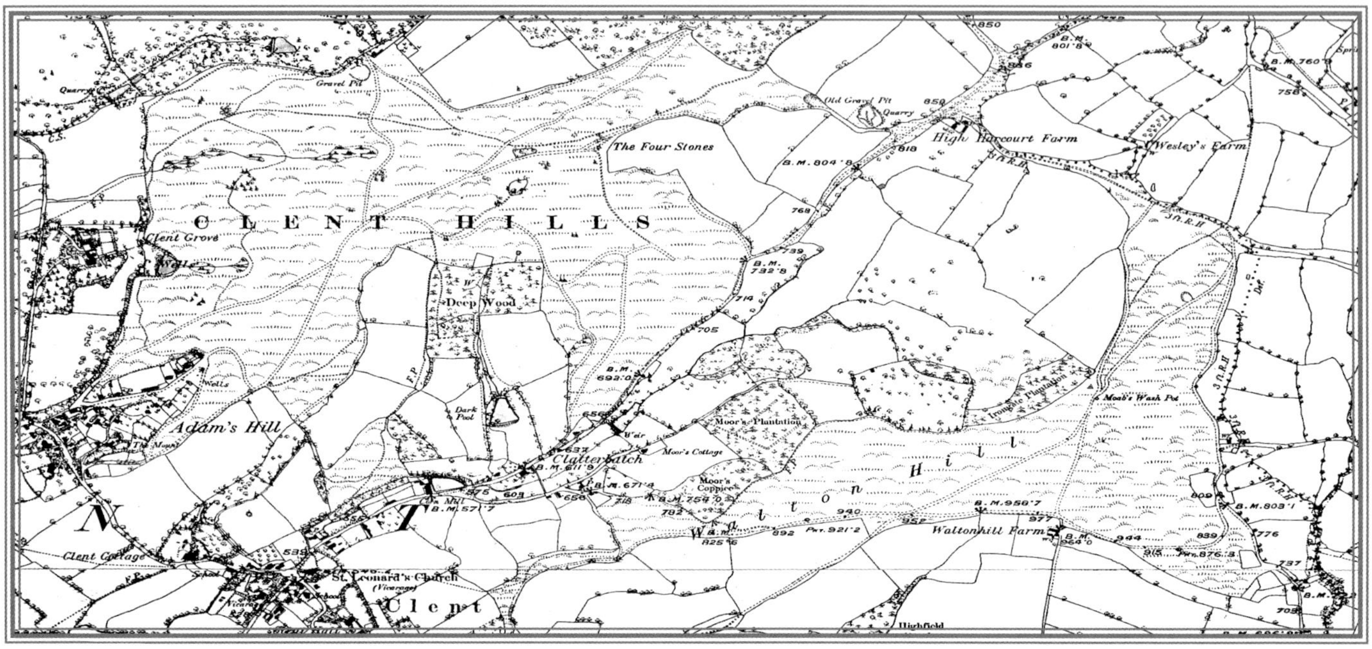

The country park has continued the recreational use of the area into the 21st century, it having for long been "the special holiday centre of Clent ... with public houses, tea gardens and the like ... (and) plenty of seats" (Worth, 1889, p. 77). The park of approximately 500 acres, is a combination of two Commons, Clent Hill Common and Walcot Hill Common. Both were acquired by the National Trust (with assistance from the John Feeney Trust) from the Worcestershire County Council and the Bromsgrove District Council in 1958. The manorial rights (i.e. ownership) had been given previously to the District Authorities by Lord Cobham of Hagley Hall which neighboured the Common on its north side. A previous Lord Cobham, as one of the Conservators, was involved in an acrimonious dispute that lasted from around 1880 to 1920 which ended up in the House of Lords. The dispute was directly caused by an escalation in the traditional use of the Clent Hills by holiday makers from Birmingham and the Black Country; booths and shooting galleries had been erected on the boundary of what was regarded as a public park in 1881. John Amphlett of Clent Grove on one side of the Common erected fences to protect his property which were regarded as encroachments by the Conservators. Conflicting surveys complicated arguments about boundary lines and arguments as to how far from the centre line should a hedge stretch with or without a ditch? In earlier years, entertainments were provided by ponies and donkeys for hire. As late as 1921, John Amphlett II contested the Conservators' right to grant permits for the sale of provisions and other articles from handcarts and baskets.

Since the advent of the railway, many came to the Common via Hagley Station. By 1900 there were several pubs and small hotels and B & Bs advertising "accommodation for teas...and apartments". Bay Tree Cottage offered two bedrooms, a sitting room, good cooking and attendance, wagonette for hire, large or small tea parties catered for." Tourist literature had developed much earlier, e.g. William Timmings's *Guide to the Clent Hills*, 1835, and Hugh Miller's *First Impressions of England and its People* of 1846. Miller found Clent to be "one of the prettiest and most characteristic of all old English villages" and its charm as a contrast to the Midlands industrial scene - "no more noisy workshops – no stir of business - nothing doing or likely to be done". Clent Hills Country Park has two centuries of public access and holiday use behind it.

Clent Historical Society, *Clent celebrated in Words and Pictures*, 1999.

K. Lewis, *Clent Remembered*, 1988.

R. N. Worth, *Tourist's Guide to Worcestershire*, 1889.

Clent House

Parish: Clent

HER Ref: WSM04937.

Grid Ref: SO 922 797.

Postcode: DY9 9PY.

O.S. 6" Map No. 9NE/SE.

Date of Map: 1884, with extent of park & gardens shaded as 1880s OS.

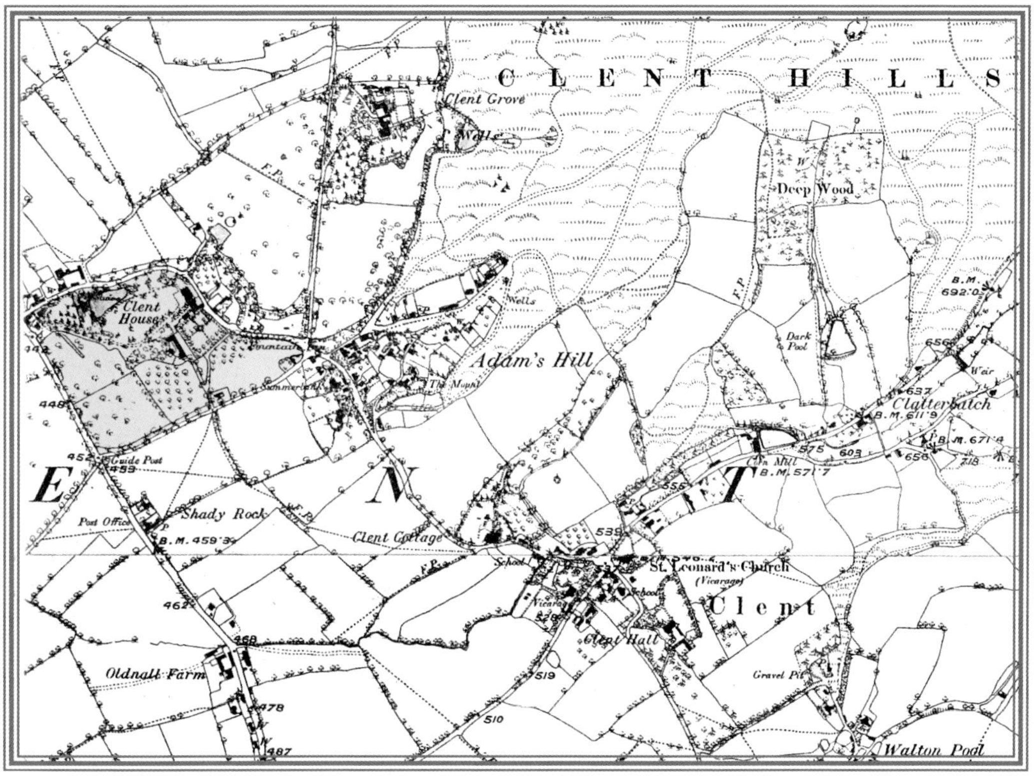

Clent House, Clent Grove, Broom House and Field House are the properties thought worthy of notice by Paterson's Roads in 1829.

Clent House, which was rebuilt in the early-18th century, was demolished in 1936, however, the Stables dated 1709 remain (BoE), now converted to residential use. A view of the House with a freestanding Conservatory is in Strong (fig. 46) and in Reid (p. 156) and the front door from the Jacobean House is now in the Crypt of Worcester Cathedral. Some grounds are discernible on Greenwood's 1822 map and Paterson in 1829 noted John Amphlett's residence. The grounds of Clent House were larger and more elaborate than those of its better-known neighbour, Clent Grove. A pool and large walled garden are prominent within a site neatly defined and contained by local roads. The intimacy of this area has been diminished by the inflated A491 but the original garden pools and walled garden survive intact within a well maintained modern garden.

R. Strong, *The Destruction of the Country House*, 1974.
P. Reid, *Burke's and Savills Guide to Country Houses*, Vol. 2, 1980.
A. Brooks & N. Pevsner, *Worcestershire*, 2007 (BoE).

Cockshoot Farm

Parish: Kenswick & Wichenford

HER Ref: WSM28899/31074.

Grid Ref: SO 923 806.

Postcode: WR6 6YL.

O.S. 6" Map No: 28NW.

Date of Map: 1883.

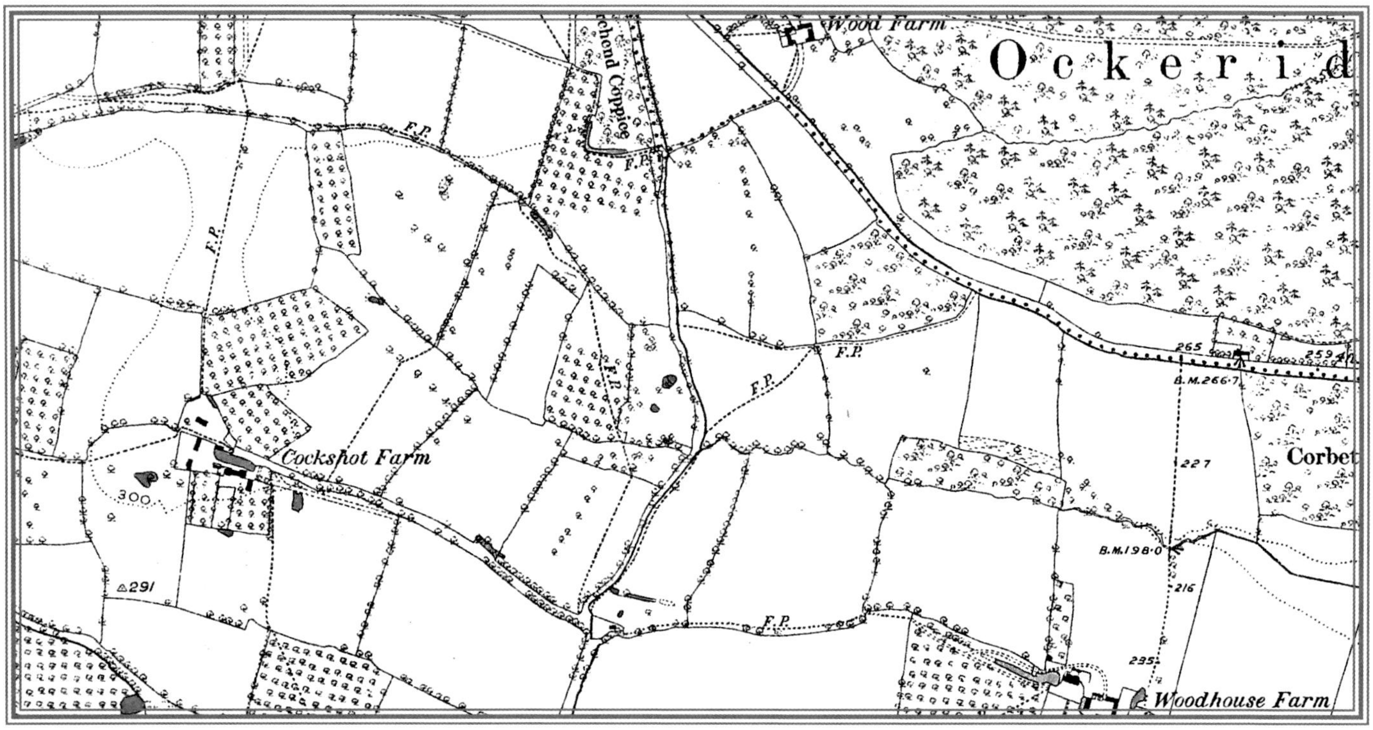

The Farm was called Cockshutt Orchard around 1730 when it is recorded in a memorandum book and some loose-leaf plans as a significant house (CRO 6134/44). The house was H shaped with two slightly projecting wings; its scale is shown as similar to that of Kenswick and the Noak but smaller than that of Wichenford Court. "The Ground Plot of the Cockshutt Orchard House" is dated 1729. One of the plans shows "The Park" (20 acres), "the further Park field" (7 acres) and "the nearest Park" (7 acres) all just north-west of the house. The most detailed of several simple maps shows an enclosure on the south side with a fence dividing this into two with probably an orchard as the outer part with a gate or steps leading to an avenue to the Martley road described as "the Front Walk". The plan has two "new proposed walk(s)" radiating south-west and south-east. Much of the detail on plan may not have been carried into effect but the intention was for the walks to be bordered by elms (front), limes (east), chestnut (west) and apple ("Back front Walk in ye Vinayd"). The residence and now Farmhouse is equidistant between Ridgend Farm on the south and Birchend Farm to the north. A memorandum in this notebook records a practical method for surveying: 50 yards equals to 90 "of my ordinary slow walking steps". At the back of the house was a pond 50 yards long and what appears to be a small canal 5 yards wide.

The Notebook is as informative about the practicalities of farming as well as garden fashion. The daily concerns of the farmer can be glimpsed: e.g. the girth of trees "in which hedge/of what sort/when measured" in 1728, 1733 and 1736! There is an estimate, dated 1738 , for "The Parts of a Waggon and the Price of each part" as well as a note that Wm. Walker of St. John's (Worcester) had been paid £5 for a new waggon in 1732. One of the accounts about the house (Bricks, Tyles etc.) "is entered in my Father Nash's own handwriting in an old poor Robins Almanack for 1679". Two rudimentary maps with thumbnail sketches include "Noke", the Noak, another property that belonged to the Nash family. These tiny sketches pick out Wichenford Court; Barbers; Kenswick.

The name of the Farm has changed from Cockshuite in 1828 to Cockshot Farm in 1897 and Cockshoot Farm today. There is no trace of parkland today.

Estate Plan circa 1730, (CRO 6134/44): Cockshutt Farm.
S. J. Price, *Cockshoot Farm*, Report to Wichenford Heritage Group, 2007.

..........continued from previous page

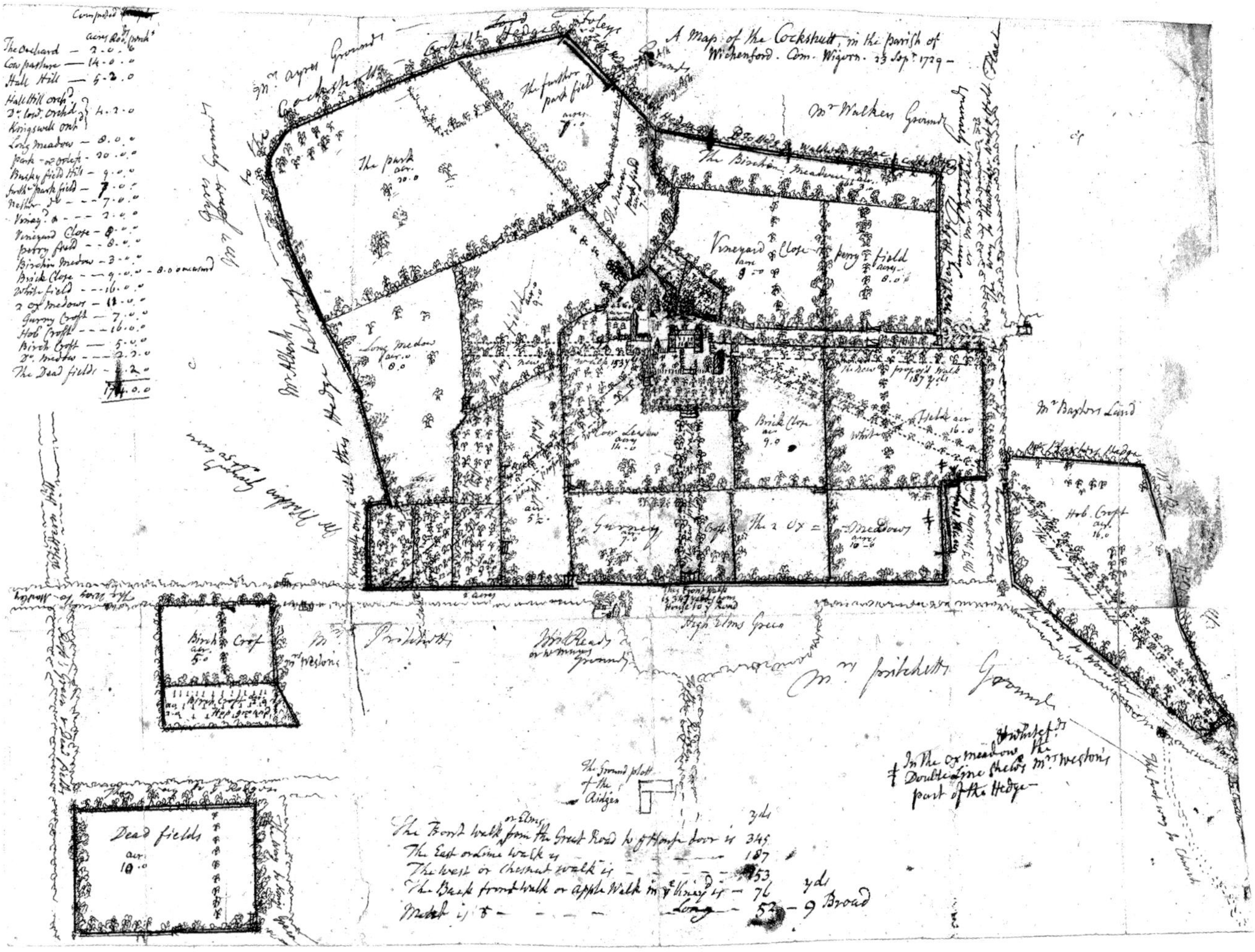

ABOVE: "Map of the Cockshutt, 1729", © WAAS 6134/44.

BELOW: Map of Cockshoot Farm with neighbouring properties, circa 1730, © WAAS 6134/44.

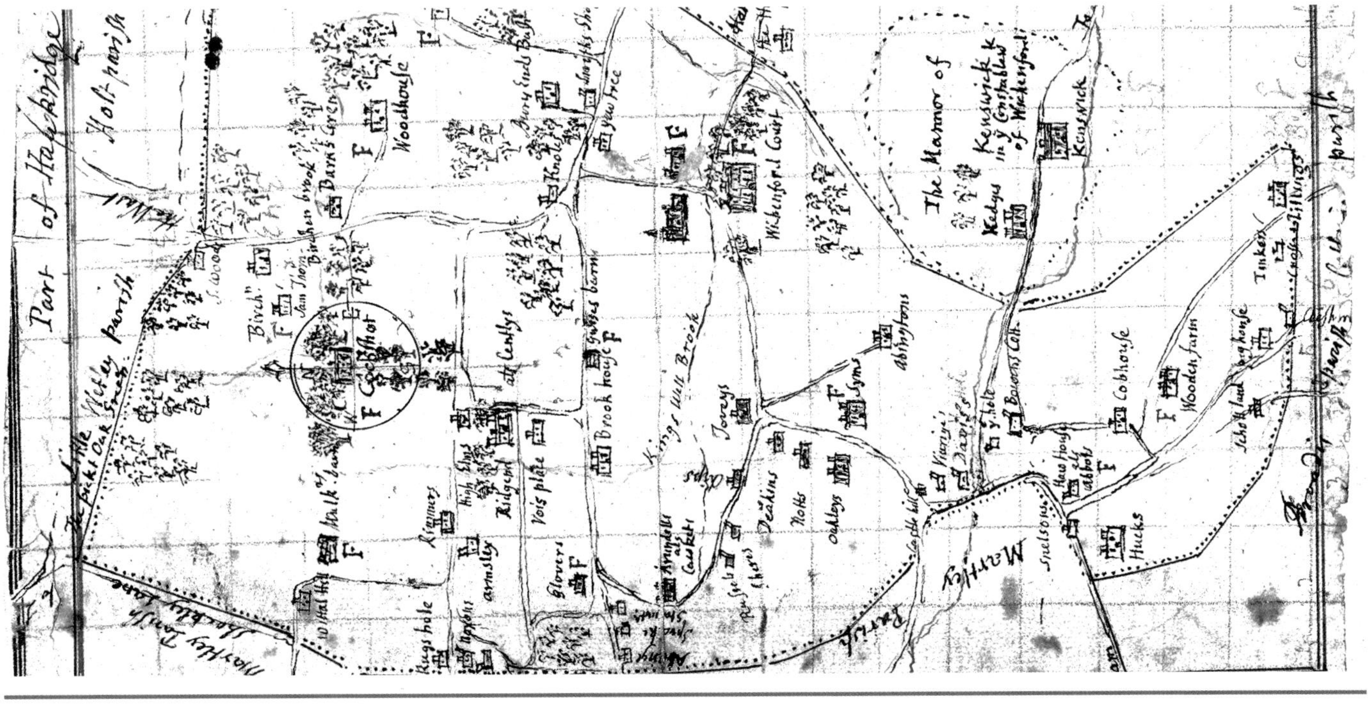

Cofton Hall

Parish: Cofton Hackett

HER Ref: WSM01869.

Grid Ref: SP 001 751. Postcode: B45 8BD.

O.S. 6" Map No. 16NW, 16NE.

Date of both Maps: 1905, with deduced extent of gardens shaded (not shaded on 1905 OS).

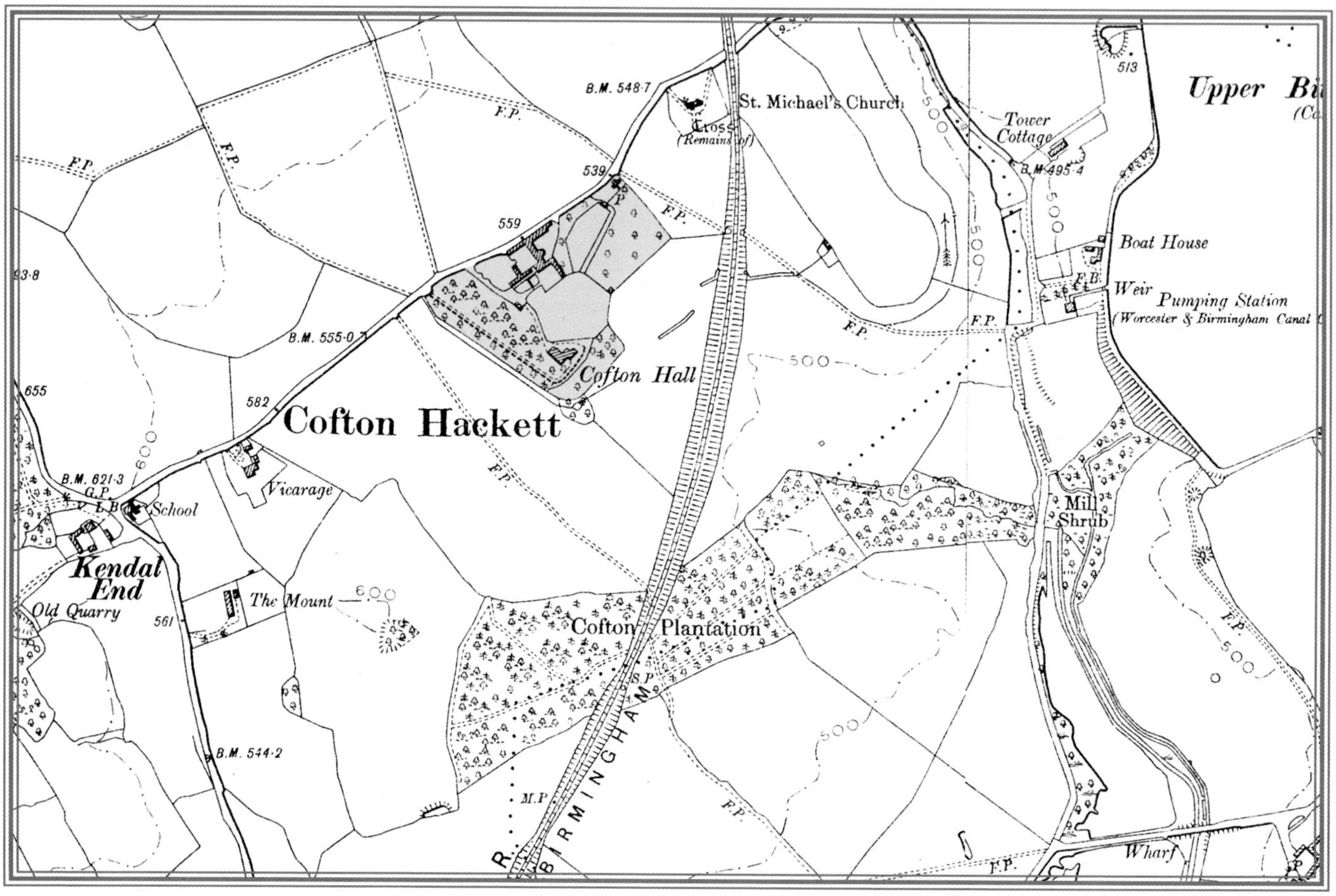

There are surviving remains of a high status mansion from the 15th century (hall) but, partly because the house was fired during the English Civil War, most of the present house and walled garden dates from the 18th and 19th centuries. Nash described the mansion as a large, convenient, manor house in 1781. Tunnicliff notes Crofton Hall as a significant residence in 1788 although George Byfield's designs for a remodelling are dated 1796. There was an estate Sale in 1809 (WAAS 4594). A small park shows on the 1816 2 inch survey for the 1st edition of the OS. By 1822, when the house is noticed by Greenwood as having grounds, it was tenanted by Mr. More "a respectable farmer" implying a diminishing in the status of the property. Bentley's Directory of 1840 refers to "a large convenient house, surrounded by a pleasant grove ... the railway runs through the grounds." The railway ran very close to the Hall on its east side, while it is confined by the B4120 on the west side under the Lickey Hills and Cofton Hill. The Upper Bittell Reservoir fills in the landscape to the east and towards the A491. To the immediate north of the Hall there is another reservoir and Cofton Park, a public park, and beyond that the now demolished Longbridge Motor Works.

P. Reid, *Burke's & Savills Guide to Country Houses*, Vol 2, 1980.

J. Bentley, *History and Guide to Stourbridge*, 1840.

C. & J. Greenwood, *Worcestershire Delineated*, 1822.

T. R. Nash, *Collections for the History of Worcestershire*, Vol I & II, 1781/2.

W. Tunnicliff, *A Survey of the County of Worcester*, 1788.

Conderton Manor

Parish: Conderton & Overbury

HER Ref: WSM04664.
Grid Ref: SO 965 372. Postcode: GL20 7PR.
O.S. 6" Map No: 55NE. Date of Map: 1884.

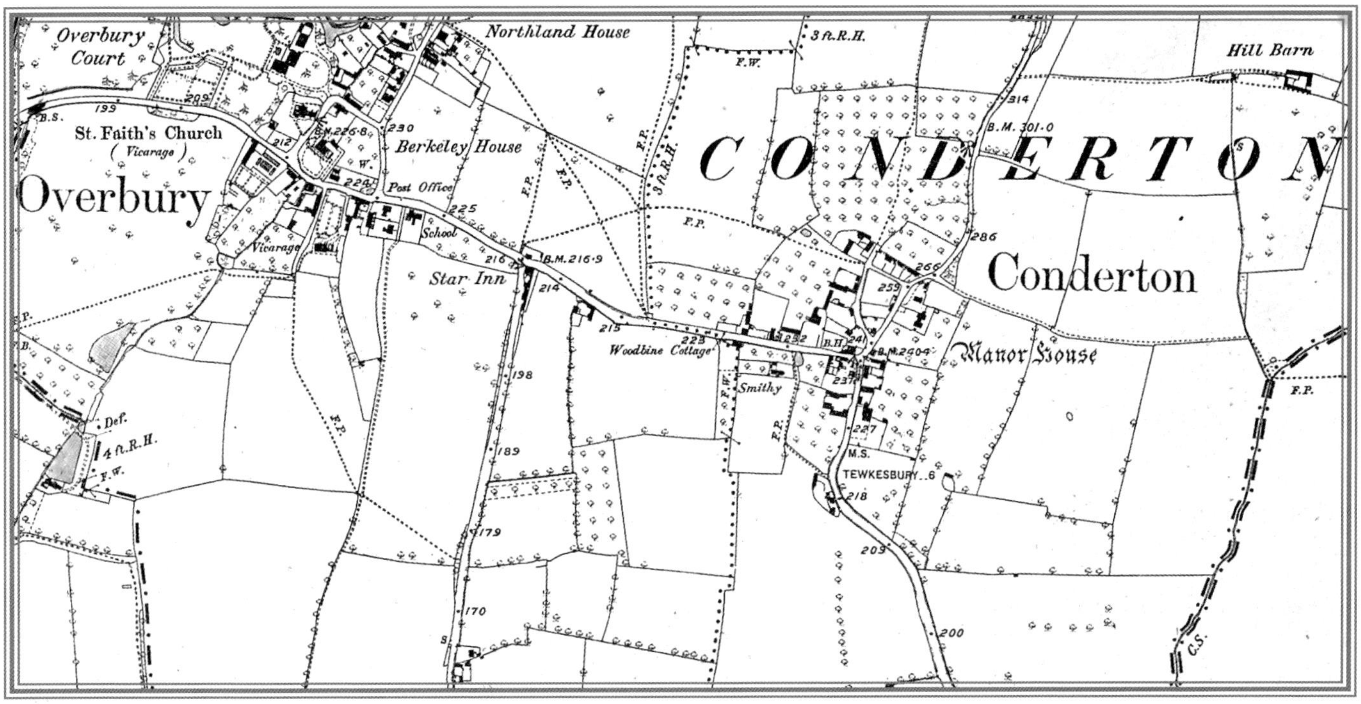

The Manor House is late-17th century with a Norman Shaw wing of 1888 (BoE). "The garden around Conderton Manor was planned by Brenda Colvin for a Mrs. Maxwell in 3 campaigns in the 1930's. Colvin laid out three vistas at right angles to each other" (Mowl, p. 75). Sidwell in 1981 says: "It must now be reckoned one of the most important collections of woody plants in our area" and mentions that some of the planting was done in the 1950s, which may be the date of the swimming pool surrounded by box hedges.

There was an early-19th century bark house in the garden which eventually succumbed to age. It has been rebuilt as a summer-house using the original floor and roof. The garden as developed from the 1990s by the present owner is fully described by Mowl (p. 156), e.g. the Kitchen garden "planted with roses and holly hocks to a cottage garden effect but on a grand scale." The garden benefits from its collection of unusual ornamental trees.

T. Mowl, *Historic Gardens of Worcestershire,* 2006, p. 75 (Colvin design).
A. Brooks & N. Pevsner, *Worcestershire,* 2007 (BoE).
R. Sidwell, *West Midlands Gardens,* 1981.

TOP: summer-house with original bark house roof and floor.
BOTTOM: steps designed by Brenda Colvin. Photos, J. Patton

Cookhill Priory

Parish: Cookhill

HER Ref: WSM29008.

Grid Ref: SP 054 573. Postcode: B49 5LN.

O.S. 6" Map No: 30SE.

Date of Map: 1884, with deduced extent of grounds shaded (not shaded on 1905 OS).

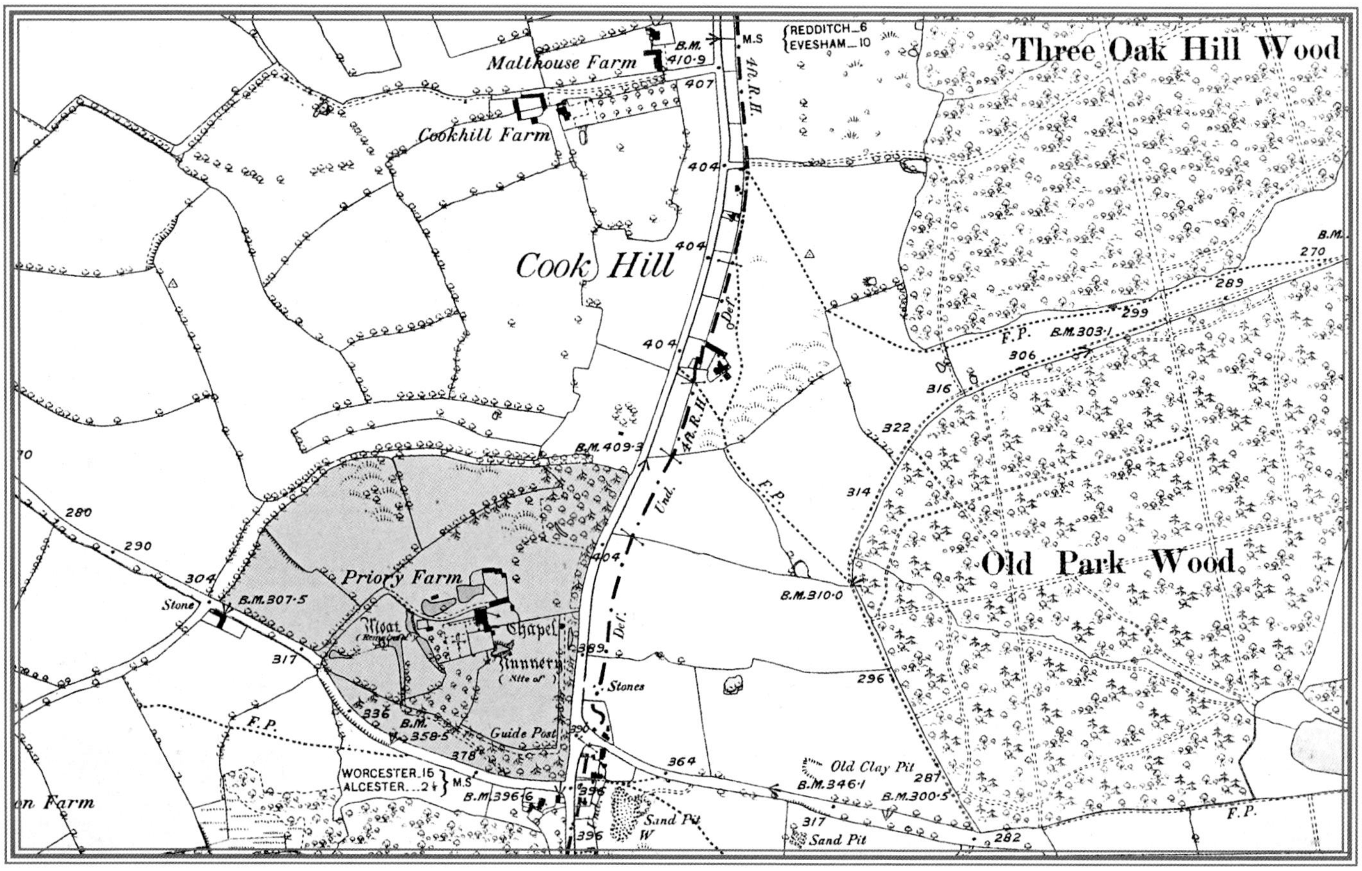

Remains of the Cistercian nunnery were incorporated into buildings of 1763 and 1783, themselves significantly enlarged in 1907 (BoE, p. 238). Reid (pp. 198-9) illustrates 3 views of the house including the castellated, gothick chapel. The Priory is included for its 18th century gazebo set above the house commanding views of the Malverns. The Mansion and Manor of Cookhill were advertised circa 1814 (London Soc. of Antiquaries, Prattinton Coll.: CRO microfilm I (xiii)) as having an excellent garden, greenhouse, summer-house, pleasure ground, rabbit warren and fishponds; moat and ponds are very visible. However, a map of the Crookhill Estate, as belonging to John Phillips Esq., made in 1824 has Nunnery Wood (31 acres) as the only notable feature. "Collections" made at the same moment, 1825, by P.P. a friend of the owner, John Phillips, notes that the house at that time had been "built, or rather enlarged, by Capt. Fortescue, the old buildings still remaining as offices" and regarding the grounds only remarks on "A summerhouse on the brow of the hill, as you turn down from the turnpike road commanded, before the trees grew up, those very extensive views which are so much admired by travellers on the ridge way" (CRO 385/80). The most informative plan of Cookhill was made for Catherine Emma Phillips by W. Endall, Surveyor, Henley in Arden, in 1877 (CRO 385/1 and 385/62). Most of the land (128 acres) was then let but Nunnery Wood was in hand; there was a large vegetable garden between the house and the pools on the west side and Old Rabbit Burrow Road to the north, which preserved the memory of the warren. Within the immediate grounds there is a circular feature with path round it called Mount Piece.

A. Brooks & N. Pevsner, *Worcestershire,* 2007 (BoE).

P. Reid, *Burke's and Savills Guide to Country Houses,* Vol. 2, 1980.

..........continued from previous page

..........continued from previous page

Croome first appears on a printed map in 1764 (Kitchen) and as a fenced, deer park, on Nash's 1781 map and William Tunnicliff's of 1788. Cary in 1805 shows Croome as the largest park in Worcestershire bar Westwood. In 1781, Nash estimated the park and pleasure grounds at 1200 acres "drained and beautified by an artificial river" (Vol. 1, p. 262). Nash reflected a campaign of work carried out for the 6th Earl of Coventry (1722-1809) which was then only at the half-way point.

Maps do not distinguish between deer parks and the landscape park created between 1750 and 1800. The grid ref. SO 867 442 is the western-most extension of the park as in the 1905 6 inch OS, short of the Panorama but still significantly west of the M5. Christopher Smith's two inch map of 1804 places the park between the B roads to the west and north, Dunstall Common to the south and the plantations on the east side where there is no road. The 1930 6 inch OS shows the park at its maximum, extending south of the Severn Stoke road, west of the Severn Stoke – Pirton road and stretching north-west to Knight's Hill and joining (at the cross-roads) the Old Park from east of the Kerswell Green road to the Pirton Pool.

The earliest survey map of Pirton Parish, made by Mark Pierce in 1623 (Croome Estate Archive; Mowl, *Worcestershire*, p. 45 and Gordon, 2000, Pl. IX), shows Pirton Pool exactly as today, with the Heath to north and west and fields to the south-east clearly connected to Pirton Court, set within moats together with a formal garden. The Old Park (marked on the Pathfinder OS) is excluded from the 1623 map being outside the Parish; this was then in the ownership of "Sir John Fouttot" (Folliot). Pirton was not added to the Croome estate until 1627. Pirton Park "called the fallow deer park" was surveyed in 1708 by John Troate in two halves. It was then a relatively new park having been established in 1687. The only surviving drawing attributable to Lancelot Brown, the creator of the 18th century landscape park, is for this part of the Croome landscape (WAAS 30046/12) but some planting "by Pirton Pool" is documented in 1746, just before Brown's arrival. It was still called the Park on the 1840 Tithe Map (WAAS 1606). Pirton Pool, as a large piece of water (about 50 acres), added another dimension to the 6th Earl's "barren landscape" before his development of the lake and serpentine river beside the mansion, which is a principal feature of the landscape today.

Mowl (*Worcestershire*, p. 48) stresses the fondness of the 6th Earl for his earlier home at Pirton Court and argues that his Croome developments in the third quarter of the 18th century were strongly influenced by the Earl's desire to connect his old and new homes with drives and walks and even some buildings. This is most persuasive when looking at John Snape's 1796 Map (WAAS 30046/15 & 405, Gordon, 2018, pp. 6/7) which extends as far north as Lickmoor Coppice which lies just short of Pirton Court. In the 1680s, the Coventry heir was advised that his Croome estate held "two large parks well stored with deer, the one with Fallow Deer and the other with Red Deer and "a lesser park for breeding of colts, various very large fish ponds besides great quantities of fishing upon the Rivers Severn and Avon and other small rivers..." (Gordon, 2000, p. 50). In other words, at that time there were 3 parks: the Fallow Deer Park at Pirton; a lesser park for the breeding of colts; the Red Deer Park. The lesser park for colts could have been situated either north of the mansion (North Lawn) or south of the mansion (South Lawn) which was called the House Park in 1719 when surveyed at 80 acres. The latter would represent the north section surveyed together with a southern section in 1708 and which formed the core of the landscape park as developed by 'Capability' Brown and as defined by John Broome's plan of 1768 (WAAS 30044/10, Gordon, 2000 p. 120). Whitaker in 1892 says that this deer park occupied 400 acres, was surrounded by a flat stone wall and contained 300 fallow deer: "The park is well timbered: magnificent specimens of elm and oak abound" (p.173). Fallow deer had been exchanged for red.

A Red Deer Park was surveyed at 180 acres in 1708 with further surveys being undertaken in 1719, 1734 and 1763. This park, also probably established in the 17th century, lay south of Red Deer Farm with The Ridings, a plantation which extended south towards Baughton Hill. This extended to the Baughton to Strensham turnpike road on the south and the Bourne Brook on the east. "The Park called the Red Deer Park ... now used in husbandry" had ceased to be a deer park or exclusively so by 1719 but the deer were reinstated when the palings were put back in 1741-4 (Gordon, 2000, p. 83). The Earl's Croome Tithe Map surveyed in 1838 (WAAS 8706) shows this area east of The Ridings as fenced and compartmented into separate fields but still calls it the Red Deer Park.

An extension of the landscape park to the north-west on which the Panorama was sited and which is now cut off by the M5 Motorway, called Cubsmoor, was acquired in the context of the 1763 Enclosure Act (WAAS 5357) in a separate negotiation with a Mr. Thorneloe of Worcester, concluded by 1773.

The first gardens at Croome were developed in the 17th century after the Coventrys acquired and then developed the estate from circa 1620 and particularly from 1627 when the 1st Baron Coventry settled the estate on his heir. However, the Court itself was said to have been burnt down in the 1620s or 1630s and again circa 1640 but was rebuilt before the disruption of the English Civil War (Gordon, 2000, passim). Expenditure on the gatehouse is recorded circa 1617 when there is also reference made to pruning the vines and apricots. This is the house recorded by Henry Beighton in 1714 (Soc. of Antiquaries, London, 1953, 1982) which Gordon (2000, p. 45, illus. p. 76) sees as advanced for its date and provincial location. (Much of the archive relevant to the 17th and earlier-18th century was taken by Lady Anne Carew, daughter of the 4th Earl, to Antony House, Cornwall)

..........continued from previous page

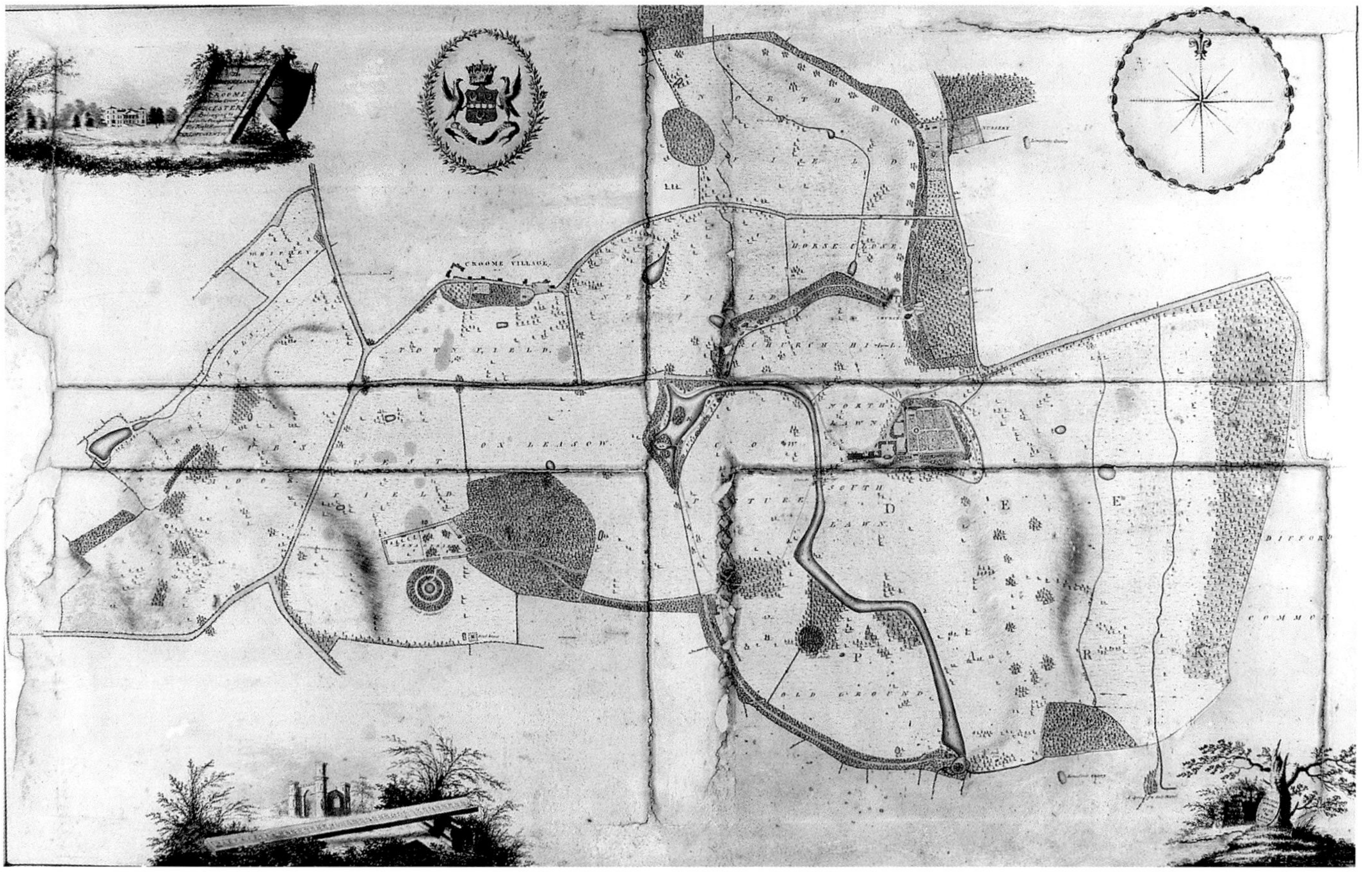

Plan of Croome Park, 1796. John Snape. © WAAS 14450/250.

Beighton's bird's eye view shows terraces on the west and east sides, summer-houses with ogee roofs on the south and *parterres de broderie* filling the radiating central section. The south boundary has metal railings which curve outwards in the centre towards elaborate iron-work gates and piers topped by eagles (the Coventry crest; piers and eagles are documented as designed and supplied between 1711 and 1717.) Gordon compares the geometric lay-out of the south garden to the contemporary garden at Hampton Court (2000, p. 77). Plants for this garden were supplied by George Adams of Stokes Croft, Bristol in 1712 and included carnations, pyramid yews and globe hollies. Adams offers to design the garden, i.e. it was not complete as claimed by the 1714 view. The central gateway with its eagle topped pillars and coats of arms and metal screens, to be supplied by Benjamin Taylor of Warwick, were not made until 1716. Henry Beighton, who was a friend of the 4th Earl, was perhaps also illustrating an aspiration rather than the achieved as in the contemporary collection of great country house mansions – *Britannia Illustrata* – published by Jan Kip and Leonard Knyff in 1707 in which Westwood rather than Croome Court was Worcestershire's sole representative.

Camilla Beresford, whose *Landscape Survey* of 1996 formed the basis for the National Trust's landscape restoration attributed a bird's eye view labelled "Croome 1750" to the Dougharty family of mid-18th century surveyors (WAAS 30044/13) (Gordon, 2000, p. 43, fig. 14), that together with a plan also circa 1750 by John Doharty junior (Croome Estate Archive) (Mowl, *Worcestershire*, pl. 5, colour) provide more potential information about Croome before Lancelot 'Capability' Brown. "Croome 1750" shows a large walled garden on the south side and raised terraces on its east and south borders, and a summer house in the centre on the south terrace with a loggia at the level of the lower central lawn. A summer-house with a vault beneath is documented in an inventory of 1719 which also refers to a Bowling Green House, Evidence House, Summer House and Garden House. The Summer House was furnished with one table, 7 chairs and a Dutch print. The main south garden is divided by 8 radiating paths with a statue in the centre. This would be the gilded *Hercules* supplied by John Nost in 1715 for 50 guineas. The Doharty plan may relate to a "final bill" of £30 in 1753 for surveying the Coventry estates. (Doharty's first bill for surveying occurs in the accounts for 1738 and is followed by others in 1740 and 1747.) This survey has an avenue going east across the north section of the park called the Lawn. The very large kitchen garden was already established in the position it occupies today but then had 3 buildings between it and

..........continued from previous page

the Court. A terrace runs west/east along the south front leading to the Evidence House (used for estate records) near a substantial piece of water, with the *Hercules* in the garden nearby. This terrace had a central section or platform which projected into the Lawn; there is no sign of the elaborate gates illustrated by Beighton. Not all this information about the earlier-18th century gardens on the south side of the Court can be reconciled. If Doharty is to be believed, the elaborate south garden adjoining the park had given way to a simple terrace.

The north side is approached through a gated wall into a grassed court called the Green Court and then through a Gatehouse into a further court divided laterally by a low wall half way to the entrance front. The old church and a pigeon house stood close to the House on the north-west. Beighton shows summer-houses or small pavilions between the Court and the inner court and omits the Gatehouse. Mowl (pp. 41-44) discusses in detail the differences between the Doharty and Beighton bird's eye perspectives (Mowl, figs. 18 & 19) and the aspirational rather than factual nature of the latter.

John Phipps is documented at Croome in the late 1740s (accounts 1749-1753) and may therefore be associated with some developments before Lancelot 'Capability' Brown (accounts 1750-1782) was responsible for a new

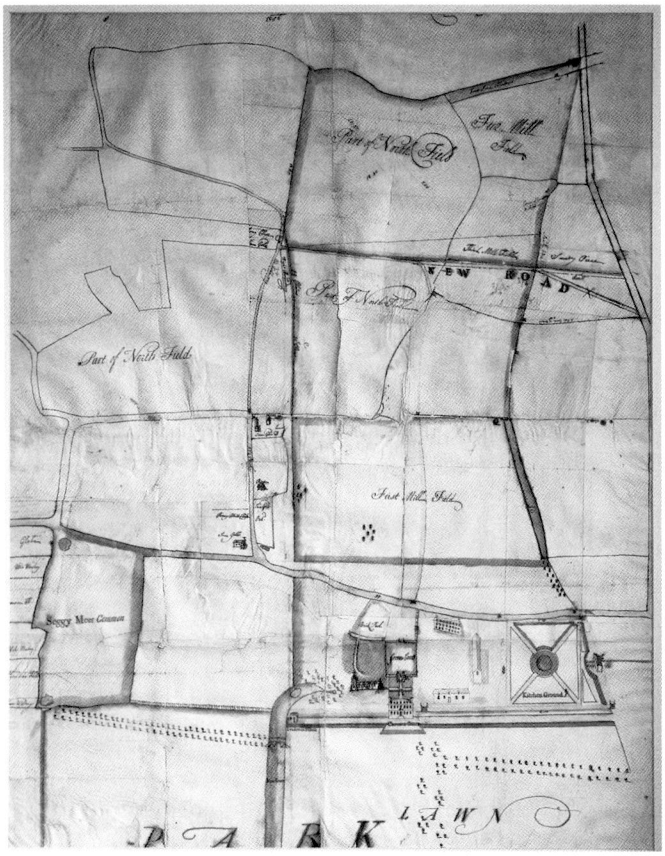

Survey circa 1751. John Doharty jnr. © WAAS 705:73 BA14450/248.

house and a new landscape. There is mention of a stone ha-ha as early as 1747, e.g. not that built by Brown in 1764 between the Lake and the Church across the north side of the park. Mowl attributes to Phipps a decisive role in pre-Brown developments as in the Doharty survey; "John Phipps was taken on to sweep away Earl Gilbert's old fashioned formal garden and create a long, serpentine canal, sleekly curved and by no means natural looking, in the park near the house." (Mowl, p. 46).

The Doharty plan shows a large piece of water or lake with a bridge to the west of the Court; the bridge was presumably the Chinese bridge published by William and John Halfpenny in their *Improvements in Architecture and Carpentry* in 1754. There are payments to Mr. Halfpenny in the accounts in 1751. The bridge (together with the Church and the Rotunda) is featured in Richard Wilson's famous 1758 view of Croome (Gordon, 2000 Pl. XIX). The bridge survived well into the 19th century, not having been replaced by any of Robert Adam's alternative designs made in the 1770s; the National Trust has returned this bridge to the landscape.

Brown's first major commission for a new landscape came after that for the mansion. His new Church (1758 – 1765), like some of the major rooms in the House, had interiors and fittings designed by Robert Adam (1761 ff.). The interior of the Rotunda (1756-1765), not certainly by Brown, is also attributed to Adam (circa 1766) and further works to it are documented in 1778-1795. Dean (1824) says that the Rotunda was fitted out as an evening apartment. The Grotto, possibly originated by Brown (1765-7), had "Derbyshire petrifactions" or spars added to it in the 1780s and further repairs in 1805. Brown is likely to have designed the two bridges to the smaller island in the Lake (Broome, 1768) which were replaced in 1806 by iron bridges from John Mackell's firm. Brown perhaps designed the first Menagerie buildings which were up by 1763, but Adam was re-designing them from 1766 and provided a new front in 1779/81. Works continued at the Menagerie throughout the 1770s and 1780s (including a new dairy) and 1790s. Dean describes the Menagerie and Aviary in 1824. Brown may have designed the first boat-houses on the lake and river although no work on these is documented until the late 1770s. The Dry Arch Bridge, to which Wyatt made alterations (1797-1807) including the Coade stone keystones and the rock works/spars, existed by 1768. So too the icehouse (by 1762) for which there are references to thatching in the 1790s. As restored, the ice-house is remarkably similar to the restored ice-house at Heveningham Hall, Suffolk where Brown was active in 1781-2. It is not clear whether or not Brown designed any gates or lodges for Croome. A building can be seen on the site of the London or Pershore gates on Broome's 1768 plan but the existing Gateway with triumphal arch was designed by Adam (1778-9); the Coade stone repairs circa 1795 were no doubt by Wyatt as in the case of the Punch Bowl gateway. The London Lodge itself was rebuilt in 1877. The Worcester Lodges are also attributed to Wyatt.

..........continued from previous page

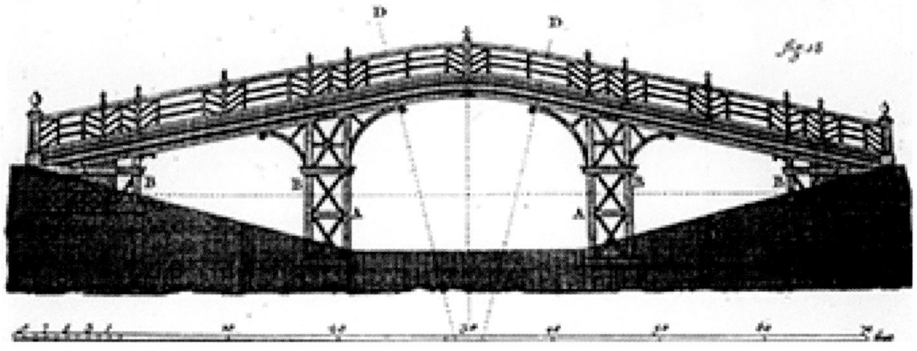

Design for the Chinese bridge at Croome from W. Halfpenny and J. Halfpenny circa 1754, from *Rural Architecture in the Chinese Taste: New Designs for Chinese Temples*, pl. VIII, fig. 18.

Robert Adam was solely responsible for the Temple Greenhouse/Orangery (1760-1767), repaired in 1784; Dunstall Castle (1764-1771); the Owl House or Park Seat (1766/7); a Dairy (1763-5). Many of Adam's fanciful landscape drawings or capricci include ruins and castles. The structure of Dunstall Castle is described in detail in BoE (p. 275) and is illustrated by Mowl (fig. 26). The Castle is on the edge of the Croome landscape but was accessed by perimeter rides through the park.

As well as work to the Lodges, James Wyatt made significant additions to the Croome landscape from the 1790s: Pirton Tower, "the Ruin in the Park" (circa 1797, see 1801 Wyatt drawing, Gordon, 2000, Pl.XVII); the Panorama (1801-7) (Wyatt drawing, 1801, Gordon, 2000, Pl. XVIII); the Saxon Tower, Broadway built 1797-9 near Springhill which was developed, Jane Bradney has shown, by the Earl's younger brother, the Hon. John Bulkeley Coventry and the Hon. John Coventry of the next generation.

As well as the various garden buildings, there were a number of smaller garden ornaments such as urns, statues and plinths. An obelisk is mentioned at the south end of the park in 1765. In the 1760s John Cheere supplied statues of *Flora* and *Ceres* (in lead for the Temple Greenhouse) and a *Camillo* and *Ganymede* and a *Vestal* and *Urania*. Richard Hayward provided vases including two bronze Volterra vases. Eleanor Coade supplied 5 stone reliefs for the Island Temple in 1778 and the *Druid*, set up near the Temple Greenhouse in 1793, came from John Sealy's Ornamental Stone Manufactory, Lambeth costing 25 guineas in 1795. The *Nymph* (**Plate 28**) at the Grotto was designed by John Bacon and supplied before 1824; Coade and Sealy provided 4 herms in 1805.

Croome is remarkable for its scale, 500 hectares at one time (HER), and for the number and wide distribution of its eye-catchers: Pirton Tower to the north; the Panorama to the north-west; Dunstall Castle to the south-west; the Owl House at the south; Baughton Hill Tower further to the south and Broadway Tower 15 miles south-east. Robert Adam's new Farm House, Inn and Cottages at High Green which date to the 1780s, represent a modest but unrecognised model village – Croome Village.

John Broome's map of 1768 (Gordon, 2000, p. 120) reflects some of Brown's planting and allows comparison with features recorded by the first 6 inch OS maps. There are also other surveys from the late-18th century, two by John Snape, one of 1796 (WAAS 30044/405) and the other of 1797 made specifically to inform the improvement of the water supply to the river, which had proved inadequate (Croome Estate Archive, Box 4). There is a further survey made by Thomas Hobcraft or Hopcraft in 1810 (WAAS 30046/15).

The shape of the planting largely survives, e.g. the wide belt along the east side of the park between Defford Common and Croome Perry Wood; the Belt linking the south end of the Lake with Westfield Wood; the planting round the Court itself and the home shrubberies; the avenue to the east Lodge; planting from the Court to the Church and then north-west to Pirton Court; the plantation or shrubbery from the Church west to and including the Lake. The larger plantations in the park south of the Court have been eroded but small clumps are still recognisable. The National Trust has undertaken an extensive programme of planting to replenish the park trees and re-create the shrubberies.

Broome shows the Home Shrubbery (round the House and the Rotunda); the Kitchen Garden just beyond the Stables (The Square); the Church and Church Shrubbery with the Icehouse sited within it; a shrubbery walk (later called the Wild Walk or Wilderness) running north from the Church to the area developed later as the Flower Garden (called the Botanical Garden on Thomas Hopcraft's 1810 estate map). Snape's 1796 plan details this Flower Garden with serpentine walks and the Nursery to its north-east and an orchard on its south boundary. Broome shows the (Temple) Greenhouse and Shrubbery with a drive through the belt of trees between the Lake and the Church.

On a visit to Croome in 1778, Sulivan commented unfavourably on the low setting of the mansion but applauded the view from the Rotunda. He praises the pleasurable walks through the shrubberies, from the Rotunda to the Church and from there to the Nursery of young trees (with greenhouses) and then to the Lake via the Temple Greenhouse "serving the purposes of a lively apartment, upon the removal of the plants into the open air." He is enthusiastic too about the Lake with its small islands and "a small boat, which, worked by the aid of pullies, carried us across the water, and landed us within a few paces of our carriage" (Mavor, pp. 75-7).

Supporting the landscape park and gardens were members of the indoor as well as outdoor staff. Indoor servants were required to remove thistles from the parks

..........continued from previous page

for example. Complete staff lists with wages exist from the mid-18th century to the early-19th century and allow for the most minute investigation of the Croome agricultural and garden economy. The Earl liked to see the weekly bills submitted by subcontractors for the heavy agricultural work (haulage, hedging, ditching, gate making, and larger scale tree planting) usually carried out by tenants. The Garden staff was divided into different departments. In the 1750s, Croome Labourers were probably part of 'Capability' Brown's work force. In 1753, £1156 was spent on the Croome Labourers as against £185 on the Garden Labourers and these ratios are typical of the 1750s as a whole. By the 1770s, the accounts distinguish Garden and Shrubbery. In the 1790s the departments are Garden (Kitchen); Shrubbery (Croome); Stables; Labourers; Plantation. In 1798, there was a team of 6 people including one woman for the Kitchen Garden, 33 Croome Labourers and 18, including 4 women, working under William Dean in the Plantation. In 1809 there is a separate Farm account.

W. Dean, *Hortus Croomensis,* aquatint, 1824.

Purchases of flowers, plants, shrubs and trees from nurseries and plantsmen at home and abroad are well documented from the 1740s. Imports from North America are listed from the 1750s and from the Far East from the 1770s. A consignment of plants was sent from St. Petersburg in 1771 when John Bush reported that "It is dangerous in these woods to collect plants there being large bears and wolves". Between 1746 and 1785 Croome was supplied by some 80 different nurseries, in 1761 alone by 16. Focussing on imports from North America and the Caribbean between 1758 and 1778 for instance, in 1758 Samuel Hewitt provides seeds from Carolina and James Gordon flowering American Bays. In 1759 George Ferne sends Swamp Pine and American White Spruce Fir and Henry Foot, Belith from Philadelphia. In 1761 79 different seeds from Carolina are supplied to Croome and in 1765 oaks also from Carolina. In 1770 the variously sourced list includes Pine apple, cork, Portuguese Broom, Japanese seeds (40) and pine cones and spruces from Canada. To support all these imports there were several hothouses in the Flower Garden and the Kitchen Garden. By 1811 there were distinct vine, pineapple, orange and peach houses. A Croome Vinery was included in a book on the latest garden buildings in 1806 (illustrated in colour by Stone, p. 46).

The Croome Estate Archive has now been transferred to the Worcestershire Archive and Archaeology Service at The Hive, Worcester and the Croome Research Plant Group has now published an analysis of some 600 plant bills dated between 1746 and 1816. Stone et al. (op. cit., 2016) have demonstrated the astonishing range of plant varieties that were sourced, e.g. for Roses, Clematis, Auriculas, Hyacinths, Ericas, Peaches, Apricots, Nectarines, Pears, Cherries, Plums, Grapes, Gooseberries, Peas, Cabbages, Lettuces, Beans. Magnolias were a Croome speciality as noted by J. Dugdale in the *New British Traveller*, 4, 1819: "To complete the character of this delightful residence we must observe ... the rarest as well as the most beautiful exotics among which are some superb magnolias flourish in the open air." Jane Bradney sees the 6th Earl's particular interest in rock plants at Croome being mirrored at Springhill, just across the border in Gloucestershire.

Numerous gardeners are recorded in the estate accounts in the 18th century, e.g. between 1772 and 1786: John Abell, Robert Mackie, John Robbie and Robert Callsie. Much better known as head gardener was William Dean because of his *Croome d'Abitot: Hortus Croomensis,* published with illustrations in 1824 and with plant lists. In 1833, the Duke of Bedford's head gardener, J. Forbes, writes to ask for plants from Croome but cannot place his order immediately but must wait until he can recover his copy of Dean's *Hortus* from the Duke!

Arthur Young's in 1801 saw Brown's plantings in their maturity. The serpentine water, about two miles long with two islands, was one of the most perfect pieces of garden scenery that he had ever seen, with fine trees bordering the water. He noted an 80ft. cedar and fine specimens of birch, turkey oak, and tripple-thorned acacia. As a botanical showpiece he placed Croome only second to Kew. The huge kitchen garden, preserving the idea of a 17th century formal garden, was a feature. He also noted shrubberies, greenhouses, hot houses, conservatory, orangery and menageries of pheasants and partridges. He specifically draws attention to an American border with azalea, kalmia, rhododendron and the arboretum which contained 25 varieties including *Quercus* and *Ginko biloba.* (Young, 37, p. 465). This description can be supplemented by William Dean's, a "Botanic Gardener", in his 1824 publication which illustrates Mansion, Temple Greenhouse, Rotunda, and Church and whose text describes the shrubberies and walks and contains his Catalogue of Plants. The prospectus for Dean's *Croome Guide* (Prattinton Collection, Soc. of Antiquaries, London – information from Stephen Price) listed amongst "the patrons of the Work" many aristocratic, clerical and gentlemen owners of parks and gardens considered in this book including Dr. Prattington (sic) and J. Williams, Esq., F. H. S., Sheriff, Pitmarston (sic), evidently the most eminent of the Worcester nurserymen and seedsmen listed!

..........continued from previous page

This factual description of developments at Croome between the mid-18th and the early-19th centuries cannot express the social atmosphere that they encouraged. Catherine Gordon (2000, pp. 98-9) refers to the fun and enjoyment associated with the Earl's second wife, Barbara St. John in the 1770s: "you (her sister) have made mine the best furnished greenhouse in this country, the seeds from Botany Bay are not yet come." Bills related to the Aviary in the 1790s refer to Snow Birds, Canada Geese, Sparrows of Paradise, Shell Ducks, redheaded Parrakeets, Chinese Geese, White Turkeys, Pied pia Cocks, Guinea Fowls, Silver Pheasants, Gold Cock Pheasants and Nunn Birds amongst other less exotic birds. The Countess's musical tastes ran to popular, Italian sheet music for the harpsichord for which the tuner's bills also survive. From this archive an extraordinarily richly-drawn picture can be made out for indoor and outdoor entertainment in this sophisticated landscape The archive is otherwise filled with the more prosaic but fundamental detail of post enclosure drainage, fencing and fertilisation, the infrastructure of a newly, productive, agricultural estate.

The restored rotunda. Photo, R. Lockett.

James Lees-Milne's *Shell Guide for Worcestershire* published in 1964 caught Croome at a low ebb, "a grave reflection of the times." Since then the principal part of the landscape park has been acquired by the National Trust (1996) and a restoration programme undertaken with Heritage Lottery support. The story from the Second World War to the present and the overall objectives behind the restoration is told by Tom Oliver in Ch. X., "Resurgam" in Gordon, 2000 (op. cit. pp. 198-202).

The walled garden (7 acres), which is in separate ownership has also been restored and redeveloped since 2000: "1 km of paths will divide the gardens into 6 discreet zones ... the paths will be 2.5 metres wide ... 140 fruit trees are to be planted "espalier" style along the primary paths. The avenues will portray... the history of apple and pears with a mixture of heritage and modern varieties from Herefordshire, Worcestershire and Gloucestershire". (Victoria Cronin).

The Croome landscape, celebrated in the literature of the 18th and early-19th century and fully discussed by 20th century garden historians, is now centre stage again. The story as told by the National Trust also embraces the significant presence of the RAF at Croome during the Second World War. An appreciation of the whole achievement, interweaving house and contents with the grounds and the landscape is given by Catherine Gordon in *Croome; a Creation of Genius*, 2018.

Dry Arch Bridge keystone, circa 1800.

W. Dean, *An Account of Croome d'Abitot: Hortus Croomensis and Observations on the Propagation of Exotics,* 1824 (4 aquatints).
J. Dugdale, *The New British Traveller,* 1819.
D. Stroud, *Capability Brown,* 1975 & 1984.
C. Beresford, *Croome Court: Historical Landscape Survey,* 1996. (for the National Trust, unpub.)
C. Gordon, *The Coventrys of Croome,* 2000.
C. Gordon, *Croome: a Creation of Genius,* 2018.
T. Mowl, *Historic Gardens of Worcestershire,* 2006. Ch. 3. "The earl, the landscaper and a morass."
T. Mowl, *Gentlemen Gardeners,* 2000, (p.155-7)
A. Brooks & N. Pevsner, *Worcestershire* 2007 (BoE),
T. Oliver, "Croome: to Thaw the Numbing Spell", *HWGT, Newsletter* 17, Summer 2001(Grotto).
J. Comins, "Developments at Croome Park", *HWGT, Newsletter* 20, Winter 2002; Newsletter 23, Summer 2004, (E. and F. Burney drawings c. 1784); Newsletter 26, Winter 2005/6.
K. Alker, "Croome Park" re recent garden developments, *HWGT, Newsletter,* 31, Summer 2008.
K. Alker & M. Smith, *Croome Parkland Plan,* 2012
L. Evans, *Worcestershire Recorder,* Autumn 2014, p. 13-4.
V. Cronin, *Friends of Croome Court, Newsletter,* Sept. 2015.
M. Stone, A. Hooper, P. Shaw, L. Tanner, *An Eighteenth Century Obsession: the Plant Collection of the 6th Earl of Coventry at Croome Park, Worcestershire,* 2015 and *Garden History Society,* 43.1, 2015.
J. Bradney, "Springhill: Part 3: George William Coventry, the 6th Earl of Coventry", *HWGT Newsletter,* 50, Winter 2017/18.
J. Lees-Milne, *Worcestershire: A Shell Guide,* 1964
HE *Register of Parks & Gardens,* 1999.
A. Young, *Annals of Architecture,* 1801.

Cropthorne Court

Parish: Cropthorne

HER Ref: WSM28951.

Grid Ref: SP 000 452.

Postcode: WR10 3NG.

O.S. 6" Map No: 42SW.

Date of Map: 1884.

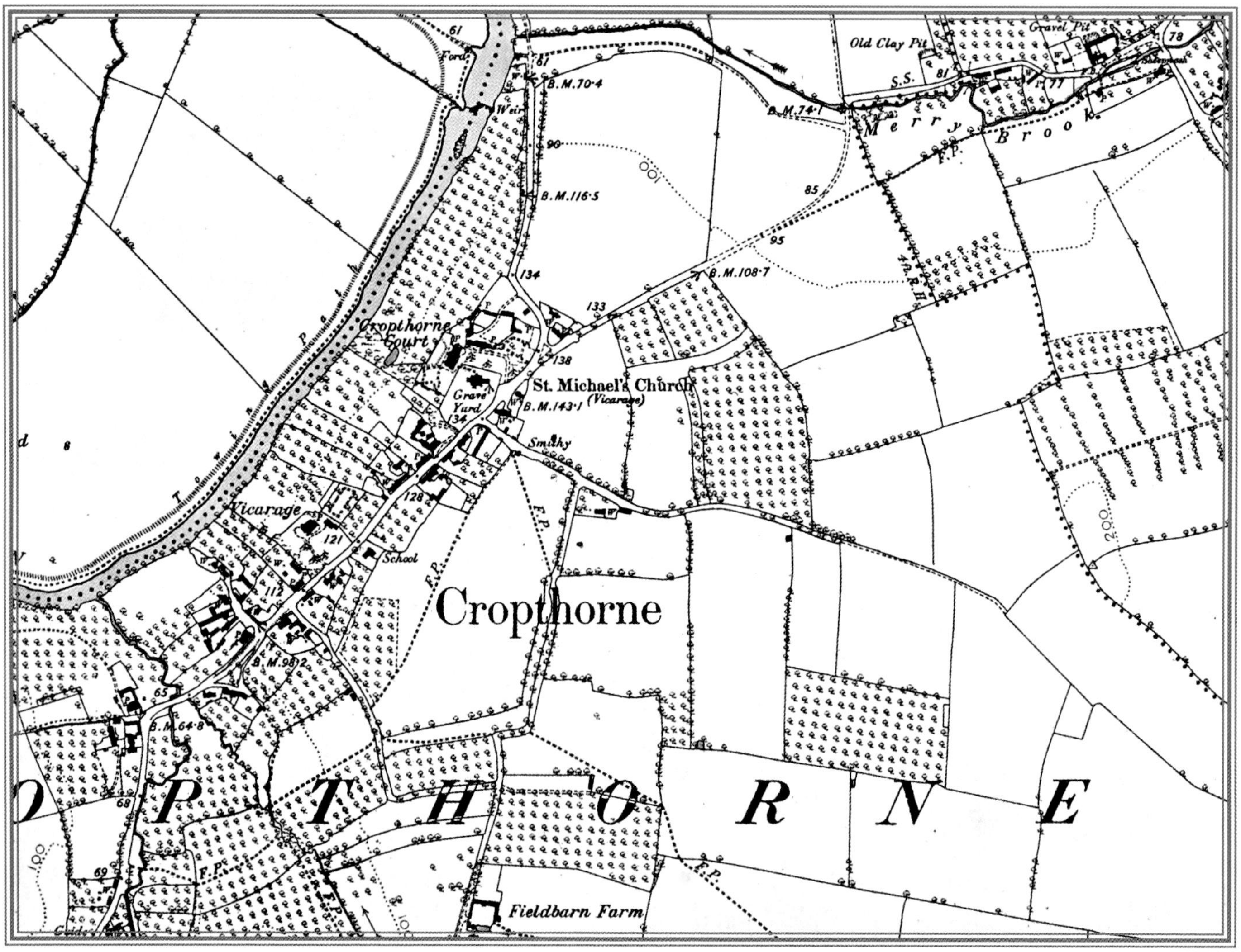

The BoE describes Cropthorne Court as mostly of the 1830s and being on the site of the medieval Manor House. The early-18th century, 6 bay, Manor is a better fit with the miniature portrait in John Dougharty senior's 1721 map of an estate called the Farm (CRO 1691/9), shewing a substantial residence with a front garden (Smith, p. 145). Only small grounds and the immediate fields, mostly down to orchards, are for sale with "the mansion house" in 1836 (CRO 5119/35). By 1920 however (CRO 5044/5) 14 acres included: "finely timbered grounds, flower gardens, terraced lawns and shrubberies sloping down to the Avon, with fine cedar, lime, chestnut, elm". This is still a private residence with a pleasant garden.

B. Smith, "The Dougharty Family of Worcester, Estate Surveyors and Mapmakers, 1700-1760", *Worc. Hist. Soc.,* NS, 5, Miscellany II, 1967.

A. Brooks & N. Pevsner, *Worcestershire* 2007, (BoE).

Crown East

Parish: Rushwick

HER Ref: WSM28870. Grid Ref: SO 810 546.

Postcode: WR2 5TR O.S. 6" Map No: 33NW.

Date of Map: 1884, with extent of park & gardens shaded as1905 OS.

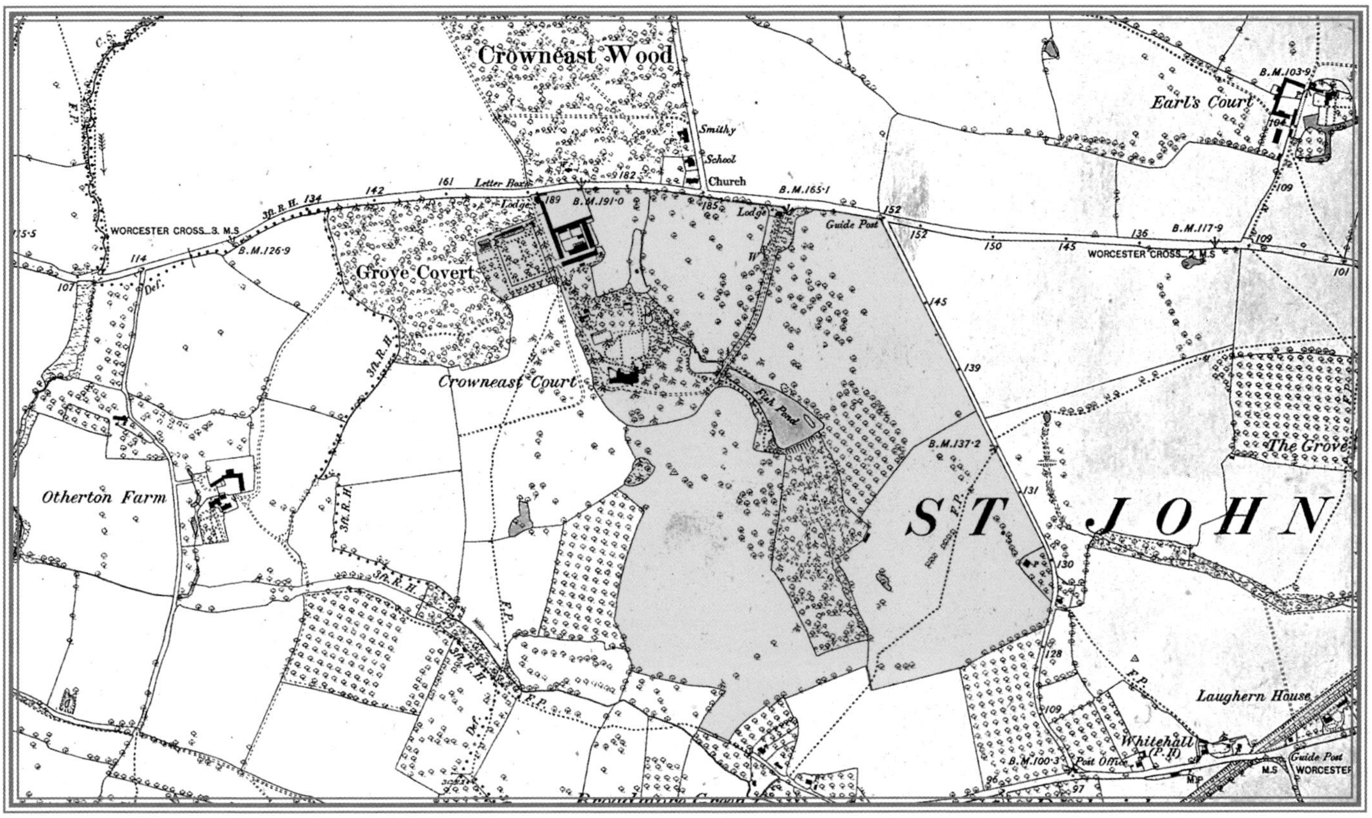

Nash refers to Crown East "now vulgarly called Crow's - nest from its high situation" (Vol. 2, 1782, p. 311) but no notice is taken of the grounds on published maps until the 1812 two inch survey for the first OS one inch which shows gardens south of the house. These grounds were probably developed by Josiah Patrick who bought 300 acres from the estate when it was sold up circa 1820 (VCH, 3, 1913, p. 504/5). At a later sale in 1855 it was described as "the pet estate of the county especially adapted for the residence of a gentleman of fortune" (CRO 5119/8). We must forgive the estate agent's licence as he provided a charming lithograph illustration with the sale particulars with a view of the mansion seen across water in park-like surroundings (CRO 5976). The approach from the Bromyard road took the visitor over a bridge across the pools. The particulars claim every variety of forest timber, ornamental water, fish ponds, plantations and woods. The area described (in parts) as park amounted to 47 acres. In the early-19th century, stables, farm buildings and a walled garden were immediately to the west of the mansion.

Changes later in the century included drying out and over planting the lower fish pond, moving the lodge from short of the main road up to it, and re-siting the Rushwick road further east thus creating an area for park east of the drive and pools as on the first 6 inch OS edition. The farm buildings, stables and large, walled kitchen garden were built to the north/north west (surviving). The house itself had been altered considerably since 1855.

The pools and house are now screened by large trees both deciduous and coniferous including Scots Pines. In 1855 the house and upper pools were more in the open and plantations were the Grove Covert running up to the Bromyard road (which has a fringe of mature trees today) and planting south of the lower pool. The 1855 plan also show conifers in the park south-west of the house a few of which survive. A footpath goes across the south-east corner of the former park. Considerable changes have happened to the southern end of this landscape as a result of the upgrading of the A4103. The substantial Crowneast Wood immediately north of the Bromyard Road must once have been a significant amenity to the mansion.

Later in the 20th century, the house became Aymestry Preparatory School but has now reverted to a private residence. The walled garden survives in good condition but in separate ownership.

Victoria County History, 1913, Vol. 3, (VCH).

T. R. Nash, *Collections for the History of Worcestershire,* Vol II, 1782.

Doverdale Manor

Parish: Ombersley & Doverdale

HER Ref: WSM28949.

Grid Ref: SO 866 671. Postcode: WR9 0PF.

O.S. 6" Map No: 21NE/SE.

Date of Map: 1888, with deduced extent of gardens shaded (not shaded on 1905 OS).

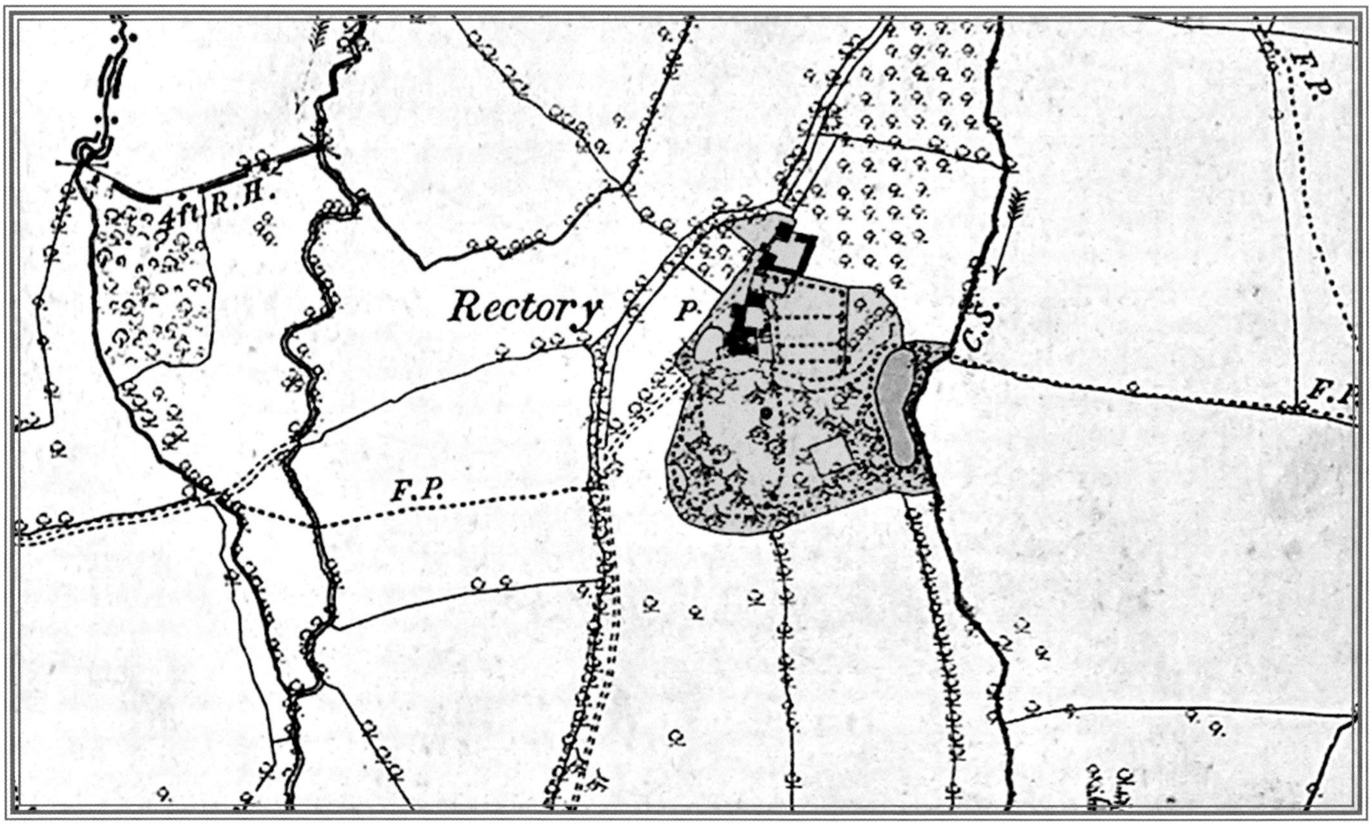

The Manor, formerly the Rectory, ("mostly circa 1710", BoE p. 260) is shown with a small park on the OS 6 inch (1882); a pool is the most striking feature but two garden pavilions are marked within the walled garden. There is a derelict 18th century icehouse in the garden. Gates, piers and flanking walls are dated to the early-19th century in the listing.

Stephen Price has established that the hey-day of the Doverdale Garden was in the 1830s when the Revd. George Larden was Rector (1831-1843). Larden was a prominent member of the Worcestershire Horticultural Society, winning prizes at their annual shows held in Worcester, e.g. in 1833 for "Stove Plants". A review of the 1834 Floral Exhibition held in July remarked on a fine American shrub – *Clethora arborea* – from Rev. Mr Larden of Doverdale Rectory. The 1838 Tithe Map indicates a House, Garden and Shrubbery extending to 7 ½ acres. The 1871 census places the gardener at Rectory Farm and much garden equipment featured in a sale that year: 3 mowing machines, lead cisterns, cucumber frames, plants in pots and minor tools.

The whole property when valued by the Inland Revenue in 1913, catalogued "good walled in kitchen garden and upper garden up stone steps, small plum orchard, pool, stoke house, lean-to vinery (glass), 2 sheds, very nice grounds prettily set out." A less matter-of-fact notice from 1999: "A glorious avenue of lime trees leads up to the house and the garden, the lawns of which are graced by centuries old trees and shrubs. A maze and an ice house had been constructed in the grounds. The ice house could be reached from the house via an underground passage" (Roelofsz, p. 194).

In 2018 the property had well maintained gardens and substantial new tree planting in the park.

A. Brooks & N. Pevsner, *Worcestershire* 2007 (BoE)

Stephen Price Associates, *Doverdale Manor, Doverdale, Worcs.*, 2015.

E. Roelofsz, *Through Changing Scenes of Life: A Millenium History of Ombersley and Doverdale*, 1999.

Dripshill

Parish: Guarlford

HER Ref: WSM28892.

Grid Ref: SO 830 454.

Postcode: WR8 0AG.

O.S. 6" Map No: 40SE.

Date of Map: 1884, with extent of park & gardens shaded as 1880s OS.

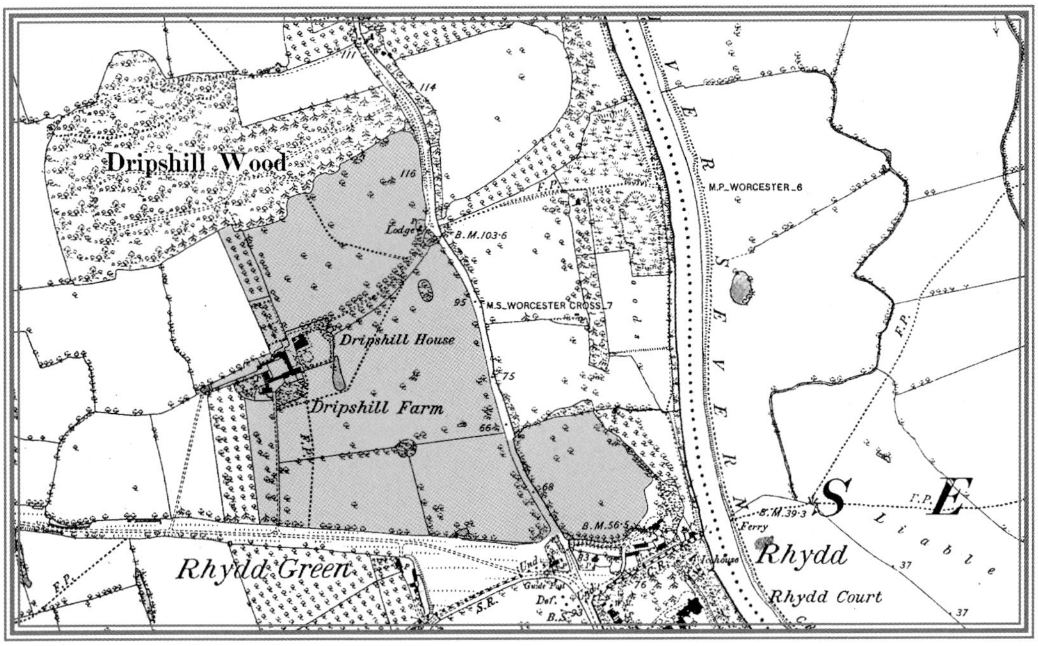

Cooke circa 1800 first notices the "agreeable seat of Sir Charles Trubshaw Withers" although he wasn't allowed in, due to the "wanton depredations of many idlers". The property is called "Trips Hole" on Cary's 1805 map. A park is shown on the 1812 survey for the first OS one inch. *Beauties* allowed the grounds to be well laid out (1814, p. 349). When sold in 1919 as an outlying part of the Madresfield estate, it was a mere 24 acres of "charming matured pleasure grounds, shaded by fine old timber and ornamental trees with tennis lawn, Dutch garden, herbaceous and flower borders, rose garden, gravelled walks etc. ... prolific kitchen garden." (CRO 4192/1). The 1884 OS 6 inch shows the park stretching from Dripshill Wood to Rhydd Green and an avenue along the drive from the Powick road. There are two pools within the grounds.

In 2016, the Lodge on the B4211 had been extended almost beyond recognition and was in separate ownership. The oak lined drive is unchanged, terminating in two mature oaks at the entrance to the surviving pleasure gardens. The stable block also survives, as does a small brick walled enclosure to its north.

Beauties of England and Wales, Vol. XV, 1814.

G. Cooke, *Topographical and Statistical Description of Co. of Worcester,* circa 1800.

Droitwich Brine Baths

Parish: Droitwich Spa

HER Ref: WSM22984.

Grid Ref: SO 901 632.

Postcode: WR9 8DN.

Droitwich Street Map.

Date of Map: 1994.

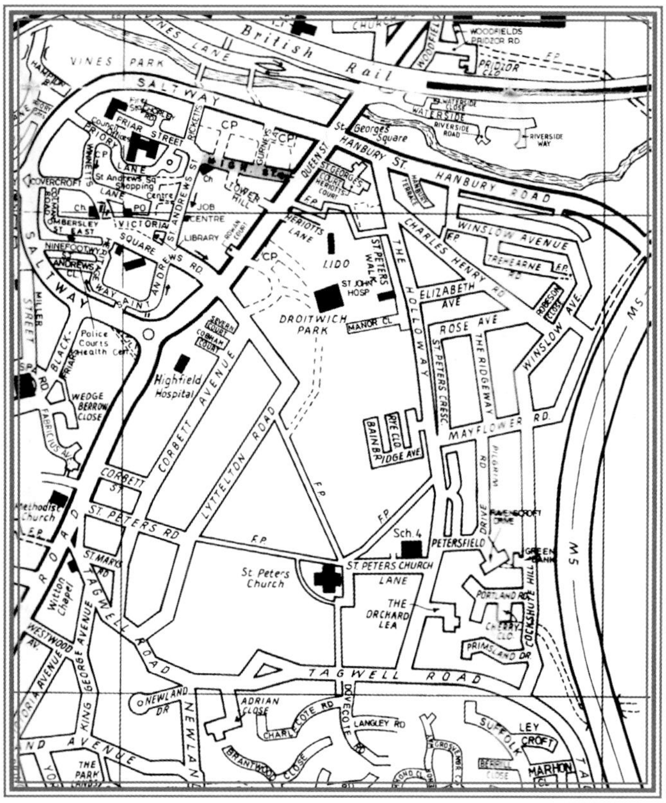

Brine Baths entrance, 1953. WAAS, Droitwich 3550.

Brine baths from the gardens, 1953. WAAS, Droitwich 3553.

The Baths were opened in 1895 funded by John Corbett, the Salt King. Large gardens with walks and a bandstand extend from the Baths to Heriots Pool (originally brine) which adjoins with the gardens of the Park Hotel to create a substantial urban park. The Park has been extended further south since the 1905 OS with the inclusion of St. Peter's Fields. The Lido itself was designed by T. H. Mawson & Sons in 1935.

Eardiston

Parish: Lindridge

HER Ref: WSM41069.

Grid Ref: SO 693 683. Postcode: WR15 8JL.

O.S. 6" Map No: 20NW.

Date of Map: 1884, with extent of park & gardens shaded as 1905 OS.

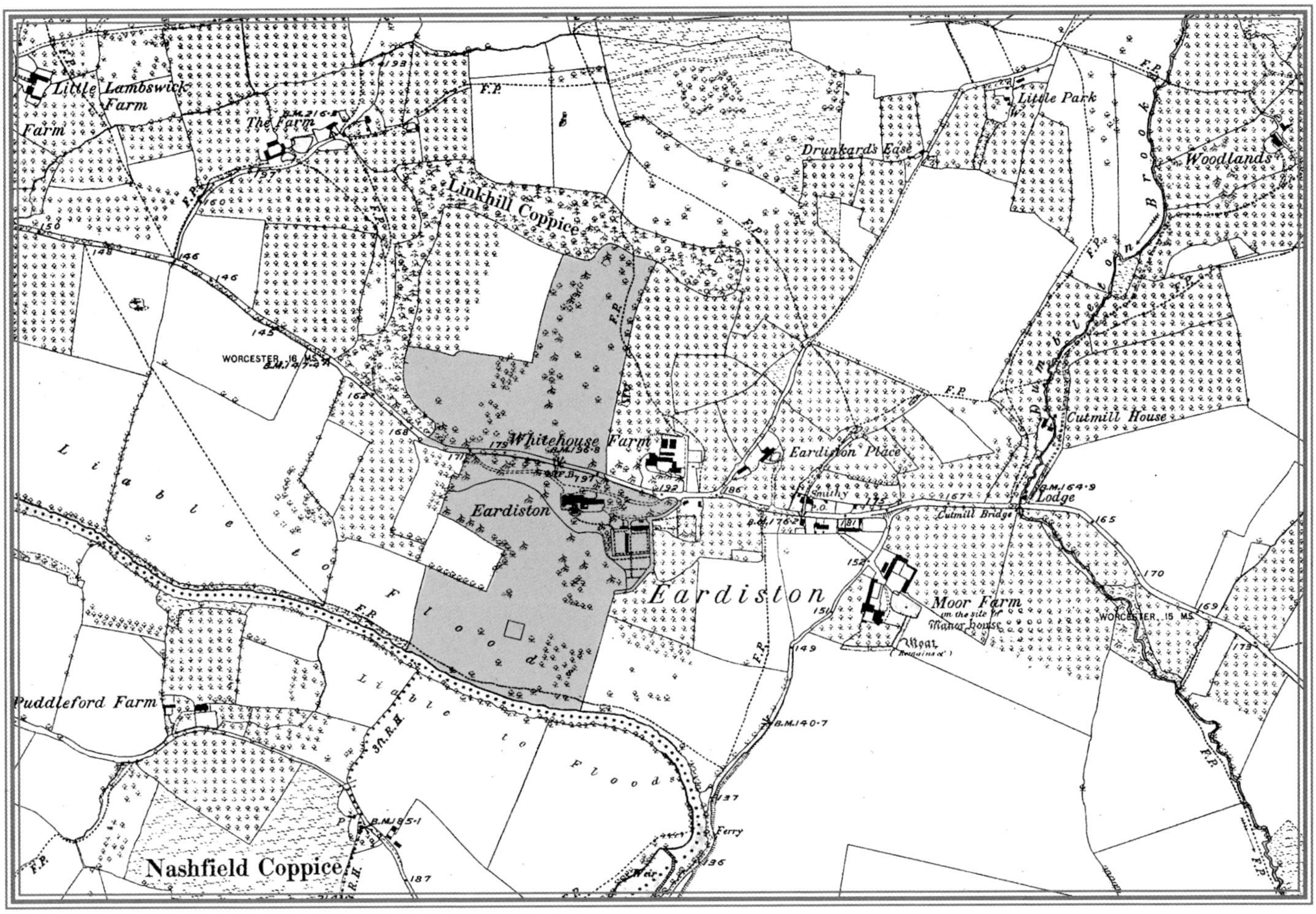

Some grounds are discernible on the earliest OS one inch of 1828 and the residence is mentioned as early as 1788 and in Directories from 1813. However, the *Beauties* in 1814 stated that "there is nothing about the grounds, however, which requires notice" not even the pleasure gardens across the road which were linked to the house by a cast-iron bridge made in Stourport in 1827 and moved to Huddington Court in 1967.

The existing House dates from circa 1830 with 1869 additions (BoE, p. 429). The 1915 sale particulars show Eardiston with a large conservatory attached to the south front and the large walled kitchen garden to the south east with freestanding and lean-to glass houses. It is shown with a park on the first OS 6 inch (1883) and the 1906 Bartholomew's between the Teme to the south and Linkhill Coppice to the north. The Woodlands was developed out of the Eardiston Estate and sold with 26 acres in 1915; this had rock and water gardens, arbour, pergolas etc. (CRO 5044/6).

Little of the original gardens survive but the walled garden is now run as a small commercial nursery. The walls are now of varying heights and the west wall has suffered a major collapse.

Beauties of England and Wales, Vol. XV, 1814.

A. Brooks & N. Pevsner, *Worcestershire* 2007 (BoE).

Elmley Castle Park

Parish: Elmley Castle, Bricklehampton & Netherton

HER Ref: WSM07681. Grid Ref: SO 980 410. Postcode: WR10 3HT.

O.S. 6" Map No: 49NW/SW. Date of Map: 1884, with extent of park & gardens shaded as 1880s OS.

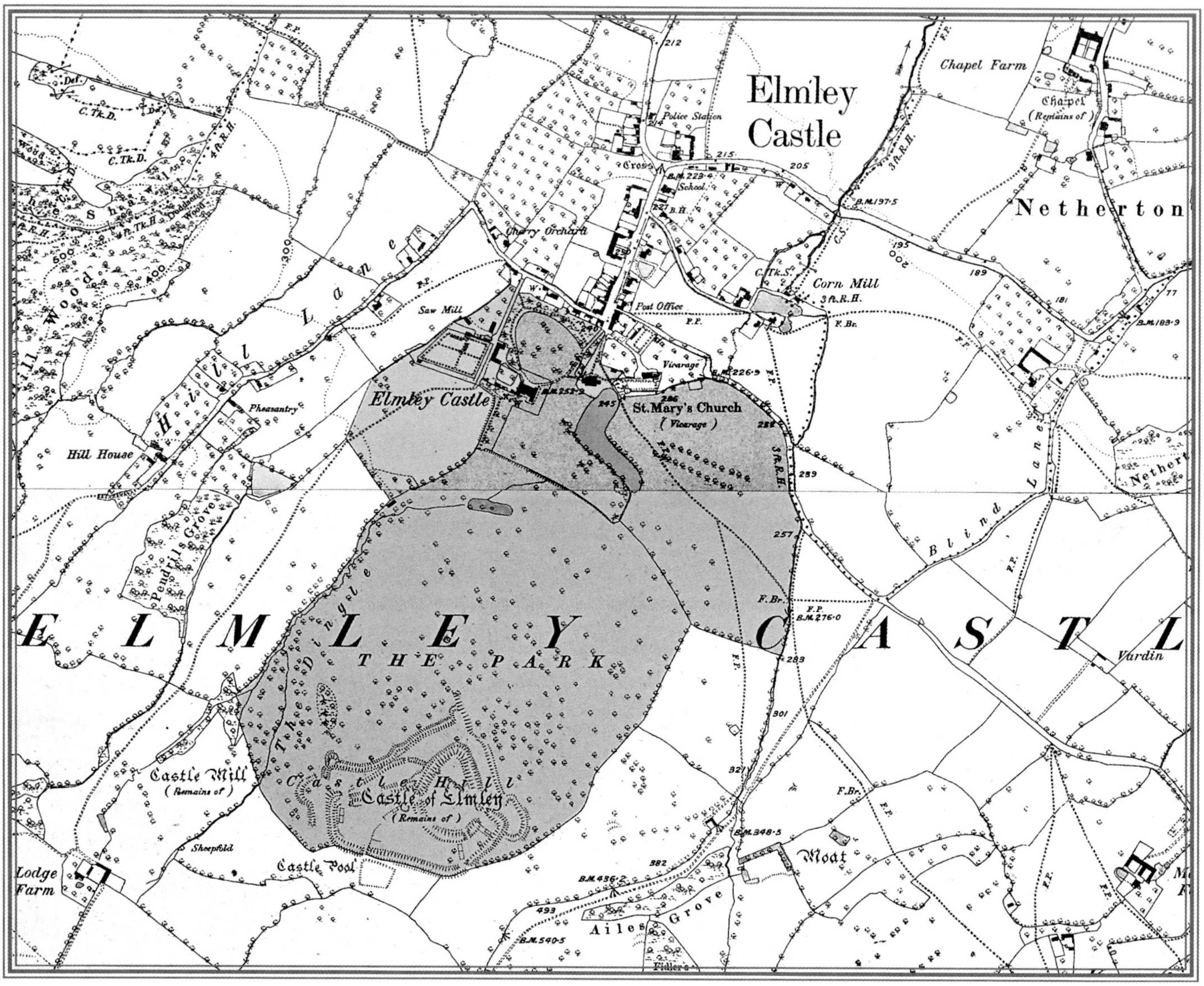

The deer park is first mentioned circa 1234 and was enlarged in 1480. The park was sold with the manor and castle to the Savages in 1544, a Savage having been Keeper of Park and Warren in 1512. In 1540 the Castle was described as "uncovered and in decay". Much new detail about the medieval park, its management and use has been gained from the publication of the *Elmley Castle Court Rolls*, 1347-1564 (Field). In this period the park was managed by a keeper and two warreners (one beside the keeper) and the rabbit warrens within the park were farmed for the benefit of the lords of the manor, the Neville Earls of Warwick. When Warwick the Kingmaker was killed in 1461, Elmley was transferred to the Yorkist Plantagenets. The Court rolls document repairs to hedges, ditches and gates and the sale of timber throughout the 15th century. Whitehead points up these and other features of park management such as the lawn, (an area of flat grassland used for fattening the deer but encroached upon from time to time) and the garden closes (attached) to the peasant cottages on the edge of the park. "Pear trees seem to have

..........continued from previous page

been a feature of these gardens ... There are still pear trees growing along the eastern boundary of the park." (Whitehead).

Park, Manor and Castle continued in Savage ownership until 1776 when house and park separated. Robert Claverley Savage still owned an estate in the Parish of Elmley Castle in 1798 (CRO 2349/5 iii) when part of the park is shown as in the ownership of Richard Browne Charlotte. It may be a simplification that Col. Thomas Davies acquired Manor, Castle and Park in 1822 (VCH. 3. p. 339) because some land was still in Savage ownership in 1840 (CRO 2349/2 ii). A fenced park at Elmley Castle is shown on the printed maps of Taylor, Nash and Cary (1772-1787) and on the 1811 survey for the first OS one inch. Whitaker gives 106 acres to the deer park in 1892 (a figure confirmed by the 1840 survey) and describes the boundaries as marked by a wall on one side, a sunk fence on another and wooden paling on the remaining two. It contained 90 fallow deer. He remarks on the supply of running water and the fine timber: oak, ash, elm, wych elm, Scotch firs, sycamore, maple; there was a great deal of tall fern. Some areas of ditch or sunk fences survive, e.g. along the north-east side of the deer park. The moat on the eastern edge of the park is now dry. Whitehead comments on the situation today: "the Park "retains a large number of veteran trees and reveals a complex pattern of planting, extending back at least to the 17th century. There appears to have been a fairly rigorous makeover in the early 19th century, with trees grouped in threes, in the picturesque manner."

The location of the deer park is immediately south of the house, Elmley Park House, running down or rather up to the remains of the medieval castle set within an Iron Age fort. The area is the same as the field named "The Park"

Lt. Col. Thomas Davies (1789 - 1846), watercolour by Richard Dighton, 1829. Private collection.

on an estate plan of 1866 (CRO 693/1) and as marked as park on the 1993 OS 1:50,000.

Elmley Park House, described in the VCH as an Elizabethan House remodelled in 1702, was demolished in 1960. There is a distant view of it in Nash, 1781. Reid (p. 223) has 4 views of this very substantial mansion including some fine 18th century plasterwork (ceiling of main staircase). The site has been redeveloped for housing. The 16th century occupier of this house, was John Breton "yeoman of the crown, park keeper and warrener" (Whitehead).

The immediate grounds of Elmley Park House were made up of kitchen garden, pools and an avenue east of the pool in the direction of the Elmley Castle - Kersoe road. The landscape park as defined by the first edition of the OS 6 inch (1883) includes the area round the house and that to the immediate north and east of the deer park. There is no evidence of the 18th and 19th century contributions to this landscape but the house is given as a residence by Cary in 1805.

Two sundials in the Churchyard are thought to be from the Elizabethan House and one of them has the Savage arms. Mowl illustrates one of these (fig. 1) and associates it with Elizabeth I's stay with the Savages in 1575.

It is illustrated by Daniel (p. 32) who dates it rather earlier to circa 1545 saying that it is "perhaps the earliest dial of its kind in England."

Division between house and grounds, e.g. shrubberies and areas of garden such as Kitchen Garden and parts of the park, may have been fluid if field names and agricultural usage are taken at face value from the 1840-6 survey. Col. Thomas Davies then had "in hand": Foxhills - Plantation; Lodge Grove – Wood (1 acre); Monument Hill – Wood (4 acres); Elmley Park – Pasture (106 acres); Kitchen Garden – Pasture (11 acres); The Lawn – Pasture (11 acres); Fish Pond – Water; Monument Hill – Pasture (45 acres). Another tenant had 24 acres of pasture known as Rough Park.

The walls of the kitchen garden survive in part and also the pool by the church. The avenue that went south-east across the north side of the park is no longer evident. There are remains of the deer fence boundary at least on the north side of the park which also contains many fine mature trees, e.g. oaks, chesnut, ash. The Long Plantation survives and has been renewed with planting and therefore continues to mark the south boundary of the park.

Victoria County History Vol. 3, 1913 p.339, (VCH).

R. Strong, *The Destruction of the English Country House,* 1974, fig. 23.

P. Reid, *Burke's and Savills Guide to Country Houses,* II, 1980, pp. 223.

C. St J. H. Daniel, *Sundials,* 2004.

D. Whitehead, "The Park at Elmley Castle, c.1400-1550", *HWGT Newsletter,* 25, Summer 2005, p. 6-7.

Elmley Lovett Lodge

Parish: Elmley Lovett

HER Ref: WSM28910. Grid Ref: SO866696. Postcode: WR9 0PU. Date of Maps: 1888, 1883, 1884, 1883.

O.S. 6" Map No. 14SE, 15SW, 21NE, 22NW with shaded extent of park & gardens deduced from text.

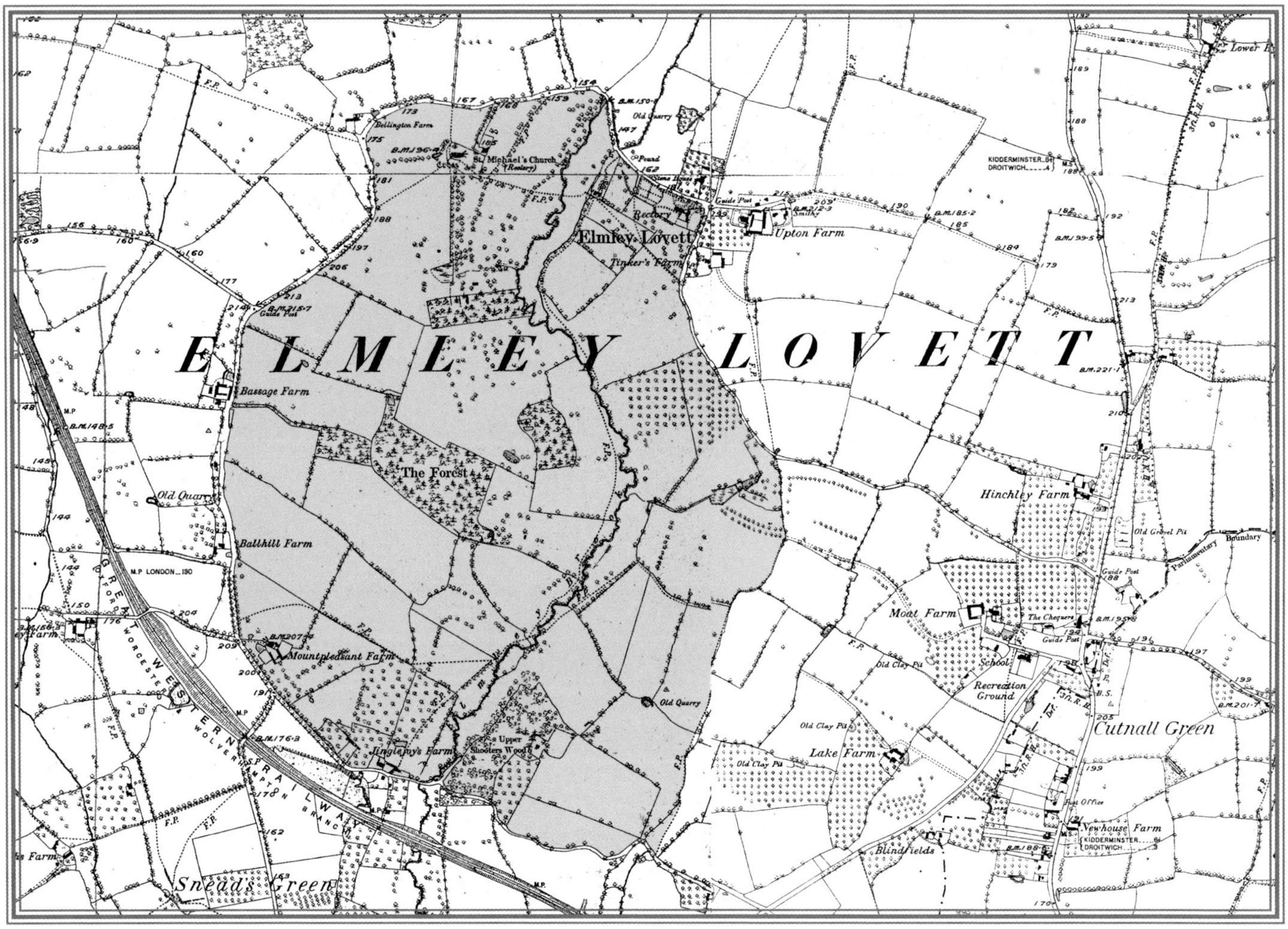

An indenture of 1628 (WAAS 11171) refers to the Manor and Lordship of Elmley Lovett and to Elmley Lodge or House and also to Elmley Park and to a mansion called The Crouch. The Lodge just south-east of the Church was a half-timbered building of circa 1635, demolished in 1890 (Reid, op. cit. p. 204), attached to which is a surviving, 18th century, brick dovecote (Pridham, op. cit.). The Lodge was approached by an avenue of elms (VCH, 3, 1913, p. 106). The house is illustrated by both Walker and Niven (op. cit.) and Niven adds that the house had a bowling green.

The house is shown as a residence on Cary's 1805 map. More detailed information can be got from an undated, rough map claiming to represent the state of Elmley Park in 1801: The Manor House, Homestead and Croft took up 5 acres; Old Orchard (1.3 a); The Park – grass (6 a.);The Park – grass (2.3 a.). Other suggestive field names are: Money Grove – arable (7 a.); The Grove – arable (7 a.); Cuckoo Park – grass (2.3 a.); Coneygree – grass (13.2 a.); Coneygree Copse – (3 a.). All of this is on a very small scale (CRO 8217/5).

The HER cites field name evidence (Boundary Bank) for a deer park. This is close to Upper Shooter's Wood on the southern border of an area defined by roads on north, west and south and by the road to Cutnall Green and a footpath taking a more southerly direction to form a likely eastern boundary (Pathfinder 974). There are no obvious park features today.

J. Severn Walker, *Architectural Sketches*, Vol. 1, 1862.
W. Niven, *Illustrations of Old Worcestershire Houses*, 1873.
Victoria County History Vol. 3, 1913 (VCH).
J. C. Pridham, *Dove and Pigeon Cotes in Worcestershire,* 1974.
P. Reid, *Burke's & Savills Guide to Country Houses*, Vol. 2, 1980.

The Elms

Parish: Abberley

HER Ref: WSM29016.

Grid Ref: SO 733 673.

Postcode: WR6 6AT.

O.S. 6" Map No: 20NE.

Date of Map: 1883, with deduced extent of grounds shaded (not shaded on 1905 OS).

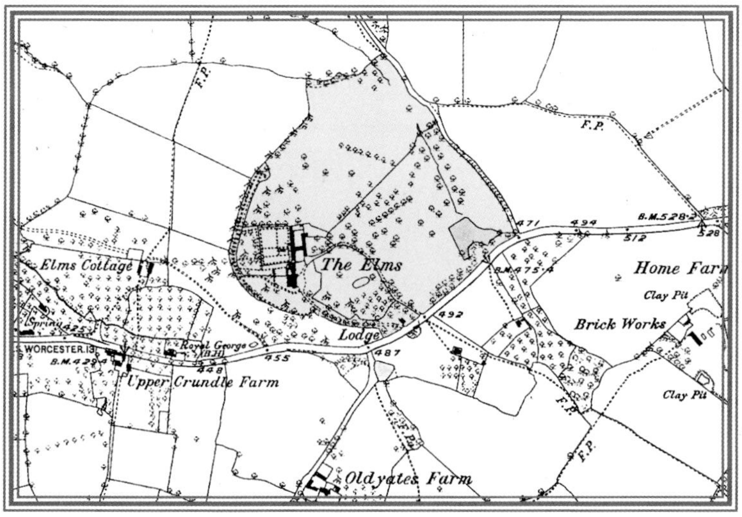

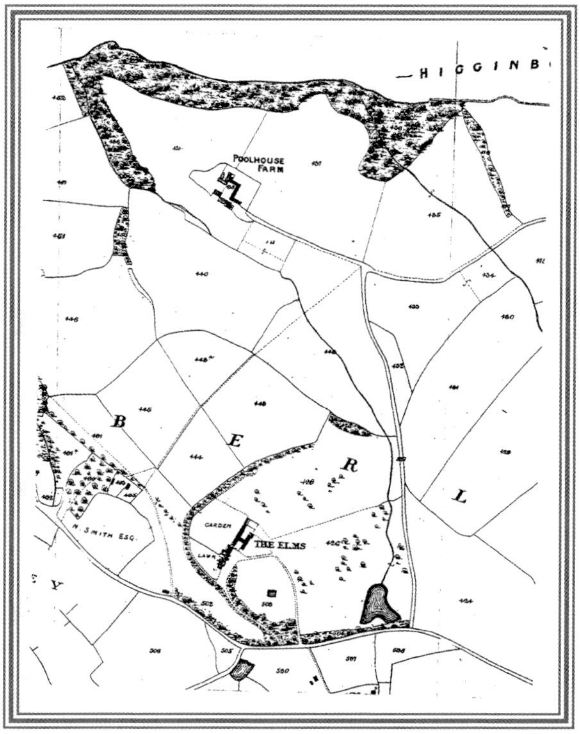

1867 Sale Plan, © WAAS 637.

Built as a country house, the mansion has been converted to an hotel. The core of the mansion is early-18th century with wings added in 1927. Isaac Taylor shows "Elms" with an avenue in his map of 1772. Its first appearance in a guide book is in 1788 as the residence of Mrs. Berry. It features on Cary's 1805 map although the *Beauties* (1814) contradict by describing the Elms as "a good seat but without any grounds" (p. 287). The 1828 OS indicates some grounds such as those now bordered by the road up to Pool House Farm on the east side and the stream from it which fed the pool just by the Tenbury road. The latter and the west and north fringes had a narrow strip of planting with a drive along it. This simple lay-out may well go back to the 18th century. When offered for sale in 1867, it was described as "a capital residence with pleasure grounds and gardens, belted with plantations and studded with timber also having a large fish pond and a walled kitchen garden, 20 acres in all" (CRO 4600/177). A conveyance of 1849 anticipates most of the amenities talked up in 1867: Lodge; walled kitchen garden; fringe plantations; pool within the lawn south of the house. The property did not have park status in the 1883 and 1905 OS.

The modern Elms Hotel underwent a number of changes to the grounds, including the loss of the walled garden to new development. The hotel is now being developed into a residential care home.

Beauties of England and Wales, Vol. XV, 1814.

The Evesham Sites

The Vale of Evesham is characterised traditionally by fruit growing and market gardening. Bretforton Manor, just to the east of Evesham itself, developed 9 orchards in the 1870's - 1890's one of which hosted 49 varieties of pear and 50 varieties of plum and among these horticultural records is an alphabetical list of 74 apple varieties! To the north-west are Craycombe and Woodnorton on the banks of the River Avon which belong in the different world of the landscape park. Closer to the town is the Abbey Manor House which combines a park with the site of the Battle of Evesham in 1265 with the Leicester Tower, a memorial of the battle which acts as an eye-catcher. Evesham is on an island defined by the River with a built-up area to the north containing the once great Abbey and the churches of St. Lawrence and All Saints and open land south and east of a west-east wall across the isthmus. The "cloister arch" (the entry to the Abbey chapterhouse) was a well-known picturesque subject painted by J. M. W. Turner amongst others.

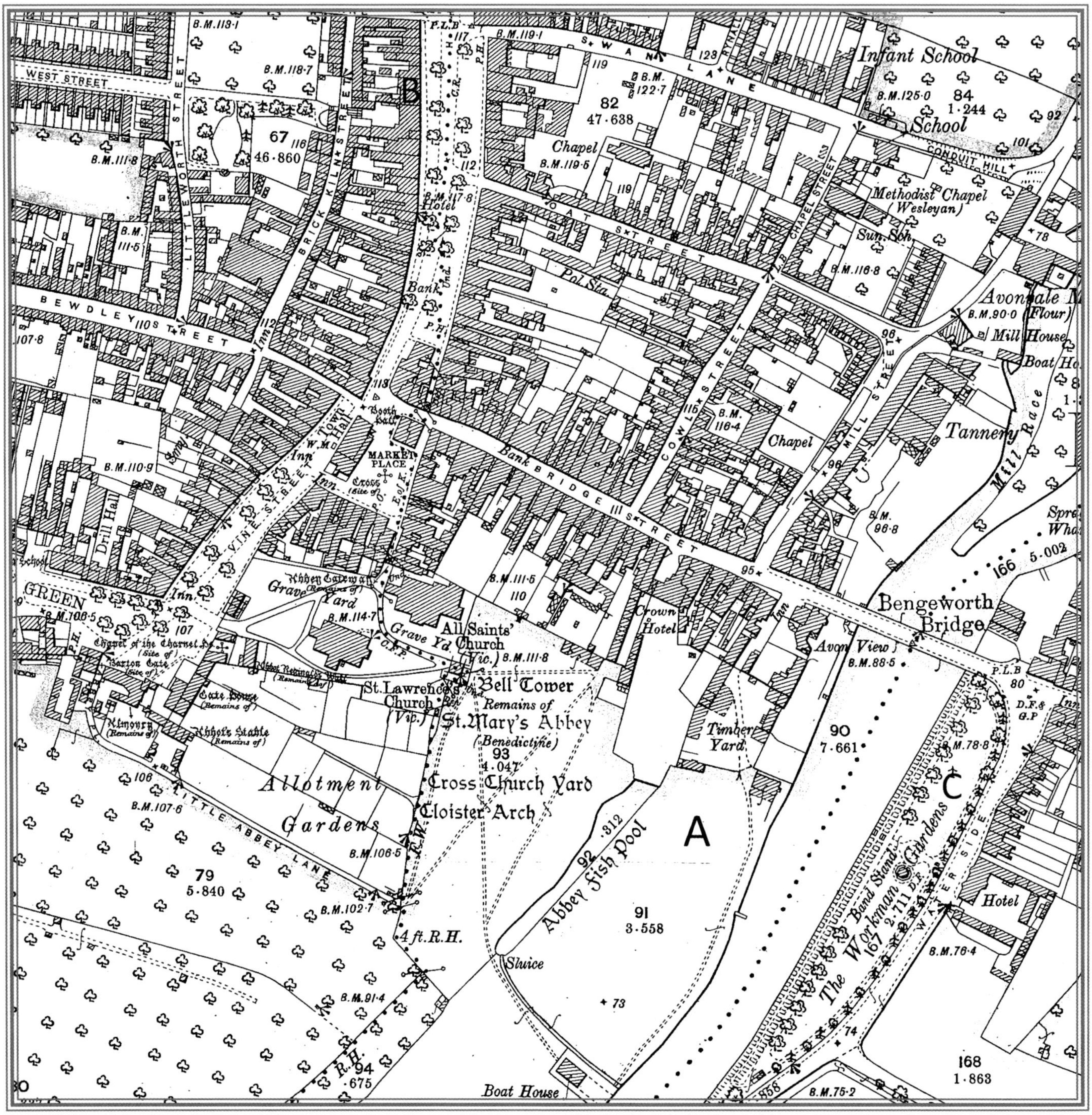

OS 25" Map No. 49-3. Dated 1904.

Farncombe Abbey

Parish: Broadway

HER Ref: WSM28992.

Grid Ref: SP 113 378

Postcode: WR10 1DT.

O.S. 6" Map No: 50SW/SE, 57NW/NE

Date of Maps: 1884.

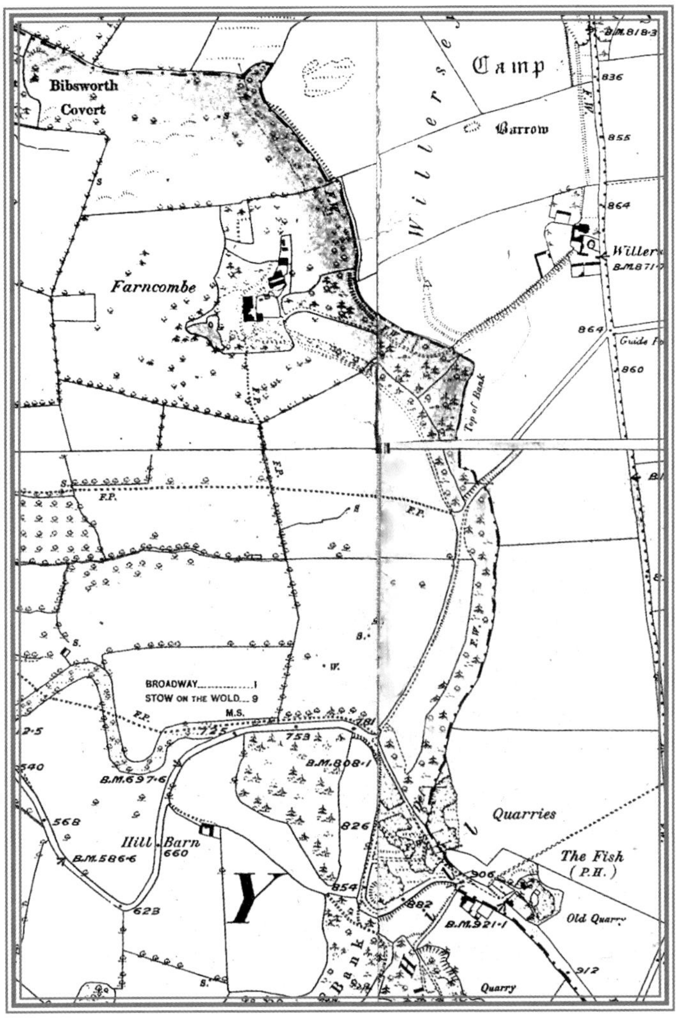

The Beauties (p. 392) describe "Farnham Abbey" in 1814 as a modern building "now well-sheltered by plantations disposed in a most pleasing style". The mansion was built in 1780 and was added to in the 19th and 20th centuries (BoE). Sale particulars of 1872 illustrate the entrance front with narrow terrace and lawn sloping down to a lake (fish pond) on the west side. "The residence, which is built of stone, is seated in a park of 42 acres with shrubberies, fish pond and pleasure grounds". The latter are arranged in a narrow belt of woods, including conifers, along Broadway Ridge. There was a large walled kitchen garden on the east side. "The gardens and pleasure grounds are quite unique and laid out with exquisite taste adorned with wild flowers and shrubs of rare and luxuriant growth" (CRO 372/1). A vinery is also mentioned. The Abbey is now a Conference Centre retaining terraced gardens with superb views (BoE). The immediate grounds of the mansion sit along the County boundary with Gloucestershire.

The Fish Inn, some way south, was built as a summer-house for Farncombe Abbey in 1771. Lord Torrington described it in his *Tour to the West* in 1781 as "the most extraordinary gaze-about house in the world"

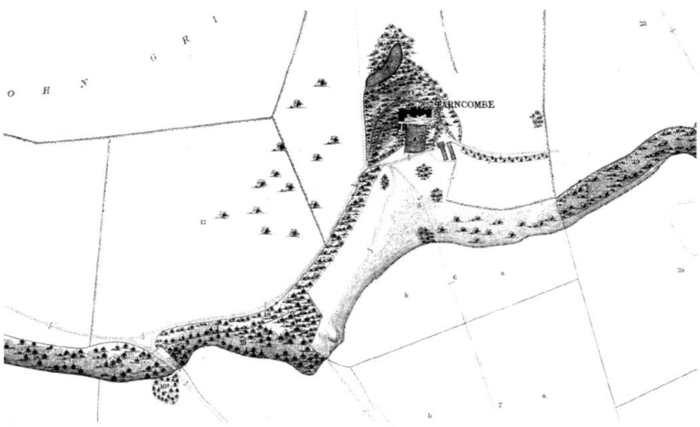

Beauties of England and Wales, Vol XV, 1814.
A. Brooks & N. Pevsner, *Worcestershire,* 2007 (BoE).
C. Bruyn Andrews, ed. *The Torrington Diaries: Tour to the West 1781,* 1954.

ABOVE & LEFT: Sale particulars, 1872. © WAAS 372/1.

Feckenham Park Lodge

Parish: Feckenham

HER Ref: WSM28911 Grid Ref: SO 967 622

O.S. 6" Map No: 29NE, 30NW. Date of Maps: 1884.

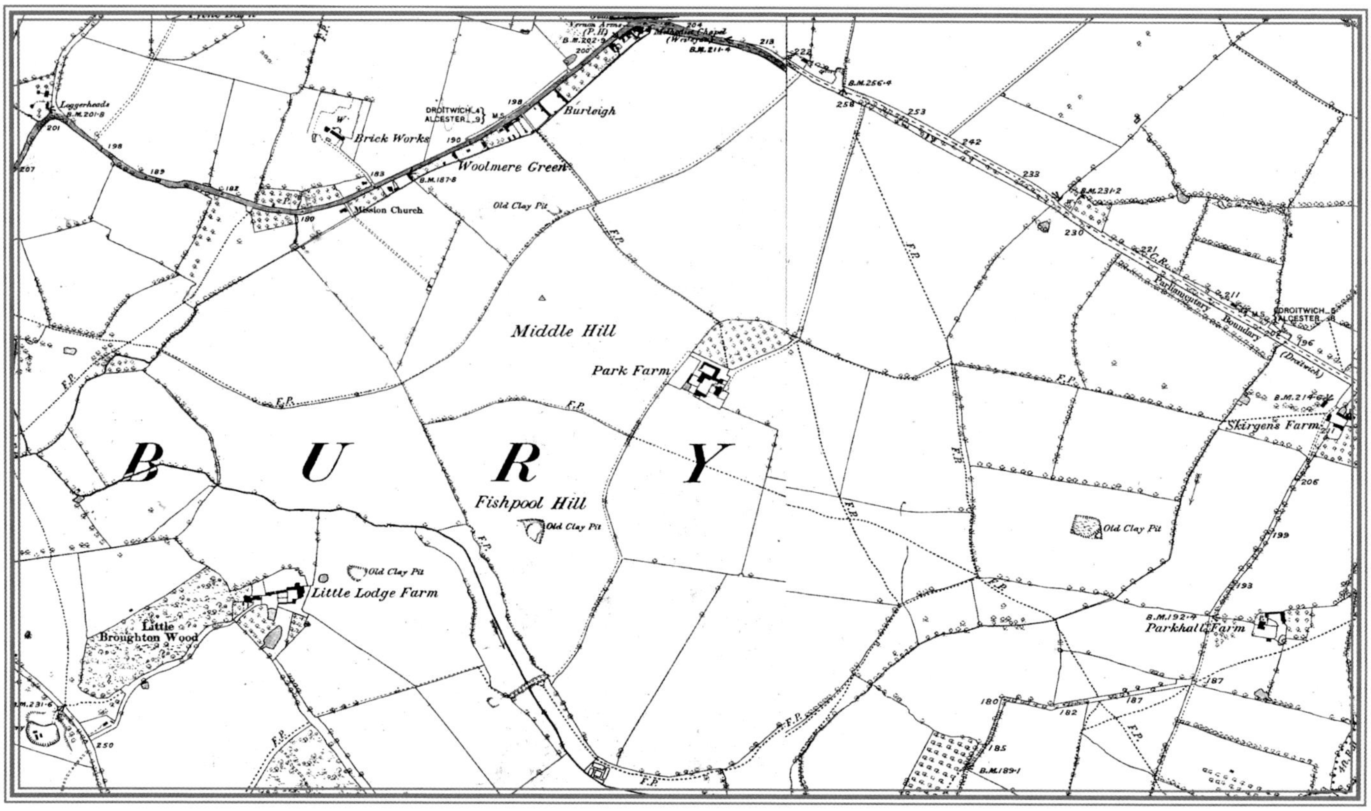

There was a royal lodge in the forest in the 12th century. There was also a royal manor house which was sold to the abbot of Evesham in the 14th century, represented now by a large moated earthwork. There are some very early references to fishponds in connection with the Royal Manor House, the building of a new and expensive fish pond in 1169 and the repair and enlargement of the fish pond in 1204 (Bettey, p. 23). This manor house was demolished and apparently not replaced since, in 1558, Sir John Throckmorton complained that he was "forced to wander up and down like an Egyptian in other men's houses for want of one of my own." Feckenham was disforested in 1629 (VCH, 3, 1923, pp. 112-117). Forest trees proved very vulnerable to Droitwich industry thereafter.

Feckenham Forest was a major constituent part of the Worcestershire landscape and grew from 34 square miles in the time of Henry II in the 12th century to 184 square miles in that of Edward I circa 1300. The growth of forests was a principal cause of grievance against a growing and arbitrary royal power (Barnard, op. cit.). Habington describes "a fair park (con)sorting in name with the King's vast forest, reaching in former ages far and wide".

The remains of the Fecknam Forest are shown as a grove of trees on Sheldon's 1590s tapestry map east of the fenced Fecknam Parke (Bodleian Library, Oxford). A copy of a 1593 map by John Blagrave (British Library, Maps M.T.6.B1 (12) by John Doharty junior (Turner, op. cit. Fig. 21), shows a "Fecknam Lodge" with two pools or fishponds and a formal garden with the "Mydle Park" and the "Further Park with ye pond" to the "south" (CRO 978). There is a 1692 reference in the Croome Archive to a Great Park, a Little Park as well as to a Feckenham Lodge. Feckenham Lodge as a house name is shown on printed maps to the north-east towards Hanbury, e.g. Nash 1781, Cooke circa 1801 and Cary 1805. Nash, however, in his text refers to Parke Hall "near the ancient park of the King" (Vol. 1, 1781, p. 548). This suggests that these sites are the same as the present Great Lodge Farm and Little Lodge Farm and that this park was centred on Middle Hill. This site is somewhat west of Feckenham village and south and east of Hanbury, as shown above.

J. Humphreys, "The Forest of Feckenham", *Birmingham & Midland Archaeol. Soc.* Trans. 45, 1919, pp. 115-129.

E. A. Barnard, "The Royal Forests of Feckenham and Hanbury", VIII, *Studies in Worcestershire History*, 1938, pp. 191-208.

B. S. Smith, "The Dougharty Family..." *Worcester Miscellany*, I, 1960, p. 38.

J. H. Bettey, *Estates and the English Countryside*, 1993.

H. L. Turner, *No Mean Prospect: Ralph Sheldon's Tapestry Maps*, 2010.

Victoria County History, Vol. 3, 1913 (VCH).

T. R. Nash, *Collections for the History of Worcestershire*, Vol I, 1781.

Finstall House

Parish: Finstall

HER Ref: WSM28859.

Grid Ref: SO 977 698.

Postcode: B60 3BU.

O.S. 6" Map No. 23NW, 16SW.

Date of Map: 1884, 1885, with extent of park & gardens shaded as 1880s OS.

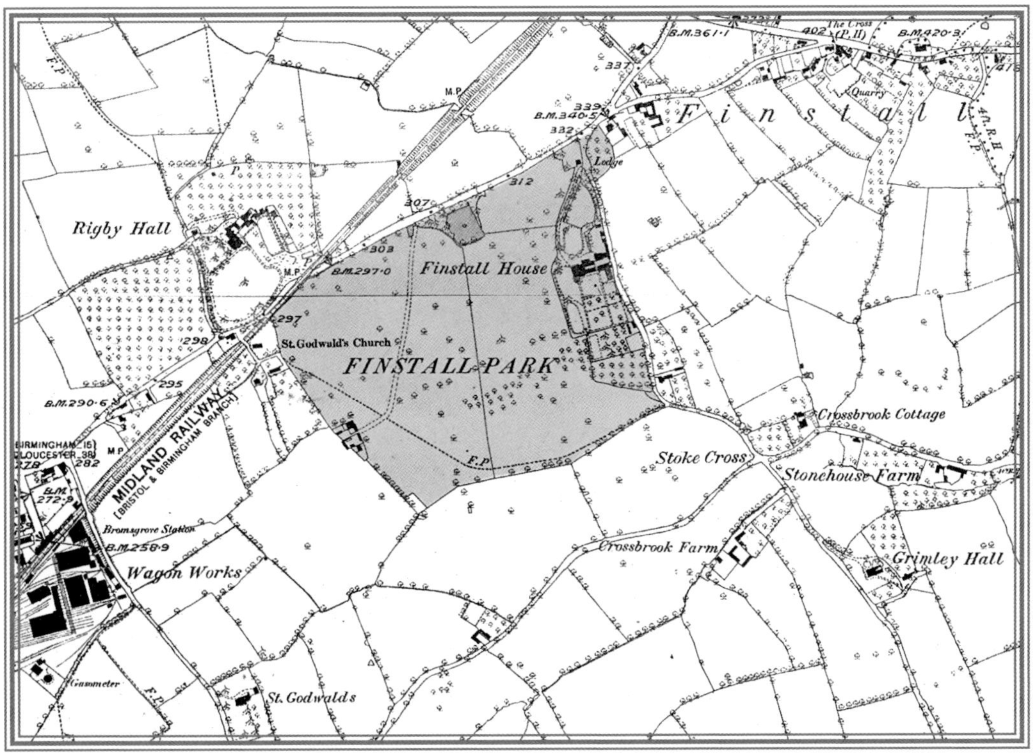

Finstall House or Park is shown as having a park on both the first two OS 6 inch editions, (1883 and 1905). By the 1905 OS the park had been extended to 120 acres with pool, boathouse and lodge (VCH. 3, 1913, p. 528). Bentley in 1840 described the house as lying amongst shady groves. A 1924 sale plan shows the park lying behind the house (which is close to the road) and extending parallel with the railway line (Bromsgrove – Birmingham) as far as Bromsgrove Station. There was a Park Cottage towards the centre of this small park (CRO 9526). The earlier-19th century house was burnt down in the 1970s and then replaced. "Much of the fine landscape park remains, a significant landscape feature south of Finstall Road" (BoE, p. 315).

A. Brooks & N. Pevsner, *Worcestershire,* 2007 (BoE).
Victoria County History Vol. 3, 1913 (VCH).
J. McGregor-Smith, *From Bromsgrove to Aston Fields,* 2008.

The Firs

Parish: Broadheath

HER Ref: WSM35420. Grid Ref: SO 808 555. Postcode: WR2 6RH.

O.S. 6" Map No. 33NW. Date of Map: 1884.

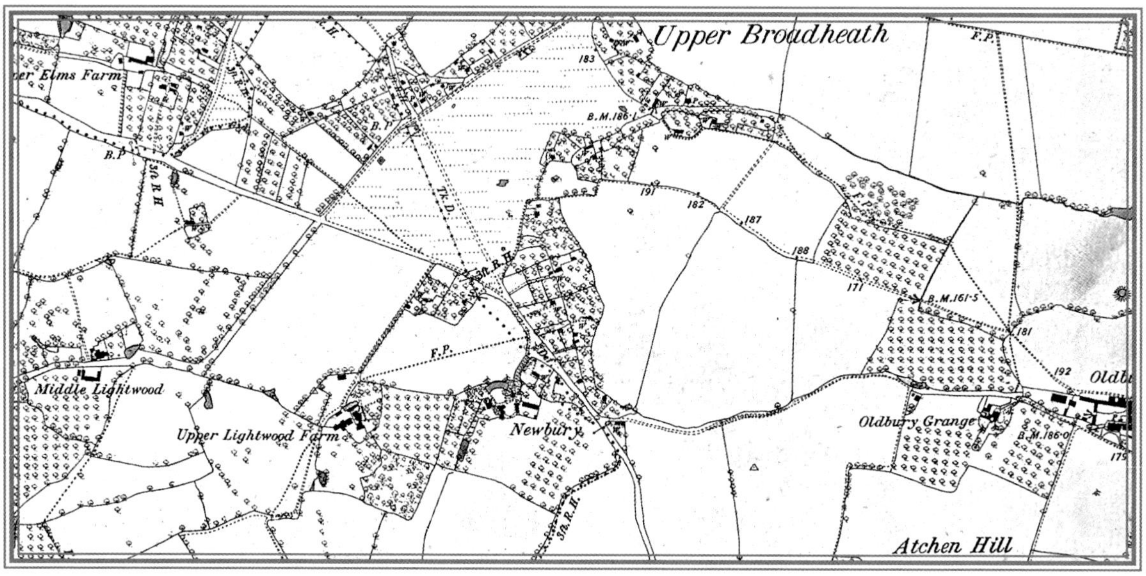

The Firs cottage was rented by Sir Edward Elgar's father as a country retreat from Worcester for the family, and the composer was born here in 1856 and lived here for 2 years. Elgar took his title from Broadheath expressing his love for the place. This is commemorated in the gardens by a life-size bronze sculpture of Elgar seated on a bench looking out towards the Malvern Hills which was commissioned in 2007 from Jemma Pearson. The gardens are "historic" in that they are based on a drawing by J. C. Buckler (1793-1894) of the cottage in the mid-19th century. Elgar's daughter Clarice Blake encouraged the City of Worcester to acquire the cottage in 1935 and she supported the development of the Birthplace as a home for Elgar memorabilia. The birthplace cottage and garden, and the visitor centre, 're-opened' in 2017 after The Firs came into the care of the National Trust. Katherine Alker, Garden and Outdoors Manager at Croome, explains that "the fairly formal layout seen in the Buckler image is an aspirational lower middle-class and rural interpretation of the gardenesque style which was popular throughout the Victorian period. This has been recreated here with a profusion of plants including lavenders, roses, honeysuckle, peonies and asters." It is as a representative of the cottage garden that The Firs is included here.

ABOVE: both photos. taken July 2019, R. Lockett.
LEFT: drawing by J. C. Buckler, 1793-1894. By permission of The Elgar Foundation.

Froxmere Court

Parish: Crowle

HER Ref: WSM28861.

Grid Ref: SO 937 559. Postcode: WR7 4AJ.

O.S. 6" Map No: 34NE.

Date of Map: 1885, with extent of park & gardens shaded as 1905 OS.

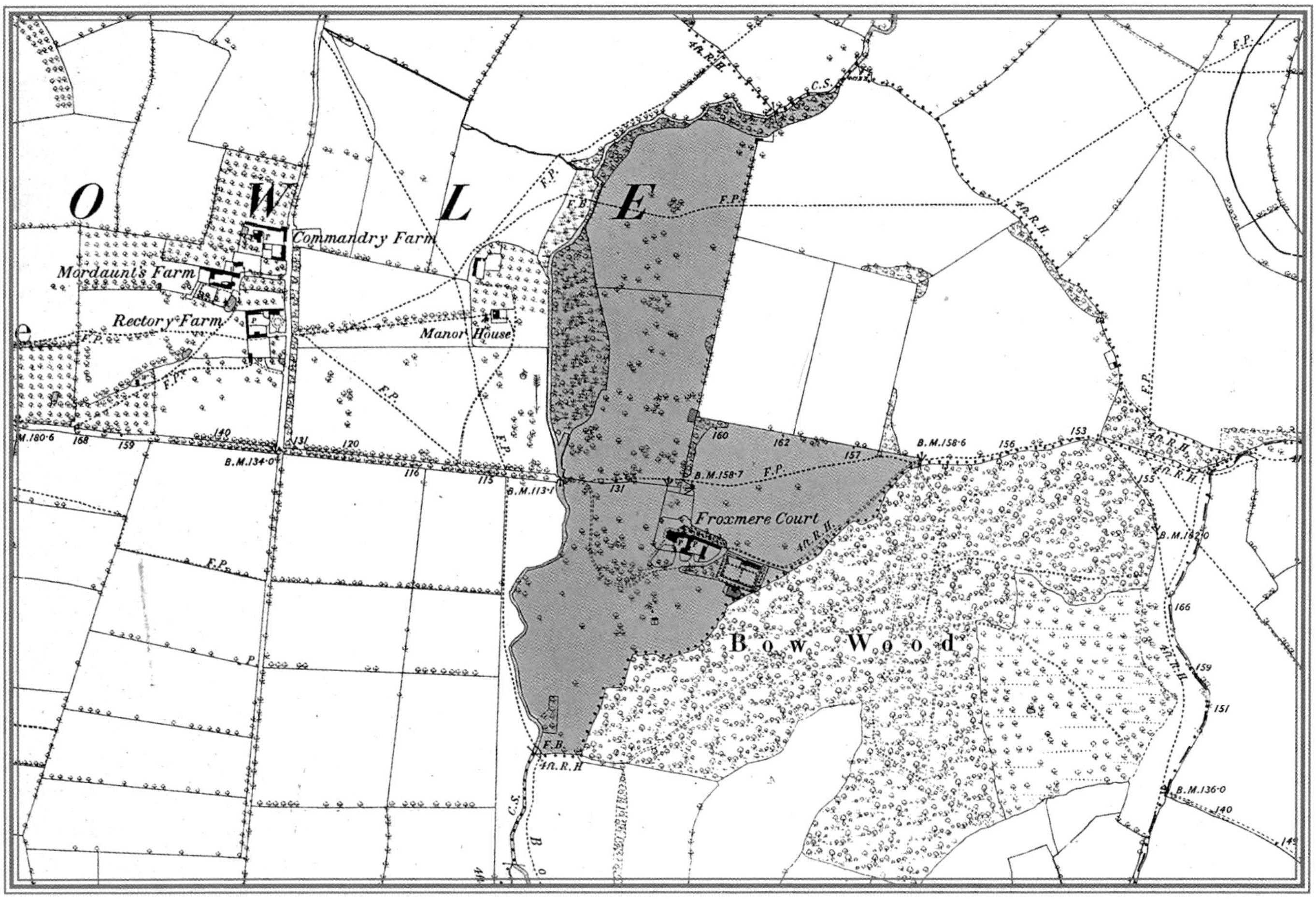

The 1905 OS shows a park arranged north/south along the ridge line, with a strip along the Bow Brook on its west side and the substantial amenity of the Bow Wood immediately south and east of the Court. There is a large walled kitchen garden and the suggestion of an avenue along the dead straight road to Crowle. BoE describes the house as circa 1836 and Tudor-bethan and as "notably picturesque" (BoE, p. 251).

The house, garden and parkland remain intact with a wealth of mature parkland trees as well as more recent planting. The various offices have been converted to separate houses and the walled garden, which is in good condition, is now within the curtilage of another dwelling.

A. Brooks & N. Pevsner, *Worcestershire,* 2007 (BoE).

Gaudywood

Parish: Mamble

HER Ref: WSM71641.

Grid Ref: SO 675 712. Postcode: DY14 9AD.

Part of sale map. Date of Map: 1919.

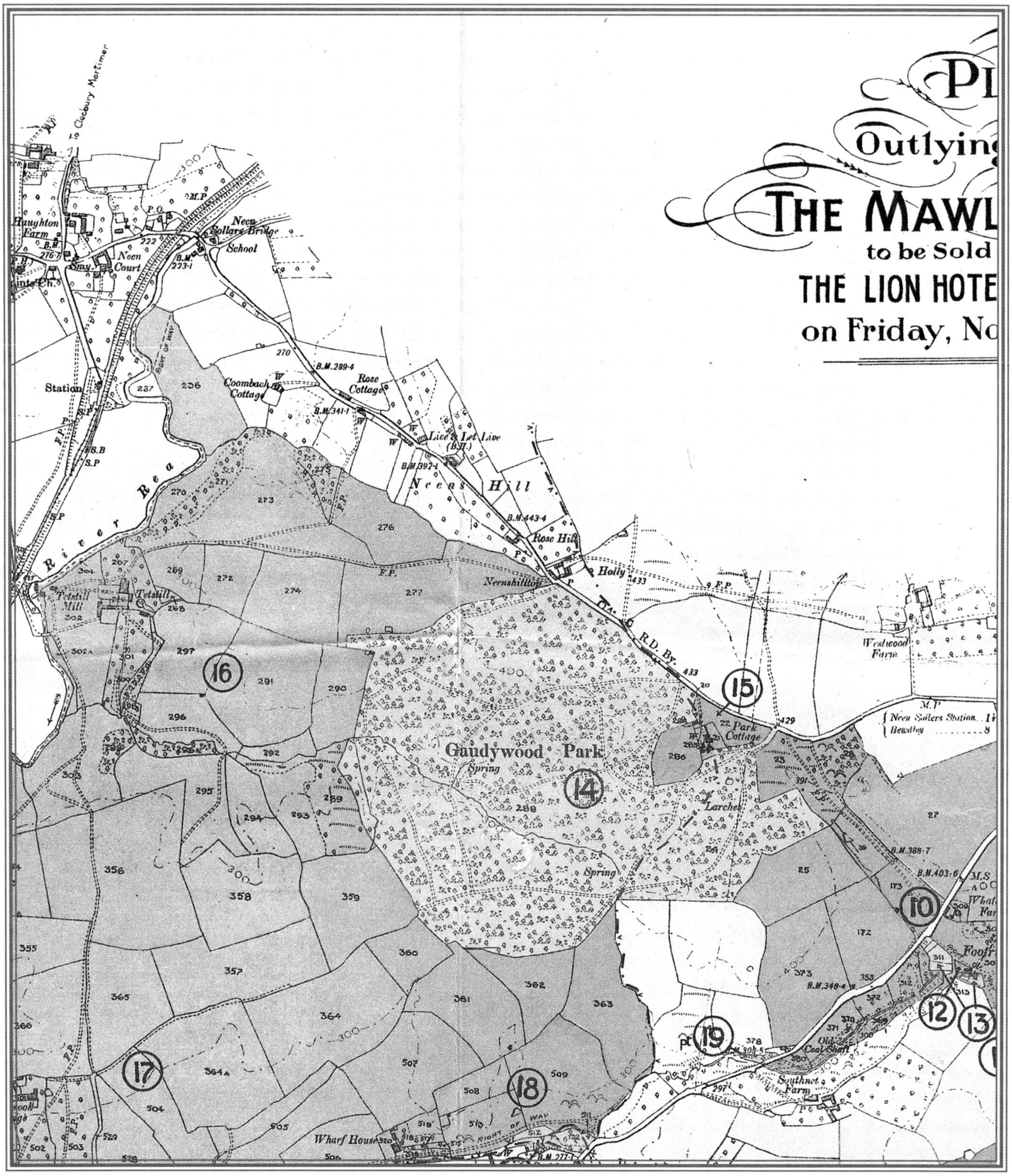

..........continued from previous page

GRAFTON PARK

John Leland visited around.1539: "I came by a park about a mile or [ere] I came to Bromsgrove on the left hand; it is called Grafton ... In this park is a fair manor place and one Talbot at this time dwelleth in it" (Toulmin-Smith, pt. IV, p. 95). There is mention in 1542 of two parks, Old and New, but none thereafter. (*VCH*, Vol. 3, 1913, p. 127). However, Morden (1695) and several 18th century followers do give Grafton a deer park. The HER identifies some earthworks south-east of the Manor House which it is suggested are related to the deer park. No doubt there was some continuity between the medieval and post-medieval parks which may be reflected in field names. The area to be considered for Leland's Old and New Parks lies between Upton Warren in the south to Dodford in the north; West Lodge and East Lodge (now west and east of the M5) may indicate other boundaries.

Both the 1837 Tithe Map and surveys of 1871/2 contain field names pointing to a park or parks. In the absence of 17th or 18th century maps, it is not safe to distinguish two or more parks (i.e. as at Croome Court) or to trace a line between a medieval or later deer park and the tiny area suggested for a landscape park in 1905. The 1813 survey for the first OS one inch sites a park south-east of Grafton Court. However, Park and Lodge field names may recall an earlier deer park rather than an 18th-century landscape park. The 1837 Tithe Map refers to: The Plain 20 acres; the Little Wilderness 13 acres; Level Park 21 acres; Park Hill 9 acres. These total about 65 acres (CRO 8181/2). These lie between Warridge Lodge (probably originally Warrener's) and the Manor and between Warridge Lodge and East Lodge. There is a Keeper's Walk near East Lodge – all this north of the Manor House.

Park Gate and Park Farm also to the north suggest the northern limit of the park as the A448 with Warridge Lodge and Monsieur's Hall to the south of it. The A38 on the east side being on the line of a Roman Road may have formed a park boundary linking East Lodge, Park Hall and Warren House to Upton Warren. The 1837 Tithe Map has the following Park field names around Upton Warren: Stony Park; Rail Park; Moat Close; Moat Field; Cold Park; Near Park; Far Park; Warden's Close; Warden's Meadow; Part of Park Meadow. These clues may fit Leland's Old Park.

The M5 now bisects the estate and divides up the areas suggested for medieval parks as well as the relatively small landscape park as shown on the 1905 6 inch OS.

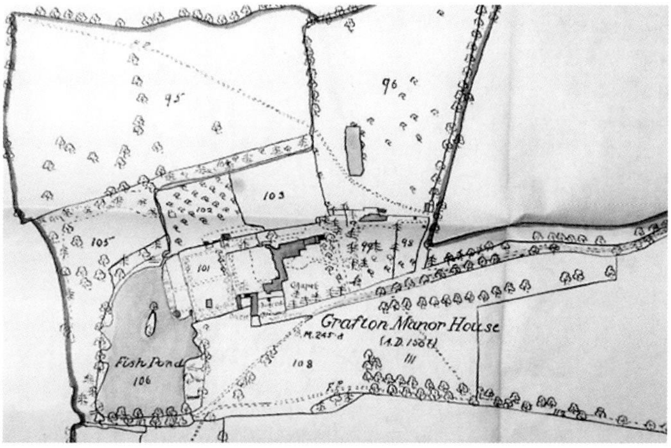

Hand coloured sale plan from OS 1884.

Views of the gardens, 1898.
WAAS, Dodford with Grafton 6890, 6895.

L. Toulmin-Smith (ed.), *The Itinerary of John Leland,* 1908.
J. Humphreys, "Sheldon Tapestry Maps of Worcestershire", *Birmingham & Midland Archaeol. Soc.*, 43, 1917.
J. Humphreys, "The Elizabethan Estate Book of Grafton Manor [1568-9]", *Birmingham & Midland Archaeol. Soc.,* 44, 1918, p. 17 ff.
J. Humphreys and E. A. Barnard (eds.)," Grafton Manor and its History", *Studies in Worcestershire History*, 1938.
A. Brooks & N. Pevsner, *Worcestershire,* 2007 (BoE).
Victoria County History Vol. 3, 1913 (VCH).

Hadzor Hall

Parish: Hadzor, Himbleton, Huddington & Oddingley

HER Ref: WSM28871. Grid Ref: SO 915 626. Postcode: WR9 7EW.

O.S. 6" Map No: 29NW.

Date of Map: 1885, with extent of park & gardens shaded as 1905 OS.

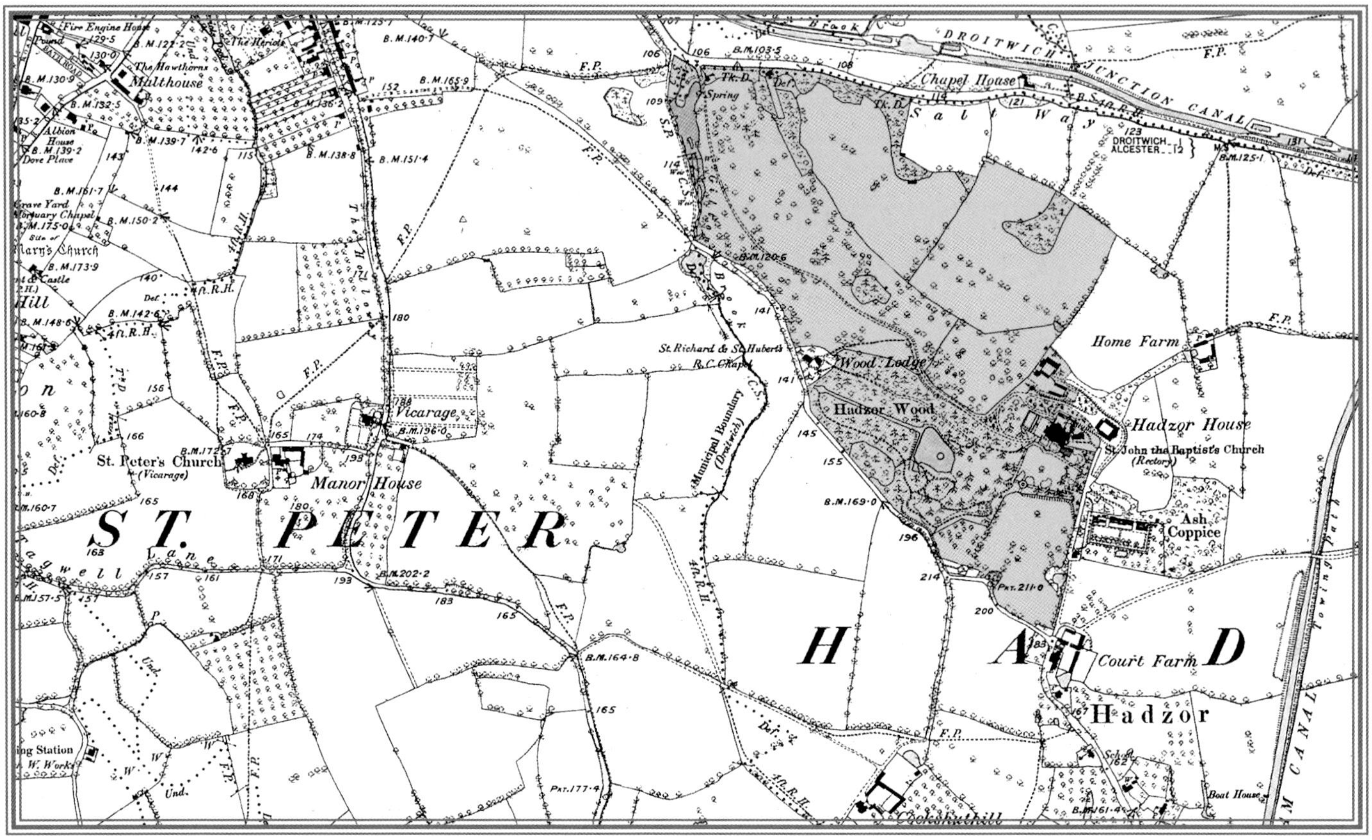

The Amphlett family acquired Hadzor in 1633 and the grounds no doubt reflected the early and late-18th century houses built circa 1702 and by John Yenn in 1769 - 1779 (Jane Bradney). The 1779 house was re-faced and extended in 1827 with later additions by Mathew Habershon for John Howard Galton of the Birmingham Banking family who acquired the estate in 1823.

Hazor [sic] is shown as belonging to W. Amphlett on Isaac Taylor's 1779 map and was regarded as a principal county seat circa 1800. Some gardens are indicated on the 1813 survey for the first OS one inch. The sale of Hadzor by the Revd. R. H. Amphlett in 1823 provides information about the pre Galton grounds (CRO 7335/7). The property was made up of 3 farms each of over 100 acres and there were 185 acres in hand. Because the property was owned by the Revd. Amphlett, the Hall served as the Rectory "a respectable Residence calculated for a large family" and the "excellent farm house" was Court Farm. The sale particulars claim exceedingly beautiful and interesting views, grounds disposed in the best possible order, a kitchen garden clothed with the choicest fruit, lawns and shrubberies leading imperceptibly to the romantic and beautiful plantations abounding with shady walks, extended drives and vistas in almost every direction. "It is here that in the oppressive heat of the weather, this incomparable retreat has been assimilated to Paradise." There is a shrubbery south of the house and a walled courtyard with lawn to the west front of the house. The Conservatory (converted into a Chapel), Dell Pool Shrine (made into a memorial to T. H. and W. J. Galton, killed in the Ist World War), walls, balustrades and gate piers all date from circa 1827. Habershon featured Hadzor, his favourite work, in his book *The Ancient Half-Timbered Houses of England* published in 1836, written he says to counter Pugin's *Contrasts* and to champion English medieval (and Tudor) domestic architecture; along the way he cites other

..........continued from previous page

local, Worcestershire examples at Elmley Lodge, Hadzor Village, Salwarpe Court and Mere Hall and his lithograph illustrations include the Woodman's Lodge, the Village and the Farmhouse at the entrance of Hadzor Village itself. The Woodman's Lodge was "built on the carriage-road in the Park, at the entrance of the beautifully-wooded dell near the House." (Stephen Price).

The development of Hadzor house, its gardens and garden buildings and other estate buildings including the church between 1823 and circa 1860, seems to have been continuous and complicated as revealed by Jane Bradley's unpublished researches. Mathew Habershon was active from circa 1827 and Alexander Roos from circa 1835 and Charles Heath Wilson circa 1838. Roos was a pupil of Schinkel and hence the BoE calling the Hadzor gardens "Schinkel-inspired". Roos was also active at Blackmore Park and Hanbury Hall.

Roos had been invited to Hadzor as a painter and decorator (ceilings) but his role was extended apparently alongside Habershon to the terrace gardens, arched gateways and urns and even an Italianate Lodge. Bradney also associates Roos with the Shrine (circular garden building) and the Conservatory (dismantled) recorded on the 1885 OS (Bradney). When travelling in Italy or more widely on the Continent, Galton kept in touch with developments to his English home for which he sent back his own design drawings to further confuse on site design decisions.

John Howard Galton formed a significant art collection which occasioned a visit from Gustav Waagen (*Treasures of Art in Great Britain,* 1854) to Hadzor in 1850 when he was treated to an archery match in the grounds (Bradney).

The photograph in Mowl (fig. 50) suggests a Roman, archaeological site. Nothing so precise or unusual in a British context is implied by Bentley's *Directory* which speaks of a well-wooded park and tastefully arranged pleasure grounds and gardens (1840). P. C. Hardwick added to the mansion in 1859 and William Eden Nesfield is on the scene before 1862 when John Howard Galton, who acquired Hadzor in 1823, died.

The high point of Hadzor's fortunes and of its gardens when tenanted by Lady Hindlip, was captured by *Country Life* in 1901 (op. cit., with 11 photographs): "There were old gardens and pleasure grounds here, but the late Mr. Galton remodelled them entirely, and they were laid out with the assistance of eminent gardeners." The reviewer remarks the broad and ample terrace with flower beds, steps to the lower gardens, finely worked balustrades and masonry walls, vases making brilliant points, the splendid yew hedge behind, and the circular garden enclosed by a box hedge (Reid, p. 205). The 1929 sale particulars (WAAS 11541) claimed that the grounds were famous for their beauty. Sale photographs show a distant view of the terrace from the other side of a stream and a large lawn leading up to it; there is another view from the terrace and another of the porticoed entrance front and from the Park. The 1929 Sale consisted of a property of 109 acres of which 68 were park. The park is defined as by the first edition of the OS 6 inch. The north-west corner of the park together with Swan Pool is now up against the M5. Earlier boundaries were made by the Droitwich - Hanbury road and the Droitwich Junction Canal and the Birmingham Worcester Canal to the east.

Most of the perimeter planting and Hadzor Wood along the west and south sides survive and contain some fine mature trees e.g. ash, oak, chesnut, and conifers. The grounds including the Kitchen Gardens have been in-filled with residential development to a substantial extent circa 2000, particularly on the north side.

P. Reid, *Burke's and Savills Guide to Country Houses,* II, 1980.
M. Habershon, *The ancient and half-timbered houses of England,* 1836.
Country Life, X, 1901, pp. 208-12.
London, RIBA Drawings Collection for a drawing by A. Roos for Hadzor.
T. Mowl, *Historic Gardens of Worcestershire,* 2006.
A. Brooks & N. Pevsner, *Worcestershire,* 2007 (BoE).
J. Bradney, Correspondence, 2016-7 (unpublished).

Photo of Hadzor Hall from the gardens. Sale particulars, 1929.

Hagley Hall

Parish: Hagley

HER Ref: WSM 01146/22983/34853/34854.

Grid Ref: SO 919 807.

Postcode: DY9 9LG.

O.S. 6" Map No: 9NW, 9NE.

Date of Map: 1887, 1884, with extent of park & gardens shaded as H. E. Register.

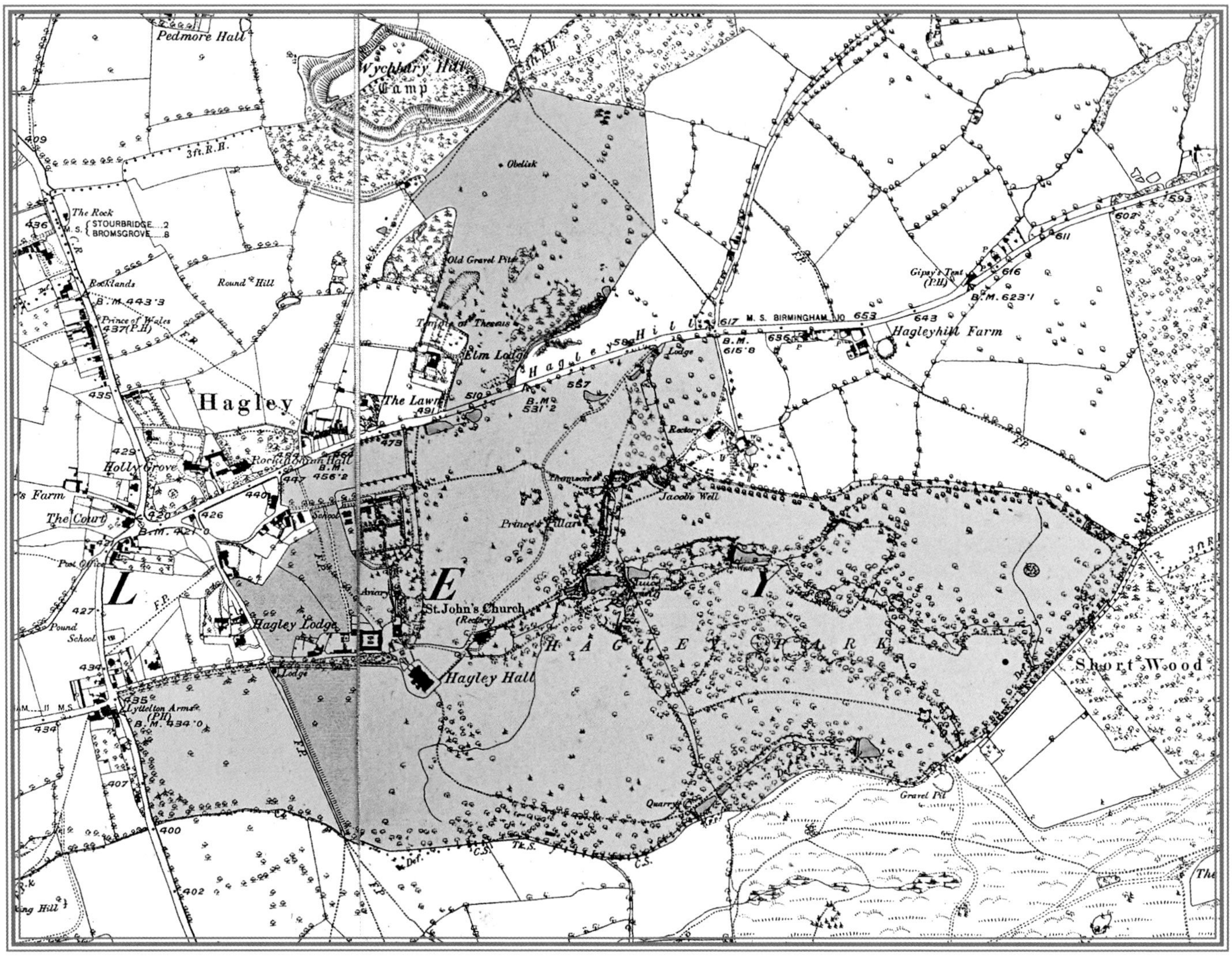

Included within Historic England's Register of Historic Parks and Gardens of special historic interest in England.

There are references to a deer park in the 14th and 15th centuries but this was not apparent in 1565 when the Lytteltons acquired Hagley nor does one appear as such in 16th and 17th century maps. However, there are earthworks that probably define a medieval park and an area equivalent to about a third of the Registered Park and nearly half that from west to east has been proposed (Askew Nelson). In 1694 Sir Charles decided to create "a little house park" of 80 acres for 40 or 50 deer contained by a post and rail fence and then added 53 acres to it. By 1703 he had 200 deer in this park and had by then built a Lodge on a hill in the middle of the park for use in part by the Keeper. The site of this lodge was later called the Castle Lawn.

Sir Charles, circa 1692, found "ye garden that was, all ruined and lyes yet wast and open" but proceeded to build walls round a new Kitchen and Flower Garden on one side of which there was a 100 yard terrace. He established a tree nursery for ash, beech, and sycamore

..........continued from previous page

and created or planned a vista through horse chestnuts. He had two acres ploughed up for groves of beech. He otherwise planted a great many trees, principally limes and elms. He had a new, skilled gardener but he died! Work on the new Hagley began in the 1730s but the Old Hall was not demolished until 1759. It is not clear how long Sir Charles's circa 1700 gardens survived and to what extent his considerable planting was subsumed into the newly formed landscape that replaced them. (Askew Nelson; Cousins, "The First Hagley Hall").

Hagley Old Hall, J. S. Walker, *Architectural Sketches*, Vol 1, 1863.

Nash and Cary indicate a fenced deer park in their published maps of 1781 and 1787. In 1892 Whitaker gives the acreage of the deer park as 200 acres surrounded by oak paling 6ft 6ins. high; besides varied timber and many old oaks, it contained 40 fallow deer. This deer park is the eastern section of the landscape park.

There is a large literature relating to the landscape park that George, 1st. Lord Lyttelton, began in the late 1740s in advance of his rebuilding of the Hall. It is the only park in Worcestershire besides that at Croome with Grade 1 status. The HE Register summarises the facts and statistics; The park is 180 hectares and the walled garden 5 hectares: "Hagley possesses many trees from the mid-C18, now in full maturity - cedar of Lebanon, chestnut, sycamore and lime". Hadfield adds: "Hagley has little water, a failing noted by contemporaries with the exception of its castle, its conceits are restrained. The sweeps of trees now contain nothing more exotic than red-stemmed pines and flat-topped cedars; it is very near cultivated nature" (1979, p. 209). Symes and Haynes (op. cit.) detail the native timber of oak, horse chestnuts, Scots pine, wych elm, ash and sycamore "often in clumps" and Lyttelton's preference for triangular clumps of cedar and Silesian larches, ("Yew and darker evergreens were used for the effect of seclusion"). They point out that Lyttelton sourced his New England pines from the Duke of Argyle and probably secured other imported species via his brother who was Governor of South Carolina in the later 1750s.

Joe Hawkins's researches have revealed new information about the water supply and its management in the 18th century: "Although the park had little water it acted as a drain for the massive catchment of the Clent hill slopes to the east and west. A 700 ft spring line throughout the east and west park boundaries has extensive 17th and 18th century stone drains supplying the water for the pools, these allowed the presence of hydro powered industry in the park until just after the re-emparkement" (corr. 2016).

The Kidderminster-Birmingham road cuts off Wychbury Hill (with the Obelisk and the Temple of Theseus) which became known as Monument Hill (1838 Tithe Map), from the main part of the landscape park. The Hill is disguised in some views such as F. Vivares' *View of Hagley Park* after J. Smith, 1749. To the west, the park stretched to Beacon Hill Meadow as today and to the east stopped short before the large Hagley Wood. To the south the boundary is the parish boundary with Clent.

Watercolour after Thomas Smith circa 1766.

Several 18th-century buildings are sited within the park: Coachhouse and Stables (late-18th century); Laundry/old Dairy, later a summer-house (Sanderson Miller, 1752); Castle using some masonry from Halesowen Abbey (Miller, 1747-8); Rotunda (John Pitt, circa 1747) originally above a small valley with cascade and Palladian

..........continued from previous page

bridge (now reconstructed) (Thomas Pitt, circa 1762-3); Hermitage (foundations located 2015 – Joe Hawkins); Prince of Wales's Column; Thomson's Seat (John Pitt, circa 1749); Obelisk on Wychbury Hill; Temple of Theseus on Wychbury Hill (James Stuart, 1758, first primitive Doric building); a mid-18th century Orangery (now a house) set within an 18th century brick, walled garden. The HER adds a grotto at SO 9232 8082. Smaller landscape features included urns to Alexander Pope and William Shenstone (of nearby Leasowes) and a seat to John Milton. The medieval church, close to the house but hidden by trees from it, was much altered by G. E. Street in 1858-65.

Rotunda and Cascade, after Thomas Smith circa 1750.

This was the most highly promoted garden of its time, a promotion that began with James Thomson's *Seasons* of 1744, written in part at Hagley, a poem that continued to be an inspiration to British painters throughout the second half of the 18th century and into the 19th century. One of the earliest tourists was Richard Pococke and his 1751 description of the newly created landscape is quoted by Mowl (*Gentlemen Gardeners*, p. 142). Horace Walpole (1753) compared the Hagley landscape to the prints or paintings of Sadeler (Jan II, re. the Hermitage) and Nicholas Poussin (re. "a pretty well under a wood") or to the poetry of Milton (Hunt & Willis, p. 313). Such comparisons could be verified by 1767 from the Old Masters to be seen in the Hall: "Admittance to see the house is by tickets from Mr. Cleeve, every Thursday during the summer" (Martyn, p. 37). Walpole's most often quoted response to the Hagley landscape concerned the Castle eye catcher : "There is a ruined castle built by Mr. Miller that would get him his freedom, even of Strawberry (Hill), it has the true rust of the Baron's Wars ... in his castle he is almost (Richard) Bentley." The Castle was nonetheless furnished for entertaining with chairs "of a Gothick form". It is worth adding Walpole's more general appreciation of Hagley Park: "As I got into Worcestershire, I opened upon a landscape of country which I prefer even to Kent, which I had reckoned the most beautiful county in England: but this, with all the richness of Kent, is bounded with mountains." Walpole is rude about the old house (still in use in 1753) but enchanted by the park: "Indeed, I prefer nothing to Hagley but Mount Edgecumbe" (Hunt & Willis, p. 313).

Mrs Elizabeth Montagu described a musical entertainment in 1762: "We had several entertainments of music in different parts of the park and adapted to the scenes ... in some places French Horns reverberated from hill to hill; in the shady parts near the cascades, the soft music was concealed, and seemed to proceed from the unseen genius of the wood." (London Soc. of Antiquaries, Prattinton I. xii). Hagley rapidly became a "must" for the tourist and was reviewed by Thomas Martyn in 1767, Joseph Heely in 1777, Richard Sulivan in 1778 and by Lord Torrington and Thomas Jefferson in the 1780s. It had its own guide books by 1800.

A step by step tour of the grounds is given in the *Traveller* (1819, p. 31): "Those who view them are first conducted among the shrubs, of which there is a great variety, and in a most flourishing state." This guidebook moves the reader from viewing station to viewing station, beginning at the church and continuing to Frederick, Prince of Wales's monument and then to "a grove from which Lord Stamford's grounds (Enville Hall, Staffs.) can be seen, and on to a pavilion dedicated to the celebrated James Thomson with an inscription to his memory. From hence you pass by a ruin, a pavilion, and a seat in an amphitheatre of wood; and then proceed by a pit of hard red stone to Jacob's-Well ... by the park pales ... parsonage-house ... hanging wood on left ... walk winding to the right, from which there is a view of the Clee-Hills: this leads into a grove, when a view of the tower breaks in. Hence you arrive at a rotunda of the Ionic order; from which you look down across water and a lawn to the Palladian-Bridge. Hence you wind down the hill, where, in a deep recess, by a purling rill, is a retired bench; from this you wind to the left up hill, and find an urn inscribed to Mr. Pope." The tour goes on to a ruined tower, to the seat of contemplation, to the root-house, or hermitage in which are inscribed lines from Milton's *Il Penseroso,* to the entrance to a wood where are more lines from Milton, to a seat that was Mr. Pope's favourite, to a lawn with steep walks, a scene that reminded Lord Anson of the island of Tinian and, however weary, one's tour continues.

Surprisingly, given this fashionable enthusiasm, Hagley did not inspire any notable pictures in the 18th or 19th centuries and the tourist literature was supported by modest engravings. But more ambitious print by Thomas Smith (1766 after a painting of 1748), from a Midlands series came at the beginning of this development in print publishing (Harris, op. cit., p. 162). Typically, a mansion would be pictured "set in its swathes of parkland". The lack of impressive "portraits" of Hagley has contributed to the difficulty of understanding the 18th century's

..........continued from previous page

enthusiasm for it. Michael Cousins's monograph of 2007 greatly increases knowledge about Hagley and presents new visual documents such as Jeremiah Mathews' Survey Map of 1828 and the 1847-8 watercolour views of Elizabeth Phipson from the Hagley Archive. From further afield, Cousins introduces thumbnail sketches of buildings by John Parnell from a *Journal of a Tour,* 1769 (British Library of Political and Economic Science) and more Romantic sketches by F-J. Bélanger of circa 1774 (Paris, École Nat. Sup. des Beaux Arts).

Restored Palladian bridge, 2014. Photo, J. Patton.

Since the first edition of this *Survey*, a major conservation of the park and its buildings has been undertaken and the *Parkland Plan* commissioned from Askew Nelson provided a comprehensive history of the grounds together with an analysis of the ecology and planting as they exist today. This, together with further discoveries made as the restoration has been progressed by Joe Hawkins, Head of Landscape, has recreated several 18th century "moments". This campaign will give meaning to the descriptive literature and allow the language of 18th century landscape theory and aesthetic experience to be appreciated once again.
Further research into Enville, Hagley and the Leasowes by Symes and Haynes, brings a 3 dimensional feel to these three associated landscapes in their differing states of preservation and details the social networks which helped shape the landscape and the buildings set within it. Their fig. 39 – "The sightlines at Hagley" – puts one in the tourist seat, able to take the views and appreciate the visual connections between individual buildings.

Somewhat isolated, to the south-east of the main landscape, are the Four Stones (Grid Ref. SO 933 803) which Lord Lyttelton perhaps intended to evoke an ancient British monument for which they were later to be mistaken (HE Register). They are now within the Clent Hills Country Park. The Registered parkland extends to about 180 hectares.

Thomas Martyn, *The English Connoisseur,* I, 1767.
J. Dugdale, *The New British Traveller,* 1819.
B. Jones, *Follies and Grottoes,* 1974.
J. D. Hunt & P. Willis, *The Genius of the Place,* 1975.
J. D. Hunt, *The Figure in the Landscape,* 1976, 1989.
David Jacques, *Georgian Gardens,* 1983.
T. Mowl, *Historic Gardens of Worcestershire,* 2006, Ch.5. " Lyttelton's Hagley and " the true dust of the barons Wars".
A. Brooks & N. Pevsner, *Worcestershire,* 2007 (BoE).
M. Cousins, "Hagley Park, Worcestershire", *Garden History,* 35, Supplement 1, 2007.
M. Cousins, *The First Hagley Hall (Grange),* 2016, unpub..
M. Symes and S. Haynes, *Enville, Hagley, The Leasowes; Three Eighteenth Century Gardens,* 2010, Ch. 4. Hagley.
Askew Nelson Ltd., *Hagley Hall Parkland Plan,* 2011.
Lord Cobham, *Hagley Hall and its Eighteenth Century Buildings, Monuments, Park and Gardens,* 2014.
J. Hawkins, *Hagley Hall; Paradise Regained,* Research and Recording Day, AGT, 2014.
J. Hawkins, "A Tale of Two Parks; Hagley Hall", *HWGT, Newsletter,* 41, Summer 2013.
J. Severn Walker, *Architectural Sketches,* Vol. 1, 1862.
M. Hadfield, *History of British Gardening,* 1979
HE *Register of Parks & Gardens,* 1998.

Restored Rotunda, 2014. Photo, J. Patton.

Hallow Park

Parish: Hallow

HER Ref: WSM01171.

Grid Ref: SO 831 579. Postcode: WR2 6PG.

O.S. 6" Map No: 28SE.

Date of Map: 1886, with extent of park & gardens shaded (also shaded on 1905 OS).

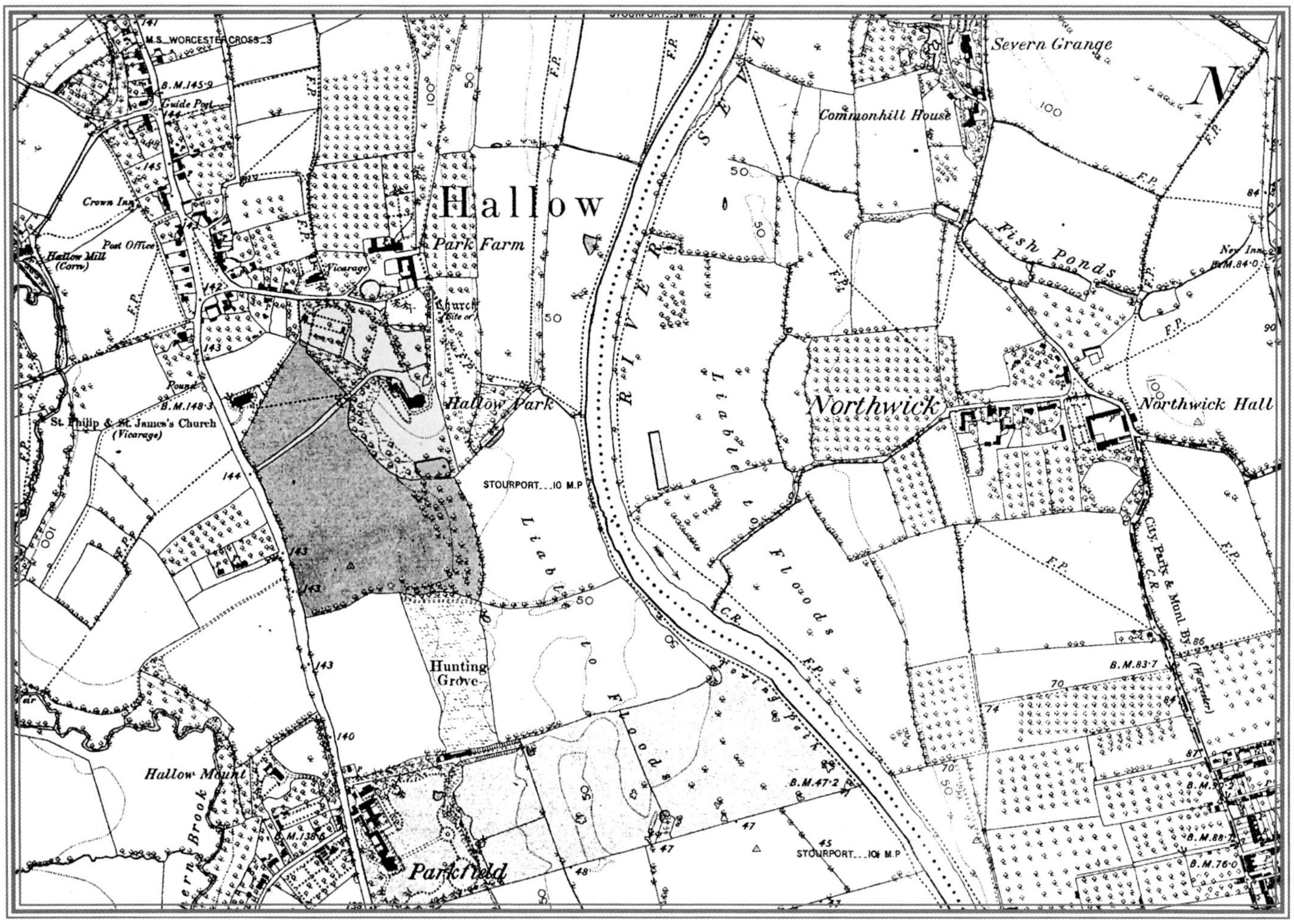

The Prior of Worcester imparked 60 acres of land and 40 acres of wood for a deer park in 1312. This imparking was violently resented by the citizens of Worcester who had fished the ponds and regarded this as common land (Hughes & Leech, p. 21). Leland circa 1530 talks of "a park without a house". Queen Elizabeth I hunted there (1575), and a wood towards the south end of the park is called Hunting Grove (surviving). Saxton recorded the deer park on his map of 1577. Park Farm to the north on the other side of the old (demolished) church may indicate that the park formerly extended in that direction. The park continued to be represented on maps into the 19th century. Thomas Habington (whose family leased the park) provides a minute description of a small park circa 1600 (*VCH*, 3, 1913, p. 367), quoted in full by Mowl (p. 299-30). To paraphrase: the house, a mile and a half up river from the City of Worcester is raised on a small hill but being so close to the river suffers from smells (contagion). Nevertheless, it has good views over the river and the city as far as Bredon Hill. It is placed in a little but most delicate park in the higher parts of which mint yielding a sweet savour abounds, so that when Queen Elizabeth was hunting the deer which "did bruise but a natural perfume" that she gave it (Hallow) "an extraordinary commendation, a dainty situation scarce second to any in England." Habington adds that Hallow was a necessary, retired place of recreation for the monks of Worcester. He also mentions that on the south side of the park there was a rabbit warren.

Perhaps the earliest visual description of the mansion and

..........continued from previous page

gardens is that in "*An Exact Map of the Manor of Hallow* ... dated 1747 by John Doharty junior, made for the Bishop of Worcester" (CRO 5403/3) which has a plan of "The Park". The house of 3 gabled bays (as seen from the east) had a small entrance forecourt with side walls and a circular lawn; an avenue connected this with the churchyard and there was a straight walk in the same direction slightly to the east with a wood on that side. Trees which might survive from these arrangements may be indicated on the 1883 6 inch OS. On the west side of the mansion, running roughly north/south was a line of 4 pools backed by woodland on the west side. The pools were separated by paths which ran west/east, separating lawns perhaps terraced down the slope to the south. Some distance to the south and south of Hunting Grove, were other buildings connected by avenues to the Worcester-Ludlow road and to the Severn. One building here has a forecourt with circular lawn. This small complex may not of course have been an extension of the Hallow Park grounds as assumed by its inclusion here.

From T. R. Nash, *Collections for the History of Worcestershire,* Vol. I, 1781

Nash (1781) illustrates a substantial mansion set up above the river as in a watercolour view by E. F. and F. T. Burney of similar date. These show the mansion set on high ground and the riverside pasture below by the river. Hallow is noticed by Tunnicliff in 1788. *Beauties* (1814, p. 171) says that, although the house had been untenanted for some time, "yet the pleasure grounds (are) still kept in good order ... the plantations are now arrived at maturity, judiciously intersected with breaks" and adds that the grounds had long been famous for a chalybeate spring. The Worcester Directory in 1820 claimed that this spring was "similar in virtue to those at Cheltenham." The OS 6 inch (1926) shows an avenue accompanying the drive to the lodge on the Worcester road and serpentine paths in Hunting Grove and the pool immediately south of the house. The grounds to the west were eroded by siting the new church there in the 1860s and were cut short to the south when the Leas, who had acquired the Hallow estate, built a substantial residence with small park at Parkfield at about the same time. Strong records that the 18th century mansion was demolished in 1920 but another source has its replacement as "built in 1914 at a great cost", i.e. earlier. The new house is illustrated in the 1924 sale particulars showing a large lawn on the north side bisected by a drive and 2 descending terraces linked by steps on the south. A large garden or kitchen garden is north-west of the mansion across the main road access and the Vicarage. This has now been developed to housing (CRO 5240/1B).

Victoria County History Vol. 3, 1913 (VCH).
T. Mowl, *Historic Gardens of Worcestershire,* 2006.
Beauties of England and Wales, Vol. XV, 1814.
R. Strong, M. Binney, J. Harris, *The Destruction of the Country House, 1875 - 1975,* 1974.
P. Hughes & A. Leech, *The Story of Worcester,* 2011.
T. R. Nash, *Collections for the History of Worcestershire,* Vol I, 1781.

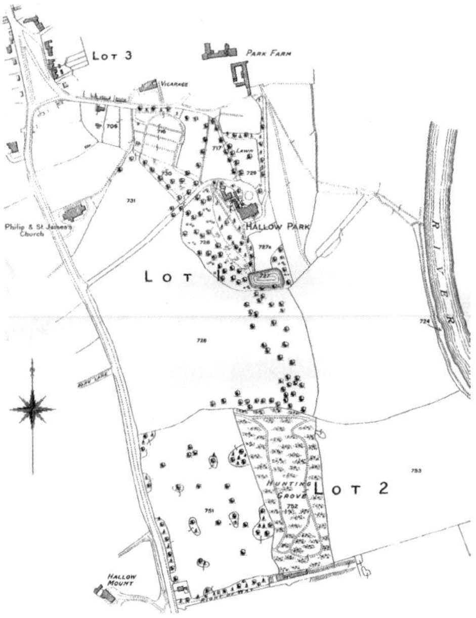

Estate Sale Plan, 1924.

Ham Castle Farm

Parish: Clifton upon Teme

HER Ref: WSM28880.
Grid Ref: SO 734 618.
Postcode: WR6 6RR.

O.S. 6" Map No: 27NE/SE.
Date of Map: 1884.

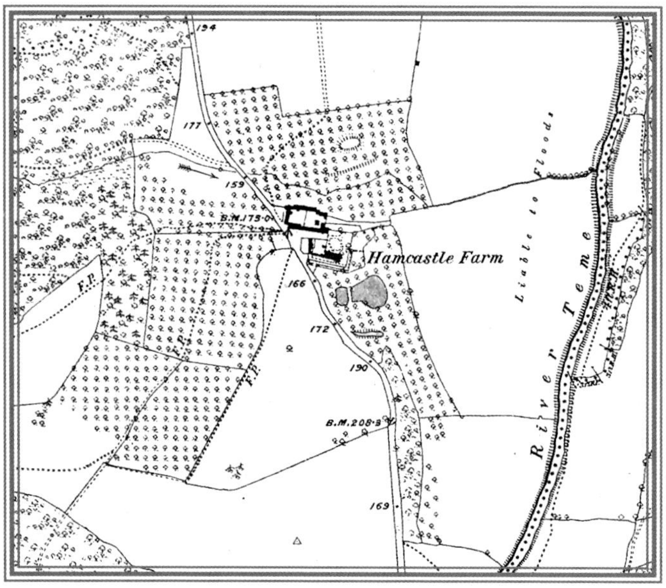

Ham Castle Farm, lithograph, 1853 from Society of Antiquaries of London, Prattinton Collection.

“The motte and bailey of a Norman Castle (first mentioned 1207)" (BoE as Homme [or Ham] Castle Farm) lies north of the Farm. Habington said it was "now ruinated" circa 1600. A double moated site south of Castle Farm indicates the medieval manor house. These moats which are shown in the 1883 OS had disappeared by the 1905 edition and are not visible today. Walker (1863) illustrates the former Farm house, which burnt down in 1887, with dates of 1677 and 1680. There is a lithograph (circa 1840) titled "Stanford Green" in the Prattinton Collection (Soc. of Antiquaries, London – information from Stephen Price) showing more clearly the late Tudor-Gothic mullions with hood mouldings but omits the half-timbering to one wing shown in Severn Walker's engraved illustration. The 1887 replacement reflects the general character of the old but only alludes to the half timbering through a gable and did not repeat a 2 storied bay window on the south side. Both have terraces on 2 sides and a walled lower terrace. According to Griffiths, the latter were "formed and the moat partially filled in, and the pools made in its place" by Joyce Jeffreys in the 1640's when she removed to Ham from Hereford which had become unpleasant due to the English Civil War. "Outside she interested herself in the garden, giving a gratuity to the two gardeners for planting the borders of the walks with sweet briar roots, and she kept Muscovy ducks".

William Tunnicliff includes a Ham Castle Park and the *Traveller* has Ham Castle as a principal county seat circa 1800. Taylor (1772), Nash (1781), and Cary (1787 and 1805) and Tunnicliff (1788) all show a fenced deer park as does the 1831 OS one inch. Indications of the deer fence boundary are visible on the north-west side of the park along the edge of Wyman's Wood. The 1831 park area is a rough triangle stretching out west and south-west from the Farm. A Survey made for Sir T. E. Winnington in 1819 (CRO 709/13) records a Deer Fold (28 acres) west of the road: Park Bank (7 acres by Wyman's Wood); Coney Green (18 acres); Leas Orchard (9 acres). Immediately west of the road from the Homestall is a larger, kidney shaped pool which had disappeared by the 1883 OS and is now only a depression filled with farm buildings. The 1819 survey further describes in a line north-east to south-west from the Farm: Lower Park (35 acres); Upper Park (40 acres) curving round Wyman's Wood above Park (18 acres) and Parkfield (9 acres). The footpath junction at SO 724 614 may mark the south-west point of the park from which the south boundary ran east to stop at the Shelsley Walsh/Shelsley Beauchamp to Ham Bridge road.

Ham Castle features in Francis Ingram's 1794/5 account of his family (CRO 438/xxxviii) which owned Stanford Court, Ham Castle, Tickenhill and Winterdyne. The Winnington–Ingrams inherited Ham from the Jefferies, an older, medieval family. Francis Ingram thought that his family name came from Ham, i.e. began as Inghamme and he valued the historical connection and the fact that his mother, Anne Winnington, had lived at Ham in the earlier-18th century with her uncle Edward Winnington Jefferyes.

A. Brooks & N. Pevsner, *Worcestershire* 2007 (BoE).
J. Severn Walker, *Architectural Sketches*, Vol. 1, 1862.
J. Dugdale, *The New British Traveller*, 1819.
Revd. R. G. Griffiths, "Joyce Jeffreys of Ham Castle; a 17th century Business Gentlewoman", *Worcestershire Archaeological Soc. Trans.*, New Series, XI, 1933, p. 1-33.
T. R. Nash, *Collections for a History of Worcestershire,* Vol I, 1781

Ham Court & The Hill

Parish: Upton-upon-Severn

HER Ref: WSM28882/29003.

Grid Ref: SO 852 386, SO 845 398. Postcode: WR8 0QZ, WR8 0SL.

O.S. 6" Map No: 47SE.

Date of Map: 1887, with extent of parks & grounds shaded as 1905 OS.

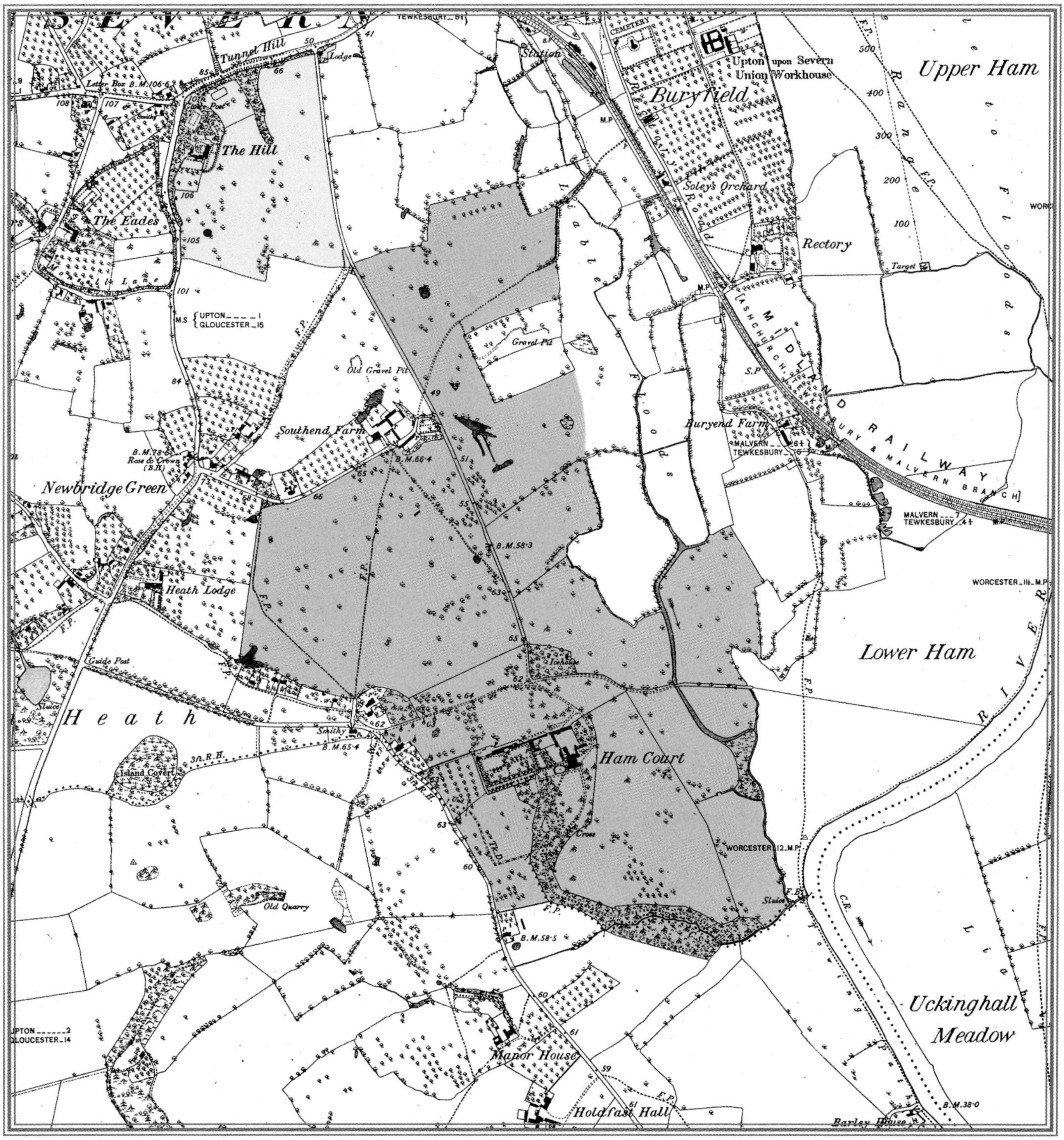

..........continued from previous page

Ham Court from T. R. Nash, *Collections for the History of Worcestershire,* Vol II, 1782.

Nash illustrates the handsome Ham Court (II, 1782, p. 444) and the plantations made by John Martin to whom the property had come by marriage with the Bromleys. This had replaced a 15th century house redeveloped in the 16th century. Ham was treated as a second house to Overbury but was still included as a principal county seat in guides circa 1800. Anthony Keck's 1772 house was demolished in 1929. A map of 1780 presumably records the grounds that went with the Keck mansion, either the gardens that went with the house that this replaced or as then new. "No landscape gardener is known at Ham Court but Keck is regularly associated with Lancelot 'Capability' Brown and his pupils" (Whitehead). Keck, in an obituary of 1797, was described as the "most celebrated architect in Gloucestershire, Worcestershire, Herefordshire and South Wales". On other occasions Keck was also accompanied by the Staffordshire landscaper, William Emes, John Davenport of Wem, Shropshire and Samuel Wheeler of Gloucester. The last laid out the grounds around the Infirmary in Worcester, soon after Keck completed it in 1775-6 (David Whitehead, *Landscape Report for Worcestershire County Council,* 1994). John Martin was a patron of the new Worcester Infirmary (Whitehead).

Field names such as Oak Ground, Broad Field and The Lawn ('Lawn' is an important indicator of parkland) do not suggest a park as such at this moment although a fenced park is shown on the two inch survey (1812) for the first OS one inch. Nash's engraving might be the view across The Lawn. *Beauties of England and Wales,* in 1814 remarked on the elegant mansion situated on a rising lawn, studied with plantations in an elegant style of improvement – perhaps meaning that it all looked quite new. The 1914 sale (CRO 5240/7) gave the well-timbered park as 90 acres. Some species of trees in the grounds are listed: *Wellingtonia,* Scotch fir, lime, cypress, *auricaria, sabiniana, picea noblis glaucum.*

The Hill to the north-north-west of Ham Court is noticed as a gentry-residence on Taylor's county map of 1772, where Ham Court is absent. This has an earlier landscape represented today by a number of veteran trees on the site that have recently been catalogued by the Woodland Trust and are estimated to date from the late-17th century. The parkland at The Hill was probably integrated into the new landscape at Ham Court, soon after its construction in 1772 and the creation of the west drive to the house. Amidst the trees on the right (north) of the Nash's engraving, The Hill appears to look down from Tunnel Hill, from its miniature park. In front of the new Court, and to the left (south), there are young plantations, planted in small clumps, which is an unnatural formation and suggests the hand of a professional landscaper. His skill was probably also necessary to thin the existing woodlands to link the Court with the Hill. The small area of parkland, close to The Hill, which exists today represents a fragment of one of Worcestershire's most important landscape parks. (Whitehead, correspondence).

The 1887 OS defines the park as part of Oak Field, exactly the same area called Broad Field and The Lawn in 1780. The principal features of the park as recorded on the 1887 OS 6 inch can be found today and earlier on a plan of Ham Court and Upton dated 1805 (CRO 2421): the Icehouse Plantation to the north; Dog Wood to the east; the large walled garden to the west of the house; the Paradise Plantation running south from the house and then turning east towards the river, and The Avenue (elm) running north-west to the Queenhill road. In 1805 a large field east of the house is called the Lawn, i.e. the 1805 survey is very similar to the 1780 plan.

The 1914 sale particulars drew attention to the old world pleasure gardens and to the ancient (century old) hedges of yew and holly e.g. the old rose garden sheltered by yew hedges. The old turf lawns were shaded by magnificent elm, plane and lime trees. The southern gardens on the main front are described as of the 18th century, perhaps referring to the shrubberies leading into the Paradise Plantation as well as to the broad gravelled terrace.

The 1926 sale catalogue has two photographs of the gardens and also notices the Fan Garden with summerhouse and the rose pergola, the outer kitchen garden and orchard, and the main kitchen garden enclosed by a brick wall. It also marks an icehouse. The Head Gardener's House is said to have 3 good bedrooms.

The walled, outer terrace between the demolished main house and the west end of the kitchen garden has gone, as has the elm avenue to the Queenhill road. However, in recent years a Palladian-style house with parterre garden has been created on the site of part of the old mansion.

D. Whitehead, "Patron and Architect: the Revd. Treadway Nash, Bevere and the Career of Anthony Keck",
Trans. Worcs. Archeol. Soc., 3rd Series, 24, 20114, pp. 237-8.
Beauties of England and Wales, Vol. XV, 1814.
T.R.Nash, *Collections for the History of Worcestershire,* Vol II, 1782.

Hanbury Hall

Parish: Hanbury

HER Ref: WSM05800/35154/35273.

Grid Ref: SO 944 638. Postcode: WR9 7EA.

O.S. 6" Map No: 22SE, 29NE.

Date of Maps: both 1884, with extent of park & gardens shaded as H. E. Register.

Included within Historic England's Register of Historic Parks and Gardens of special historic interest in England.

A deer park at Hanbury was established at some time within the Royal Forest of Feckenham, to which officials were appointed into the 18th century, e.g. Richard Baylis in 1722 as warriner in the manor of Hanbury, the manor of Astwood Court and the Forest of Feckenham (CRO 7335/48). Park Hall relates to the medieval park and the Royal Feckenham Forest and belonged to the hereditary Keepers of the Forest (VCH, 3, 1913, p. 372). The oldest parts of Park Hall Farm House (Hollowfields Road) are circa 1600. Nash referred to it "as near to the ancient parke of the King". Christopher Saxton marks the deer park on his 1577 map and so does Nash in 1781. The Dougharty's "An Exact Terrier to a Book of Maps" (CRO 7335/154-5), compiled 1731/3, gives the Park 127 acres and "all within the park pales and walk" 139 acres. Whitaker surveyed the deer park in 1892 when it extended to 63 acres, was fenced with wood and iron and held 150 fallow deer as well as cattle and horses, and noted the trees as elm, oak, ash, chestnut (both horse and Spanish), hawthorn, maple. He pointed out that the ancient deer park had been obliterated temp. Charles I but that it had been re-established circa 1720 by the Vernons. A keeper's account book for 1797-1801 shows that the deer park was then in commercial use with the keeper averaging 10 bucks in July – August and a dozen does in November – December; regulars from the local gentry were supplied with half carcases, haunches or sides (CRO 7335/3).

Jackson-Stops (p. 12) illustrates two early views of the post-1700 formal garden and landscape arrangements as recorded by Sir James Thornhill (circa 1710) and Joseph Dougharty (1732) which are consistent with two undated designs for Hanbury by George London (CRO 8041/1). Forward of the main front of the mansion were two forecourts each with metal railings and gates; these had side walls screening off farm buildings on the edge of the park on one side and the principal front garden on the other. This was arranged around a central oval with statue

Hanbury Hall

..........continued from previous page

in the centre and was divided by paths set in a Union Jack, cross pattern. To the furthest side of this was the bowling green (with energetic players in Thornhill's drawing). Beyond, behind hedges or wall, lay the Wilderness and another parterre garden both of which have been restored from bare lawn recently, as has the garden with two pavilions beside the Orangery. Ground archaeology which revealed some of the structural design as in the early-18th century views and plans (Currie) did not reveal which 18th century plants were preferred so that within a generally Dutch mode the approach to planting is free (Neil Cook).

Sir James Thornhill, *Hanbury Hall from ye Bowlingreen*, drawing circa 1710. Courtesy of Trustees of British Museum.

The Dougharty prospect shows linear planting to the north and east (The Lime Walk) and a wide double avenue stretching out north-east (The Long Walk) towards a raised viewing platform (The Semicircle). George London intended an amphitheatre 365 feet wide related to the wider landscape by views or vistas between the planting. These would be as finely calculated as the geometrical plan would allow and be open to: Malvern Hills; Berrow Hill; Woodberry Hill; the Brown Clee; Wooverlow; Kinver Edge; Upton Steeple; Clent Hill; Lickey. The radiating views are tree-lined alleys and this feature compares

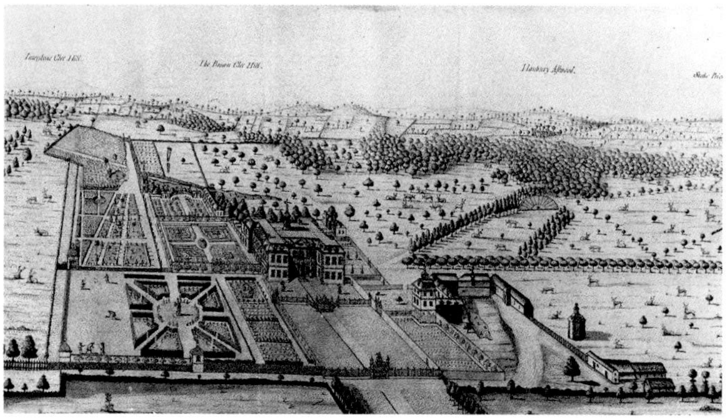

Joseph Dougharty, Prospect of Hanbury Hall, drawing 1732. © WAAS 7335/155.

generally to Dougharty's 1732 survey drawing. Only one of the slices of the cake is annotated: "Nursery/ all the quarters be filled with trees". Jackson-Stops (p. 156) illustrates Robert Furber's *Twelve Months of Flowers,* 1730 which lists Bowater Vernon as a subscriber to this, the first, illustrated, nurseryman's catalogue to be published in England. Furber's 1727 tree catalogue may have been relevant to Hanbury Hall as well. Vernon was a major patron of the Dougharty family of surveyors whose *Book of Maps* recorded his principal estates.

The mansion was designed with a cupola set on the roof from which a bird's eye view could be had of the formal, parterre garden beside the house, the angled lines of planting in the semi-natural Wilderness beyond and the further park with avenues and Semicircle.

There is a very rough Memorandum of circa 1729 which gives a down-to-earth idea of the management required by a steward and his reminders to himself begin "To get a cider mill made; some new wheelbarrows made; the sun dial here carried to Hanbury and fixed there by Doharty (instrument maker as well as map maker); the dials of the Great Clock new gilt; to take down the range of iron rails next the House and fixed on the side next the Park; the trees on the Commons and in the Park planted and fenced; to have the ground under the Mulberry trees grassed." He had to see to repairs to Sir John Thornhill's staircase murals as well (CRO 7335/3).

There are similar records of maintenance nearly a century later in 1803-9 by James Brasier and then Theophania Vernon. Theophania's maintenance diary for 1809 (going back to 1804) is incredibly detailed and shows the most thorough surveying and ordering of maintenance works to the Hall, the buildings, the gardens and grounds as well as to all the tenanted farmhouses and agricultural buildings on the estate, not forgetting the Shrawley Wood property. The palisading between house and park and around buildings in the grounds and park are repaired or replaced by brick walls; the Green House, the Menagerie House, the Grain House are stripped and tiled with Broseley tiles and other major repairs to windows and glazing and pulleys and roofs. The Exotic House and Hot House are deemed to be beyond repair.

The inner forecourt has pavilions designed by R. W. Billings in 1856; the original gates which went off to Mere Hall in 1790 were replaced at the same time (**Plate 31**). Surviving garden buildings or hard features include the mid-18th century Orangery with its adjoining walls and nearby sundial. A late-18th century walled garden to the north- east of the house encloses 7200 sq. yards. There is an 18th century icehouse.

Jackson-Stops characterised the gardens at Hanbury as a compromise between French and Dutch taste as laid out by George London about 1700: "There are no less than six gazebos or pavilions terminating walks or flanking vistas" (p. 13). The ha-ha from the north to the south-west is part of a late-18th century movement towards greater informality. Evidently much landscaping continued in the

Hanbury Hall

..........continued from previous page

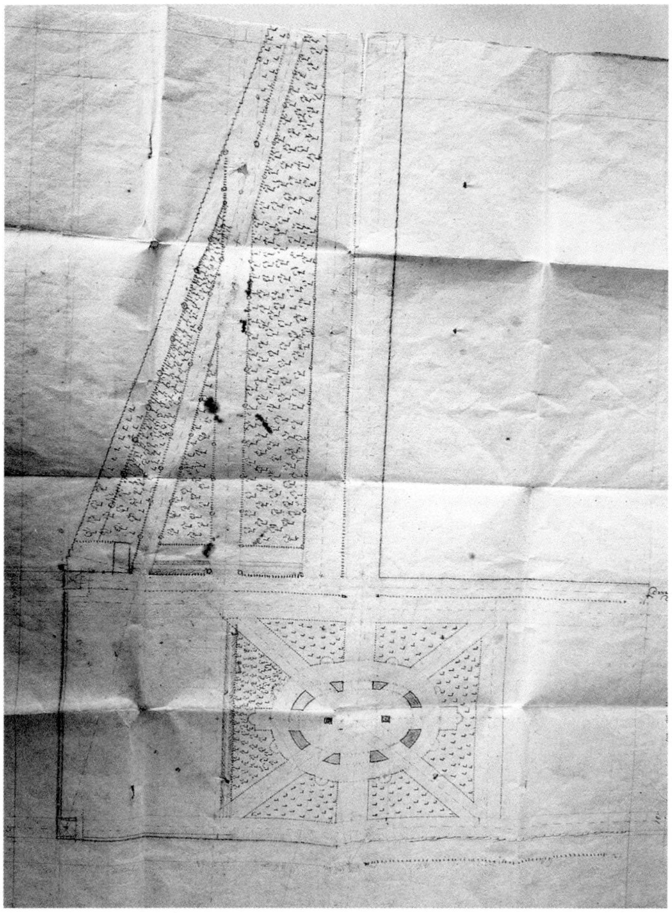

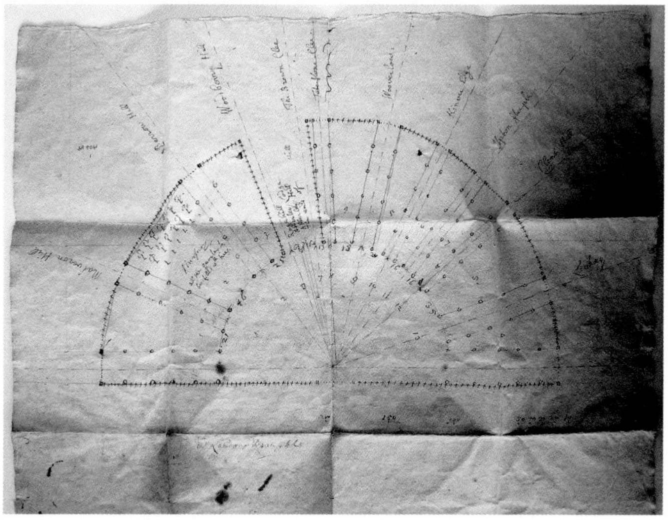

ABOVE: design for parterre and Wilderness
ABOVE RIGHT: design for Semicircle.
Drawings by George London, circa 1710. © WAAS 8041/1.

From T. R. Nash, *Collections for the History of Worcestershire,* Vol. I, 1781

later part of the century, e.g. £40 spent on 1000 young oak trees from a Birmingham nurseryman in 1779 (Harris) and 8 tons of slate for the Menagerie. The BoE summarises that George London's gardens as in Dougharty's 1732 bird's eye view were "swept away later in the 18th century." A portrait of Bowater Vernon hunting, painted by John Wootton in 1734, agreeing closely with Dougharty, shows the house in its landscape setting with formal gardens on one side and the hills in the background as George London understood could be an important aspect of an otherwise formal lay-out (illus. in Haworth and Jackson-Stops), swept away in the late-18th century.

The 1883 OS 6 inch shows some belt planting on the west side (Belt Covert) and regular linear planting or avenues directed roughly north-west, south-west and south-east from the house. The wide avenue towards the main entrance (elm and lime in 1968, J. Lees-Milne, *Country Life*, CXLIII, p. 19) extended a considerable distance in a south-east direction and can be seen extending well beyond the 1883 limits of the park. The south-west avenue leads to the "West Lodge".

George London's formal sunken garden is one of only three in the country, the most famous being the Privy Garden at Hampton Court, London. The National Trust's millenium reconstruction of the London/Dougharty grounds - sunken parterre (**Plate 18**), Grove and Wilderness, has given Worcestershire an early-18th century mansion in its original setting.

H. Avray Tipping, *Country Life*, XXXIX, 1916.
J. Lees-Milne, "Hanbury Hall", *Country Life*, Vol. 143, 4 and 11 January, 1968.
A. & E. Harris, *Hanbury Hall Estate*, 1980.
G. Jackson-Stops, *An English Arcadia: 1600 - 1990,* National Trust 1990.
C. K. Currie, "Excavations at Hanbury Hall, Worcs.," 1991 & 1993 *Worcs. Archaeol. Soc. Trans.*, 3rd Series, 15, 1996.
J. Haworth & G. Jackson-Stops, *Hanbury Hall,* 1998, Guide Book, Ch. 2. "The Garden and Park" (2003 ed.).
A. Brooks & N. Pevsner, *Worcestershire,* 2007 (BoE).
Victoria County History, Vol. 3, 1913 (VCH).
T. R. Nash, *Collections for the History of Worcestershire,* Vol. I, 1781.

Hanbury Rectory

Parish: Hanbury

HER Ref: WSM28889

Grid Ref: SO 958 645

Postcode: B60 4BT

O.S. 6" Map No: 22SE

Date of Map: 1884

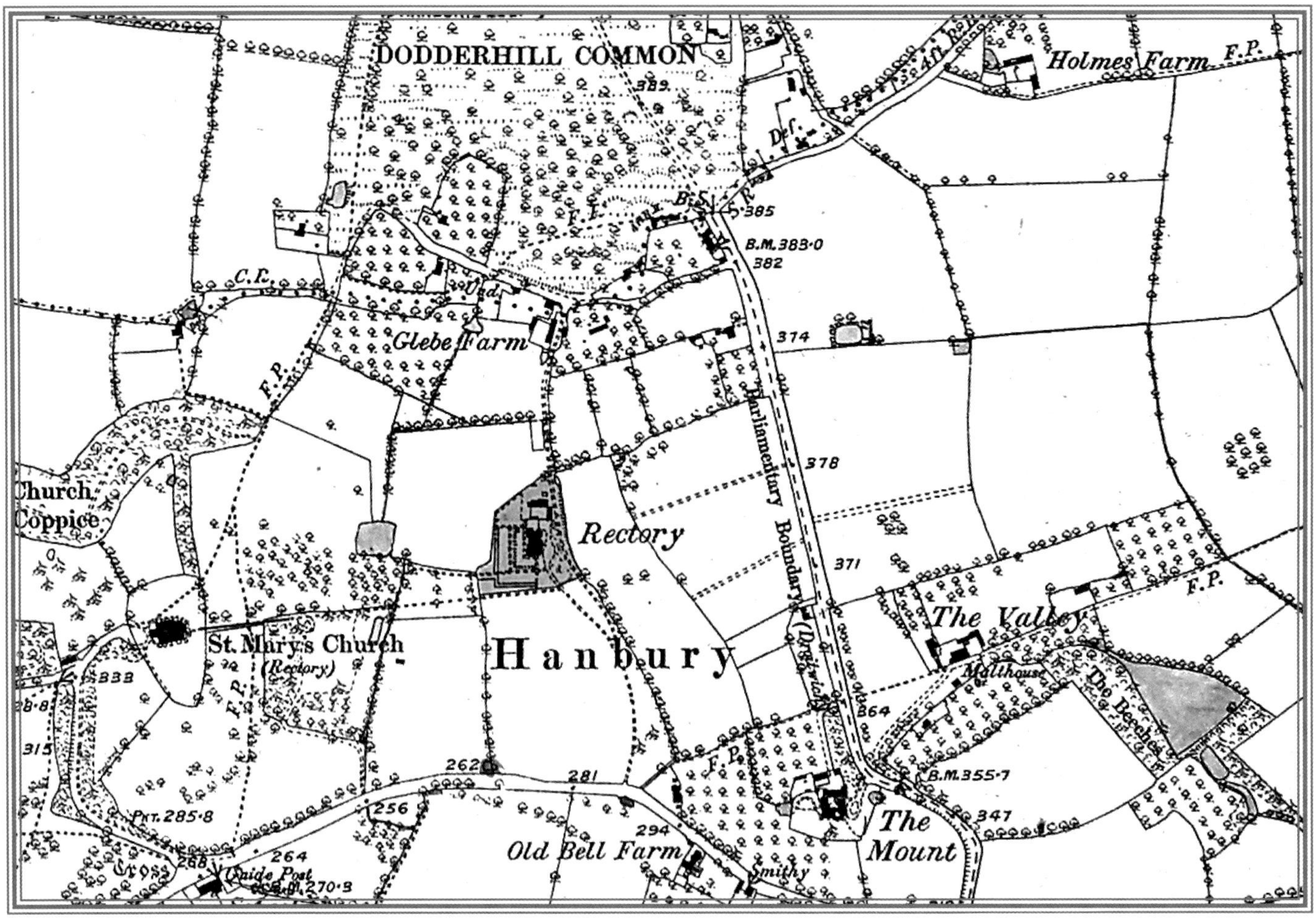

The present Rectory was designed by David Brandon in 1862 (Pevsner, p. 187). The Rectory is included here on the strength of two maps of the Vernon estates dated 1733 (CRO 7335/154) that illustrate a small but quite elaborate garden as existing at that date. Steps, as today between Church and Rectory, are shown as 3 separate flights. The garden was all east of the house beginning with two parterre beds with perhaps fruit or vegetables beyond, with 3 rectangular pieces of water to the east and a mini canal or moat. Just south-east of the house were outbuildings, possibly stables, and beyond them a straight hedged path leading to a gate, parallel to the east side of the canal and within it. Beyond the east side of the canal was a narrow plantation boundary. Set across the first break in the canal at the north end was an arbour/summerhouse/gazebo. North-east of all this was an extension to the garden made up of a 4 bed square with a tree-lined walk on its west side and a rectangular pool at an angle off its north-west side. This had some elaboration, possibly a grotto, on its northern end. This reading of a minute drawing is made with hesitation. The scale is given as 10 chains to 2½ in., "the scale to which all estates surveyed".

Susan Dalton, "Landscape and Gardens: the Estate Maps of the Dougharty Family of Worcester 1716-1764", Notes on Lecture by Brian Smith, *HWGT Newsletter*, 2000, pp. 16-7 (illus. of John Doharty jun.)

Hartlebury Castle

Parish: Hartlebury

HER Ref: WSM07075/35179.

Grid Ref: SO 836 713.

Postcode: DY11 7XX.

O.S. 6" Map No: 14SE.

Date of Map: 1888, with extent of park & gardens shaded as H. E. Register.

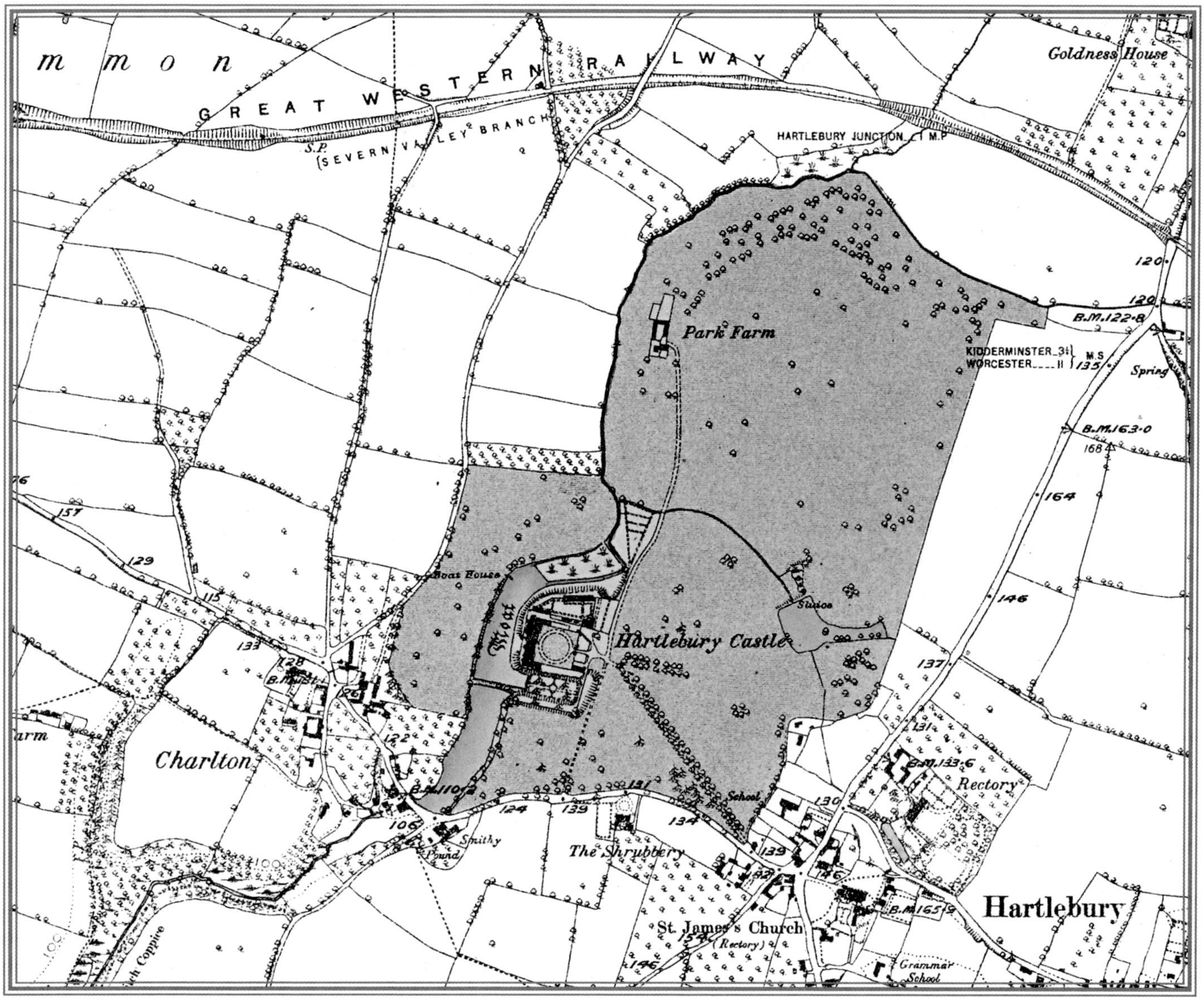

Included within Historic England's Register of Historic Parks and Gardens of special historic interest in England.

Hartlebury was given as a defensible site to the Bishop of Worcester circa 854 AD and continued to belong to the Diocese until 2014 AD. The possibility therefore exists of gardens if not a deer park at any moment through the Middle Ages. Domesday Book shows that Hartlebury was Bishop Wulfstan's most valuable property in the County although nothing is said about hunting. The Castle was upgraded perhaps from wooden defences to stone and given a moat by Bishop Walter de Cantelupe in 1255 and it sounds as if Hartlebury was made into a proper castle by Bishop Godfrey Giffard in 1268; he entertained Edward I here in 1282 when the King was en route for Wales. Significant building works are recorded in the 14th century (Great Hall). A Gatehouse was built on the east side in the 15th century which argues for a moat on that

..........continued from previous page

side of the castle as on the other three. There may have been gardens within the moat or indeed without during the later Middle Ages.

The deer park was first licensed in 1339 (English Heritage, 2000). There is a continuous history of the deer park from the time of the Protestant Reformation. John Leland casting his eyes about England for Henry VIII around 1539 says: "There be fair ponds; there is a park with deer and a warren for coneys; but the soil about the castle is barren" (VCH IV, p. 89). Fifteen years later a more calculating eye, that of William Green, made a Survey for the Augmentations Office in 1554 for the benefit of the Duke of Northumberland who had been granted Hartlebury "by way of exchange". This was just prior to the Duke's unsuccessful attempt to secure the Royal Succession for Lady Jane Grey, his daughter-in-law. "There is a fair manor place called the Castle of Hartlebury wherein the Bishop for the time being hath used off times to lie (a description of the castle follows) ... Also there is a moat and a pond adjoining to the said Castle well stored with fish as is reported by the tenants there ... Also there is a little park containing one mile about by estimation wherein be 76 deer of all sorts ... Francis Blount now Keeper there had yearly ... pasture for one horse and 2 kine and pasture for 5 kine within the said park ... There is a little wood within the said park not above 40 or 50 timber trees nor very little other wood saving bushes and thorns." Green then advises that the woods upon the Waste "should be saved and reserved as well for the reparation of the Pale of the said Park as for the repairing of the Castle and tenements there." "Also there be certain Copses or Spinneys: one Coppice of 24 years growth – one Coppice of 10 years growth – one other of 21 years growth - one little grove of 3 years growth." (WAAS 2636/50). The Bishop of Worcester only regained the park with the manor of Hartlebury in 1579 (Molyneux).

North East View of Hartlebury Castle. Pen and wash by J. Sherriff, 1780. Reproduced by permission of the Church Commissioners and the Bishop of Worcester.

Nearly a century later, in 1647, Hartlebury is described again by a Parliamentary Survey (WAAS 2636/50) or valuation: "Lords of this Manor have the Royalty within the same as Hunting, Hawking, Fishing and Fowling and particularly Fishing." The Manor contained the ferry at Redstone Ferry. "To this Manor of Hartlebury belongeth a strong Castle situate upon a Rock with a Moat round about it full of water which filleth several great ponds stored with fish ... To this Castle there is adjoining a fair park which has been measured by us and containeth 86 acres, 20 perches of pasture ground, the yearly value £20 There is also belongeth to this Manor a Warren of Coneys being on the waste called Hartlebury Heath and called by the name of Charlton and Torton Warrens There is also upon Hartlebury Heath one fair Fishpond. The Castle, the Court, the Storehouses and the buildings belonging to the same Gardens and several fish ponds worth to be let £23 ... All the Pales and Hedges of the Park by reason of the late distraction are pulled up and carried away, the Trees cut down and the Wood called Lynall Wood impaired and great store of fish in the ponds taken away by the soldiers, lately quartered in the parts near thereunto."

An additional Survey defines the tenancies relating to some small pieces of the park (WAAS 2636/50). Referring back to 1630: Edmund Edwards was salaried at £3. 6s. 8d. plus pasture in the park for one gelding and 4 cows for Keeping the Park. The Bishop's cook was then paid 20 shillings and had a room in the Gatehouse and pasture in the park for one gelding and 2 cows. In 1647 "The Castle, the Park, the Meadow and the Wood called Lynall and the Warren of Coneys was let to Edward Smith, Gent. "in £45 rent of the Park". It was estimated that the inclosing and fencing of the Park and putting it into tenantable repair would cost £20. The deer park is marked on Robert Morden's map of 1695 and when Bishop Edward Stillingfleet died in 1699 he had 125 deer in his park. An inventory made in 1700 breaks the numbers down into 10 warrantable bucks, 20 sores and sorrels, 31 prickets, 50 female deer, 35 fawns. There were 58 casualties from the hard winter that year (VCH, 3, 1913, pp. 380-383).

There is a lot of information to show how the deer park, which included some farmed areas as described in 1554 and 1647, was gradually changed into a landscape park. Bishop Stillingfleet planted the lime avenue leading to the main lodge, a successor to which survives today. A plan of 1801 by Richard Hurd junior (WAAS 12098) records a stunted avenue aligned directly opposite to the entrance court to the Castle. There is therefore just a hint that a modest radial planting scheme was attempted at this time, as was then fashionable (e.g. Westwood and Severn End). Bishop Hough (1717-1743) planted a Holly Grove and an Elm Grove and Bishop Maddox (1747-1759) "planted the Cedar Trees in the Park and the Beech Grove and also the Plantation of Planes, Chestnuts, Walnuts, Hawthorns, Oaks, Mountain Ashes, Beeches etc. between the Horse

..........continued from previous page

Pond and the Great Oak" as shown on the 1801 Map. Hurd defines the areas directly used by the Bishop for the pleasure grounds which included the park proper and 5 additional fields, on the west beyond the moat and on the east adjoining the park pale. The latter are named: Wheeler's Park Meadow; (Rector's Orchard); Bishop's Lower Park Close; Wheeler's The Middle Park Close; The Upper Park Piece or Stanford Close. Clearly marked are 2 avenues, 5 groves and 6 pieces of water in a line.

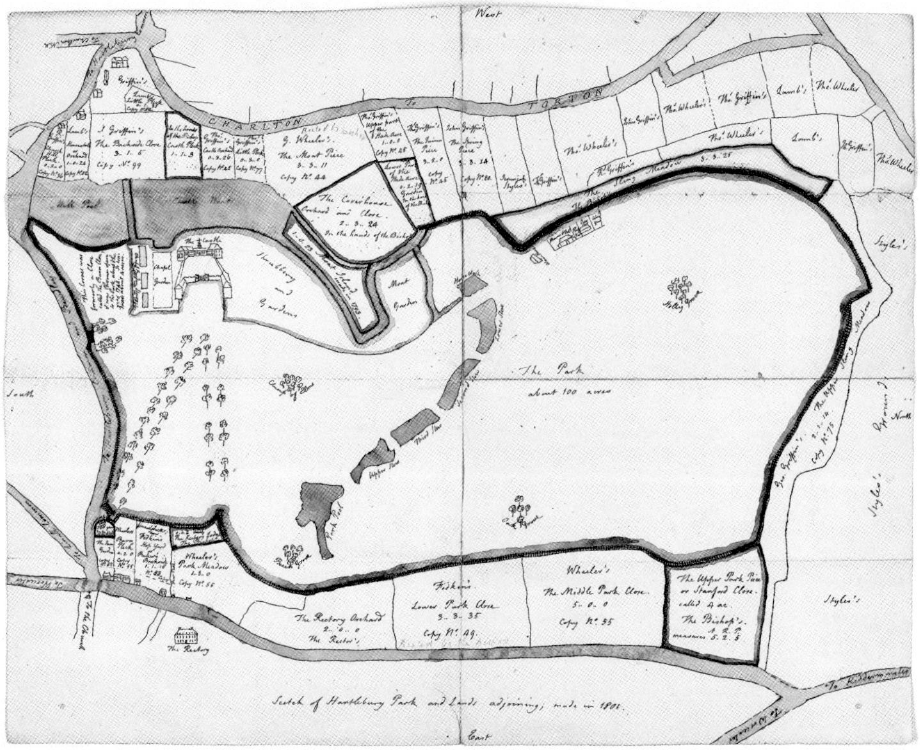

Hartlebury Castle plan by Richard Hurd junior, 1801. © WAAS 12098.

A note on the map says that the ground south of the Chapel (Sunk) Garden had just been "thrown into the park". Bishop Hurd had otherwise to concentrate on the infrastructure of the park, e.g. the repair of the Keeper's Lodge and the Deer Cote and the park paling. The park as today can be related generally to this map and although the park is now "dry", the lost line of ponds has been traced by geo-physical survey. (Pearce, op. cit. compared the 1801 map to the park as it was in 1926).

Work on the park carried out for Bishop Johnson in 1774, included drainage and dredging of the ponds and new park pales and gates, and new park pales (fences) between the park and the garden. Work at this time included the Keeper's Lodge (Molyneux). This may also have been the moment when the Sling, a meadow adjoining the west side of Hartlebury Park (formerly granted with Charlton Mill)" was taken into the Park.

The Hurd plan of 1801 (WAAS 12098) can be supplemented from a finely drawn survey with terrier of 1821 (WAAS 7105) made to record the Inclosure Award as it effected the Bishop of Worcester. The Hartlebury Manor Estate of 4431 acres (excluding 216 acres of Hartlebury Common) breaks down into 716 acres of Freehold, 847 of Leasehold and 2652 of Copyhold (WAAS 2630/50). Hartlebury Castle with its appurtenances, Yards, Gardens, Plantations, Pools etc. amounted to 12 acres. The marking of the deer park fence is not quite complete on the west side, stopping some way north of the line of the moat and Castle with the moat as its western boundary down to the road and bridge by Charlton Mill. From that point it goes east along the road towards Hartlebury Village as far as the Lodge Gates (present main entrance) and then goes north to define the eastern boundary of the Park before turning west along the north side. – all this as on the 1801 map. These are the same boundaries as on the 1905 OS together with a consolidation of some fields on the west side of the moat which in 1821 were named, south to north: Backside Close, Moat Orchard, Castle Orchard, Castle Pleck, Pool Tail Meadow. In 1821 The Park, including Game and Gatekeeper's Lodges, Fold Yard etc. amounted to 94 acres.

The English Heritage Register of Parks and Gardens (1997) estimated the landscape park as circa 20 hectares "at its most extensive, the park covered circa 40 ha, mainly on the northern and eastern side of the Castle. Much now used for agriculture. The moat extends 300m north-south on the western side of the Castle, being divided by a tree-covered causeway 50m to the south-west. A tree-lined avenue leads from the south-east to the gatehouses."

The history of the pleasure grounds or gardens as distinct from the Park cannot be described in such detail. The major building periods known for the castle in the 13th, 14th and 15th centuries can only be pointers to likely moments of activity within and without the moats. It must be remembered that the Bishops of Worcester had several other major residences such as Kempsey and Alvechurch, and in Worcester itself, all of which are likely to have had gardens. Post Reformation gardens are not recorded, for example in 1553 when Hartlebury is called "a fine manor house" nothing further is said. The oldest supposed relic of the 16th century, Queen Elizabeth's Walk (**Plate 23**), the

..........continued from previous page

terrace overlooking the south arm of the moat, was created by Bishop Fleetwood as documented by accounts from 1680-1683 (WAAS 2636/7 - Edgar, *Conservation Management Plan*). This terrace overlooks the south moat, filled in and developed as gardens in stages from the early-18th century. The moat was still full of water when Elizabeth I arrived hot foot from Kenilworth Castle in 1575, escorted by the Earl of Leicester who had created a new garden for the Queen (recently re-created by English Heritage). Six hundred people are said to have cheered the Queen from across the moat. Bishop Nicholas Bullingham's widow claimed that her family was bankrupt when her husband died in 1576; any investment in the gardens at Hartlebury for the Queen's visit must have been kept to a minimum and was probably of a temporary nature (David Kendrick). The Bishop did not recover full possession of the Manor of Hartlebury, granted away at the Reformation, until 1579 (Molyneux).

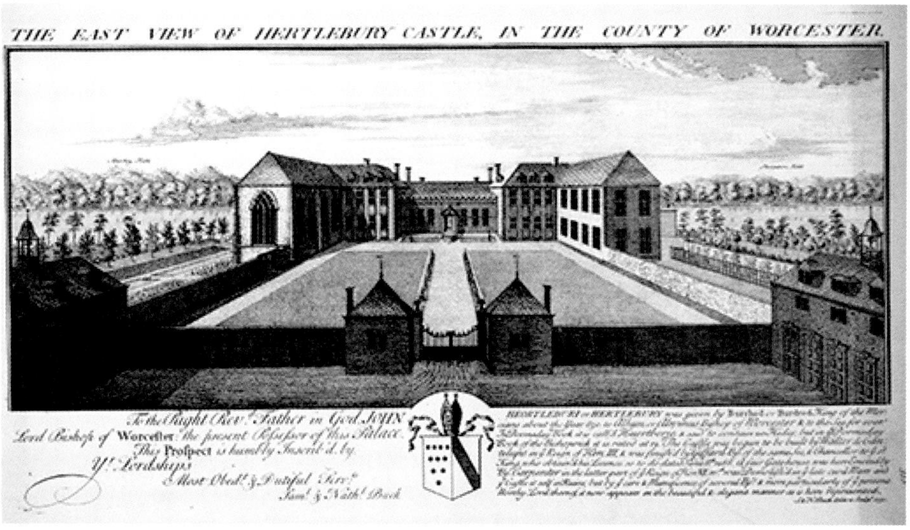

S. & N. Buck, The East View of Hartlebury Castle, engraving, 1731.

One way or another, the English Civil War cannot have been good for any gardens although the Castle was not slighted before being sold to Thomas Westrowe for £3000 in 1647. In the 1670s, when Hartlebury became the Bishop's principal residence for the first time, Bishop Fleetwood (1675-1683) demolished redundant parts of the castle such as the remains of the Gatehouse and perhaps of the Warwick Tower at the north-west corner of the Castle. Fleetwood established the front court with a pair of lodges and walls to north and south and a central path between the front door and the filled-in, east, dry ditch. The accounts refer to much removal of rubble and the re-distribution of good soil to the forecourt and to terraces. Fruit and other trees were planted on the terraces and in the park and seats of "Willow Sally" sited around the moat (which was also fenced) (Edgar, op. cit..). Fleetwood may also have established terrace gardens on the north side of the Castle above the Great Pool.

The next phase of development at Hartlebury was undertaken by Bishop John Hough who spent £7000 leaving little to be "superadded" by his successors according to the Revd. Smallbroke's *Some Account* published in 1743 (Edgar). Hough built Stables and a Coach house and in 1731 filled in the south arm of the moat "a tedious work that makes no show at present but of rubbish and disorder; yet, I flatter myself that when it comes to be laid out in something of regular form, the idea of which is only in my head, my pains will not appear to be ill disposed; for I shall then have an acre of ground, in a garden of whimsical, and unusual, but not I hope disagreeable figure" (Hussey, 1951). The much repeated and plagiarised view of the Castle from the east by Samuel and Nathaniel Buck, also published in 1731, has been taken by Edgar (op. cit.) to be reliable about garden details for the Queen Elizabeth's Walk terrace and the sunken garden below, for the forecourt and for the grounds to the north. There is a slight difficulty in using Buck so definitively as Hough's works were begun in 1731 and the engraving is dated to the same year; sometimes, particularly for the grandest mansions, engraved views are aspirational rather than realised. However, the partial view of the south side shows two parterres of different design on the terrace with 2 out of the probable 3 basins of water (the stews filled up in 1806 according to Richard Hurd – WAAS 12098) and the raised terrace above the "sunken" garden with regularly planted trees. This far terrace slopes down towards the moat (out of sight). The castle forecourt has gravel paths divided by an entrance drive to the front door which has small lawns flanking it. On the north side trees or shrubs are shown against the court wall with a gravelled space beyond and then some formal planting before the ground slopes down to the moat depicted as a lake.

Price & Walker (op. cit.) have investigated the sundial signed "Dougharty fecit" and engraved with the arms of Bishop Hough, on a stone baluster until recently sited on Queen Elizabeth's walk. This must relate to Hough's circa 1731 works and to John Dougharty, senior (1677-1755), the mathematician and teacher who was a dial maker. Edgar (op. cit. Appendix 1) associates the sundial with a seat and a pyramid placed at the east end of the Walk mentioned in an inventory of 1781 (WAAS 2012). The great moment for the Queen Elizabeth's Walk and the terrace on the other side of the sunken garden came in 1788 when George III and Queen Charlotte were visiting

..........continued from previous page

their friend Bishop Richard Hurd and were seen by the crowd walking there in the garden.
The sunken garden had been dramatically redeveloped by Bishop Isaac Maddox in 1748 as part of his gothick transformation of the Castle's Great Hall and Chapel. Maddox built miniature castle walls with two bastions and a mulberry tree in each, with ditches separating walls and park. This was the moment for taking the field to the south of the moat into the Park as recorded by Richard Hurd's 1801 map. There are earlier and grander 18th century examples of castellated walls being pushed into the park such as the "Grimsthorpe bastion", as drawn by William Stukeley circa 1714, or Vanbrugh's massive curtain walls at Castle Howard circa 1720. Maddox however most likely got his ideas from his university background, e.g. College Gardens on a miniature scale as seen in David Loggan's *Oxonia Illustrata,* 1675.

Revd. Edward Waldron, South West View of Hartlebury Castle, pen & wash, 1788, Reproduced by permission of the Church Commissioners and the Bishop of Worcester.

Richard Hurd junior's *Memorandum* of 1796 (WAAS 12098/1 xv) further documents Maddox's impact on the Hartlebury scene: "He made the Walk by the Mill Pool and the Moat (i.e. the two pieces of water separated by a causeway) and also the Kitchen Garden at the end of the Moat (possibly where the sunken garden adjoins the moat)...And there was another Kitchen Garden where the Beech Grove now is. Both these Gardens he destroyed."
Maddox's successor Bishop Johnson was responsible for the development of the gardens beyond the north wall of the court: "The Hot Houses, Green House and rooms behind, were erected by him; as also the Waggon House and Deer Shed. And he built the North Wall in the Hot House Garden; the fence till then was a yew hedge." Some of these changes can be deduced from 18th century engravings. Another source quoted by Molyneux (p. 154) describes the Johnson works: "An intire kitchen garden made, enclosed by a fine brick wall; well planted. The hot house with a succession house at one end, and a green house at the other, built. A room behind it, and another for the use of the gardener." More work included "a very large piece of water, mudded and made quite clean in 1773; the mud laid upon the garden and park ... New gates to the bowling green, which in the year 1773, was made for carriages to drive in, with a sweep to the hall door." This then was how the surviving circular bowling green in the centre of the forecourt originated.
Not necessarily attributable to Bishop Maddox but noticed in a map made for him, was the Hermitage near the Redstone Ferry. This perhaps had some tourist value but the map's concern is with fishing rights on the River Severn.
Hurd was a keen gardener long before he became Bishop of Worcester in 1781. In 1759, when Rector of Thurcaston in Leicestershire, he writes to his friend, the poet William Mason: "When may I expect you here. The season is now come for planting and I want you exceedingly to superintend some improvements for my garden". In 1765 Hurd writes: "This dry weather has made sad havoc with my clumps. But as you know, I have little passion for shrubs, this does not affect me. The best is my forest trees thrive well. Beside this my walk is sanded and proceeds in so easy and sinuous a trace to the *latebrae dulces*, I am quite satisfied with it." In 1781 Hurd had to deal with dilapidations to the Park but also set to on the pleasure grounds round the Castle; work was needed on the flood gates between Mill Pool and Moat, to the boat houses, to the piling and stanking and the walk beside the Mill Pool, the posting, railing and paleing to the garden and round the Mound Shrubbery (WAAS 12908/1 xix). His tidying up of this part of the gardens can be seen in a monochrome watercolour by James Ross of circa 1790.
If Hartlebury Castle could ever boast that it had a landscape garden, it would have been circa 1800 when the *Traveller* commented on the "spacious rooms and fine gardens". *The Beauties of England and Wales* published the Castle's most picturesque view, from across the moat, taken by J. P. Neale (1814).
In 1781 as incoming Bishop, Hurd had to buy hundreds of potted plants and any unbroken sheets of glass for the hot houses as recorded in a view by James Ross. The quantity of glass is recorded for each relevant building – Green House, Fruit House, Succession House, Forcing Pits, Melon Pits, Pine Pits. "The Fruitery" and "Hot House" were measured to have 540 feet of crown glass. An invoice dated 1820 addressed to Mr. Suttle the Head Gardener at Hartlebury indicates a huge range of vegetables grown in the Kitchen Garden; seeds and plants were sent by Knight's Scotsman's Exotic Nursery, Chelsea, London. There were a 100 different varieties of vegetables (WAAS 13852 - information from Virginia Wagstaff). (The 1781 inventory revealed that the gardener kept the seed press in his bedroom!)
Walker (op. cit.) provides a valuable picture of the Castle

Hartlebury Castle

..........continued from previous page

and Village and something of the atmosphere of living in the castle in the later 19th and first half of the 20th centuries. Walker illustrates the "Moat Garden" as before the 2nd World War. Bishop Henry Pepys (1841-1860) did much to develope the formal gardens in particular the Chapel Garden to which Bishop Huyshe Yeatman-Biggs (1905-1918) added a bog garden at the moat end which was removed by Bishop Mervyn Charles-Edwards (1956-1971). There was a garden at this point at the lower level by the later-18th century, as illustrated in a watercolour of 1789 (Hartlebury Castle, Hurd Library). Bishop Perowne (1890-1905) put a circular basin into the centre of the Chapel Garden to commemorate Queen Victoria's Jubilee in 1897. Joan Cash, daughter of Bishop William Cash (1941-1955), gives us glimpses on the gardens in her father's time (Walker) and Mrs Charles-Edwards has left detailed notes of the planting in the years following (Edgar).
In 2015, the Hartlebury Castle Preservation Trust acquired the Castle from the Church Commissioners and a conservation campaign is currently underway which will include the pleasure grounds and perhaps the park. The most comprehensive account of the park/gardens is James Edgar's *Conservation Plan* made in the context of the related Heritage Lottery Bid. Plans have now been drawn up to replant the Carriage Circle and Queen Elizabeth Walk.

After J. P. Neale, engraving from *Beauties of England and Wales,* 1814.

J. Nankivell, *Letters of Francis Evans, Secretary to Bishop Lloyd, 1699-1706*, 1903.
J. Nankivell, *Letters of Richard Hurd to William Mason,* 1950.
D. Robertson, *The Diary of Francis Evans, Secretary to Bishop Lloyd, 1699-1706*, 1903.
L. Toulmin-Smith, *The Itinerary of John Leland*, Vol. IV, 1908.
E. H. Pearce, *Hartlebury Castle*, 1926.
C. Hussey, *Country Life*, Vol. LXIX, 1931, p. 161.
J. Lees-Milne, *Country Life*, Vol. CL, 1971.
C. J. Bond, *Moated Sites in Worcestershire,* 1974.
R. O. Walker, *Hartlebury, Worcestershire: A Record of A Parish,* 1987.
HE *Register of Parks & Gardens,* 2000.
R. Lockett, *Hartlebury Castle; its Park and Gardens,* Report for Hereford and Worcester Gardens Trust, 2008, Hartlebury Castle Preservation Trust website 2014.
R. Lockett, "Hartlebury Castle: Park and Gardens", *Worcester Civic Soc. Newsletter*, Spring 2009.
N. Molyneux, "Hartlebury Castle; an architectural history of a bishop's residence.", *Worcs. Archaeol. Soc. Trans.,* 3rd Series, 22, 2010, pp. 129-167.
M. Arden-Davis, *Hartlebury Castle Garden Tours,* 2018.
M. Arden-Davis & V. Wagstaff, "Our Gardening Bishops", *HWGT, Newsletter*, 37, Summer 2011.
V. Hopkinson, "The Garden (Sunken or Moat Garden)" *HWGT, Newsletter*, 37, Summer 2011.
S. Price & P. Walker, *"The Sun Dial at Hartlebury Castle",* 2012. *Worcs. Archaeol. Soc., Trans.*, 3rd Series, 22, 2010, pp. 129-167.
James Edgar, *Hartlebury Castle: Conservation Management Plan;* Report for Heritage Lottery Submission, "A History of the Garden, Park and Outbuildings", 2014.
Ryder Associates, *Hartlebury Castle Gardens Options Report,* 2018.
J. Dugdale, *New British Traveller*, 1819.
Victoria County History Vol. 3, 1913 (VCH).
Victoria County History Vol. 4, 1924 (VCH).
Beauties of England and Wales, Vol. XV, 1814.
D. Miller, "Archaeological Fieldwork at Hartlebury Castle", *Worcs. Archaeol. Soc. Trans.*, 3rd Series, 21, 2008.
A. Hart, *William Lloyd: 1627-1717,* 1952.
C. J. Bond, *Moated Sites in Worcestershire,* 1974.
A. Emery, *Greater Medieval Houses of England and Wales,* Vol. II, 2000.
P. Moore, "An Inventory of Hartlebury Castle", *Worcs. Hist. Soc.*, Miscellany I, 1960.

Harvington Hall

Parish: Chaddesley Corbett

HER Ref: WSM28967. Grid Ref: SO 878 744.

Postcode: DY10 4LR.

Chaddesley Corbett Estate Map, 1745-6.

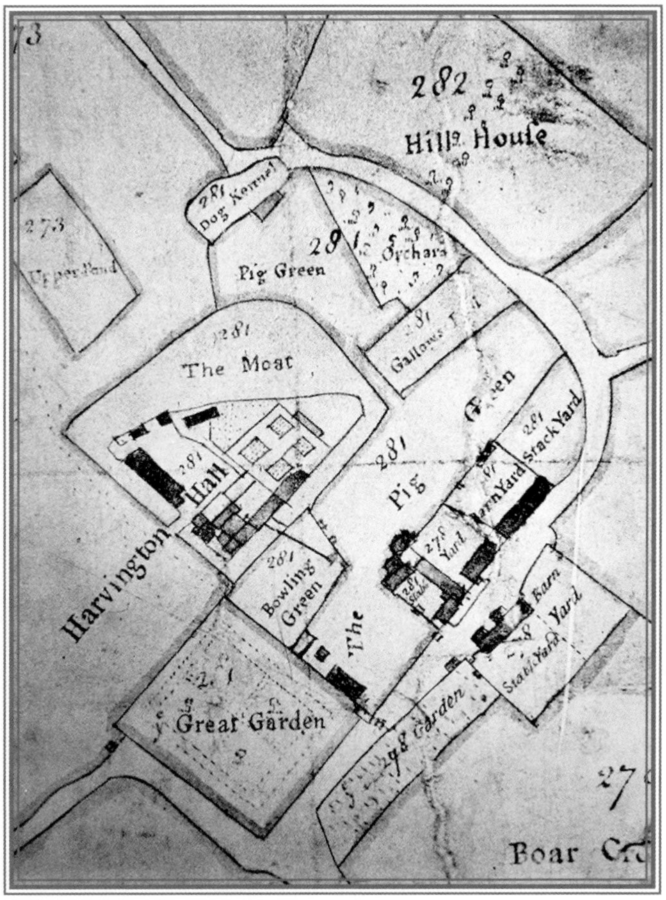

Harvington Hall is a significant example of a moated manor house and the triangular site is entirely surrounded by water with further water (Gallows Pool) nearby. The medieval house was rebuilt by Sir John Pakington between 1569 and 1578. In 1873 Niven described Harvington Hall as "a ruin inhabited by swallows" although a hundred years earlier it was still of sufficient status as a residence to appear on Nash's 1781 map and indeed continues to have a presence on 19th century maps. An Album put together by H. R. Hodgkinson (CRO 11561) has several views of the house with one side almost completely hidden by ivy. This was removed circa 1930. The Hall was separated from its supporting land when it was sold from the Throckmortons' Coughton Estate in 1934.

A Survey of the Manor of Chaddesley Corbet by James Fish was made in 1697 to show "the lands belonging to the Corporation of Warwick" (the medieval manor had belonged to the Beauchamps) and this gives some information about the Hall and property then owned by Lady Yate, celebrated for having given refuge at Harvington to Father John Wall, the Jesuit Martyr. This survey has 3 Park field names- Watchwood or Watch Oak Park, Packington Park and Dyall Park (CRO 2927).

The EH Listing specifies the garden wall as circa 1600 with later repairs "enclosing the west, east, south sides of the garden west of the Priest's House. This wall enclosed "The Great Garden" where the greater double blush anemone was recorded in 1629". A map dating from 1745-6 of the Throckmorton estate in Chaddesley Corbett shows the "Great Garden" with paths going round the square within the wall and a division of the centre of the garden by paths into 4 compartments. A more obvious arrangement of 4 parterres is shown immediately beside the Hall on its north-east side. Immediately beside the Great Garden is the Bowling Green (CRO 844). The principal area which links the Great Garden, Bowling Green, and Yards (Stable and Stack) stretches round the Moat to link with the Dog Kennel and Dog Kennel Quarry on the north side – all this is called Pig Green. An Orchard and Gallows Pool are taken out of this part. These arrangements approximate to the 1882 first edition of the OS 6 inch. Middle Pool and Little Pool are shown as rectangular pieces of water on the 1745 plan. The brick wall of the Great Garden survives but only the part that serves as garden to the Priest's House is used as such, the rest being car park. The Bowling Green is now used for car parking and the Green is part of the field to the north-west of the moats. There has been much work done in recent years to restore the gardens including the addition of a small knot (herb) garden (Scott).

Harvington Hall from the south-east, taken from *Victoria County History* Vol. 3, 1913, (VCH).

C. J. Bond, *Moated Sites in Worcestershire*, 1974.
D. Whitehead, "An Elizabethan Herb Garden at Harvington Hall", *HWGT, Newsletter*, 9, Summer 1997.
G. Scott, "Harvington Hall", *HWGT, Newsletter*, 36, Winter 2010/11.
A. Emery, *Greater Medieval Houses of England and Wales,* Vol. II, 2000.

Hawford House

Parish: North Claines

HER Ref: WSM29045.
Grid Ref: SO 848 599.
Postcode: WR3 7SQ.
O.S. 6" Map No: 28NE/SE.
Date of Map: 1886.

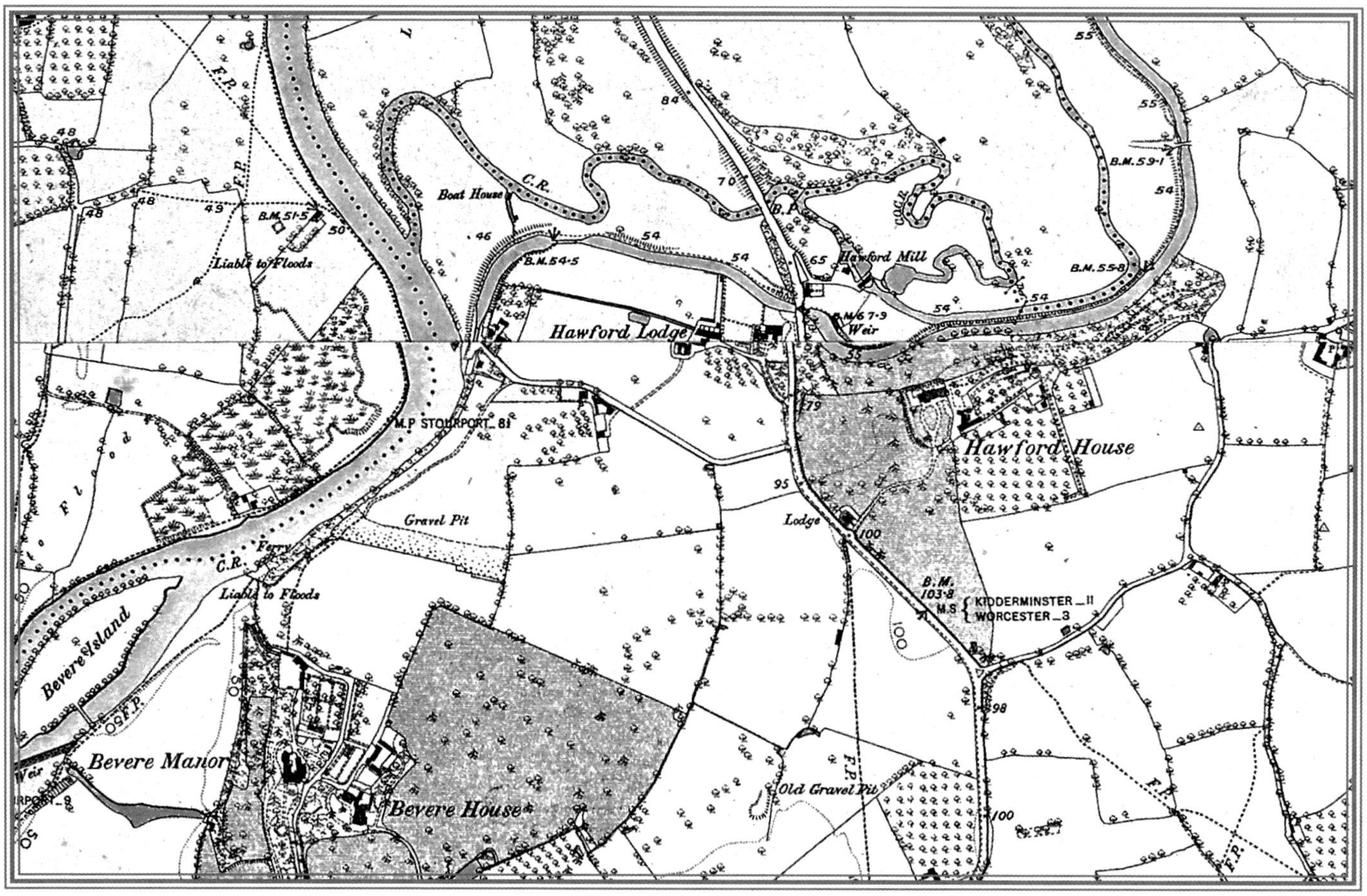

The 1929 sale particulars are particularly informative through photographs of the grounds and garden, tennis courts and rock garden showing lawns, woodland walk (overlooking the Droitwich Canal and the Salwarpe) and the gravelled terrace also overhanging the water below (CRO 5240/36). The woodland walk (300 yards long) is perhaps one of the plantations mentioned by the *Beauties* in 1814 (p. 189). The place had been noticed earlier in 1788. Clumps were also mentioned, presumably in the park bounded by Egg Lane. The park only covered the south-west part of this area by the 1926 OS 6 inch. The western edge of the park has now been cut by the A449.

Beauties of England and Wales, Vol. XV, 1814.

Hewell Grange

Parish: Tutnall & Cobley

HER Ref: WSM07080/WSM00027/35180.

Grid Ref: SP 006 690. Postcode: B97 6QJ.

O.S. 6" Map No. 16SW, 23NW.

Date of Map: 1885, 1884, with shaded extent of park & gardens informed by 1905 OS.

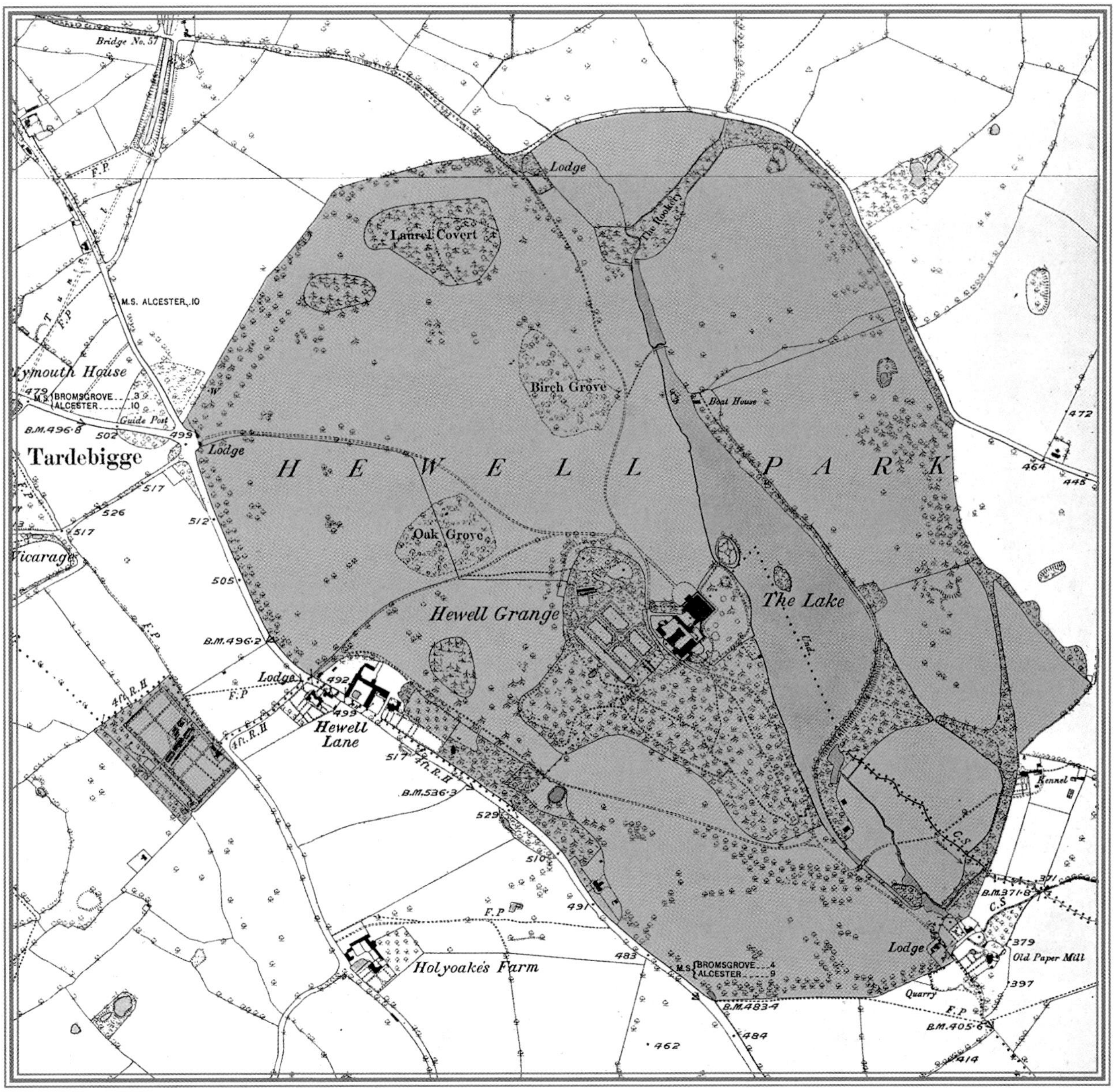

Included within Historic England's Register of Historic Parks and Gardens of special historic interest in England.

Hewell Grange began life as a Grange of the Cistercian Abbey at Bordesley and came into the ownership of the Windsor Family by exchange with Henry VIII in 1542, i.e. immediately after the Dissolution of the Monasteries. The large lake developed for the later landscape park grew from the monastic fish ponds. (David Whitehead, 2005).

Lord Windsor was granted a licence to impark 1000 acres in 1561 in Bordesley and Tardebigge and this may have

..........continued from previous page

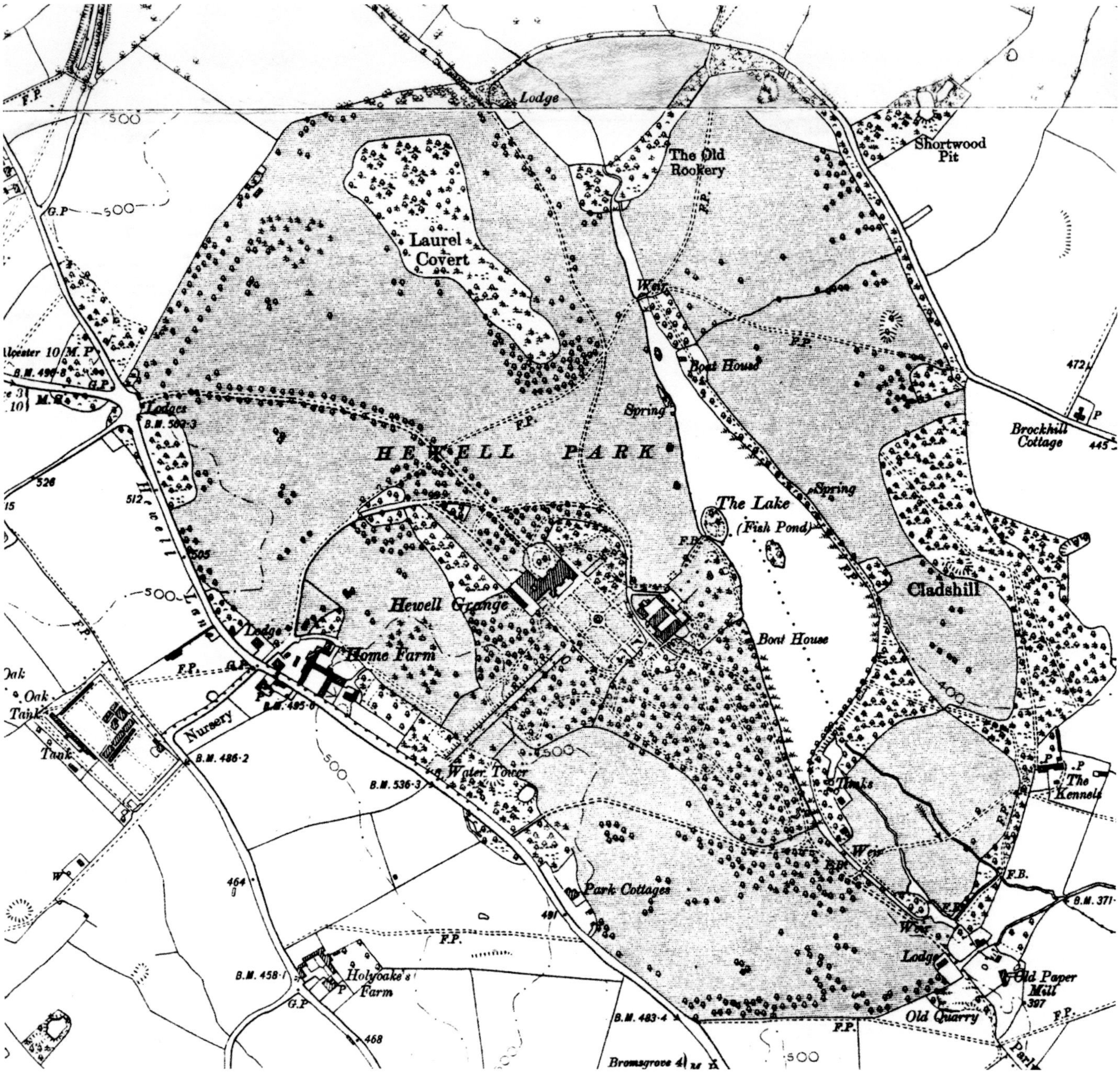

1905 OS 6 inch map showing the changes in the landscape resulting from the Bodley and Garner mansion set on a new site on higher ground above the lake. Note the new formal gardens, the loss of some of the old coverts and the establishment of the larger Laurel Covert as well as new avenues and parkland planting.

included Hewell. A fenced deer park is marked on Taylor's 1772 map for the first time. In 1913 the VCH described the park as about 850 acres containing a large piece of ornamental water.

Michael Cousins (op. cit.) cites an inventory of 1576 referring to a house with a courtyard and separate gatehouse that probably developed from the buildings of the monastic grange; the house is named Hewell Grange on Speed's 1610 Map of Worcestershire. There is reference in 1689 to bleaching courts. In 1649 the Great Poole was measured at 30 acres which Cousins believes may have been reduced over the next century. According to Nash in 1782, the re-development of Hewell for the 5th Earl of Plymouth spared some of the old buildings. By 1737-8 there is mention of a bowling green "paled round and planted about with elms" and a nursery, hop garden,

..........continued from previous page

west of it is a big orchard and nut plantation. At the far end of the bowling green a pleasant garden-house ... has been built against the southern garden wall, and a lawn and formal garden are linked by a double flight of steps." The most prominent trees in the landscape today are mature poplars and cedars on the west side of the Castle. Brick walls with sandstone coping are typical of the boundaries to the Churchyard and the Castle gardens.

J. Dugdale, *New British Traveller*, 1819.
Victoria County History, Vol. 3, 1913 (VCH).
T. Mowl, *Historic Gardens of Worcestershire*, 2006.
Country Life, LXXXVIII, 1940.
C. & J. Greenwood, *Worcestershire Delineated*, 1822.
M. Salter, *Castles of Herefordshire and Worcestershire*, 1989.

Holt Castle, west front, taken from *Victoria County History* Vol. 3, 1913, (VCH).

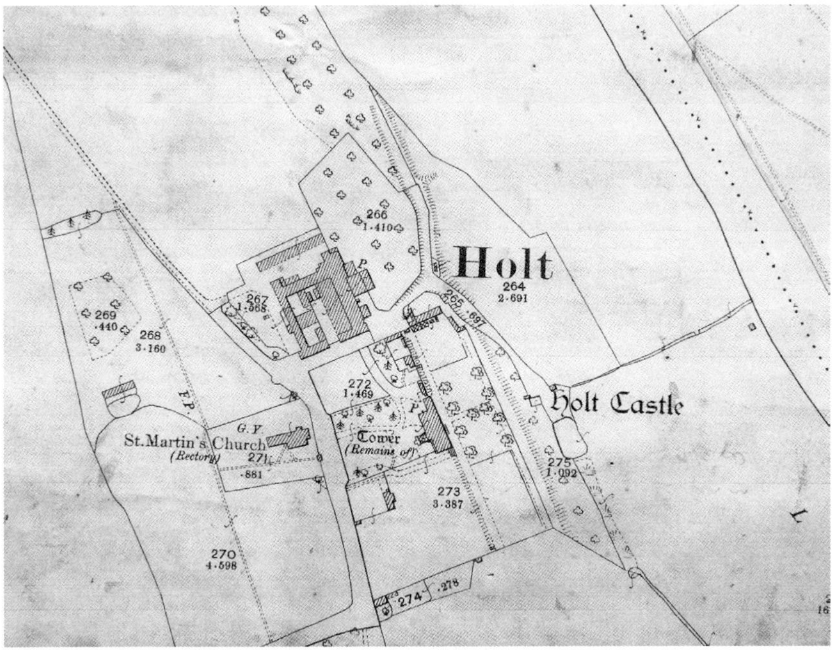

OS 2nd edition 1905.

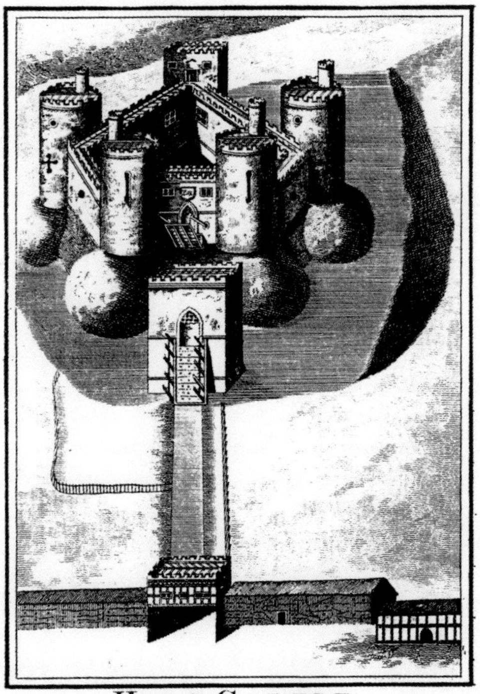

HOLT CASTLE.

ABOVE: fanciful 18th century engraving of a fortified Holt Castle with castellated towers.

LEFT: drawing of Holt Castle and the Tilt Yard, 1721, Bodleian Library, Oxford.

Hopton Court

Parish: Leigh & Bransford

HER Ref: WSM28864.

Grid Ref: SO 758 524. Postcode: WR6 5HP.

O.S. 6" Map No: 32SE.

Date of Map: 1884, with extent of park & gardens shaded as 1905 OS.

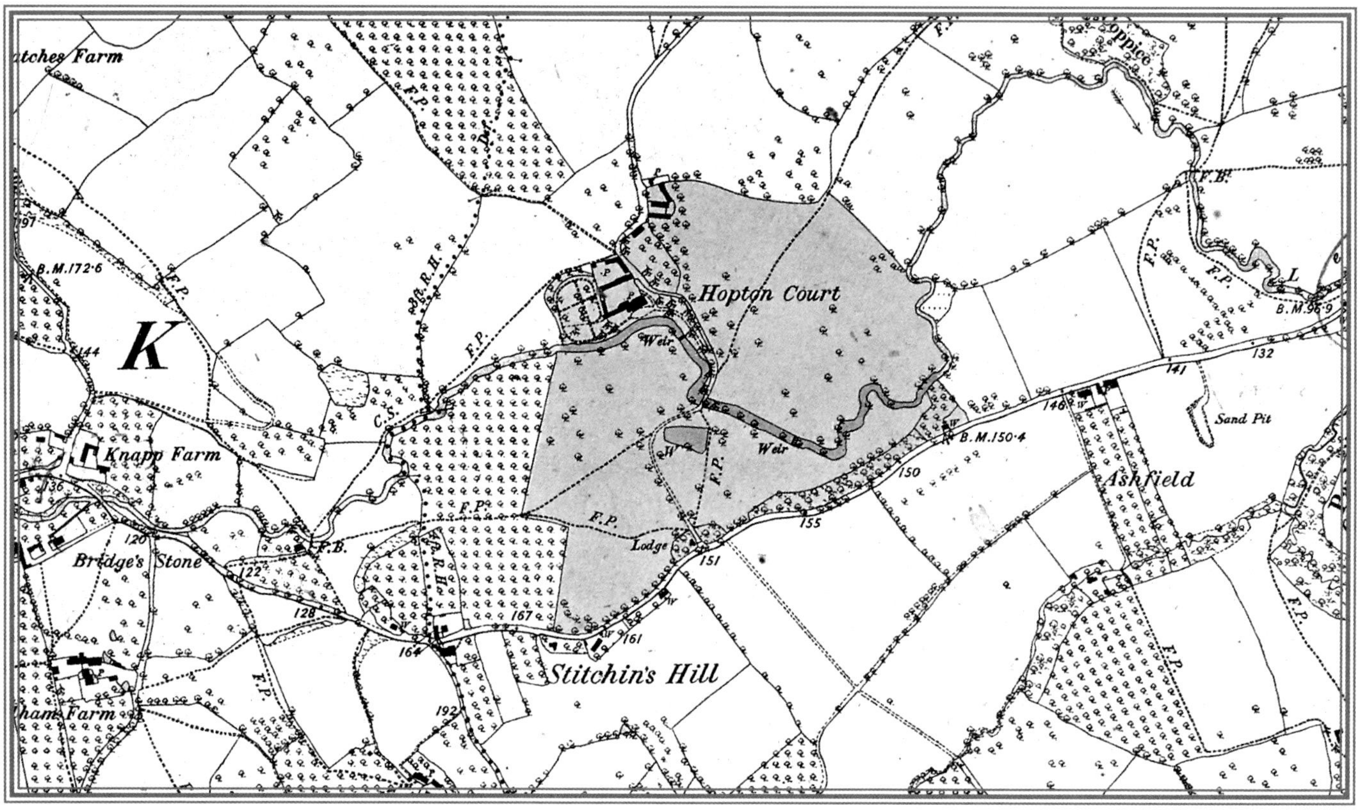

The house is early-19th century and the grounds were presumably laid out from that time. John Nash is said to have made alterations to the house after 1803. The park is shown on the 2nd edition of the OS 6 inch together with a Lodge and the Leigh Brook running through the centre of the park. A road and footpath go north and west through the park area. The lodge, stable block and walled garden survive.

Huddington Court

Parish: Hadzor, Himbleton, Huddington & Oddingley

HER Ref: WSM07966.
Grid Ref: SO 942 573.
Postcode: WR9 7LL.
O.S. 6" Map No: 29SE.
Date of Map: 1884.

The grid ref. for the documented deer park (HER) is near Huddington Hill Farm, south-east of the Court. A "parke close" is recorded by the 1651 Parliamentary Survey of the Court. The status of the property (and the existence of a park) no doubt declined after the involvement of the Winters in the Gun Powder Plot in 1605. A tenanted property does however rate as a residence on Cary's 1805 map. A Plan of the Huddington Estate of 1790 (CRO 11768/10) marks two fields as "Park" towards Huddington Hill.

.........continued from previous page

The earliest part of the surviving manor house has been dated to 1493 and stands on a platform within a double moat enclosing 0.83 acres. Price & Molyneux summarise the complex building history of the manor house: "what survives today represents only about one third of the buildings which occupied the moated site as late as 1697." There are other small pieces of water on the south and east sides and a larger, rectangular piece of water, that might indicate a second moat on the north-west side. The foundations of a circular, probably medieval dove-cote were found in 1905. Moats hold the promise of gardens or stock enclosures in the medieval and later periods. The inventory of 1535 for a house with 22 rooms however, does not have anything to say about the gardens.

The Parliamentary Survey of 1651 following Sir George Winter's support for the King in the English Civil War, gives no details about gardens to a mansion house "very much out of repayre." Besides several outbuildings; brew house, barns, pigeon house, court house, stable, the 4 acres with the mansion contained one "orchard a green Corte and one small hopyard ... bounded by a close called the Park close on the south, a Croft called the Oake Croft on the west, Huddington streete on the North and a Close called the Piggs Close on the East." (Price & Molyneux). Later 16th, 17th and 18th century alterations and developments to the manor house do not suggest any contemporary developments to the gardens such as an extension of gardens beyond the moated site although Oswald proposed that there was a forecourt outside the moat – "old cobbled paving, carefully arranged in patterns, was found under the turf."

By the later-19th century, apart from a kitchen garden, formal or other gardens had been abandoned and there are photographs of the house and grounds in this decayed but picturesque state in the Benjamin Stone Collection (Birmingham City Library) (Humphreys, op. cit.). The gardens today, within the moated site, are as created by the Edmondson Family after they acquired a very neglected property from the Shewsbury Estate Sale in 1918 (CRO 4460/30). Twentieth century additions or replacement buildings and other features include the two dovecotes from Abbots Morton and the Stourport-made, iron bridge dated 1827 moved from Eardiston in 1967. The Orangery of circa 1824 moved to Huddington in 1971, was previously an entrance lodge to Strensham Court. Some balustrading and statuary is also from Strensham. Other listed features are the 16th century brick bridge and 18th century piers and gates (from Yorkshire).

Huddington Court is featured by Mowl as "the county's true garden museum ..." (pp. 166-8) and he eloquently describes the gardens and their atmosphere. There are two moats, one dry, and within the inner moat "a pleasaunce of low box hedges, a pampas clump and the first scatter of more than 20 stone urns". Across the outer moat is Lady Winter's Walk noted as an avenue of trees by the VCH in 1913. Three topiary peacocks stand guard along the entrance front. Comins describes "an ample area of lawns, shrubs and beds ... fine plantings of specimen trees ..." (op. cit.).

Plate 27, 17th century Dovecot.

A. Oswald, "Huddington Court", *Country Life*, LXXX, 1936, p. 119.

J. Humphreys, "The Wintours and the Gunpowder Plot", *Studies in Worcestershire History*, 1938.

J. Comins, "Huddington Court", *HWGT, Newsletter*, 32, Winter 2008/9.

S. Price & N. Molyneux, "Huddington Court; the History and Architectural Development of Worcestershire's 'Most Picturesque House' ", *Worcs. Archeol. Soc. Trans.* 3rd Series, 23, 2012, pp.. 139-175.

T. Mowl, *Historic Houses of Worcestershire*, 2006.

Victoria County History, Vol. 3, 1913 (VCH).

Impney Park

Parish: Droitwich Spa

HER Ref: WSM28863. Grid Ref: SO 911 640. Postcode: WR9 0BN.

O.S. 6" Map No: 22SW.

Date of Map: 1888.

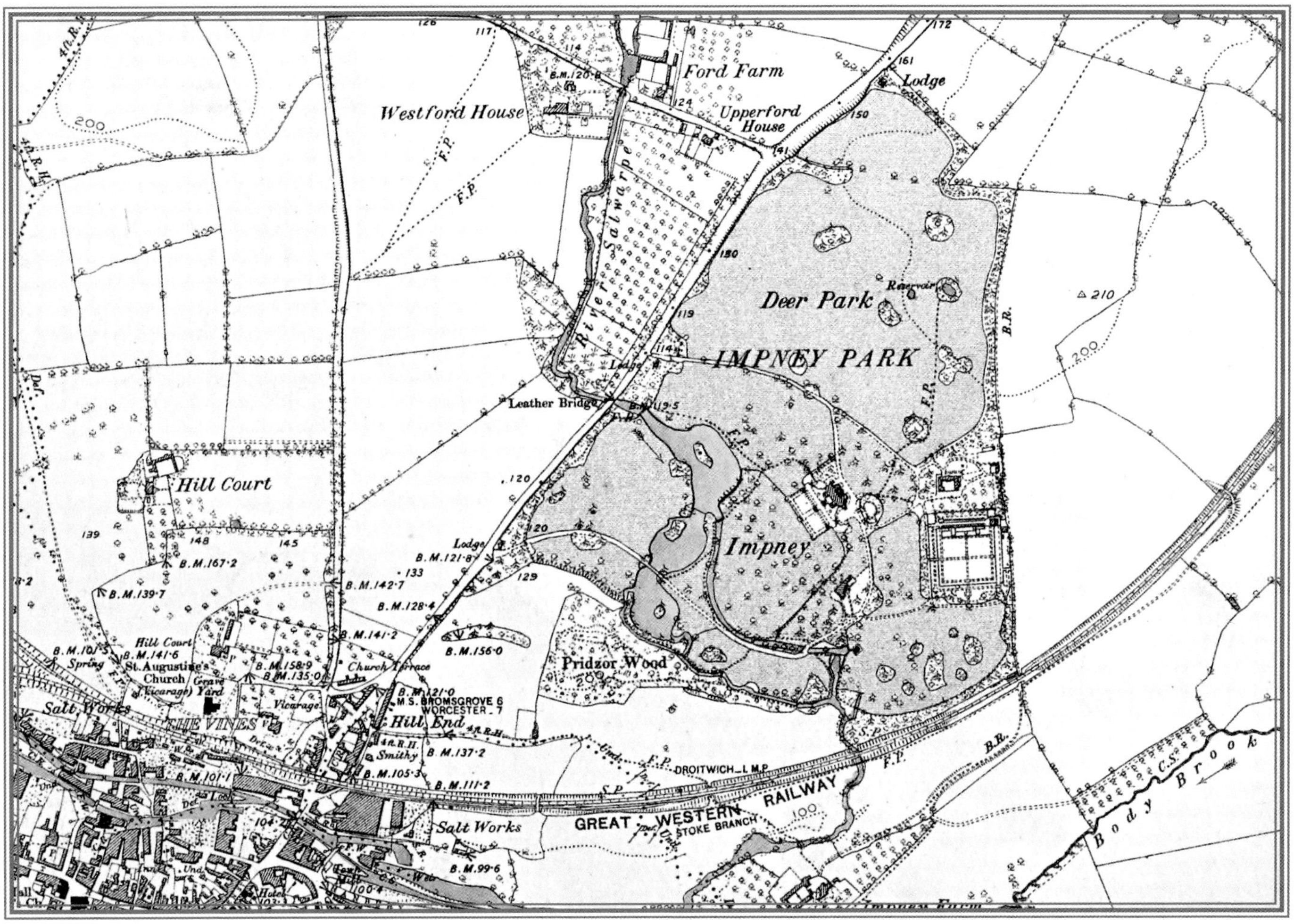

A mansion was built on a green field site, Impney Manor, for John Corbett by Auguste Tronquois (with R. P. Spiers as site architect) between 1869 and 1875 (**Editorial** illus.). Corbett, the Salt King of Stoke Prior, also sponsored several community facilities, including Brine Baths, hotels and hospitals in Droitwich and beyond. Apart from the Chalet (Ravenscrest) built in 1891, the gardens and garden buildings were also built at this time: the upper terrace with steps leading to the lower terrace with balustrading and busts of Roman Emperors and the cast iron fountain by the British Iron Foundry of Derby and James Forsyth's statue of *Flora* (1888). The iron foot bridges in the grounds were supplied by Hardy & Padmore of Worcester. The gardens, still looking very stark and new, are well-illustrated by *Country Life* in 1901 (IX, pp. 592-596) which describes the lower and upper lake divided by a pretty waterfall, a "bronze" fountain "good enough for Versailles", and the white marble figures on the terraces. "The fern dell is one of the features of the garden ... formerly a natural hollow where common British ferns grew. Then a roof was erected over the dell and the interior was at once transformed into a substantial rock garden ... and species flourish as if in a New Zealand valley ... A new rose garden was recently added ... herbaceous borders are exceptionally fine ... holly hocks, lillies, wild rose, paeonies, larkspurs ... good effect of white marble busts on grey balustrades contrasting with the Irish yews ... large leafed foliage plants are bedded out in great quantities and mixed freely with the brilliantly-coloured geraniums and begonias."

Hodges features the Indoor Fernery which ran the length of the house, was accessed via a grotto made of imported

.........continued from previous page

tufa and accommodated a stream for the "golden carp luxuriating here". The Conservatory on the north-east side was celebrated for its camellias. The considerable, square-shaped Kitchen Garden had a range of glass houses, with a small octagonal fernery in the centre, providing space for peach houses, vineries, a fig house and also a frame ground with pits 250 ft long.

Photograph taken circa 1900, courtesy of R. Spollen.

Hodges (op. cit., particularly Ch. 3, "The Park and Gardens") gives a full picture from the beginning to the present quoting the contemporary gardening press such as the *Journal of Horticulture and Cottage Gardener* for April 1884 and September 1903 and the *Gardener's Chronicle* in 1901 and 1904 and the Sale particulars of 1925. The press remarked on the succession of well-known head gardeners such as Owen Thomas (from Chatsworth) and William Goldring and Mr. Jordan. William Crump of Madresfield reviewed the Impney gardens in 1890. Mowl (op. cit., pp. 114-5) describes the gardens as they are today and "the modern Water Garden ... added below the set-piece floral terrace and, unlike so many water gardens, it enjoys a generous bubbling flow down small cascades". Mowl corrects the characterisation of Impney as Louis XIII or "Gardenesque" to "pure Napoleon III, and of Second Empire date".
The creation of a brand new deer park underlines the owner's wish to recreate the essential parts of a grand landscape on a relatively small site but with a difficult-to-beat French château as its centre-piece. To create the necessary acreage to turn Impney Manor into Impney Park meant the acquisition of land from different owners principally from Lord Somers whose forebear had inherited the property from Dr. Nash of the *History of Worcestershire* (1781-2) (Blewitt, op. cit.). The VCH (1902, p. 58) estimated the whole deer park at 200 acres. The amount of the landscape park that was allotted to the deer is no doubt accurately stated by Whitaker in 1892 as 58 acres. The deer park was fenced with iron railings and contained 69 fallow deer: "The park is planted with Scotch firs, Austrian pines, sycamore, and horse-chesnuts". Since 1900, Impney Park has had to respond to two world wars, the first requiring the deer to share the park with other more productive stock and the second for the grounds to accommodate a prisoner of war camp with Nissen huts while the tropical grotto was used as a gas chamber for the testing of poisonous gas (Hodges, op. cit., p. 300). There was considerable damage and what survived is due to restoration post 1949 after the house was released by the MOD in 1942 and the mansion, already a hotel before the 2nd World War, returned to hotel use as Chateau Impney. New buildings, a golf course, tennis courts and other leisure and conference uses have led to further building within the grounds. The deer park now also hosts Highland Cattle and rare breeds.
There were 3 lodges, all to the west where the park is bounded by the road. The Railway forms an impenetrable boundary on the south and east sides and the water tower (The Folly) and walled garden are sited hard up against it. Pools were created by using the Salwarpe which ran through the centre of the park. The landscape retains its perimeter woods and park-like appearance, e.g. clumps of Scots Pine in the north part and beeches near the south boundary below the old kitchen gardens. There are some fine trees in the immediate surroundings of the mansion. Chateau Impney is illustrated in colour by both the BoE and Mowl.

View north-west across the terrace parterre towards Hill End. Photo circa 1900, courtesy of R. Spollen.

J. R. Hodges, *Chateau Impney*, 2009, Ch. 3 "The Park and Gardens".
L. Blewitt, "From Manor to Mansion; the 19th century ownership of Impney", *Dodderhill Parish Notes*, 2006.
Country Life, IX, 1901, p. 592 (12 photos.).
A. Brooks & N. Pevsner, *Worcestershire*, 2007 (BoE).
T. Mowl, *Historic Gardens of Worcestershire*, 2006.
Victoria County History, Vol. 2, 1902 (VCH).
pulham.org.uk: *The Pulham Legacy*, August 17th Newsletter
parksandgardensuk.wordpress.com.*Owen Thomas.2.*

Ismere House

Parish: Churchill & Blakedown

HER Ref: WSM28941.

Grid Ref: SO 865 796. Postcode: DY10 3NY.

O.S. 6" Map No: 8NE.

Date of Map: 1882, with extent of park & garden shaded as 1880s OS.

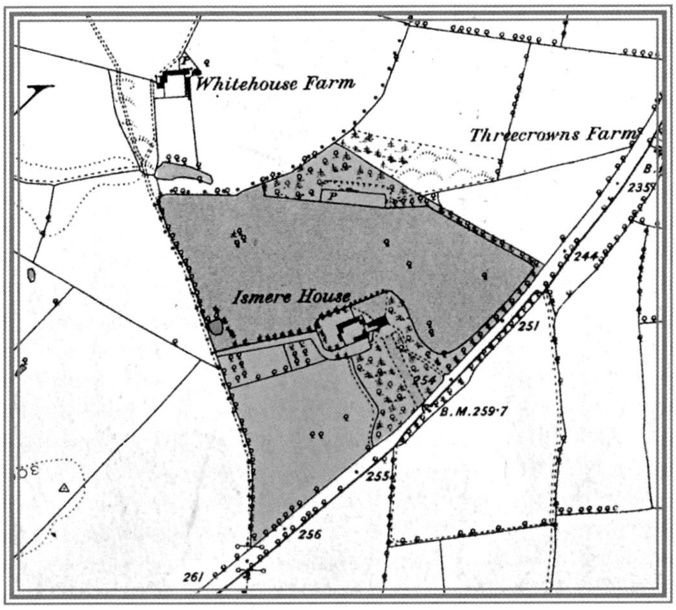

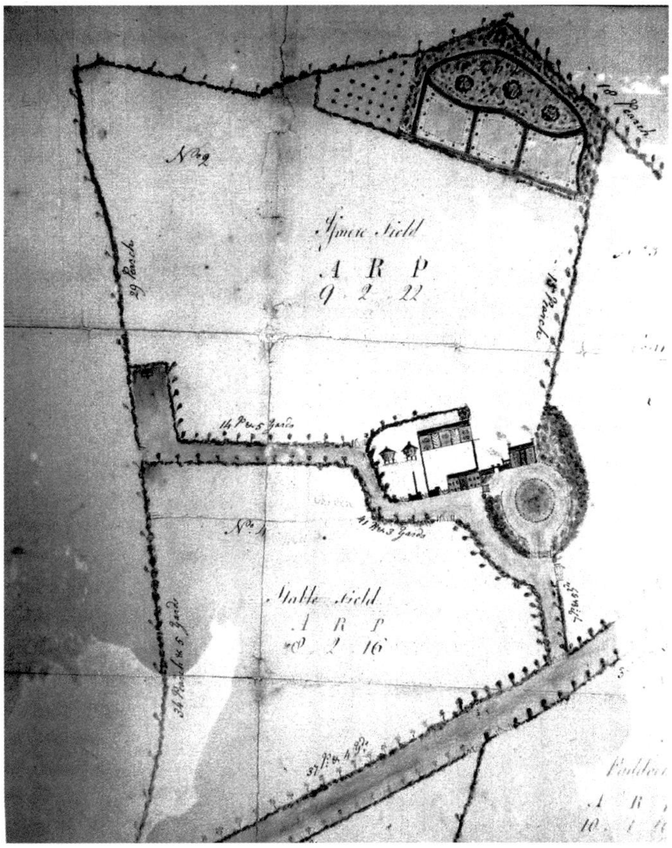

ABOVE & LEFT: details from Benjamin and William Cope's estate plan, 1788. Courtesy of David & Sarah Houle.

The House is shown with grounds on 19th century printed maps and with a small park on the first Ordnance Survey of 1831. The BoE attributes the building of the house to John Smith and gives a date of circa 1775. The house does not appear on a Toll Map of 1770 but does appear on one dated 1780. The house was built in 3 phases as shown by the use of 2 or 3 courses of brick (David Houle). A library bay was added circa 1950 and the conservatory was replaced more recently. The Listing describes a small country house "with associated barn". There is in fact a courtyard of farm buildings including Stables and a piggery next to the house, a 3- sided, walled

..........continued from previous page

garden some distance from the house and formerly a Dog Kennels beside a piece of water also some way from the house. All of this is found on a *Plan and Survey of the Estate of Mr. John Smith of Ismere in the County of Worcester* made by Benjamin Cope, Surveyor, 1788 and drawn and coloured by William Cope. Ismere represents in miniature the amenities of grander country houses, this one of modest scale and construction was suitable for a gentleman who enjoyed hunting. Ismere may already have been tenanted by a hunting man; Mr. William Trow of Kidderminster commissioned a fine portrait of himself and eldest son with horses and hounds by William Williams in 1789. The Trows were tenants of Ismere through much of the 19th century.

The arrangements as shown on the Plan of house, out buildings, gardens and approaches remain virtually unaltered to the present day apart from the entrance from the A451, the Stourbridge road, which was changed at some time between Sales of 1864 and 1922. (The drive was moved to the west and the more central approach route was made into lawn and described as Pleasure Ground on the 1840 Tithe Map). In 1788 the entrance gate opened to a short drive ending at the front door with a turning circle. This drive was sheltered by planting extending into a shrubbery to the right of the entrance front. Metal railings ran along the outside of the drive and protected the circle of lawn. This drive branched to the left towards the Barn Yard etc. and then on down a tree-lined drive to the pool and dog kennels. The plan minutely describes gates into the Stable Yard and Rick Yard and into Ismere Field (9 acres), Court Field (6 acres) and Stable Field (8 acres); Ismere Field and Court Field are defined as the park on the 6 inch OS 1882. Although not defined as park in 1788, the plan does show a wall with piers, i.e. a formal entrance into Ismere Field from the main entrance to the house. The Stables are given some architectural presence with a centre bay of 3 stories with a curved, Dutch pediment. There are walls too with asymmetrically arranged gates into the yard between the Stables and a magnificent barn and into the Rick Yard containing two round, thatched ricks raised off the ground.

Ismere House, according to the 1788 Plan didn't have any garden immediately beside it but opened directly onto Ismere Field. The two acre garden presumably refers to the gardens at the far side of Ismere Field which have a small orchard on one side and a small plantation round it, all hedged off from the field. The gardens were divided by hedges into 4 parts: a serpentine hedge between one planted area and three compartments filled with paths and eccentric beds or lawns. By 1840, when Ismere Field was called Garden Field, this garden had been formalised with brick walls on 3 sides and a greenhouse on the south side and a boiler house on the north side with a well which connected with the hothouse through horizontal ducts in the wall. An old espaliered pear on the wall suggests its earlier use. This walled garden is set on a lower level than the house and enjoys better soil and the topography explains its unusual location.

The Dog Kennel was also unusually sited and given a relatively grand approach from which some Scots Pines survive. It was set at one end of a rectangular pool which has been naturalised. The Pool and Kennels are at a lower level than the house. In 1788 the drive/avenue from house to kennels had Ismere Field on the north side and stable Field on the south side. A section of the latter next to the Kennel drive had been developed into gardens by 1840 when the pleasure grounds had also extended into Ismere Field (lawn) and between the Yards and the field as continues today. The 1840 Tithe Map put these gardens at 4 acres.

The original garden layout is now much simplified but the house still looks out across its small park to the south facing walled garden. The ha-ha still survives intact between domestic garden and park.

Ismere is known for the "Ismere Charter", a land grant written in Latin in 736 A.D, remarkable as surviving in its original form. It is also significant for describing Aethelbald, King of the Mercians as King of the South English and as King of Britain.

A. Brooks & N. Pevsner, *Worcestershire,* 2007 (BoE).

Kemerton Court (Lower Court)

Parish: Kemerton

HER Ref: WSM28990

Grid Ref: SO 942 368 Postcode: GL20 7HY

O.S. 6" Map No: 55NE

Date of Map: 1884 with extent of designed landscape superimposed, including 20th century additions.

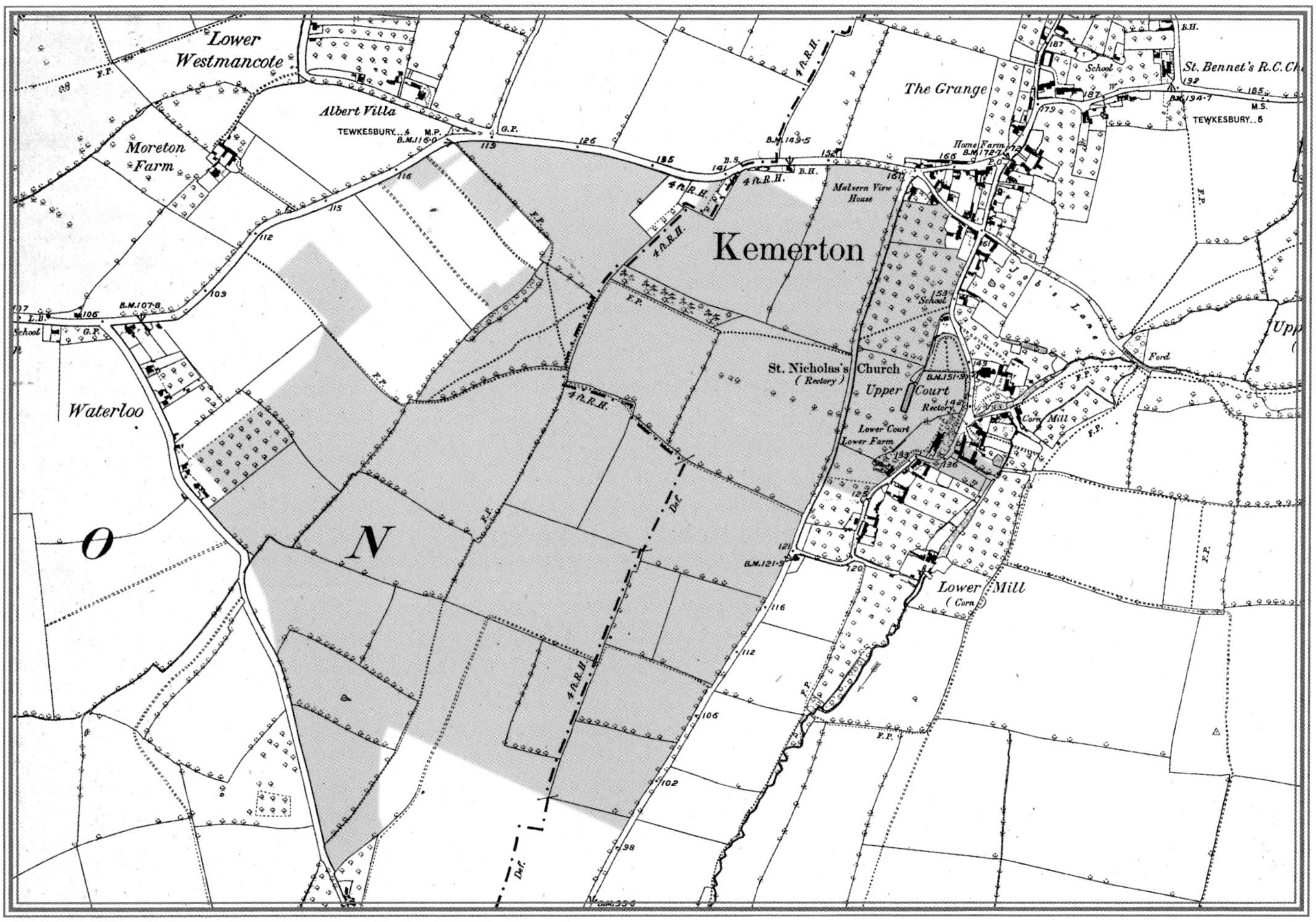

Kemerton Court (Listed grade II*) is the principal of two manor houses in Kemerton built for the interrelated Lygon, Parsons and Hopton families. The house is of 16th century origin and received a Baroque, west façade in the early-18th century variously attributed to Thomas White of Worcester and the Smiths of Warwick. Since 1949, the house has been in the possession of the Darby family, descendants of the original owners. The parish of Kemerton was in Gloucestershire until 1931.

There is evidence of an early-18th century formal landscape contemporary with the west front. Prior to 1825, the main approach to the house was from Kinsham Lane via a 180m lane which ran perpendicular to the west front ('Walk End Lane' or 'The Walk'). This was bordered by an avenue of elms, some of which survived until mid-20th century. From the intersection of Walk End Lane and Kinsham Lane, a footpath led westwards to the county boundary.

450m west of the house and precisely aligning with its axis, a long, narrow wood (220m x 30m) was planted post-Inclosure (1772). Several ridges or shallow banks run lengthwise through the wood at right angles to the pre-Inclosure plough pattern. The wood fits awkwardly into the Inclosure field layout. Both factors suggest the wood may have been planted on the remains of an axial (possibly tree-lined) approach road, later made redundant by the Tewkesbury-Overbury turnpike in 1756.

In the second half of the 18th century, a stone tower ('Parsons Folly' or 'Bredon Tower') was built at the summit of Bredon Hill for squire John Parsons MP (1732–1805), 2.3

..........continued from previous page

miles to the north. This acts as an outer eyecatcher from multiple locations within the grounds. The northern part of the walled garden was constructed sometime before 1825. In the later-18th and early-19th centuries, informal Brown-style parkland was developed between the house and Kinsham Lane (the Near Park). This is recorded in the 1828 OS one inch map and a number of trees survive from this period.
During the second quarter of the 19th century, extensive changes to the house and grounds were undertaken for Rev. William Parsons/Hopton (1749-1841) who adopted the name Hopton on inheriting the Canon Frome estate in 1817. In 1825, Walk End Lane was closed by court order and the public road diverted east of the house, with a new main entrance created on the east front. Yew trees planted alongside the new road largely survive. A second elm avenue was planted along Kinsham Lane north of the house which was photographed in 1905 (the elms survived until the mid-20th century and were replaced with limes in 2009). A mid-19th century drawing shows the west front in its parkland setting, with haymaking taking place on the site of the former lane. Post-1838, the Far Park was created west of Kinsham Lane by combining two fields enclosed in 1772 and retaining mature hedgerow trees.
By 1883 (OS County Series 1:2500 survey), an ornamental

The west front of Kemerton Court from the park. mid-19th century. Courtesy of Adrian Darby, OBE.

Kemerton Court in 1918. WAAS, Kemerton 2161.

lake had been made in the Near Park and a wet ha-ha built along the east side of Kinsham Lane. The walled garden had been enlarged to the south and a barrel-vaulted ice house constructed. A series of hoggin paths were built in the grounds, several of which survive including the Church Walk between the house and walled garden, and the path to the Stables, both of which were edged with surviving box, laurel, yew and holly. Additional 19th century planting includes cedar of Lebanon and *Liriodendron*. Pine and spruce from this period was mostly felled in the 20th century. In the early-20th century, an avenue of horse chestnuts was planted in the Far Park, which has recently been affected by phytophthora.
Early in the 21st century, the Far Park was enlarged to 56 acres for Adrian Darby to designs by his son Matthew Darby. Three additional arable fields were incorporated, and intervening hedges removed while retaining mature hedgerow trees. Several hundred young trees were planted, principally oak, beech, lime, ash, elm and chestnut, either individually or in clumps, groups and belts, forming an extensive area of informal parkland in the Brown style.
West and south of the Far Park, woodland and an arboretum collection extends over some 110 acres (mainly planted 1970-2010). This encircles Kemerton Lake to the south, a 45 acre wetland complex created on the site of a former gravel pit, 1989-99. The woodland has been laid out in an early-18th century style to designs by Matthew Darby. It is enlivened by a series of intersecting rides which align with distant eyecatchers in the form of hilltops and notable structures (Cleeve Hill, Oxenton Hill, North Hill, Worcestershire Beacon, Dumbleton Hill, Parsons Folly, Gloucester Cathedral, Bredon Church, Kemerton Church and Kemerton Court). This is certainly one of the most ambitious and significant landscape garden developments in the County.
The gardens today extend over 7.5 acres. The bell-shaped walled garden, designed by Meriel Darby, contains a wide double border around the perimeter, and a central cross path planted with apple trees and irises and with a sundial in the centre. The gardens are spectacular in spring; "The newly restored walled garden is a triumph of colour and texture within the constraints of a formal layout" (Patton, op.cit.).

C. Elrington (ed.), *Victoria County History: A History of the County of Gloucester*, Vol. VIII, 1968.
J. Lees-Milne, *English Country Houses: Baroque*, 1970.
P. Reid, *Burke's & Savills Guide to Country Houses*, Vol 2, 1980.
T. Mowl, *Historic Gardens of Worcestershire*, 2006.
A. Brooks & N. Pevsner, *Worcestershire*, 2007 (BoE).
J. Patton,"Visit to Kemerton Court", *HWGT Newsletter*, 29, Summer 2007.
Kemerton Estate Archives.

..........continued from previous page

Included within Historic England's Register of Historic Parks and Gardens of special historic interest in England.

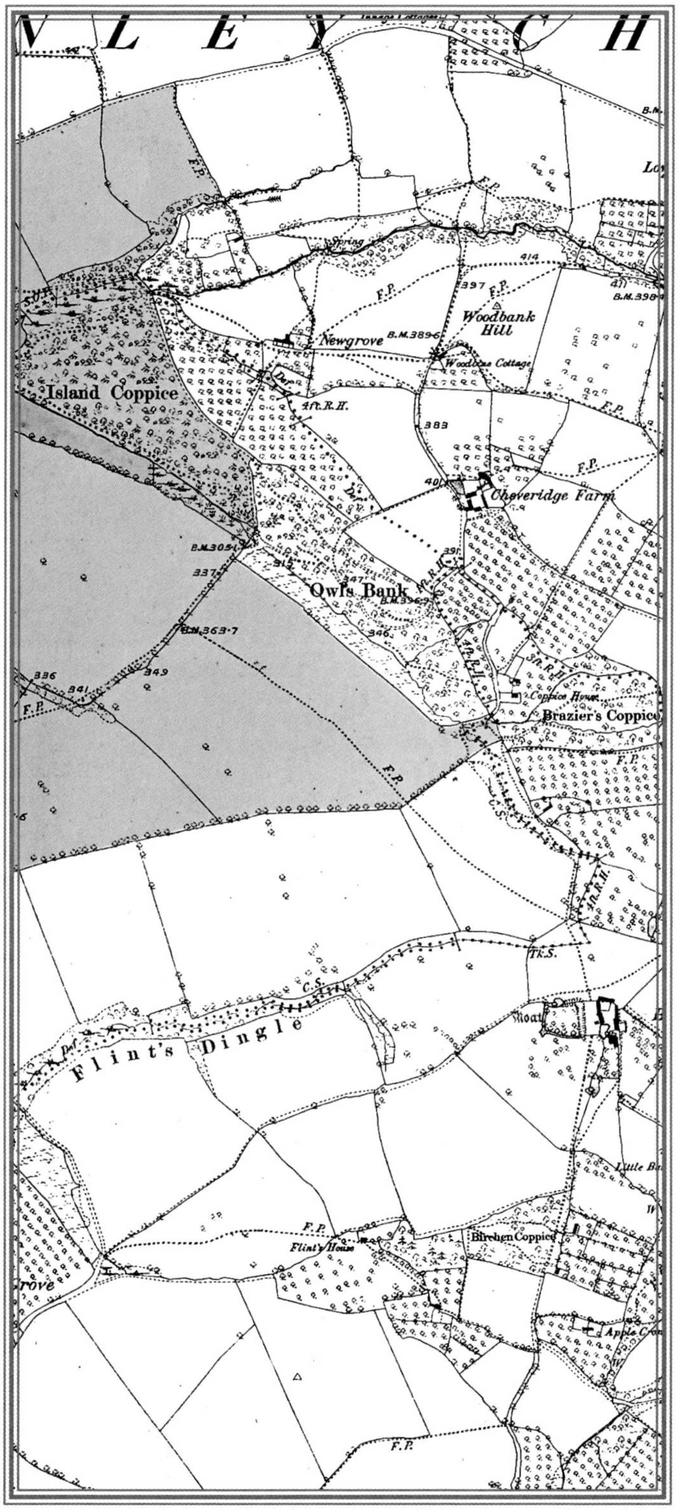

John Wyard was licenced to impark his woods at Kyre Wyard in 1329 and there are references to the park from the 15th century. The park was famous for its oaks as early as the 16th century (Leland). Habington praised it similarly: "The park of Kyreward is not to be shut up in silence for it is adorned with so many and mighty oaks as scarce any ground in England within that quantity of acres can show so many." The property declined under the ownership of Lord Compton (like others in Worcs.) until revived circa 1585 by Sir Edmund Pytts. (VCH, 4, 1924, p. 283). Saxton (1577) shows a deer park as does Sheldon in a tapestry map (1590s). They are followed by Blome (1673), Morden (1695) and some 18th century printed maps. Cary still shows a deer park in 1805. Nash says that the park of 500 acres had been reduced by the later-18th century to 180 acres. A deer park of 170 acres of which 60 were pasture, still existed in 1892, was fenced with old paling and contained 60 or 70 fallow deer. Whitaker remarks then of the ancient avenues of oak and beech (and the existence of a heronry). Avenues are prominent on the first edition of the OS 6 inch (1883) which restricts the park definition to the deer park. This is separated from the grounds of Kyre Park house by the Kyre Brook and stretches from Nineveh in the north-west towards The Grove and Bannall's Farm to the south-east and, in 1883, stopped short of the natural boundary of Flint's Dingle just beyond Lodge Barn. The park as shown in 1905 had contracted by 3 large fields along its south-east side. The avenues suggest that they led to the pool in the north corner and to the large Kyre Pool in the north-east. The latter was made by Sir Edmund Pytts in 1583. The EH Register suggests a 17th century contribution to this part of the landscape but rather tentatively. The character of the deer park has been altered by much planting in its northern half including conifers and poplars. The pools here have also contracted.

It is not always easy to know whether commentators are referring to the area of the deer park above or to the grounds round the house which were physically separate and in their day elaborate. These grounds were bounded by the Bromyard road to the north and east and the Perry Brook in the south-east and extended south-west to the Pigeon House and the Gate House. This is the landscape park and lake illustrated by James Ross and "the water and pleasure ground" described by Nash in 1781 (Vol. II, p. 70 & p. 473) and believed (by the family) and mentioned in 1924 to have been arranged by 'Capability Brown'. The 1753-56 architects were, however, William and David Hiorne. Whitehead has considered Noake's claim in his 1868 *Guide to Worcestershire* that the grounds were laid out by the celebrated 'Capability' Brown "of whose style it

Kyre Park

..........continued from previous page

is probably one of the best examples". Whitehead has found that John Davenport of Wem "worked for many years for Mr. Pytts of Kyre Park" and therefore proposes that Davenport, a known assistant of Brown, locally managed a Brown contract. "The key feature at Kyre is a 13 acre water garden where a modest stream is persuaded to produce rills, cascades and sinewy lakes before it disappears into the Kyre Brook. This looks very much like Davenport's work, rather than Brown's." (op. cit. p. 15). Mowl dates Davenport's involvement at Kyre to the 1760s (i.e. much earlier than his plan for Hanley Court of 1786) and discusses the garden buildings lost, surviving or recently reconstructed (pp. 90-92).

Conifers are prominent around the water and the house in the Ross view. Nothing remains of the formal gardens that Pytts laid out beside his post-1586 house or of the 17th century contribution. Avray Tipping (op. cit., p. 252 and p. 276) says that another Edmund Pytts in the mid-18th century removed formal gardens on the south side occupying 2 courts at different levels. "His ponds, grottoes and groves remain" and the lakes and serpentine lawns. There are remains of cascades between the lakes. A boathouse has been demolished in living memory.

Plan of the Parish of Great Kyre taken from a Survey of Mr John Brittains "made about 30 years ago. By J. Davis. 1804. Scale 6 chains to an Inch", (Prattinton Collection, Soc. of Antiquaries, London – information from Stephen Price) records something of this elaborate if small-scale landscape park. It claims to record the status quo in 1774 and something of the "ponds, grottoes and groves". The water is very similar to what is there today. A bridge and boathouse are with the fish pond in the north-east corner of the immediate grounds; there is a small building either side of the bridge over the serpentine pool now called the River. The Hermitage appears on the map as 2 small buildings even then labelled "ruin". Meandering paths and some planting are concentrated round the River. A Walk is marked running east/west along the run of pools on the north side of the grounds. None of the waterfalls or grottoes, some of which have been recovered in recent restorations, are shown. The 4 acre walled garden to the south together with a gardener's house in one corner is marked out into 8 compartments.

The 18th and 19th centuries have bequeathed a formidable arboretum including fine specimens of yew, cedar, cypress, beech, oak, ash, plane, alder, acacia, horse chestnut and Scots Pine. Yews are quite dominant and were probably used to mark the boundaries of these pleasure grounds; yews also link together the garden with the mansion, the Stables, the Church etc. Kyre is justly celebrated for its trees and a cut leaf beech is "apparently the largest girthed specimen in England" (*Kyre Park Garden Tour of the Garden and Shrubbery*). A HWGT Survey remarked particularly upon Ironwood, *Zelkova crenata*, Cedars and rare *Ruscus Hypoglossum* (Alexandrian Laurel).

HE *Register of Parks & Gardens,* 1998.
L. Toulmin-Smith, *The Itinerary oif John Leland,* 1908.
H. A. Tipping, *Country Life*, XLI, 1917, p. 252, 276.
T. Mowl, *Historic Gardens of Worcestershire,* 2006.
D. Whitehead, Was 'Capability' Brown Here?, *HWGT, Newsletter,* 46, 2015/6.
Victoria County History, Vol. 4, 1924 (VCH).
T. R. Nash, *Collections for the History of Worcestershire,* Vol. I 1781.

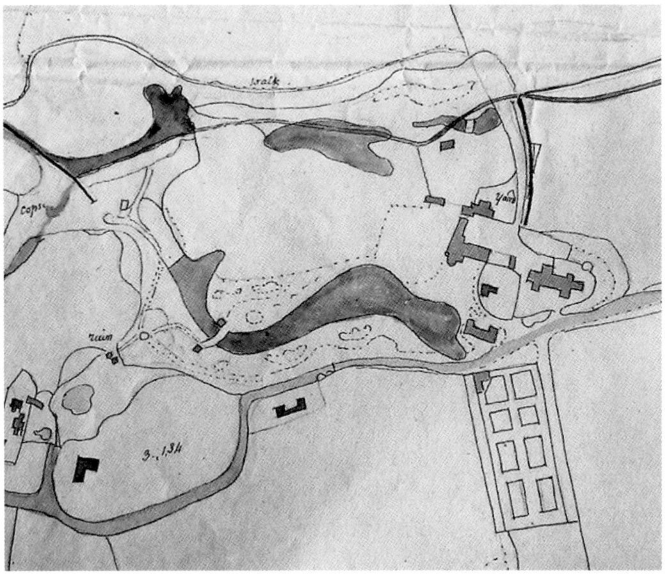

ABOVE: James Ross, engraving from T. R. Nash, *Collections for the History of Worcestershire,* Vol. I, 1781.
LEFT: J. Davis, detail of estate map, 1804, Society of Antiquaries of London, Prattinton Collection.

Kyrewood House

Parish: Tenbury

HER Ref: WSM28851.

Grid Ref: SO 605 680.

Postcode: WR15 8SG.

O.S. 6" Map No: 19NW.

Date of Map: 1884, with shaded extent of park & gardens deduced from text.

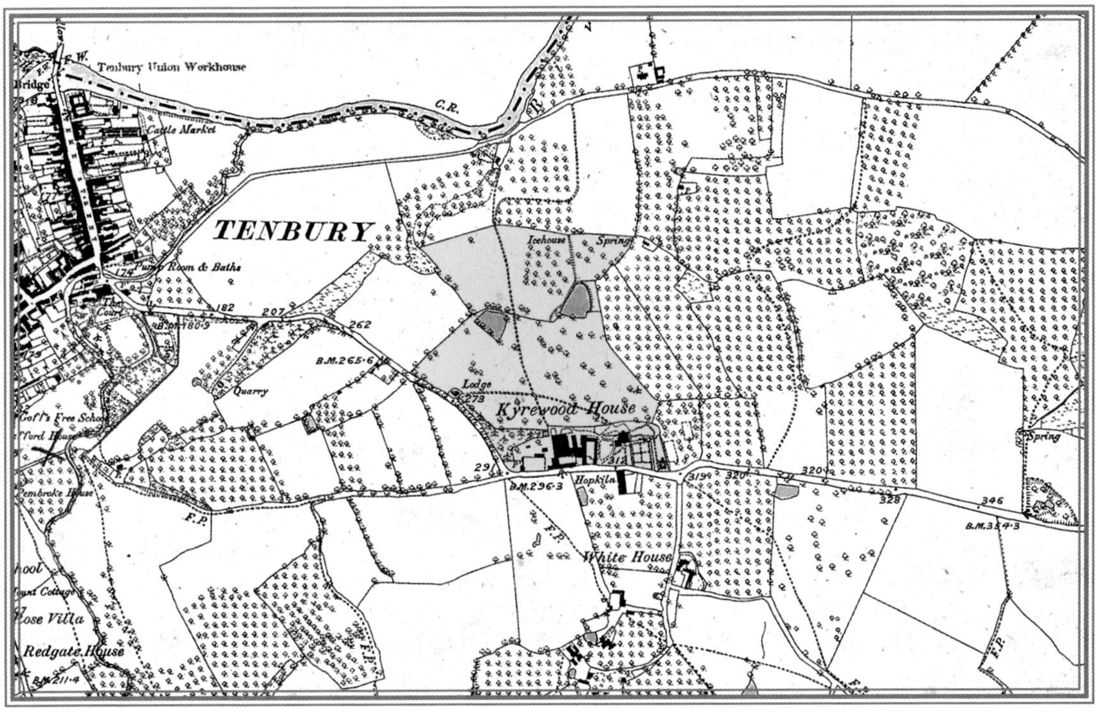

The small park shown on the first edition of the OS 6 inch (1884) and on the 1906 Bartholomew is bounded on the south and west by two roads to Tenbury. It perhaps extended further north towards Rise Lane at least to include the icehouse within the park. Surviving mature trees support this theory. Kyrewood is mentioned in early-19th century directories and the house is dated to 1721 by Pevsner (1968, p. 279).
The walled garden has been laid to lawns and has lost its paths and glasshouses. Three of the four walls survive, in good condition.

N. Pevsner, *Worcestershire*, 1968.

Lea Castle

Parish: Wolverley & Cookley

HER Ref: WSM28847. Grid Ref: SO 841 793. Postcode: DY10 3QB.

O.S. 6" Map No: 8NE/8SE.

Date of Map: 1888, with extent of park & gardens shaded as 1880s OS.

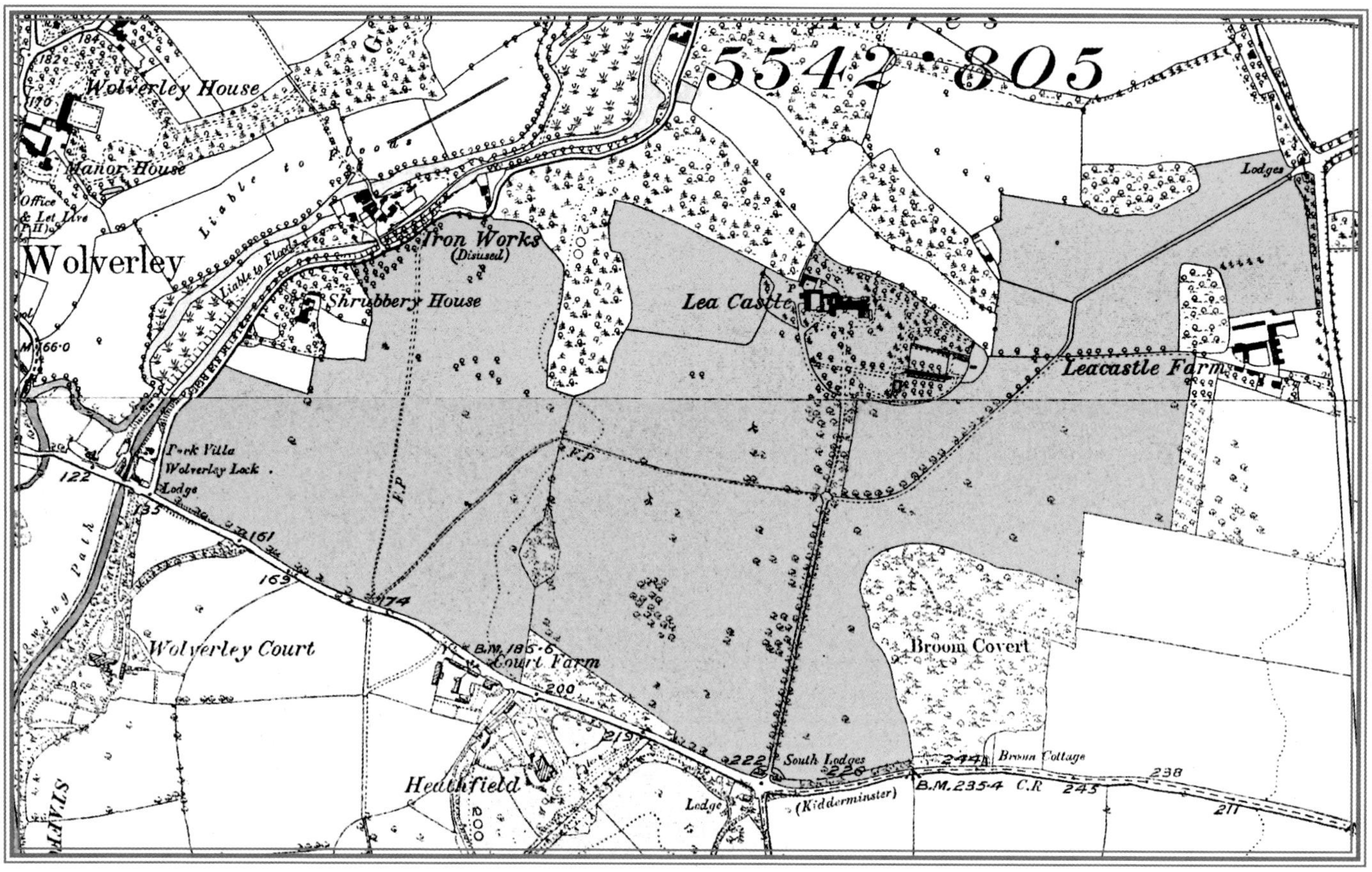

In the later-19th century, Lea Castle was part of the same estate as the Manor of Wolverley. They were sold as two estates totalling 1,072 acres in 1823 when the mansion, garden, park and plantations amounted to 133 acres. The gardens included hot houses and there were also an ice house, a Dwelling House with water, Corn Mill and several pools then leased from the Dean and Chapter of Worcester Cathedral.

The Lea Castle estate remained undisturbed by the expansion of Kidderminster into the early-20th century and is shown as a park on the first OS 6 inch. Much of the area defined then as park is still green, albeit put down to arable. It was bounded on the west by the Staffordshire-Worcestershire Canal, the B4189 to the south (south lodge), with an east lodge on the Cookley-Broadwaters road near Lea Castle Farm. An avenue connected the house with the south lodge.

The house as "Cookley" is noticed on Isaac Taylor's 1772 map. The Castle of circa 1812-16, attributed by the BoE to the antiquarian writer John Carter, was demolished in 1945. This neo-gothic castle (illus. Reid, p. 215) should have attracted a picturesque landscape setting like that of Downton Castle which was also a Knight family property. There is a pen drawing of it by James Ward. Landscape details cannot be made out from early or mid-19th century printed maps and the grounds today lack any special quality except for a vale between two woods close to the site of the demolished mansion on the north side. The mid-19th century, castellated lodges and the brick boundary wall survive (BoE, p. 241). Lea Castle Hospital is not on the Lea Castle site, but to the east of it.

P. Reid, *Burke's & Savills Guide to Country Houses*, Vol 2, 1980.
A. Brooks & N. Pevsner, *Worcestershire*, 2007 (BoE).

Lower Wick Manor House

Parish: Wick

HER Ref: WSM28996.

Grid Ref: SO 838 521. Postcode: WR2 4DA.

O.S. 6" Map No: 33SE.

Date of Map: 1884, with deduced extent of grounds shaded (not shaded on 1905 OS).

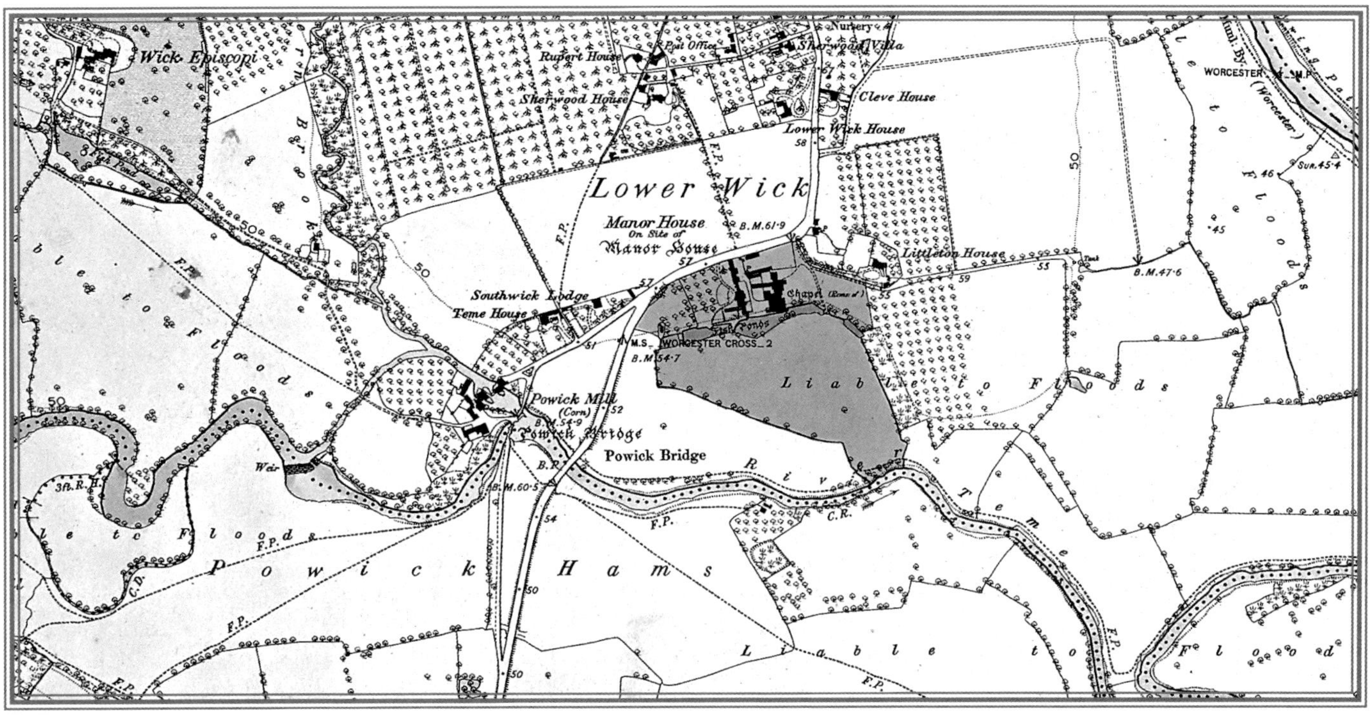

The present house is of 16th and 17th century origins but circa 1800 for the most part (BoE, p. 776). This is on the site of a more ancient manor house from which survive a line of 3 fish ponds along the south border of the buildings and the remains of a Norman chapel, St. Cuthbert, (restored 2012) among the farm buildings.

The manor house belonging to Bishop Giffard of Worcester is recorded in 1299 and was used by him to entertain Archbishop Winchelsey in 1300. This house had garden, curtilage and 2 fishponds. A deer park is mentioned in 1339 (VCH, 3, 1913, p. 50). Whether this park lay north and north-west of the manor house or in the flood plain of the Teme and Severn to the south and east is not known.

The 1916 sale of 312 acres included hop gardens, fruit plantations, nice walks and rock gardens and fish ponds connected by a rustic bridge leading "to nicely laid out pleasure grounds and walks ... there is a Conservatory, Vinery and Potting Shed." (CRO 5240/7).

There are now no traces of either park or gardens but the fishponds are still prominent but with large-scale development on the north side. The chapel has been conserved.

A. Brooks & N. Pevsner, *Worcestershire,* 2007 (BoE).

Victoria County History, Vol. 3, 1913 (VCH).

Madresfield Court

Parish: Madresfield

HER Ref: WSM08936/35182

Grid Ref: SO 809 475

Postcode: WR13 5AJ

O.S. 6" Map No: 40NW/SW, 40NE/SE

Date of Maps: 1885, 1884, with extent of park & gardens shaded as H. E. Register.

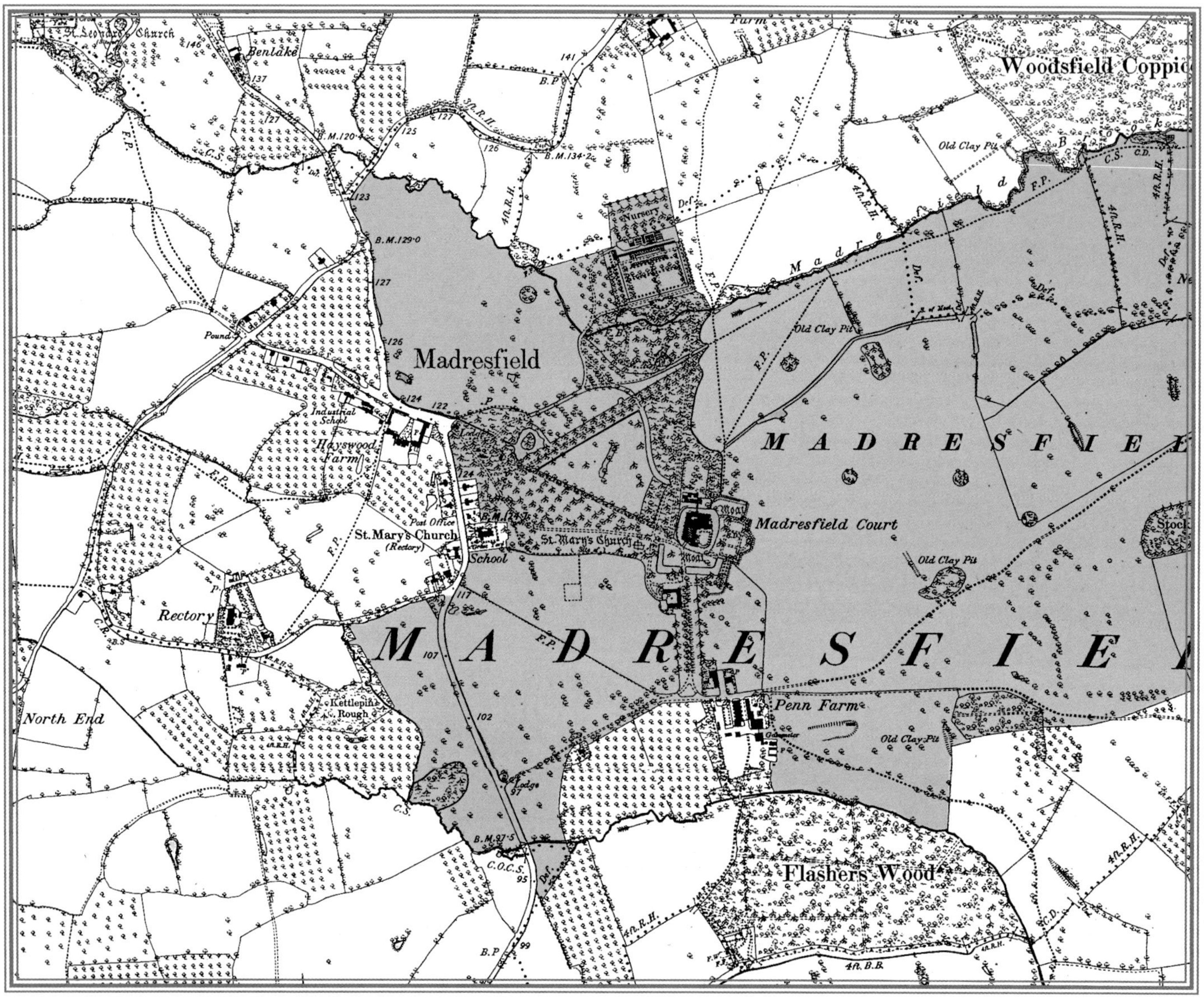

Included within Historic England's Register of Historic Parks and Gardens of special historic interest in England.

The building history of the Court is summarised by the BoE and taken back to the 13th century: "By 1451 it had developed into a substantial manor house … rebuilt from 1584 … NE wing by George Byfield 1799… remodelling begun by P. C. Hardwick … in 1863 … only completed c. 1890." All these were possible moments for activity in the gardens and park.

It can be assumed that the relatively large 15th and late-16th century buildings set within a double moat had gardens immediately adjoining them. A John Doharty junior map of 1744 gives some indication of the gardens at that time (WAAS 9663/2).

It is also presumed but undocumented that a medieval park on the fringe of Malvern Chase lies behind the later park and grounds. The HE Register suggests that

Malvern Chase

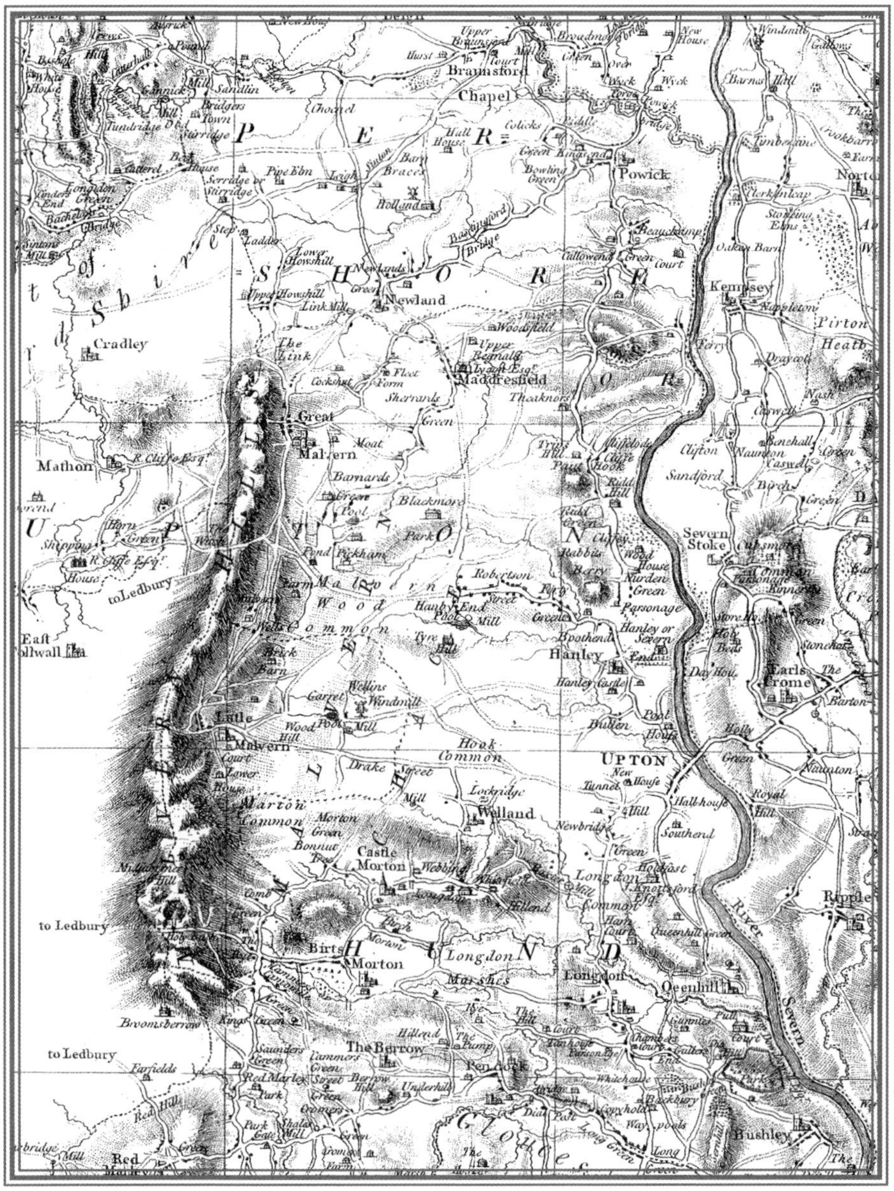

Isaac Taylor,
Map of the County of Worcester, 1772.

The creation of Malvern Chase as a Royal Forest by William the Conqueror was the first stage in the subsequent development of parks within it – Hanley Park, Blackmoor Park and others. It extended from the River Severn in the east to the Malvern Hills and beyond in the west and so contained many future sites discussed in this book. Sections of Isaac Taylor's 1772 map and Christopher Greenwood's 1822 map, showing the extent of the Chase are illustrated side by side by Pamela Hurle (op. cit. figs. 54 & 55). King John, who is famously connected with Malvern Chase and Hanley Castle, inherited the Manor of Hanley through his first wife before, as King, he became owner of the Chase. When John and Isabella divorced in 1201, Isabella retained the Manor and John kept the Chase and the Castle. The Royal Forest was granted to Gilbert de Clare in 1290 but reverted to the Crown circa 1500. The Chase was disforested in 1632 following a Survey in 1629, i.e. before the English Civil War and this accelerated centuries of erosion by assarting (intakes for agriculture) and the development of private parks within it. The greater landowners within the Chase rather than the commoners at large got the lion's share of the farmable land, e.g. the Hornyolds of Blackmoor Park and the Russells of Little Malvern and others who bought the third share assigned to the Crown. Later changes to land ownership and land use within the former Malvern Chase resulted from enclosure acts in the 18th century. The landscape was made up of wooded glades, moors and heaths for the most part rather than forest.

E. A. Barnard, "Survey of Malvern Chase", *Worcs. Archaeol. Soc. Trans., NS VI*, 1929, p. 187 ff.
B. Smith, *A History of Malvern,* 1964 and 1978.
P. Hurle, *The Forest and Chase of Malvern*, 2007.
G. Demidowitz, *A guide to the c17 banks and ditches of the North Malvern Hills*, 2018.

Parish: Great Malvern

O.S. 25" Map No: XXXIX-12, XXXIX-16, XL 9, XL-13

Date of Maps: 1904, 1905, 1927

The development of Malvern as a Spa town created the larger houses with grounds and public parks. Smith (op. cit.) begins the medieval story with the Hermitage sited between St. Ann's and Hay Wells and a late-13th century court reference to a well or wells perhaps in the same location. Wikipedia locates the Hermitage on the

Malvern Wells, The Dell

Parish: Malvern Wells

HER Ref: WSM71640.

Grid Ref: SO 775 422. Postcode: WR14 4HU.

O.S. 6" Map No: 46NE. Date of Map: 1885.

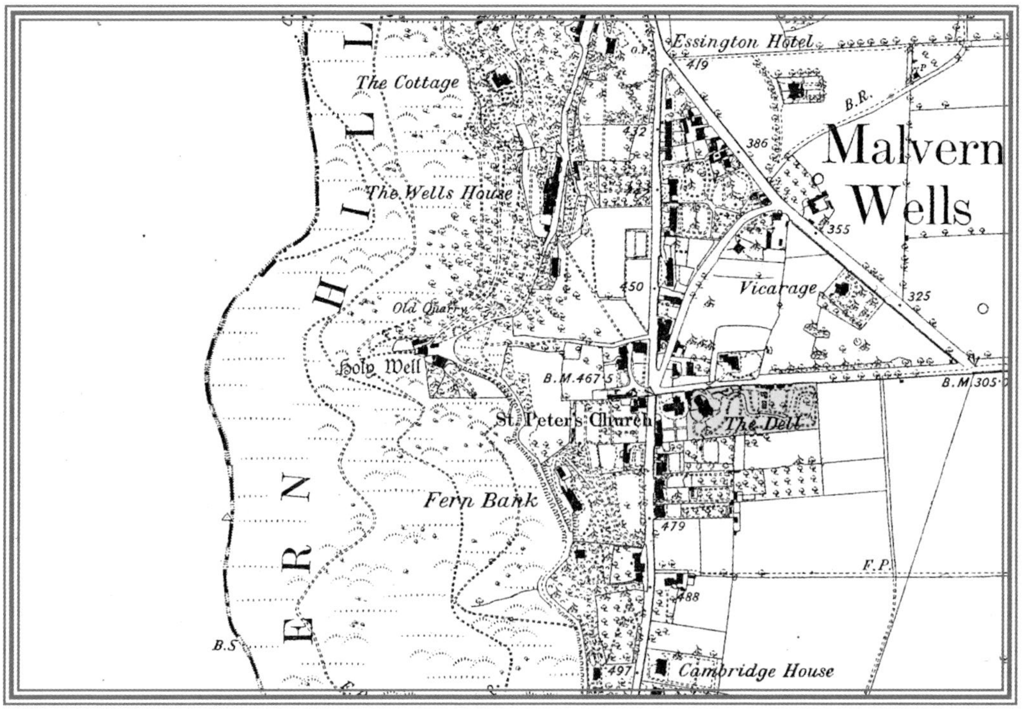

The House is of several 19th century dates and owes much, including its tower, to the Revd. Francis Hopkinson (ob. 1898), Rector of St. Peter's Church nearby. Hopkinson was responsible for the summer-house which was the only garden feature noticed in the previous edition of this *Survey*. The summer-house, relocated within the garden and now beside Green Lane, was rebuilt in 2001 by Peter Knight whose large chess pieces were then a feature of the garden and which are now echoed by a recent adjacent tree carving of a giant Lewis chessman (2019). The interior decoration of the summer-house was restored by Meriel Hodgetts in 1976, i.e. the lettering and coats of arms which refer to major local, medieval families (**Plate 16**). A quotation from John Milton's *L'Allegro* appears on the walls. The map on the ceiling represented the prospect as from its original orientation at the Dell House by naming some notable, local places (Jane Bradney).

The tiered garden features many specimen trees from the 19th century. Where trees have died, chainsaw carvings have been commissioned from Steve Elsby of Hereford by the current owners, Kevin & Elizabeth Rolph, as part of the current restoration and development of the garden.

The original garden is indicated on the 1885 OS 6 inch and is now fragmented into the gardens of four properties.

J. Bradney, correspondence 2017.

K. & E. Rolph, correspondence, 2019.

The summer-house with its decorated interior. Photo, J. Patton (see **Plate 16**, Berkeley of Spetchley coat of arms).

Malvern Wells, Essington Hotel

Parish: Malvern Wells

HER Ref: WSM28971
Grid Ref: SO 773 427
Postcode: WR14 4LQ
O.S. 6" Map No. 46NE
Date of Map: 1885

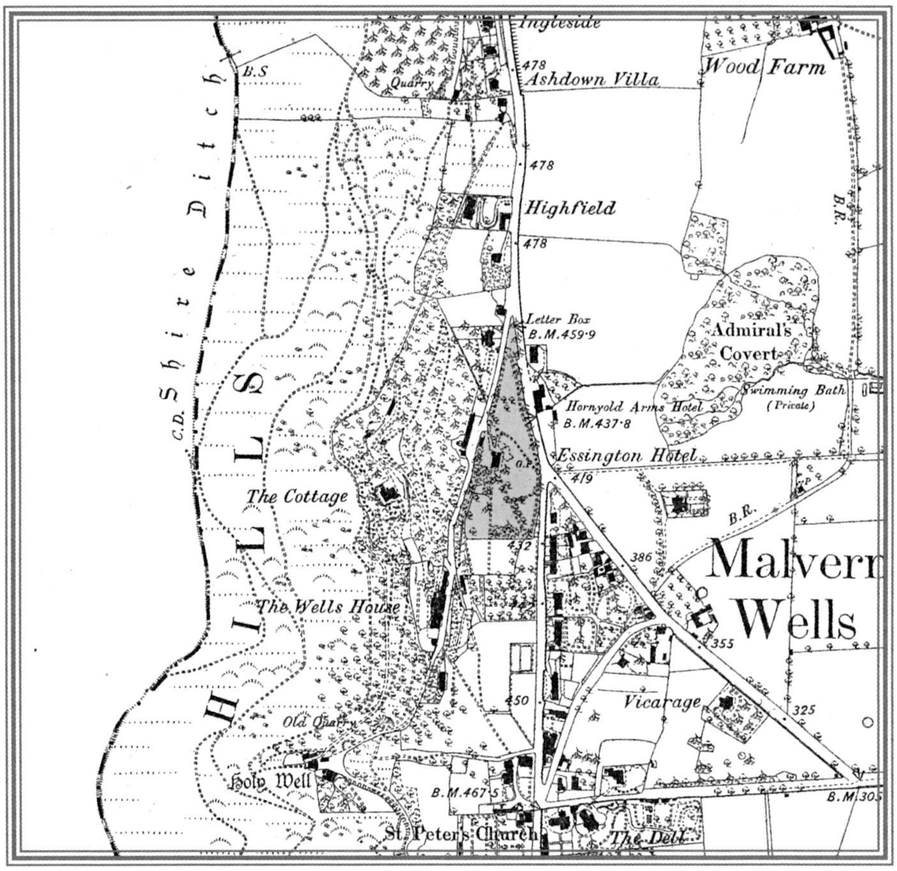

This was built for visitors to the Holy Well circa 1800. Chambers in 1817 advertised the amenities attached to the house as hot and cold baths, a wood, a garden and a hermitage (p. 186). Lewis's 1820 *Directory* illustrates the garden with a gardener and potted plants. Granville, in 1841, praised the Hotel's commanding aspect "and all around enlivened by pleasure grounds thickly clothed in many parts with luxuriant plantations" (op. cit., p. 264). A *Visitors Guide* of 1861 describes the Hotel as pleasantly situated above the main road, having a pleasure garden, with a number of pleasant walks attached to it. The grounds of the Hotel were approximately 5 acres when sold from the Hornyold Estate in 1919. The Hotel is now apartments and most of the grounds have been developed for residential use.

J. Chambers, *A General History of Malvern* , 1817.
A. B. Granville, *Spas of England, 2, Midlands and South,* 1841 (1971).
K. Smith, *Around Malvern,* 1905.

Malvern Wells, Holy Well

Parish: Malvern Wells

HER Ref: WSM36907. Grid Ref: SO 770 425.

Postcode: WR14 4LE.

Holy Well to the west of Malvern Wells is set within an indent in the Hills (see map for Essington Hotel). It was recorded by the 1633 Survey of Malvern Chase and its water was analysed by Dr. John Wall in his *Experiments and Observations on the Malvern Waters,* 1757 which promoted the medical qualities of Malvern water generally. J. Dugdale's *New British Traveller,* 1819: "The Holy Well is the most frequented; probably on account of the beautiful scenery through which it is approached, and of the numerous villas, boarding-houses, and walks, gay with company... The Spring itself has a convenient pump-room with several cisterns, and pumps for the enjoyment of the bath." "Some enterprising projectors have built a neat gothic structure over the spring" (Powell, 1858). The bottling of Malvern Water by Schweppes started at Holy Well in 1850 and the Holywell Water Co. Ltd. bottles Malvern Spring Water today. The mid-19th century guidebooks describe a prominent and popular ash tree as a resting spot nearby, an amenity for those prescribed exercise as well as cold baths!

Dr. J. Wall, *Experiments and Observations on the Malvern Waters,* 1757.
J. Dugdale, *The New British Traveller,* 1819.
J. Powell, *Malvern as I found it.*, 1858.

Postcard image of Holy Well in 1901.

Malvern Wells, Wells House

HER Ref: WSM28972. Grid Ref: SO 770 425. Postcode: WR14 4LH.

The Well or Wells House was revived in 1761 as a Hotel after a decline in the Spa's general fortunes for visitors to the Holy Well just south of it. When Lord Torrington visited Malvern in 1781, he stayed here along with 25 other visitors (with their servants) and was given to understand that it had been built 40 years earlier; he remarked on the long room added "16 years ago". Nash, also in 1781, may have been referring to the Wells House when describing "a large house with all the conveniences for the reception of those who come to drink the waters." An engraving of 1789 shows a substantial building of 7 bays and four stories including dormer windows. The *Beauties* in 1814 said that the boarding house had a garden, gravelled walks, shrubs, flowers and seats, i.e. it was one of the better establishments. The property was redeveloped by T. C. Hornyold after 1843. In Charles Dickens' *Household Words,* 1851, Harriet Martineau described coming down from the Hills through the back door of the Well House and going up to the drawing room on the third floor to enjoy coffee and the view with friends. The Hotel was sold from the Hornyold Estate in 1919 and became Wells House School with 19 acres; the house is now divided into apartments.

Beauties of England and Wales, Vol. XV, 1814.
C. Dickens *Household Words,* 1852.
T. R. Nash, *Collections for the History of Worcestershire,* Vols. I & II, 1781-2.

Guests staying at Wells House could choose between a gentle stroll in the well-tended gardens in front of the hotel or a more challenging excursion out onto the Malvern Hills. Modern reprint of circa 1830 engraving, courtesy Malvern Museum.

West Malvern, St. James & the Abbey School

Parish: West Malvern

HER Ref: WSM29004.

Grid Ref: SO 762 461.

Postcode: WR14 4AY.

O.S. 6" Map No. 39SE.

Date of Map: 1906.

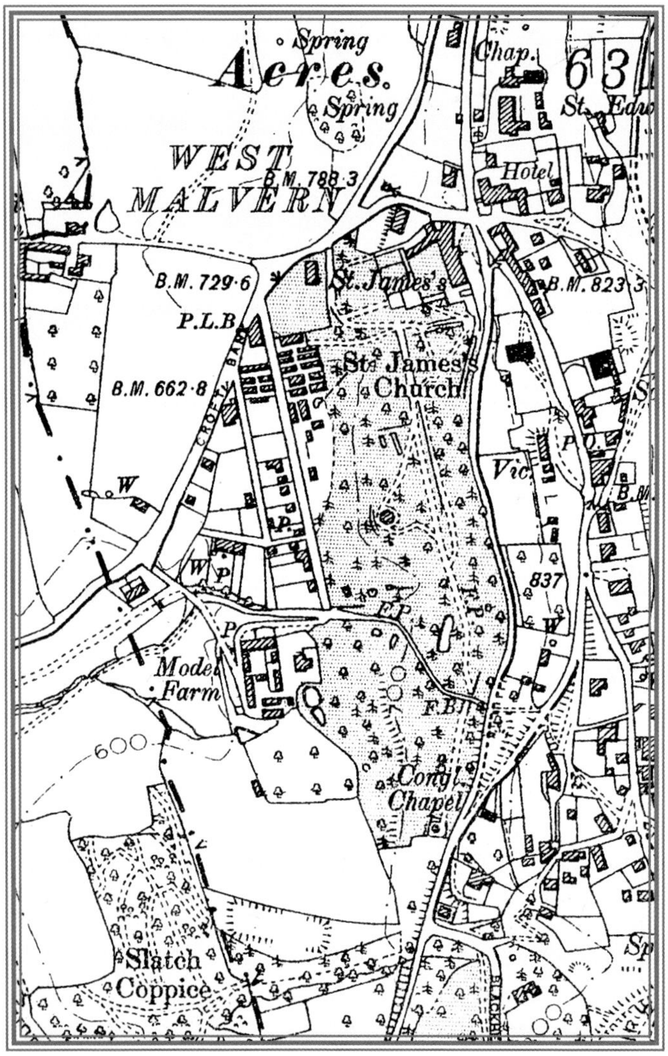

The original house was built circa 1850 and "spectacularly enlarged by the Dowager Lady Howard de Walden" (Pevsner, p. 285) who acquired the property in 1890. The terraced gardens were supported by 70 gardeners (Smith, p. 231). Model cottages were built for the workers as well as a model farm. Lady Howard de Walden created further walks on the adjoining Malvern Hills. The house was leased as a School in 1899 and purchased in 1902, continuing as a School until 2010. The 1905 OS 6 inch shows the grounds in some detail as a park set between Croft Bank and West Malvern Roads.

The mansion with its grounds stretching north/south is set on a magnificent site on the west edge of the Malverns. Most of the late-19th century terracing and some garden buildings (Summer House, Pools, Bridges) survive and the plantings have now produced many mature trees of great variety, e.g. cedar, yew, holly, Wellingtonia, cypress, pine and fir. The gazebo on the upper terrace to the mansion has been converted into a Chapel. The Chief's Shelter of 1928 (**Plate 25**) takes its name from its use by Baden-Powell, the founder of the Scout Movement, whose daughters were at the School. Yew hedges define principal paths and some areas which were given over to particular shrubs etc. There are topiary yews and shrubs have been used to create compartments or smaller spaces, rose garden etc. The terraces are built of rusticated stone. The property is now the Regents Theological College.

J. Patton, "October Visit" (St .James and the Abbey School), *HWGT, Newsletter*, 20, Winter 2002.

B. Smith, *A History of Malvern*. 1978.

N. Pevsner, *Worcestershire,* 1968.

West Malvern, Royal Well Spa/Royal Spa Lodge

HER Ref: WSM71700. Postcode: WR14 3HB.

The Spa with Baths and Pleasure Grounds was built in 1883 and adjoined the Spa Hall which housed a permanent exhibition. This closed in 1895 and was demolished circa 1940 (Smith, p. 211). It lost out to the Assembly Rooms built in 1888. Royal Spa Lodge, on West Malvern Road, is marked by a pillared entrance to the road and some ruins in its garden. The rest of the site is filled with 20th century housing.

B. Smith, *A History of Malvern,* 1978.

Mere Hall

Parish: Hanbury

HER Ref: WSM28842.

Grid Ref: SO 952 618. Postcode: WR9 7EE.

O.S. 6" Map No: 29NE.

Date of Map: 1884, with extent of park & gardens shaded as 1880s OS.

Images taken from *Victoria County History* Vol. 3, 1913, (VCH).

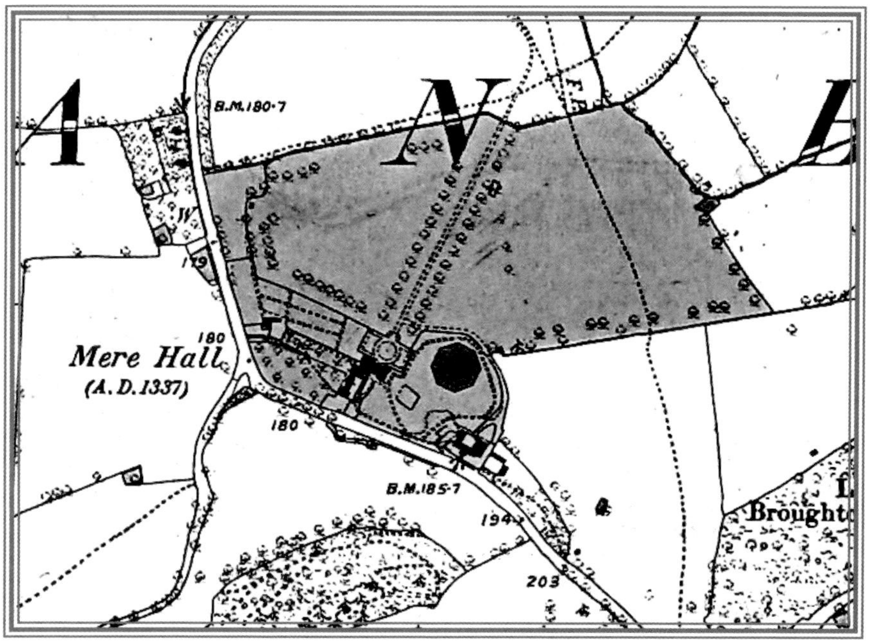

The house goes back to the mid-16th century but received significant alterations and additions in each of the next 3 centuries, e.g. in 1828 by Habershon (BoE, p. 351). The walls, gates, piers and pavilions surrounding the forecourt are dated circa 1700: "The layout of the forecourt is an interesting example of the Queen Anne period" (VCH, 1913). The gates themselves are 18th century and said to have come from nearby Hanbury Hall. The VCH mentions that "The fine avenue of trees (elms) which leads up to the entrance is no longer used for the drive" (3, p. 373). This avenue was old by 1853 (Burke) and is described as ancient by Niven in 1873. There is a large fishpond near the house. Significant renovations have been made to the pavilioned, entrance forecourt in recent years. Habershon described Mere in 1836 as "beautifully situated at the termination of an avenue; and has a large and lofty hill in the rear, covered with wood, which forms a handsome and picturesque background."

The gardens are illustrated in two bird's eye views on Maps 3 & 4 of 1731/3 in the *Book of Maps* of the Vernon estates surveyed by the Doughartys (CRO 7335/154). These show a walled court on the south (Broughton) side with a small gate. A simple garden was laid out to the west. The front (north) court with its pavilions at the north-west and north-east corners has handsome piers with gates in the centre; gates and an ironwork screen are situated at the end of the long, wide avenue going north.

The house is marked as a residence on Cary's 1805 map as Mere Green with a lodge to the south-east.

The grounds are first described as a park on a Parliamentary Constituency map of circa 1840 and later on the first two editions of the OS 6 inch in 1883 and 1905 and on Bartholomew 1906. *Country Life* describes the broad sweep of the park and the truly splendid trees in an illustrated article of 1908 (VIII, p. 808).

However, there was a deer park here at a much earlier date as farm and buildings names suggest: Keepers Lodge (Broughton Green); Little Lodge Farmhouse; Park Farm, the last two immediately east of the Hall. Madam's Hill immediately south of the Hall might indicate some park or garden feature.

The main (north) avenue to the house has been replanted with poplar and more recently limes have been interleaved. This avenue was originally elm. There are the remains of ridge and furrow in the field north-east of the house; it is in this direction that some mature oaks create the most park-like atmosphere in the old park areas today.

A. Brooks & N. Pevsner, *Worcestershire,* 2007 (BoE).
Victoria County History, Vol. 3, 1913 (VCH).
Country Life, VIII, 1908.
J. B. Burke, *A Visitation of Seats of Great Britain,* Vol. 2, 1853.
W. Niven, *Illustrations of Old Worcestershire Houses,* 1873.

Middle Hill

Parish: Broadway

HER Ref: WSM29021.
Grid Ref: SP 110 353.
Postcode: WR12 7LA.
O.S. 6" Map No. 57NW/SW.
Date of Map: 1883.

..........continued from previous page

J. P. Neale gives a full description of the history of Middle Hill (*Seats*, 1824): "The House is built on a slope of the Cotswolds ... As a proof of the extensive prospect afforded, thirteen counties are visible from a tower (Broadway Tower) on this estate." Neale goes through the change of ownership from William Taylor's 1724 house; "Four avenues of ash-trees were planted by him of which only one is left ... On the principal eminences adjoining, clumps of fir- trees were planted, which still exist."

Nash (Vol. 1, 1781, p. 144): "Mr. Savage is building a very handsome house on his estate at Middle Hill". Neale says that Thomas Phillips (ob. 1818) "added considerably to the estate by various purchases, and adorned the sloping hills with numerous plantations." The resulting landscape is perhaps recorded with artistic licence in oil by John Glover in 1825 (exhibited at the London, Society of Artists) characteristic of "quintessentially English parks bathed always in an eternal English summer" (Harris, op. cit., pp. 344-5).

The circa 1800 landscape improvements can be checked on a "Plan of an Estate in the Parish of Broadway and County of Worcester" (CRO 1069). Several features of this map can be followed to a printed estate map by Gordon M. Hills of 1872 (CRO 3278/4) and to the first OS 6 inch of 1883, and even to the 1990 OS Pathfinder. The circa 1800 manuscript map records a belt of trees between Middle Hill and Dornap enclosing the Stables. These were subsequently demolished and replaced with single storey cottages. The plantation along Coneygree Lane was then a drive to St. Edburga's Church and Broadway Court. On the south side the planting led to Kite's Nest and to the northern tip of Dulverton Wood. The road from the church to Snowshill then had a lower status and the footpath or drive was an avenue. The drive from Middle Hill to "The Rookery" was also an avenue, still strongly marked in 1872 and less obviously in the OS 6 inch but now retained with ornamental conifers.

There was no garden or elaborate grounds round the mansion shown in Neale's 1824 engraved view and the house was set directly into the landscape, open only on one side and closely shrouded by trees on the other three. Drawings in the Prattinton Collection (Soc. of Antiquaries, London, 965 – information from Stephen Price) support this but add an entrance around a small circular lawn to the front door, all very modest.

Works to the main house and its subsidiary buildings were carried out in the 1870s and 1880s as well as in the 1980s. The Octagon, a substantial building immediately north-east of the mansion has an inscribed date of 1886 (BoE, op. cit., p. 180). Some work on the grounds was done for Miss L M. Hingley in 1921 by Milner and White. The house has terraces on three sides and a detached garden building on the south-east side where a new formal garden has been created.

The landscape to the south and west is magnificent and well wooded with fine mature trees and open clumps. The beech hangers are a particularly dominant feature of the landscape, while the ornamental cedars planted below the house add a strongly contrasting element.

This has been a changing landscape due to the extent and nature of sequential new woodland planting throughout the last three centuries.

A. Brooks & N. Pevsner, *Worcestershire,* 2007 (BoE).
J. P. Neale, *Views of Seats of the Nobility and Gentry,* 1824.
J. Harris, *The Artist and the Country House,* 1985.

ABOVE: south-east view of the house taken in 1951. Courtesy of Birmingham Post.
LEFT: anon, View of Middle Hill from south-east, watercolour, circa 1820, from Society of Antiquaries of London, Prattinton Collection.

Monks

Parish: Chaddesley Corbett

HER Ref: WSM28922.

Grid Ref: SO 883 757. Postcode: DY10 4NA.

O.S. 6" Map No: 15NW.

Date of Map: 1883, with deduced extent of park & garden shaded (not shaded on 1905 OS).

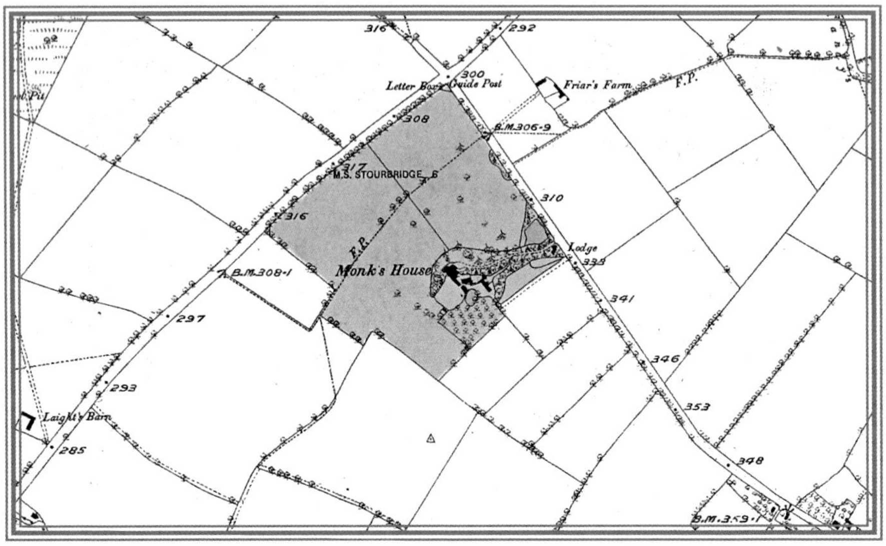

The property takes its name from Harvington or Monks Common (1745/6 estate map - CRO 844).
Grounds are shown on mid-19th century maps and it is upgraded to a park on the 1st edition of the OS 6 inch in 1882 which marks a lodge and pools.
Today, it is still a private residence with a well maintained garden separated from its park by a ha-ha. There are a number of fine parkland trees.

Moor Hall

Parish: Stourport-on-Severn

HER Ref: WSM28923. Grid Ref: SO 805 715. Postcode: DY13 8SQ.

O.S. 6" Map No: 14SW. Date of Map: 1888, with extent of park & gardens shaded as 1905 OS.

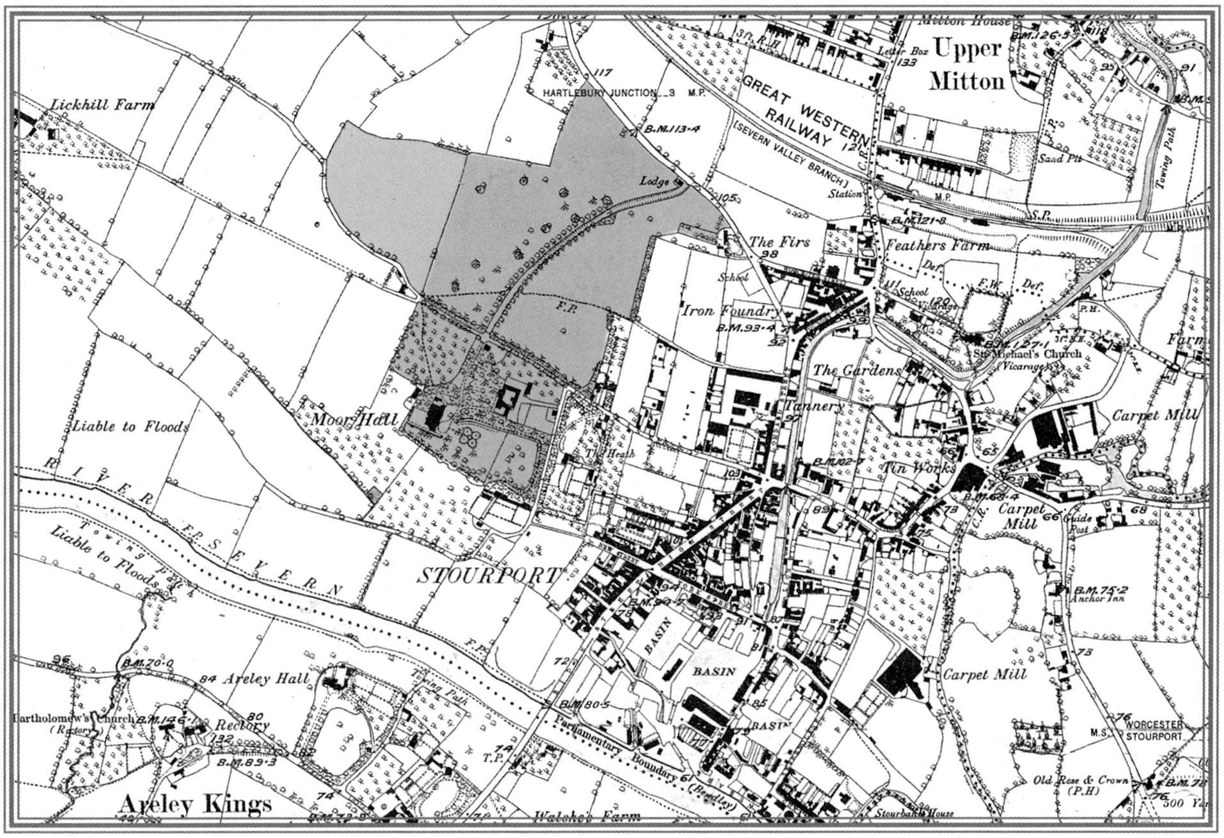

Moor Hall is called Moor Hill by Paterson in 1829 and shown with grounds on the first OS one inch in 1828. As a mansion it had been mentioned in the *Cambrian Guide* of 1808. A sale in 1844 described the property of 105 acres: "a mansion of importance, seated on an eminence in park-like grounds" (Reeves). The house, which has been demolished, was set on a raised terrace on the west and south sides and sported a splendid, attached Conservatory.

The park on the first OS 6 inch of 1882 relates to fields immediately next to the main avenue drive with lodges between the Lickhill and Bewdley roads as developed by John Brinton who acquired the property in 1871. "He erected 3 pairs of ornamental iron gates" (Reeves). When the property was put up for sale in 1917, it was advertised as having gardens, lawns and grounds inexpensive to maintain with a walled kitchen garden of an acre and a vegetable garden of similar size. The house was described as set on high ground surrounded by woods (CRO 5240/6). Of the 28 acres which made up the estate in 1917, 2 fields of the park to the north/north-east of the Lickhill Road were purchased circa 1924 by Stourport as its Memorial Park.

Jean Reeves, "Moor Hall", *Stourport –on–Severn Civic Society Newsletter,* 13. 6. 1994.

D. Whitehead, "The Memorial Park, Lickhill Road, Stourport", *HWGT Newsletter,* 8, Winter 1996/7.

Moor Hall, sale particulars, 1917. © WAAS 5240/6.

The Nash

Parish: Kempsey

HER Ref: WSM29000.

Grid Ref: SO 859 474. Postcode: WR5 3PB.

O.S. 6" Map No: 40NE.

Date of Map: 1884, with deduced extent of park & gardens shaded (not shaded on 1905 OS).

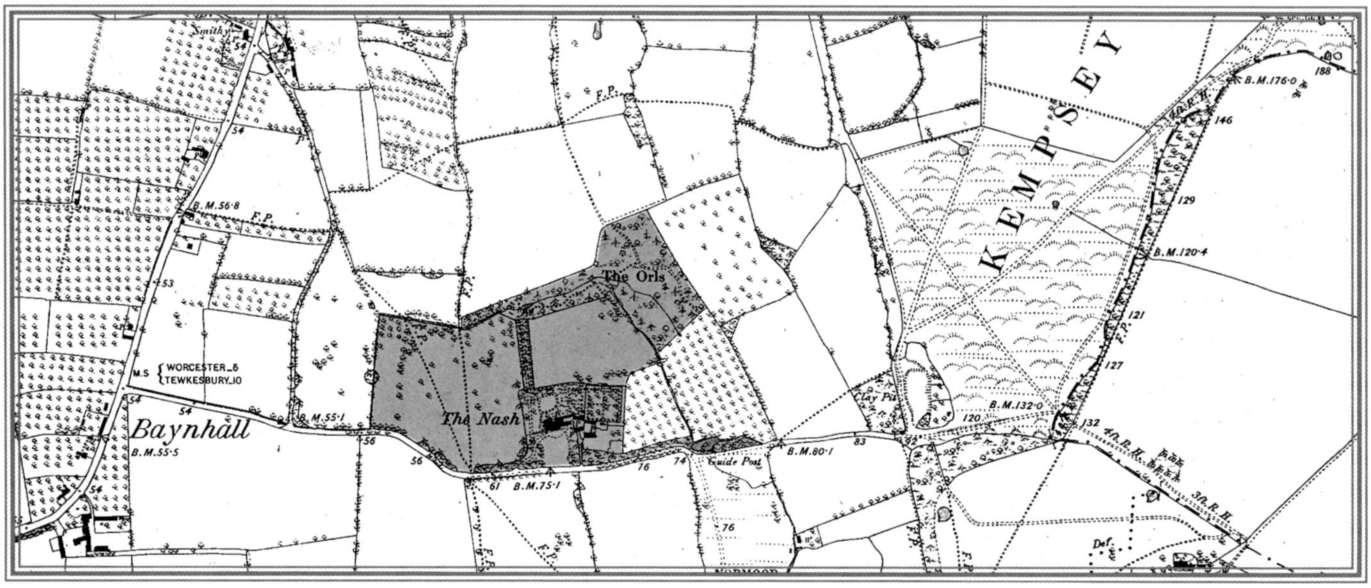

The house of circa 1600 (VCH – as 3 independent half-timbered blocks) had significant works done to it in 1831 and circa 1900. It appears as a residence on Cary's map of 1805. The planting of the fields to the west of the house, an avenue of trees up to the drives in the wood (The Orls or Owls Wood) supports the 1923 sale particulars (WAAS 5240/7) re. "magnificent old grounds" of 5 acres and a small park of 17 acres, walled kitchen gardens, spreading lawns etc. The park with mature trees survives to the west of the house and is crossed by public footpaths. The walled garden appears to be in good condition, adjacent to the modern vineyard.

Victoria County History, Vol. 3, 1913 (VCH).

ABOVE: The Nash, image taken from *Victoria County History* Vol. 3, 1913, (VCH).
BELOW: photograph taken 1974, WAAS, Kempsey 51140.

Nash's Plantations/Abbotswood

Parish: Drakes Broughton & Wadborough with Pirton

HER Ref: WSM71783.

Grid Ref: SO 886 492.

Title page from T. R. Nash, *Collections for the History of Worcestershire*, Vols. II, 1782.

The title page of Vol. 2 of Nash's *History of Worcestershire* (1782), similarly used by Mowl (2006), has an engraving of some speculative planting laid out by his elder brother from whom he inherited considerable property in Worcestershire. Whitehead's researches into Nash's pocket books has revealed that Nash began to build a Hermitage in the centre of Abbot's Wood (as it was also known) in 1766; the wood covered 200 acres and he estimated contained 15,000 trees. The wood was permeated with drives; Whitehead sees this as "Nash's foray into landscape design". Abbot's Wood is probably the same as that located between Norton and Pirton on Nash's County Map in Vol. 1 (1781). If so, this is confirmed by the first edition of the 6 inch OS as east of Stonehall Common. The *Beauties* in 1814 (p. 359) describes "a range of woodlands, the principal of which is near to Wadborough, and is now called Nash's Plantations, but formerly Abbots Wood ... 30,000 good timber trees disposed in regular rides and walks."

D. Whitehead, "Patron and Architect: the Revd. Treadway Nash, Bevere and the Career of Anthony Keck", *Trans. Worcs. Archaeol. Soc.*, 3rd Series, 24, 2014, pp. 225-248.

T. R. Nash, *Collections for the History of Worcestershire*, Vols. I & II, 1781-2.

T. Mowl, *Historic Gardens of Worcestershire*, 2006.

Beauties of England and Wales, Vol. XV, 1814.

Newnham Court

Parish: Knighton on Teme

HER Ref: WSM09921.

Grid Ref: SO 643 688. Postcode: WR15 8JF.

O.S. 6" Map No: 19NE.

Date of Map: 1884, with extent of park & gardens shaded as 1905 OS.

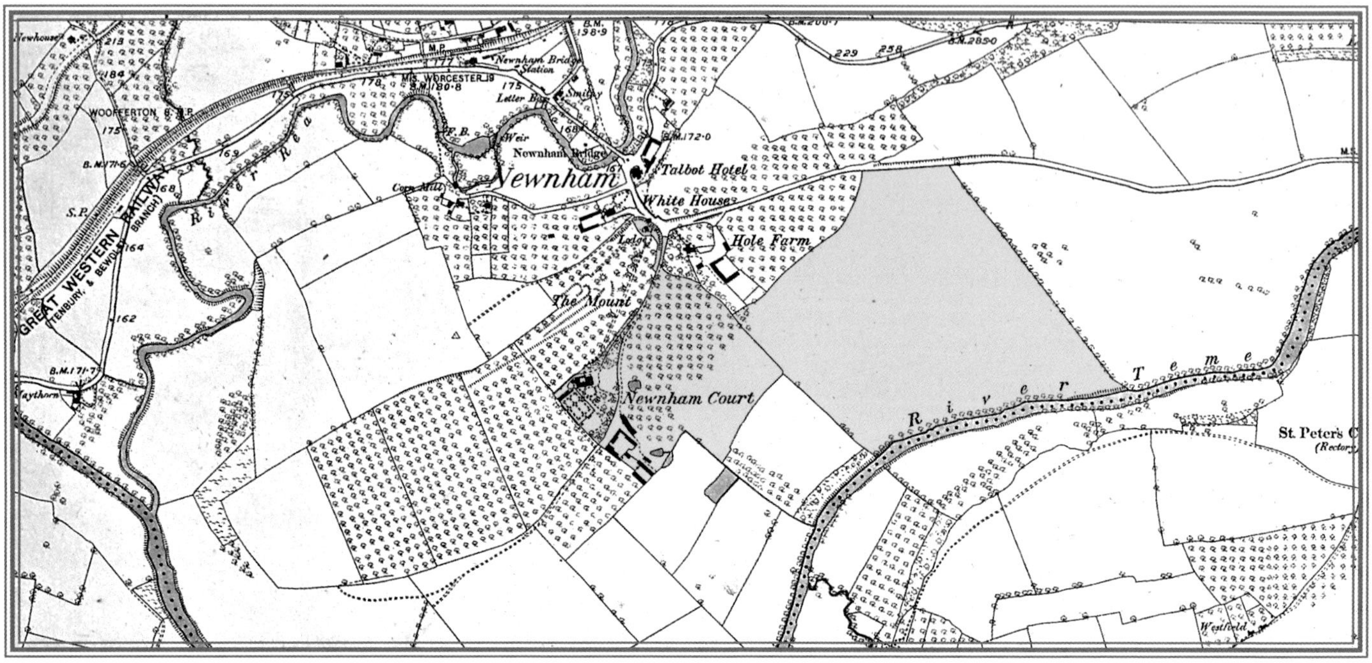

The house dates from the 1820s and 1830s (BoE). Grounds rather than a park are shown on the 1828 OS one inch. Today, there are magnificent cedars which were probably planted by then or earlier. The house is noticed in 1788 (Tunnicliff) and 1814 *(Beauties)*. The walled garden was revived along old lines in the 1990s.

A. Brooks & N. Pevsner, *Worcestershire,* 2007 (BoE).
Beauties of England and Wales, Vol. XV, 1814.
W. Tunnicliff, *A Survey of the County of Worcester,* 1788.

The Noak

Parish: Martley

HER Ref: WSM28841.

Grid Ref: SO 751 604. Postcode: WR6 6PD.

O.S. 6" Map No: 27NE.

Date of Map: 1884, with extent of park & gardens shaded as 1905 OS.

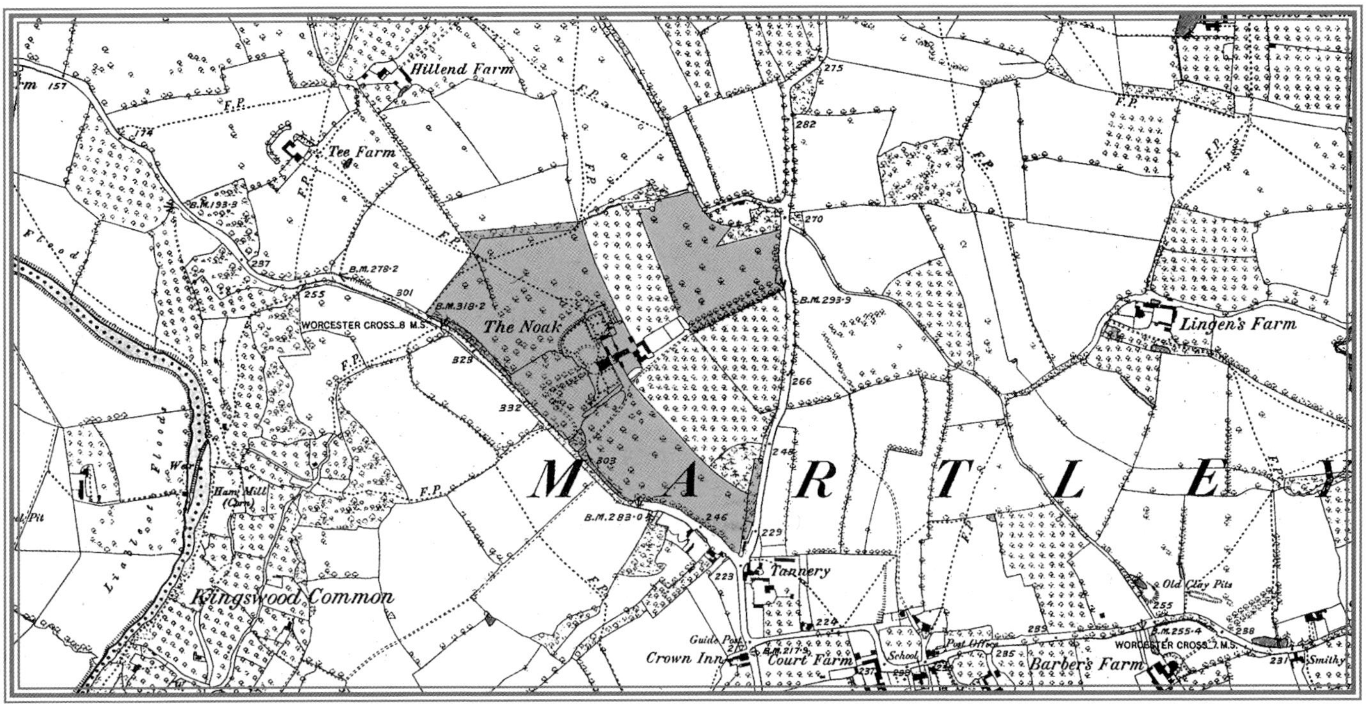

The house is of 17th and mid-19th century date and was the principal residence of the Nash family until the 19th century. Before that, according to Francis Ingram in 1795 (CRO 438/xxviii), the Noak had belonged to the Ingrams from the Reign of Elizabeth I. It is first noticed in map form on a very rough map of 1730 related to Cockshoot Orchard Farm (CRO 6134/44). A Survey of 1780 by John Perkins records an avenue between the mansion and the road (CRO 4935/xxxv). Nash as county historian, includes the house on his 1781 map and it is shown with grounds on printed maps in the first half of the 19th century. Niven selected the house as one of his venerable, county mansions in 1873.

Its park is defined on the OS 6 inch in 1883 with pools and avenues, some of which survive. There was a short avenue south-west towards the Teme, which appears to have been re-planted, and another (now a farm drive) north-east to the Great Witley road. The lawn linking house and kitchen garden is embanked towards the park. Noak Farm lies to the west on the other side of the River Teme, a significant distance away. Footpaths cross the area of former park which is now devoid of trees.

W. Niven, *Illustrations of Old Worcestershire Houses,* 1873.
T. R. Nash, *Collections for the History of Worcestershire,* Vol I, 1781.

The Noak from the north-east, taken from *Victoria County History,* Vol. 4, 1924, (VCH).

Norgrove Court

Parish: Feckenham

HER Ref: WSM29006/50185.

Grid Ref: SP 007 654. Postcode: B97 5UH.

O.S. 6" Map No. 23SW.

Date of Map: 1884, with deduced extent of park & gardens shaded (not shaded on 1905 OS).

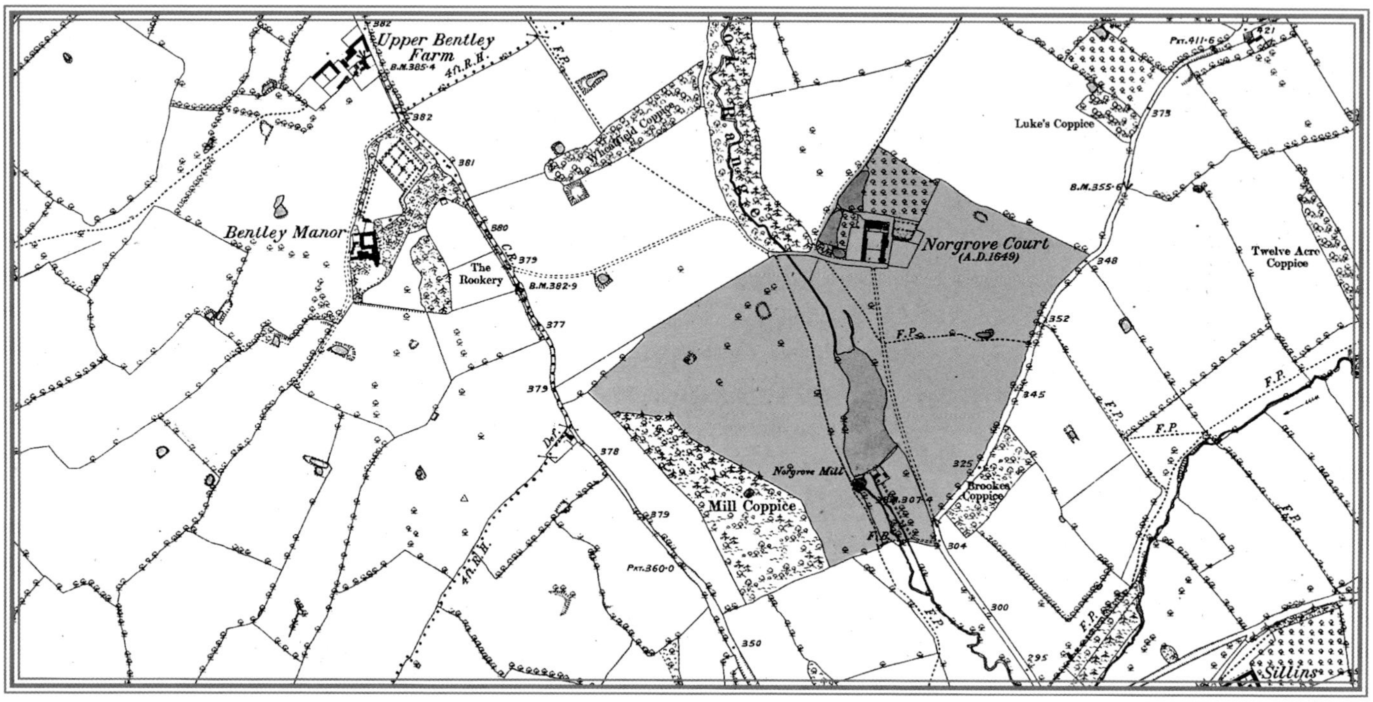

Norgrove Court is a substantial 17th century house with mid-19th and late-20th century work.

The main part of the house is associated with William Cookes, High Sheriff of Worcestershire in 1651 who was developing an earlier building. Any garden works that Cookes may have carried out in association with his mansion, would therefore have been contemporary in Worcestershire terms with Judge Lechmere's terraced gardens at Severn End.

Two blocked first-floor windows once gave onto staircases leading down into a garden and, it may be presumed, one of some ambition although no part of this survives (*Country Life*, 1994, p. 4558). The 1905 OS 6 inch shows a boathouse on the Mill Pond (regarded by Whitehead, p. 5, as part of the formal, 17th century gardens) between the house and Norgrove Mill; the brook runs north/south along the west side of the property. There is an orchard of fruit trees to the rear of the mansion.

The house has been restored in recent years and the 3 lakes shown on the 1883 OS 6 inch have been recovered with some other lost parts of the grounds. These restorations were illustrated by Cornforth in 1984. The park, however is much reduced and mainly put to arable.

J. Cornforth, Norgrove Court, Worcestershire, *Country Life*, 27. 12. 1984.

Country Life, CLXXVI, 1994.

D. Whitehead, *"Artist in Paradise"*: Exhibition at Hanbury Hall, HWGT, 1997.

Norgrove Court, south front by Laurence Davies from *Victoria County History* Vol. 3, 1913, (VCH).

Norton Hall

Parish: Norton Juxta Kempsey

HER Ref: WSM28840.

Grid Ref: SO 889 251. Postcode: WR5 2QU.

O.S. 6" Map No: 34SW.

Date of Map: 1884, with extent of park & gardens shaded as 1905 OS.

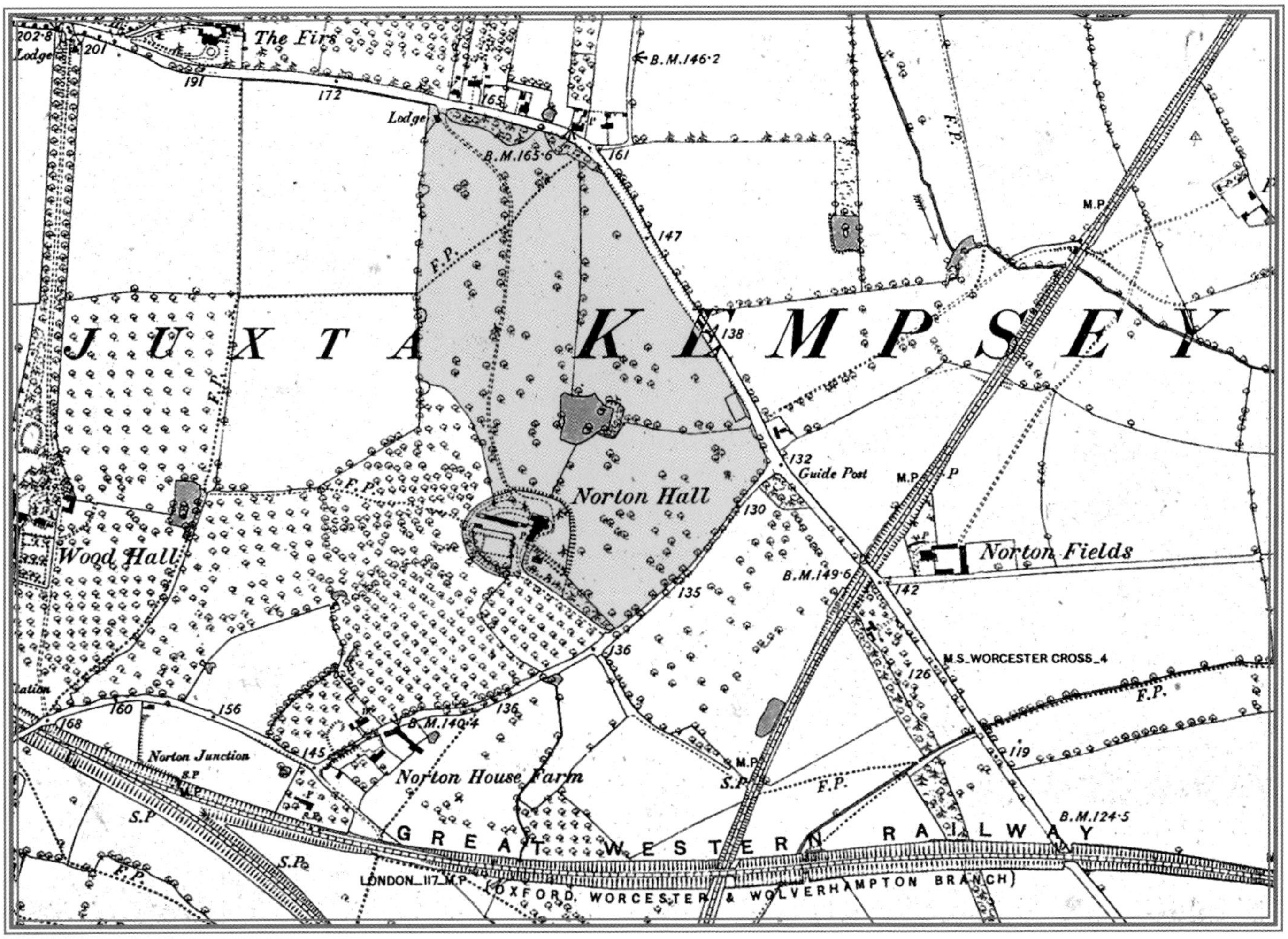

This is shown as a small park in the 1st edition of the OS 6 inch (1883) when it had a lodge and a fishpond. The immediate circle of grounds round the house is surrounded by a ha-ha. The drive is to the lodge on the Pershore road. The 1916 sale catalogue (CRO 5240/6) has photographs illustrating the park (36 acres), the south terrace with formal laid out lawns and beds, the rose garden and the house with a conservatory.

The house is now a residential care home with most of the gardens lost to modern development. The park remains as agricultural land and retains a park-like character with its surviving fish pond and scattered trees. The original access from the northern Worcester-Pershore Road has been lost to a modern access off Woodbury Lane to the south.

Norton Park

Parish: Bredon, Bredon's Norton & Westmancote

HER Ref: WSM28839. Grid Ref: SO 936 391. Postcode: GL20 5HA.

O.S. 6" Map No: 48SE.

Date of Map: 1883, with extent of park & gardens shaded as 1905 OS.

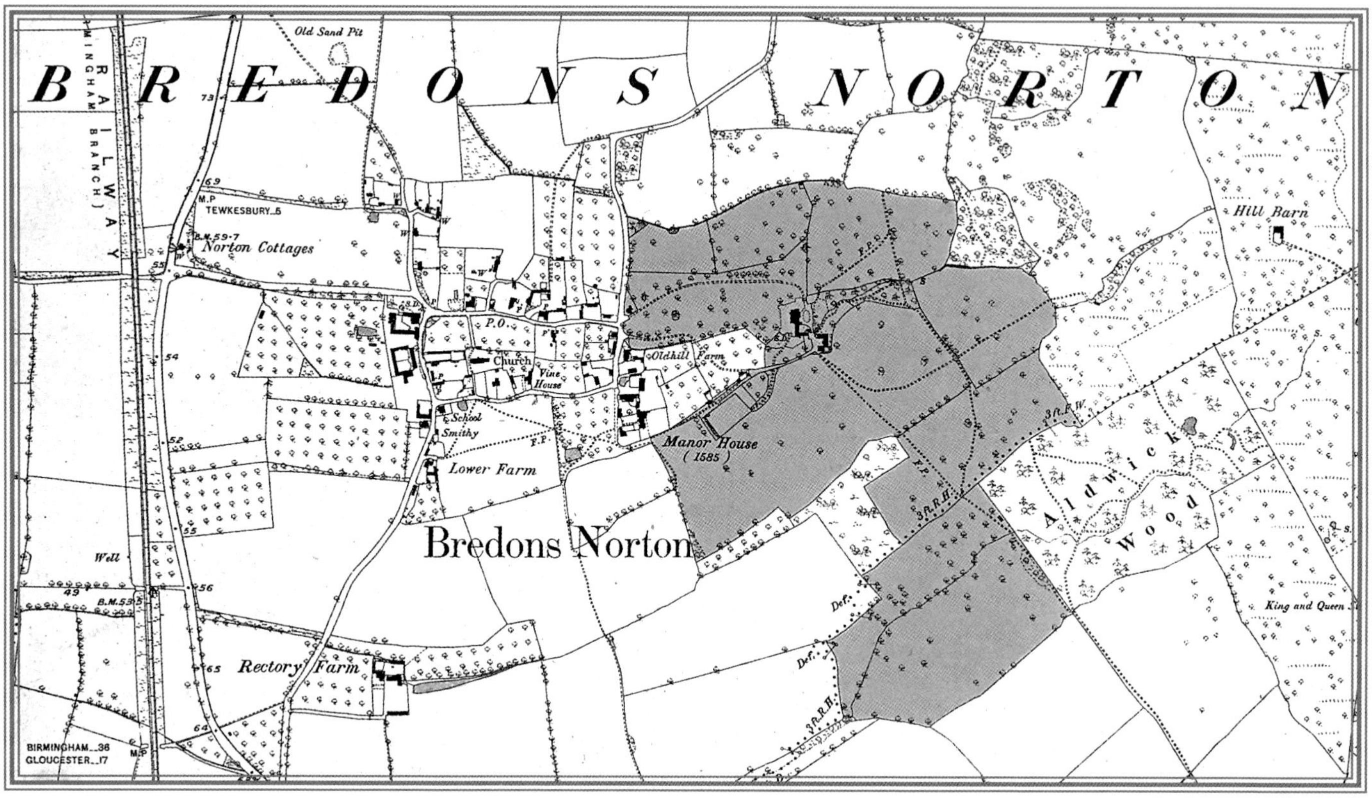

The house was finished for the Misses Martin in 1839; the lodge is dated 1865. The park is shown on the 2nd edition of the OS 6 inch (1903) as Norton Court when *Country Life* found "the gardens and grounds (to be) full of English loveliness" and illustrated them profusely. There was a main terrace on the west side as developed by Mrs Woodhull Martin in 1902 and an "extraordinary variety of the trees and shrubs near the house and the beds are radiant all the summer long". Apparently the secluded quiet suggested to Mrs Martin's guests the alternative name of "Brainrest"! Drives extended the grounds into Aldwick Wood on the south-east corner of the park. The woodland paths were named after the poets Tennyson, Longfellow and Swinburne. Mature trees and a few clumps of oaks and beeches today give the house a park-like setting on all sides. The gardens were much reduced 20 years ago and the planting also greatly reduced. The walled garden survives and has been put down to grass.

Norton Park, circa 1900. Private collection.

"Norton Park, Worcestershire", *Country Life*, XI, 1902, p. 776.

Oakhampton Manor

Parish: Astley & Dunley

HER Ref: WSM28838.

Grid Ref: SO 791 691. Postcode: DY13 0TZ.

O.S. 6" Map No: 21NW.

Date of Map: 1885, with extent of park & gardens shaded as 1905 OS.

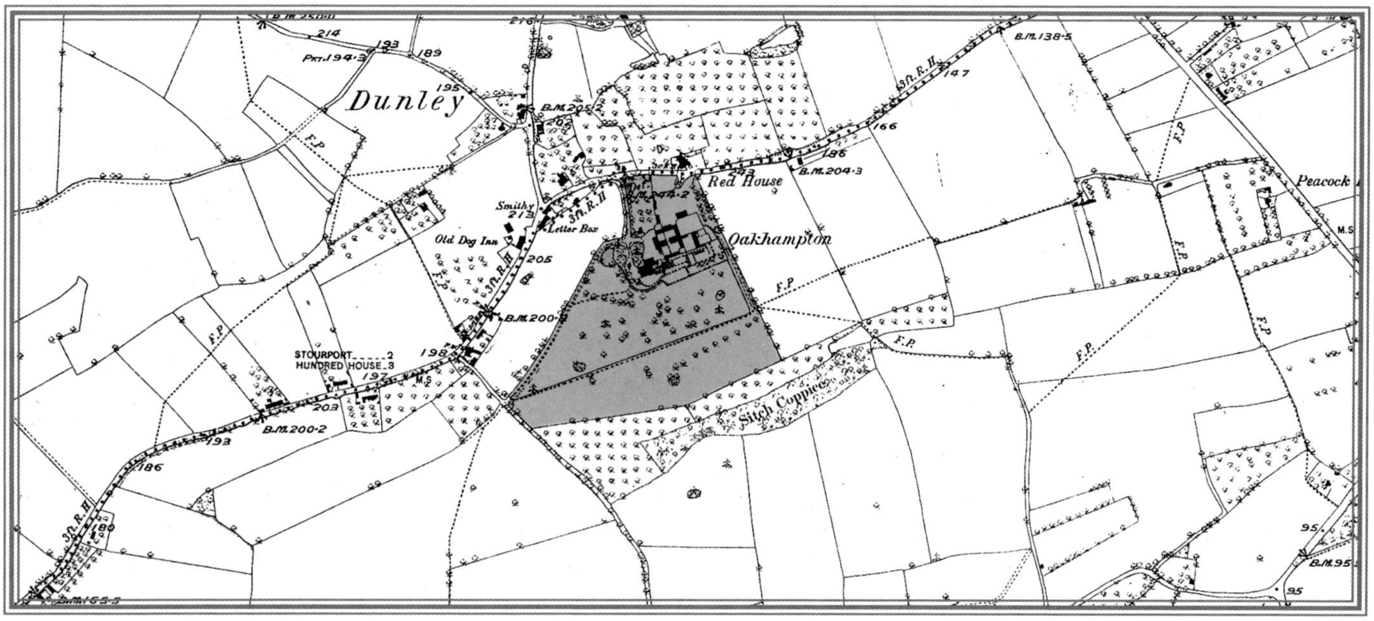

The House, as Oakhampton is described by the BoE (p. 116) as early-19th century, sub-italianate, unsubtly enlarged in similar style in the later-19th century. According to *Country Life,* the house was modernised in the 1840s and again in 1883 by J. P. St. Aubyn. While the owner was away fighting in the Boer War, his wife built a Roman Catholic Chapel and Priest's House which the husband demolished on his return! The house is given a small park on the 1904 edition of the OS.

The property, when sold in 2010, was described as having "65 acres of formal gardens, a vinery from the late-1800s and an arboretum of 27 acres of wooded parkland" (Churchill). A few parkland trees still stand.

P. Churchill, *Country Life,* 18. 10. 2010, p. 74.
A. Brooks & N. Pevsner, *Worcestershire,* 2007 (BoE).

Ombersley Court

Parish: Ombersley & Doverdale

HER Ref: WSM12433. Grid Ref: SO 842 634. Postcode: WR9 0HH.

O.S. 6" Map No: 21SE, 28NE.

Date of Map: 1888, 1883, with extent of park & gardens shaded as H. E. Register.

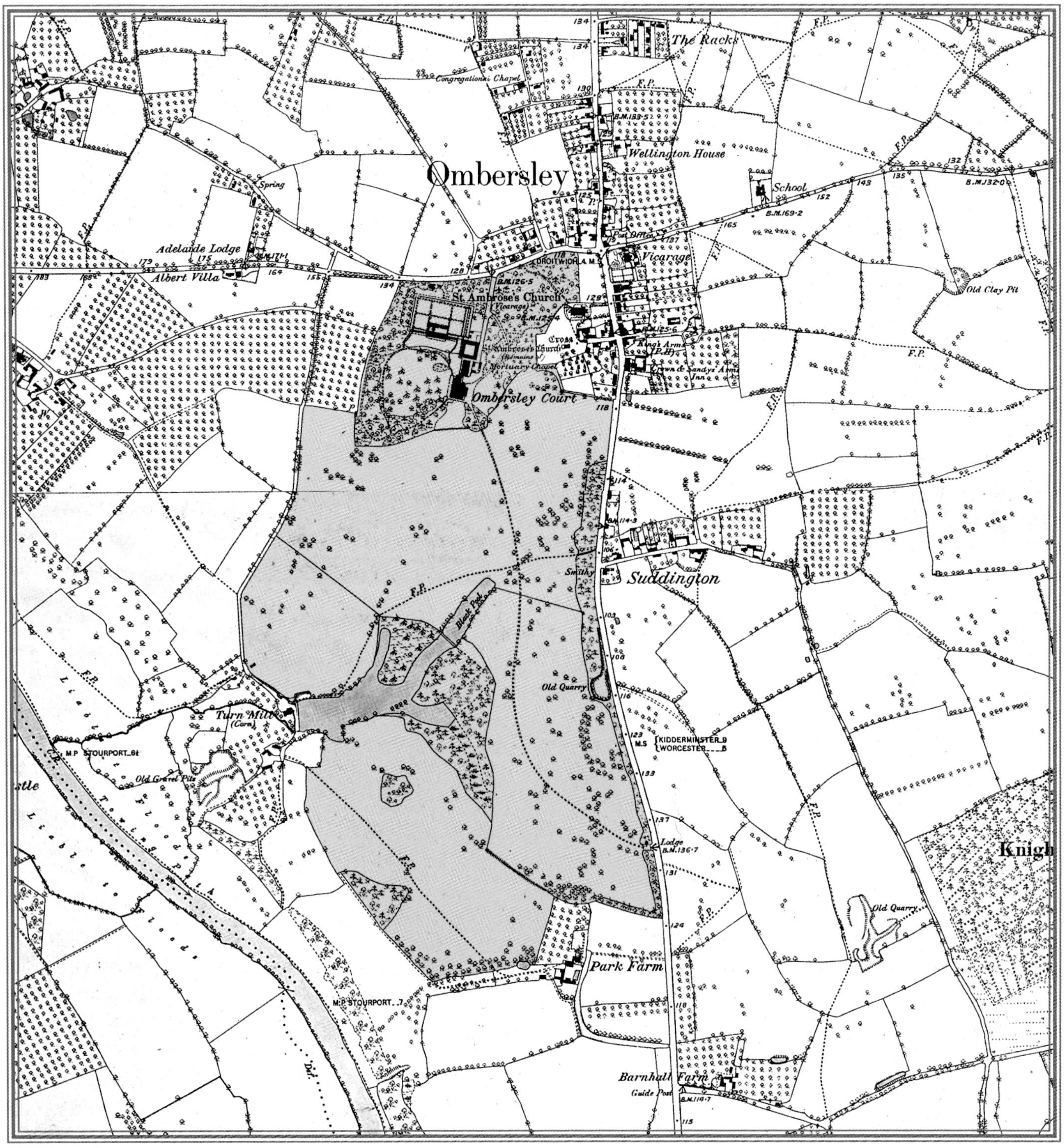

..........continued from previous page

Included within Historic England's Register of Historic Parks and Gardens of special historic interest in England.

The manor of Ombersley belonged to the Abbey of Evesham before the Dissolution of the Monasteries and the *Valor Ecclesiasticus*, made for Henry VIII, showed it to be by far the abbey's most valuable asset. It was acquired for the Sandys family by Sir Samuel Sandys, eldest son of Bishop Sandys of Worcester, later Archbishop of York. The deer park was within the Wyre Forest before this was effectively disforested in 1229. Licence to impark 300 acres was granted in 1376 (VCH, 3, 1913, pp. 461-464). Field names in the Inclosure awards (D. Guyatt, Ombersley Survey, 1995) would refer to this park: Pale Coat; Pale Piece; Park and Farm Field. These are all north-west of Ombersley Court and Park, towards Boreley House and beyond Uphampton. An Extract of Fines from the Manorial Court (CRO 3972/9) provides much information about the park/warren between Edward I and James I (i.e. circa 1300 – 1600). In the time of Edward III, punishments were handed out for killing hares and rabbits and any dog had to carry a weighty clog "that he may not hunt in the Lord's Park or Warren". The Vicar of Holt killed a hare in the reign of Richard II! A licence for a warren of conies was sought as late as 1751 (WAAS 7335) and a Coney Green is marked on a rough map of 1801 on the west side of the mansion at which time the "Parke" near Sinton Pool lies south in the centre of the modern park area.

Ombersley's later park does not appear on printed maps until 1830 (Murray) but can be defined as the triangle of land between the Holt road (before its early-19th century replacement) and a thin strip of planting parallel with the Severn and Bournes Dingle where the river and the A449 meet at the south end. Maps do not suggest any particular park planting and the principal features are the large pools connecting back to the river. Descriptions of the park are vague, e.g. Cooke circa 1801 "a handsome building well situated in a well wooded park". The Revd. William Gilpin wrote of "the sweet groves of Ombersley" in 1809 (p. 202). An evaluation of the park before any improvements were carried out was given by John Britton in his *Beauties of England and Wales* in 1814: "In the midst of extensive but very flat grounds, except towards the river where they are picturesque, being well wooded, stands the seat of the Marchioness of Downshire." (Roelofsz, op. cit., p. 141).

The Park as defined by the 1905 OS is marked by a trackway, today a footpath, that starts on the Holt road and then runs north/south, strongly marked for much of its length by mature trees, principally Turkey oaks (*Quercus cerris*). The track continues and descends to the foot of the dam across the Fish Pond. There are impressive sandstone rocks by the track where stone may have been quarried and also at the higher level of the dam where it outflows steeply down to the Turn Mill and eventually to the River Severn. Footpaths come together at this point which is a natural, picturesque moment. One footpath then continues towards the fringe of trees that skirts the River Severn which was perhaps the earlier boundary of the park, with open grassland between that and the 1905 park boundary. Roelofsz (op. cit. p. 27) suggests that this corn mill known as the Trypole Mill may have had medieval origins and Whitehead cites a reference to it in 1406 (op. cit.).

The 1905 OS extends the park east of the Worcester/Ombersley Road with the remains of a widely spaced avenue of trees shown on the much earlier 1772 Taylor map and indicated in the 1782 illustration in Nash's *Worcestershire* (op. cit.). This park area is now truncated by the A449 and the remaining part, now treeless, is the Ombersley Cricket Club ground. That the park stretched across the road, is still suggested by surviving stone walls on either side.

V. Green, *Ombersley Court*, mezzotint from T. R. Nash, *Collections for the History of Worcestershire,* Vol II, 1782.

The mansion (Grade 1) by Francis Smith of Warwick dates from 1724-1732 and was remodelled in 1812 – 1814 by John Webb of Lichfield. The only ancillary building from the 18th century is the later-18th century ice house situated in the south-west corner of the plantings on the west side of the mansion (restored in the 1980s). Other buildings such as a game larder, stables, walls, gate piers and gates are from the Webb period, except for the Sinton Lodge and its gates which date from circa 1830. John Nash was consulted and produced drawings (3) for Ombersley in 1808, the year of a visit from the Prince Regent, but nothing came of them (Roelofsz, op. cit., pls. 37, a,b,c). Immediately afterwards, John Webb was invited "to reshape the grounds incorporating trees and forming a woodland glade or arboretum around the Court and its

..........continued from previous page

adjacent Park" (Roeloftsz, op. cit., p. 134). A plan by James Wadmore junior made in 1811 (Sandys Archive; Roelofsz, op. cit., p. 130) shows the two pavilions to the entrance front already demolished and other new buildings such as the dining-room wing and the portico to the entrance front already built. Webb's arrangement of the pleasure grounds are recorded by a survey by Albert R. Jackson, Surveyor of Gt. Malvern, based on the Inclosure Award of 1827 (CRO 3962/40). Out of a total of 6,962 acres surveyed, the Marchioness of Downshire was owner occupier of 414 acres: Mansion, Stabling, Outbuildings and Lawn amounted to 16 acres. In hand were further plantations, a 15 acre grove, the Big Wood of 61 acres and the Bournes Dingle of 21 acres.

The extension of the park area south of Park Farm is attributed by David Whitehead (op. cit.) to Webb who no doubt added his own favourite variations of tree planting to the enlarged park, much of which survives.

Characteristic of Webb, may be single trees or short lines of trees planted in preference to clumps, and the in-planting to the shrubberies. The principal landscape feature according to Wadmore and Jackson, was a lake with 3 fingers or inlets, still shown at its full extent on the 1884 OS but which had apparently shrunk back by the 1905 edition to the Fish Pond at the south-west end and the Black Pool at the north-east end, with everything in between, including the boat house site, silted up and, as today, partly filled with reed beds. This water was not visible from the mansion and therefore not part of a typical landscape park; views towards the mansion and the church have to be taken from above the Fish Pond rather than from the mansion towards the lake. Both Fish Pond and Black Pool have been further reduced since 1905 and the Black Pool hardly now exists. The 1905 OS suggests that further pools lay beyond Black Pool closer to the village. Jackson in 1827 shows more water than Wadmore in 1811 agreeing with the OS. Wadmore and the OS both show a small causeway across the Black Pool.

Whitehead's analysis (op. cit.) relates the present landscape to the Wadmore Map of 1811 which perhaps anticipated rather than recorded the status quo. How much the 18th century contributed to the landscape as it is today or as

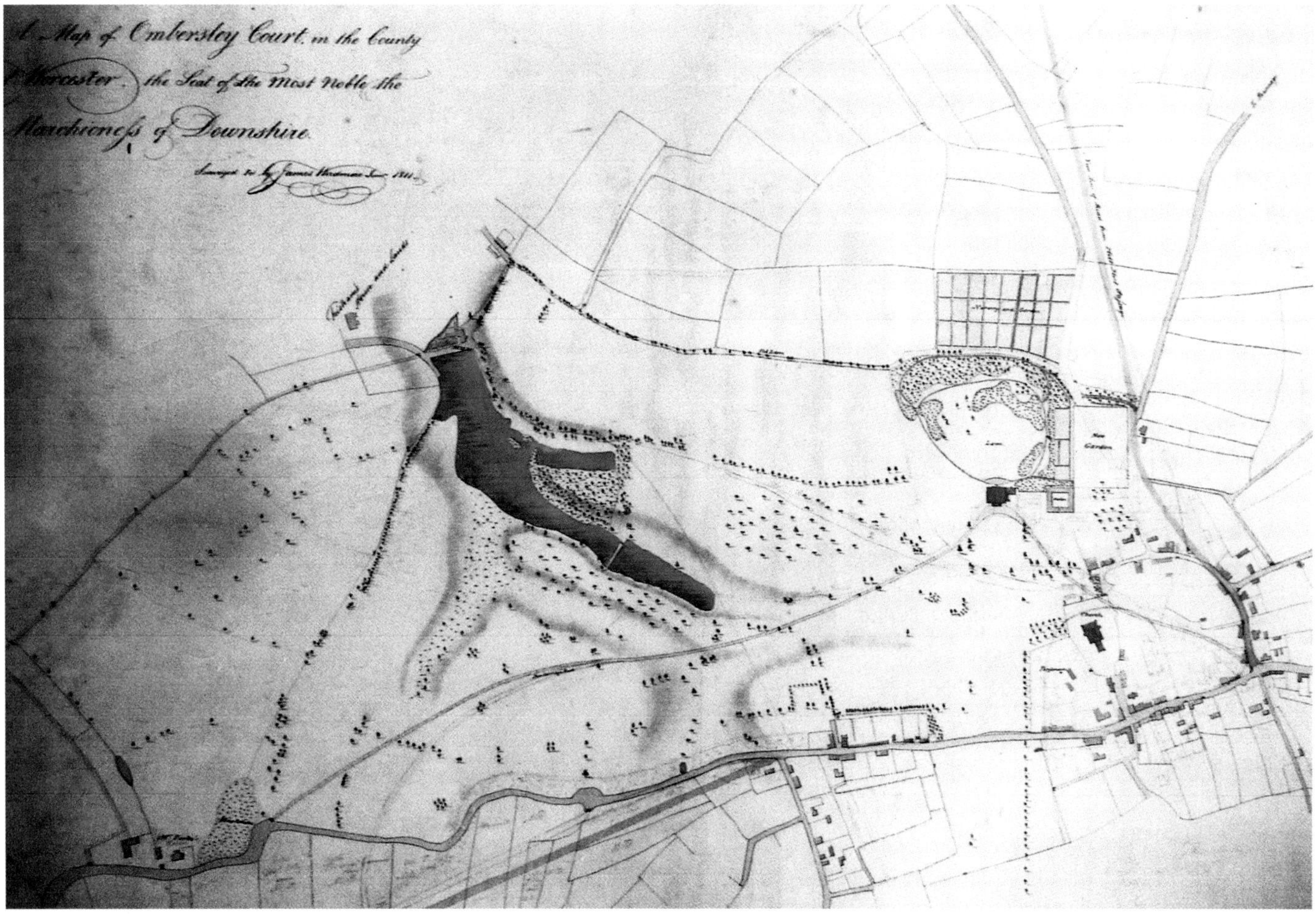

James Wadmore junior, *Map of Ombersley Court*, 1811. Courtesy, Trustees of the Sandys Archives.

..........continued from previous page

re-shaped in the early-19th century has become a more interesting and relevant question due to Jane Bradney's discovery of a reference to Richard Jones (1740-1831) who worked as a foreman for Lancelot 'Capability' Brown on the Royal Gardens in London. Jones was recommended by Brown to Lord Sandys circa 1766 and worked at Ombersley apparently for 3 years before migrating to Somerset (*Gardener's Magazine*, 1831). This information was annotated by J. C. Loudon. The obituary describes the contract "to superintend the gardens attached to Ombersley Court, Worcestershire" which does not clarify whether his remit extended beyond the immediate grounds to the further park with its surviving picturesque features and water. Neither of these maps nor the 1905 OS clearly indicate Brownian features such as clumps or perimeter belts; how the water was managed and developed from medieval to modern via the 18th century is undocumented.

Valentine Green's drawing, engraved by Francis Jukes for Treadwell Nash circa 1780, of the view from the east shows figures (and sheep) enjoying the park beyond the road. In between park, road and mansion there is a formal area of square lawns divided by paths separated by a pillared fence from the gravelled area by the front door. (This view was reproduced on a Flight & Barr plate (Roelofsz, op. cit., p. 151)). Early-19th century maps (1811 & 1827) show the formal garden removed in favour of a gravelled forecourt with a drive round a circular lawn (WAAS 1294). Present arrangements are hardly changed from those established by Webb.

There is no evidence for 18th century arrangements on the west or garden front; Wadmore (1811) shows a small gravelled area by the access through a full-height ground floor window. Jackson (1827) does not show this. Wadmore shows islands of shrubs and a belt of trees along the west side as proposed by Webb. Jackson has no islands but does have trees along the west side and around the walled garden. This garden was fondly remembered by Dr. Samuel Johnson in September 1784 when he recalled that he had "never had quite as much as he wished of the wall-fruit except once in his life, and that was when we were all together at Ombersley" (Balderston, op. cit., p. 186). Brown's foreman perhaps concentrated his efforts on the grounds immediately around the mansion rather than on the surrounding park.

Whitehead's analysis (op. cit.) relates the present landscape to the Wadmore map of 1811 which may anticipate rather than record the status quo. Whitehead values Ombersley as "probably the best surviving landscape by John Webb to be found in England". The landscape of park, grounds and mansion went with a redeveloped rural village of new houses and a new church (1825-9); the Marchioness of Downshire even funded the new bridge over the Severn at Holt. Webb began his career working for William Emes, a serious rival to 'Capability' Brown, before he established his own independent practice; "Webb can now be associated with nearly 40 projects and during the first three decades of the 19th century and was frequently viewed as either a substitute or successor to (Humphry) Repton" (Whitehead, op. cit.). He was well placed to supplant John Nash for the planned developments of house and grounds at Ombersley Court after 1808. Webb was skilled with water and Whitehead compares the lake at Ombersley to that at Crewe Hall, Cheshire, of circa 1804 (a project carried out with Emes).

To return to the immediate surroundings of the mansion, Webb created a back drive with gates and stone side walls leading to the Stables and the side of the house or curving towards the front entrance through a wooded area as required by the Marchioness. The Wadmore plan shows how the west or garden front opened on to a lawn and small gravelled area via one of the full-height French windows. "The style of the garden with its island beds, easy curves and circulating paths is essentially gardenesque and similar to designs promoted by John Claudius Loudon" (Whitehead, op. cit.).

Wadmore and Jackson both show the principal drive running south to the road along the east side of the lake. Wadmore but not Jackson shows another projected drive from the main entrance going north-east and past the old church to the cross roads in the village, an idea that was not realised.

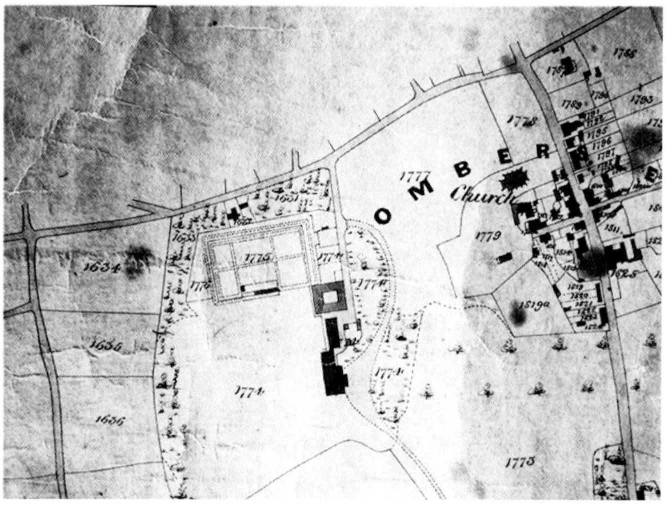

A. R. Jackson, detail of Ombersley estate map, 1827. © WAAS 3962/40.

The Marchioness of Downshire's ideas for the redevelopment of Ombersley expressed in 1819 are known: "The entrance into the Park from the Worcester side where the Lodge shod (sic) be, to commence at Bourne's Dingle carried as Mr. Webb may judge best to secure the distant views of Malvern & the Surrounding Country. Any trees that are wished to be taken down to be only marked this Autumn, The Railing near the house to be properly placed accordingly as I have staked it. ... Respecting the Kitchen Garden & Hot Houses I am decidedly of opinion that the upper Garden may be done

..........continued from previous page

away with & laid into pasture. The new Kitchen Garden giving a sufficient supply for myself and family. I wish likewise to lessen the Hot Houses & save the expense of building a Green House by having only two houses for Pines, & the other turned into a Green House. The Houses are at present much more for shew than for profit" (information from Martin Davis). Wadmore's 1811 plan shows a large Nursery and Garden marked off into 24 compartments (like allotments) on the west side of the Lawn garden occupying fields which the Jackson Survey numbers 1634, 1635, 1636. This means that the Marchioness's views were respected and this managed area was returned to field.

Wadmore details the walled "New Garden" overlaying the old roads within the estate including that to Holt Fleet. This walled garden was laid out by Webb in line with the Stables. Wadmore appears to show glasshouses along the whole of the south wall facing on to the Lawn but the existing glasshouse only occupies the central section of the south wall as in Jackson in 1827. Jackson documents the buildings on the north face of this central section of the wall and the inner walled garden behind it as today and as recorded by the 1884 OS. Jackson shows the Kitchen garden divided into 6 plots. He also records the walled areas east of the garden linking with Webb's drive off the Holt Road. Flues and chimney pots for heating are sited on the north and south outer garden walls. The gardener's house (Vine Cottage) is positioned between the north wall and the road. The substantial, arcaded walled structure which supports the glasshouse facing south was understood to be Webb's work when restoration work was done to the walls in 1984. The construction details of the glasshouse are comparable with those of the hothouse at Rode Hall, Cheshire with its cast iron rafters and fixed roof lights (Whitehead, op. cit.). A relatively early-19th century date is supported by Jackson's 1827 plan.

Although the planting around the mansion is worthy of being called an arboretum and derives in principle from Webb's early-19th century design, the specimen trees are in fact of varying dates; some Listed trees were planted later, e.g. the 124 ft Wellingtonia in 1853. The European Larch is said to date from the 1720s (Martin Davis). The Listing identifies the latter as the second largest larch in the British Isles. Mowl (op. cit. pp. 103-5) has coined an alternative to the arboretum, "a garden of trees" in which he singles out a Swamp Cypress, a Golden Larch, the Wellingtonia, a Golden Ash (planted in 1860) and two "apprentice" trees, a lime compounded with a hawthorn, and a copper beech. Much work was done on the trees in the 1990s.

Ombersley Court was added to Historic England's Register of Historic Parks and Gardens as a "garden and park laid out c. 1812 - c. 1820 by John Webb for the Marchioness of Downshire, remodelling an earlier C18 park" (2017).

Revd. W. Gilpin, *Observations on Picturesque Beauty,* 1809.
A. Oswald, "Ombersley Court", *Country Life,* CXIII, 1953, pp, 34, 94, 152.
M. Mainsbridge, *John Nash,* 1991.
E. Roelofsz, *Through Changing Scenes of Life: A Millenium of History in Ombersley and Doverdale,* 1999.
K. C. Balderston, *Thraliana: Diary of 1776-1789,* 1951.
T. Mowl, *Historic Gardens of Worcestershire,* 2006.
D. Whitehead, *Submission to Register of Historic Parks and Gardens,* June 2016.
Beauties of England and Wales, Vol. XV, 1814.
Victoria County History, Vol. 3, 1913 (VCH).
T. R. Nash, *Collections for the History of Worcestershire,* Vol II, 1782.
HE *Register of Parks & Gardens,* 2017.

The remains of the glasshouse on garden side of walled garden, 2018. Photo, R. Lockett.

Overbury Court

Parish: Conderton & Overbury

HER Ref: WSM35183. Grid Ref: SO 951 375. Postcode: GL20 7NP.

O.S. 6" Map No: 48SE, 55NE. Date of Map: 1883, 1884, with extent of park & gardens shaded as H. E. Register.

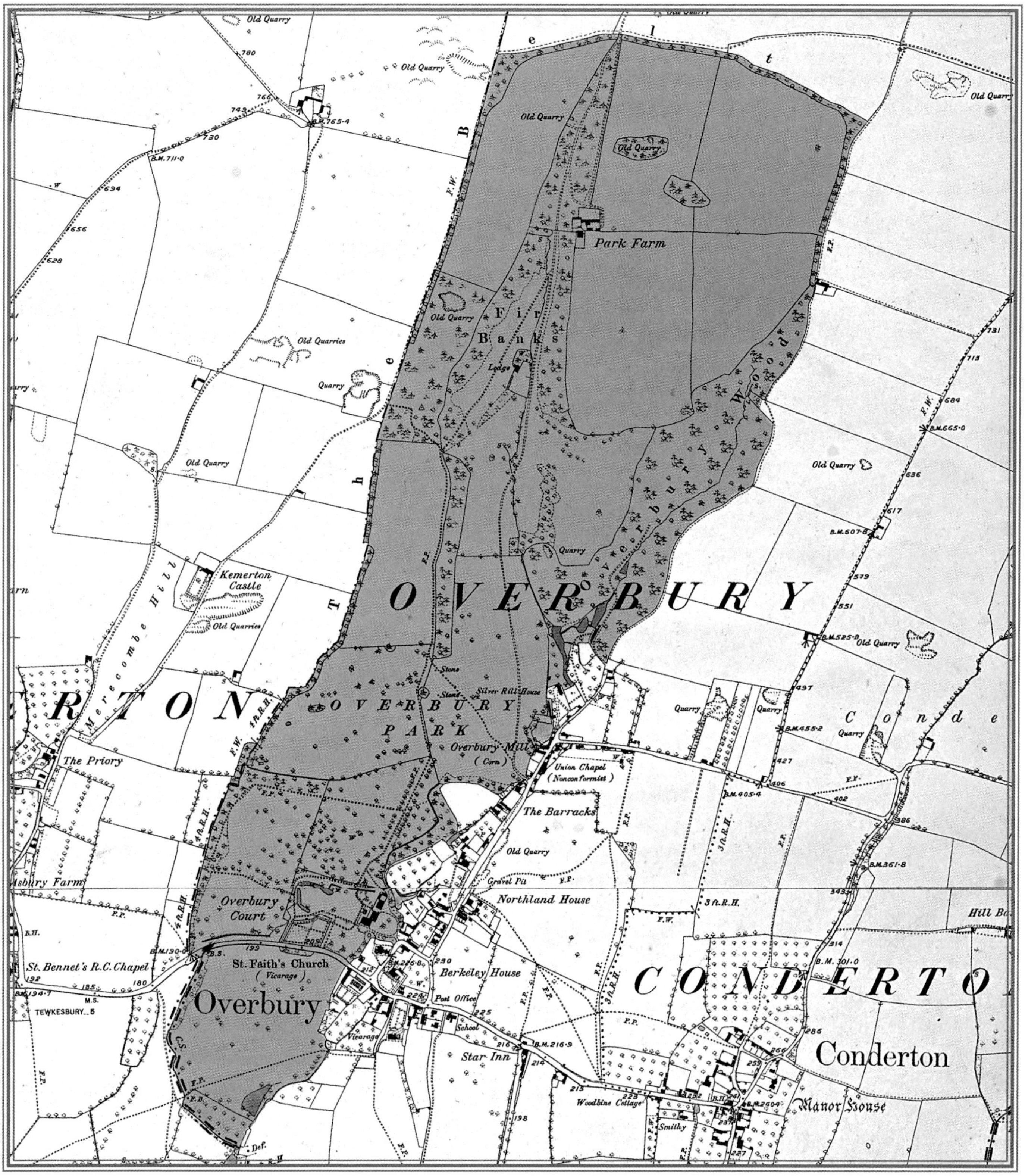

Overbury Court

..........continued from previous page

Included within Historic England's Register of Historic Parks and Gardens of special historic interest in England.

The Court was "rebuilt after a major fire in 1739-43, perhaps by the younger William Smith" (BoE, p. 513). Richard Norman Shaw in 1887 and circa 1897, Ernest Newton circa 1910 (N E Lodge) and Sir Herbert Baker circa 1925 and Victor Heal circa 1959 did architectural work at Overbury without necessarily contributing to the gardens or further landscape. To quote the BoE (p. 514): "The formal 19C GARDENS were simplified by Guy Dawber, 1923; his pyramid-roofed GAZEBO, SE corner, is said to be a reconstructed C18 building from Burford. Further rearrangements by Russell Page, 1968." Mowl (p. 53) adds Brenda Colvin and Peter Coats to this list of garden designers; he further attributes the "winter garden of sinuously curved reflecting pools" to Geoffrey Jellicoe in the 1930s. Mowl sums up by saying "Overbury's gardens were not laid out in a single year but several decades, from 1923 to 1968, and the work is ongoing." (p. 156).
The known history of Overbury Court and its landscape park does not go back beyond the 18th century.
Taylor in 1772 names the park and shows an avenue. Nash's illustration (Vol I, 1781, f. p. 559) is taken from beside the approach drive from the south with its avenue. It is difficult to decide whether or not he shows some clumps/planting in the park near the house to support Sidwell's feeling of Brownian style. The early-19th century directories refer to "a seat surrounded by some very fine groves." Cary in 1787 and 1805 makes the park a deer park. Overbury Park is marked on the first edition of the OS one inch (1828) and on earlier-19th century printed maps and was regarded as a principal county seat circa 1800.
The HE Register puts the gardens at 7½ hectares and the park at 60 hectares.: "Overbury Park extends mainly n.wards, and to the w., from Overbury Court, with thin belts of trees along the western boundary, woodland 1 km to the n.e. Traces remain of a formal avenue northwards from Overbury Court in otherwise mainly open country. Some areas now returned to agricultural use. Two artificial pools and a cascade, possibly of 18th c. origin, and shaded by mature planes, lie between the park and the formal gardens, which are on the western and southern sides of the house. Approach drive to e. of house, with small shrubbery and lawn. To w. of house, main lawn leading to the pools and cascade. 19th c. formal gardens laid out to s. of house, much simplified and altered in 20th century, lastly by Russell Page in 1968. This rectangular area now contains a swimming pool in the eastern half and a crocquet lawn to the w., with a double row of Irish yews between. Gazebo in south-eastern corner, 1923. To the e., scalloped edge border of alternating gold and silver planting fronted by a gravelled edge along the wall of St. Faith's churchyard, with a line of junipers rising up beyond the wall. To the w., the Kemerton Walk, running n./s., with borders on each side."
Sidwell (pp. 76-78) mentions that the enlarged Victorian conservatory had been demolished and that the swimming pond replaced a sunken lily pond.

Overbury, the seat of John Martin Esq.

Overbury from T. R. Nash, *Collections for the History of Worcestershire,* Vol I, 1781.

T. Mowl, *Historic Gardens of Worcestershire,* 2006.
A. Brooks & N. Pevsner, *Worcestershire,* 2007 (BoE).
R. Sidwell, *West Midlands Gardens,* 1981.
T. R. Nash, *Collections for the History of Worcestershire,* Vol I, 1781.
HE *Register of Parks & Gardens,* 1997.

Parkfield

Parish: Hallow

HER Ref: WSM29025. Grid Ref: SO 830 573. Postcode: WR2 6PJ. O.S. 6" Map No: 28SE, 33NE.

Date of Maps: both 1886, with extent of park & grounds shaded as 1905 OS.

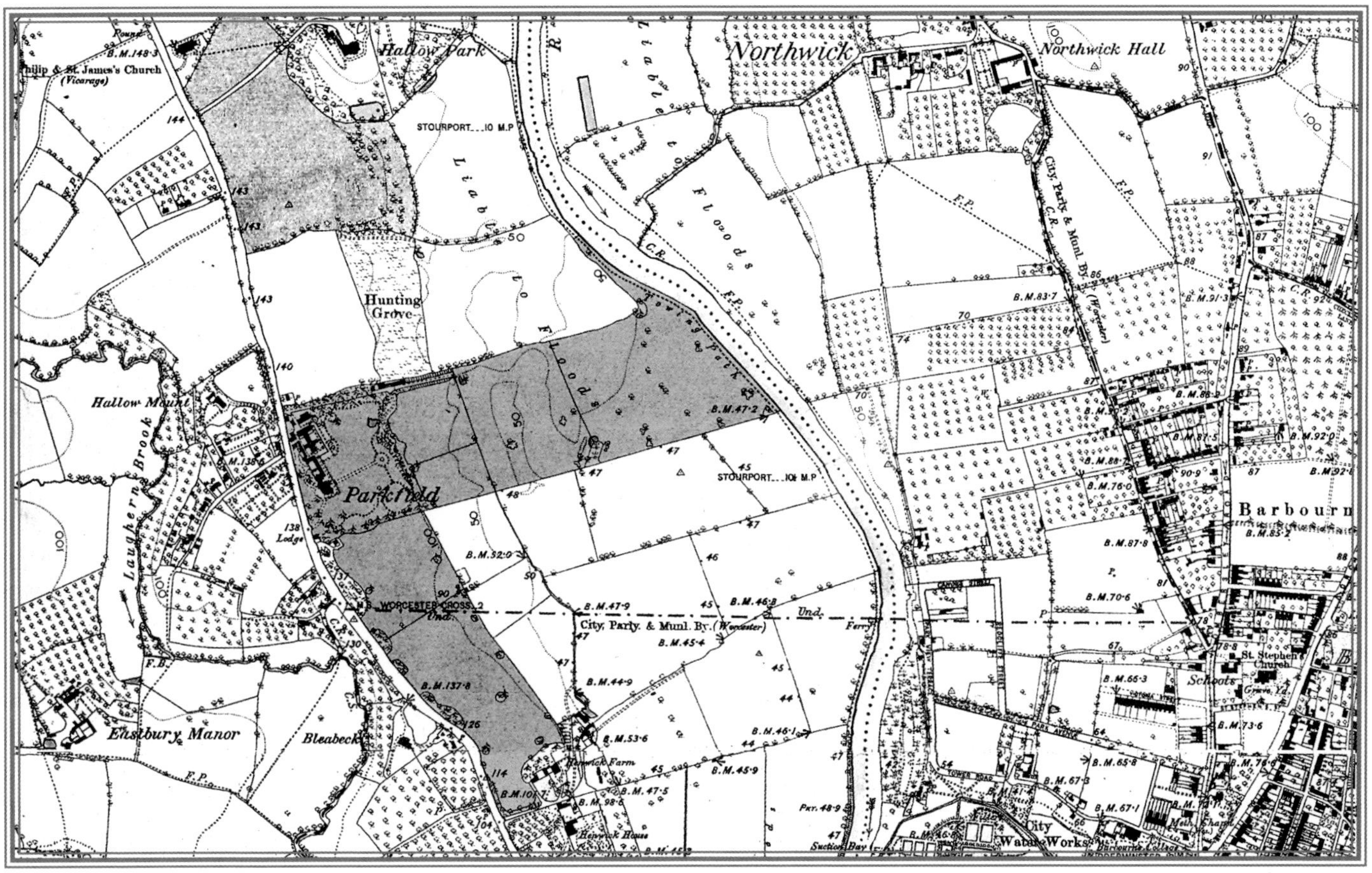

Parkfield, formerly called Bohun Court, was built in the 1860's by W. J. Hopkins for C. Wheeley Lea who acquired much of Hallow including Hallow Park. The *Worcestershire Chronicle* described the architectural style of the new residence as Middle Pointed or Decorated English of the 14th century. The house was replaced in 1932.

The park and grounds of Parkfield were taken out of those of Hallow Park (VCH, 3, 1913, p. 367) as a narrow, rectangular strip between the Hallow-Worcester road and the River Severn and a narrower strip continuing south along the road (OS 1905 6 inch as parkland). The walled garden with gardener's house is on the west side of the main road. This was featured in 1866 by the *Worcestershire Chronicle:* "an extensive kitchen garden surrounded by lofty walls and containing various vineries, peach-house, and other horticultural appliances. The hot-houses and the laying out of the gardens and pleasure grounds were designed by Mr. Kemp (Edward Kemp 1817-1891), the landscape gardener. At the entrance of the grounds is a picturesque lodge..."

The BoE notices as surviving from the Hopkins period, the South Lodge, terracing on the garden side of the house, a Coalbrookdale iron fountain topped by a swan set within a polygonal basin and two "remarkable timber-framed GARDENS PAVILIONS of c.1870". One of these, a games room, has tiled decoration by W. B. Simpson & Sons illustrating the sports of archery, crocquet and badminton.

Between 1882 and 1905, the gardening press reported that Mr. and Mrs. Charles Wheeley Lea's garden was notable for flowering plants, especially orchids. The impressive glasshouses are still visible from the road.

The House (Bohun Court), its immediate grounds and kitchen gardens are shown in great detail in a sale plan of 1925 (CRO 9526/46). The gardens on the west of the road became commercial nurseries thereafter.

Much of the original planting, including mature conifers survives and can be seen from boundary roads and footpaths.

Worcestershire Chronicle, June 6th, 1866.

Gardener's Chronicle, 17th Dec. 1892, p. 744 (Gardener given as Mr. A. G. Catt); 17th March, 1894, p. 366; 12th May, 1894, p. 589; 21st Jan., 1905 (re an American Aloe). Information from Jane Bradney.

A. Brooks & N. Pevsner, *Worcestershire,* 2007 (BoE).

Park Hall

Parish: Churchill & Blakedown

HER Ref: WSM61690.

Grid Ref: SO 972 782. Postcode: B45 9AT.

O.S. 6" Map No: 8SE.

Date of Map: 1888, with extent of park & gardens shaded as 1880s OS.

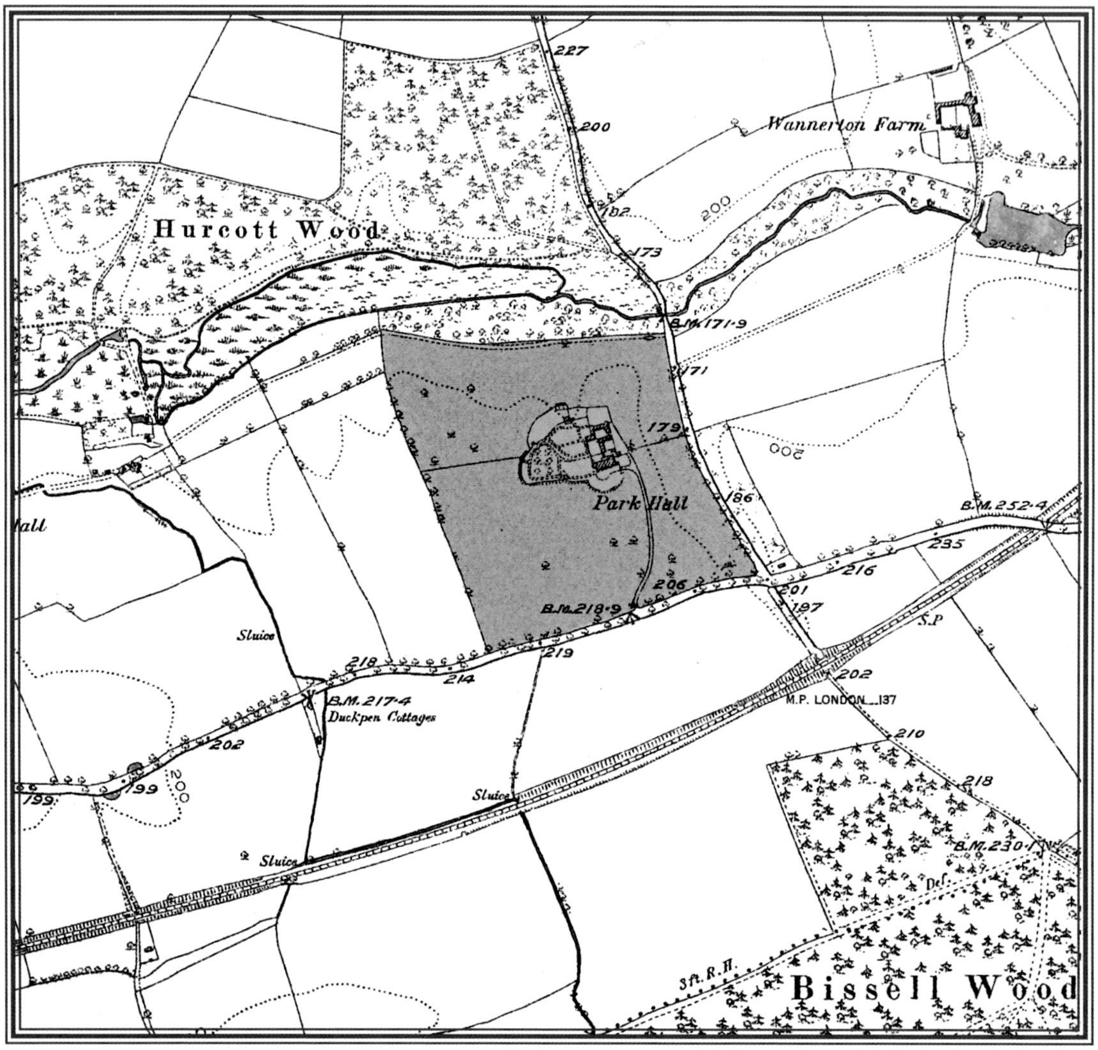

The early-18th century house was greatly enlarged circa 1833 (BoE, p. 156) when the estate (2,560 acres) was sold (CRO 4813). It is noticed as a residence by the *Beauties* in 1814, Greenwood in 1822 and Paterson in 1829.

A ha-ha surrounds the immediate gardens to the south and west of the house. How much of the landscape with 3 large linked pools went with Park Hall is unclear; the Banqueting Pool in Hurcott Wood (a marshy area bounded by the river) certainly did in 1833. A park is marked on the 2nd edition of the OS 6 inch.

The house is now in multiple ownership; the park is intact with some fine trees.

A. Brooks & N. Pevsner, *Worcestershire*, 2007 (BoE).

Beauties of England and Wales, Vol. XV, 1814.

Pensax Court

Parish: Pensax

HER Ref: WSM28837.

Grid Ref: SO 725 690. Postcode: WR6 6XJ.

O.S. 6" Map No: 20NW, 20NE.

Date of Maps: both 1884, with extent of park & gardens shaded as 1905 OS.

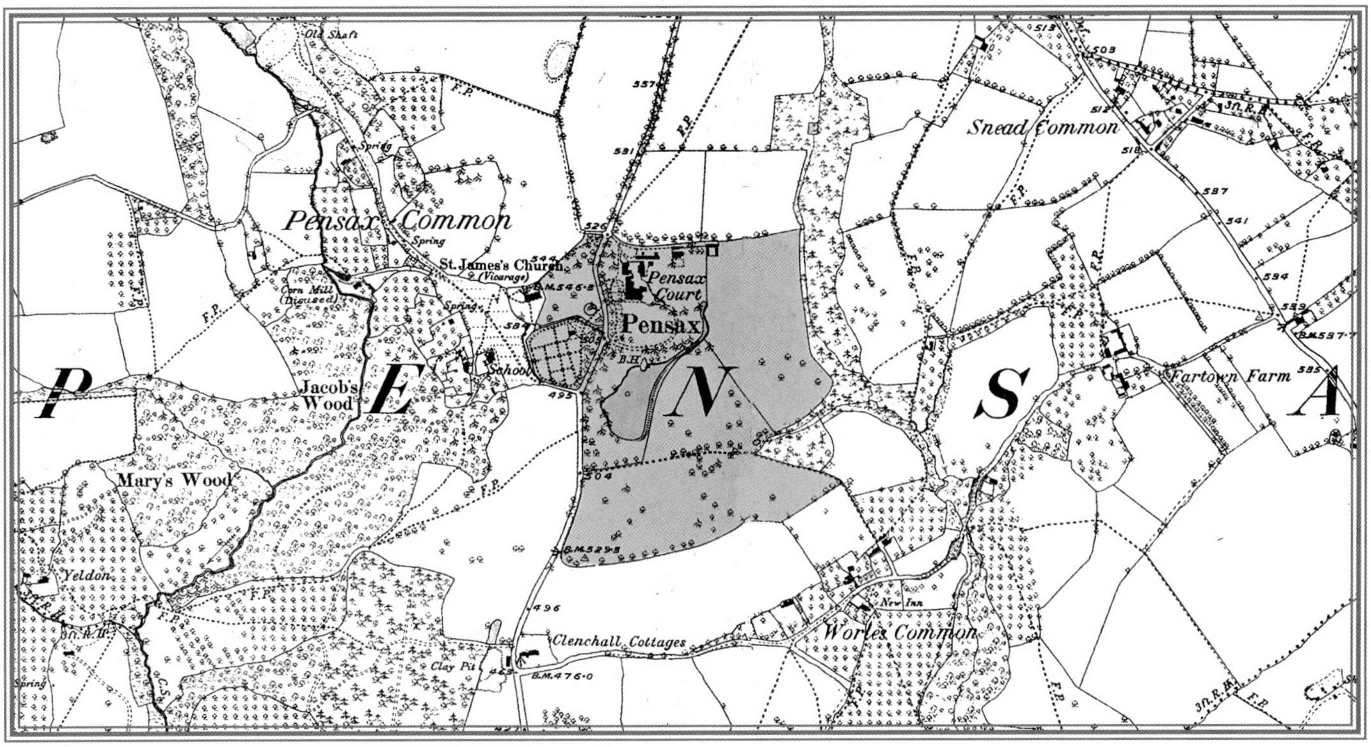

The present house is of circa 1840 and 1882. Grounds are indicated on the 1828 OS one inch and these are shown as a park on the 1883 OS 6 inch. The walled kitchen garden west across the Stockton road was 4.9 acres; a large pool with boat house was south-west of the house which is embanked on its east side. Rowley Coppice was north/south on the east side of the park and there were clumps at the south end. The estate sold in 1946 amounted to 745 acres (CRO, 3762/148); the sale particulars talked up the pleasure grounds with spacious lawns, shrubberies, flower gardens and a collection of specimen, coniferous trees.

Modern housing development around the Court has disrupted its setting, although a couple of mature Wellingtonias survive to the south-west of the house and there is other planting suggestive of the late-19th century. The parkland is now down to arable but some parkland trees survive in good condition to the east and south of the lake. The walled garden is now attached to a separate modern house.

Pirton Park

Parish: Severn Stoke & Croome D'Abitot

HER Ref: WSM34808. Grid Ref: SO 875 470. Postcode: WR8 9EE.

O.S. 6" Map No: 40NE/SE, 41NW/SW.

Date of Maps: both 1884, with extent of park & gardens shaded as H. E. Register.

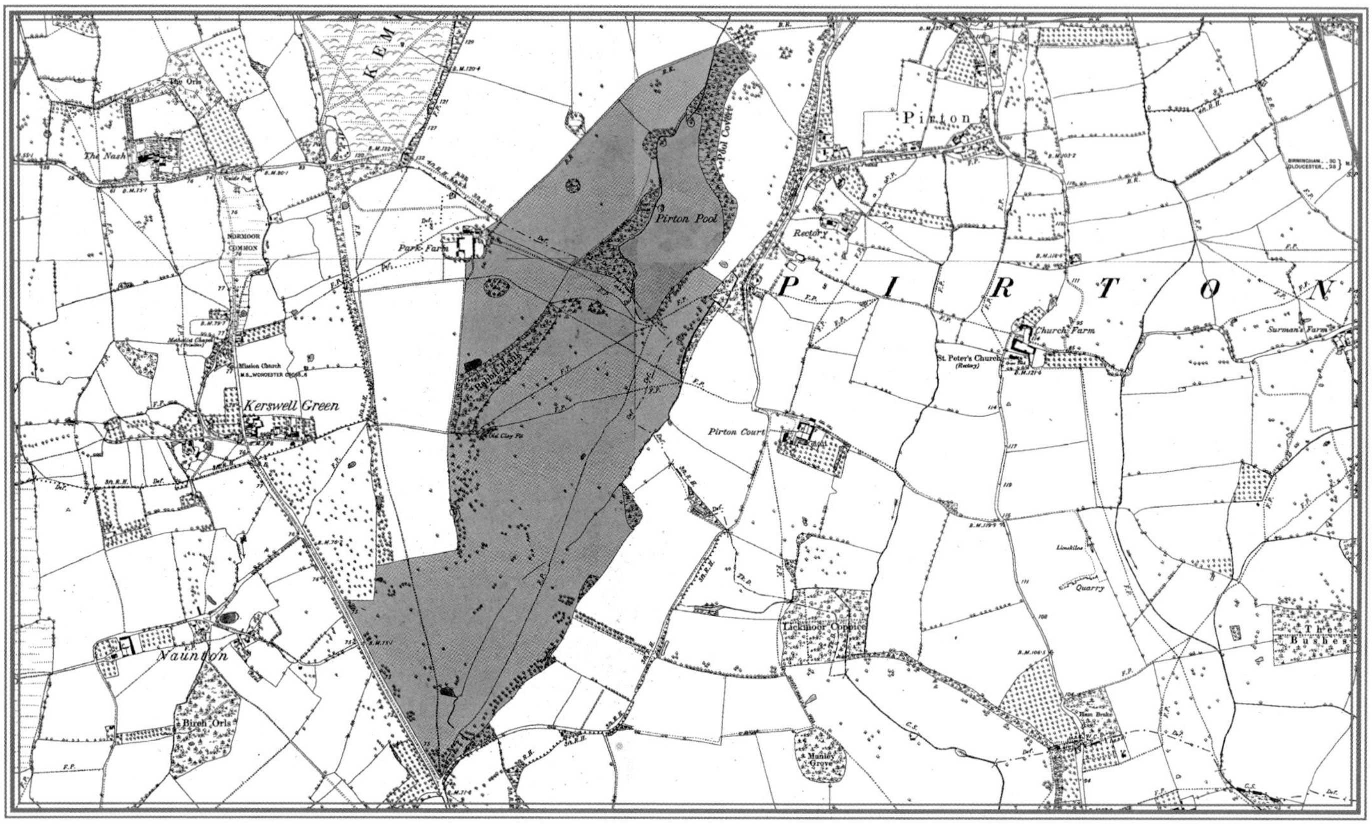

Included within Historic England's Register of Historic Parks and Gardens of special historic interest in England.

The medieval owners of the moated Court or Manor House were the Folliotts. Parts of the 17th century, half-timbered house survive with a wing added in the 19th century for the Coventry heir. Viscount Deerhurst was living there in 1924 (VCH 4, p. 180, photo). According to a *Survey Map of the Parish of Pirton* by Mark Pierce dated 1623, the moated house had a formal garden but the land to its west and south is not defined as a park (Gordon, Pl. IX). The area later known as the Old Park (still so-called on the OS Pathfinder), to the west of the Court apparently still belonged to the Folliots (Fouttot on the map) in 1623 and lay outside the parish. The eccentric shape of Pirton Pool is almost exactly the same in 1623 as it is today; this medieval fish pond is about 50 acres (Gordon, p. 22).

The Croome Estate was acquired bv Sir Thomas Coventry in 1592 but Pirton Court was not added until 1627 which confirms the 1623 Parish Map information. In the early-18th century Pirton Park was called the Fallow Deer Park and was surveyed at 80 acres in 1719. It was one of three deer parks at Croome from the mid-18th century. Some tree planting in the park is recorded in 1746, before 'Capability' Browns arrival on the scene. This is the only part of Brown's landscaping at Croome (circa 1764) for which a drawing by him is known (WAAS 30046/12). Brown's map shows the park pale and the Keeper's House. This is still called the Park on the 1840 Tithe Map (WAAS 4270/1).

Mowl in his discussion of Croome Court, argues that the Croome garden and landscape developments in the mid-18th century were designed in part to maintain the sentimental and topographical links between Pirton as the old home and Croome as the new (p. 48). The landscape of the Park contains the Pirton Tower of 1797 by James Wyatt, an eye-catcher to Croome Court which competes with some prominent, mature cedars and oaks. These have recently been augmented with new planting by the HWGT.

C. Gordon, *The Coventrys of Croome*, 2000.
T. Mowl, *Historic Gardens of Worcestershire,* 2006.
Victoria County History Vol. 4, 1924 (VCH).
HE *Register of Parks & Gardens*, 1999.

The Priory

Parish: Kemerton

HER Ref: WSM28991.
Grid Ref: SO 950 378.
Postcode: GL20 7JN.
O.S. 6" Map No: 48SE.
Date of Map: 1883.

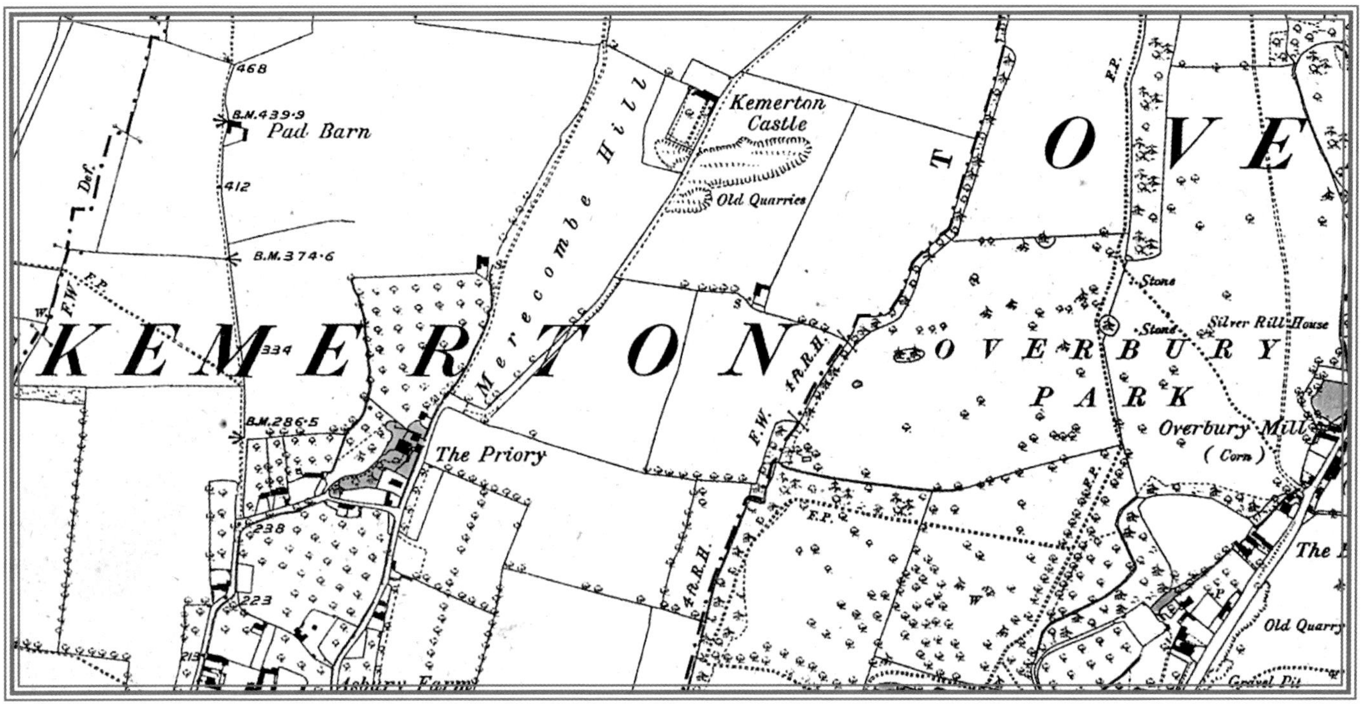

Sidwell (p. 81/4) describes a garden of 3 acres as being an essentially Victorian garden until 1938 and a post 1946 development by Peter Healing of a yew-hedged "New Garden" in the earlier kitchen garden. This garden goes with a house of late-17th, early-19th and mid-19th century date. Mowl (pp. 159-60) features the garden circa 2006.

Peter Healing described the garden created by himself and his wife in 1982: "The garden lies on the southern slopes of Bredon Hill ... with views on a clear day to the Bristol Channel and the Welsh Hills ... four acres under cultivation, bounded on either side by small swift running streams." It is rare to have a detailed picture of a garden at a specific moment described by its creators border by border and the process of creation with its seasonal variety, all "caught" (Lees-Milne and Verey). The Healing garden featured rare plants. Yew hedges continue to frame or provide a back drop to borders and there is a striking sweep of yew standards edging one side of the circular path to the main entrance. The sunken garden is on the site of an old woollen mill (also described as a stocking factory). On the other side of the house beside an ancient yew, is a ruined building with re-set mullion windows looking into the garden.

A. Lees-Milne & R. Verey, *The Englishman's Garden*, 1982, pp. 72-5 & pls. 80-4 and vignette.

M. Forsyth, "The Priory, Kemerton", *HWGT, Newsletter,* 46, Winter 2015/16.

R. Sidwell, *West Midlands Gardens,* 1981.

Pull Court

Parish: Bushley

HER Ref: WSM28835.

Grid Ref: SO 862 361. Postcode: GL20 6AH.

O.S. 6" Map No: 54NE/SE.

Date of Map: 1884, with extent of park & grounds shaded as 1905 OS.

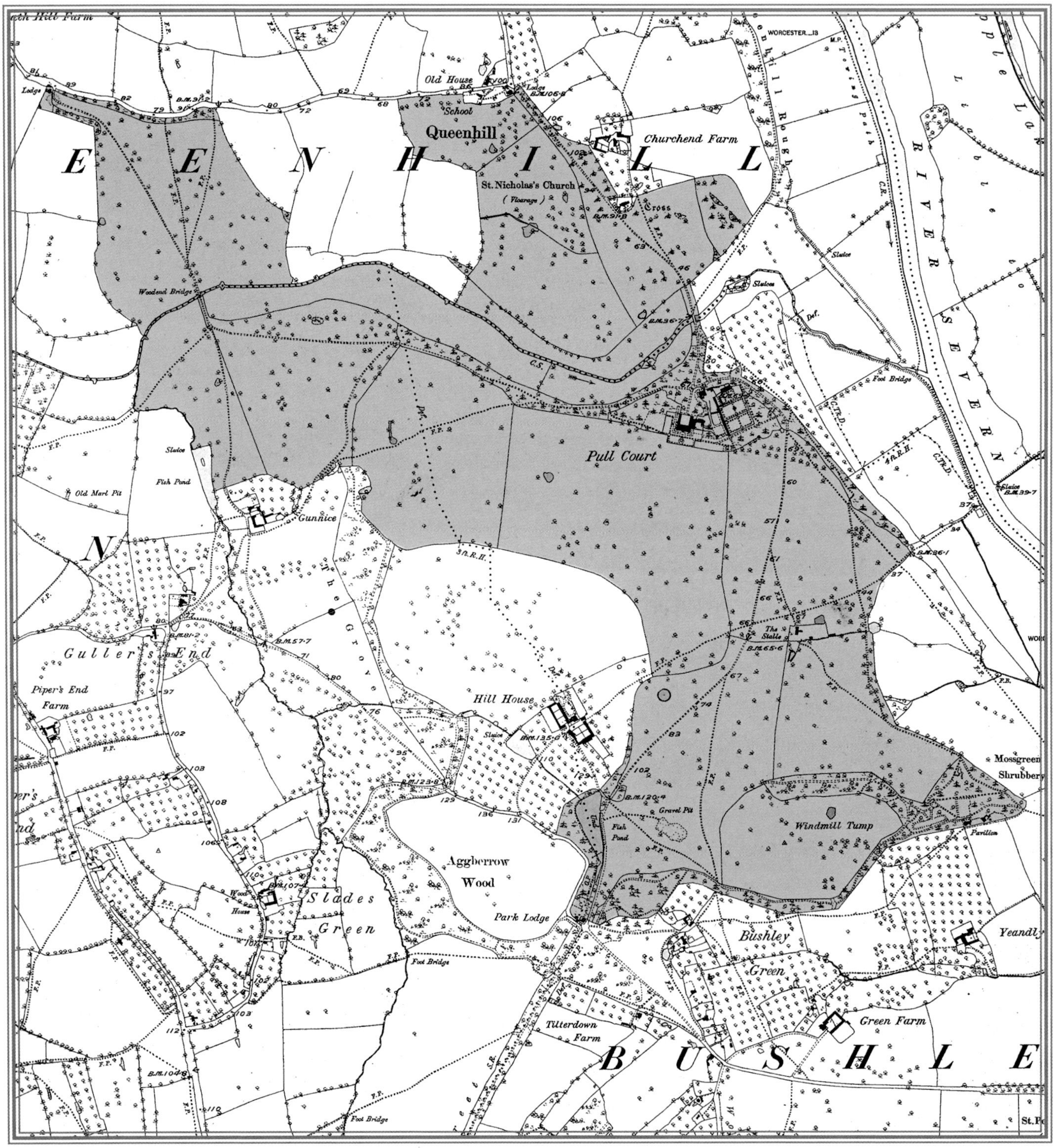

Pull Court

..........continued from previous page

According to the Revd. E. R. Dowdeswell, Pull Court was purchased by a Roger Dowdeswell in 1628 from the Rouse family. Before the Reformation, the manor belonged to the Abbey of Tewkesbury. It is found in Doomsday Book as "La Pulle" (Dowdeswell, op. cit.).

The deer park appears for the first time on printed maps, Taylor in 1772 and Nash in 1781. Taylor marks a fenced park to the south of the mansion. Bushley Park, sited further to the south, was an older deer park and "Bushley Park" is sometimes given as the property name circa 1800, e.g. in the *Traveller*. A fenced park is shown on the 1811 survey for the first OS one inch. The landscape park is somewhat larger on the first, 1883 edition of the OS 6 inch than on the 1905 edition.

A Map of an Estate situate chiefly in the Parish of Bushley ... the Property of General Dowdeswell (Private Collection) "enlarged from Maps ... made about the year 1792" shows the location of the older park centred on Bushley Park Farm separated by a substantial block of other Dowdeswell land from the park at Pull Court (information from John and Vincent Yorke). Bushley Park Farm extended further south towards the River Severn than today's County boundary with Gloucestershire. The Farm was contained on the north and east sides by a road or track as from "Corse Lawn" (also Dowdeswell property) which as "Park Lane" linked south to the River and the Upper Lode river crossing to the Tewkesbury Ham, itself largely acquired by William Dowdeswell in 1773. 424 acres were let with Bushley Park Farm in 1792 (Gloucestershire Archives, D 9051).

Pevsner (p. 114) mentions a tradition that the landscape park of Pull Court was designed by 'Capability' Brown in the 1770s when he was working for Lord Coventry at Croome Court. Since Brown was working at Croome from circa 1750 and Dowdeswell had inherited Pull Court as a minor in 1728 and was of age by then, a connection between them could have been established earlier. (William Dowdeswell was briefly Chancellor of the Exchequer in 1764/5 and died well before Brown in 1775). The tradition that Brown worked at Pull Court has been supported most recently by David Whitehead (op. cit.). This undocumented tradition was first mooted by Burke (pp. 122-3) in 1855: "The pleasure-grounds and plantations are extensive and picturesque, exhibiting the peculiar taste of the celebrated Launcelot Brown ... In front of the mansion is a magnificent park, that slopes from it with a gentle descent, and affords a beautiful prospect from the terrace" (Richard Webb).

There are two Survey Maps which can help document landscape developments at Pull Court in the third quarter of the 18th century: A 2 ½ x 4 ft. Map enlarged from two 1792 originals around 1811-1824 for General Dowdeswell (Private Coll., above) and *A Survey & Particular of Pull Court and other Estates of Thomas Dowdeswell Esqr in the Parishes of Bushley and Longden* (sic) *and in the Hamlet of Queenhill in the County of Worcester & also in Tewkesbury and Forthampton in the County of Gloucester, 1792*

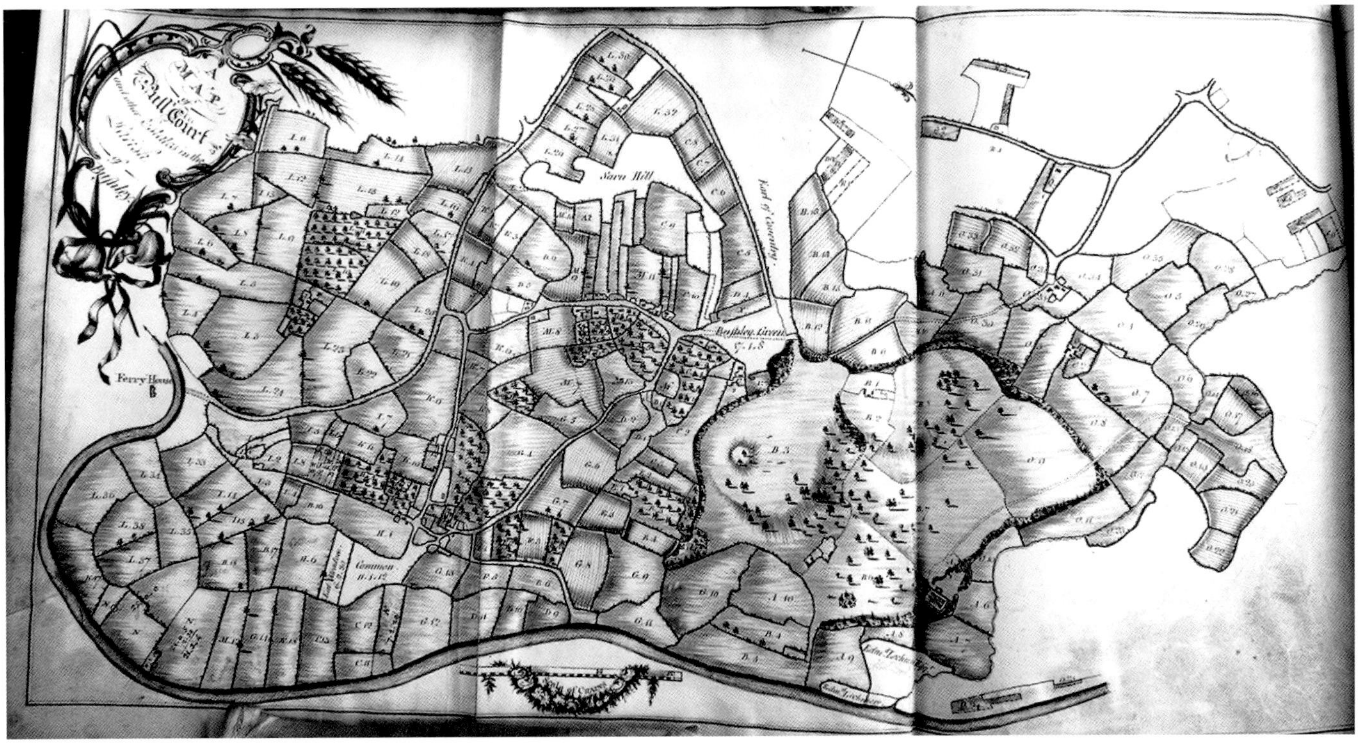

A Survey & Particular of Pull Court, 1792, Gloucestershire Archives (D 9051).

..........continued from previous page

(Gloucestershire Archives, D 9051). The latter, a small, bound volume measuring only 9 x 15 ins., has a brief *Introduction* which describes the scene without naming any designer: "Pull – Court Estate is situated about three Miles south of Upton – and comprehends the whole of the Parish of Bushley The Mansion House stands upon an eminence in the park commanding a view of the greatest part of it – it is an old building with suitable offices, an excellent garden and about 35 acres of pleasure grounds. The Park contains about 350 Acres new divided into several closes by sunk fences in which are many beautiful swells and uneven Grounds – well dotted with Oak and Elm; timber trees and the Hills covered with Plantations. Encircling the whole is a border of various trees and curious shrubs planted in general 20 years since, some longer and a part (about a quarter of a mile) only 2 years, all in a kind of growing state."

The terrier to the 1792 Survey gives further information about the division between Court and park: The Pull Court Demesne - House, Offices and Folds 3 acres; Grounds - Garden, Shrubbery and two Plantations (24 acres) 33 acres. Hill Farm (which included the "Park", an 104 acre field of old pasture) had with it 409 acres let at £457. The breadth of the estate "is about a Mile and a half and consists mostly of Pasturage and Meadow with Orcharding on all the Home Closes the Rents are principally made by the Dairy and Seeding the Tillage being little more than sufficient for the Consumption of the Families – The Soil is of various qualities, the Meadowing along the Severn is a deep fine Loam ... the higher Grounds is in general flat and cold on a stiff clay over which the Severn frequently runs rapidly and washes off the good Soil and Manure and causes the Land to throw up a hard flat Grass called by the farmers Gillbent which no Beast will eat". On other grounds there is a very strong healthy soil on a marl bottom "not much to their improvement". It is suggested that lime stone, available on the estate, fired from coal imported at 10s 6d a ton was preferable being "next to Dung, the best Manure the Farmer can make use of". The location of the Pull Court Estate was in the vicinity of Gloucester, Tewkesbury and Upton and produce could be conveyed to more distant markets "on the Navigable River Severn".

The fold-out plan shows planting around the presumed borders of the park (perimeter planting) as in later maps and as largely remaining today. Using names not on this plan but applicable to it, the borders could be described generally as located between the River Severn and the Court (east), continuing west to Woodend Bridge parallel to, but south of the Bushley Brook (north) and then turning south from the Grove to Aggberrow Wood and Bushley Green and then striking east to Windmill Tump and Mossgreen Shrubbery (OS Explorer Map 190, 1:25000). The fringe planting in both the 1792 and 1811-28 maps ends at the Mossgreen Shrubbery at the south-east corner of the park and so there was no complete circuit drive as on the 1905 OS 6 inch. The north boundary from west to east has Pull Court itself towards the centre and Park Lodge in the centre of the south boundary. The major alteration to the historic park has been caused by the M50 which has sliced off the northernmost section of the park between the Severn, the Bushley Brook and Gunnice Farm; this cuts through some planting of exotics (cedar, Wellingtonia) along the drive from Pull Court to Queenhill Church.

The convention for representing trees in the 1792 Survey implies that the park boundaries were planted exclusively with conifers and the park within with deciduous trees (oak and elm according to the earlier quotation) aside from one clump of firs (in Clover Piece) south of the Court's south plantation; this was no doubt an over simplification. The plan suggests one or two clumps only and a belt of trees on the east side of Windmill Tump.

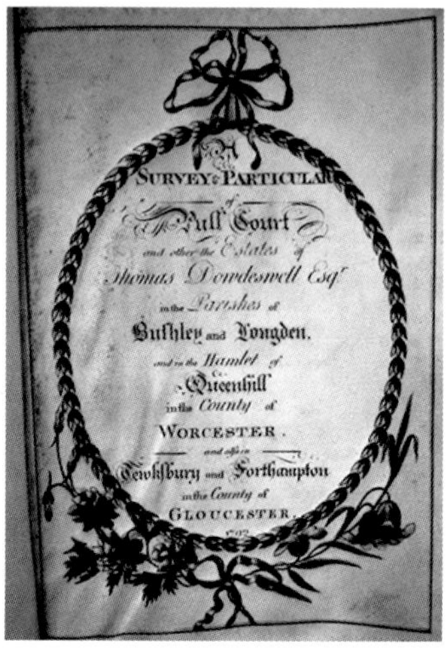

Cartouche from 1792 Survey.

For further information on the park, besides these two watercolours (gouache) painted on vellum, there are among 5 illustrated pages: *South West View of Pull Court*; *A View of Pull Court Park*; *Hill Court Demesne with Lands in Longden* (plan); *A Map of Pull Court and other Estates in the Parish of Bushley*; *A Survey and Particular* (Title Page) as above. The decorative frames for titles in vignettes and the two landscape views are delightful but old-fashioned even naïve, attributable no doubt to the surveyor who has turned his hand to view painting without owning Humphry Repton's pictorial skills. The *South West View of Pull Court,* i.e. the view of the Court from the south-west towards the Court shows a conventional post and rail fence around a 64 acre field (Pulling) which was let with Hill Farm, the principal farm set within the park. The view shows a few single trees which agrees with the plan. The *View of Pull Court Park* looking south from the mansion has a small piece of flower garden in the left foreground (which slopes down towards the park) and single, double and one clump of 7 or 8 trees comparable to grazed parkland today. This particular section of the park therefore contained no characteristic Brownian features.

General Dowdeswell's 1811 Map, on a much larger scale, generally confirms the 1792 Survey as to field divisions, whether sunk fences or conventional post and rail fences, between the tenanted farms. Most of the park was let with Hill House Farm including the 104 acre field called "The Park". The latter included Windmill Tump and extended as far as Mossgreen Shrubbery. The 1792 Survey shows

..........continued from previous page

TOP: *South West View of Pull Court*, from 1792 Survey.
ABOVE: *View of Pull Court* from 1792 Survey.

some closer planting than the usual isolated trees along the east side of Windmill Tump which in the 1811 plan has a regular form – rows of trees. The trees in the perimeter belts are not specified in 1811 but deciduous trees, including 3 clumps and some short lines of trees (not avenues) are shown within the park. Both maps share the convention of trees with shadows. In 1792 only one drive to the Court is drawn which was from the west in the direction of Woodend Bridge. In 1811 this had been developed with an exit drive going west across the centre of the park just south of Hill House Farm between Aggberrow Wood and Bushley Green; this drive remains today.

Another passage from the 1792 Survey Introduction might be read as pointing away from Lancelot 'Capability' Brown towards the anonymous surveyor himself: "The peculiar situation of this Estate did not escape the Attention of the late Owner (William Dowdeswell) for in the year 1773 He with an able assistant Carefully survey'd it, and being aware of the advantages attending it's vicinity to the Manufacturing Town of Tewkesbury etc then laid it out in convenient Farms and advanced the Rents much above those of other Properties in that Country". Was the surveyor also a tenant farmer? The *Survey* makes clear that William Dowdeswell, an erstwhile Chancellor of the Exchequer associated with austerity, was intent on maximising rental returns and therefore it seems unlikely that he would have employed an architect-landscape designer considered by some to be extravagant with client's money. Dowdeswell may of course have taken advantage of professional advice and then avoided placing a commission.

There is one aspect of the Pull Court landscape, its lack of water which argues against Brown's involvement. No water is shown on the 1792 Survey within the park and no landscape use is implied for the fields that lay between the perimeter planting on the north side of the park and the Bushley or Longdon Brook which runs west to east before entering the Severn. General Dowdeswell's Map however shows a small pool beside the Court and other water close to Hill House Farm between the Farm and Aggborough Wood. These pools at the western exit drive from the park between Aggborough Wood and Bushley Green are there today.

The General's Map perhaps indicates more landscape interest in the fields adjoining the Bushley Brook, some of which were in hand: The Tinnings; Grove Meadow; Lower Pleck (in hand); Thistley Piece (in hand); Queen Ham (in hand). But this does not amount to a managed landscape element. It also seems that the Severn itself was taken for granted and the only view of it, from a distance, was through the substantial gap in the perimeter planting on the south-east side between the Moss Green Shrubbery and the belt south of the Court. The 1792 Survey names a field on the river bank as "The Walk".

Both documents have information about the mansion that preceded Edward Blore's redevelopment of the 1830's, said to be ancient in 1628 (*VCH*, 4, 1924, p. 45) and described by Nash as a 15th century building with a good park in 1781. *South West View of Pull Court* (1792 Survey) shows the old mansion in the distance and so with another house set back and to its left and the substantial stable block with cupola to its right. The west front of the mansion has 5 windows at ground and first floor level and dormer windows to the attic. The main front facing south towards the park has 4 gabled bays with a porch entrance to the third bay. The plan shows that the stables, a little south-east of the mansion, were set in front of the large walled garden then divided into 4 squares. The walled garden seems to have kept its position and size from this time onwards and survived the 1830s redevelopment. This watercolour therefore adds to information about the pre 1830s mansion. The ground plan can be glimpsed from the 1792 Survey and the 1811 Map and the differences between them might be due to the difference in scale of the two plans or to development between 1792 and 1811-24. The latter suggests that the house was extended

..........continued from previous page

to create an inner courtyard. The lawn between mansion and stables had by 1811 been eroded for an additional drive and a small pool is placed by the east corner of the mansion. The stables on the west side of the walled garden are now shown as divided into 8 compartments with possibly a gardener's house or glass house on the north side.

Edward Blore's mansion of 1834-9 (BoE, p. 210) was Blore's first "Elizabethan" country house which Girouard describes as having a "weedily symmetrical front" and it may have "impressed" less than its predecessor. Its situation is not as elevated as commentators suggest and the mansion demands a higher platform and more visual support from its balustraded terraces. (Two of the estate lodges are also Blore's work).

Sketch taken from Women's Federation of Women's Institutes, *The Worcestershire Village Book*, 1988.

The large formal garden first laid out in the 1830s received other interventions in the 19th century prior to 20th century infill buildings. The grounds contain an ornamental ruin dated 1843 that incorporates two 14th century windows from the old church. It is said that W. A. Nesfield and his son A. M. Nesfield did some work at Pull Court in the later 19th century (John Borron, 1998 quoting Shirley Evans). The Pavilion, in the south-east corner of the grounds in the Shrubbery was built in 1864 (BoE, p. 202, "now Moss Green House") and was used to extend leisure facilities for his tenants by the Revd, Canon Richard Dowdeswell, the squire from 1893 (Webb).

The terraced gardens to south and west now exist only in outline and to appreciate the Victorian gardens one must visit via the 1932 Sale Particulars (Gloucestershire Archives, D 9051) when the estate amounted to 2450 acres and had "delightful Pleasure Grounds, Walled Gardens, etc. in all about 32 acres", i.e. almost exactly as in 1792. The mansion was "approached by a charming drive, through well-timbered parkland." "The Dignified Old Gardens comprise Formal and Flower Gardens, Rose Gardens & Lawns... A Beautiful Magnolia Walk guarded by wrought iron gates, lily pond, summer house and aviary ... Three Matured Kitchen Gardens (i.e. 3 divisions of) all being completely walled and covering about 1 acre each. Some of the walls being hollow and heated by pipes for forcing wall fruit ... Vine and Peach House ... 4 Divisions, Lean-to Glass House and Useful Forcing Houses together with Bathing Pool and Extensive Shrubberies and Plantations affording pleasant woodland walks, giving an area of about 31a. 3r. 35p." The estate agent's description represents the height of Pull Court's fortunes circa 1900 and the Park, particularly along its boundaries, has survived better than the Court, except for its truncation by the M50 which divides the Court from the Church and some now isolated cedars and Wellingtonias. South of this modern boundary there are veteran trees - oak along with Wellingtonia, cedar, sweet chestnut, yew, lime and Portuguese laurel. Pull Court itself, now Bredon School, has suffered the familiar intrusion of modern development in the walled garden and throughout the immediate grounds.

Sir B. Burke, *Visitations of Seats and Arms*, 2nd S., 2, 1855.
J. Noake, *Guide to Worcestershire*, 1868.
Revd. E. R. Dowdeswell,"Sketch of the Parish of Bushley", *Assoc. of Archaeol Socs.*, 24 (1), 1897.
M. Girouard, *The Victorian Country House*, 1979.
A. Brooks & N. Pevsner, *Worcestershire*, 2007 (BoE).
N. Pevsner, *Worcestershire*, 1968.
R. Webb (ed.), "Pull Court and the Dowdeswell Family" in *Bushley through the Great War*, 2015.
D. Whitehead, "Was 'Capability' Brown here?", *HWGT, Newsletter*, 46, Winter 2015/6.
Victoria County History, Vol. 4, 1924 (VCH).
Gloucestershire Archives: information from Jane Bradney & Sandy Haynes.

The Rhydd

Parish: Hanley Castle

HER Ref: WSM07771/28834. Grid Ref: SO 837 450. Postcode: WR8 0AD.

O.S. 6" Map No: 40SE. Date of Map: 1884, with extent of park & gardens shaded as 1880s OS.

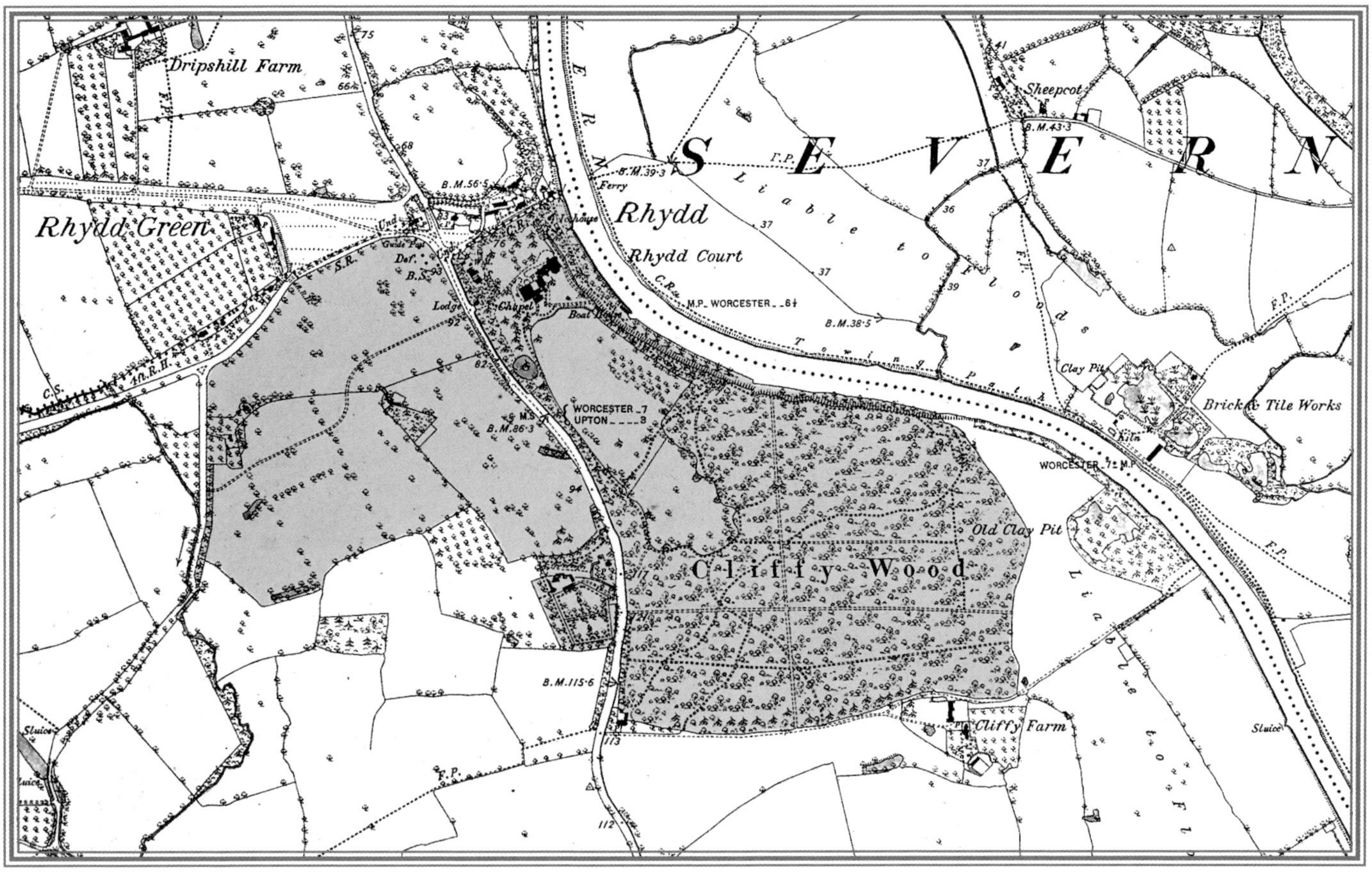

The early history of the Rhydd was no doubt associated with Cliffy Wood and a ferry station on the River Severn. This was the eastern boundary of Malvern Chase which stretched from here to the west side of the Malverns. Early-19th century guide books suggest that the Rhydd, for which the Lechmeres briefly left Severn End in 1805, was relatively undeveloped in landscape terms : "as yet little embellishment has been given to it" (*Beauties*, 1810, p. 347); "much remains to the hand of art to contribute to the embellishment of this spot" (Cooke, circa 1801, p. 117). Paterson in 1829 however, could refer to the agreeably diversified grounds. The 1812 survey for the first OS one inch defined the Rhydd as a park. It is shown as a residence on Cary in 1805 as Kidd Hill (possibly a confusion with Dripshill) and Ridd-Hill in a guide book of 1788: a miniature landscape is recorded by a "Map of the Rydde Estate" made by Thomas Buckle (CRO 1531/68) in 1803. There was a perimeter plantation (the Coppice) with rides along and high above the River Severn returning along the south border of "the Orchard" to the road on the west. Across this road was a field running up to the road by Rhydd Green with clumps. This looks more park-like than the Orchard. Also mapped are the Mansion House, Yards, Pleasure Grounds (4 acres), Orchard with Dairy House, Plantations and Water (i.e. Pool) (14 acres). The distinctive feature of the Rhydd was the setting of the house hard by and dramatically above the River Severn.

The 1st edition of the OS 6 inch (1884) records the park and grounds of Rhydd Court with lodge, boathouse and icehouse and much as in 1803. Features common to both were the boundaries of Rhydd Green (north) and the Severn (east) with a park area west of the road stretching south to the existing walled garden (Rhydd Gardens).

The considerable expenditure on bricks in the period 1818 - 1824 (CRO 1531/51) is most likely to refer to the building of the walled garden and nearby Gardener's House. The Orchard of 1803 is in 1884 also park and has been extended into Cliffy Wood; the latter is rich in oak, sycamore, ash and beech.

The early-19th century house was enlarged in 1863 and the gardens developed after that to the point recorded in

..........continued from previous page

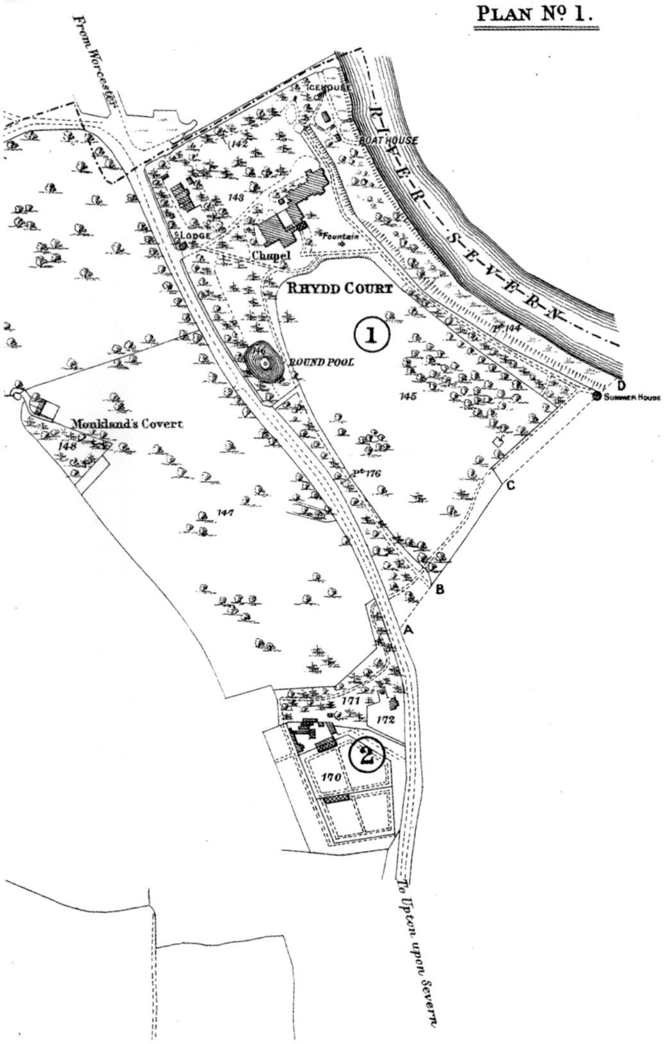

Rhydd Court sale particulars, 1919 (© WAAS 4192/1).

Sir Anthony Lechmere Bart. (1766 - 1849), watercolour by Richard Dighton, 1831. Private collection.

Croome Hunt meeting at Rhydd Court, 1886.

1884 and are documented by sale particulars of 1919 (CRO 4192/1). A later-19th century watercolour and print shows the large parterres set into the lawn on the west side of the house (Hurle, fig. 10). There is a fountain on the south lawn. A boat house and landing stage on the river are shown in 1884.
The landscape is essentially the same today as far as its plantations are concerned and something of a park atmosphere exists in the north-west corner of the park, west of the road from the Rhydd itself. The plantations stretching north/south along the river contain some fine trees including cedar.
The walled kitchen garden and its glasshouses also survives in separate ownership; the walls well maintained and enclosing tennis court, paths with pergola and the original central dividing wall.

Aalps College now occupies the main house and has erected additional ancillary buildings.

P. Hurle, *Malvern Chase*, 1978.
Beauties of England and Wales, Vol. VI, 1805.
G. Cooke (ed.) *Topographical & Statistical Description of the Co. of Worcester,* circa 1800.
Patersons Roads, 1829.

Ribbesford House

Parish: Ribbesford

HER Ref: WSM28833.

Grid Ref: SO 786 738.

Postcode: DY12 2TG.

O.S. 6" Map No: 14NW.

Date of Map: 1888, with extent of park & gardens shaded as 1880s OS.

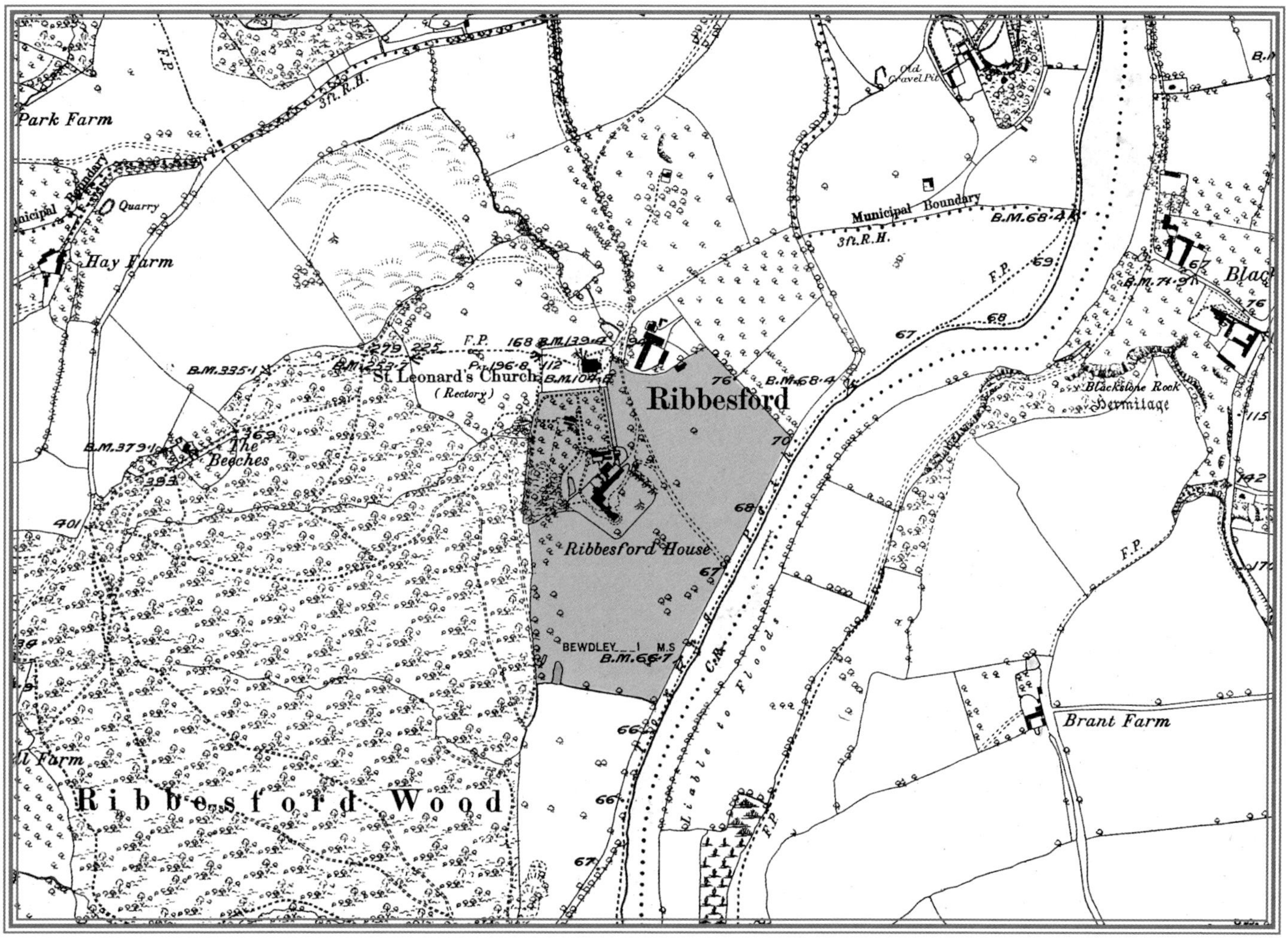

A sale in 1900 (CRO 5240/7) says that the moated, medieval house was rebuilt circa 1535. The Stables date from 1669. Further works belong to 1787 and 1830. Two gateposts to the drive are Jacobean (set at the house end of the entrance drive). J. Severn Walker (1863, p. 27) quotes a reminiscence from the 1820s of the house as it was in the 18th century, presumably before the alterations to the gardens that would have followed from the filling in of the moat circa 1790: "the moat included within its circuit a lawn or bowling green and many small gardens of parterres and alleys, laid out with rule and compass. Over the moat were two bridges ..." Another historical memory, which may or may not have topographical fact behind it, was "The Poet's Walk" said to recall George Herbert's connection with the property in the 17th century when this belonged to Lord Herbert of Cherbury.

Walker's reminiscences are supported by a map and watercolour drawings of the house in the Prattinton Coll. (Soc. of Antiquaries, London, information from Stephen Price). An 1813 copy of a 1771 map (**Plate 7**) shows the moat on all sides of the mansion broken by the gatehouse on the north side. The moat extends into a pool at the south end from which point the garden wall runs north-west with an inner wall parallel to it with a possible summerhouse halfway along at the entrance to a 3 sided walled orchard. To the north are 3 small paddocks containing the Church and the Lady's Bower. On the east side, also walled and linked back to the north-west end of

..........continued from previous page

the moat and house are 3 small straight- edged pools. The lawn within the moat on the south side was surrounded by a hedge – "South West View of Ribbesford Hall. 1771 by J. Slater" (also a copy) and another drawing shows it in use for bowls.
Nash (Vol. 1, 1781, f.p. 38) illustrates the substantial mansion in the later-18th century, a distant view from the river showing the church behind but no details of the gardens or landscape.
The later-18th and earlier-19th century landscape encompassed Blackstone Rock just to the north across the River Severn. (William Stukeley published an engraving of Blackstone Hermitage with a view back towards the Ribbesford bank in his *Itinerarium Curiosum* of 1712, p. 74).
By 1900 there was a wharf on the west bank of the river a little south of the mansion with a boat house beside the tow path. The landscape must always have included drives into and round Ribbesford Woods.
Ribbesford was regarded as a principal county seat circa 1800. Greenwood reported the grounds to be extensive in 1822 soon after "considerable additions" to the house had been made for the Revd. E. Winnington Ingram.
By the early-20th century, a large walled kitchen garden with glass-houses had been established north of the house. An ancient appearance had again been given to the gardens by a restoration of the house "in the Elizabethan style" in the mid-19th century (Niven, 1873). The north-east side of the house had a terrace with a ha-ha that continued round to the south side where it had a low wall and gates in the centre; the 1910 sale catalogue warned that the tenant might remove these gates! The 1914 Sale particulars state that the Elizabethan Mansion had recently been re-arranged and modernised at considerable cost; "The House is lighted by Electric Light". The Pleasure Grounds were then estimated at 6 acres within a total estate of 1,541 acres (CRO 5723).

The park as defined by the 1930 edition of the OS 6 inch, was a triangular wedge of land between the church at the north, the Woods to the west and the river and road on the east. A sale in 1910 (CRO 5240/7) refers to a fine avenue of ancient sycamores going north to the Bewdley-Cleobury Mortimer road. The park area, now arable, is bare of trees except for one large clump or coppice. An avenue of horse chestnut runs along its north side ending at the junction with the Church and the 17th century Stables.

J. Severn Walker *Architectural Sketches,* Vol II, 1863.
W. Niven, *Illustrations of Old Worcesteshire Houses,* 1873.
T. R. Nash, *Collections for the History of Worcestershire,* Vol I, 1781.
W. Stukeley, *Itinerarium Curiosum,* Vol. 1, 1726.
C. & J. Greenwood, *Worcestershire Delineated,* 1822.

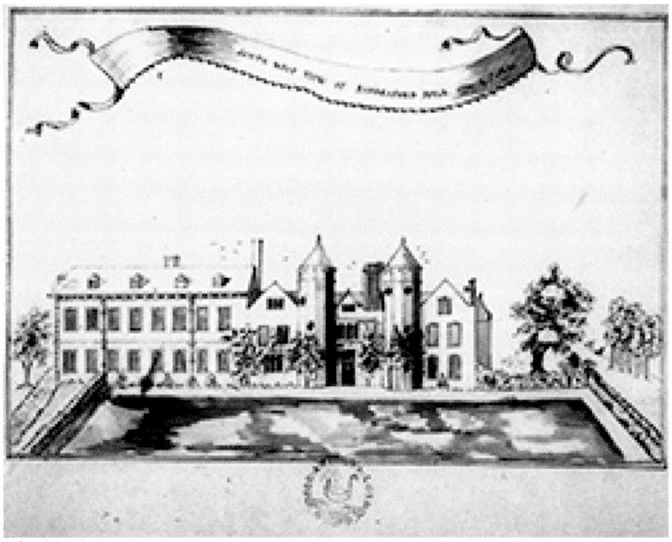

After J. Slater, 1771, *South West View of Ribbesford Hall,* Society of Antiquaries of London, Prattinton Collection.

J. Severn Walker *Architectural Sketches,* Vol II, 1863.

Rochford House

Parish: Rochford

HER Ref: WSM28832.

Grid Ref: SO 631 676. Postcode: WR15 8SN.

O.S. 6" Map No: 19NE.

Date of Map: 1884, with extent of park & gardens shaded as 1905 OS.

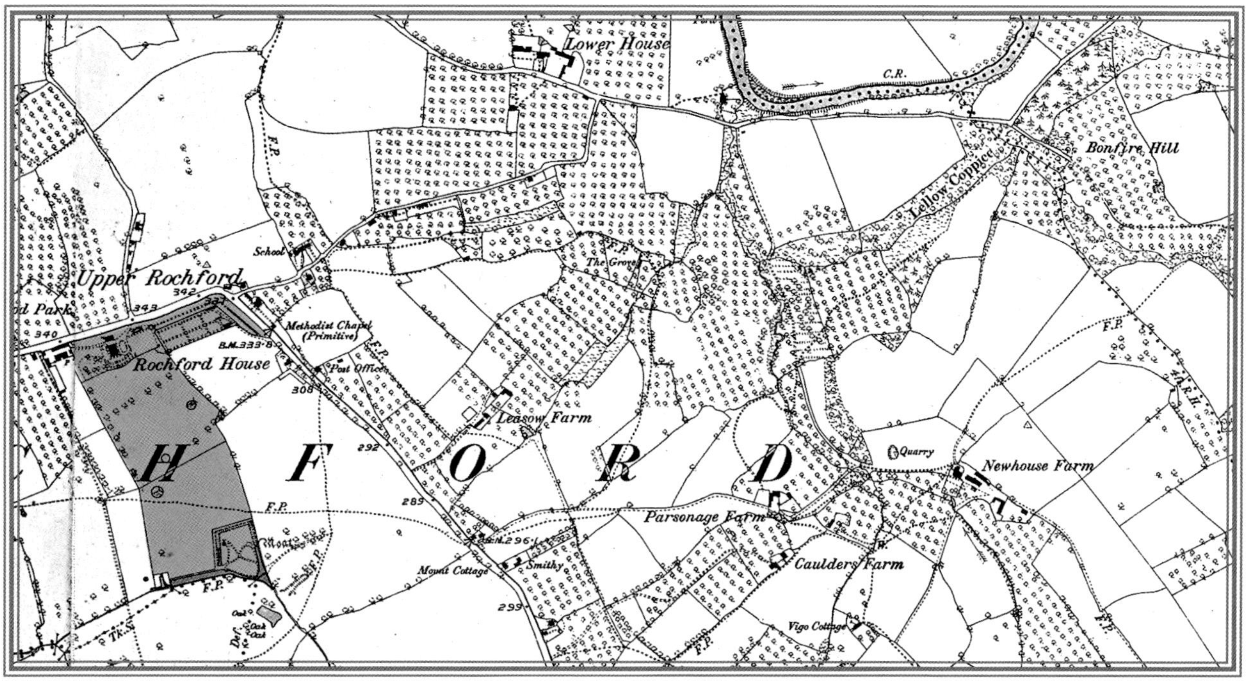

A small park is shown on the first editions of the OS 6 inch with an icehouse, fishpond and moated site gathered together at its south end. Only small grounds are shown on the first edition of the OS one inch (1828).
In 2016 the walls of the surviving walled garden are in good condition and there are a number of specimen trees, including cedars. There is no surviving park.
The property is referred to as Rochford Court House in the VCH.

M. Salter, *Medieval Castles of Herefordshire and Worcestershire,* 1989 (no. 62).
Victoria County History, Vol. 4, 1924 (VCH).

Rosedene

Parish: Dodford with Grafton

HER Ref: WSM71784.
Grid Ref: SO 930 731.
Postcode: B61 9BU.
O.S. 6" Map No: 15NE.
Date of Map: 1884.

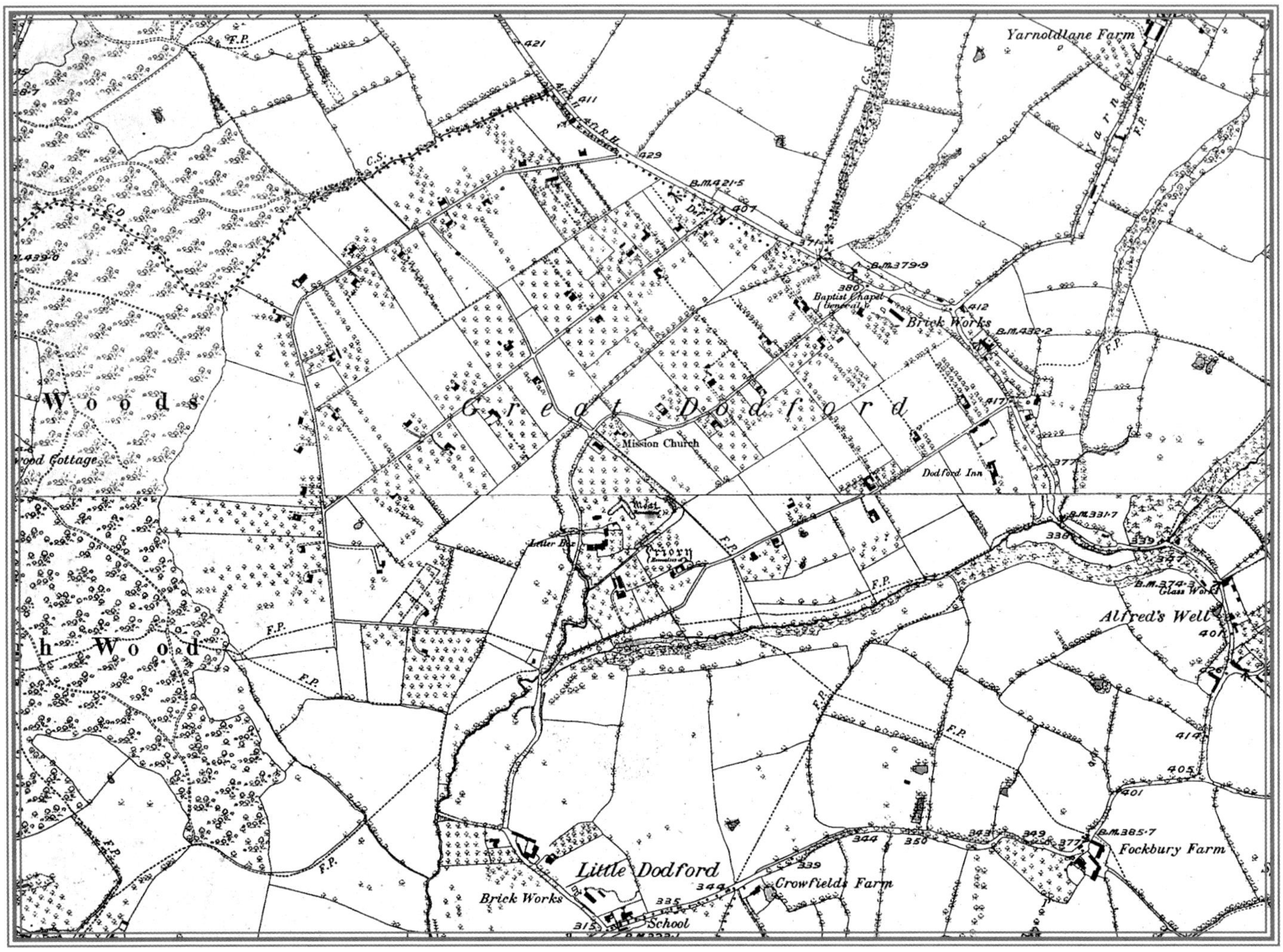

This cottage, in Dodford, is a survivor of the Chartist project of 1848-50 (National Land Company). It was acquired by the National Trust in 1997 and subsequently restored to the original concept with 4 acres of organic garden, vegetable plot and orchard. Dodford was the most successful of 5 Chartist settlements and the cottage is a survivor among 11 Listed buildings from among the original 40 cottages built on 273 acres acquired by Fergus O'Connell in 1848. Rosedene was already occupied by 1849 (Plot 29). The 1884 OS map shown above illustrates the distinctive enclosure pattern.

Despite the poor soil, a red clay for which a special digging fork made in Stourbridge was manufactured, Dodford developed a successful vegetable and fruit business (strawberries a speciality) and was able to take advantage of the neighbouring industrial towns and markets and sustain a viable business until after the Great War. A stable and a piggery were added in the 1880s, a sign of commercial success.

The garden behind the house is cultivated today to produce fruit and vegetables.

W. Bond, *From Hamlet to Parish*, 1872.

D. Ross, "Britain Express", *National Trust Archeological Review*, 1999-2000.

Rous Lench Court

Parish: Rous Lench

HER Ref: WSM09168/33862. Grid Ref: SP 019 530. Postcode: WR11 4UJ.

O.S. 6" Map No: 35NW/SW, 35NE/SE.

Date of Map: 1884, 1885, with extent of park & gardens shaded as H. E. Register.

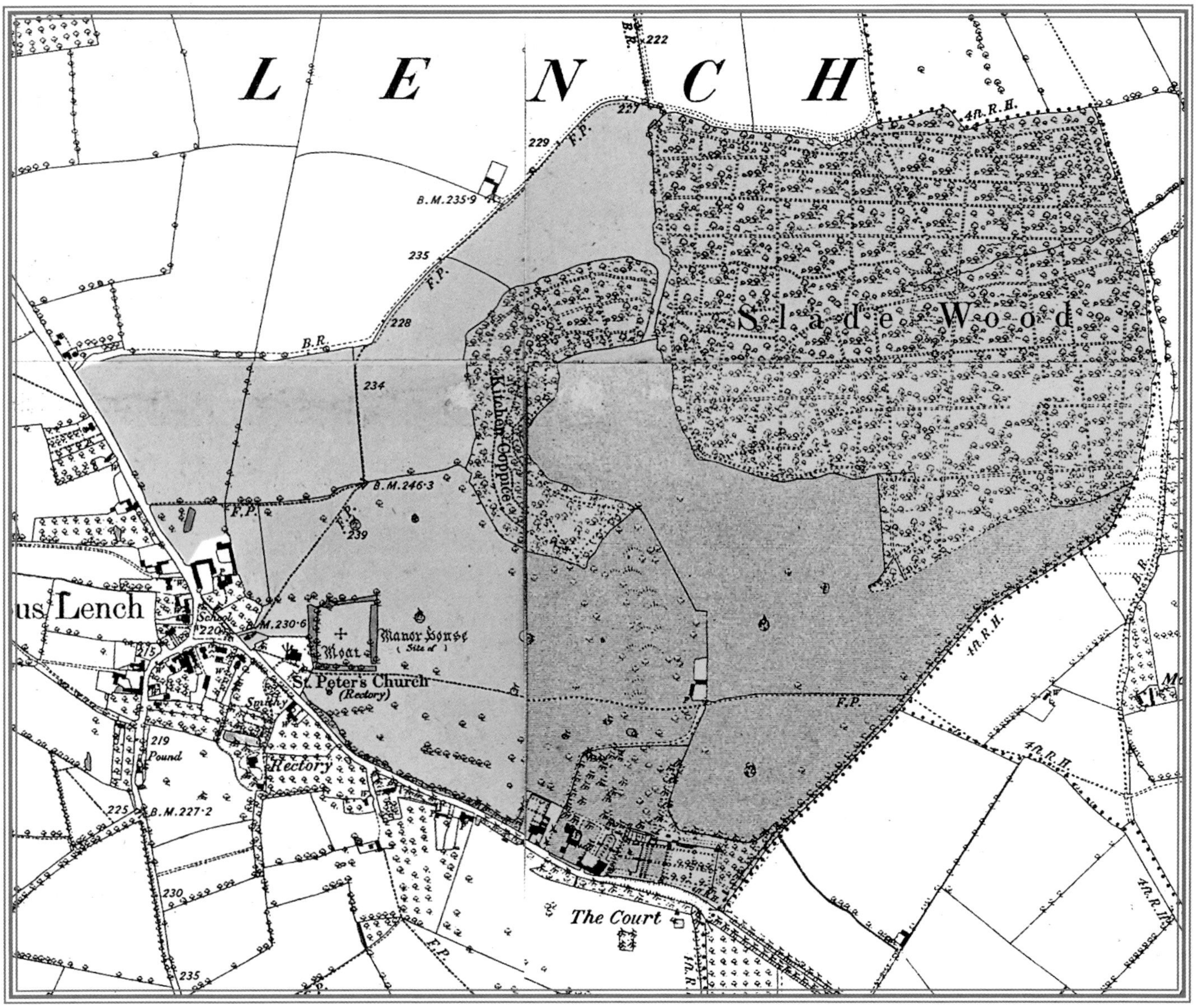

Included within Historic England's Register of Historic Parks and Gardens of special historic interest in England.

The house dates from the 16th, 17th and 19th centuries. Nash in 1782 mentions: "The summer-house at the top of the garden, from whence you have a pleasant prospect, still remains". (Vol. 2, p. 84). This had gone by 1873 when Niven recorded the house and the clipped yews. The property is listed as a principal county seat circa 1800.

The HE Listing dates steps, terrace, retaining wall, balustrade and Italianate tower to the 1850s and 1860s; the BoE gives 1881 as the date of the Tower as a commemoration of Richard Baxter of Kidderminster with a possible attribution to William Burges. The estate was put up for sale in 1875 when it was acquired by the Revd. Dr. Chafy and the sale particulars then described the garden as Italian and illustrated a terrace with small cypresses set in the lawn; the yew hedges were only

..........continued from previous page

Rous Lench Court, image taken from *Victoria County History* Vol. 3, 1913, (VCH).

Rous Lench Court looking remarkably unchanged in 1980. Courtesy of Berrows Journal.

illustrated in plan (CRO 1775). The Revd. Chafy extended his imaginative development of Rous Lench to include the village where he placed half-timbered pillar boxes (Jones, p. 341).

This famous, substantially 19th century garden, has been well recorded, e.g. by *Country Life* in 1899 (VI, p. 336) and discussed by garden historians such as Christopher Hussey, Avray Tipping and Miles Hadfield. The VCH in 1913 gave a detailed description: "The terraced gardens with their clipped yew hedges, laid out under the direction of The Revd. Dr. W. Chafy, form an almost unique example of topiary art. The splendid yew ring surrounding a summerhouse on the south east side of the house, together with a few single trees here and there and a fine avenue, remain as survivals of the original garden, which could never have been large. The whole now covers about 7 acres. In the park is still to be seen the moat which surrounded the old manor-house. It includes an area of about half an acre in extent."(Vol. 3, p. 497). The HE Register adds: "The main topiary features are shaped as tall towers, battlemented walls and gateways, emphasising the fall of the terraces, with a massive domed circular yew arbour near the centre ... in the lower part of the gardens the terraces contain a formal area of paths, pool, lawns and bedding to the north of the house. A further balustraded terrace with steps faces west from the house. Ornamental woodland in the north-western area, with mature conifers from the late 19th century."

Dr. Chafy's own description in his 1901 *Short History* has some charming illustrations by Gwendolin Chafy: Yew Hedge on Site of old Baronial Hall; Rous Lench Court from the Italian Garden; Lower Pleasaunce Tower in the Garden; Yew Avenue planted 1480; The End (gateway in gardens as end piece). His text explains that the garden, extended by himself to 8 acres, is "laid out in formal style in a succession of 10 terraces most clipped in various ways, some buttressed and pierced, some scalloped, and with many gateways of yew architecture, that on the site of the Baronial Hall being divided by an archway lofty enough to admit of carriages driving beneath it, and flanked by massive piers terminating in Peacocks with spread tails – the Chafy Crest." "Standing beside the lower gates and looking up towards the House, the view is "scenic and Baronial". Immediately in front is a square Lawn, parted up the middle by a broad gravel path bordered with golden yews, and terminating in a flight of 19 stone steps 20 feet wide, right and left of which at the top is an ornamental stone balustrade like that at Haddon Hall, where a Rosary has been made with a fountain throwing up jets in the form of a cage." The tour continues to the Italian garden "intersected by brick walks and prim flower-beds, with another fountain in the centre ... the yew avenue ... the Lower Pleasaunce in the midst of which stands the historic yew circle, 37 feet in diameter ... 19 more steps ascend to the next level which is edged by a dense thickness of massive yews ...".

Country Life returned to Rous Lench in 1921: "Mr. H. E. Chafy ... has considerably increased the extent of the old garden ... he sticks to the English fashion of not distracting the eye with peacocks, ships and evangelists" (Vol. LI, p. 758). In 1959, Hadfield said :" It seems to me that it (the garden) has evolved over the centuries into the finest topiary garden in Britain. The shapes are simple and without the eccentricity that Alexander Pope ridiculed in Queen Anne's day" (Vol. CXXVI, p. 532).

In many ways the best and most evocative description of Rous Lench is by Ethne Clarke (op. cit.) who describes the Revd. Chafy's developments (including perhaps those of H. E. Chafy) and takes the story on to the Burns's, father and son, and their head gardener, Mr. Newman, and Mrs. Houghton, the manageress of the nursery garden, the eventual legatees. Clarke captures the moment of the

..........continued from previous page

ABOVE: The entrance to the Yew Garden, 1954. WAAS, Rous Lench, 8073.

mature garden retreating towards nature but with all its essentail structure intact. "Rous Lench Court as we see it today is an early example of the Italianate English garden; its hedge-enclosed rooms, dramatic vistas and manipulation of the natural terrain pre-date the garden at Hidcote Manor and Sissinghurst. For this, and for its 15th century *alléé*, it should be respected and if possible preserved" (Clarke op. cit.).

The 1875 sale details remind us that the park as well as the garden was of some age. Lots connected with Court Farm have park field names: Far Park Hill (10 acres); Middle Park (18); Park Hill (7); Meadow Park (14). The first and second editions of the OS 6 inch show slightly different areas for the park. The 1884 park apparently extended south-west into the village; the 1905 park did not, but overlaid more fields to the north and stretched north-west from the Court to beyond Grange Farm.

The Lavender Terrace with statue of Mercury. Photo taken 1954. WAAS, Rous Lench, 8077.

B. Jones, *Follies and Grottoes*, 1974.
Country Life, Vol. VI, 1899, p. 336.
C. Hussey, "Of Yew Hedges", *Country Life*, Vol. LI, 1921, p. 756.
H. A. Tipping, "Evergreen Hedges", *Country Life*, Vol. LVIII, 1925, p. 796.
M. Hadfield, "Yews in Garden Design", *Country Life*, Vol. CXXVI, 1959, p. 532.
Victoria County History Vol. 3, 1913, p. 497 (VCH).
W. K. W. Chafy, "The History of Rous Lench", *Assoc. Archit. Socs., Reports and Papers.*, 1899, (Worcester Diocesan Architectural Soc.), p. 182 ff.
W. K. W. Chafy, *A Short History of Rous Lench,* 1901 (reprinted 1983), with illus. by G. M. Chafy.
A. Brooks & N. Pevsner, *Worcestershire,* 2007 (BoE).
P. Hunt, *The Shell Gardens Book*, 1964.
G. Jekyll & C. Hussey, *Garden Ornament,* 1918, ed. 1927, Topiary Work, p. 155, figs. 17 - 19.
T. R. Nash, *Collections for a History of Worcestershire,* Vol I, 1781.
HE *Register of Parks & Gardens,* 1997.

Woodcut by G. Chafy from *A Short History of Rous Lench,* 1901.

E. Clarke, "Times Glory: The mystery and chance of Rous Lench Court", *Hortus,* No. 11, Autumn 1989 (with 4 etchings by Simon Dorrell).

Severn Bank

Parish: Severn Stoke & Croome D'Abitot

HER Ref: WSM29002. Grid Ref: SO 856 432. Postcode: WR8 9JG.

O.S. 6" Map No: 40SE, 47NE.

Date of Maps: 1884, 1885, with deduced extent of park & gardens shaded (not shaded on 1905 OS).

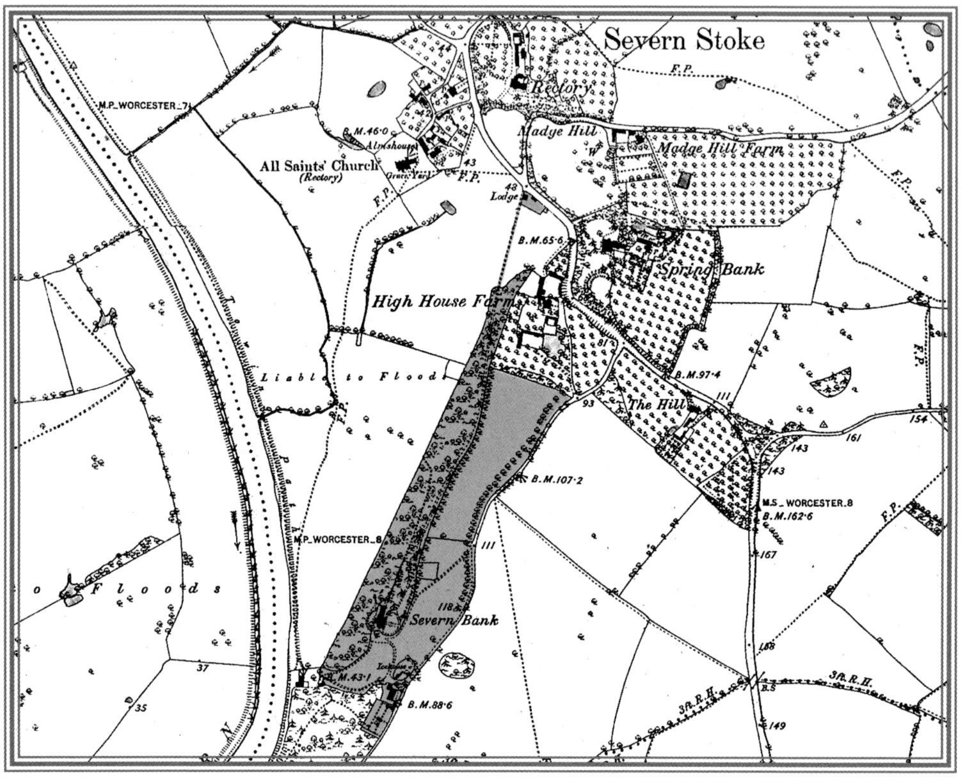

Richard Dighton, "The Noble Viscount", (Lord Deerhurst 1784 - 1843), print, 1828.

This early-19th century, stuccoed and castellated house is described in *Beauties* as "a place of pleasure for fishing parties" (1814, p. 346). It was used by Lord Deerhurst, heir to the Earl of Coventry, and was an outlying part of the Croome Court estate situated close to the landing stage which was very important to estate management; two American Deer were delivered there for the Croome Menagerie in 1776. The garden wall with gothic panelling, the gate- piers and cast-iron gates, and a small curved belvedere, are all from the early-19th century and the lodge is circa 1840 (HE Listing).

The grounds as shown on the 1884 OS 6 inch, are made up by a narrow strip of land with wood on the river side and a drive from the house north-east to Severn Stoke. There was an icehouse immediately south-east of the house and a boathouse south-west on the river bank. Cliff Wood borders the grounds to the south. All this is on the plan made by Thomas Hopcraft for Lord Coventry in 1810 (CRO 849). Two views through the wood were evidently cut through for sight of the river and a third was added later.

These details of the landscape and architecture of the house may need to be dated back to the 18th century from evidence relating to the Croome estate, e.g. tree felling recorded in 1782, a new boat house in 1789 and a sunk fence proposed in 1790. Some work was going on at Severn Bank as early as 1771 and continued at intervals until 1791 (Croome Estate Archive). Robert Adam made a design for altering the front in 1779 and this front was stuccoed in 1781. Further stucco work was carried out circa 1820 and circa 1840 (BoE p. 592).

A public footpath follows the east boundary of the park. When sold in 2009 the property was described as standing in 22 ¼ acres of formal gardens, woodlands and paddocks on the east side (*Country Life*). The walled kitchen garden is now the private garden to a separate residence.

Country Life, 26. 8. 2009.

Beauties of England and Wales, Vol. XV, 1814.

A. Brooks & N. Pevsner, *Worcestershire,* 2007 (BoE).

Severn End

Parish: Hanley Castle

HER Ref: WSM05772.

Grid Ref: SO 846 426. Postcode: WR8 0BW.

O.S. 6" Map No: 47NE.

Date of Map: 1885, with deduced extent of park & gardens shaded (not shaded on 1905 OS).

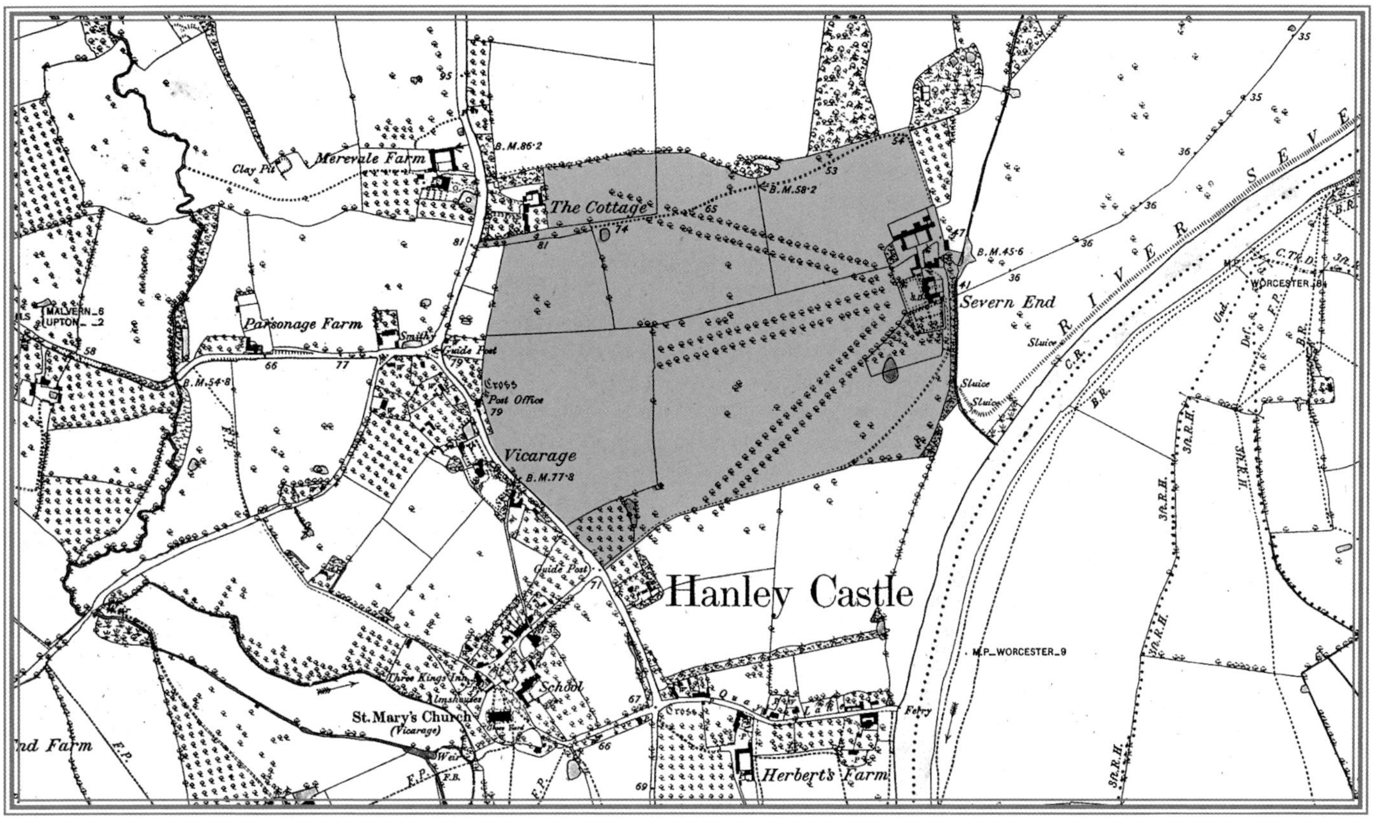

The medieval background for a park at Severn End is the park associated with Hanley Castle which was also within Malvern Chase. "The pleasant seat of the Lechmeres" (Nash, 1, 1781, p. 559) had a small deer park in the 18th century but this was disparked circa 1790 (VCH, 4, 1924, pp. 90-98). This was presumably sited in the area of the park-like land west of the house called The Park. The most evident features of the landscape park were 3 avenues which radiated west from the house as shown on the 1884 OS 6 inch map but not on the 1812 survey for the first edition of the OS one inch. These avenues no doubt represent late-17th century landscape fashion and augment the remarkable, small, terraced walled gardens developed next to the mansion by Sir Nicholas Lechmere from 1656. The 3 avenues are still shown on the 1930 OS 6 inch. The central avenue of limes is the best surviving, the other two being much degraded. The *Beauties* in 1810 mention the fine oaks (p. 346) but by 1975 (*Country Life*, op. cit.) the avenues were horse chesnut, lime, and Norway maple replacing wych elm. None of these avenues followed the line of the drive from the house to the Lodge on the Worcester-Upton road established at the time of the post-fire restoration of 1896.

In 1889 the Revd. Wood recorded some family tradition about the park trees. In 1641 Judge Lechmere "began to plant a crescent of elm trees in the park on the western side of the house and which he completed in 1650. A few of these trees still remain. The avenues of trees which supply the place of those removed were planted about 20 years ago. Where it was found to be possible the few old trees remaining were incorporated into the new lines, thus forming a connecting link between the past and the present" (op. cit, p. 123). Wood's article includes an engraving of the river frontage of the house before the 1896 fire.

The house is shown as a residence (Hanley End) on Cary in 1805 but by 1814 the Lechmeres had moved to the Rhydd and in 1822 Greenwood reported that Severn End was "now occupied as a grazing farm on a large scale". Niven in 1873 said that the house was occupied by

Severn End

..........continued from previous page

Sir Edmund Lechmere's farm steward "but well kept up". In the interval, Severn End was sold in 1830 only to be bought back in 1849. There was a devastating fire in 1896 so that much of the present house is a replica of a 17th and 18th century house. The Listed Lodge Gates go with this late-19th century moment.

Sir Nicholas Lechmere's diary allows his gardening to be followed precisely. The north wall was put up in 1656, two more along the west and south sides a year later, and a garden pavilion (restored 1858) was erected in the south-west corner in 1661. Lechmere used this pavilion as a study. Between 1657 and 1662 he raised a terrace within the east walk (known as the Mount Walk) with steps at either end. In 1677 he built a pigeon house and in 1681 a malt house. *Country Life* points out that Lechmere left no description of his garden on the west side of the house but that a great-great grandson remembered a formal parterre with beds edged in curious patterns. The south garden was no doubt also formal and had fruit trees (p. 266). Nash's illustration of the mansion from the river (Vol. 1, 1781) shows an east wall to the south garden of considerable length, with a pavilion at the south-east corner, perhaps an exaggeration of the facts.

Photo dated 1891. WAAS, Hanley Castle 6740.

A full interpretation of the gardens related to the Lechmere Diary is given by Lewis Sheppard, the architect who superintended the post-fire restoration of Severn End, and is the source for "the parterres in patterns of curious design, some of them edged with box" within the garden on the west side (Sheppard, op. cit). He attributes the chestnuts in Upper Lechmere Field to 1658 "some of which remain" (1899). He also tells the story of the gardener's ghost, the gardener who occupied a room in the north-west corner of the mansion on the first floor.

The timber for the post 1896 restoration of the house came from the estate.

A Day Book (CRO 1531/31) recording minor expenditure on the park and gardens for the years 1754-1764, refers in the park to: dung, the Keeper, man killing a buck, pletching the Church Park Hedge, thorns, hedging in the Walk ground, the Pool on the Green. In the garden, money is spent on Guernsey Lilly roots, Rhubarb, and amounts of between 11 and 18 shillings for "gardners" - Baldwin and Luke in the 1750s, Baldwin, Cullorne and Cole in the 1760s.

Severn end, the seat of Edmund Lechmere Esq.

Severn End from T. R. Nash, *Collections for the History of Worcestershire,* Vol I, 1781.

Nash noticed the *sorbus ancapania* (sic), perhaps relevant to the 17th century and in 1822, Greenwood remarked on a quicken pear tree. Horace Walpole visiting Severn End in 1753 (apparently arriving by river) commented: "About a mile from Worcester you break upon a sweet view of the Severn. A little farther on the banks is Mr. Lechmere's house, but he has given it strict charge of a troop of willows never to let him see the river. To his right hand extends the fairest meadow covered with cattle that ever you saw; at the end of it is the town of Upton, with a church half ruined, and a bridge of six arches, which I believe with little trouble he might see from his garden" (Information from Jane Bradney).

Revd. T. W. Wood, "Severn End", *Assoc. Archit. Socs. Reports & Papers,* 1889, 1. (Worcester Diocesan Architectural Society).
Lewis Sheppard, "Severn End, Worcester", *Assoc. Archit., Socs., Reports and Papers,* 1899, Worcester Diocesan Architectural Society, p. 172 ff.
R. Bentley, *The Letters of Horace Walpole* ..., Vol. 3, 1840, p. 22.
Victoria County History, Vol. 4, 1924, pp. 90-8 (VCH).
Country Life, Vol. CLXXVIII, 1975.
P. Hurle, *Malvern Chase,* 1978.
T. R. Nash, *Collections for the History of Worcestershire,* Vol I, 1781.
C. & J. Greenwood, *Worcestershire Delineated,* 1822.

Shakenhurst

Parish: Bayton

HER Ref: WSM28831/45670.

Grid Ref: SO 673 730. Postcode: DY14 9AR.

O.S. 6" Map No: 12NE/SE, 13NW/SW.

Date of Maps: both 1884, with extent of park & grounds shaded as 1905 OS.

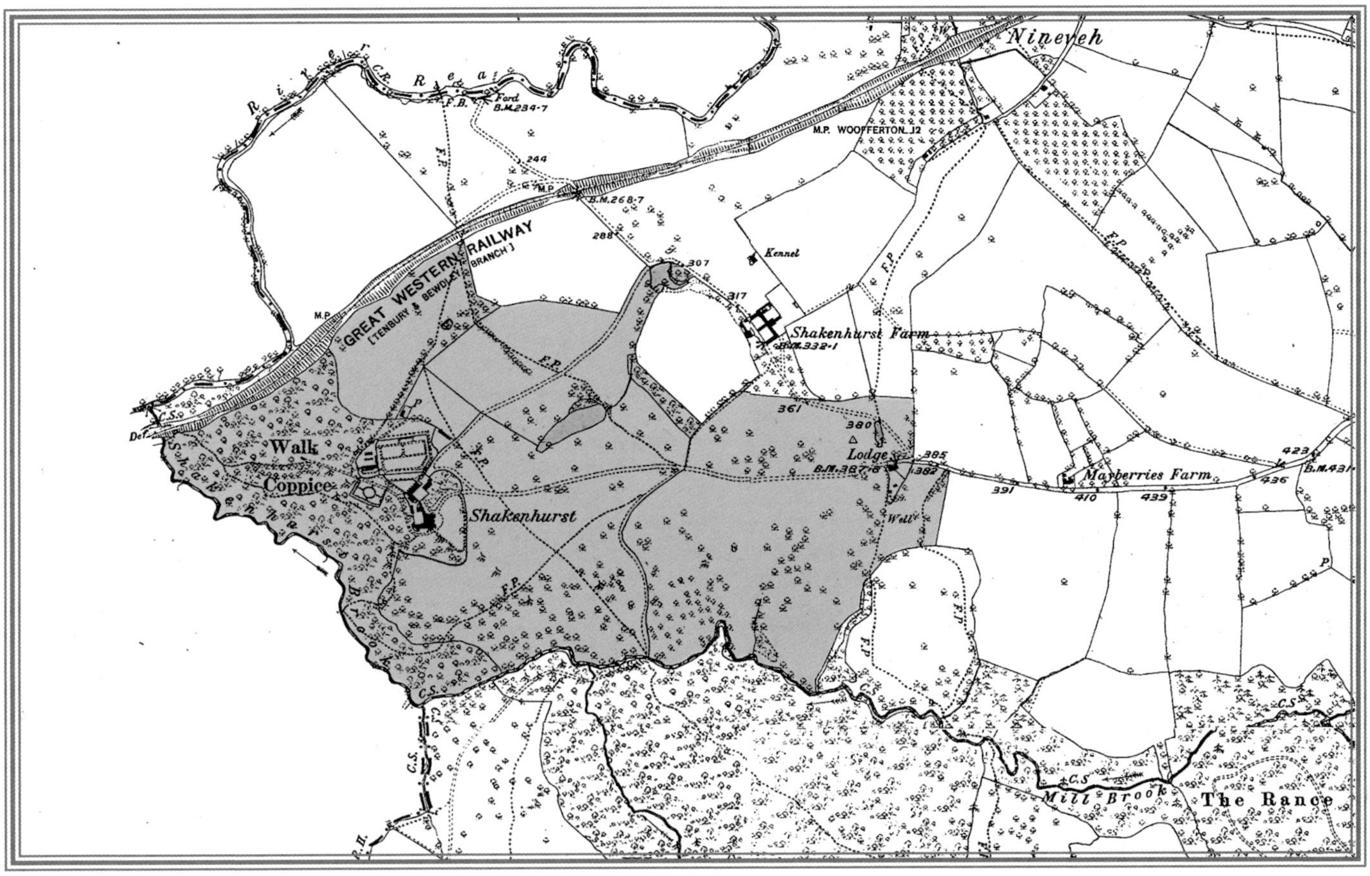

The house is of circa 1700 and 1804 and the park may therefore be of 18th rather than 19th century origin; the site is much more ancient. It is first shown as a park on Walker's map of 1835. The park as on the 1882 OS 6 inch is restricted to the west by Walk Coppice and the Great Western Railway, with the Shakenhurst Brook running along the south side. The area then designated as park didn't extend very far down the drive to the lodge towards Bayton, but no doubt once did.

Shakenhurst is marked as a residence on Cary in 1805 and the *Beauties* in 1814 and Bentley in 1841 both speak of a handsome seat and the latter of extensive grounds. In 1884 there was a formal garden set in the Walk Coppice and a large kitchen garden immediately north of the house where there is also a large pool.

In 2017 the gardens and park were substantially intact with most of the tree cover and the park grazed.

Beauties of England and Wales, Vol. XV, 1814.
Bentley's History and Guide to Dudley, circa 1841.

Sherridge House

Parish: Leigh & Bransford

HER Ref: WSM28829.

Grid Ref: SO 772 514. Postcode: WR13 5DB.

O.S. 6" Map No: 32SE.

Date of Map: 1884, with extent of park & garden shaded as 1905 OS.

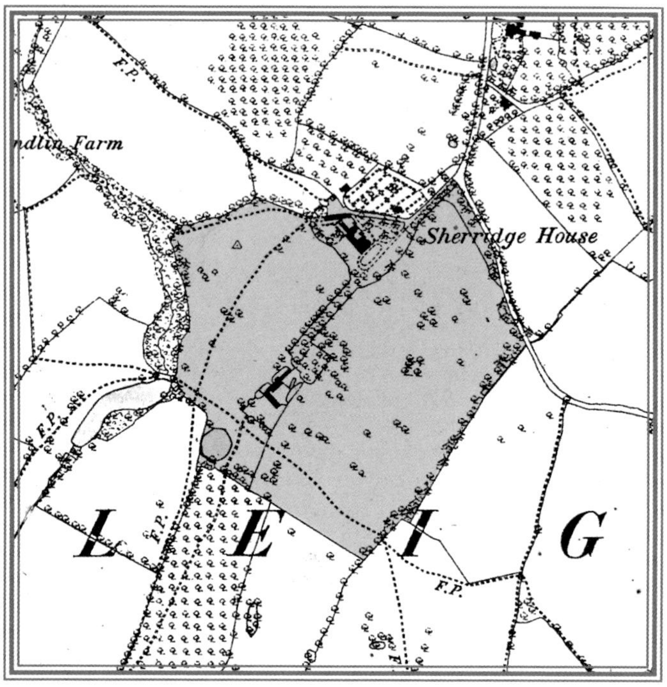

Worcestershire Archery Society Fete, 1855. *Illustrated London News.*

Some grounds are shown on early to mid-19th century printed maps and a park is marked on the 2nd edition of the OS 6 inch in 1905 and on Bartholomew's in 1906. The house is known to the family as Sherridge, to the BoE in 2007 as Sherridge House and to the *Illustrated London News* in 1855 as Sherridge Court.

The creation of the Sherridge landscape as it is today, began in 1723 when Benjamin Johnson, Town Clerk of Worcester purchased it. He acquired the old Court House which was an E shaped, half-timbered building which he developed into its present form (Peter Norbury). At this time, Sherridge Lodge to its north-east was the more important estate. This remained the case according to an estate map of 1822. The rise of the Court followed from its acquisition by Thomas Jones circa 1832 who took the name of his wife, Mary Anne Norbury whom he had married in 1828; acquisitions of adjoining land were made in the 1830s and 1850s and 1870s. Charles Crisp's 1832 survey (Family Archive) documents an estate just beginning to be formed. The fields then called the West Meadow, the Big Meadow and a small part of Barn Meadow represent the Park as on the 1905, OS 6 inch. The Big Meadow (Park) seems the likely site for the "Fete of the Worcestershire Archery Society, at Sherridge Court, near Worcester" shown in the *Illustrated London News*.

In 1832, the Mansion was approached from a drive off the Leigh Sinton to Worcester Road having a fence to Big Meadow on the left, the drive continuing up to the front door around a piece of oval lawn. The drive branches to the right towards the yard and Stables and is fenced off from the gardens of 2 cottages and parallel strips (belonging to other tenements); one half-timbered cottage remains as the Old House. All these arrangements have survived except that these gardens were later absorbed into a large un-walled, kitchen garden. An orchard was beyond the gardens. A small plantation along the right had side of the entrance drive is today represented by an avenue of limes and chestnuts.

The entrance drive continued past the principal front of the house towards farm buildings used as part of intensive fruit farming at Sherridge in the 19th and 20th centuries; one of these was the packing shed. This route is marked by an avenue of trees. There is a pool a little beyond the farm buildings made in the early-20th century. The Fish Pond to the north of this was an old landscape feature adjoining the Dingle, the two elements linked by some rock work. The whole forms a miniature and unassuming landscape park.

Beside the east front there is a short, arched avenue of yews known as Worms Alley. On the lawn at this point there was until the 1960's a large water clock made by Prisoners of War during the First World War.

Shrawley Wood House

Parish: Shrawley

HER Ref: WSM12686/28828.

Grid Ref: SO 804 654.

Postcode: WR6 6TT.

O.S. 6" Map No: 21SW.

Date of Map: 1884, with extent of park & grounds shaded as 1905 OS.

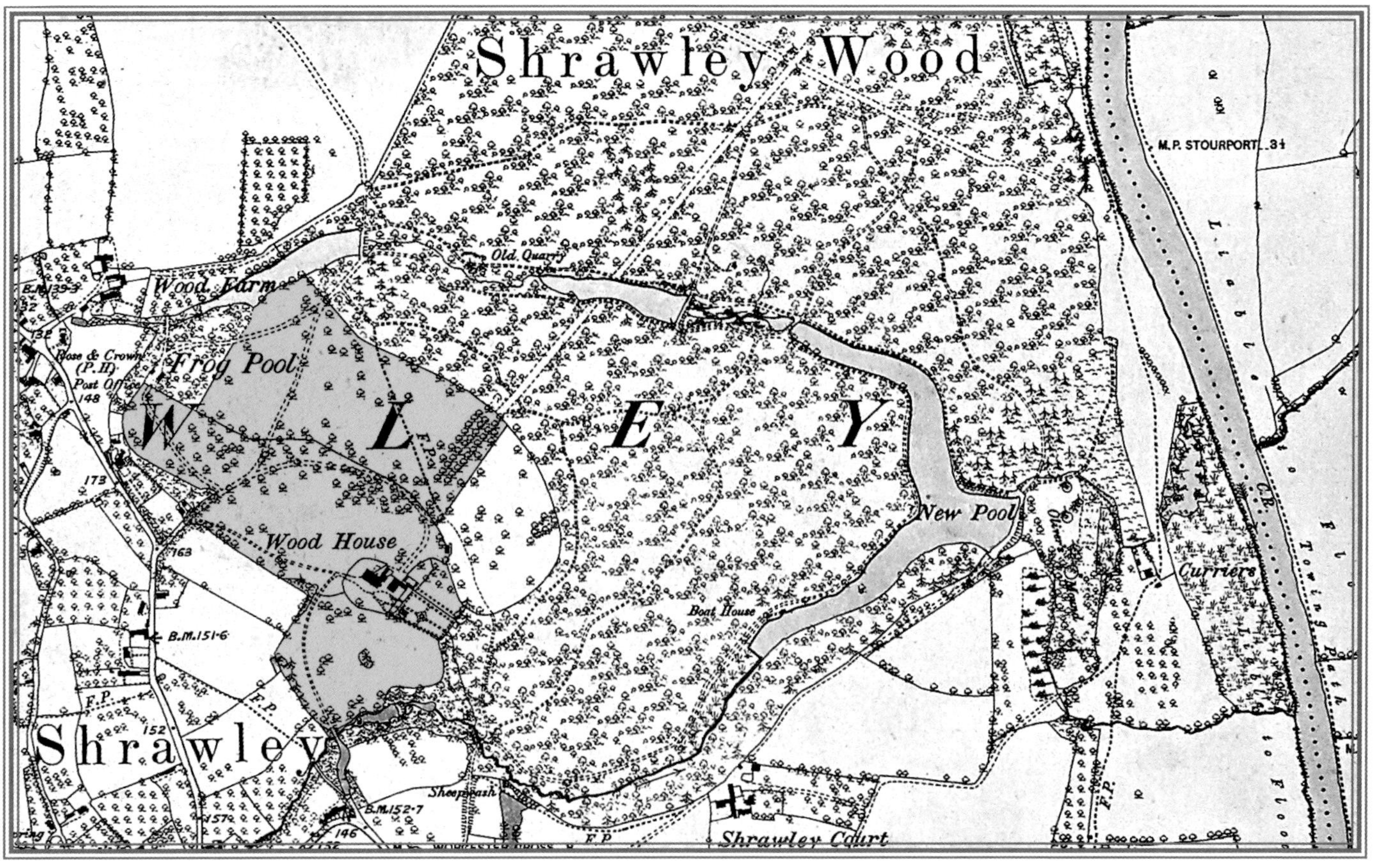

The circa 1800 house (stuccoed) replaced an earlier house illustrated on a Dougharty Map of the Vernon Estates made in 1731-2 (CRO 7335/154) when as Wood Hall it was leased to a Captain Vernon, and used as a lesser Vernon residence to Hanbury Hall. This house had a modest, formal garden with trees or shrubs either side of a central path. There is an early-19th century wash drawing of the later house (CRO 7335/47) showing the back of the house and one end giving on to a large lawn with a glimpse of the veranda which ran along the main front. An annotation explains that, in order to illustrate the house, some fine trees have been excluded from the view. The Listing gives a date of circa 1850 for the gate and piers to the garden enclosure but does not mention the large central feature, which may be a fountain, recorded by the 1883 OS. The park is shown on both OS 6 inch maps of 1883 and 1905 along with 3 large pools, a boat house on New Pool, and 2 Lodges. The east reach of the New Pool runs up to Oliver's Mound set above the River Severn.

The site now attracts many visitors to see the bluebells lining the public footpaths that cross to the south of the house. The walled garden in 2017 is used as a pleasure garden with the slips as orcharding. Some 18th and 19th century trees survive and the New Pool appears to be substantially unchanged.

Sion Hill House

Parish: Wolverley & Cookley

HER Ref: WSM28979.

Grid Ref: SO 837 786. Postcode: DY10 2YY.

O.S. 6" Map No: 8SE.

Date of Map: 1888, with extent of park & gardens shaded as 1880s OS.

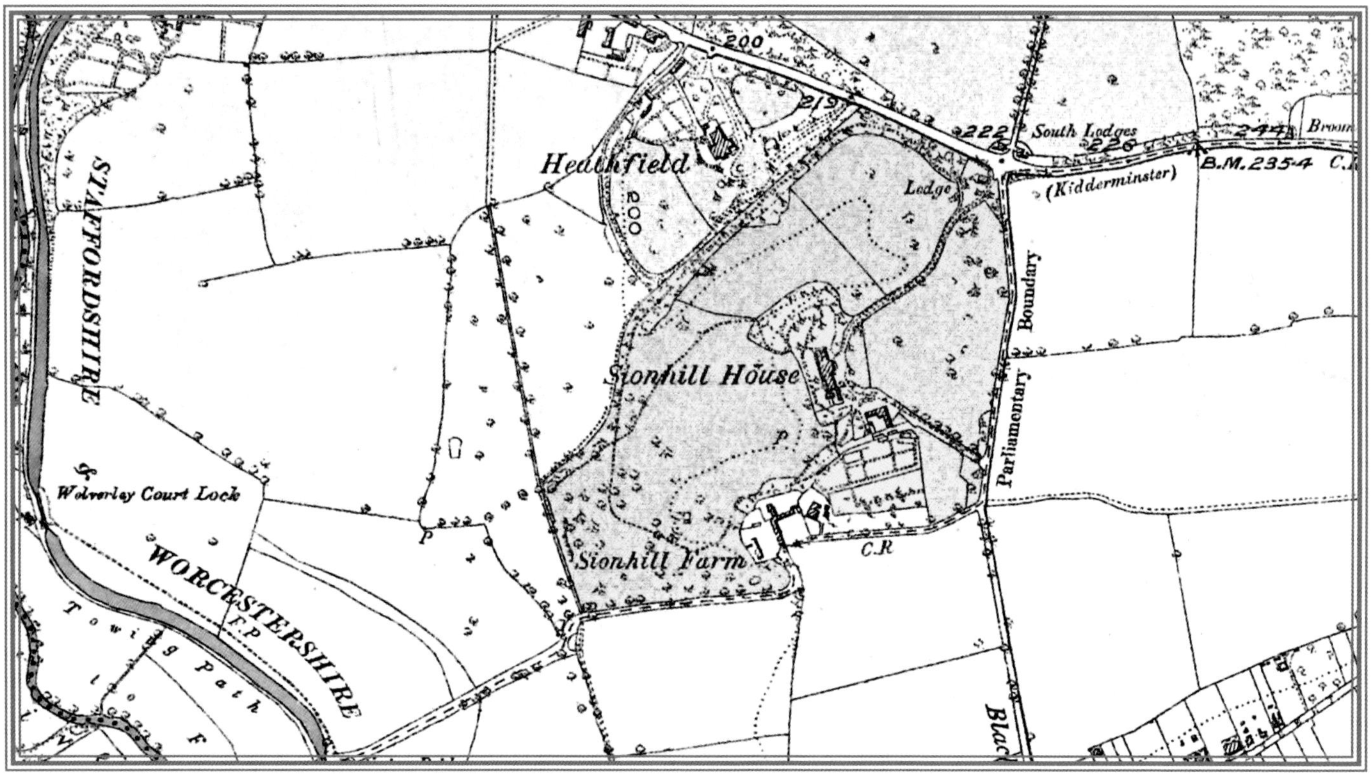

THIS PAGE AND OVERLEAF: lithographs by Thomas Underwood, 1836 from Sale Particulars. © WAAS 5278/44.

General View of Entrance Front & Drive.

The first edition of the OS 6 inch describes a small park with fringe planting, a lodge, kitchen garden away from the house and the farm. This early-18th and 20th century house is essentially a villa in scale, divided by the planting from Heathfield adjoining on the north-west. It has its lodge at the north-eastern corner facing the south lodges of Lea Castle. Nash noticed it as a pleasant house in 1782 (Vol. 2, p. 471) and grounds are shown on early-19th century maps, e.g. on the 1815 survey for the first OS one inch.

The landscape is excellently described in sale particulars of 1836 (WAAS 5278/44) which are illustrated with no less than 6 tinted lithographs by Thomas Underwood of Birmingham (e.g. "Garden Front from the Old Yew Tree"), as well as by a plan. The lithographs show the yew tree in the park fenced off and with a circular seat round it and in the same view the ha-ha dividing the terrace with a path round a circular lawn, the large conservatory attached to the house and a veranda. Other vignettes show the Temple (summerhouse), the lodge and views of

..........continued from previous page

the Dingle. The grounds "laid out as a park" amounted to 30 acres. Broadwaters has now expanded up to its south boundary.

The property has remained unchanged in all major respects with a park-like atmosphere on the north side, the old main approach and a young lime avenue to the present main entrance from the east.

The south part of the park is full of mature trees, e.g. oak, beech, pine, chestnut, merging into a wooded fringe on the south and west boundaries.

The 1836 sale particulars give an unusually detailed insight into the requirements of a desirable property at this date: "This excellent mansion house affords every accommodation to a family of high social position.... billiard or book room, lighted from above, and well adapted for a picture gallery...double coach house, stables for 10 horses...the lawn and flower gardens in which is a Conservatory or Orange House are well stocked with flowers and shrubs and the grounds around the house (30 acres of meadow land) are laid out as a park ... scarcely surpassed for picturesqueness ... diversified by hill and dell and glen."

T. R. Nash, *Collections for the History of Worcestershire,* Vol II, 1782.

TEMPLE IN THE GROUNDS.

THE LODGE ON THE WOLVERLEY ROAD.

VIEW OF THE GARDEN FRONT FROM THE OLD YEW TREE

Sion House

Parish: Chaddesley Corbett

HER Ref: WSM23034/29001.

Grid Ref: SO 896.764. Postcode: DY10 4PE.

O.S. 6" Map No: 9SW.

Date of Map: 1885, with deduced extent of park & grounds shaded (not shaded on 1905 OS).

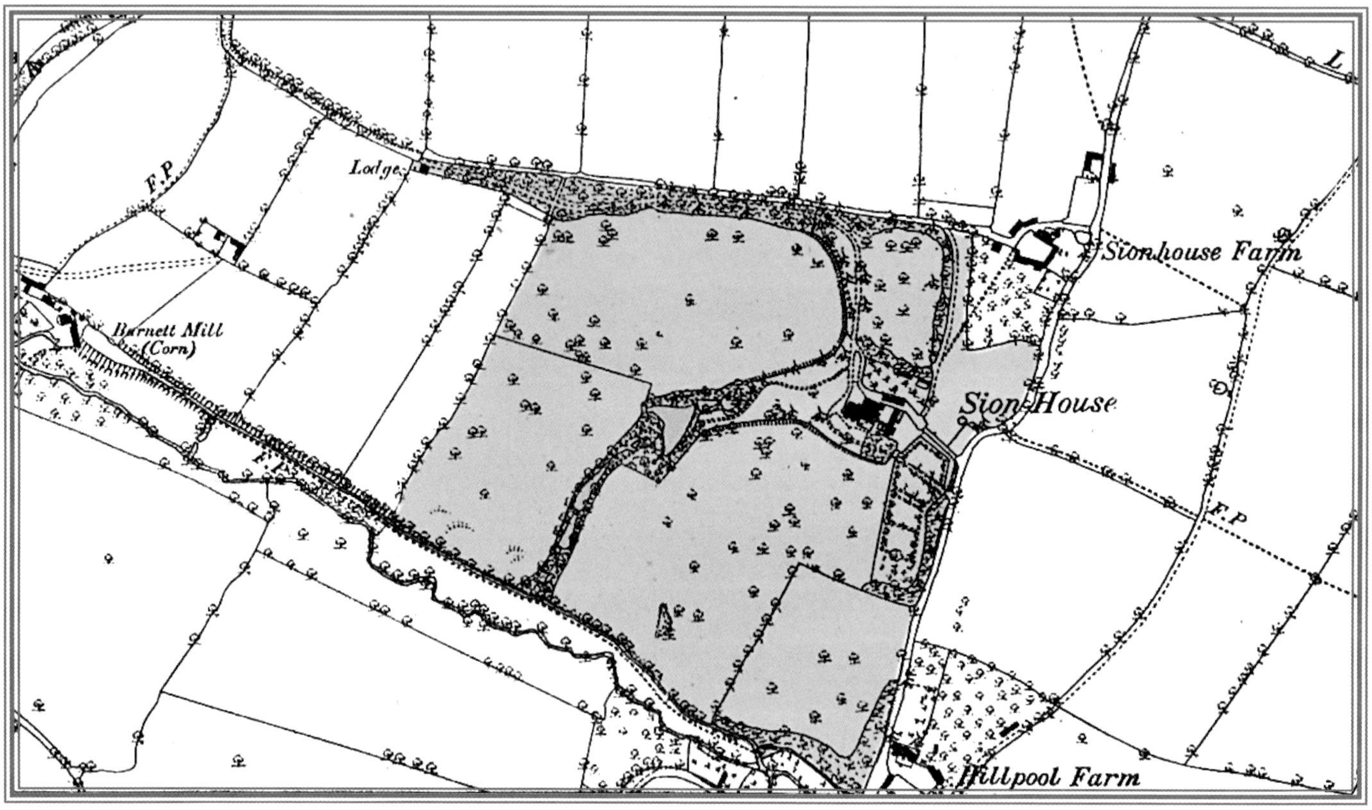

A residence is marked at Hillpool by Cary in 1805. The house is shown with grounds on earlier-19th century, printed maps and with a park and lodge on the first edition of the OS 6 inch in 1882. The BoE (p. 221) notes that the house has been rebuilt since 1995; e.g. the characteristic stucco has been removed.

A sequence of small linked pools in the centre of the park is the main feature. A little more detail can be found on the 1838 tithe map for Chaddesley Corbett, e.g. a ride into the fringe planting (CRO 4000/867). The south boundary of the park is made up of a narrow wood with yew, sweet chestnut, beech, oak, alder. A dry ditch connects this and the brook below it with the pools in the centre of the grounds. A pool has been made in the south-east corner of the old, park area.

A. Brooks & N. Pevsner, *Worcestershire,* 2007 (BoE).

Sodington Hall and Mamble Park

Parish: Mamble

HER Ref: WSM29011.
Grid Ref: SO 693 710.
Postcode: DY14 9JY.
O.S. 6" Map No: 13SW.
Date of Map: 1884.

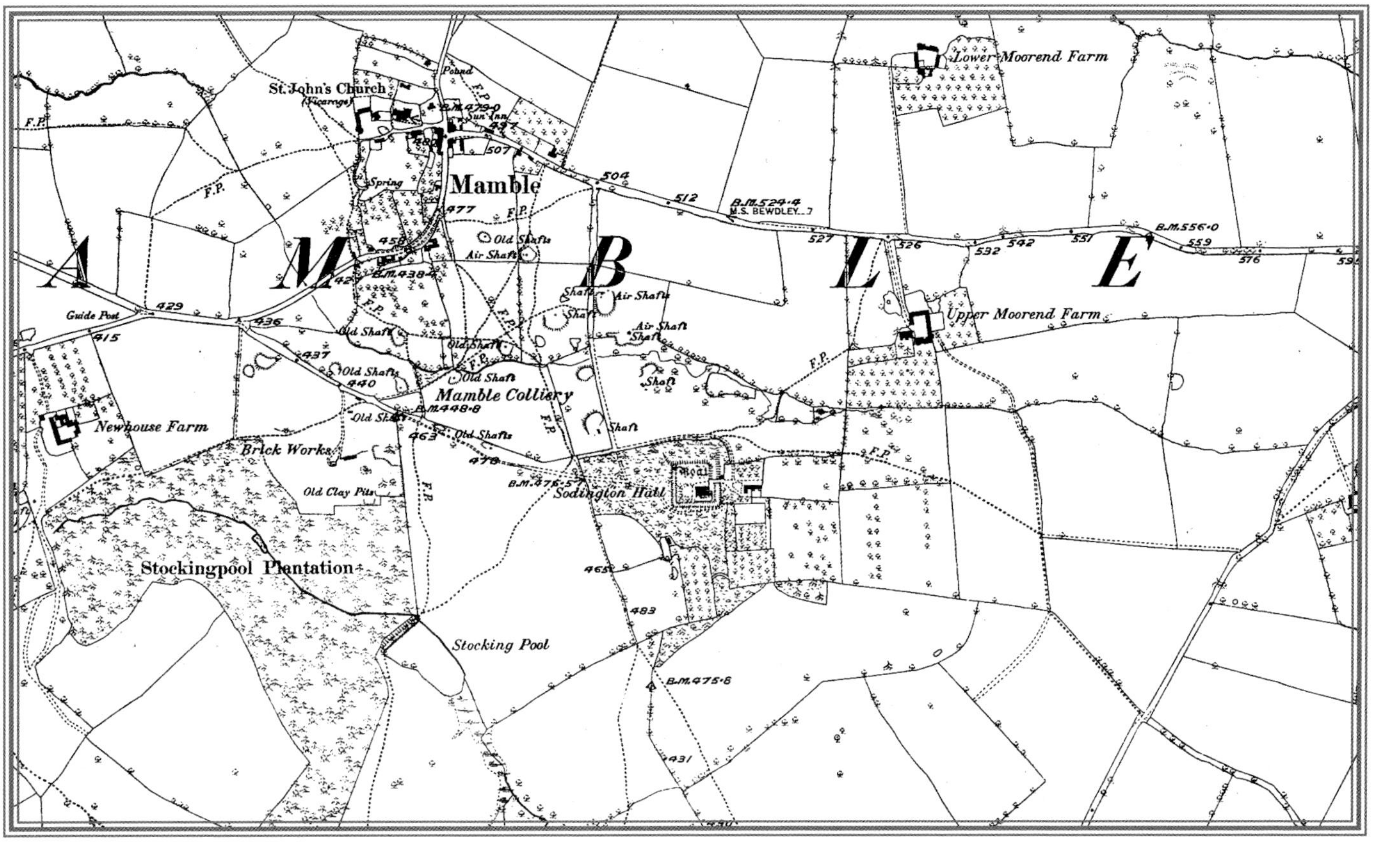

Sodington is shown as a residence by Taylor in 1772 and described by Nash in 1782 (Vol. 2, p. 159) as having " a very pleasant summer situation, on a gentle eminence moated round with four drawbridges". It is among 28 sites given principal seat status for the county in the *Traveller* circa 1800. This house was pulled down in 1807 and immediately replaced by a house described as neat and modest but worthy of notice by the BoE (p. 59). (The redevelopment revealed a Roman brick kiln and 10,000 bricks "the greater part well burn't" – *Gentleman's Magazine,* 1807). Grounds are shown on earlier-19th century maps but no park until Walker in 1835. It has lost this status by the OS 6 inch circa 1900. The 1883 OS records a moated site with two ponds nearby of which a fragment of a moat is noticed by Salter. When sold in 2010, the property was described as having 16½ acres of gardens, paddocks and woodlands.

Early maps show in preference a deer park at Mamble and the 1835 park may have been the same although there is a gap in the map evidence between circa 1790 and 1830. Mamble is shown as a deer park on Saxton's map of 1577 and continues to be shown as such in Blome and Morden in the 17th century and by Bowen in 1778 and Haywood in 1789. However, the park was not apparently associated with any major residence and the survival of the park in maps may simply represent the laziness of the mapmakers.

Another suggested park is Gaudywood (see), which was another Blount property adjoining Sodington and may also have been part of the Sodington Estate. There are park field names in an early-18th century map relating to Sodington, Gaudywood or Mamble (WAAS 6442). "The Demeans of Soddington" has a Hunt House, Dear Park and Cunny Park. More modest names apear next to Sodington in the 1838 Mamble Tithe Award: Lower Owl Park; Middle and Upper Owl Park. The Blounts attached the baronetcy, granted for support to Charles I in the English Civil War, to Sodington. The estate was confiscated during the Commonwealth and restored to the family at the Stuart Restoration.

Gentleman's Magazine, 1807.

J. Dugdale, *The New British Traveller,* 1819.

T. R. Nash, *Collections for the History of Worcestershire,* Vol II, 1782.

M. Salter, *Medieval Castles of Herefordshire and Worcestershire,* 1989.

Spetchley Park

Parish: Spetchley

HER Ref: WSM28825/35184. Grid Ref: S0 896 539. Postcode: WR5 1RS.

O.S. 6" Map No: 34NW/SW.

Date of Map: 1885, with extent of park & gardens shaded as H. E. Register.

Included within Historic England's Register of Historic Parks and Gardens of special historic interest in England.

Licence to impark any part of the parish for deer, rabbits and pheasants was granted in 1625 (VCH, 1913, p. 524). The deer park is shown on Nash's 1781 map. Whitaker in 1892, in his national survey of deer parks, says that this one covered 116 acres, was fenced by cleaved oak with wooden pegs or with iron "and is extremely picturesque", and contained 200 fallow deer and some splendid oaks (800 to 100 years old) and elms (250 years old): "There is an oak in this park in which a summerhouse large enough to seat 20 people is built in the branches." Whitaker publishes a photograph of the "Great Oak in Spetchley

..........continued from previous page

Park". David Smith has found further evidence of the deer stock as in 1908: 14 stags; 3 prickets; 5 calves; 11 hinds (Spetchley Archive).

The part of the park that was the deer park is shown on the Ist edition of the OS 6 inch (1883) and represented more than the southern half of the whole; it had the large fishpond with boathouse on its south-east side. There is another large fishpond towards the north-east near the house grounds and flower gardens. There is little fringe planting and this is restricted to the northern road boundary and to the south-west corner of the deer park. The only obvious avenue planting follows the line of a footpath running from the north-west corner to half-way down the east boundary of the park. This corner of the park has been cut off by the M5. This west/east avenue, as well as an avenue going south across the park, are shown on the 1811 survey for the first OS one inch. Spetchley only features as a landscape park on printed maps from circa 1835. David Smith notes some basic maintenance to the park circa 1900 and the re-stocking of the park pool with 1000 trout in 1913 (Smith, 2014).

Until relatively recently, there seemed to be little documentation for the gardens that went with the pre-19th century house. There was a Tudor manor house which may have been improved or replaced after purchase by Rowland Berkeley in 1605. This was burnt down during the English Civil War. David Smith, however, has greatly extended what was known of the gardening interests shared by Robert Berkeley of Spetchley and John Evelyn from their meeting on October 13th 1683: "a most virtuous and religious Gent, seated neere Worster, very curious in gardening etc." (De Beer, p. 757). From letters between the two men (B.L. Mss. Add. 15857 & 78299) Smith (2013) has shown that they exchanged detailed information about the importing and planting of exotic species of trees and shrubs, as well as the husbandry of fruit and vegetables. Berkeley was evidently in the forefront of fashion in planting cypress, ilex, holly, laurel, yew, juniper, pine, pyracanthus, rosemary, orange and lemon trees, the latter "secured by keeping them underground". "I have some cedars to set out but am loth to expose them till I know yours have endured this winter". Cedars were introduced to England around 1670 (Smith) and the letters related to Spetchley were written between 1684 and 1691; cedars remain a prominent feature of the Spetchley landscape: "these are cathedrals of trees with vaulting boughs that frame vistas of the Malvern Hills" (Griffiths).

The letters show a shared interest in garden technology such as "Mr. Boyle's (vacuum) pump for irrigating fruit and flowers" and in contemporary Dutch experiments with glass-house design providing protection against severe weather "without stove or fire" (Smith, 2013). In 1693 Berkeley tells Evelyn that "I am now making a conservatory something in imitation of yours but with this addition, having each side of it wings, in the manner of your ruin on casks where we keep our Indian plants" (Smith, 2013). It is frustrating that there are no illustrations of the Spetchley gardens and grounds circa 1700; a watercolour by E. F. Burney of 1784 (WAAS 2432) shows only high walls with fruit trees behind.

The present Greek Revival mansion was designed by John Tasker in 1811-18 and the BoE (p. 599) gives a detailed description of the "fine Reptonian landscape park", i.e. as going with the new mansion but with the moat from the earlier house forming a western boundary to the grounds "crossed by a pretty wrought-iron FOOTBRIDGE, with ornate spandrels".

Maps of the Estates of Robert Berkeley, Esquire by James Webb, Surveyor, Worcester, dated 1837-8 (Spetchley Archive & **Plates 14 & 15**) has one map for the park, mansion and grounds which records the status quo before the development of the gardens begun by Ellen Willmott and Rose Berkeley circa 1900. For the grounds (which extend across the A422 to include Round Hill and House) and gardens, there is apparently little if any change between 1837 and the 1905 OS 6 inch. The southern section of the park in 1837 had the same west and east boundaries which then continued north excluding a new area of park east of the mansion garden and grounds and also excluding a large, new area of park on the north west, a small part of which is now cut off by the M5. The footpath shown in 1905 which stills goes through the park from west of the M5 to the Railway line on the east, was, in 1837, a wide avenue with intermittent planting which is more strongly marked at the later date. Other park planting is very similar including copses on the periphery.

The 1837 survey shows the same front drive curving across the park from the porticoed entrance of the mansion to the road now exiting just short of the M5. Sinuous paths make their way around the Round Hill extension north of the road as well as around the grounds of the main house on all sides and towards the pool, the walled garden and the area south of it which contained a garden house/glass house. A canal connects the south-west corner of the walled garden and the pool, with a bridge at that point. The walled garden with its walls splayed going south, is impressively large. It is set out into squared compartments and has a central water basin. Similarly laid out is the vegetable garden on its east side. There is a glasshouse on either side of the north wall and a partly walled melon yard on the north-east corner, i.e. the infrastructure is as today, unchanged by later developments. The plan shows paths and fencing around the whole of the walled space. Whether or not the shaped, yew hedges, which are such a dominant feature of the gardens today, are represented in their infancy is debatable. The 1837 survey shows a ha-ha or metal fence stretching from the road on the north-west boundary between grounds and park, continuing to the junction of canal and pool.

Overall, the 1837 survey and the 1885/1905 OS 6 inch maps are in such agreement, that it is clear that the redevelopment of the gardens and grounds, first by Ellen Willmott and Rose Berkeley and then by other members of the family, retained the basic ground plan set out by

..........continued from previous page

Rose Berkeley and her daughter Betty weeding, circa 1916, Spetchley Archive.

Fishing on the lake circa 1910, Spetchley Archive.

the mid-19th century or even earlier, contemporary with John Tasker's rebuilding of the main house from 1811.
Spetchley is most celebrated in garden terms for the work done in the later-19th and early-20th centuries. To quote the HE Register: "Main gardening activity from 1891 onwards, directed by Mrs Rose Berkeley with the collaboration of her sister Miss Ellen Willmott (1858 – 1934). The plant collection which they began was augmented after 1922 by Captain R. G. W. Berkeley. Walled formal gardens of 1½ ha, 150m east of the Hall, with cross paths and espaliered fruit trees. Small central pond. Walled kitchen garden in south west corner, now used for sales of plants. Herbaceous borders on outer west, east and south sides. To the south is the Fountain Garden, quartered by paths and yew hedges, and with central pool and fountain; this area is attributed to Ellen Willmott. To the east 17th century Lebanon cedars, 19th century Conservatory to south and, beyond, the Rose Lawn. 19th century Root House, with pebble floor. Ornamental woodland extends along the eastern boundary, and beyond the Cork Lawn,

The view to the fountain, circa 1916, Spetchley Archive.

the Pond closes the southern and south-western side of the gardens." Tipping mentions the Doric Temple beyond the kitchen garden wall (p. 74) built as a memorial to Rose Berkeley.
Griffith (in an interview with John Berkeley) argues that the Fountain garden is a flourishing survival of Ellen and Rose Willmott's circa 1900 creation "as an ornamental botanic garden ... 36 beds, each focussed on a different plant group and contained within four yew-hedged compartments centred on a fountain". The Root House is illustrated by Headley and Meulenkamp (op. cit.) and Hunt (op. cit.). The Spetchley Archive contains much information about the re-making of the infrastructure to the gardens (walks and paths and fences) circa 1899 and also of the planting of bulbs and flowers and fruit trees in the same period; "During the 1920s bulbs were grown commercially" (Smith, 2014).
An ambitious *Conservation Management Plan* (2012) for Spetchley's 30 acres of gardens is in progress and there is a busy, interactive website in support of it.

H. Avray Tipping, *Country Life,* Vol. XL, 1916.
M. Griffiths, "Spetchley's world of botanical treasures", *Country Life,* 27. 6. 2012.
P. Hunt, *The Shell Gardens Book,* 1964.
B. Jones, *Follies and Grottoes,* 1974.
G. Headley and W. Meulenkamp, *Follies: a National Trust Guide,* 1986.
D. J. H. Smith, *John Evelyn's Influence on Spetchley gardens and pleasure grounds,* 2013, unpub.
D. J. H. Smith: *Improvements to Spetchley gardens and grounds: evidence from the archives,* 2014, unpub.
Victoria County History, Vol. 3, 1913, (VCH).
A. Brooks & N. Pevsner, *Worcestershire,* 2007 (BoE).
HE *Register of Parks & Gardens,* 1998.
J. Whitaker, *Descriptive List of the Deer Parks and Paddocks of England,* 1892.
D. de Beer (ed.), *The Diary of John Evelyn,* 1959.

THE DOUGHARTY MAPS

John Dougharty senior and his sons Joseph Dougharty and John Doharty junior were the leading surveyors in the County between 1725 and 1755 when John senior died and John junior left Worcester for London. All 3 contributed to a *Book of Maps* made for Bowater Vernon of Hanbury in 1731-3. John senior was a celebrated mathematician and set up a school, first in Bewdley and finally in the Edgar Tower where he taught members of leading county families. Among the Dougharty's principal clients were the Earl of Coventry, Lord Foley and the Bishop of Worcester. Dougharty senior was also a dial maker and a sundial made by him for Bishop Hough survives at Hartlebury Castle. The Diglis Pleasure Grounds situated beside the Castle and the River, their principal commercial venture, offered a bowling green, a banqueting house and a riding school. John Doharty junior was responsible for the majority of the family's surveys as well as for the printed maps of Worcester (1741) and Kidderminster (1753).

B. S. Smith, 'The Dougharty Family, Eighteenth-Century Mapmakers', *Worcs. Archaeol. Trans.* 3rd Series, Vol. 15, 1996.

Malvern

Plate 1. Panorama of the Malvern Hills from Foley Estate Map, John Doharty junior, 1744. © WAAS 1101.

Plate 2. Detail of map shown in Plate 1.

Witley court

LEFT: Plate 3. Witley Court, John Doharty junior, 1745. © WAAS 974/1.

BELOW: Plate 4. Lithograph circa 1873.

Worcester Sites

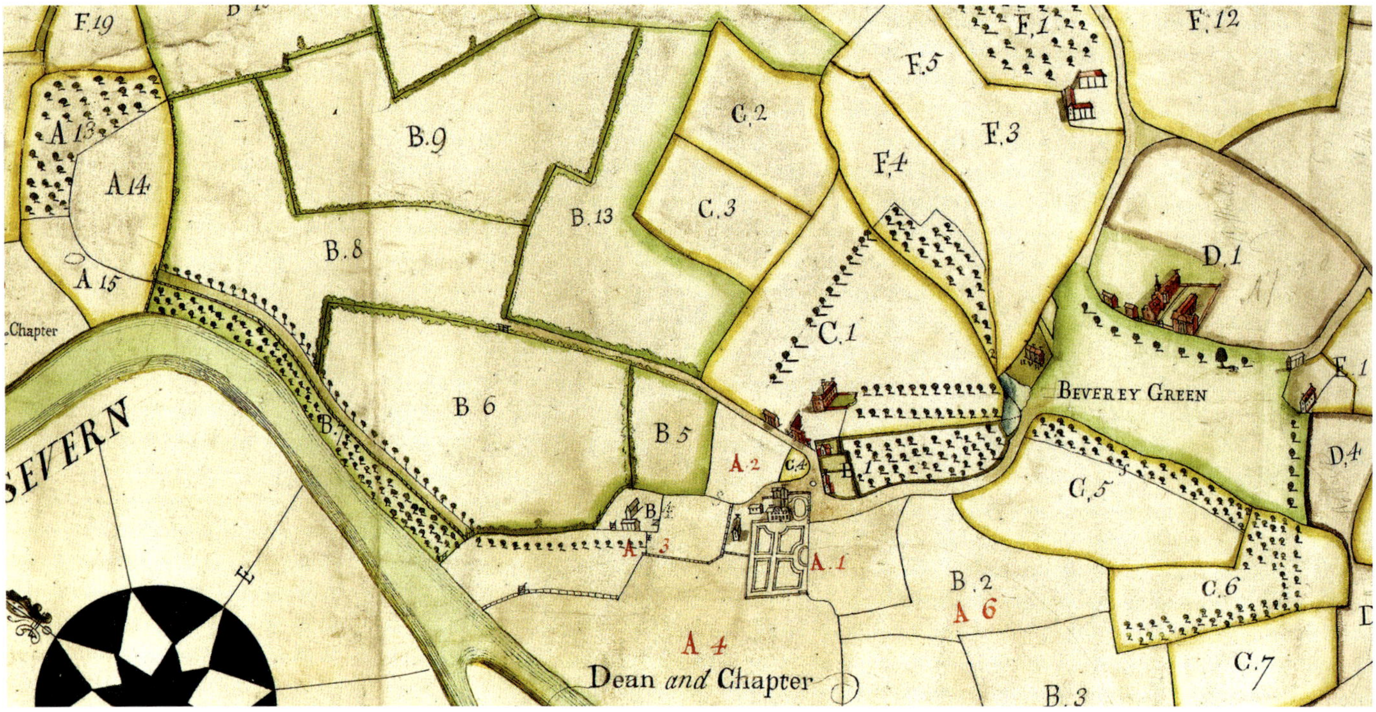

ABOVE: Plate 5. Bevere from Map of Claines, John Doharty junior, 1751. © WAAS 5403/10.
BELOW: Plate 6. Barbourne from Map of Claines, John Doharty junior, 1751. © WAAS 5403/10.

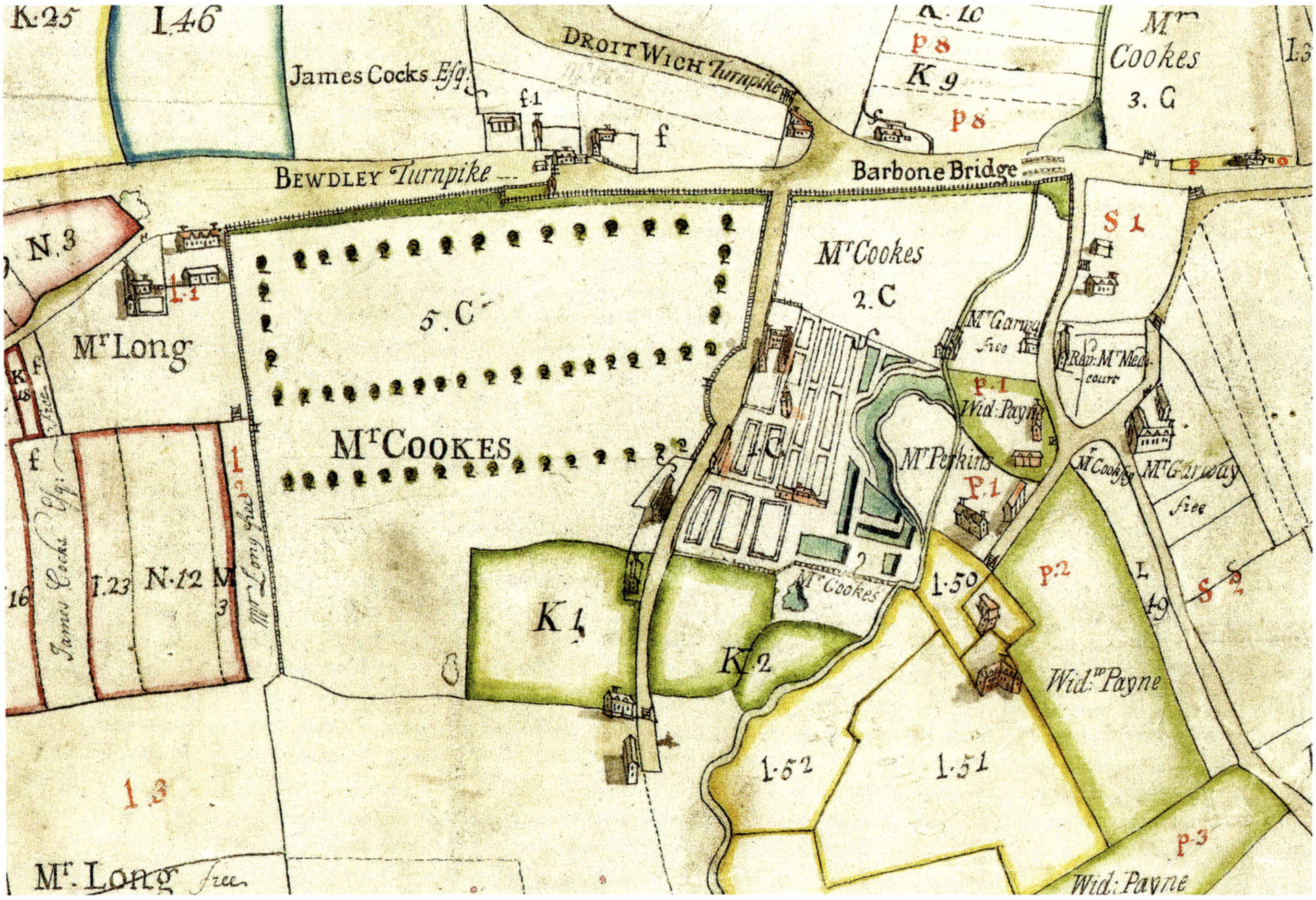

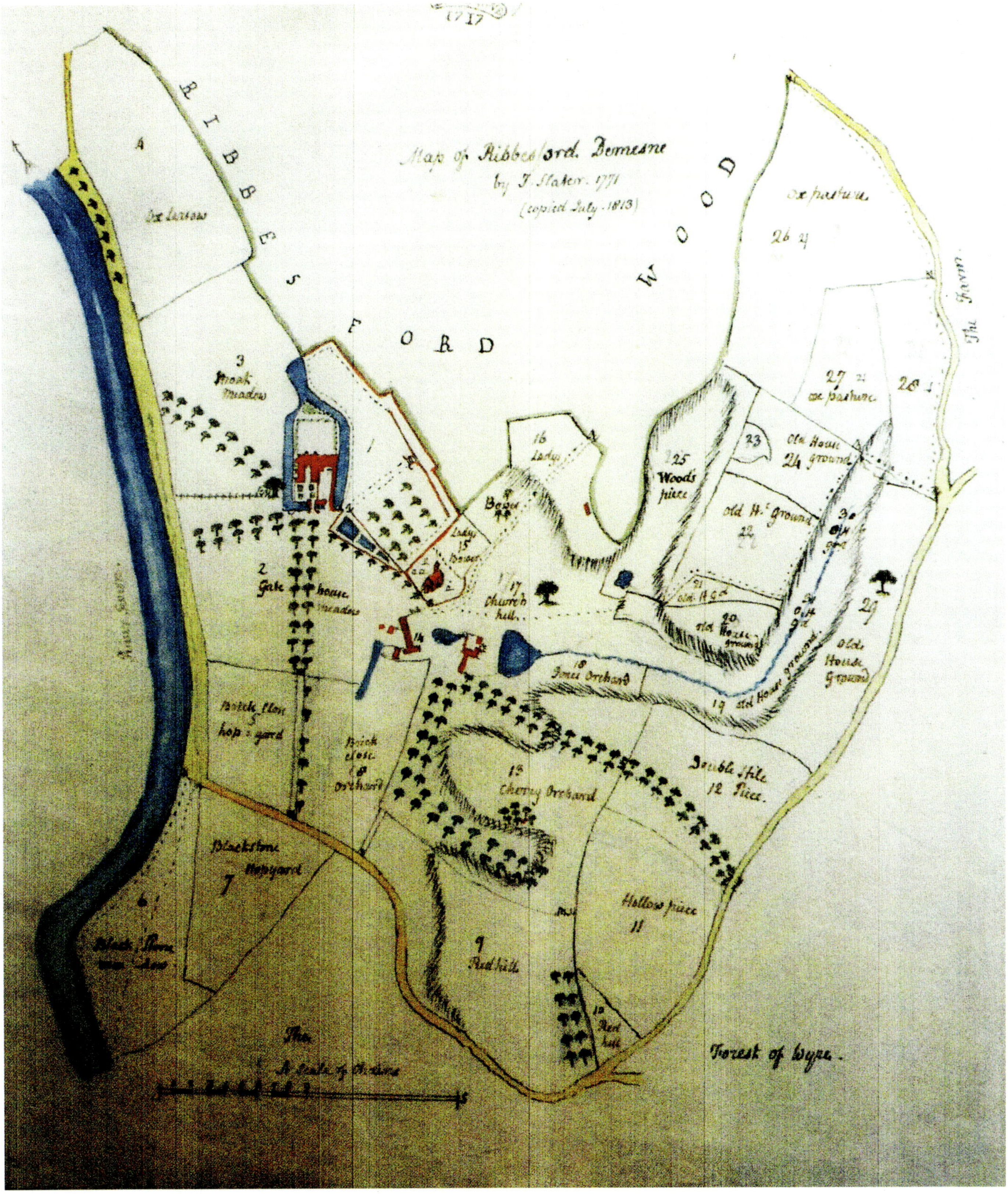

Plate 7. After J. Slater, 1771, *Map of Ribbesford Demesne,* 1813. Society of Antiquaries of London, Prattinton Collection.

HUMPHRY REPTON'S RED BOOK FOR HEWELL GRANGE

Humphry Repton (1752 - 1818) came late to landscape gardening after several disastrous failed business ventures. He started as an exponent of the 'Capability' Brown style, promoting tranquil parkland and eschewing old fashioned formal gardens but as he grew older he altered his thinking to suit his clients and ended pursuing a distinctly Gardenesque style. His greatest selling point were his site reports containing advice and recommendations, often as watercolour sketches with cleverly constructed folded windows that could be opened to show the anticipated effects of his proposals. The books were bound in red vellum, hence the name Red Books and he produced over 200 that have been identified. Five sons and two daughters survived into adulthood and his eldest son, John Adey Repton, an architect and later antiquarian, joined him in his practice and produced many of the drawings found in later Red Books. Selected drawings from the Hewell Grange Red Book are shown here with permission from Lord Plymouth. They were photographed by Derek Foxton who also gave his permission to use the images.

D. Whitehead & J. Bradney *In the Enemy's Quarters: Humphry Repton in the West Midlands*, 2018.

Plate 8. This view, with the slide closed shows the unimproved view of the house standing behind the visible scar of the ha-ha supplemented by ugly fences to prevent stock circumventing it at the water's edge. The precise rendition of the architecture suggests John Adey Repton as the artist. He emphasises the shallow interrupted reflection of the mansion in the lake.

Plate 9. The companion illustration to Plate 10 has the slide raised to reveal Repton's suggested improvements with the addition of a promontory, trees removed to expose the skyline of the stables and flowering shrubs running down the line of a light fence from the mansion to a new pedimented boathouse and urn.

Plate 10. The east side of the house with the private lawn and pavilion. Dense woodland with conifers cloaks the bank and a farm cart suggests this is a somewhat functional landscape, not dedicated entirely to private pleasure. The square structure is presumably also utilitarian. There is no access to the lake, which continues to be boring and uninviting.

Plate 11. The after-view showing Repton's recommendations is now an inviting pleasure ground. New steps from Lady Plymouth's terrace descend on the right and a dry, easy path of gravel or hoggin encourages the visitors beyond the light fence around the lake, which has an inviting inlet. Trees on the slopes of the sheep-walks have been thinned so that their changing shadows can now be enjoyed.

PLATE 12. Bevere Manor Estate Map, 1937. © WAAS 5240/5.

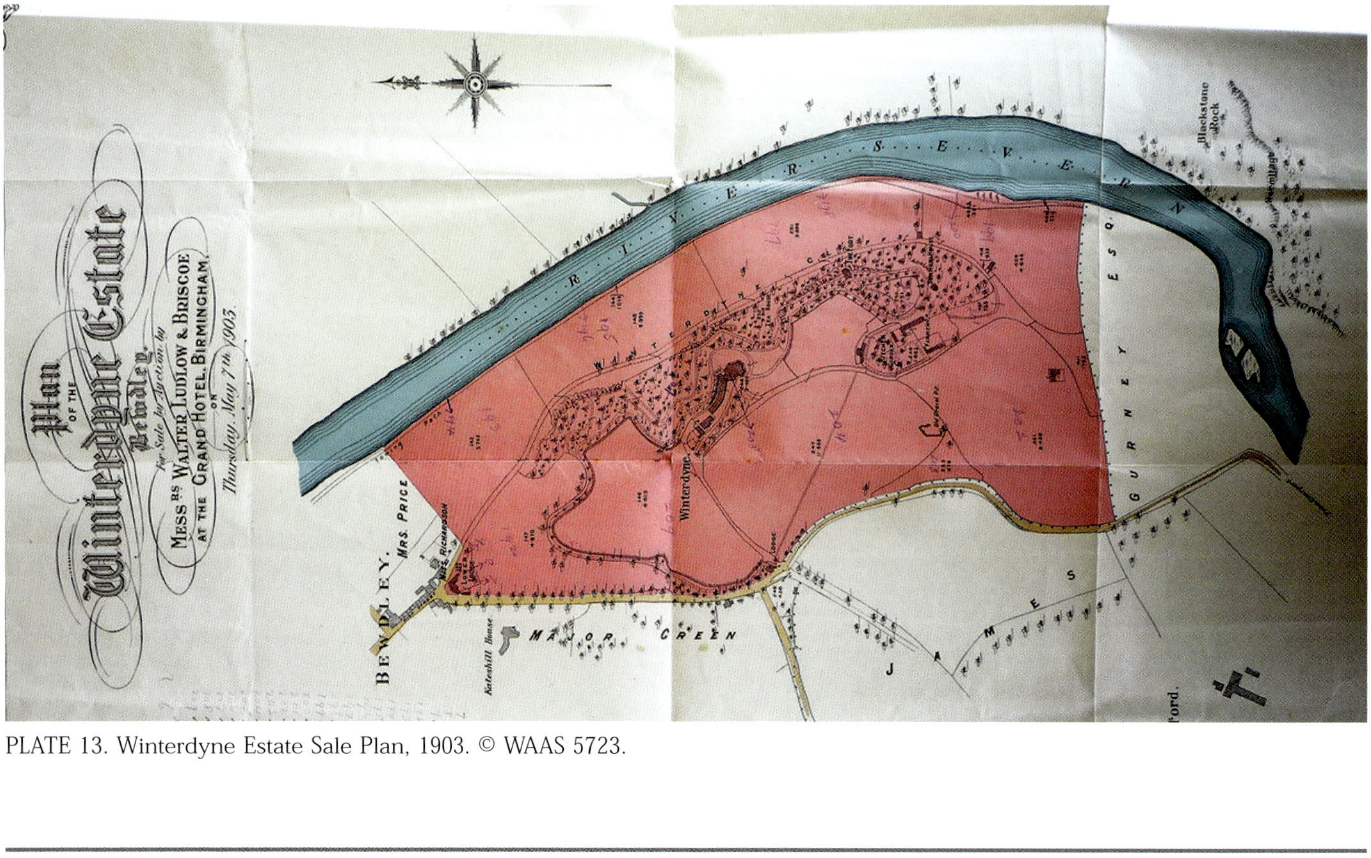

PLATE 13. Winterdyne Estate Sale Plan, 1903. © WAAS 5723.

GARDEN ORNAMENTS

TOP LEFT: Plate 29. Hewell Grange, *The Fallen Gladiator*, photo circa 1902. Courtesy of Country Life.
TOP RIGHT: Plate 30. Croome Court, *Sabrina*. Photo, J. Patton.
MIDDLE LEFT: Plate 31. Hanbury Hall, entrance gates. Photo, R. Lockett.
ABOVE RIGHT: Plate 32. Davenham, Malvern, stone urn. Photo, J. Patton.
BOTTOM LEFT: Plate 33. Davenham, Malvern, well-head. Photo, J. Patton.

Spring Grove

Parish: Bewdley

HER Ref: WSM28824.

Grid Ref: SO 802 756. Postcode: DY12 1LF.

O.S. 6" Map No: 14NW.

Date of Map: 1888, with extent of park & gardens shaded as 1905 OS.

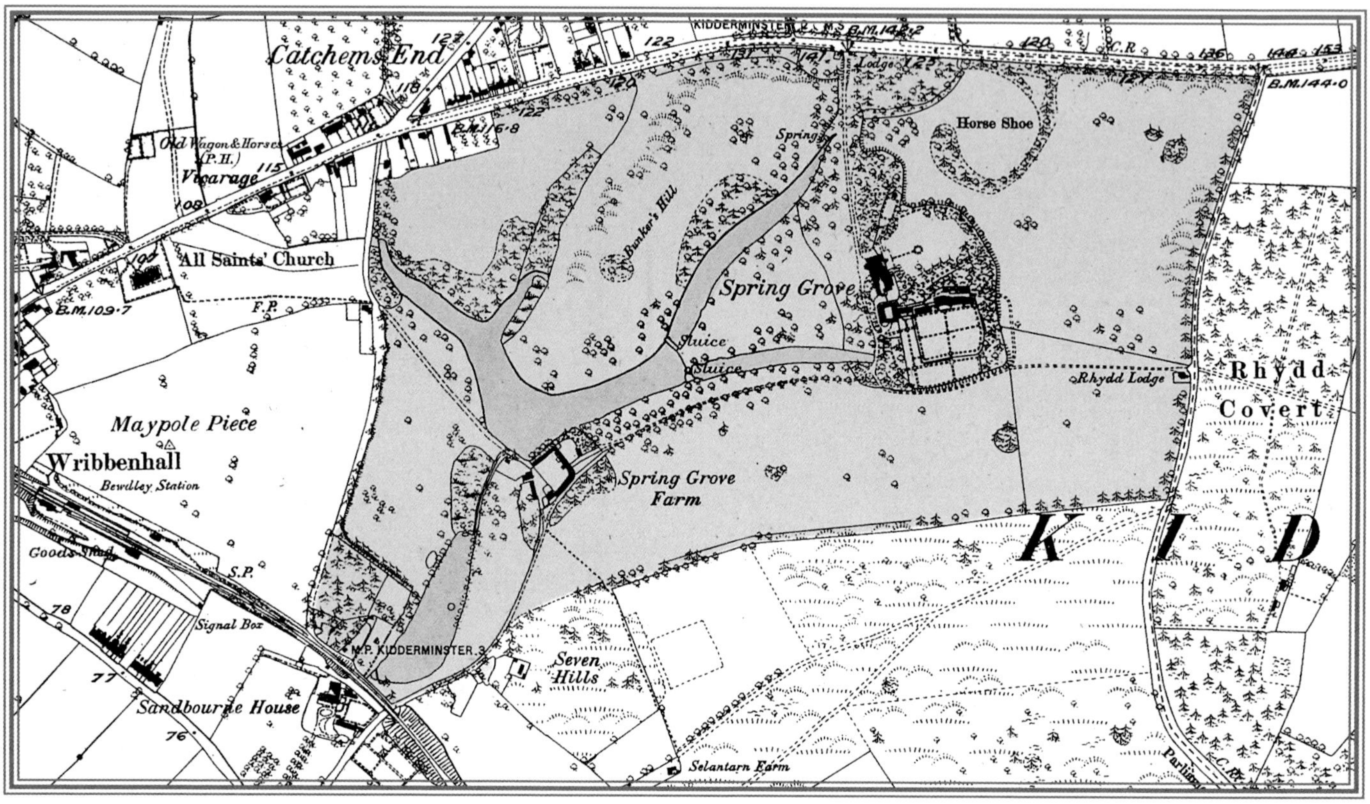

Spring Grove takes its name from the springs situated either side of the main drive from the Wribbenhall-Kidderminster Road which fed the pools in the south-west quarter of the park. The property was developed out of barren heathland. The Farm buildings were partially excavated out of solid sandstone (Richard Webb).

The present house was built 1787-90 for Samuel Skey, a former town bailiff of Bewdley (ob. 1806) and there were additions circa 1840 (BoE, p. 781). Spring-grove is marked on Tunnicliff's 1788 map as Skey's residence.

Spring Grove is shown as a large park on the 1815 survey for the first OS one inch map and suggests that the main features as recorded by the first OS 6 inch in 1883 had been established at least 70 years earlier. This was the house and landscape that John Constable enjoyed when he visited Maria Bicknell, Sarah Skey's half-sister, in December 1811. Constable claimed that some of the happiest hours of his life were spent at Spring Grove "mix't as they were with moments of unutterable sadness". S. Skey, Esq. is given as owner in the *Beauties of England and Wales* in 1814 but by Greenwood's county map of 1822, John Taylor was in residence. (In 1822 Taylor was reported to be about to build a new house at Strensham Court).

Spring Grove temp. "Buonparte" is unctuously described in *A Pastoral Descriptive Poem* dedicated to Samuel Skey junior "as this pleasing villa", "the haunt of fairies and the muses kind" and compared to Stowe! The writer's botanical descriptions are hopefully more prosaic: odifrous shrubs from far, weeping willow; well-trained firs; hawthorn; lilac; myrtle green; sweet briar; thorny rose; laurel; beech; cypress shade. "Go Hatchett, first rate artist, try thy best", probably J. P. Hackert, a German painter admired by British Grand Tourists for his Claudeian landscapes such as may have inspired Skey senior. More local references in the poem are made to "Firm Blackstone Rock and modern Winterdyne, the seat of neatness".

The poet reaches the walled garden: "The gard'ner op'd a door to feast my eyes/A spacious piece of ground that's near a square". A list of fruit trees follows: nectarine; peach; apricot; fig; Orlean's plum; grape from Gaul; pear;

..........continued from previous page

damson from Damascus; apple. The walled garden as fully developed included a boiler house, heated walls and a Camelia house growing very tall camelias. The garden had a cruciform layout with fruit trees down the centre. " What attracts the eye most is that prolific hot-house ... form'd just like a lady's fan ... pines; lemons; oranges; grapes; melon; cherry; strawberry; cucumber; French beans; green peas ... potato; radish; asparagus; cabbage; Windsor bean; balm; mint; marjoram; sage; thyme; parsley; turnip; carrot; onion. "Linnaeus would much enjoy the feast." (Richard Webb). In 1829, Mr. Skey drew the attention of the *Gardener's Magazine* to his oranges and lemons and "this year one lemon of 110 oz." (Vol. 5, p. 213) (Jane Bradney). There was an auction at the Springrove Nursery in 1833 of "choice fruit trees, forest trees and shrubs" (London Soc. of Antiquaries, Prattinton Coll. 9142.141) (Stephen Price).

The 1883 map describes an elaborate landscape with 2 pools, 2 lodges, boat house, some fringe planting and planting round the pools, a kitchen garden and an avenue from it to the Farm. There is an icehouse not shown.

The park's western boundary stretched from the Bewdley-Kidderminster road to the GWR track. The eastern boundary was the Rhydd Covert and the road to the Racecourse. Most of this park is now the West Midland Safari Park, established in 1973. The Bewdley by-pass has cut off the north and west edges of the park and a reduction of the pools has lessened the original character of the landscape. The animal enclosures now create their own divisions of the internal landscape. The 1913 Sale Particulars with photographs record the mature parkland with trees and water before modern changes. The mansion suffered a serious fire in 2006 and was restored by 2015.

Anon., *Spring Grove: A Pastoral and Descriptive Poem,* n.d.
Beauties of England and Wales, Vol. XV, 1814.
I. Fleming-Williams, *Constable,* Tate Gallery exhibition catalogue, 1976.

ABOVE & LEFT: Spring Grove from sale particulars. 1913.

Stanbrook Abbey

Parish: Powick

HER Ref: WSM11934.
Grid Ref: SO 835 499.
Postcode: WR2 4TY.
O.S. 6" Map No: 40NE.
Date of Map: 1884.

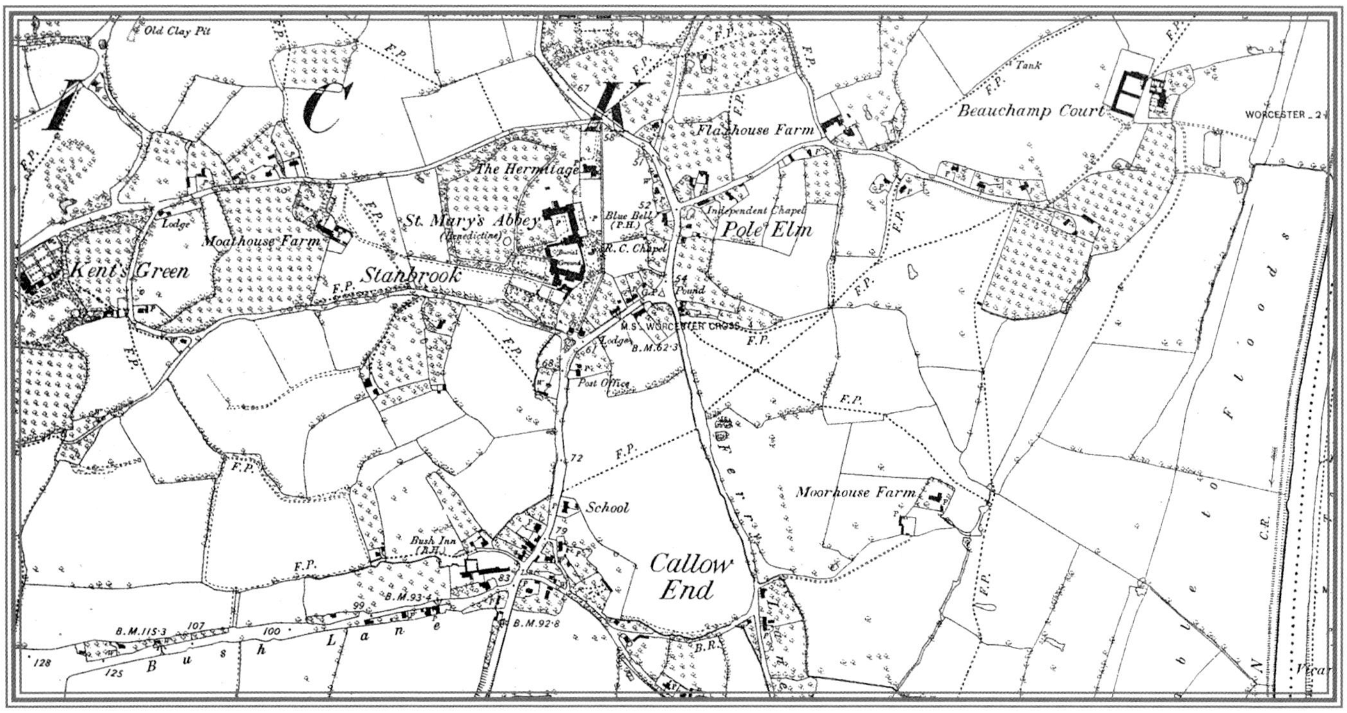

An estate plan of circa 1700 shows a formal garden to a house at "Stansbrooks End" which may be on the site of the later house (CRO 940/1). This was at one time the residence of Dr. John Wall. Stanbrook House or Hall is on Greenwood in 1822 and is shown on early-19th century maps with grounds, i.e. before the arrival of Benedictine Nuns in 1838. An 1837 *Guide to Worcester* anticipates this date describing Stanbrook Hall as formerly the residence of Abraham Thompson Esq., but recently sold to a community of nuns. The two Lodges, which probably predated E. W. Pugin's post-1878 Abbey, are described by the Listing as early to mid-19th century. The grounds or small park have fringe planting round much of 3 sides and a walk inside the planting with The Hermitage on the north-east side of the site. The 1835 sale particulars included stabling, a double coach house and walled gardens. The main house was demolished in the late-19th century.

Sale particulars of 2005 show a formal arrangement of beds within a walled garden on the north-west side and a total acreage of 21 ½. (*Country Life*). The hotel and wedding business now owning Stanbrook Abbey has altered its setting with the addition of modern buildings and car parking. However, the two Lodges (much extended) and The Hermitage survive, along with vestiges of other garden features.

Country Life, 1. 12. 2005.
1919 Sale Plan (CRO 4192/1).

Stanford Court

Parish: Stanford with Orleton

HER Ref: WSM28823.

Grid Ref: SO 707 657. Postcode: WR6 6ST.

O.S. 6" Map No: 20SW.

Date of Map: 1884, with extent of park & grounds shaded as 1905 OS.

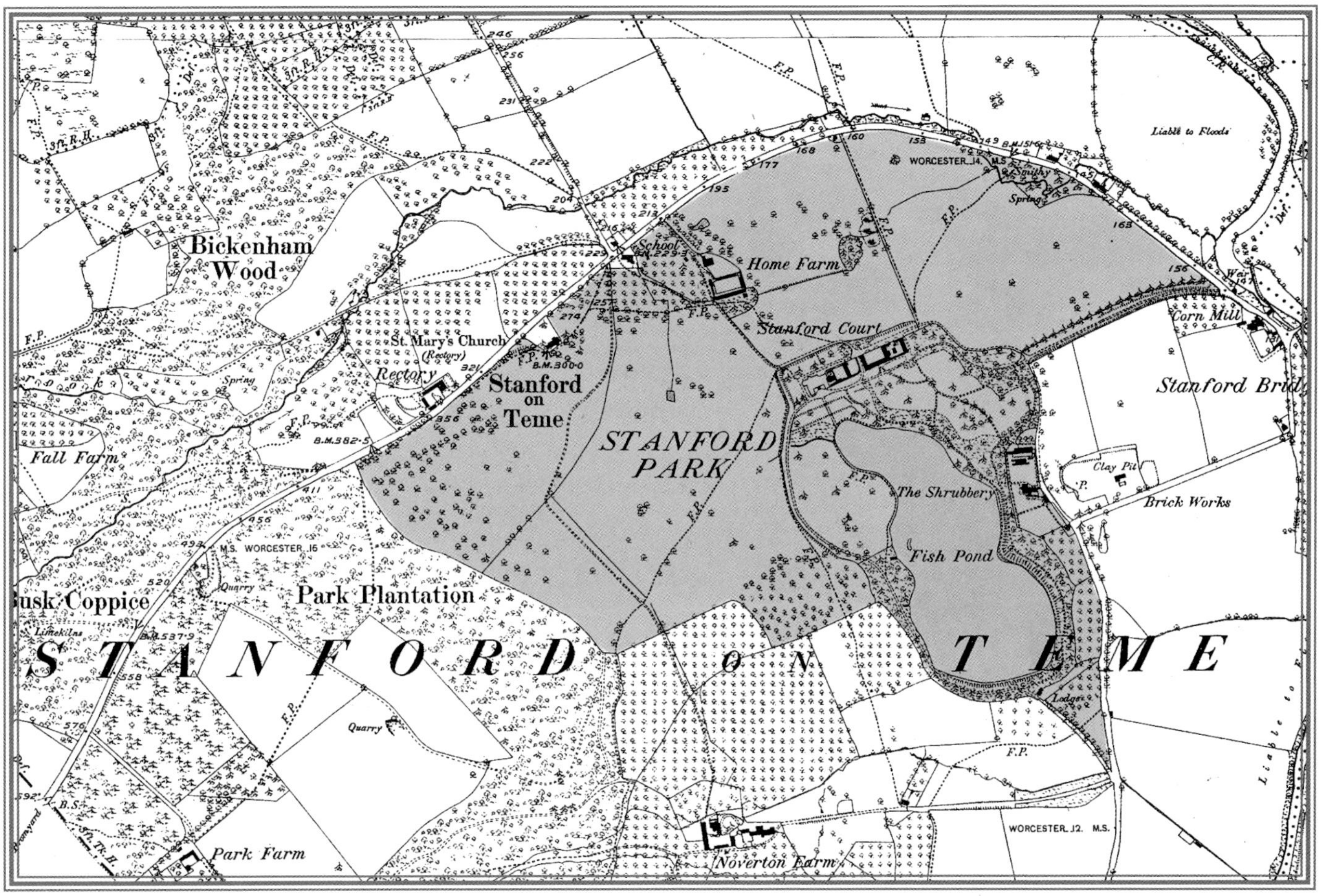

A fenced deer park appears on later-18th century maps. An 1803 Survey by T. Davis, *A Plan of the Parish of Stanford* … the property of Sir E. Winnington Ingram, Bart, shows the landscape as at the end of the 18th century (WAAS 709/12). Warden's Grove and the Warren on this map may suggest the original west boundaries of the deer park. Today, Park Farm and Park Plantation are well to the west of the Court. The Deer park in 1803 amounted to 90 acres and the lake was calculated as 21 acres. Ash Grove and Linacre Grove along the south side of the landscape park in 1803 had drives and there was a wide drive going due north through Oakley Leasowes. There was an icehouse directly east of the house on the far side of the Stanford road. The 1813 survey for the first OS one inch gives some detail of field divisions and plantings. The *VCH* in 1924 (Vol. 4, p. 342) estimated the park as 75 acres and the lake as 25 acres, i.e. fairly close to the size of the park etc. in 1803.

The mansion of early-17th century and 18th century date was largely destroyed by fire in 1882 and was rebuilt in Georgian style in 1886-8 (Reid, p. 228); the Stables survive from the 18th century development. The BoE dates the basic lay-out of the landscape park to the 1760s (p. 601). Nash gives quite a full description of the park in 1782 (Vol. 2, pp. 367/9). " Stanford Court ... is situated in a very extensive park ... delightful prospects ... fine groves of oak ... two large pieces of water, made by Sir Edward Winnington ... a cedar of Libanus, planted ... only 28 years ago, that is now more than 3 yards round." Nash's illustration of Stanford is particularly elaborate and shows a pleasure boat on the lake and details some plantings of conifers across the lake and south-east of the house.

There are or were a few park buildings of performing as eye-catchers such as the Church of 1768-9 by James Rose. There is also a classical temple (now ruined) in Temple Dingle some way south-west of the house and

Stanford Court

..........continued from previous page

Noverton Farm (marked on the OS 1905 6 inch). This would have been visible from the house, and its open portico overlooked the park before the trees took over. Some years ago, I was told that the Keeper occupied the Temple and would be summoned to the big house by running up a flag! Whitehead has noticed that it is marked on Greenwood's 1822 County map and that it functioned as a banqueting house in the guise of a Doric Temple; he attributes to James Rose of Bewdley who was responsible for the new church. Stephen Price has found John Hayward doing stonework at Winterdyne for James Rose in 1768-9 (op. cit.) and suggests that he may have worked at Stanford also. The OS 6 inch maps record a waterfall a little way to the west of the Temple linking with the Park Plantation. A surviving part of this 18th century landscape is the model Farm set below the Church. Commentators in the early-19th century also remark on the Southstone Rock Hermitage, a monolith, about a mile south of the park boundary but said by Paterson in 1829 to be within it. The *Beauties* in 1814 chose to pick out: oak, water, church, hermitage and stone house hewn out of solid rock.

There are 2 maps by John Broome in the London Society of Antiquaries, (Prattinton Collection) (information from Stephen Price), one of which is dated 1759 (Prattinton 115) shows the fenced deer park given over to plantations and fields and the individual agricultural uses specified as arable, meadow, close, pasture, coppice, grove, leasow, nursery, batch-hield. (The terrier is in the Winnington archive, WINN 2/2). The other, "A Map of Stanfords Court Farm" (Prattinton 91) shows some garden features although the Court itself, not being part of the Farm, is omitted and has to be presumed to be in the void between the lake and mansion. This map shows a very small fountain and 2 pavilions on the north side of the lake connected via a possible walled conduit to a stream in the park. Sited east of the lake and north of the old church and close to the old Court was a more significant, formal, probably terraced, walled garden with fountain and a small walled area with pavilion within it. Taking the Broome map at face value, the 1759 gardens were east of the mansion rather than west or south-west between mansion and lake as on Davis's 1803 map.

Stephen Price has discovered evidence that Sir Edward Winnington, Ist Bart., was importing from North America in the 1760s and therefore that the development of the Stanford grounds was ambitious in its time. A "List of Plants and Shrubs" "sent to England in the Ship Billericay" from New York in October 1765 specifies a dozen of 20 items: Larch Firr; Magnolia Tulip; Laurel leav'd Tulip; Allspice Wood; Hemlock Spruce; Magnolia Berry; Sweet Bay or Swamp Magnolia; White Spruce; The five leav'd pine; Mountain Laurel; Honey Suckle; Black Spruce; Cranberry plants; Red Cedar; White Cedar; Decidious Magnolia; Great Bird Cherry; Myrtle; Saussafras; Large Mountain Tulip. A footnote adds 1 oz of large magnolia Seed (WINN 2/3 a-b).

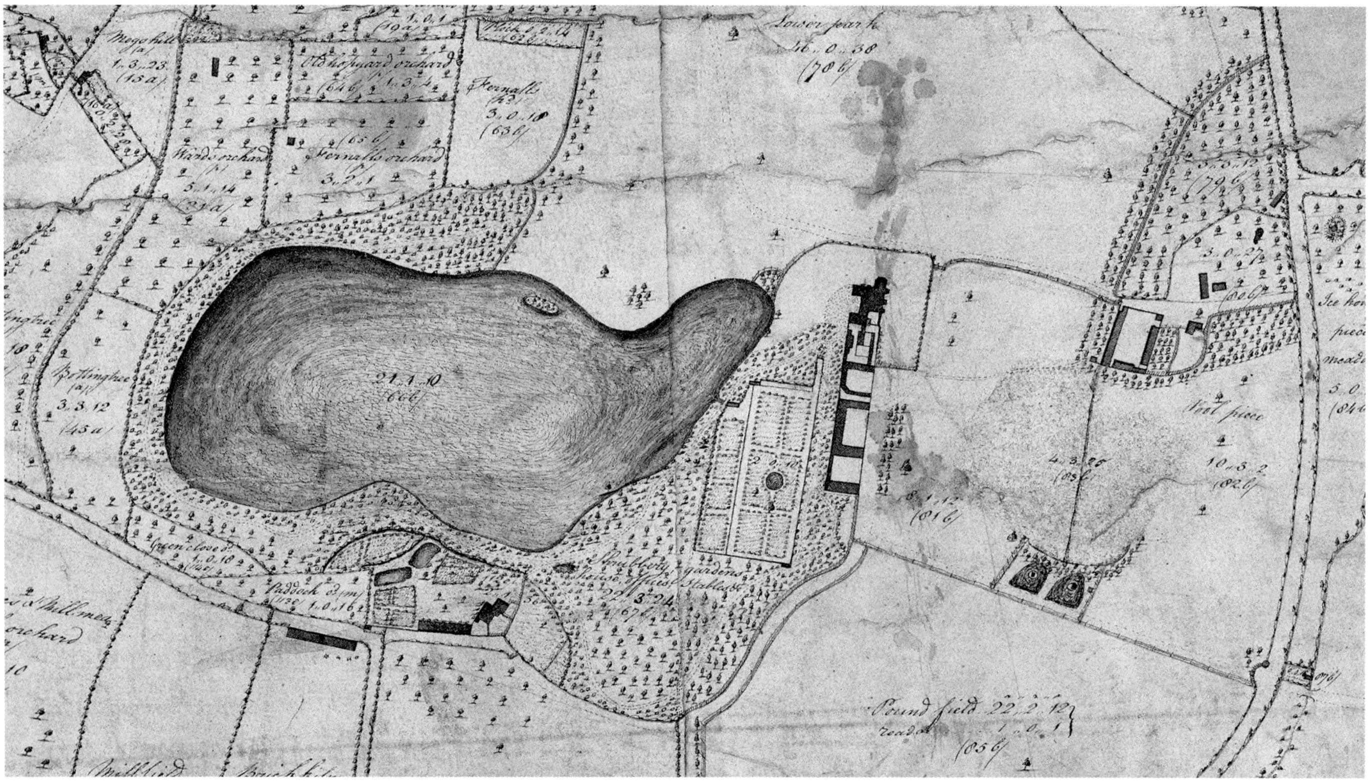

Detail of central section of 1803 parish survey by Thomas Davis showing Stanford Court, the lake and garden.© WAAS 709/12.

Stanford Court

..........continued from previous page

Davis's 1803 Survey records the park and pleasure grounds immediately around the mansion house. The house and ancillary buildings such as the Stables are laid out in a line with a formal and probably terraced garden on the same axis set between the mansion and the lake. This garden had a central water feature and perhaps gazebos at each end of a long terrace parallel with the house and a third pavilion on the further corner of the garden close to the lake. The bones of this 18th-century landscape can be recognised today with the Church occupying the high ground at the north-west tip of the park and the lake and the Shrubbery next to the large walled kitchen garden surrounded by mature trees (cedar, umbrella pine, Scots pine), extending down most of the east side. William Cobbett stayed here in 1830 and gives a long and lyrical description of the park and tempts himself with the prospect of abandoning politics for it (Martin, pp. 393-5). In particular he picks up the bumpy character of the park fields: "on another side there rise up beautiful little hills, some in the form of burrows or downs, only forty of a hundred times as large, one or two of which with no trees on them, and others topped with trees; but on one of these hills, and some yards higher than the lofty trees which are on this little hill, you see rising up the tower of the parish church ... " (Whitehead, op. cit.). Nothing of the formal gardens by the mansion are visible in Nash's view across the lake.

A. Brooks & N. Pevsner, *Worcestershire,* 2007 (BoE).
Paterson's Roads, ed. E. Mogg, 1829.
W. Cobbett, *Rural Rides*, ed. E. W. Martin, 1958.
D. Whitehead, "The Temple at Stanford-upon-Teme, Worcestershire", *HWGT, Newsletter,* 23, Summer 2004.
S. Price, *The Winnington Archive.: An Introduction,* 2015, (unpub).
T. R. Nash, *Collections for the History of Worcestershire,* Vol II, 1782.
Victoria County History Vol. 4, 1924, p. 342 (VCH).
Beauties of England and Wales, Vol. XV, 1814.

TOP LEFT: James Ross, Stanford Court from T. R. Nash, *Collections for the History of Worcestershire,* Vol II, 1782.
BOTTOM LEFT: lithograph circa 1851 showing the same view as Nash.
TOP RIGHT: lithograph circa 1851 of the Temple, both lithographs from Society of Antiquaries of London, Prattinton Collection.
BOTTOM RIGHT: the ruined Temple in 2016, note the changes to the frontage. Photo, R. Lockett.

Strensham Castle

Parish: Strensham

HER Ref: WSM28982.

Grid Ref: SO 904 404.

Postcode: WR8 9LJ.

O.S. 6" Map No: 48NW/SW.

Date of Map: 1888.

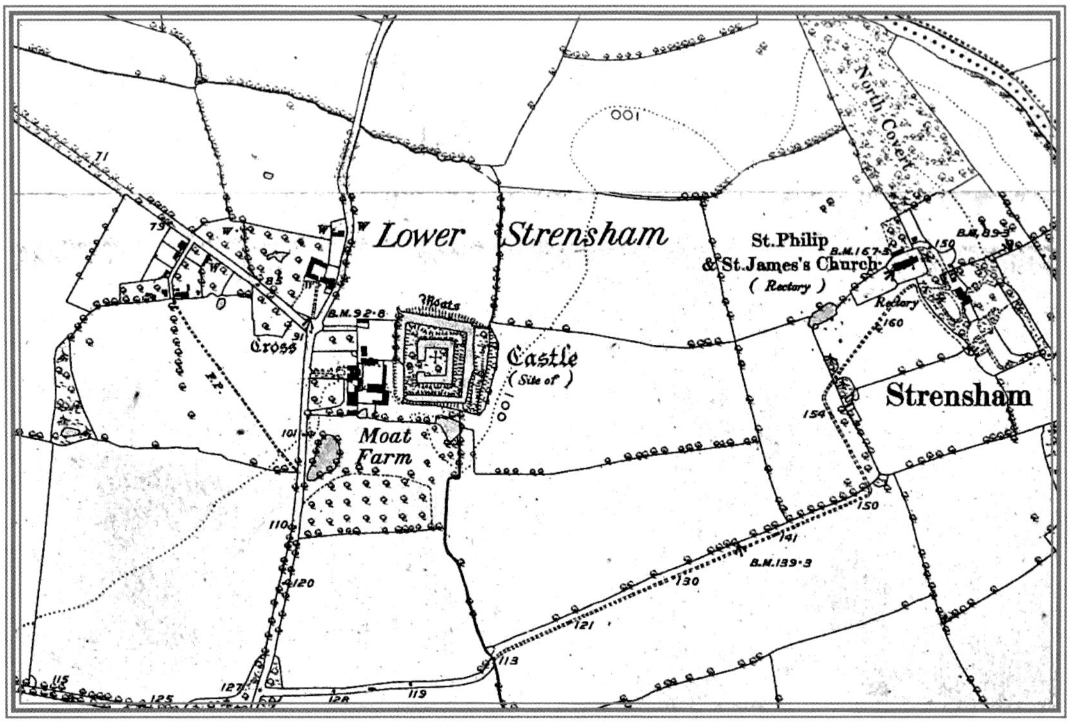

Licence to crenellate was granted to the Russells in 1388 and nearly a century later, in 1483, Richard III was anxious that Elizabeth Russell's park at Strensham should be replenished with game, presumably because it had suffered from some depredations (VCH, 4, 1924, p. 202). This must be the deer park shown in Saxton's map of 1577 and Sheldon's tapestry map of the 1590s (Oxford Bodleian Library) and in Blome's 1673 map. It is still being marked in the 18th century but perhaps being mistaken for Croome, e.g. in Bowen (1778). This park has not been precisely located and the grid reference given is for the surviving castle with double moat. Nash's view of 1776 shows a large house apparently on this site of which the *Beauties* in 1814 says, that even in its best days (obviously departed), it was "a struggling pile of confusion " (pp. 350/1).

Beauties of England and Wales, Vol. XV, 1814.
Victoria County History, Vol. 4, 1924, p. 202 (VCH).
T. R. Nash, *Collections for the History of Worcestershire,* Vol II, 1782.

Tickenhill Palace and Park

Parish: Bewdley

HER Ref: WSM28984.
Grid Ref: SO 785 751.
Postcode: DY12 2ER.

O.S. 6" Map No: 14NW.
Date of Map: 1883.

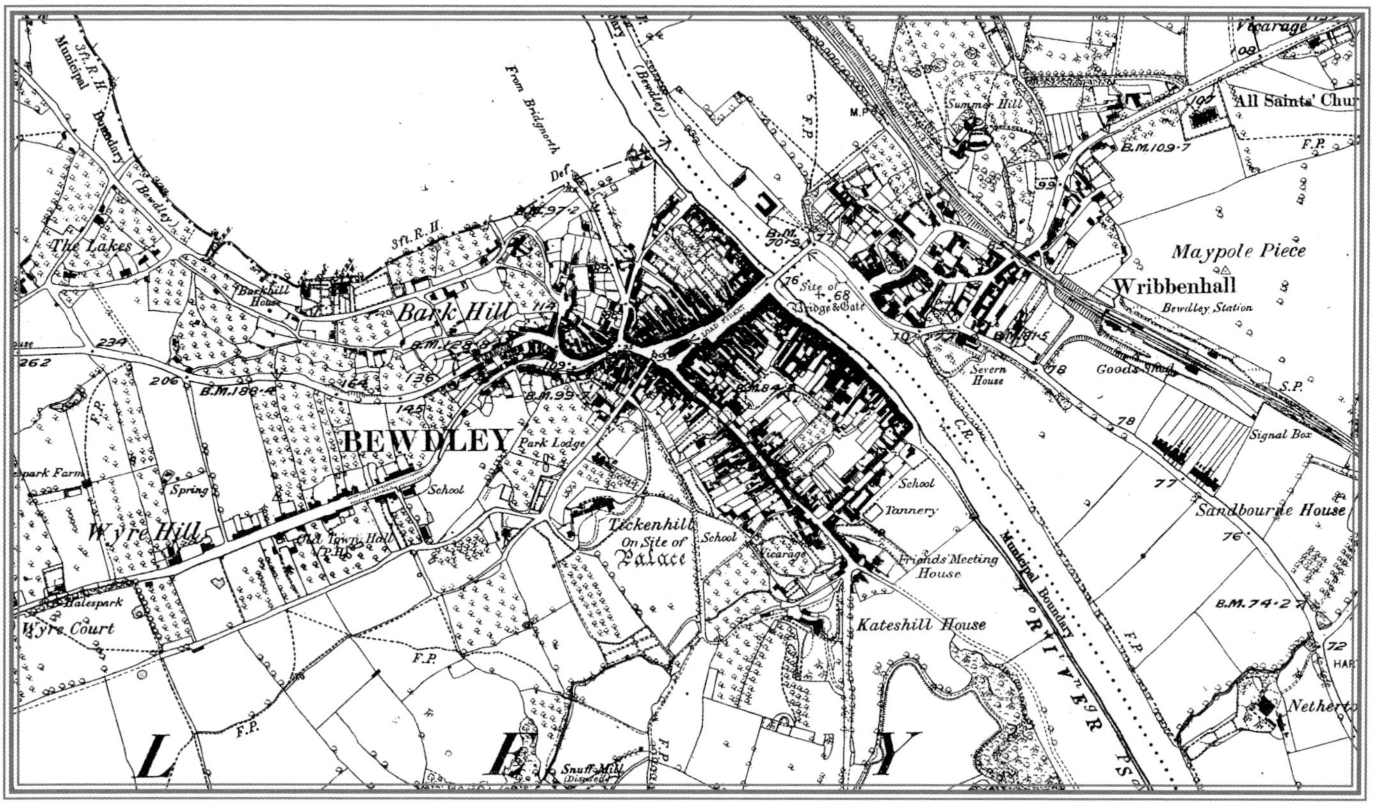

Tychnell is the name that Christopher Saxton gives to a fenced deer park in 1577 and this location is retained by his imitators John Speed, 1610 and Richard Blome and Robert Morden in 1673 and 1695. There is perhaps mention of more than one park in the 14th century according to the VCH which proposed a park both at Bewdley and at Tickenhill. Dr. Stuart Davies has interpreted these same sources as referring to a single park at Tickenhill beginning with the grant of free warren in 1301 to the Mortimers. In 1304 there was "a park of which the underwood and herbage and pannage is worth 8 shillings yearly". In 1336 "there is a capital messuage situated within the park" and another document mentions "a great park combining 600 acres of great oaks" There were rabbit warrens within the park. The deer park was presumably taken out of the royal Chase of Wyre a royal forest and after the granting of a charter to the town in 1472, rhe manor is generally called "BEWDLEY" and the park "Bewdley Park" (Davies, correspondence, 2017).

Around 1539, Leland described the "fair manor place ... standing in a goodly park well-wooded on the very knapp of a hill that the town standeth in" (part iv, p. 88). Nash in 1782 associated Habington's late-16th century description contemporary with Saxton, with Tickenhill, a park famous for spreading oaks that had been damaged in the Civil War and repaired by Mr. Ingram (who demolished most of the surviving Palace). A 1785 map of the Winnington estate (CRO 4600/737) has "Park Lane" immediately north of the house, "Park Lands" to the south-west, "Ticknell Ground" immediately south of a fence and two small fields both called "The Park" between the house and the river.

The deer park did not develope into a landscape park and by the early-19th century seems to have been used as an amenity by Bewdley Town. The *Beauties* in 1814 say: "the park is open as a general promenade ... though the park is not very extensive, it possesses a variety of hillside and dale, and of romantic dells, that renders it susceptible to the highest and most picturesque improvement" (pp. 272-3).

Stuart Davies (op. cit.) has described the economic use of the park in the 17th century by the Crown, the Keepers of the Park, the lessees and the towns people of Bewdley, e,g, for wood and grazing for a variety of livestock and even for popular entertainment. In 1623 the park was estimated at 400 acres, half of which was heath, containing 3500 old trees and 100 deer. In 1623 the walls and pales were in ruins and there were no deer (Lea, op. cit.). In 1609 coppicing was required to make repairs to the Palace and to repair the park fences (Parker, op. cit.). By 1721 the deer park was a memory and Dr. Stukeley then observed:

..........continued from previous page

"here was a park too, part of the Wire forest".
Tickenhill Palace was one of the places used by the Council of the Marches circa 1500; this had come to the Crown via the Mortimers. Prince Arthur and Catherine of Aragon were married by proxy at Tickenhill in 1499 and Prince Arthur was at Tickenhill on and off between 1493 and 1502. The Palace presumably had some gardens that Princess Mary might have enjoyed when housed here in 1525. Instructions were given that the Princess should "at all times serve God" and "at Seasons convenient to use moderate exercise on taking open air in the gardens sweet and wholesome places and walks which may confer on her health, solace and comfort as by the said Lady Governess (Countess of Salisbury) shall be thought most convenient" (Barnard, p. 7). In 1582 Sir Henry Sidney made repairs, brought in a water supply and set up "a fair large fountain made with limestone and lead" decorated with the Royal Arms (VCH). Tickenhill was recommended to Prince Henry (Charles I's elder brother) for his health but he died on the way from Ludlow in 1612. A bower in the park is documented in the early-17th century but this may have belonged to the Tudor age.
A century later the gatehouse and much of the old house was still standing but substantially pulled down in 1738. A memoir of 1795-6 by Francis Ingram (CRO 438/xxxviii), whose father resided at "Ticknell, the manor house of Bewdley belonging to the Winnington Family" says that it was "repaired and nearly rebuilt by my father". Francis Ingram himself did some works at Tickenhill in order to provide himself with a view of Winterdyne which, with Ribbesford and Stanford Court were other family houses.
Tickenhill was rescued from further decline by Joseph Tangye who bought Tickenhill from the Crown in 1873. The BoE describes what remains from the 15th and 16th centuries (p. 148) but nothing now remains on site to evoke the gardens that served the Palace between the 15th and 19th centuries.
Today, this is a large tract of rolling, open countryside on the southern borders of Bewdley, It is deeply incised by the narrow valley of the Snuffmill and Park Dingles with stream, pools, woodland and ancient hedges. A section of the northern part of the park has been developed for residential use, the western part is a golf course and it has been bisected by the A456, Bewdley by-pass. However, the greater part is still intact.

Dr. W. Stukeley, *Itinerarium Curiosum*, Iter 4., 2nd ed. 1776 (1721).
J. Severn Walker, *Architectural Sketches*, Vol. 1, 1862.
L. Toulmin-Smith (ed.), *The Itinerary of John Leland ... and Collectania,* 1908.
G.E.D., *Notes on Tickenhill*, n.d., (WAAS 8041/10).
Victoria County History, Vol. 4, 1924, (VCH).
Revd. E. Lea, "Notes on the History of the Wyre Forest", *Worcestershire Naturalist's Club,* 1923, pp. 63-80.
E. A. Barnard, *A Vanished Palace; Tickenhill,* 1948.
J. F. Parker, *An Account of Tickenhill House, Bewdley,* 1979.
A. Brooks & N. Pevsner, *Worcestershire,* 2007 (BoE).
Beauties of England and Wales, Vol. XV, 1814.
S. Davies, "There having beene then a great wynde"; trees, deer and conflict in Bewdley Park in the 17th century, 2017 (unpublished).

·:· Old Tickenhill Palace ·:·

J. Severn Walker *Architectural Sketches,* Vol 1, 1862.

Wadborough Park

Parish: Drakes Broughton & Wadborough

HER Ref: WSM28907.
Grid Ref: SO 897 488. Postcode: WR7 4RH.
O.S. 6" Map No: 41NW. Date of Map: 1884.

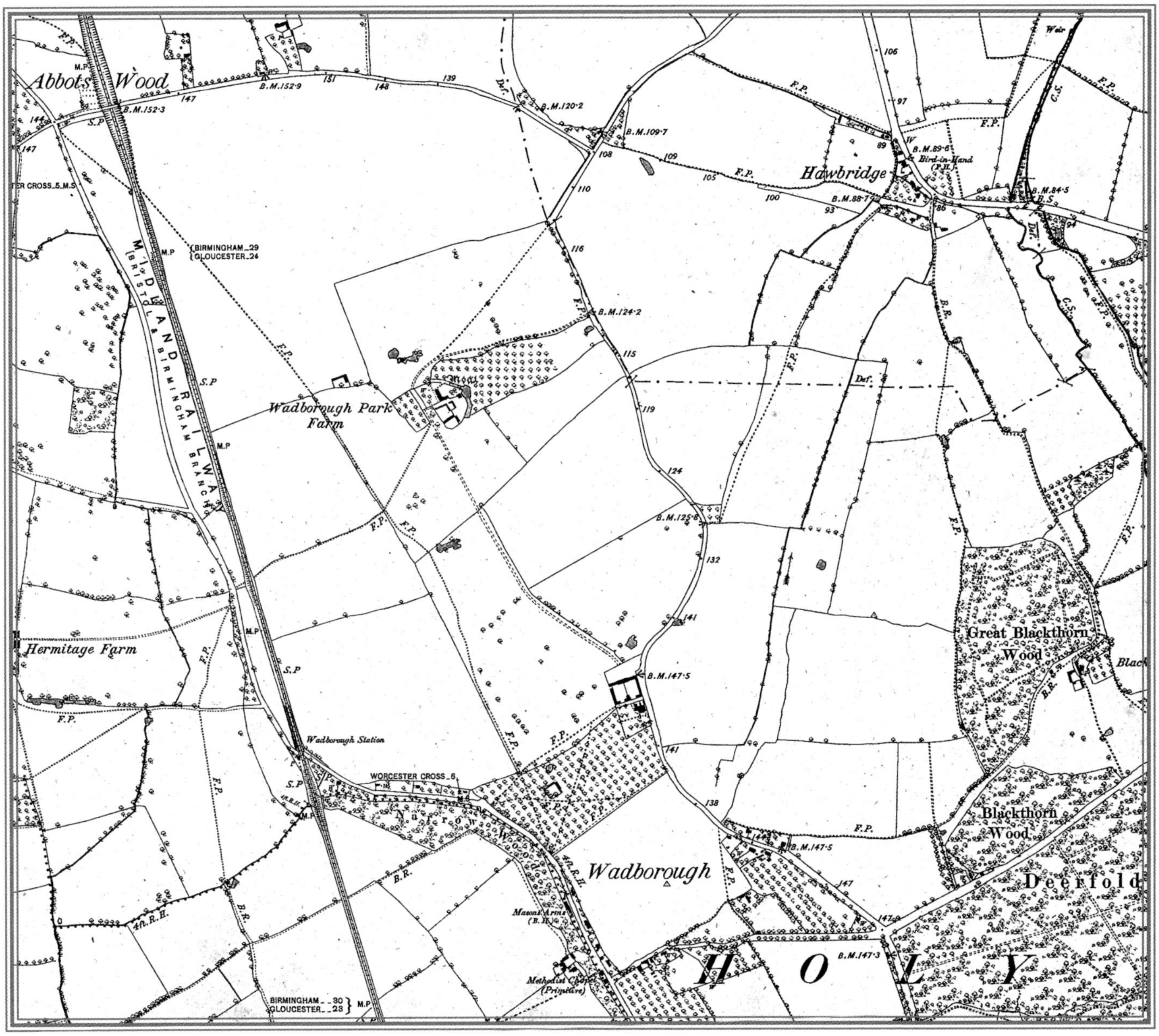

Wadborough is documented as a park temp. Edward III and the VCH (1924) thought that this park might date back to the 12th century. It is shown as a deer park on Saxton in 1577 and repeated by his 17th century followers, e.g. Morden (Holberow) and retained in many 18th century maps including Haywood in 1789 (as Wallborow). However, Nash makes it clear that as a park and manor it was only a memory by 1782 (Vol. 2, p. 249). The Wadborough Park Farm, which is moated, no doubt represents the manor house site and Deerfold Wood to the south-east might indicate the extent of the park in that direction. The grid ref. is taken from the Farmhouse which is described by the BoE as a dramatic ruin (p. 261). The railway goes through the area of the park suggested by the map centred on Wadborough Park Farm and also separates this area from Abbotswood. Park Farm was sold in 1917 with 502 acres as part of the Stoulton (Somers) Estate (WAAS 5240/6).

A. Brooks & N. Pevsner, *Worcestershire,* 2007 (BoE).
Victoria County History Vol. 4, 1924, (VCH).
T. R. Nash, *Collections for the History of Worcestershire,* Vol II, 1782.

Waresley House

Parish: Hartlebury

HER Ref: WSM28830.

Grid Ref: SO 845 699. Postcode: DY11 7XR.

O.S. 6" Map No: 14SE, 21NE.

Date of Maps: both 1888, with extent of park & gardens shaded as 1880s OS.

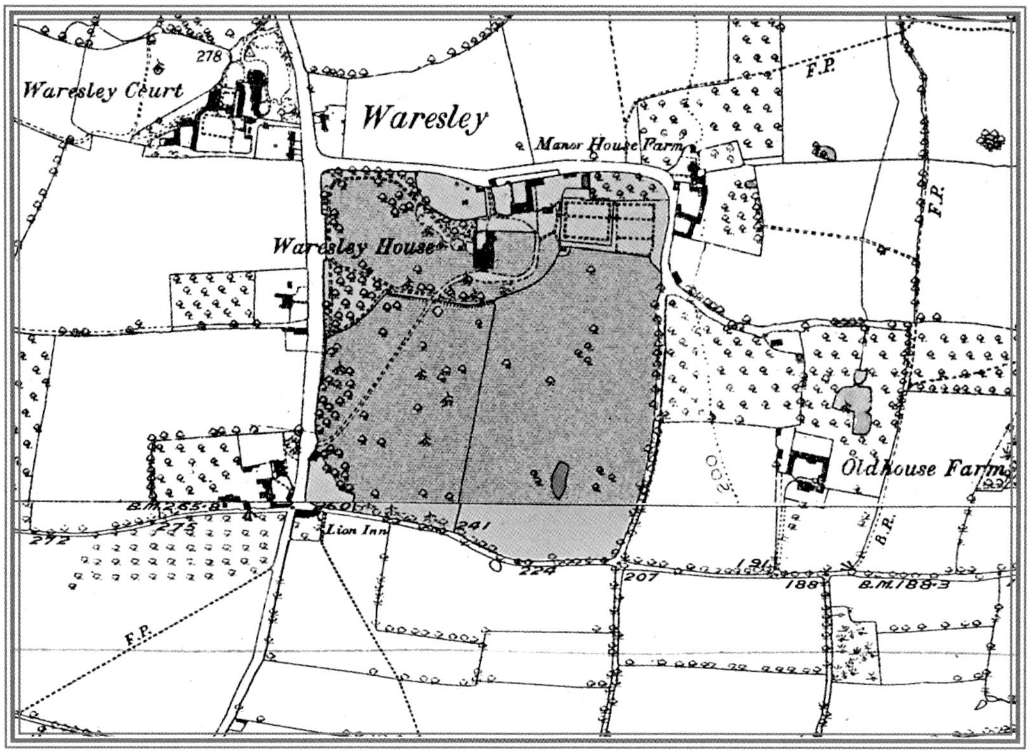

Waresley House is noticed in a guide book of 1788 and is still being shown as having a park on the 1938 OS.

This small rectangular site is bordered by roads on all sides and remained unchanged from at least circa 1840 (when it became the country residence of the Dean of Worcester, the Very Revd. John Peel) until recorded by the 2nd edition of the OS 6 inch in 1905. *Bentley's Directory* circa 1841 comments on Peel's "very tastefully planted grounds". There was a large, walled kitchen garden east of the house and a lodge in the south-west corner and some fringe planting on the west and south. The 1912 sale particulars claim "a special garden mainly planted with rhododendrons and azaleas ... an old-fashioned Georgian Conservatory ... rustic summerhouse"; the ground and gardens were put at 11 acres out of a total of 36 acres (WAAS 4600/142). These details are the same as sale particulars of 1874.

The house and gardens are now occupied by the buildings and playing fields of St. Gilbert's school. Much of the park has been developed for housing and the walled garden eradicated.

J. Bentley *Guide and Directory to the City and Suburbs of Worcester,* 1841.

Waresley House from 1912 sale particulars.

Wassel Grove

Parish: Hagley

HER Ref: WSM28994.

Grid Ref: SO 933 824. Postcode: DY9 9JP.

O.S. 6" Map No. 4SE, 9NE.

Date of both Maps: 1884, with extent of park & garden shaded as 1905 OS.

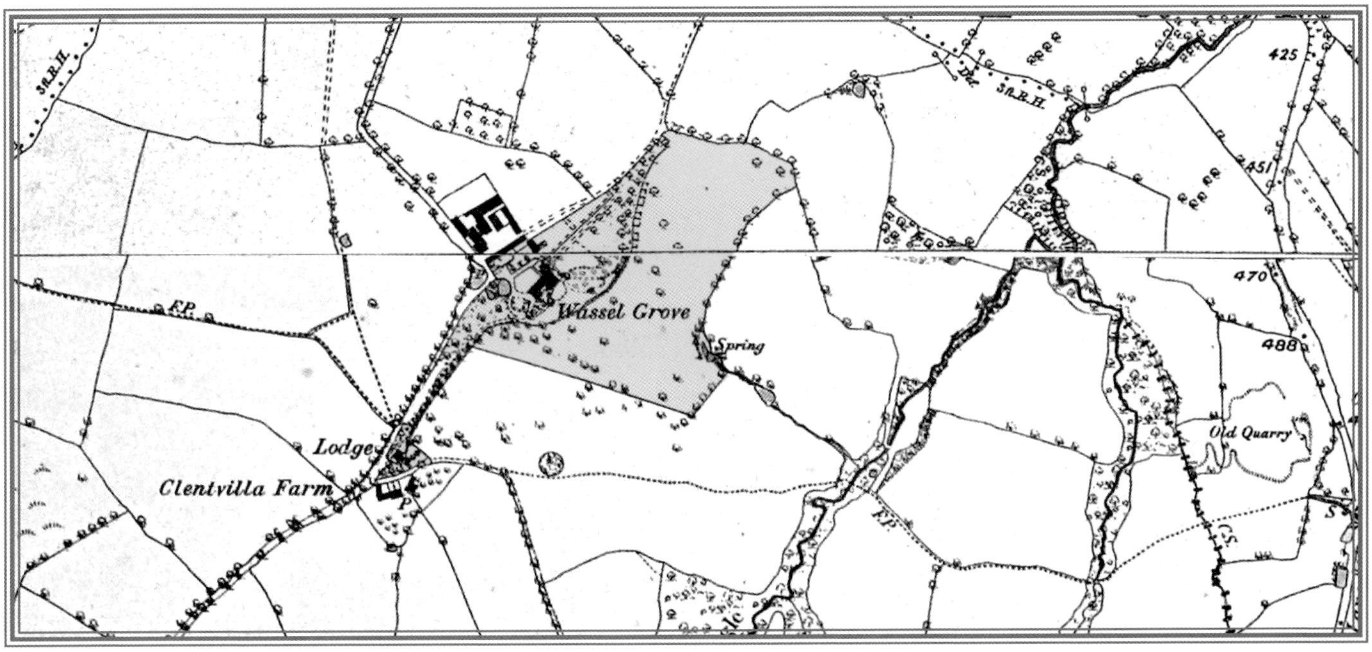

Greenwood's map shows the Grove with some grounds in 1822; a small park with lodge is shown on the 1905 OS 6 inch and the Listing refers to a small enclosed garden with gateway and piers. The park was related to a large classical villa of 1831 which was demolished in the 1970s (BoE, p. 340). This entry relates to the surviving Farm House of similar date. The park has some fine veteran trees.

A. Brooks & N. Pevsner, *Worcestershire,* 2007 (BoE).

Wassel Grove, 1908. Postcard image, Haddon series.

Wassell Wood House (Warshill)

Parish: Kidderminster Foreign

HER Ref: WSM28995.

Grid Ref: SO 795 773. Postcode: DY12 1LD.

O.S. 6" Map No: 8SW.

Date of Map: 1889, with deduced extent of park & grounds shaded (not shaded on 1905 OS).

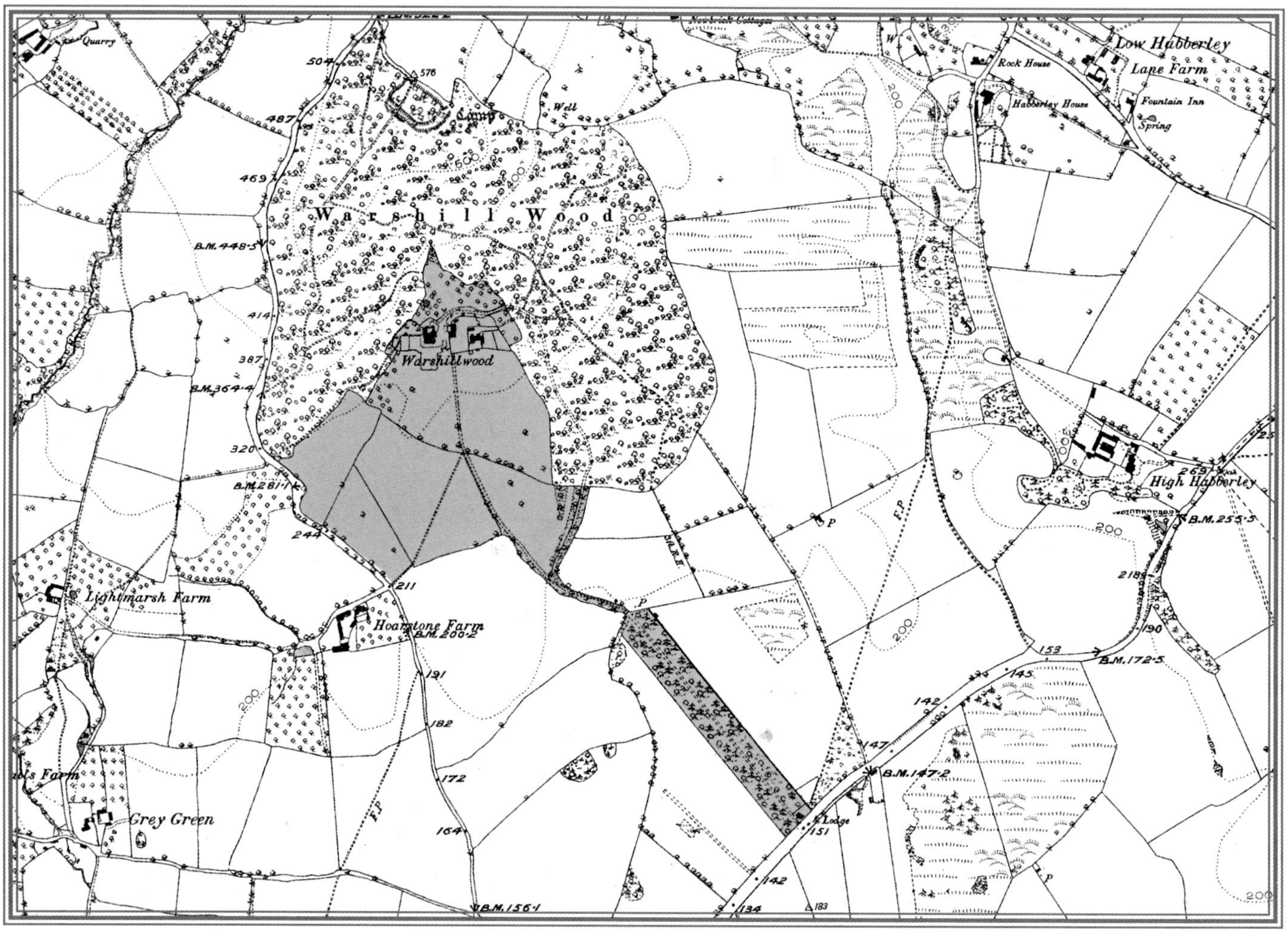

Wassell House is marked as a residence on Cary in 1805. The present house was built in the 1840's (BoE, p. 781). A small park with a lodge is shown on the first OS 6 inch edition of 1881/2. The house is situated in a wedge opening out to the south cut out of Wassell Wood which otherwise envelopes it. The name was changed from Warshill between 1889 and 1903.
This is now a working farm with the Lodge in separate ownership. The park remains with some fine trees.

A. Brooks & N. Pevsner, *Worcestershire,* 2007 (BoE).
P. Reid, *Burke's and Savilles Guide to Coutry Houses,* II, 1980.

Weatheroak Hall

Parish: Wythall

HER Ref: WSM03139.

Grid Ref: SP 062 744. Postcode: B48 7ED.

O.S. 6" Map No. 16NE, 17NW.

Date of Map: 1883, 1884, with extent of park & gardens shaded as 1905 OS.

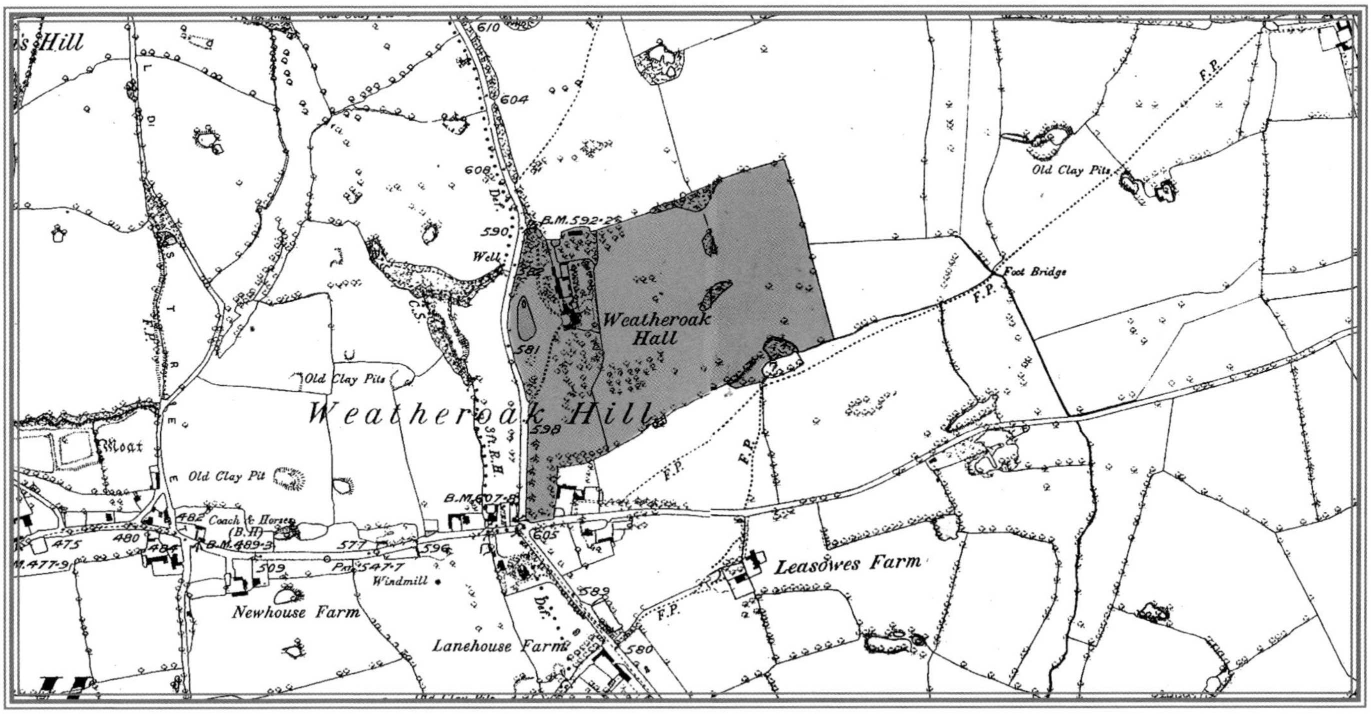

Countryside Treasures identifies the moated site and fish ponds within "a small medieval park, the boundary of which can be traced as a prominent bank and ditch". Grounds are mentioned by early-19th century guidebooks. The grounds were no doubt developed by James Mynors, a successful Birmingham surgeon, who built the house in the late-18th century. A fine conversation piece of the Mynors family by James Millar, dated 1790, implies a park-like setting (Birmingham Museum and Art Gallery). The BoE notes "brick GAZEBO by W. A. Harvey, 1911" which was actually built by the Revd. T. H. Mynors in 1884. The 2nd edition of the OS 6 inch shows the park with lodge and fishponds (1905).

Weatheroak Hall is now the King's Norton Golf Club. The ornamental pond and some tree clumps remain but there is no trace of the park.

Worcestershire Register of Countryside Treasures, 1973, revised 1984.
A. Brooks & N. Pevsner, *Worcestershire*, 2007 (BoE).

Westwood Park

Parish: Hampton Lovett & Westwood

HER Ref: WSM12962/21263. Grid Ref: SO 829 531. Postcode: WR2 5SY.

O.S. 6" Map No: 21SE,22SW, 28NE, 29NW.

Date of Maps: 1888, 1888, 1883, 1885, with extent of park & gardens shaded as H. E. Register.

..........continued from previous page

Westwood Park

..........continued from previous page

Included within Historic England's Register of Historic Parks and Gardens of special historic interest in England.

F. B. Andrews sums up the history of the landscape: "Habington speaks of Westwood Park as a "vast and solitary wood" but now it is nothing more than a well-timbered pasture land ..." (op. cit. p. 72). Westwood House caught the imagination of the Romantic period and featured in volumes which sought to evoke the appearance and atmosphere of Tudor and Jacobean houses, e.g. in Joseph Nash's *Mansions of England in the Olden Time*, 1839 (with figures in 17th century dress) and S. C. Hall's *Baronial Halls*, 1848 (tinted lithographs).

A watercolour by E. F. Burney of circa 1800 titled in the saleroom as *The return from the chase, Westwood House,* anticipates Joseph Nash by imagining Westwood in its 17th century dress (Christie's, London, 7. 7. 2015 (78)); the Burneys were local to the City of Worcester.

Lithograph from Joseph Nash, *Mansions of England in the Olden Time*, 1839.

Lithograph from S. C. Hall, *Baronial Halls*, 1848.

An 1837 *Guide to Worcester* views it more distantly: "It is seen from the Kidderminster Road lifting its numerous turrets and pinnacles in the midst of a large and magnificent park". Earlier, circa 1720, Daniel Defoe noticed Westwood "in a most agreeable situation, the mansion a seat of Sir John Packington, a baronet of very ancient family" (Vol. 2, p. 43). It had been erected by a particularly showy Elizabethan at the end of his days who was licensed to create a park of 1000 acres at Westwood, Hampton Lovett and elsewhere in 1618. He impaled 2 great parks called Westwood Parks and stocked one with red and the other with fallow deer and planted the avenues which radiated from the house (VCH, 3, 1913, pp. 236-7). Because the deer park was created post-Saxton (1577), it does not feature on the 17th century maps which depended on him and first appears on Bowen's map of 1772. Apparently before the Reformation, the nuns had a licence to make a park but never activated it; archaeological finds supported the belief that the nunnery was on the site of the later walled garden. Whitaker inventoried the deer park in 1892 as 278 acres with a 60 acre lake, surrounded by a brick wall and iron and wood fences and stocked with 110 fallow deer. The current Registered park area is circa 240 ha. (Historic England).

Mowl (op. cit.) links the design of both house and park to the presence of a group of dispossessed Anglican clergy (Non-Jurors) at Westwood during the Commonwealth and Protectorate (1649-1660) under the patronage of Dorothy Packington (sometimes thought to be the author of *The Whole Duty of Man*). A theological interpretation follows for the four diagonally-set towers representing the four Evangelists and the ten radiating drives through the plantations for the ten Commandments, an idea first proposed by Hussey (op. cit.) and characterised by Mowl as "a religious hunting garden". This would be an example on a huge scale of the more familiar shaped yews in contemporary topiary gardens as at Cleeve Prior or Rous Lench.

Recent evaluation of the structure has however focussed construction dates for the mansion around a documented date for carpentry work in 1612 and a likely second campaign for the tower wings set diagonally to the corners in the 1620s. The interior decorations would be dated to the Stuart Restoration (Maguire op. cit. and BoE, pp. 653-4). This is not to say that the Anglican divines should not have cast a theological interpretation over an existing landscape as first proposed by Hussey.

There was a late-17th century cadenza written by another dispossessed Anglican divine - George Hickes (Dean of Worcester 1683-1691), a prominent Non-Juror, a clergyman who, having taken an oath of allegiance to James II, felt unable to take another to William and Mary and so had to give up his benefice. Hickes dedicated his *Grammatica Anglo-Saxonica* (1689) to the same Sir John

Westwood Park

..........continued from previous page

Pakington who embellised Westwood in the 1660s and in the Latin dedication acknowledged the comfort and relief that the architecture, gardens and landscape of Westwood gave to a mind burdened with a life of letters: "There are porches, vestibules, columns, gardens, walks, covered and open, straight and winding, all contributing to literary thought; there are groves, woods, shrubberies, meadows, fields, lawns, pastures, nor is there anything there that is not restful and pleasing to the mind in any way out of harmony with literary pursuits, either reading, hearing or any of the arts of learning" (quoted by Andrews, op. cit., *Country Life*, 1902, previously by Hall, op. cit. in 1848 and first by Nash, op. cit. in 1781). "The revival of the practice of meditation within the Anglican tradition led to a new function for gardens, which were to be the prime places for such religious reflections" (Strong, p. 108).

Put these 17th century thoughts together with the bird's eye view by Jan Kip and Leonard Knyff in *Britannia Illustrata,* (1714, pl. 65) with further help from Nash and Hall, and one can imagine the four pavilions (of which two survive) and the Gatehouse, linked together by walls and fences surrounding a large area of formal flower, fruit and other productive gardens. There are a number of other buildings, certainly Stables and what has been described as a tilting ground and perhaps a deer house and a viewing station or grandstand. Is there a hunt in progress? If *Britannia Illustrata* is to be believed, Westwood had unusually irregular and varied gardens immediately adjoining the mansion; as with other properties promoted by this ambitious book, the plates may be aspirational rather than factual but the peculiarities at Westwood may imply the latter.

Lord Torrington, who visited Westwood in the 1780s, cast an experienced eye over "the house very antient, with lofty turrets, placed in the midst of a wood, in which great avenues are cut, and thro' one there is a view of the great pool of water, now much contracted from its former largeness; and the timber is also greatly diminished. Here is a striking appearance of wood and old grandeur, but the house is sadly improved with modern glazing; and the trees being at some distance afford not immediate shade. The approach to the house is bad and formal, not leading (as it ought to do) thro' the wood. It is surrounded by gardens, and walls, in the old taste..." (Bruyn Andrews, p. 51). The gardens immediately around the house as illustrated in *Britannia Illustrata,* may now have to be dated to the 1620's rather than post English Civil War when the Pakington's manor house at Hampton Lovett was destroyed (BoE, pp. 653-6).

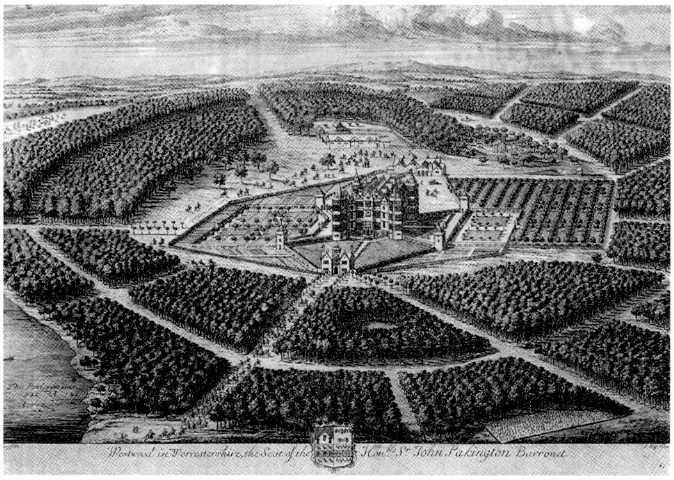

Bird's eye view by Jan Kip and Leonard Knyff from *Britannia Illustrata,* 1714.

W. Niven, engraving in *Illustrations of Old Worcestershire Houses,* 1873.

Nash, who was sufficiently impressed by the house to compare it to the Chateau of Madrid, Paris and to Holland House, London, the latter for its turrets and gables (Vol. I, p. 351, 1781); he includes 2 illustrations of Westwood, one pirated from Kip, and the other, a view across the Great Pool (reduced from 120 to 60 acres) with a pleasure boat. When Miss Fanny Burney visited Westwood in July 1777, "Sir Herbert was so obliging as to plan a water excursion every day; for he was desirous to shew me his barge, and to display all the beauties of his large Pool, which is reckoned the finest in England, being more than two miles long and proportionally wide. However, the weather never allowed of any such scheme being put into execution" (Pakington, pp. 104-5). After recording that "Lady Pakington produced some coins that she had very lately dug out of the Nun's Chapel" she continues "yet she shewed so much ignorance of History as to render her researches truly ridiculous" ... "she always took it for granted that every king of the same name followed in regular succession; and so, when we had examined the coins of Henry II, "Now", said she, "we'll come to Henry III: but happening instead to meet with Richard the First, with the same correctness she looked for Richard the Second ..." (Pakington, op. cit. pp. 102-105).

Westwood Park

..........continued from previous page

Only four avenues cut through the Great Wood on the 1813 OS surveyed at 2 inch scale. However, Hall, in 1848, suggests an all-round benefit: "The principal front of the house commands a view of this lake, and being situated in the centre of the park, commanding on all sides, the vistas produced by the fine old trees whose radiating avenues surround it; it is as happily placed as any mansion in the kingdom".

The HE Register details one of the three surviving avenues as being composed of Irish and golden yew, deodar, Wellingtonia. The OS 6 inch of 1905 does not show these avenues at all clearly. The woodland, (i.e. Nunnery Wood, the thin west strip on Warren Bank, Broadfield Plantation in the south point and the plantation along the south side of the Great Pool up to Boycott Wood) survived relatively unchanged from 1905 to the 1950s (Whitehead, p. 5).

Westwood from T. R. Nash, *Collections for the History of Worcestershire,* Vol I, 1781.

The HE Register interprets the existing formal garden of 6 ha as 19th and 20th century and the walled, kitchen gardens of 1 ha also as 19th century. These gardens are said to be on the site of the Nunnery which gives its name to the largest surviving area of woodland of 40 hectares to the north-west near which are 2 small pools of 2 and 1 hectares. There are belts of trees also along the north-east, east and south-east boundaries of the park. Other garden buildings include an icehouse and a 19th century (post 1883) summer-house. The HE Listing includes the later-19th century Jacobethan boathouse and Middle Lodge (post 1883) in similar style, the Droitwich Lodge (by 1883) with gateway and gates and the Ombersley Lodge (in Picturesque style) with gateway and gates; photographs of the Lodges feature in the 1902 sale particulars. Philip Hardwick was involved at Westwood Park as he was at Madresfield and Sir Reginald Blomfield was active at Westwood circa 1883 and 1900.

The whole of the park (and mansion) was parcelled into 26 lots for sale in 1902. In 1952 it was included in a single lot amounting to 439 acres (CRO 11541/4) except for the mansion with 8 acres of Pleasure Gardens and Walled Kitchen Garden. The 1952 particulars picks out some garden features: "formal rose garden with artistic summer arbour all enclosed by clipped yew well-stocked with walled fruit, espalier trained and standard, apple and pear trees and soft fruit borders. Gravelled pathways with dwarf box hedges intersect the gardens, whilst in the centre is an ornamental lily pond." In addition the particulars detail Plant House, Vinery, Tomato House (5), Peach House, Forcing House, Cucumber House, Cold Frames and a vegetable garden enclosed by yew hedges. What, if any of this was the work of Milner and White who worked at Westwood for Lord Doverdale in 1945, is unclear. The Listing dates the chinoiserie summer-house to the mid-18th century, a date given to some of the walling immediately around the mansion and to the kitchen garden to the west.

The mansion was divided into separate apartments in the 1980s.

S. C. Hall, *Baronial Halls,* 2 vols., 1848, "Westwood House, Worcestershire".

C. Hussey, *Country Life,* Vol. 12, 1902, p. 696.

Country Life, LXIV, 1928, p. 50, 94.

M. Beckett, "The Butterfly House", *Country Life,* 24. 10. 2012.

F. B. Andrews, "Westwood", *Birmingham & Midland Archeol. Soc.,* 43, 1917, p. 63.

C. Bruyn Andrews, *The Torrington Diaries,* 1970, Vol. 1.

H. & R. Pakington, *The Pakingtons of Westwood,* 1975.

A.Tinniswood, *Country Houses from the Air,* 1994.

T. Mowl, *Historic Gardens of Worcestershire,* Ch. 2, 2006.

Oxford Dictionary of National Biography, *Dorothy Pakington.*

R. Strong, *The Artist and the Garden,* 2000.

A. Brooks & N. Pevsner, *Worcestershire,* 2007 (BoE).

A. Maguire, "Droitwich, Westwood Park", *Soc. of Architectural Historians of Gt. Britain,* September 2000 Conference, pp. 99-101.

Victoria County History, Vol. 3, 1913, (VCH).

J. Nash, *Mansions of England in the Olden Time,* 1839.

T. R. Nash, *Collections for the History of Worcestershire,* Vol I, 1781.

Guide to Worcester, 1837.

D. Whitehead, *Artists in Paradise, exhibition in Pictures,* HWGT Exhibition 1997.

W. Niven, *Illustrations of Old Worcestershire,* 1873.

HE *Register of Parks & Gardens,* 1998.

Wick Episcopi

Parish: Rushwick

HER Ref: WSM29005.

Grid Ref: SO829 531. Postcode: WR2 5SY.

O.S. 6" Map No: 33SE.

Date of Map: 1884, with extent of park & gardens shaded as 1905 OS.

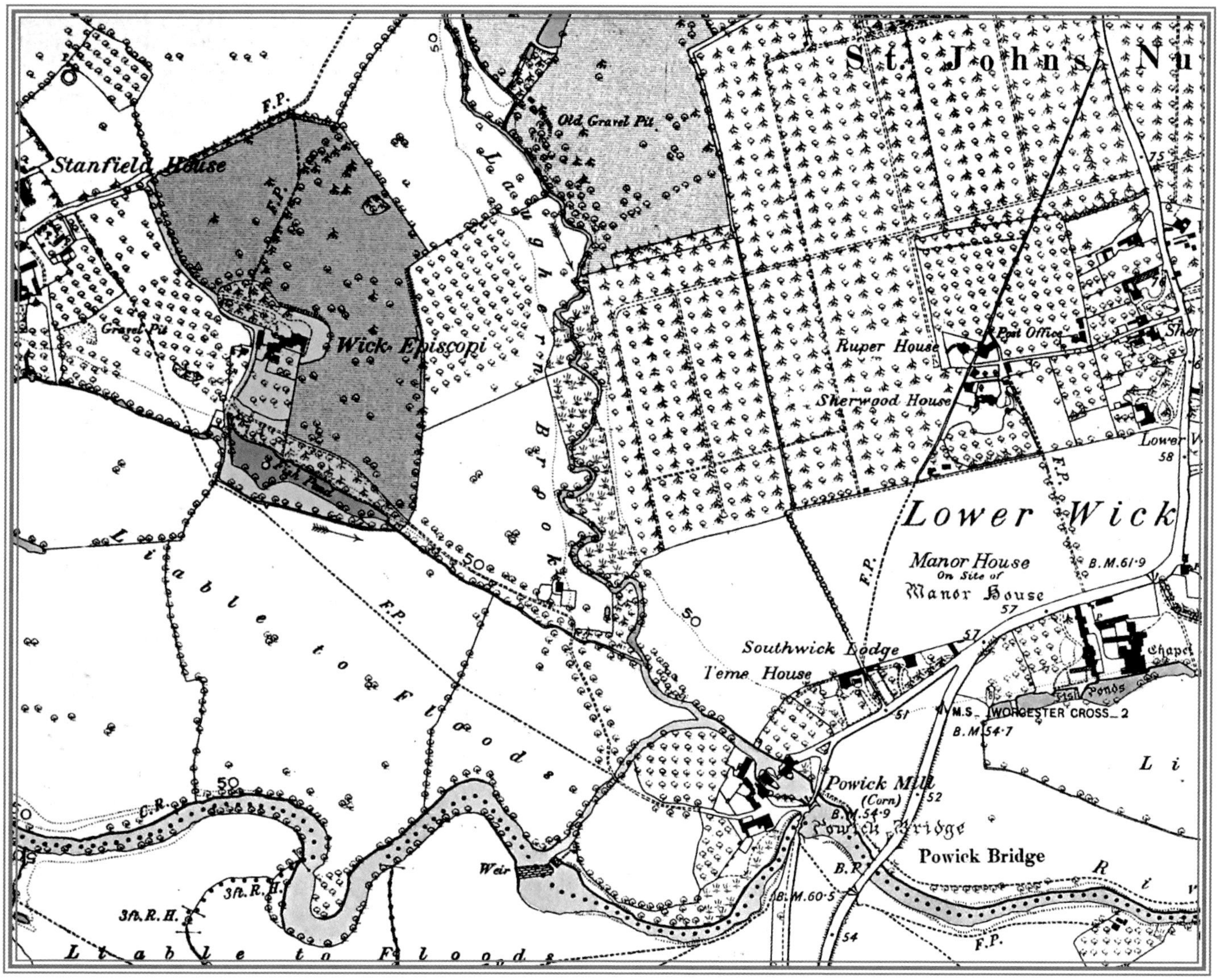

The house is of late-17th and late-18th century date (BoE, p. 252). A small park and fish pond are shown on the first OS 6 inch. A narrow strip of surviving planting runs along the north side of the large fishpond which has now been reduced. An 1836 map of the Upper Wick Estate by Samuel Barnett gives the area of House, Gardens, Lawns, and Plantations as 6 acres and the pool as 4.6 acres (CRO 438/12). The park is shown as more substantial on small-scale, printed maps of 1830 (Murray) and 1835 (Walker) when it extended further south and south-west towards the Teme. The parkland is still substantially intact with fine parkland trees but is now bordered by the Worcester A440 ring road.

A. Brooks & N. Pevsner, *Worcestershire,* 2007 (BoE).

Wick House

Parish: Wick

HER Ref: WSM28981.
Grid Ref: SO 952 451.
Postcode: WR10 3NT.
O.S. 6" Map No. 41SE.
Date of Map: 1905.

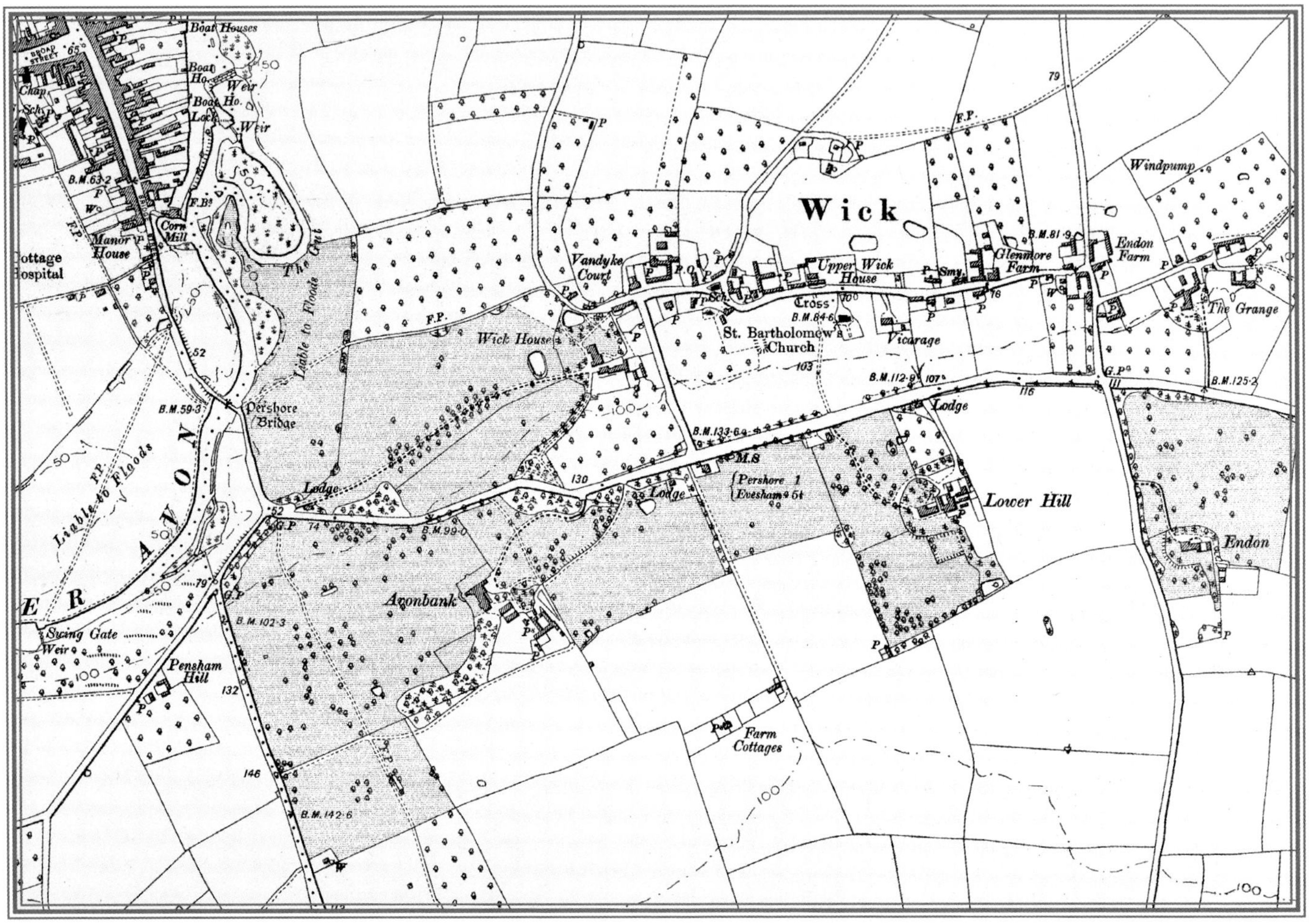

A Wick House and grounds are noticed in guides from Tunnicliff in 1788 to Greenwood and Paterson in 1822 and 1829. The very substantial 18th century house (illus. Reid, p. 231) was demolished in the 1950s and its site is now occupied by Wick House Close. A recent Village History (typescript in WAAS) identifies trees along the Pershore - Evesham road as remains of 1780 plantations. The park as shown on the 1905 OS 6 inch extended across the Pershore - Evesham road, to include the later parks of Avon Bank and Lower Hill or Bryn Issa. Its south-west point would have been at SO 953 443 as in the 1811 survey for the first OS one inch. Around 1820 the land that went with Wick House north of the Pershore/ Evesham Road belonged to Richard Hudson and Henry Hudson and the land to the south of the road to Thomas Hudson. There is a manuscript *Plan of the Estate of the late Henry Hudson Esq.* covering the Pershore side of the estate dated 1849 (WAAS 5240/14). Hall (op. cit.) clarified the family history in 2012 explaining that from the 18th century the house was known as Upper Wick House and that it was acquired by Richard Hudson in 1764 with a division between 3 sons in 1804 (i.e. pre 1820). A Chapel was built in memory of Lt. Alban Hudson, M. C., killed in action in 1917. The house was "transformed" by Cecil Hare and was known as Wyke Manor prior to its demolition.

Anon. *A Short History of Wick Village*, n.d.
Michael Hall, *Country Life*, 8. 12. 2012.
W. Tunnicliff, *A Survey of the County of Worcester*, 1788.
C. & J. Greenwood, *Worcestershire Delineated*, 1822.
Paterson's Roads, 1829.
P. Reid, *Burke's and Savilles Guide to Coutry Houses,* II, 1980.

Winterdyne

Parish: Bewdley

HER Ref: WSM28980.

Grid Ref: SO 790 747. Postcode: DY12 2TE.

O.S. 6" Map No. 9NW/9SW.

Date of Map: 1887, with deduced extent of park & gardens shaded (not shaded on 1905 OS).

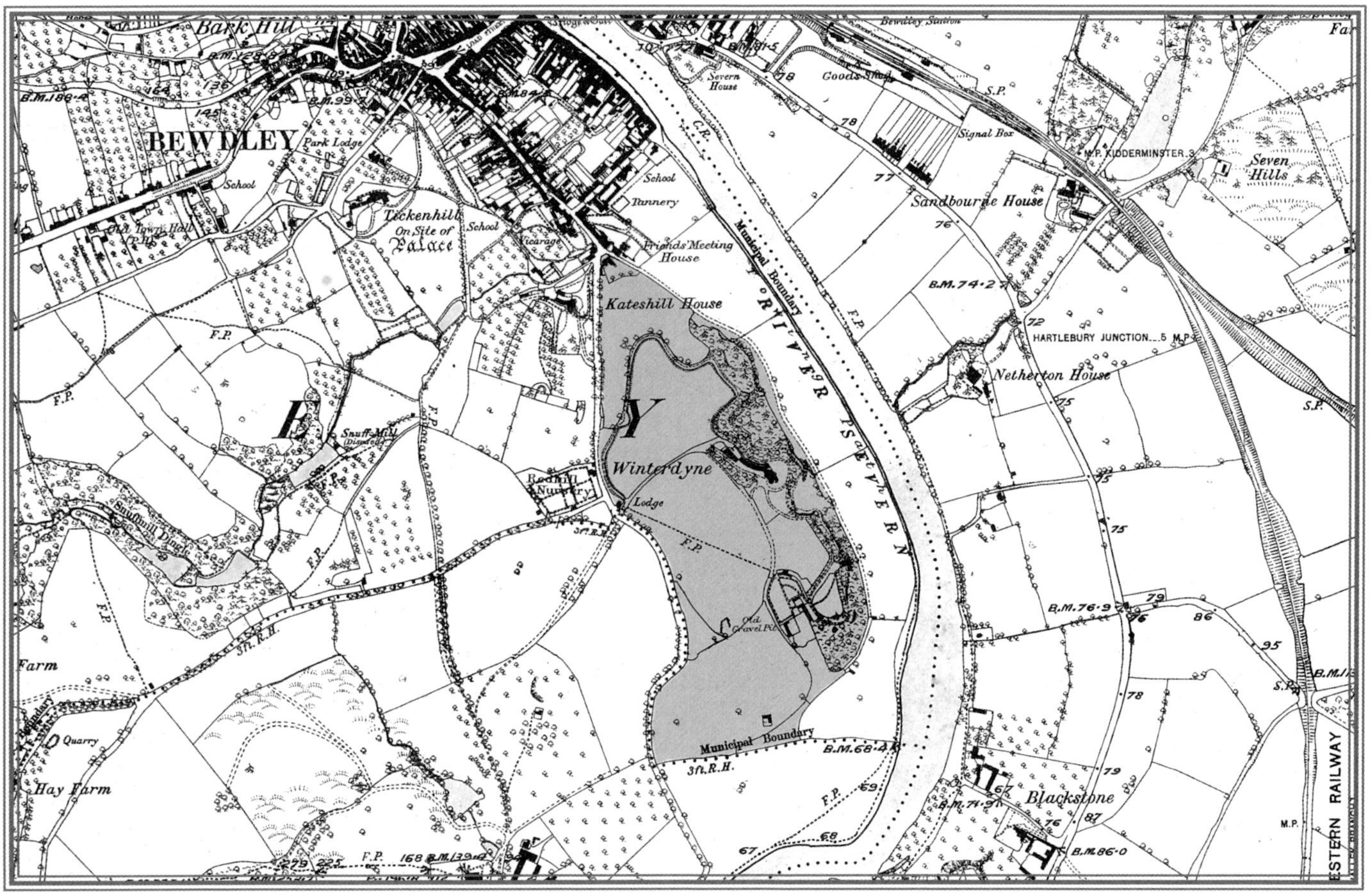

Nash in 1782 (Vol. 2, p. 275) says that Sir Edward Winnington, Bart. " has lately built a new manor or mansion house, on a hill near the town (of Bewdley), called Winterdyne, which commands a delightful view of the Severn, with its pendant rocks and woods ...". Stephen Price has found an invoice for stonework done in the garden by John Hayward (working for James Rose) in 1778, including work to garden walls, the Battery and the coping to the parapet and Shrubbery wall (Winnington Archive, Winn5/6). A little later, in 1814, the *Beauties* commends "a most elegant villa surrounded by ornamental walks, interspersed with Gothic towers, and seats, hermitages etc." (pp. 259-60).

The VCH (4, 1924, p. 301) gives a later description: "The grounds, which slope steeply down to the river, are beautifully laid out with winding paths and terraced walks on the face of the hill, which is in parts almost precipitous." These general descriptions can be supported from a manuscript map of 1785 (CRO 4600/737) and sale particulars of 1903 (CRO 5723). The 1785 map shows the longitudinal planting as today, starting north of the house and running south parallel with the river, to a short return west to the walled kitchen garden and a fold yard. The Park lying between the west and east boundaries of the small estate is called The Lawn in 1785. The drive from the house west to a lodge on the Stourport road is in place. The narrow serpentine planting along the north side of the park (Lodge Piece in 1785) is there too but not evident on the 1905 OS. The only vanished section of planting is between the Lodge and the south boundary of the park now dominated and overhung by the by-pass/road bridge. Perhaps this planting was never established.

Winterdyne

..........continued from previous page

The 1903 particulars show a North Lodge at the extreme tip of the property; the old castellated building called "The Fort"; the summer-house at the south end of the estate "on a bold cliff facing the celebrated Blackstone rocks ... formerly used as a billiard room." The particulars point out that the property had a 1000 yards frontage along the Severn. "There is also a rustic tea house and two stone seats cut out of the sandstone rocks ... the whole estate lies in a ring fence containing 72 acres".
Francis Ingram (1795-6) enlarges on the exact circumstances of the development of Winterdyne by Sir Edward Winnington of Stanford Court: "In the year 1776 Sir Edward Winnington on the marriage of their son came to be resident at Winterdyne". Ingram has explained that the Winningtons had handed over Stanford Court to their son on marriage and that he himself was living at Tickenhill nearby "from the consideration that Sir Edward Winnington was preparing to build near me on the Rocks of Winterdyne where he soon erected a very elegant villa which he adorned with delightful walks and pleasure grounds and told me he intended it as the place of residence for my sister Lady Winnington after his death" (CRO 438/xxxviii).
The major changes to the landscape since the descriptions of it above, result from the making of the south arm of the Bewdley by-pass along the southern boundary of this small estate which has impacted on the Farm. The kitchen gardens which were set next to it have gone. Only the Fort can be seen from the river bank, and the stone ridge on which the house is set, is now completely dominated by its trees.
Prints by J. W. Williams and James Ross circa 1784 illustrate the relationship within the Bewdley landscape of Tickenhill and Winterdyne as described by Ingram and the original setting of Winterdyne with open views over the river and the Fort below it to the south. Williams's print is titled "The Winterdyne Rocks with the Seat of Sir Edward Winnington Bart" (Winnington Archive).

Plate 13, Plan of the Winterdyne Estate, 1903.

Winterdyne, drawn and engraved by James Ross 1784

The Winterdyne Rocks with the seat of Sir Edward Winnington, Bart, by J. W. Williams, circa 1784. from the Society of Antiquaries of London, Prattinton Collection.

Victoria County History, Vol. 4, 1924, (VCH).
Beauties of England and Wales, Vol. XV, 1814.
T. R. Nash, *Collections for the History of Worcestershire,* Vol II, 1782.
S. Price, *The Winnington Archive: an Introduction,* November 2015, unpub.

Winterfold House

Parish: Chaddesley Corbett

HER Ref: WSM10306.

Grid Ref: SO 894 739. Postcode: DY10 4PW.

O.S. 6" Map No: 15NW.

Date of Map: 1883, with extent of park & gardens shaded as 1905 OS.

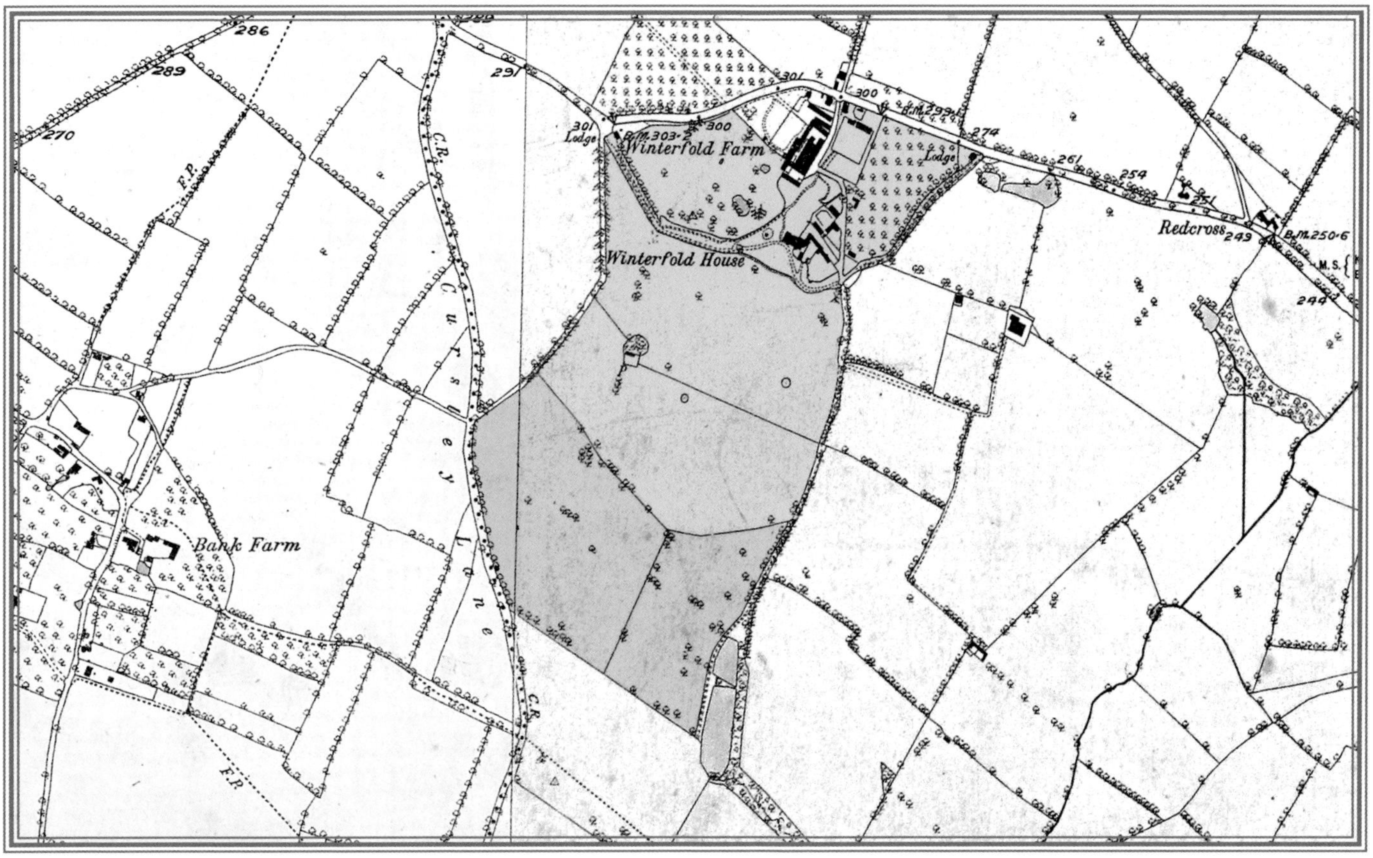

The house is first noticed by guidebooks in 1814 and shown with grounds on early to mid-19th century maps. The BoE has the house as mostly rebuilt circa 1800 (p. 369). The VCH in 1906 described a red brick mansion standing in a well-wooded deer park which once formed part of the forest of Piperode, which was later absorbed into Feckenham Forest. A 1745 map of the Throckmorton estate in Chaddesley Corbett does not show any park or any park field names on "Winterfold Yield" (WAAS 844) and it is not clear when the deer park was established before it is shown as a distinct part of the landscape park on the 2nd edition of the OS 6 inch in 1905. There was then a small area of park with the Farm and 2 lodges to the north of the house and the deer park to the south. It is in fact shown as a park on the 1815 survey for the first edition of the OS one inch. Whitaker (op. cit.) describes the deer park in 1892 as 52 acres, fenced with iron and wood paling, containing 34 fallow deer and some West Highland cattle amid natural oak and elm.

The house is now a school and much of the garden and orchard lost to development, although there are still some fine trees. The park is under arable.

Victoria County History, Vol. 2, 1906, p.36, (VCH).
A. Brooks & N. Pevsner, *Worcestershire,* 2007 (BoE).
J. Whitaker, *A Descriptive List of the Deer Parks and Paddocks of England,* 1892.

Witley Court

Parish: Great Witley & Hillhampton

HER Ref: WSM05756/35187. Grid Ref: SO 766 652. Postcode: WR6 6JT.

O.S. 6" Map No: 20SE, 21SW. Date of Maps: 1884, 1883, with extent of park & gardens shaded as H. E. Register.

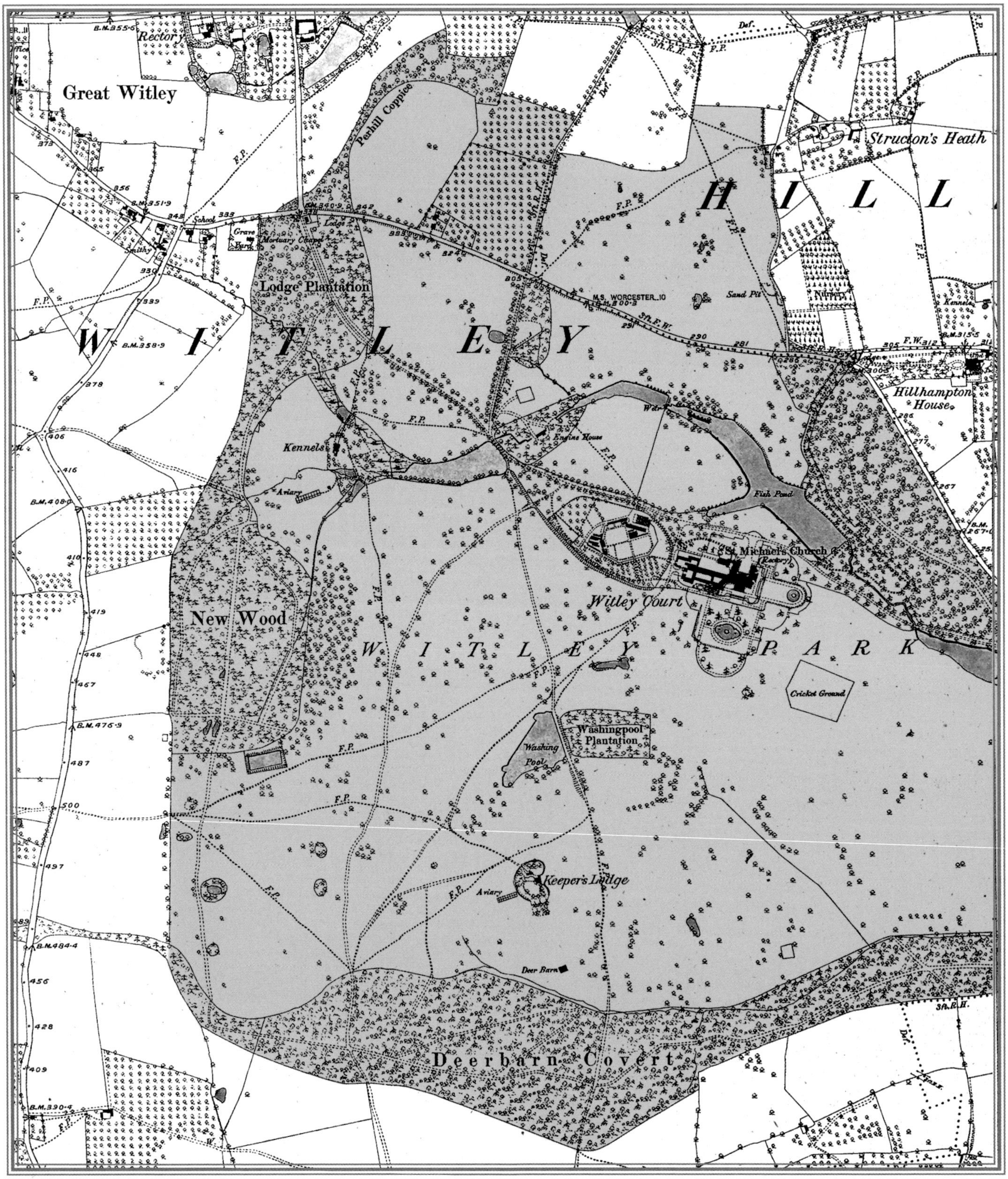

Witley Court

..........continued from previous page

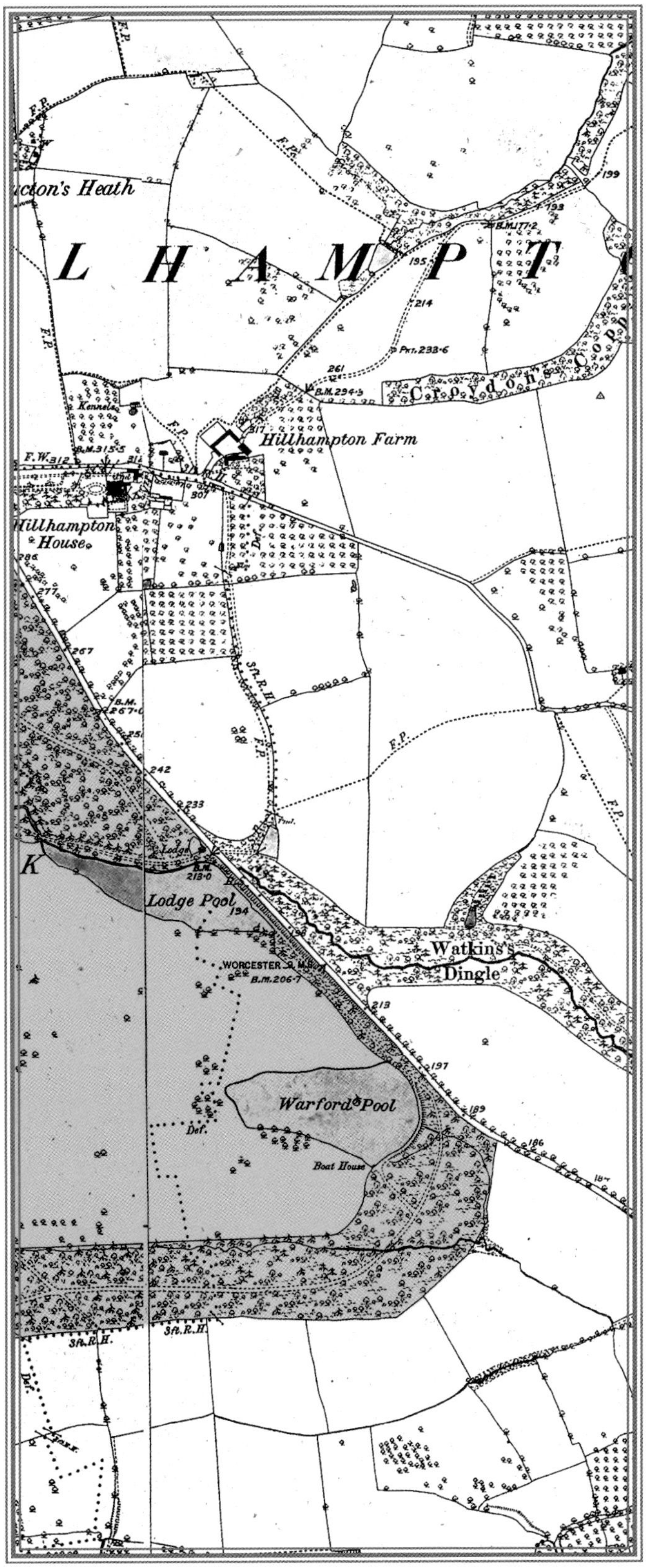

Included within Historic England's Register of Historic Parks and Gardens of special historic interest in England.

A deer park is shown by Saxton in 1577 and on 17th century maps and by Taylor (1772), Bowen (1778) and Smith (1804). Whiteley (sic) Park is shown with a deer fence on the Sheldon tapestry map of the 1590s (Oxford Bodleian Library), as it is on the 1813 survey for the first OS one inch.

The development of the deer park between the 16th and 19th centuries has been demonstrated in Reports for English Heritage by the Hereford Archaeology Unit (documentary research by Dr. Pat Hughes).

There is reference in 1664 to "impaled ground called Witley" (Hughes, 1997). A manuscript by C. Price of 1732 (WAAS 11976), shows that the park was restricted to an area between the Court and "New Wood", the only part of substantial woodland at this time and which in outline survives today (illus. in EH guide, 1997). The east boundary of the park in 1732 ran south from the west corner of the Kitchen Garden to Deerbarn Covert on the line of the track east of Washing Pool, the Keeper's Lodge, and the Deerbarn. The park was extended east in stages during the 18th century and had reached Lodge Pool, Warford Pool and the turnpike road by 1793. Deerbarn Covert, the large strip of woodland along the south boundary, was planted in the early-19th century but was almost entirely felled post 1938. The 1938 Sale (CRO 460/30) pointed up "magnificent timber, mainly mature oak". Most of the later-18th century planting within the park has disappeared. Whitaker gives a snapshot of the deer park as in 1892: 422 acres including water, fenced with flat bar iron (largely surviving on the west and south sides) and containing 500 fallow deer. The most notable trees then were oak and Spanish chestnut.

The Reports made for English Heritage describe the probable 13th century remains of a medieval manor house on the site beneath the circa 1600 house (Camden's "fair new-built house"), redeveloped in the mid and late-17th centuries and revealed by the 1937 fire. The crop marks revealing a large formal garden layout south-east of the Court are surprisingly distant from the mansion in its 17th century phase. A painting of the early-18th century shows 2 terraces of formal gardens on the south side linked by steps in the centre, leading to gates and further steps down (Pardoe). Price in 1732 shows large formal gardens on the south side. A thumb-nail sketch on a map of 1745 by John Doharty junior (CRO 974/1) shows a rectangular garden with an oval lawn fringed with trees to the west and another rectangular lawn to the south, with a semi-circular extension and larger curved fence, wall or ha-ha, forming the border with the park (**Plate 3**). A ha-ha between the park and the 19th century, walled kitchen garden may be of 18th century date and the kitchen garden was on this site before 1793 (Hughes).

Witley Court

..........continued from previous page

Early-18th century developments to the house included the addition of wings in the Palladian fashion on the north side and the building of the Church in 1733-5 in the Baroque style. These developments will have had implications for the gardens. The crucial date however, established by Hughes, was the purchase in 1718 from the Hillhampton estate of the land between the stream and the turnpike road which allowed the development of a typically mid-18th century landscape on the north side, with a line of pools (the Cascade, Weir, Front Pool), a new approach from the road to the north front and the slightly later creation of the "Wilderness" (1780s). Some 19th century buildings and rhododendron walks survive in this area, otherwise redeveloped post-War for agricultural or residential uses (e.g. Pool House). Taylor's 1772 map and Nash's 1782 view illustrate the mid-18th century Front, the Pool and the approach via causeway and bridge.

Sulivan, making a tour in 1778, found the grounds "evidently neglected" (Mavor, p. 81) but by 1814 the *Beauties* describe an "improved and improving seat" (p. 290) and a "magnificent park, modern plantations, venerable avenue, fine ornamental pieces of water, temples, seats, cottages, lodges". A watercolour of circa 1784 by E. F. Burney (CRO 2432) illustrates the only significant 18th century garden building, the Keeper's Lodge (illus. EH, 1997) that survived until the 1950s and replaced an earlier lodge documented in 1664 and 1732 (Hughes). This was of 3 stories and attic, with porthole windows on one elevation and more portholes behind the pedimented, 4 column portico on the principal front. The latter was set above a rusticated base and 3 arched openings into the basement, with steps either side. The Lodge, attributed to Henry Flitcroft, was noticed by William Shenstone in 1762. It was a grander building than the Temple at Stanford Court, but also in its last years housed the game keeper. Other and lesser garden buildings such as bridges, boat houses etc. were added in the 19th century. The Red House by George S. Repton of 1828 (Hughes), built as Dog Kennels, is made up of 5 small octagons and is worthy of notice in landscape terms.

Lord Foley consulted with Humphry Repton circa 1805 at the same time as he commissioned John Nash to improve his mansion. Repton's impact on the landscape can be seen in a watercolour view of the north front attributed to George Repton, which shows a projecting lawn with balustrade and ha-ha with raised steps to Nash's portico (York Univ. and Mainsbridge, p. 86). C. R. Cockerell made a plan of the house circa 1821 which shows an L-shaped, formal, parterre garden to east and south. This was within a balustrade on both fronts (illus. Whitehead & Bradney). Whitehead and Bradney suggest that Repton's influence may be seen in the existing drive system "and its serpentine approach from the east ... the belts around the extensive deer park were all in place c.1840".

A Parish Map of circa 1841 (CRO 974/2) outlines east and south terraces and a narrow terrace along part of the south side. Drives went into the park and perimeter planting everywhere. All this was before Lord Ward took up residence in 1846 and shortly thereafter began the redevelopment of the house by Samuel William Daukes and the gardens by William Andrews Nesfield.

It is the Daukes/Nesfield works which are reflected in the 1906 OS 6 inch map and the ruins of Witley Court today. Samuel Daukes added the curved west wing with Orangery, Pavilion, Stables and Coachhouse (1854-6). The HE Listing gives a slightly earlier date to the Gardener's House and the Villa Fiore. It is not clear whether Daukes or Nesfield (1854-60) was responsible for the gardens' retaining walls etc. or for the south-east and south-west pavilions. The fountain sculptures (*Perseus and Andromeda*

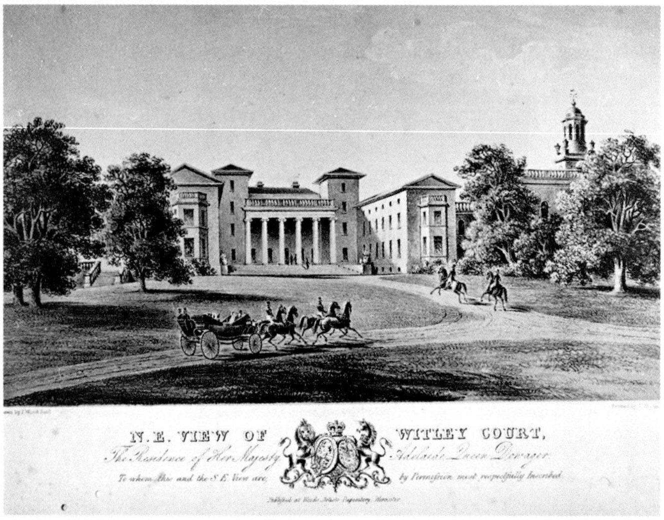

Lithographs after J. Wood jnr., 1843, published at Woods Artists Repository, Worcester. © WAAS, Great Witley 50461, 50462.

..........continued from previous page

TOP: Postcard image, 1920.
ABOVE: Valentine & Sons' postcard image of the Italian Garden, 1900.

and *Flora and the Tritons*) both by James and William Forsyth (1858-60), required major hydraulic works and the construction of a reservoir and engine house (Brown and Stansfield). The Stourport and Worcester Lodges replaced earlier lodges by Henry Rowe in 1884.

The Nesfield gardens at Witley were justly celebrated and minutely described in *The Gardener's Chronicle* of 1873 although it said that Witley's formality was by then unfashionable (**Plate 4**). The reviewer describes the *Flora* fountain as surrounded by a trellis or chain of jets. He details the shrubs and plants and scrolls of box: "I have never seen a geometrical garden that could bear so much green without distraction". Mr Westland " sometimes whips out the box altogether and carpet beds the entire space to the tune of 20,000 plants of *alternantheras, golden feathers, echeverias, semper vivreus* ... And then again the Box is replaced." A lot of bulbs would go in for the Spring. He noted Westland's success with camelias (Conservatory). The kitchen garden was in transition, growing pines with difficulty. The *Chronicle*'s reviewer suggested adding some heaths and an American plantation to link the gardens with the park.

In 1945 Christopher Hussey could still describe the view from the south portico: "a broad vista formed by yews, Portugal laurels and cypresses" (*Country Life*, p. 1038). Pardoe has several photographs of the gardens in their Edwardian hey-day as does the English Heritage Report in 1997.

The house suffered a devastating fire and was put up for sale together with the garden furniture, including the *Perseus Fountain* (Lot 76) in 1938 (CRO 3762). Mowl remarks on "the astonishing beauty of its Perseus Fountain. Chatsworth has nothing to equal it and nothing in Versailles is superior."(p. 12). Alfrey anticipated the effect: "Nesfield had painted Niagara Falls in his early years as an artist and several decades later would go on to create the extraordinary fantasies of falling waters for Lord Ward at Witley Court, Worcestershire. According to the *Illustrated London News*, the necessary waterworks by Mr. Easton and the 40 horsepower steam engine cost in excess of £20,000. Gates, dated 1862, are now in Lake Havasu City, U. S. A. (Wikipedia).

Witley Court house and part of its grounds were acquired by HE in 1972 and opened to the public since 1984. Historic England has embarked on a major restoration of the Nesfield gardens to the south and east of the mansion with a restoration of the *Perseus Fountain* and a partial restoration of the *Flora Fountain* with parterre.

W. Mavor, *The British Tourists,* 3, 1798, (J. Sulivan).
Gardener's Chronicle and Agricultural Gazette, 21. 6. 1873.
"Witley Court", *Country Life,* Vol. II 1897, p. 126.
C. Hussey, "Witley Court", *Country Life,* Vol. XCVII, 1945, p. 992, p. 1036.
M. Whiffen, "Witley Court", *Country Life,* Vol. XCVIII, 1945, p.76.
M. Hadfield, "Witley Court", *Country Life,* Vol. CXLIII, 1968.
J. Harris, "C. R. Cockerell's Ichnographia Domestica", *Architectural Hist.,* 14. 5, 1971, figs. 24 & 25a.
York Univ. Design , *The Conservation of Witley Court, Worcestershire,* Feasibility Study, 1974.
B. Pardoe, *Witley Court,* 1986.
M. Mainsbridge, *John Nash: A Complete Catalogue,* 1991.
M. Brown and G. Stansfield, *The Fountains of Witley Court,* 1992.
Report to English Heritage, 1994. Appendix B, Documentary Research Dr. Pat Hughes.
Hereford Archaeology Series, 215, *Witley Court...Archaeological Landscape Survey.*
Hereford Archaeology Series, 275, *Witley Court...Landscape Survey of the Southern Park,* ditto 1996.
English Heritage, *Witley Court,* 1997.
N. A. Alfrey, *The Art of the Garden,* Tate Gallery, 2004.
T. Mowl, *Historic Gardens of Worcestershire,* 2006.
A. Brooks & N. Pevsner, *Worcestershire,* 2007 (BoE).
J. Whitaker, *A Descriptive List of the Deer Parks and Paddocks of England,* 1892.
D. Whitehead & J. Bradney "*In the Enemy's Quarters: Humphry Repton in the West Midlands*", 2018.
HE *Register of Parks & Gardens,* 1998.

Wolverton Hall

Parish: Stoulton

HER Ref: WSM28827.

Grid Ref: SO 930 507.

Postcode: WR10 2AU.

O.S. 6" Map No: 34SE, 41NE.

Date of Map: 1883, 1885, with shaded extent of park & grounds deduced from text.

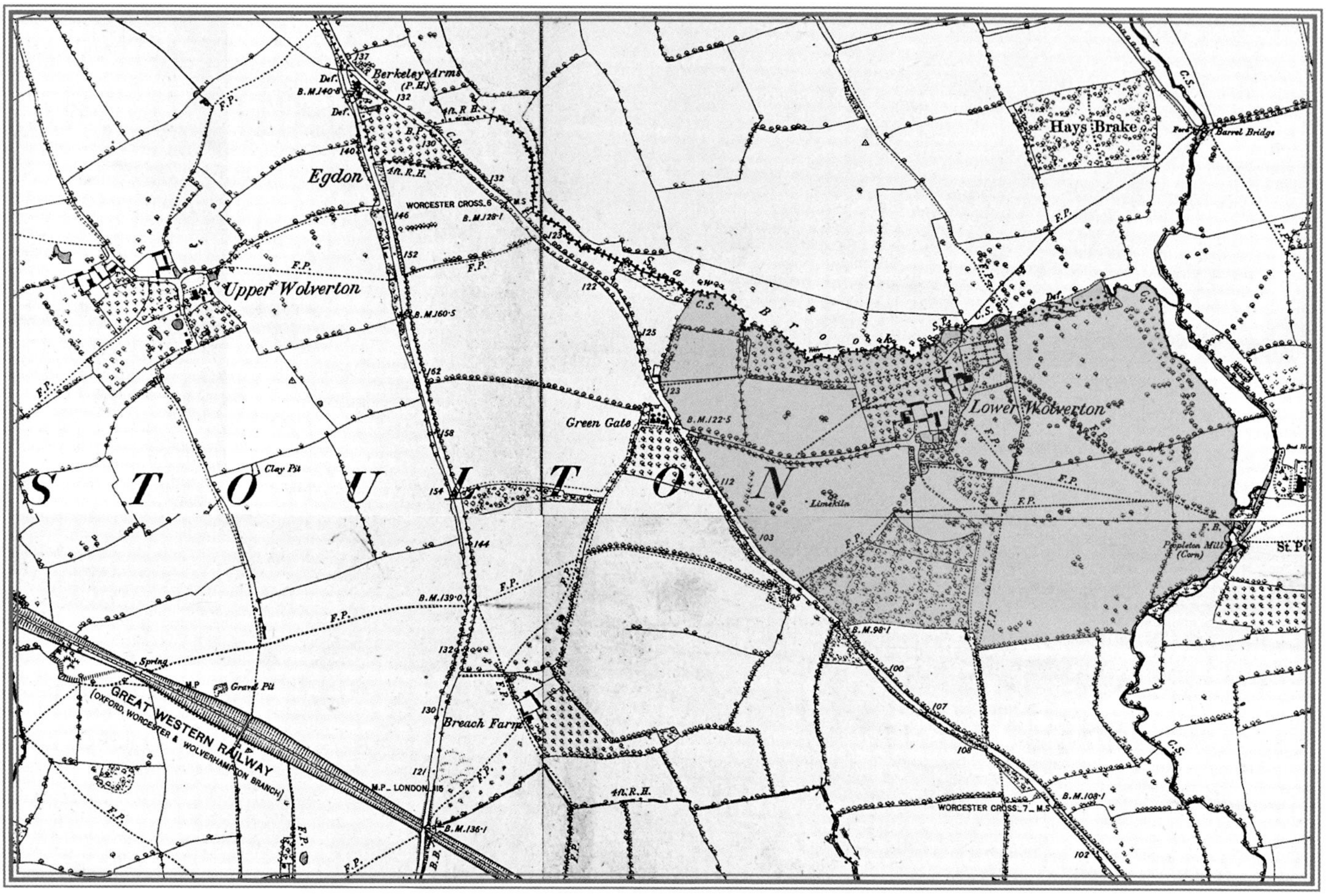

There is no park shown on the first OS 6 inch maps circa 1900 but there are strong suggestions of avenues from the house south-east towards Peopleton and west from the Farm to the Worcester - Evesham road. There are fishponds north-east of the house. Taylor in 1772 marks the house as a significant residence; the house is early-18th century but has a substantial later-18th century porch (Pevsner, p. 268). Grounds are shown for Lower Wolverton Hall on the OS one inch (1831) which has the avenue going south-east and another going due south as on the 1891 OS 6 inch. Home Covert to the south-west is marked (surviving). Any park is likely to have extended east to the Bow Brook and west perhaps to the Worcester - Evesham road.

It is possible that Wudmerton (Saxton, 1577), Widmerton or Wodnerton (Speed, 1610, Janson, 1647, Blome, 1673) might refer to Upper Wolverton (Farm) situated west of Egdon Lane/B4084. But Wodverton on Tunnicliff (1788) and Wilverton on Smith (1804) certainly refer to Wolverton Hall. Taylor in 1772 clearly marks both sites as Woferton for Upper Wolverton and Woolverton for Lower Wolverton.

The western avenue and much of the boundary tree planting still exist, as does the walled garden with its ornamental pond and planting. However, the surrounding land which may once have had a parkland character is now farmed intensively with no remaining individual trees.

N. Pevsner, *Worcestershire*, 1968.

Woodfield House

Parish: Ombersley & Doverdale

HER Ref: WSM28938. Grid Ref: SO 837 656. Postcode: WR9 0JU.

O.S. 6" Map No: 21NE.

Date of Map: 1888, with extent of park & gardens shaded as 1905 OS.

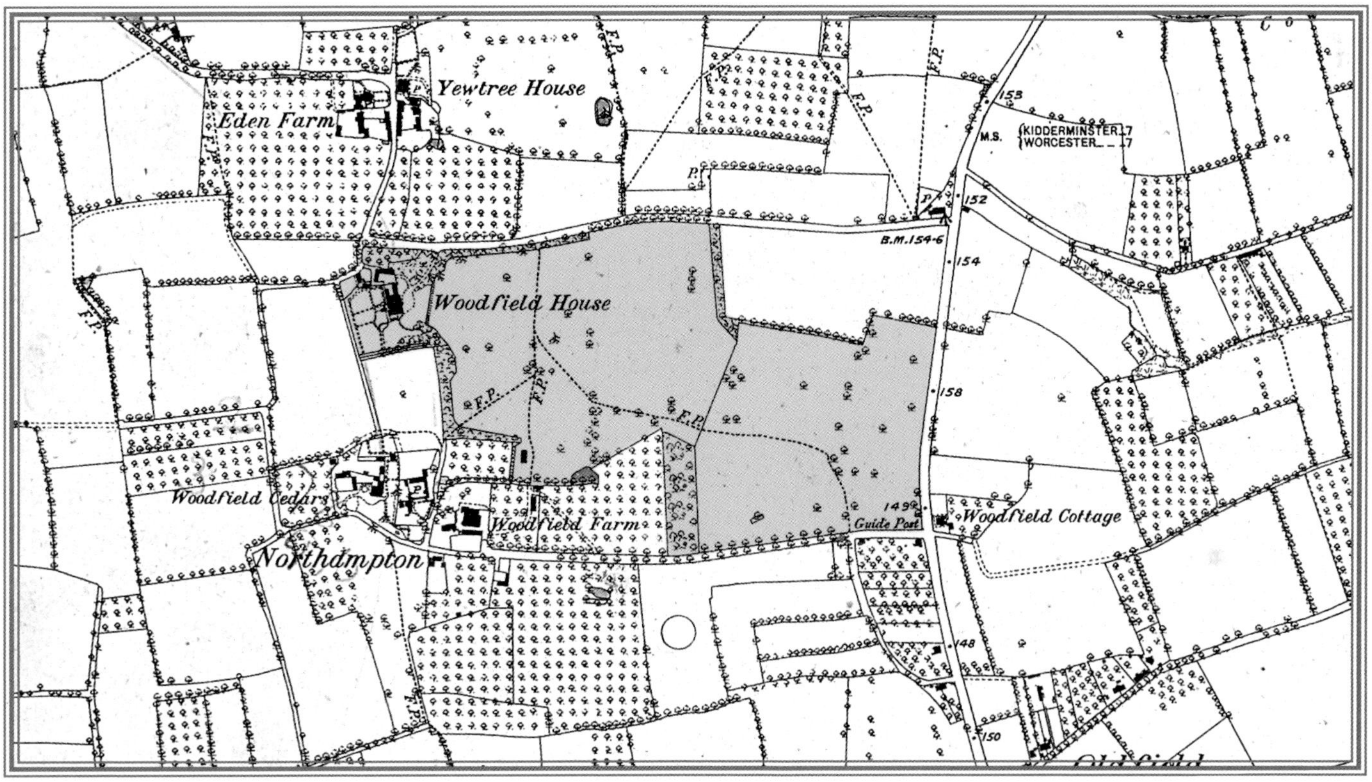

The house is late-18th century in origin and was extended circa 1800 and again circa 1850. A park is shown on the 2nd edition of the OS 6 inch. This part was sold as a lot of 58 acres in 1920 (CRO 4788/1) out of an estate of 874 acres. A small section of the park was known as the Grove in 1841 (CRO 3740/8) when Bentley (p. 105) described a house "surrounded by fertile lawns, shady groves, and pleasant walks interspersed with flowers and laurels".

The park shown on the 1905 OS 6 inch can still be seen clearly from the A449 from where a fine avenue of oaks leads to the property. The park has been extended in recent years and there is much new parkland tree planting as well as a new avenue. The gardens are immaculate.

Bentley's Guide and Directory to Stourbridge, 1840.

Wood Hall

Parish: Norton Juxta Kempsey

HER Ref: WSM29017.

Grid Ref: SO 882 513. Postcode: WR5 2RR.

O.S. 6" Map No: 34SW.

Date of Map: 1884, with extent of park & gardens shaded as 1905 OS.

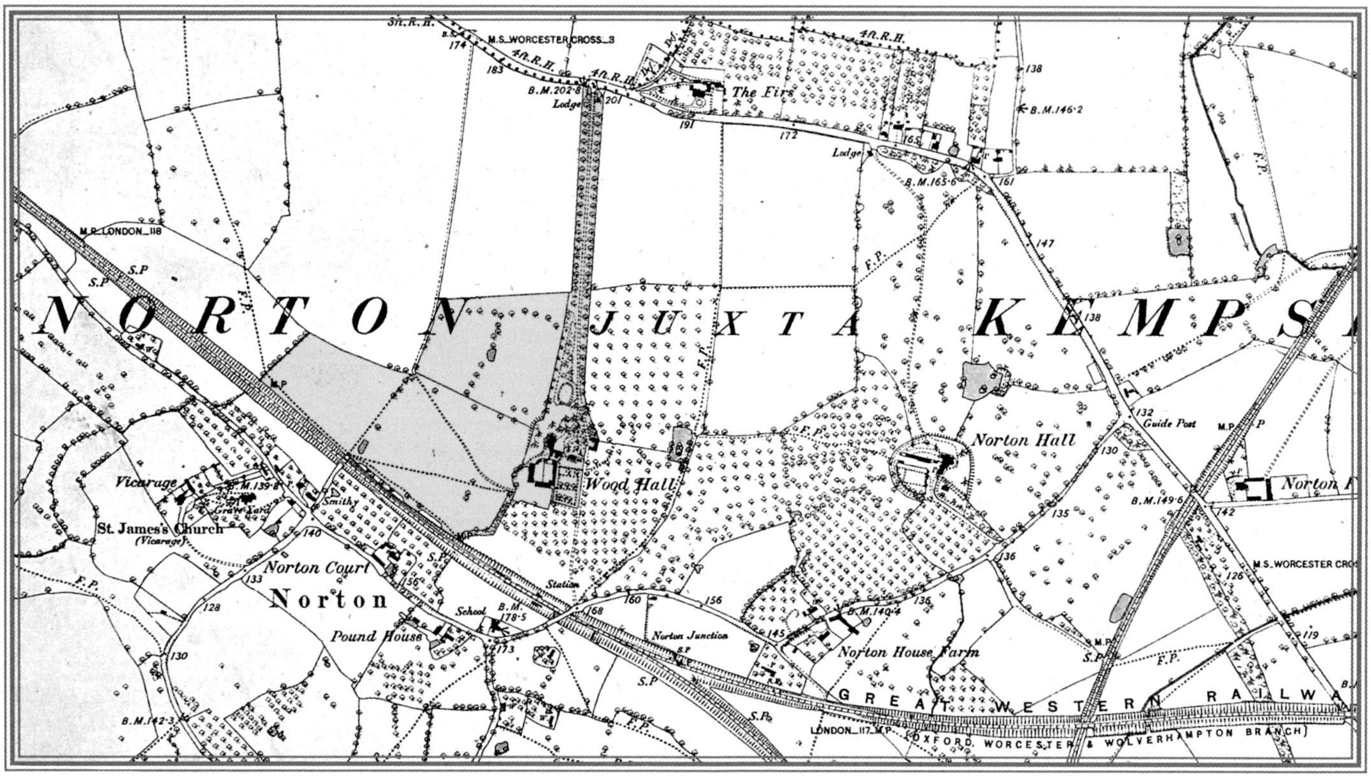

A strong avenue from the Worcester-Pershore road south to the house, as today, is marked on the 1811 survey and on the 1828 OS one inch. There is a photograph of the elm avenue, which is a ¼ mile long, in the 1924 sale particulars (CRO 5240/6). The 1924 grounds amounted to 8 acres and the sale photographs also illustrate a balustraded wall and ha-ha separating the grounds from the field on the west side, the sunk rose garden and a small formal garden with lily pond. Other garden amenities included a stone summer-house, a walled kitchen garden and a wild garden. Maps suggest that Wood Hall was more significant at an earlier date; it is shown as a residence on Taylor's 1772 map and on Cary's 1805 map and as a park on Murray in 1830. Perhaps the railway, which separated the house from Norton Hall, reduced its status. The pasture land with the Hall in 1860 extended west to SO 875 515.

The avenue eventually succumbed to Dutch Elm disease but has been re-planted with different species. The gardens, with most features intact, still survive, albeit overgrown with part of the walled garden in a ruinous state.

Wood Norton

Parish: Norton & Lenchwick

HER Ref: WSM28819. Grid Ref: SP 017 471. Postcode: WR11 4YB. O.S. 6" Map No:42NW/SW, 42NE/SE.

Date of Maps: both 1887, with extent of park & gardens shaded as 1905 OS and deduced from text.

The Duc d'Aumale, a son of Louis Philippe lived at Wood Norton from 1857 and bought the property in 1872.

His heir, the Duc d'Orléans built a large new house in 1896-7 designed by G. H. Hunt in Jacobethan style, an attractive mix of red brick, stone and a little half-timbering. This was on the site of a previous Keeper's Cottage. There are 2 late-19th century Lodges and 18th century style wrought-iron gates probably by J. Starkie Gardner circa 1864 (BoE, p. 503).

The establishment of the deer forest does not seem to be documented. In its late-19th century hey-day, the Wood Norton Property included Craycombe House and extended from Craycombe in the west to Lenchwick in the east with Wood Norton more or less in the centre. The B4084 forms a southern boundary. Wood Norton post the Bourbons has been a School and then BBC training centre and the grounds immediately north-west of the main house have been extensively built over. The gardens between the main house and the road were never of great interest. When offered for sale in 1925 (769 acres), it was apparently an attraction that there were "no costly gardens or glass houses." Lodges, gardens and grounds occupied 29 acres and a logwood Pavilion had 106 acres attached. There were 2 carriage drives "bordered by fine specimen trees and shrubs" (CRO 5240/7). The pleasure grounds depended principally on drives into the very extensive woods which enclosed the mansion except on the south-east side. A lawn surrounded by a balustrade separated the house from the woods on the west and south sides. The (logwood) Pavilion or Highclere was set between Blue Bank and Craycombe Coppices, the westernmost extension of the property.

The property is being converted to an hotel and retirement village (2018).

A. Brooks & N. Pevsner, *Worcestershire,* 2007 (BoE).

Woollas Hall

Parish: Eckington

HER Ref: WSM28818.

Grid Ref: SO 947 406.

Postcode: WR10 3DN.

O.S. 6" Map No: 48NE/SE.

Date of Map: 1884, with extent of park & grounds shaded as 1905 OS.

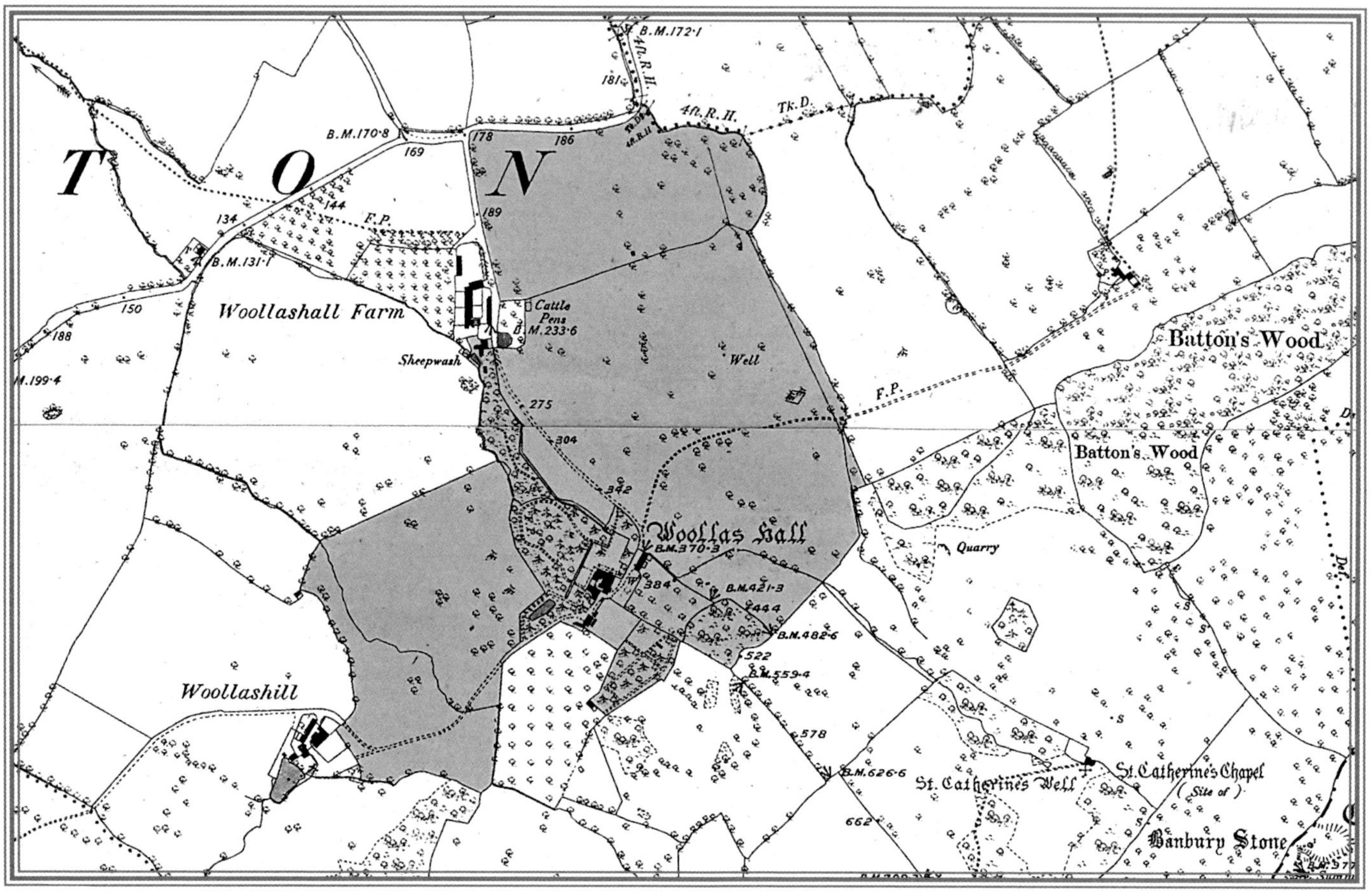

Woollas was an important residence and is marked on maps from Saxton in 1577 onwards. There is a date of 1611 on the house. A thumbnail sketch on a map of 1712 (CRO 950/74) suggests a balanced facade, i.e. 2 bays on each side of the entrance bay. A formal garden will have accompanied this Jacobean mansion but only a green lawn is shown on the north side. Otherwise, field names suggest that it had a park which probably stretched south to the "Warren" on Bredon Hill. Another survey is dated 1711: *The Manor of Woolleshall described, part of the possessions of Compton Hanford esq.* 1711 (CRO 950/73): 1. The Mansion; 2. The Garden; 3. The Hop Garden; 4. The Upper Orchard; 5. The Pigeon Close. Farming concerns were evidently uppermost.

An account book (ins: *Edward Hanford, his book*, 1711) notes expenditure (£5 14s. 3d.) in 1724 on fruit trees: peaches; apricots; plums; pears; apples; dwarf cherry; vines; sweet water; mates. This all sounds like an old-fashioned fruit garden (CRO 950/65). By the 19th century, Woollas was regarded as "a good picture of ancient domestic arrangements" (*Beauties*, p. 361) which may mean that some formal gardens had survived. *The Gentleman's Magazine* for 1811 (op. cit.) reviewed Woollas at some length: "A small stream of water rises just under the brow of the hill and turns a wheel which roasts the meat in the great kitchen". There is specific mention there of the bowling green. "It would be difficult to select a finer situation for a house than this ... he who would have the most complete view of the Vale of Evesham must take it from somewhere near this house." The further landscape amenities discovered as one mounted the hill were: the foundations of the Chapel of St. Catherine of the Rock; a camp with double trench enclosing about 20 acres of ground (British or Roman); a stone prospect house which from the Vale appears like a

..........continued from previous page

square pillar, "but it has two rooms, one above the other, capable of receiving 20 persons; near this an immense stone, called the "Bramsbury Stone".

A 1798 map (CRO 445) has grounds adjoining the Hall labelled as Lower Garden (NNW), pig yard (with fountain!) (W), Upper Garden (SSE) and Drying Yard (Stable yard) (SSW). A Wilderness (2 acres) and Coningree (13 acres) lay south and further south. Many of these details are confirmed by another map of the Hanford Estate (1593 acres) made in 1844 (CRO 960/58).

The 1828 OS one inch shows a park area stretching from the Eckington - Great Comberton road, immediately east of Woollas Hall Farm to the Hall but not as far south as St. Catherine's Farm as on the 1884 OS. Even at its greatest mapped extent (OS 1919), the park does not extend as far south as the Warren (between Bredon Hill Nature Reserve and Banbury Stone Tower), a reference to a medieval park.

Burke in 1853 (illus. and p. 59) includes within his description of "Woolers Hill" the bowling green (presumably a terrace of the garden), the foundation of a chapel, i.e. St. Catherine's Chapel and the two-storied, stone prospect house on the brow of the hill, i.e. Bredon Tower (summer-house) which was set inside a pre-historic earthwork.

In recent years Deer Park Hall, a group of new buildings, has been developed as a Conference Centre adjoining the Hall.

J. B. Burke, *A visitation of Seats of Gt. Britain,* 1853.
The Gentleman's Magazine for 1811 (II, pp.209/10).
Beauties of England and Wales, Vol. XV, 1814.

Woollas Hall, the north front, taken from *Victoria County History* Vol. 4, 1924, (VCH).

WOOLLAS HALL.—Seat of Charles Hanford Esq.r

Engraving, 19th century.

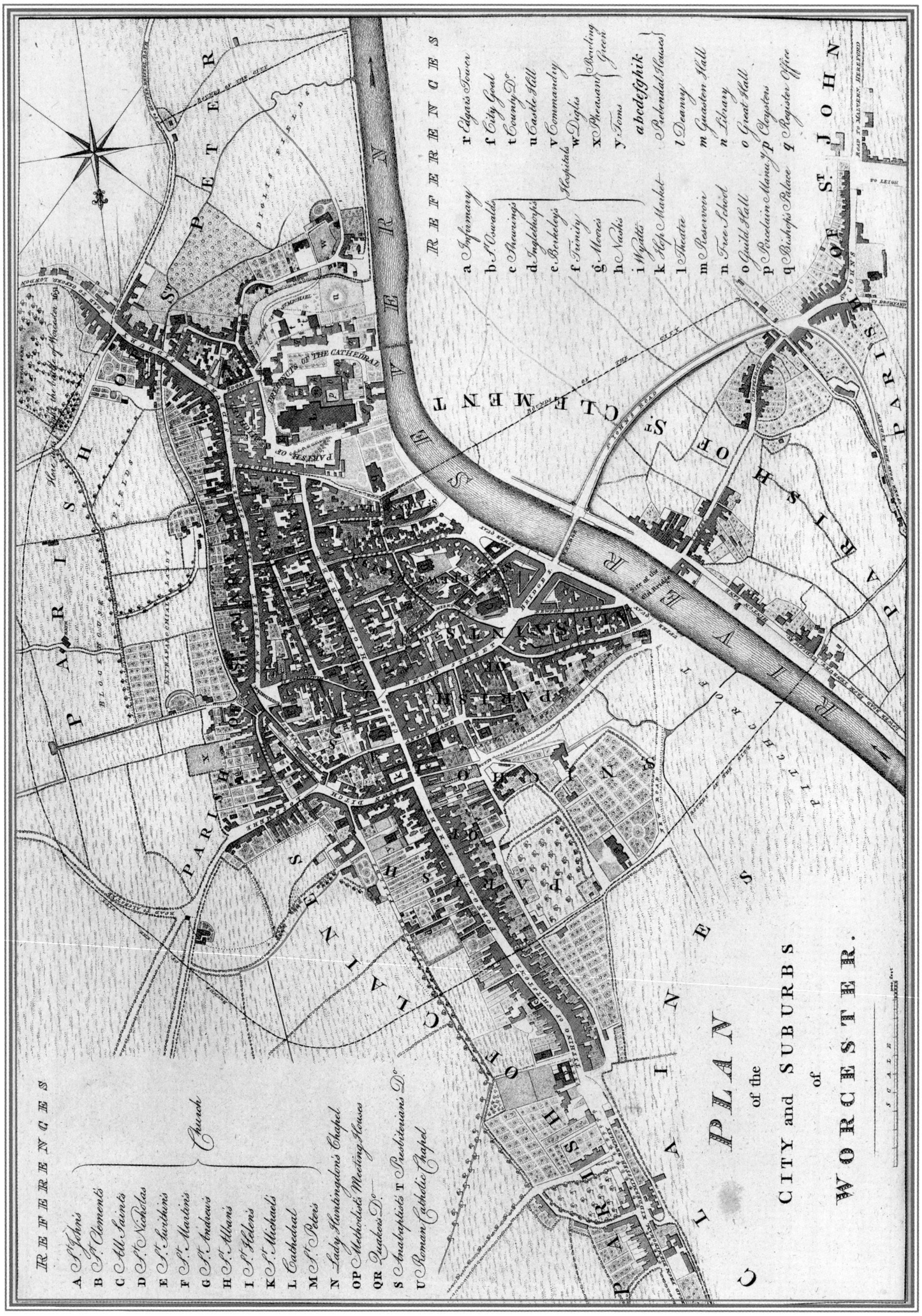

Worcester City Plan from T. R. Nash, *Collections for the History of Worcestershire*, Vol II, 1782.

The Worcester City Sites

The presence of gardens within the City from the medieval to the modern period has to be presumed rather than documented from maps, the underlying methodology of this *Survey*. Gardens as represented on printed maps from the early-18th century can only be regarded as schematic except for a few sites. Charles Crisp's 1832 City map provides precise information on gardens for the first time.

Most of the city's medieval monastic establishments and those of the Minor Orders as well as medieval hospitals would have had gardens within the City Walls (e.g. College Green, Commandery). The Protestant Reformation and Dissolution of the Monasteries led to a redevelopment of these sites under secular ownership. "The other main physical change was one of growth. Speed's plan (1610) still shows considerable areas of open ground used as gardens or just left waste within the walls; this was particularly true of the Black Friars by the northern wall. These garden areas were gradually built over during the late-16th and early-17th centuries" (Dyer, p. 18).

Whitehead has drawn attention to the development of the City suburbs and the perceived need to escape the "pestiforous odours" noting particularly the Foregate suburb and the popular use of orchards and promenades which were akin to public gardens such as Lovesgrove and Dr. Wall's Walk. The 1816 edition of W. R.'s *Concise History of Worcester* expands on the raison d'etre : "since its population has increased, and the town has been enlarged, many of the more opulent ... have adopted the London plan of having small suburban villas, for the purpose of breathing a more pure air, and as a retirement in the evening from the noise and bustle of the City, as well as to indulge their families in the enjoyments attendant on a rural and retired life; and as most of these residences are newly erected, and finished in their accompaniments of gardens, shrubberies etc., with some portion of taste, the effect produced thereby, is highly pleasing and ornamental and makes the Public Walks by these retired villas, agreeable Promenades; but the principal and most favourite Public Walk, lies parallel with the Foregate-street and is called Sansome Fields ... The Walks over Rainbow Hill, and near Perry Wood ... The banks of the Severn, and along the line of the new Canal, afford many varied and agreeable Walks. Pitchroft, where the Races are held, and the Moors adjoining, by being so near the City, are frequented as Promenades ... and the tea gardens at Henwick Hill". "In the summer evenings, a handsome imitation of the tea gardens of the metropolis may be met with at the Porto Bello" according to James Dugdale in his *New British Traveller* in 1819. The gardens were still in use in 1848.

The river bank was a relatively unsung place for promenading. The landscape painter, John Constable, writes shortly before Christmas in 1811 to his future wife whom he had been visiting at Spring Grove: "I was at Worcester two or three hours before the Mail (coach) set off – which gave me an opportunity of seeing the Cathedral and most of the Town & I had a very beautiful walk down to the river" (Tate Gallery, *Constable*, Exhibition, 1976, p. 40 with drawing of Worcester Cathedral from the river bank). The Worcester Pleasure Grounds, known today as the Arboretum, was a short-lived attempt in the mid-19th century to create a public park with sports facilities as were developed in Malvern for its full-blown tourist industry.

The small scale of 18th and 19th century gardens and the lack of relevantly-scaled printed maps generally excludes them from this *Survey*, but *The Story of Worcester* by Hughes and Leech in their overview of the City from medieval times to the present shows the mix of buildings and gardens from printed and manuscript sources particularly for the 18th and earlier-19th centuries. Manuscript surveys document private gardens and gardens operated on a commercial scale, for instance "*Ground Plans of the Houses etc. held by Lease under the Corporation of Worcester* measured and planned by J. Aird, begun in 1771" (1771-1775), another dated 1794 but surveyed by Aird in 1784 and a third by William Bailey and Thos. Corfield, Surveyors, Worcester, 1824 (WAAS 9360) "particularising the whole of the Corporation Lands and Premises within One Mile of the City"; all these are available on CD at The Hive. The surveys record significant areas occupied by gardens near Dolday, around Frog Lane and Castle Hill, between the City Wall and the Town Ditch and gardens along the Severn by and belonging to the China Manufactory; Messrs Hopley and Shinton had 35 gardens near the Cornmarket. Gardens were attached to the City's Almshouses (Charities) some of which had been taken over or leased by others, e.g. Sir Anthony Lechmere Bart. (senior partner of the Berwick Bank) who leased a garden from the Inglethorpe's Charity on Sansome Walk as well as Walnut House, the Artichoke Field nearby (4 acres) and Wheelers Gardens (2 acres) which adjoined the Royal Infirmary.

These surveys reveal a patchwork of tenements, warehouses, factories, churches, ministers' houses, coal yards (9 acres) and a cold bath (1 acre). Many of the open spaces are described as orchards. The word "pleasure ground" is rare but can be found, e.g. at Netherton House. Some of the 18th century public spaces have survived, such as Pitchcroft and Fort Royal Hill although Sansome Fields was developed post 1840. Cripplegate Park and Gheluvelt Parks have survived from the early-20th century, the latter extended recently. Development of public space in the 21st century has concentrated on the River Severn, linking the two sides with additional pedestrian bridges.

A. Minoprio & H. Spenceley, *An Outline Development Plan for Worcester*, 1946.
A. D. Dyer, *The City of Worcester in the Sixteenth Century*, 1973.
D. Whitehead, *The Book of Worcester*, 1976.
P. Hughes & A. Leech, *The Story of Worcester*, 2012.
C. & T. Wardle, *The History of Barbourne*, 2007.
J. Dugdale, *New British Traveller*, 1819.

(A) Worcester, Barbourne House

HER Ref: WCM91083 Postcode:WR3 7AA area O.S. 25" Map No. 33.3 Date of Map: 1904

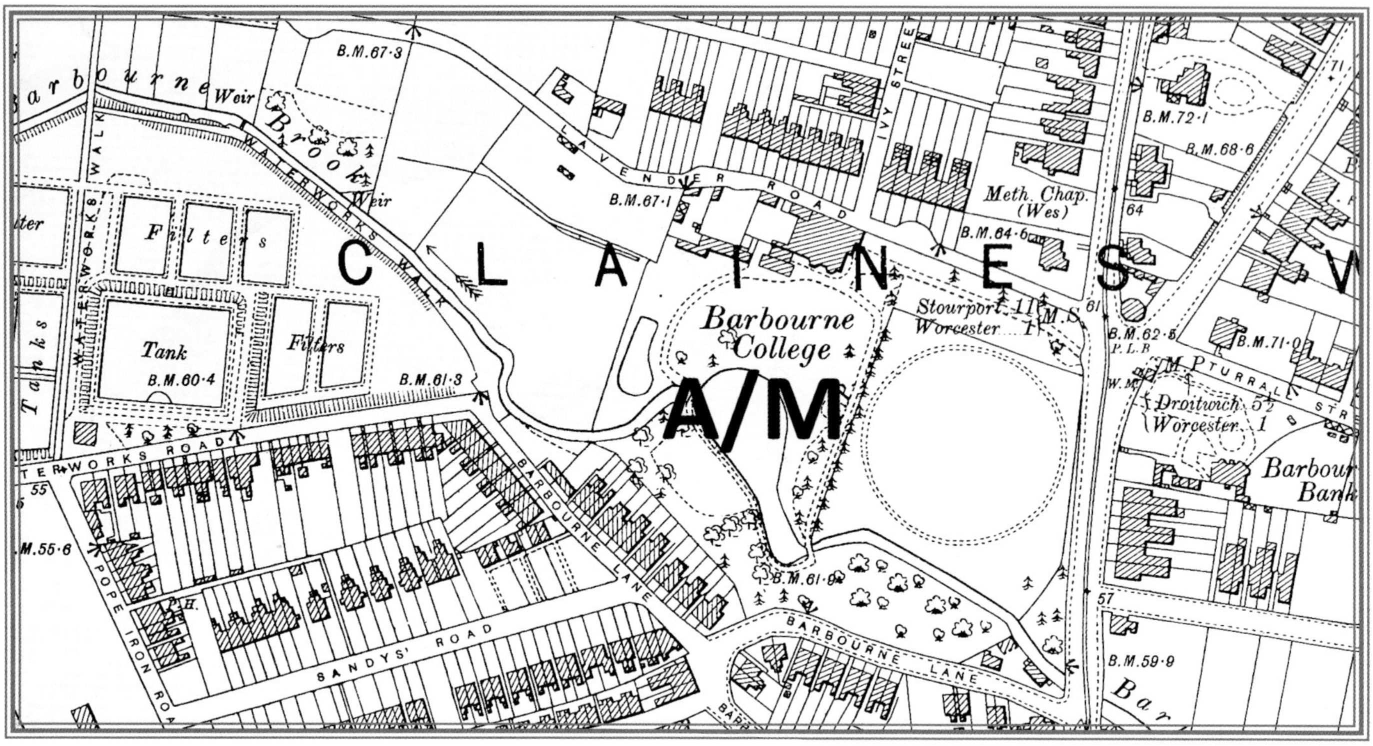

The residence is noticed by Tunnicliff (1788) when occupied by the Revd. Thomas Cookes. Paterson in 1829 (op. cit. p. 149) commented that Sir Edward Denny Bart. had "a very neat and commodious residence, situated amongst grounds possessing very considerable elegance". The mansion was sited close to the turnpike and the toll house between the Bewdley and Birmingham roads. It was north of the Barbourne Brook which was the major feature of its grounds and its south boundary. The Brook formed a large fishpond at the bottom of the garden on its way to the waterworks and the Severn. At its greatest extent circa 1800, there was a field or meadow, perhaps used as a park, to the north of the access carriage road, which became Lavender Road.

Several maps show the arrangement of the grounds between 1751 and 1838. John Doharty junior's 1751 *Map of Claines* (**Plate 6**) shows that Mr. Cooke had a large field with barn across the carriage way on the north side with a semi-circular recessed and gated entrance. The house had courts on west and east sides, one separating the house from a meadow along the main road and down to the Barbourne Brook. There were apparently several formal pieces of water (possibly fish tanks) in the grounds, and formally arranged gardens on the south side of the house with perhaps a pigeon house in the centre. The garden area to the west of the house was probably kitchen garden. Maps of 1774 and 1826 show the arrangement and use of lands along the Barbourne Brook, an area where water and drainage were contested at law. James Webb's map of 1838 (WAAS 3706/14) illustrates the grounds at a moment of sale between T. H. Cookes and J. P. Lavender. This map shows that the formal garden as in 1751 had given way to lawn and shrubbery. The property extended south of the brook to 3 small pastures and 3 small tenanted houses with gardens. Little of this miniature landscape had changed by the 1904 OS.

Barbourne House itself was sold again in 1879 (Wardle, p. 129) with "lawn and pleasure grounds tastefully laid out, fish ponds, bridges, shrubbery with leisure walks and summer houses." The House then became a School and later College and when sold again in 1909 was described as having "attractive grounds, well–timbered with oak, elm, birch, beech, poplar, ash, chestnut, fir and other trees." The Barbourne Brook was "a stream of exceptionally clear water". Other features added for school and college use were tennis and croquet lawns, lake and open-air swimming bath with diving board. House and grounds were eventually sold in 1918 to the City of Worcester (and the House demolished) for the creation of the Gheluvelt Memorial Park containing houses for First World War veterans.

T. Mowl, *Historic Gardens of Worcestershire*, 2006.
C. & T. Wardle, *History of Barbourne*, 2007.
W. Tunnicliff, *A Survey of the County of Worcester*, 1788.
Patersons Roads, 1829.

(B) Worcester, Battenhall Mount

HER Ref: WCM98712 Postcode:WR5 2HN O.S. 25" Map No. 33.8, 33.12 Date of Maps: both 1904

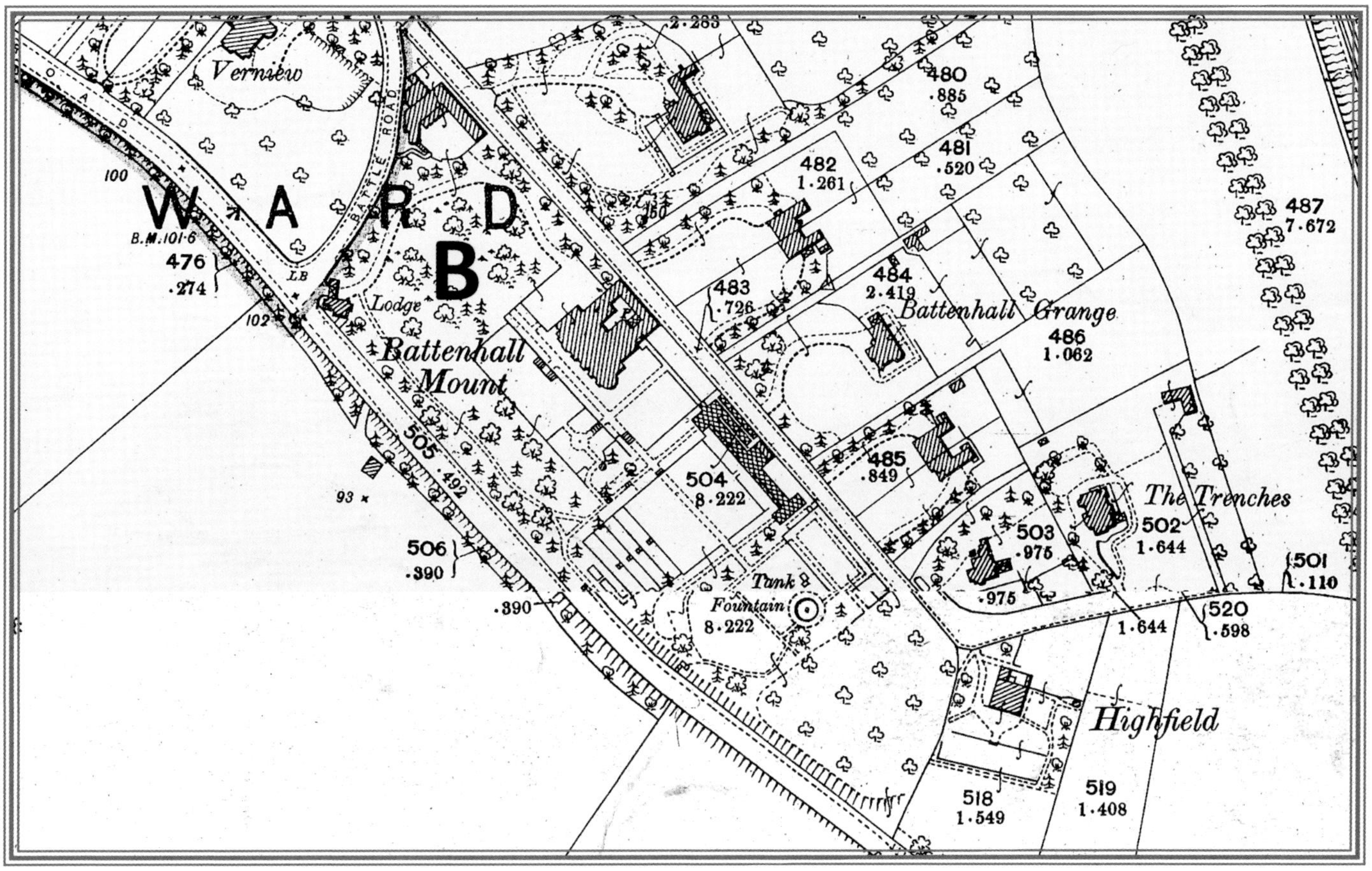

The original house of circa 1867 (later St. Mary's Convent) was redeveloped by the Hon. Percy Allsop in the 1890's through two architects, J. H. Williams and R. S. Briggs. The gatehouse Lodge and Stables, now Listed, are by J. H. Williams. (BoE, p. 771). Williams and Briggs together were responsible for mansion and its interiors and the BoE attributes different parts to each architect with metal work by Starkie & Gardiner and stained glass by J. H. Hardman. H. H. Martyn of Cheltenham who worked for Briggs, sponsored by Allsop, on the Jesus Chapel in Worcester Cathedral, perhaps also contributed. The designation of the Mount and Gardener's Cottage was raised from Grade II to Grade II* in 2015.

The Mount is a relatively rare survival of a late Victorian house within its garden setting laid out in the 1860s and 1890s. In his obituary, Allsop was praised generally for "his taste and judgement in the planning and planting of the gardens." More specifically, the obituary referred to "flower parterres and borders with pergolas, sundial, ornamental fish pool with fountain and picturesque draw-well and water tanks in the Moorish style" (*Worcester Herald*, 2. 3. 1929).

When the estate was put up for sale in 1918 and again in 1921 (WAAS 5240/ 6) the sale particulars were illustrated with photographs and plan of the Italianate garden with its steps and balustrades. The plan shows the serpentine access from the Lodge via the Stables to the mansion and the lay-out of the terraces at different levels linked to a large number of glasshouses, some of them supplanted by 20th century buildings.

The gardens survive in outline as laid-out in ascending terraces linked by staircases set along the line of the escarpment above and parallel with Battenhall Road on which the Mount is set. The layout is shown at 1:2500 scale in the *Conservation Area Appraisal* adopted by Worcester City Council in 2010. These gardens have become increasingly overgrown since St. Mary's, originally a Convent and then a convent School, closed in 2014 but they survive in their essence except for the intrusion of car parking and tarmacked surfaces around the main entrance and on the first terrace immediately below. The natural divisions between the gardens as they ascend are reinforced by trees, some of them specimen trees. There is a major scheme for the reuse and redevelopment of the Mount and its gardens being progressed (2018).

A. Brooks & N. Pevsner, *Worcestershire*, 2007 (BoE).
Worcester City Council, *Battenhall Villas Conservation Area*, (CA 20), 2010.
C. & T. Wardle, *The History of Barbourne*, 2007.

(C) Worcester, Battenhall Park

HER Ref: WCM91029 Postcode:WR7 4RU O.S. 25" Map No. 33.12 Date of Map: 1904

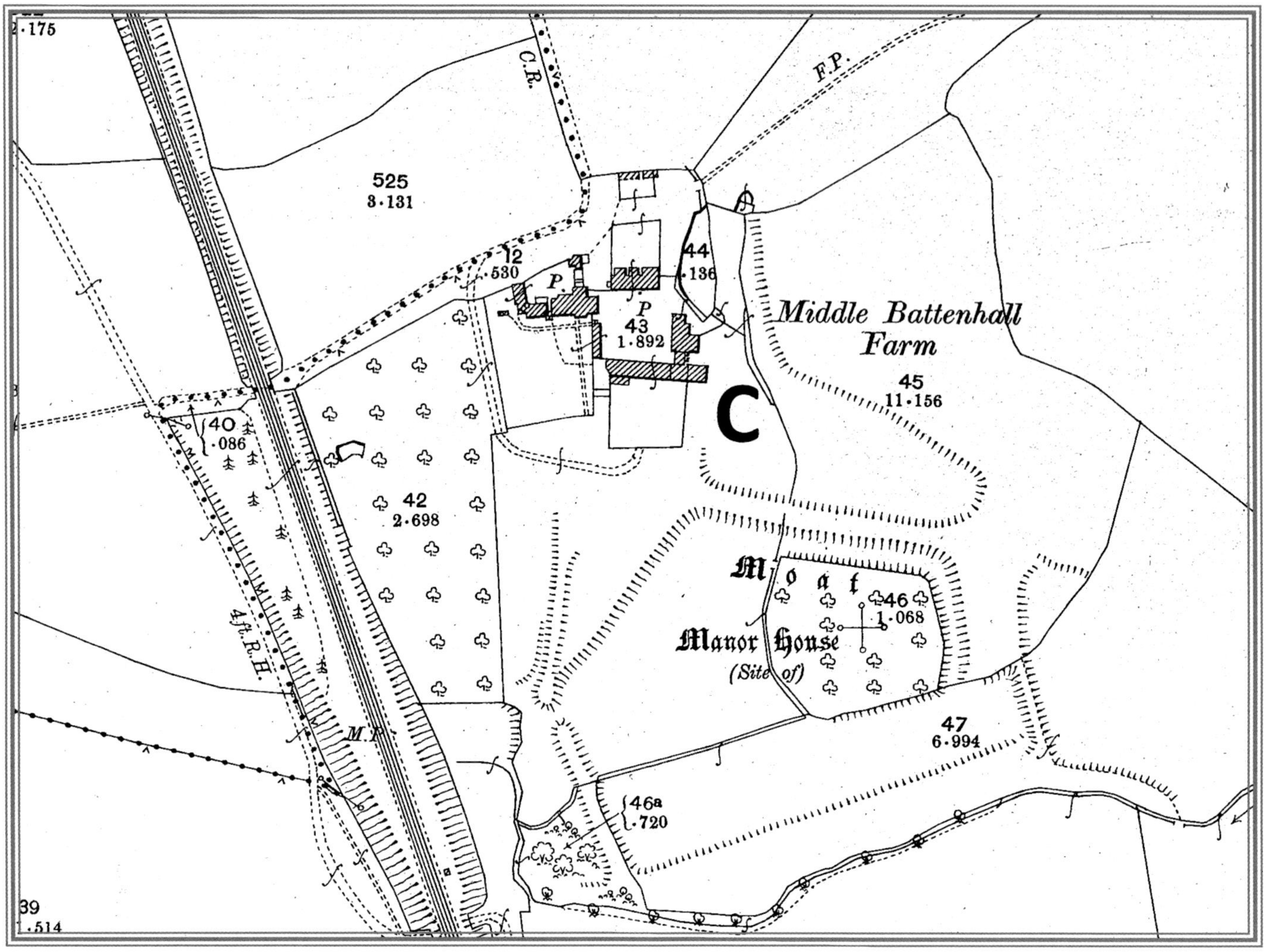

Battenhall was an important park and manor attached to the Priory of Worcester (VCH., 3, 1913, pp. 514/5) and a favourite residence of Prior William More who invested in its fishponds up to the moment of the Dissolution (Bettey p. 23). The BoE describes the present Farm House, Middle Battenhall as "partly 17th century, on the site of the Priory Grange ... with some timber framing perhaps relocated from Prior More's 16th century house." The property ceased to be part of a larger estate following a sale in 1930.

The park was granted with the manor at the Dissolution. It is marked as a deer park on Saxton's printed map of 1577 and on Sheldon's tapestry map of the 1590s (Oxford Bodleian Library). Blome (1673) and Morden (1695) continue this status still given by E. & T. Bowen as late as 1767 and 1778. Battenhall park was distinct from Crookbarrow park which had also disappeared by the end of the 18th century (Nash, Vol. 2, 1782, p. 327). The moat near Middle Battenhall Farm marks the site of the manor house. Elizabeth I visited the Park on her visit in 1575: "And on Friday the 19th day of August, in the afternoon her Majesty rode to Battenhall Park intending to hunt there, but for that finding the game very scarce, she returned again without hunting at all." On leaving Worcester she departed "through Battenhall Park, through made ways, with a great train both before and behind, and so to Elmley Bredon." (Noake, pp. 184-5).

The manor boundaries as marked circa 1830 (WAAS 351/55) stretched from the Severn at its south-east corner up to the boundary of Spetchley Park in the north-west. Hughes & Leech (p. 18 and plan) have suggested the boundaries of the 16th century Park contemporary with the ownership of Sir John Bourne.

J. Noake, *Worcester in Olden Times*, 1849.
J. H. Bettey, *Estates and the English Countryside*, 1993.
P. Hughes and A. Leech, *The Story of Worcester*, 2011.
A. Brooks & N. Pevsner, *Worcestershire*, 2007 (BoE).
Victoria County History Vol. 3, 1913, (VCH).
T. R. Nash, *Collections for the History of Worcestershire*, Vol II, 1782.

(D) Worcester, Berkeley's Hospital

HER Ref: WCM96069. Postcode: WR1 3QG.

George Young's map from Valentine Green's *The History and Antiquities of the City and Suburbs of Worcester,* Vol. II, 1796.

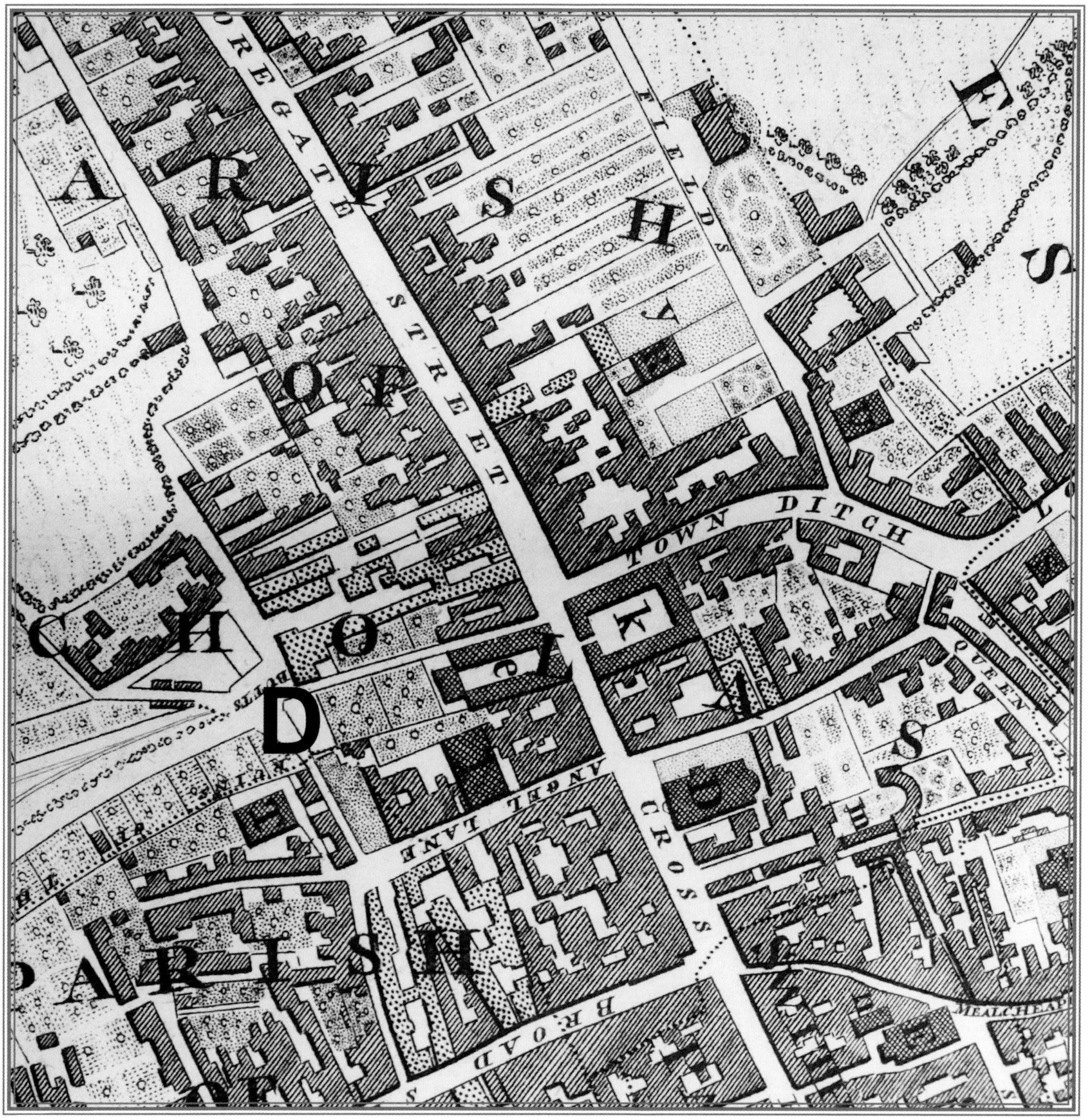

The site for the Hospital became available when the Foregate was demolished in 1702. The layout of this 1703-1710 courtyard building (Chapel dated 1703) created the space for a garden in the centre. Although very small in scale this is obviously a garden site. In 1896, it was laid out with a row of 6 trees on each side and when listed there was a "delightful avenue of Japanese double pink cherries". This seems to reflect the spirit of the planting recorded by mid-18th century maps, e.g. John Doharty junior's of 1742 and Broad's of 1768. The land immediately to the west of the Chapel was laid out as gardens until the later-18th century (1780's map, WAAS 372/1); this is now used for car parking.

(E) Worcester, Bishop's Palace

HER Ref: WCM96015 Postcode:WR1 2LA O.S. 25" Map No. 33.8 Date of Map: 1904

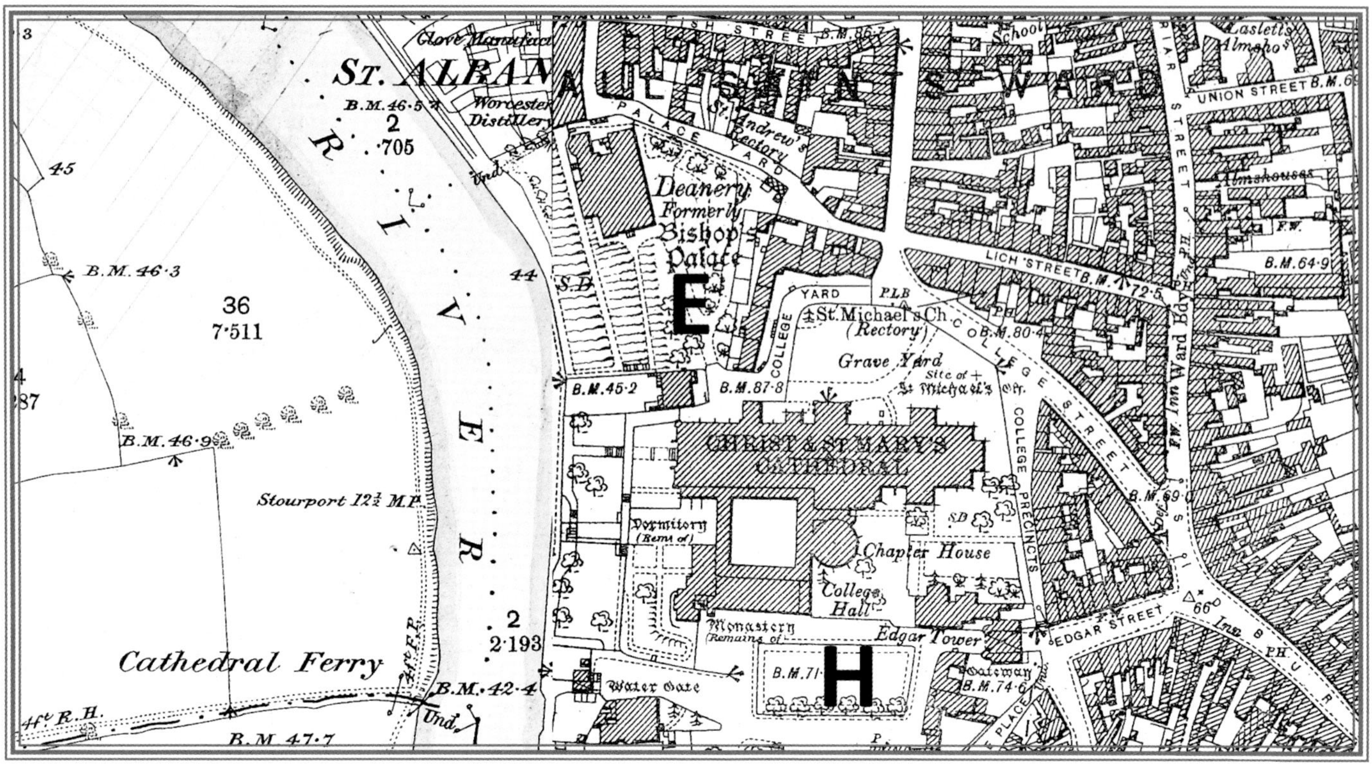

The site of the Palace was established for the anglo-saxon bishops of Worcester circa 900 AD (Baker & Holt, fig. 14.1) and parts of the surviving buildings date back at least to the 12th century. The bishop was granted licence to crenellate in 1271 which probably resulted in a substantial wall and gatehouse surrounding a precinct of 2 acres (Salter, p. 64). Hughes & Leech (p. 89) illustrate a detail from a printed map made in 1651 relating to the Battles of Worcester which shows some formal gardens and radiating walks but, given the scale of the map, should be taken with a pinch of salt. Nash quotes the Parliamentary Survey of 1648: "Before the palace was a fair green, containing an acre at least, with a bowling alley"; "There were diverse fine walks and prospects on the leads and tops of the palace" (Nash, p. 319). 18th century plans show formal gardens between the 18th century gateway and the north porch of the Cathedral and also on the east side, e.g. 2 shaped beds in a 1741 plan by John Doharty junior (WAAS 5403/10). Palace Yard, was eroded by the creation of Deansway (the Palace had become the Deanery) in the later-18th century when it became a drive way or forecourt as illustrated by Green in 1796. Coach house and stables survive from the 18th century as well as the entrance from the road: "The former Bishop's Palace is set back from Deansway behind a C18 brick wall with gate piers with stone urns, on a site sloping steeply down to the Severn" (BoE, pp. 704-5).

The most detailed visual description of the gardens and forecourt is to be found in George Young's 1796 map of Worcester; this follows his earlier map of 1779. A general description of the gardens is given in a *History of Worcester* by W. R., published in 1808: "The gardens, which are laid out on a gentle declivity, near to the water, command a delightful view of the Severn, and a fine range of country, terminated by the Malvern Hills, and other fine distant objects." The walled gardens between the palace and the river were used for fruit trees but later-18th century views imply a relatively natural scene of trees and shrubs. However, in 1819, the gardens are described as "neat, with a fine prospect of the river." By the time of Charles Crisp's map of 1832, the terraced layout of the grounds towards the River had been established.

In 2009 a landscape scheme was developed to share the grounds of the Old Palace with the new Bishop's Palace at 10 College Green. The division of the Palace garden between an upper lawn and a lower lawn with some hard landscaping remains with new fenced boundaries including one dividing the lower lawn along the riverside.

M. Salter, *The Castles of Herefordshire and Worcestershire,* 1989.
N. Baker & R. Holt, *Urban Growth and the Medieval Church: Gloucester and Worcester,* 2004.
P. Hughes & A. Leech, *The Story of Worcester,* 2012.
V. Green, *History and Antiquities of Worcester,* 1796.
T. R. Nash, *Collections for the History of Worcestershire,* Vol II, 1782.
A. Brooks & N. Pevsner, *Worcestershire,* 2007 (BoE).

(F) Worcester, The Blanquettes

HER Ref: WCM98624 Postcode:WR3 8BN area O.S. 25" Map No. 28.15, 28.16 Date of Map: 1904, 1889

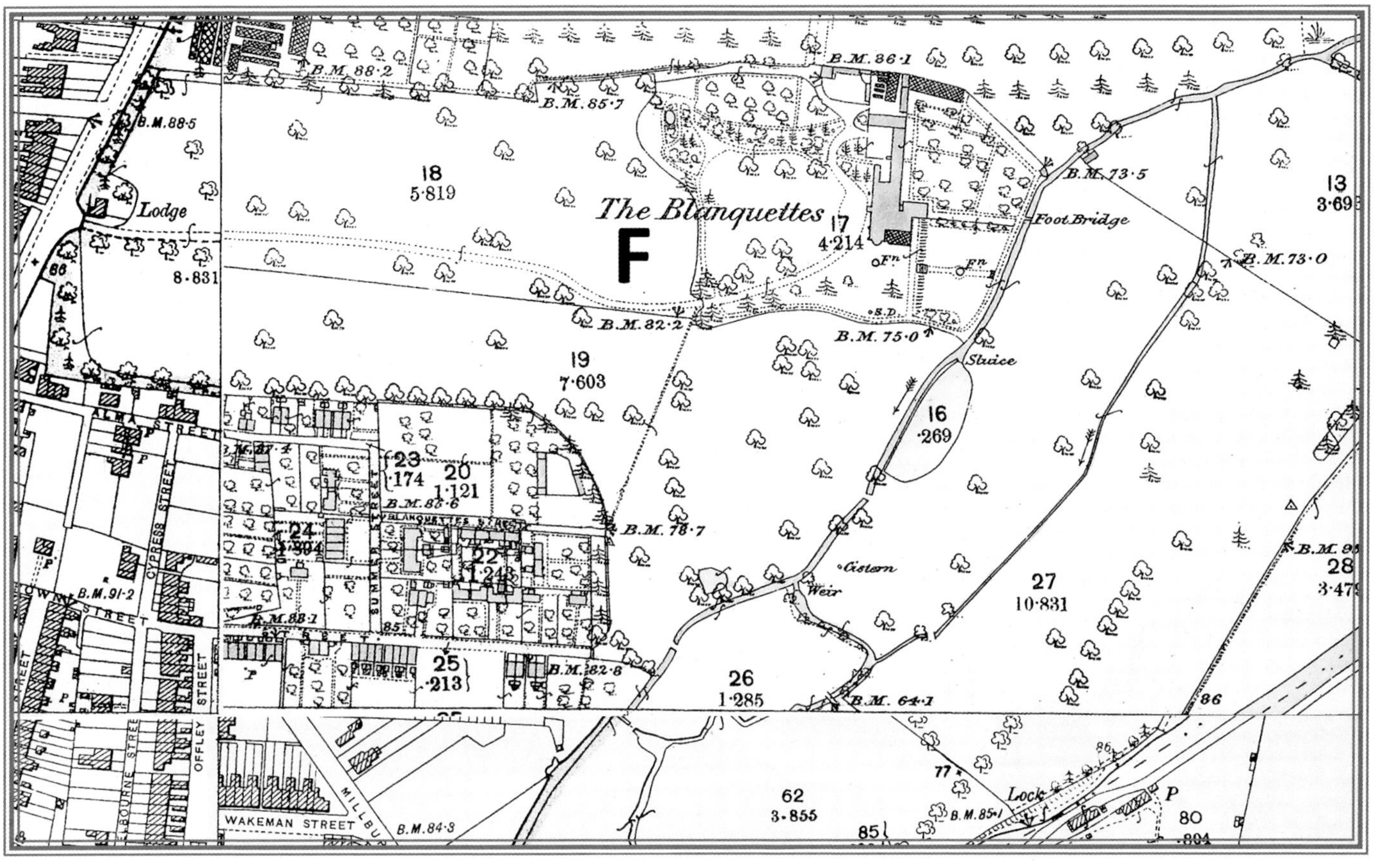

The 18th century estate belonging to the Dean and Chapter is shown as let to Mr. Amphlet on John Doharty junior's Map of 1751 (WAAS 5403/10) (Hughes & Leech, p. 87, illus.). The estate included land either side of the Barbourne Brook to the east, most of the land up to the Brook on the south and west to the Droitwich Turnpike Road. Doharty shows a particularly grand entrance with fine wrought-iron gates behind a semi-circular recess off the road giving on to a wide, rectangular field with a double line of trees on each side of the carriage drive, with rectangular pools at the end – The Walk (5.1 acres). The house with a small forecourt, surrounded by farm buildings including a pigeon house, was set in about 4 acres.

The VCH, published in 1913 (Vol. 3. p. 301) reported the moment of change: "The Blanquettes in Barbourne, standing in large grounds, watered by the Barbourne Brook, is being cut for building." The part of the estate in question was The Walk which became Blanquettes Avenue. The rest of the estate, amounting to 26 acres (as shown on the 1930 OS 6 inch) was equivalent to a small park. The 1932 Sale particulars (WAAS 5240/4a) illustrate a Regency house with large attached conservatory: "The House is surrounded by charming grounds, nicely planted with handsome specimen Shrubs and Trees with spacious Lawns, Sunk Italian Garden, Rose Borders, Fountain, and pretty walks. The large walled-in Garden with a southern aspect is well planted with choice sorts of Fruit Trees; another Kitchen Garden, range of Vineries and Peach House, Span-roof Greenhouse, Forcing Frames and Potting Sheds. Stabling, Garages, small Farmery, excellent Pasture Land, Orcharding, the whole extending to 26a." The principal feature of the gardens was the lower lawn beside the Barbourne Brook with a central fountain which was set on a lower level to the house.

The Blanquettes is treated generously in this *Survey* because it represents a small estate typical of the country rather than the town and one that can be documented over nearly 2 centuries with grounds characteristic of their period. Despite its situation on the edge of the City, it was recognised as a significant residence (Blankets) on Isaac Taylor's one inch to the mile County map of 1772. It did not receive park status until the 1905 OS 6 inch which included the Walk on the west side and land to the east and south between the Barbourne Brook and the Canal. Barbourne Nurseries occupied the land immediately to the north. Apart from the Walk, the park was still represented as such on the 1930 OS. The whole site is now occupied by residential development.

P. Hughes & A. Leech, *The Story of Worcester,* 2012.
Victoria County History Vol. 3, 1913, p. 301, (VCH).

(G) Worcester, Boughton Park

HER Ref: WCM91080 | Postcode: WR2 4EZ | O.S. 25" Map No. 33.7, 33.11 | Date of Maps: 1888, 1904

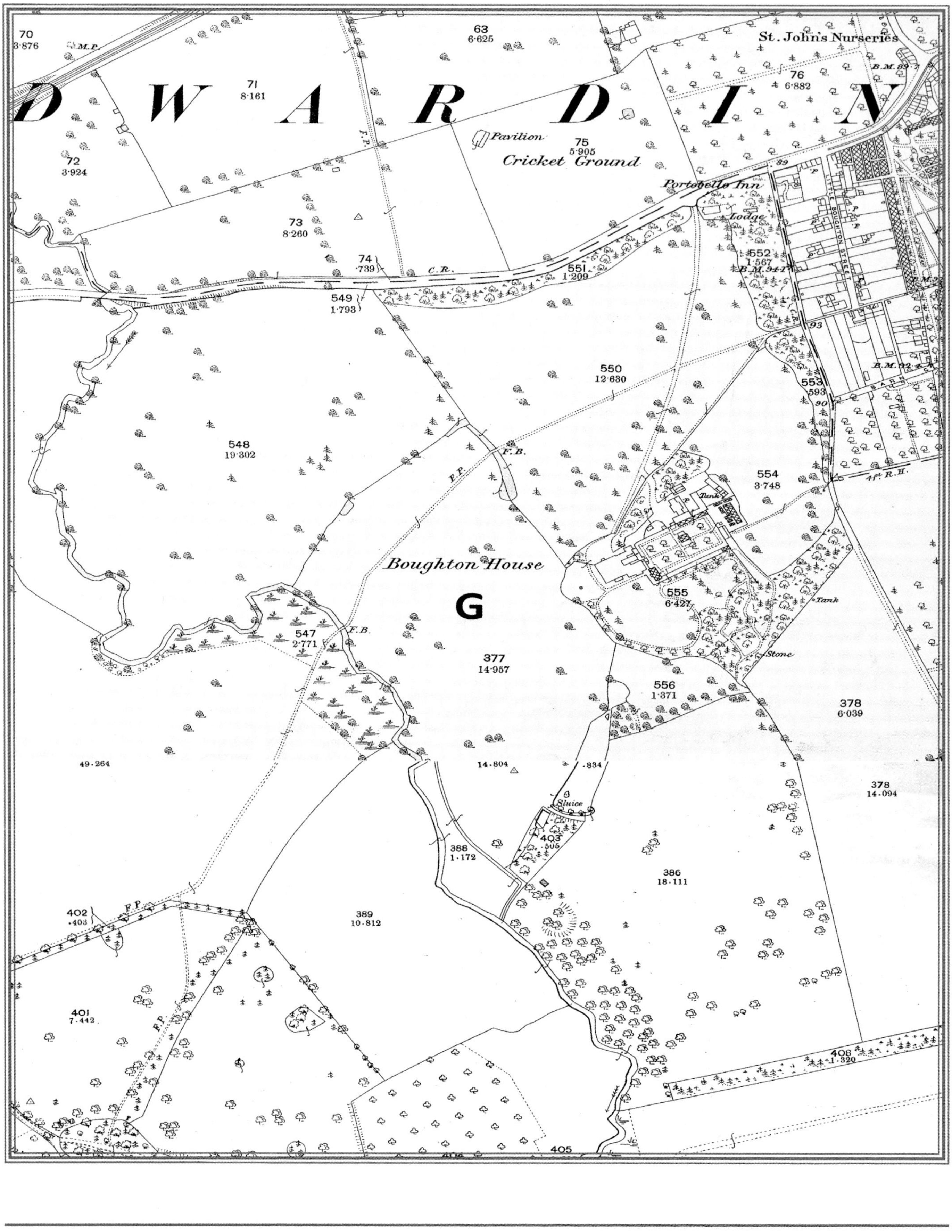

..........continued from previous page

Boughton House is Listed but is much modified from the house built by Elias Isaac circa 1814. In particular the mansard roof was not re-made after a devastating fire in 1948. This is now the Worcester Golf and Country Club House.

Around the mansion, some small remains of gardens known as the Italian garden date back to the later years of Isaac family ownership. The lake remains a landscape feature no doubt from the earliest time but has lost its boathouse marked on the 1905 OS 6 inch.

There is no evidence for significant grounds or park as mapped in 1905 before the 1820's when the site was called Boughton Fields on City maps. Only 2 large fields as part of Boughton Farm are shown on a 1777 survey map by George Young (WAAS 5589/138) but an early-19th century sale advertised a "Manor or capital messuage, gardens and fish pools stored with carp" (WAAS 4600/26). The house is marked on Greenwood's map of 1822 and described as a pleasant mansion in a Worcester Guide of 1837.

Historically, Boughton was part of the manor of Wick Episcopi where a house was built for Henry Gower in 1429; Boughton remained in Gower ownership until 1730 (R. J. Henderson in Robertson, op. cit.). John Leland noticed "a fair house" in the early-16th century.

The estate was divided when sold in 1778 but was reintegrated by Elias Isaac, a partner in Berwick & Co, the Worcester Bank in 1814, from which time the Club House originates. Some estate buildings such as stables and walled garden (occupied by 4 tennis courts from the earliest days of the Club – 1928) go back to this period. A Lodge (demolished) is shown on a tithe map (WAAS 5589) at which time the property belonged to J. Whitmore Isaac, Esq. who inherited in 1841 and lived here until 1884. He re-ordered the agricultural estate and introduced and planted a considerable variety of trees many of them from Europe and North America. Henderson and Denyer (op. cit.) say that Isaac intended to have a belt of trees around the entire estate featuring Corsican Pines. Elsewhere the planting included limes and grey poplars along the northern edge of the estate plus a Douglas fir, an Atlantic cedar and a Wellingtonia. The sweet chestnuts by the main entrance to the house are much more ancient. J. S. Isaac, a son of J. W. Isaac, gave Worcester its first Cricket Ground in 1865 taken out of the Boughton Estate which became the County Ground until 1896 (Gwilliam op. cit.). "By 1935 ... the Club bought and planted 3000 new trees around the course" (Robertson op, cit.). Further planting was carried out by Abbey Forestry with a grant from the Forestry Commission in 1984-5 when adjoining land was added from the Wick Episcopi estate (Stuart Denyer). Planting of specimen trees continues.

Richard Williams, who came to Boughton as a jobbing gardener around 1820 and married an Isaac daughter, developed the nursery from which the Worcester Pearmain was marketed in 1876. The family ran a seeds business from premises on the corner of High Street and Broad Street, Worcester (Gwilliam, pp. 189-90).

The Worcester Golf and Country Club, the present owners, formerly the Worcester City Golf Club founded in 1898, started life at the Tolladine Links as tenants but by forming a Joint Stock Company in 1926 was able to acquire the Boughton site and be back in action by 1928. The grounds were first laid out as a golf course by the celebrated Dr. Alister Mackenzie (1870-1934), 'The Course Doctor' whose last design was for the Augusta National, the home of the USA Masters, in 1934. The Mackenzie Course at Boughton is substantially that played on today and is therefore 'historic' and represents a latter-day landscape park, uniquely in this *Survey*.

A temporary interruption in this landscape succession came with the 2nd World War when 15 obstacles to troop-carrying aircraft were set up on the course and land was ploughed up for potatoes or given over to sheep grazing. The grounds were not returned fully to golf until 1949 (Robertson op. cit.).

The Club grounds are bounded by the Bransford Road, the Laughern Brook, Swinton Lane and Columbia Drive and amount to over 100 acres.

H. W. Gwilliam, *Old Worcester People and Places,* 1977.

S. Robertson, *Worcester Golf and Country Club: 1898 – 1998,* 1998.

Worcester Golf and Country Club (illustrated brochure), n.d.

R. J. Henderson & S. Denyer, *An Account of the Trees in Boughton Park*, n.d. (unpublished).

Boughton Park golf course, 2019. Photo, S. Denyer.

Worcester, Bowling Greens

HER Ref: not allocated.

Bowling Greens were a prominent feature of Worcester in the 18th and 19th centuries and were found throughout the County, not always as part of the gardens of the greater houses (e.g. the Bowling Green at Powick). In towns they were important open spaces for recreation alongside unofficial public gardens like Sansome Fields and Lovesgrove. The bowling green at the Diglis Pleasure Grounds was part of a commercial, recreational complex including a Riding School. Hughes and Leech (p. 143) illustrate John Doharty junior's watercolour drawing of it as in 1754. Nash's map (Vol. II, 1782) singled out the Pheasant and Tom's which were attached to Public Houses. They are more clearly mapped on George Young's larger scale 1790 map. The Pheasant Bowling Green lay in Pheasant Street between Silver Street and the open field on the eastern boundary of the City. There is a plan of this dated 1759 (WAAS 1026). In 1849, in the back of J. Noake's *Worcester in Olden Times,* W. Daniels, the proprietor of the Pheasant Inn, New Street "begs to thank the public and his friends in general for their kind support since the opening of the Bowling Green, and hopes, by strict personal attention, to merit a continuance of their favours." Tom's was sited between Foregate Street and Sansome House. The Diglis bowling green was still in business in 1832 as was the Pheasant close to the Cornmarket outside the City Wall (Crisp 1832). Later the Pheasant was described as a Croquet and Archery ground on *The Visitors' Map of Worcester,* 1868.

By 1832, Tom's had gone from the map but a bowling green behind the Saracen's Head on the Tything has appeared; a coloured aquatint by Joshua Gleadah for James Clements "dedicated to the Subscribers" shows the latter in full social swing. A key provides names, occupations and addresses: Harvey Skelton, Accountant, Britannia Square; Joseph Skelton, senior, Lay Clerk (of the Cathedral), Sansome Fields; Wm. Cole, the boy, Green Scout; Wm. Bass, Agent for Pickford, Rain Bow Hill Terrace; Thos. Butler, Victualler, Saracen Hd., Tything; Gilbert Jones, Land Surveyor, New Street; J. N. Lavender, Gov. City Gaol, Salt Lane; Wm. Blind, Lawyer, Foregate Street; John Phillips, Hop Merchant, Sansome Street; John Bristow, Currier, Sidbury; Wm. Lamb, Gentleman, Henwick Hill; Wm. Manning, Jeweller, 20 Cross; Wm. Browning, Glover, Factory Walk; Walker Swan Holdsworth, 2nd son of Wm., Sansome Street; Jo. Pitman, Artist; Wm. Young, Artist, 14 Foregate Street; Abm. Pemberton, Plumber, 50 Broad Street; Captain Ottey, Indian Officer; John Portmann, Malster, 56 Tything; Jn. Shuck, son of Sword Bearer, Green Man, Tything; Jo. Churchill, Retired House Painter, 23 Foregate Street; Wm. Newport, Coach Builder, 9 Tything; W. V. Holdworth. Junr., Lawyer, Foregate Street; Danl. George, Maltster & Baker, Friar Street. Later in the 19th century the bowling green and other land beside it was used for circuses and religious preaching, boxing and hot air balloon events (Wardle, p. 36).

P. Hughes & A. Leech, *The Story of Worcester,* 2011.
C. & T. Wardle, *The History of Barbourne,* 2007.
D. Whitehead, *The Book of Worcester,* 1976.
C. Crisp, *Map of the City and Suburbs of Worcester according to the new Act of Parliament,* 1832.
T. R. Nash, *Collections for the History of Worcestershire,* Vol II, 1782.

Aquatint by Joshua Gleadah for James Clements's *Bowling,* circa 1820. Private collection.

(H) Worcester, College Green

HER Ref: WCM96378 Postcode:WR1 2LH O.S. 25" Map No. 33.7, 33.8 Date of Map: 1888, 1904

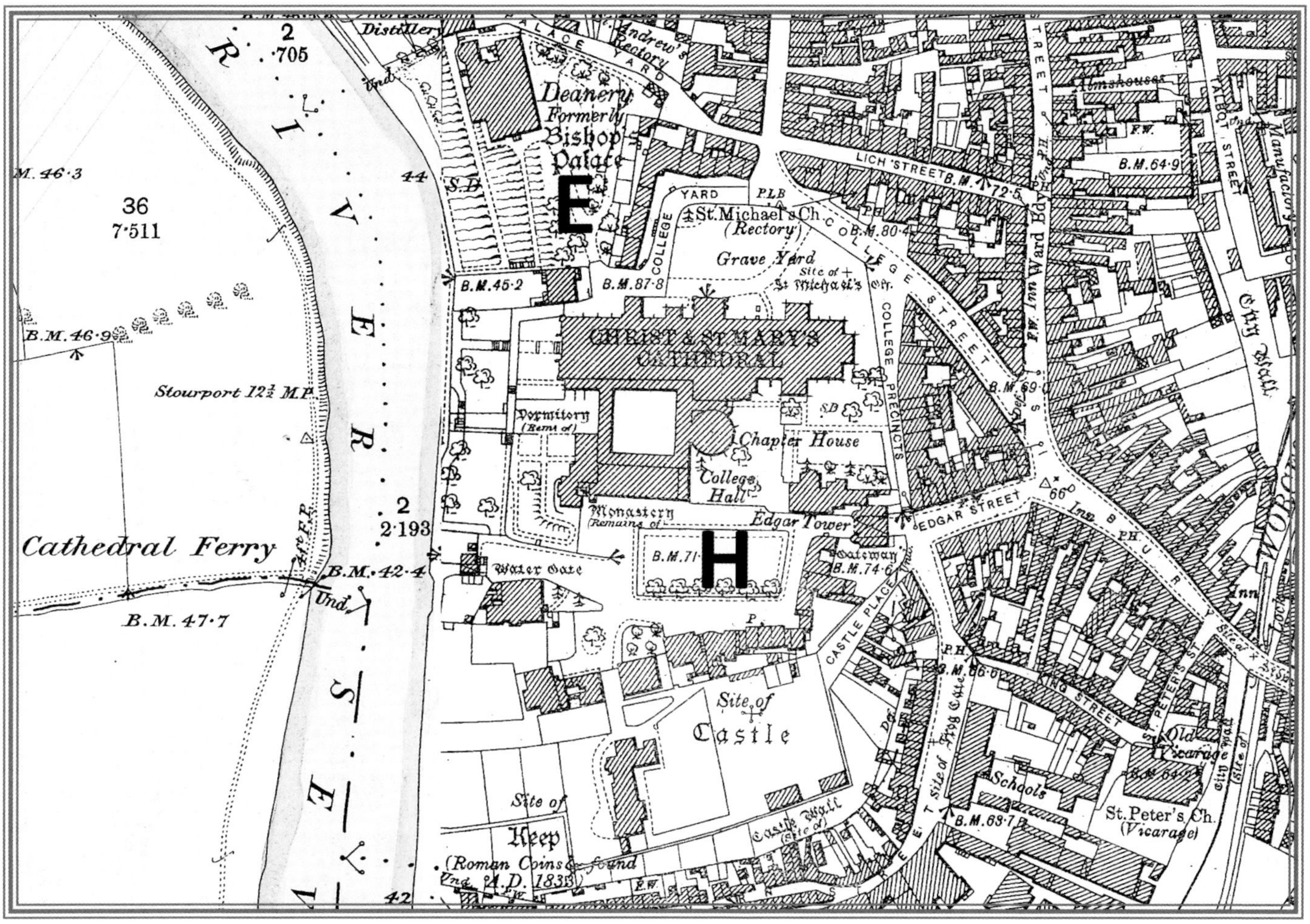

College Green, lying between the Cathedral Refectory (College Hall) and Guesten Hall on the north side and the Chapter Stables and houses on the site of the castle on the south side, had become a relatively public and social place by the Reformation and no doubt more so when the monastic community gave way to Secular Canons' houses and the King's School. Today this space is filled with a bare lawn with a few trees and sometimes with a marquee or two.

Pat Hughes (op. cit. 2016), in a recent study of the houses around College Green and their occupants in the 17th century, says that it "was a grassed space, although in 1608 it was plagued with nettles. By the 1670s it was regularly mowed and laid out with walks, and posts and rails are mentioned as needing repair" (*A Look at College Green*). There are references in the late-17th century (Receiver General's Accounts, Worcester Cathedral Library, A 27) to tree planting and garden furniture. In 1678 3 shillings are paid out for bringing lime trees to the Green; in 1681 reference is made to the Globe in the Green; in 1690 20 walnut trees are sourced from Oxford (information from David Everett).

By the mid-18th century, there existed an elaborate, formal garden of shaped beds and standard trees as in the printed maps of John Doharty junior (1741) and Nash (Vol. 2, 1782). (The cathedral cloister was also laid out with 4 square beds and a central feature). At some moment this formal garden was removed and printed city maps of 1779, 1795, 1822 and 1829 show a rectangular and perhaps fenced space lined with trees, either on 4 sides or only on 2. The mid-19th century Green had fencing with brick piers as in a watercolour of circa 1790 viewed from the Edgar Tower (Hughes & Leech, p. 204). The Green became a potato field during the 2nd World War and today has returned to a lawn with a few trees on the north side.

N. Baker & R. Holt, *Urban Growth and the Medieval Church; Gloucester and Worcester,* 2004, (p. 308, plan of Cathedral Precinct).

P. Hughes & A. Leech, *The Story of Worcester,* 2011.

P. Hughes, "A Look at College Green in the 17th Century", *Archaeology at Worcester Cathedral*: Report of the 26th Annual Symposium, March 2016, pp. 4-6.

T. R. Nash, *Collections for the History of Worcestershire,* Vol II, 1782.

(I) Worcester, The Commandery

HER Ref: WCM96001 Postcode:WR1 2HU O.S. 25" Map No. 33.8 Date of Map: 1904

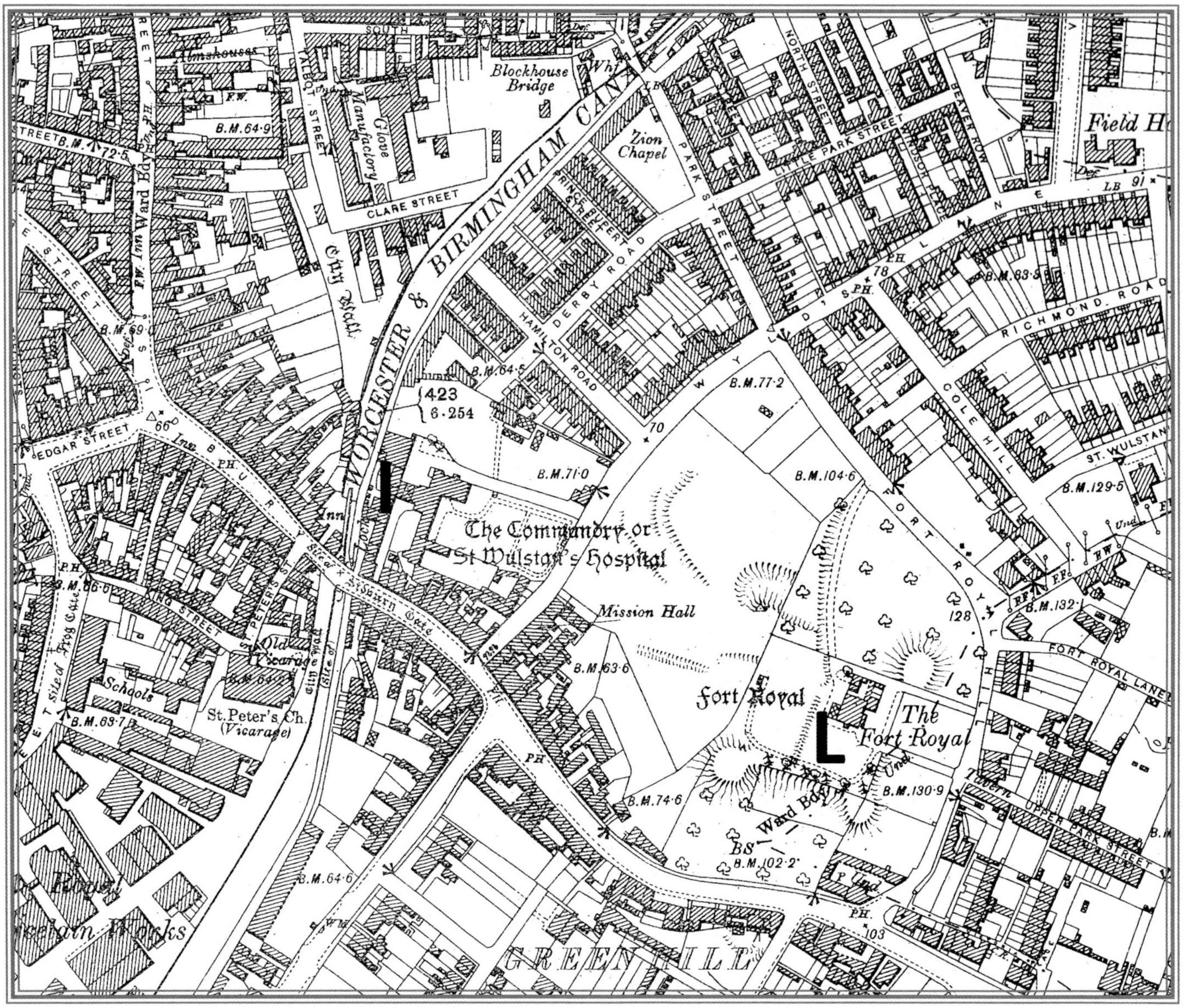

The Commandery belonged to a leading draper in the 16th century, Robert Wylde (ob. 1608) whose tomb is in the Cathedral. No doubt his gardens were inherited from the medieval hospital that was disestablished at the Reformation. John Doharty junior's 1741/2 *Plan of the City* shows some formal gardens between the Commandery and Wylde's Lane and a wide avenue of trees leading up to Fort Royal Hill (illus., by Latta, p. 13). Latta quotes a marriage settlement of 1776 indicating that at this date Fort Royal Hill was enclosed and stocked as a deer park i.e. that the Commandery was enjoyed as a country house and estate. "The commandery ... is a fine old house of timber, in the form of a court ... Above in the park is to be seen a great work of 4 bastions, called the Royal Mount, whence a vallum and ditch run both ways to encompass this side of the city" (*Traveller*, p. 130). Nash's 1781 map exaggerates the scale of the gardens but shows the formal lay-out of beds and the avenue and park-like treatment of the ground below Fort Royal Hill. There is further confirmation in George Young's 1790 map made for Valentine Green's 1796 *History*. For a photograph of the gardens circa 1900 "towards Fort Royal" see P. Harrison, *Images of England: Worcester*, 2005.

T. R. Nash, *Collections for the History of Worcestershire*, Vol II, 1782.
V. Green, *History and Antiquities of Worcester*, 2, 1796.
C. Latta, *The Commandery*, 1977.
J. Dugdale, *The New British Traveller*, 1819.

(J) Worcester, Cripplegate Park

HER Ref: WCM98800 Postcode:WR2 4QG O.S. 25" Map No. 33.7, 33.8 Date of Map: 1888, 1904

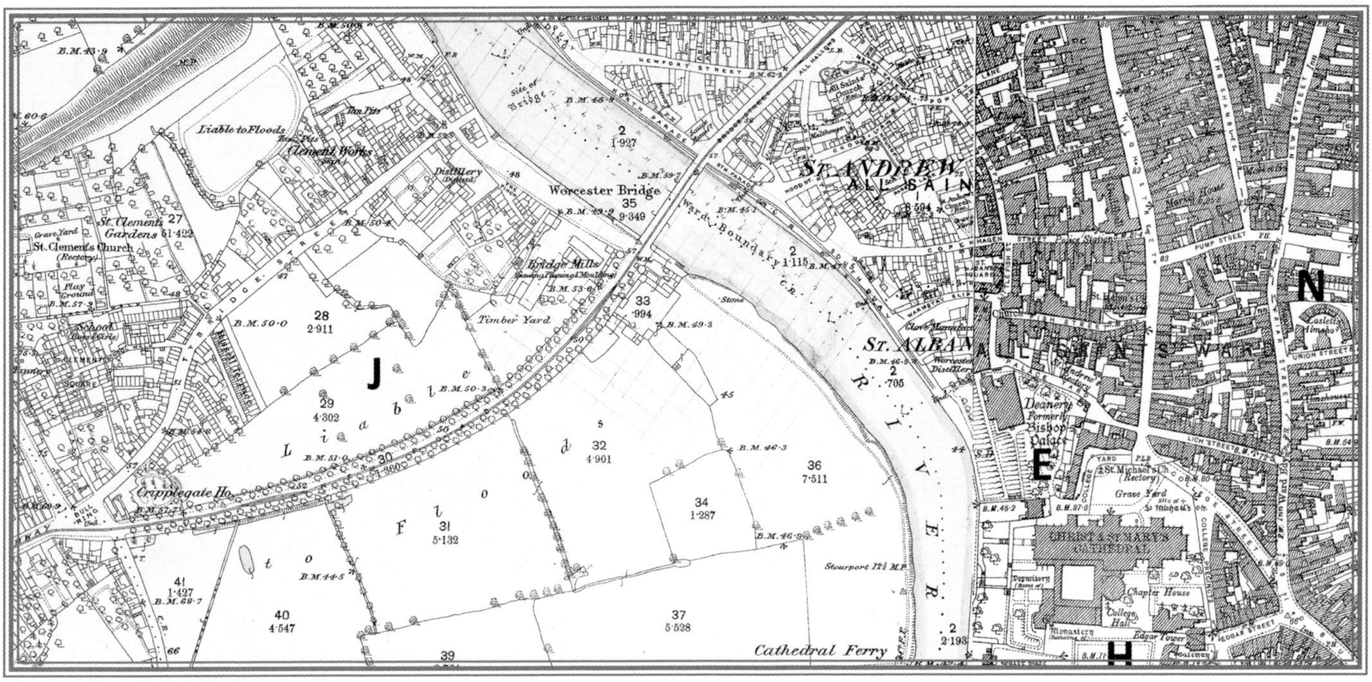

A *Souvenir Guide* to mark the re-opening of the Park in 1932 by the future King Edward VIII, gives a start date to the Park as 1912 when 3½ acres were acquired by the City but, being liable to flood, the site was raised to the level of New Road by tipping. Cripplegate House was bought in 1919 and the Park first opened in 1922 with a Bowling Green, 2 grass and 4 hard tennis courts and a childrens' recreation ground. The purchase in 1929 of the timber works then on the site, together with some road widening allowed the Park to extend to Hylton Road. The lay-out of the extended Park was designed by the City Surveyor. The cast-iron fountain by Hardy & Padmore was given by Richard Padmore to the City and is Listed (BoE, p. 774).

The 1885 OS 6 inch shows the oval space occupied by the gardens partially filled with industrial buildings. The situation pre-19th century development can be found on earlier maps such as George Young's of 1790.

Cripplegate Park, 1933, courtesy of Francis Frith Collection.

Souvenir Guide, *Visit of His Royal Highness Edward, Prince of Wales, Oct. 28th, 1932.*

A. Brooks & N. Pevsner, *Worcestershire,* 2007 (BoE).

Cripplegate Park flooded in 1933 with the Power Station and other industrial buildings before they were demolished. Private Collection.

(K) Worcester, Diglis Pleasure Grounds

HER Ref: WCM96656 Postcode:WR1 2NF

George Young's map from Valentine Green's *The History and Antiquities of the City and Suburbs of Worcester*, Vol. II, 1796.

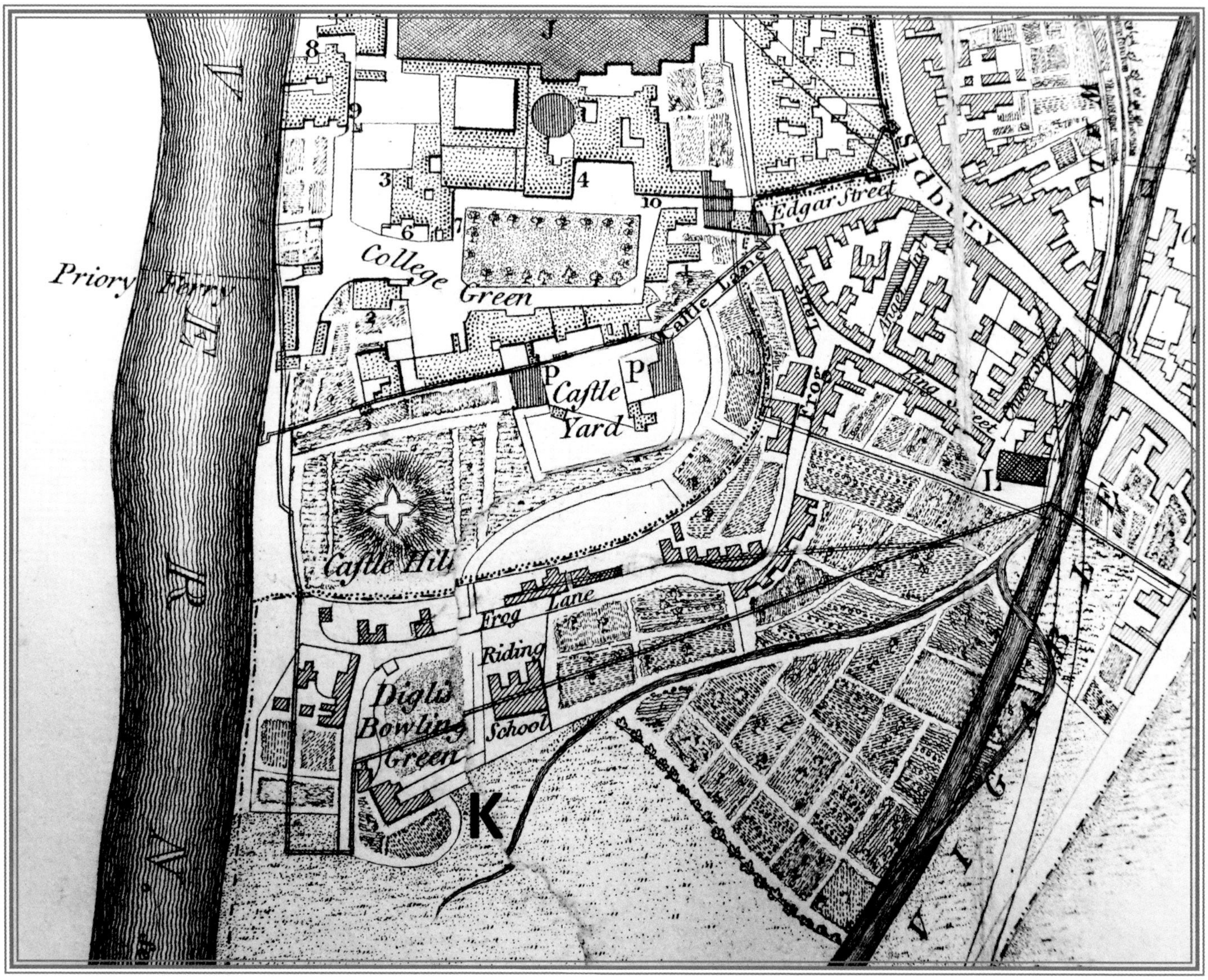

The pleasure gardens, situated on Frog Lane just south of Castle Hill, were developed around one of Worcester's several bowling greens between 1741 and 1755 by John Doharty junior (**Plate 19**). A banqueting house, sundial, globes and a weather vane "embellished" the bowling green gardens (Smith, p. 253). Young's 1779 printed map shows the site generally, with the Riding School on the east side and Diglis Meadows expanding south (illus. Hughes & Leech, p. 186). The 1780's printed *Plan of the City and Suburbs of Worcester* details the small shrubberies. The continuing history of the pleasure grounds can be followed on Crisp's map of 1832 and the bowling green is still recorded in the 1906 OS beside Diglis House, now a Hotel. This ground is now used for marquee events. The banqueting House is contained within one of the Kings School's Buildings (Smith, op. cit.).

Following his father's death in 1755, Doharty totted up the income from the pleasure grounds as £25p.a. for the bowling green and banqueting house; £21 for the riding house garden and the riding ground; £38 10s. for Diglis House and several cottages. Doharty left Worcester not long after (Smith op. cit.).

B. S. Smith, "The Dougharty Family, Eighteenth-century Mapmakers", *Worc. Arch. Soc. Trans.*, 3rd S. 15, 1996, 245.

P. Hughes & A. Leech, *The Story of Worcester*, 2011.

S. Mainley & C. Crisp, *Plan of the City and Environs of Worcester*, 1828.

Charles Crisp, *Map of the City and Suburbs of Worcester according to the new Act of Parliament*, 1832.

(L) Worcester, Fort Royal

HER Ref: WCM96141 Postcode:WR5 1BT O.S. 25" Map No. 33.8 Date of Map: 1904

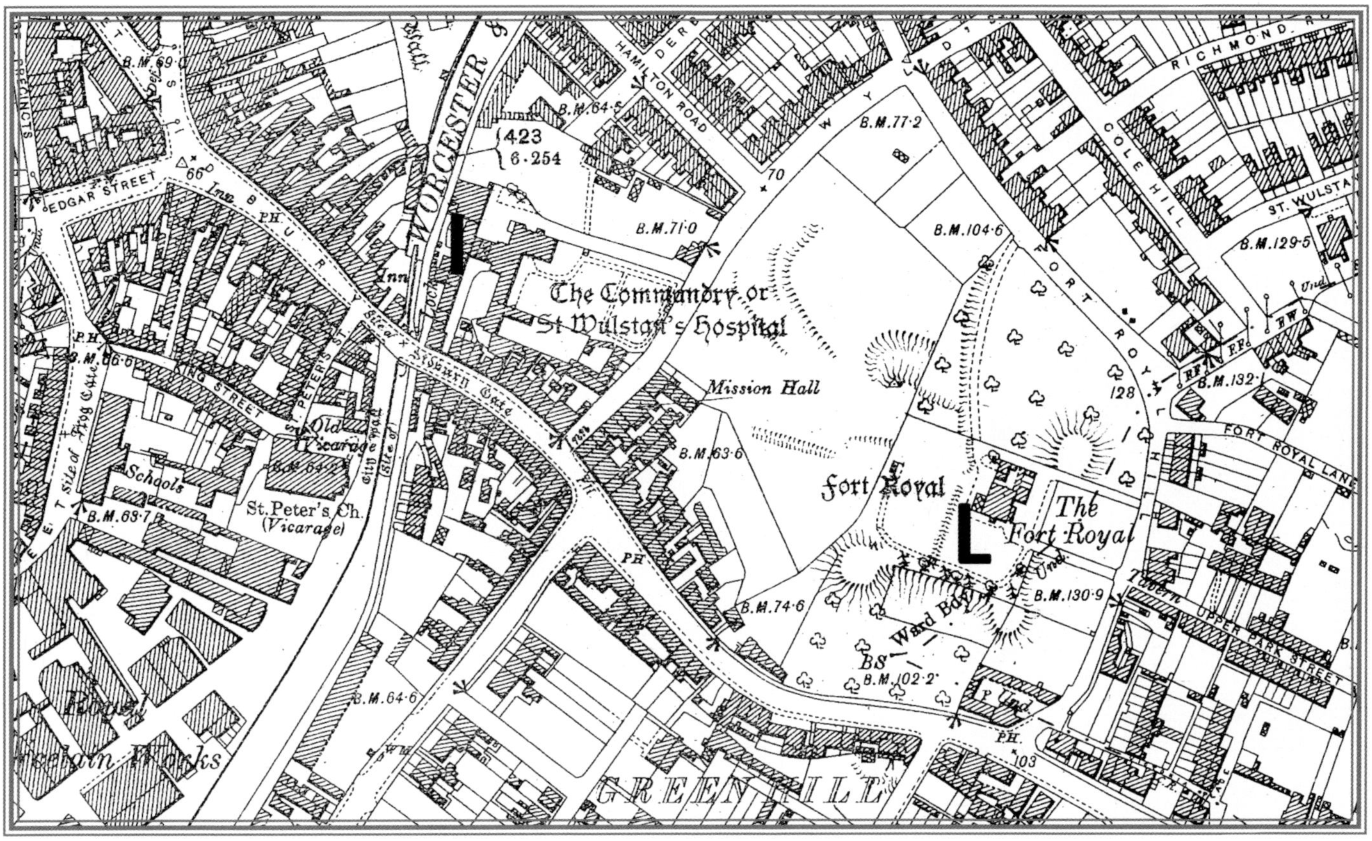

Fort Royal with all its Civil War associations has been used as a public space at least since the 18th century. The Royalist post was overrun by Parliament's troops in 1651 and the guns were then turned on the City. Some of the fortifications survive but are substantially eroded from the star-shaped bastions recorded on 18th century City maps such as George Young's of 1790 in Green (op. cit.). Coming down the hill to Wylde's Lane and the Commandery, a wide avenue of trees is shown on all 18th century maps. The *Traveller* circa 1800 (p. 130) describes the Royal Mount: "Above in the park is to be seen a great work of 4 bastions..." The 1837 *Directory* called this area the Park.

V. Green, *History and Antiquities of Worcester,* Vol. II, 1796.
J. Dugdale, *The New British Traveller,* 1819.

G. BAILEY, DEL. ET SC.

THE "FORT ROYAL" FROM ONE OF THE COMMANDERY WINDOWS.

Published by Littlebury & Company, The Worcester Press.

The "Fort Royal" from one of the Commandery Windows. Published by Littlebury & Company, The Worcester Press. © WAAS 22274.

(M) Worcester, Gheluvelt Park

HER Ref: WCM91085 Postcode:WR3 7AA Photo, Gheluvelt Park in 1936, courtesy of Francis Frith Collection.

Included within Historic England's Register of Historic Parks and Gardens of special historic interest in England.

Barbourne House (see above) and its grounds formed the basis of the public park Listed Grade II in 2015. Originating as a country house on the edge of the City, belonging to the Cookes family, it was sold to J. P. Lavender in 1838 and then by the Misses Lavender in 1881, to become a School and finally Barbourne College. The house and grounds are recorded in the 1902 6 inch OS.

The estate was purchased by the City for a Memorial Park in 1918 and the park was opened by Field Marshal Sir John French in 1922. It is now recognised as "a good and representative example" and as "a relatively rare landscape type, displaying a significant attention to layout, created ... by the noted local architect Alfred Hill Parker"; "the park has remained largely intact" (Historic England, op. cit.). The park covers 9.7 acres and is bounded by Lavender Road, Barbourne Lane and Waterworks Road.

The principal features include the 1919/1920 retirement homes sited on the north along Lavender Road, which extend the idea of a public amenity space. Notices attached to the Arch recorded that the " Homes for disabled Sailors and Soldiers were erected to commemorate the Battle of Gheluveldt in which the Worcestershire Regiment played a very distinguished part" (**Plate 26**).

The engagement of the 2nd Battalion on October 31st 1914 is celebrated in the park every year. The Memorial Arch (1924), a small-scale echo in brick and stone of the better-known memorials by Sir Edwin Lutyens and others in Belgium and Northern France, is derived ultimately from the tradition of the Roman triumphal arch.

The pool survives from the earlier fishpond but was not originally planned to be the site for the Bandstand which therefore required a bridge (1923). The Barbourne Brook continues to meander through the grounds but has been marshalled into a concrete channel; another watercourse runs along the north side of the park. A children's playground and 6 tennis courts were part of the original concept to which a putting green and a miniature railway were early additions. An army tank was placed in the centre of a large circular flower bed in the north-east corner of the park and remained there until 1940. Alderman Alfred Hill Parker was the driving force and overall designer of the park. William Crump, the head gardener at Madresfield is said to have given horticultural advice, presumably before he died in 1919. A Park Keeper's House and a building for the Sons of Rest were added in 1939 and 1953.

Parker's principal alteration to the 19th century grounds was to raise the level on the north side with 4 terraces as an amphitheatre to face the Bandstand (Historic England, op. cit.); this area has been modified over the years with planting and hard landscape. The planting today is made up of mature deciduous trees and younger specimen trees. The play area has been refreshed with new equipment and the striking Regimental War Memorial by Plincke Landscapes is a new and prominent feature in the south-east corner of the park (2010).

D. Lambert, "Memorial Parks of the First and Second World Wars", *Garden History*, 42, Supp. I, 2014, pp. 34-57.

C & T. Wardle, *The History of Barbourne,* 2007.

HE *Register of Parks & Gardens,* 2015.

Worcester City HER Monument Report, Gheluvelt Park, WCM96655.

(N) Worcester, Greyfriars House

HER Ref: WCM96466 Postcode:WR1 2LZ

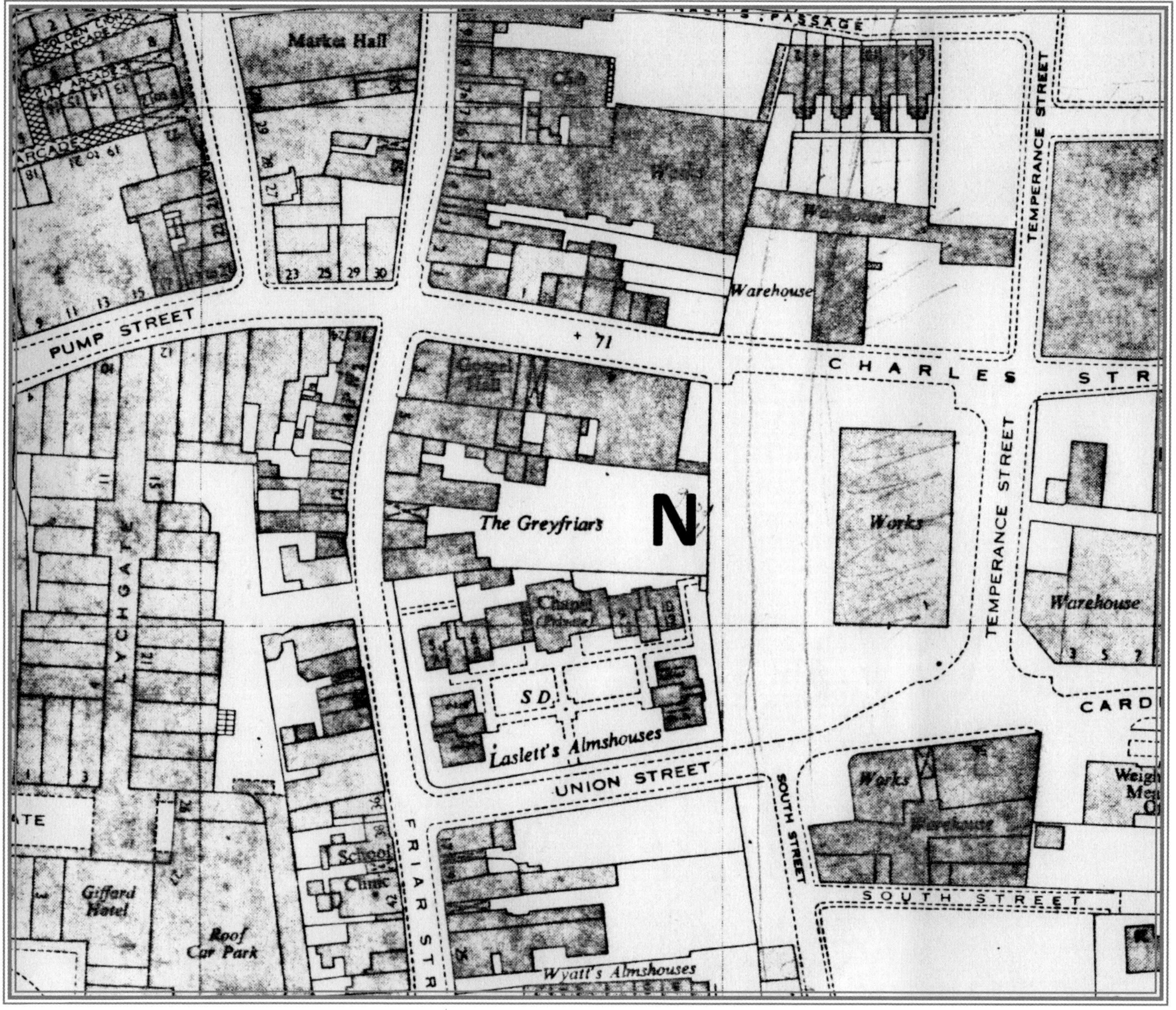

Demolition of buildings created a space for a garden up against the City Wall, which does not relate to the half-timbered building from the 1480's now thought to be a merchant house rather than anything to do with the Franciscan Friary. 18th century maps imply that gardens with houses in Friar Street extended across the City Wall ditch. The BoE (p. 743) notes "Beautiful enclosed garden re-created from 1955, with small brick summerhouse decidedly of the 1950's." This, like the Greyfriars itself, was the creation of Elsie and Matley Moore who gave their home to the National Trust.

Country Life, CXLVI, p. 1390.
A. Brooks & N. Pevsner, *Worcestershire,* 2007 (BoE).

Photo, J. Patton, 2019.

(O) Henwick Lodge

HER Ref: WCM91236. Postcode: WR2 5NZ. O.S. 25" Map No. 33.3. Date of Map: 1884.

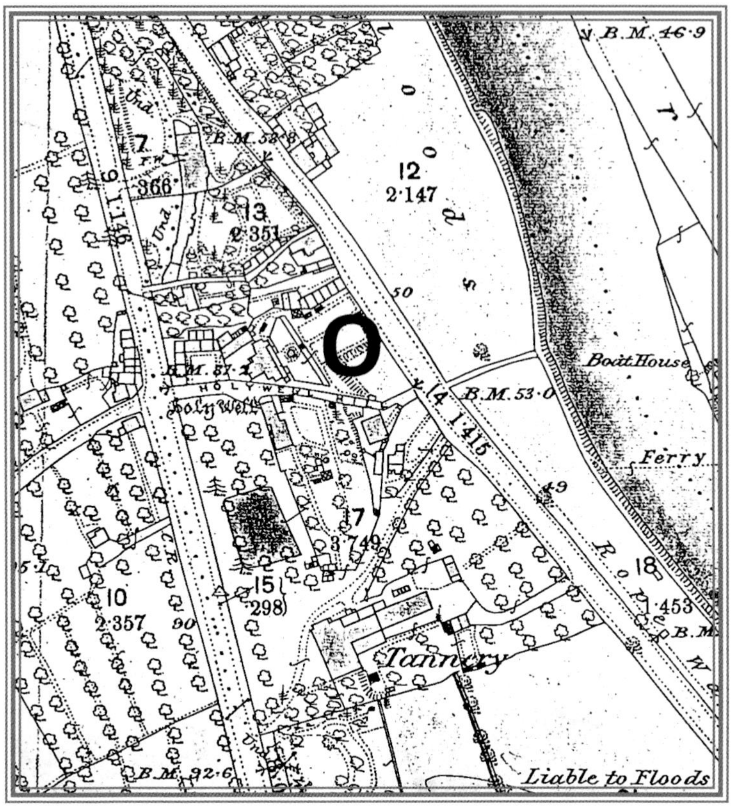

Henwick Lodge was the name given by John Doharty junior to a house advertised for let or sale in 1746 as recently built, with a cold bath and convenient for water for business use, e.g. for a distiller, tanner or skinner, or for a gentleman of considerable fortune (Smith, op. cit.). Crisp's 1832/3 printed map plots a brewery (which had become a tannery on the 1902 OS 1:2500) by the south-west corner of the gardens on a lane that connected the upper and the lower roads. These maps which define the site of Henwick Lodge and its once, elaborate gardens, agree with 2 drawings of them made by John Doharty junior in 1747 (WAAS 5403/3) and 1755 (Powell-Cotton Museum, Quex Park). Smith (op. cit.) identified the site as at Tripleton Cottage and 1, Holywell Hill with the gardens east of the Henwick Road and south of Holywell Hill Lane. The lane, no longer continuous, formed the boundary on the south side.

House and gardens lay in the south-east quadrant of a cross roads formed by the Oldbury Road, Henwick Road and Holywell Hill Lane. A field, still undeveloped in 1902 on the west side is now developed with houses along the Henwick Road. It is not clear if this field went with Henwick Lodge in the mid-18th century. House and gardens occupied a narrow terrace at the point at which the ground slopes down to the Hylton Road (the Ludlow Road in 1747/55). By 1902, a terrace of houses had been developed along the Hylton Road towards the Bridge. Open grounds remain between these developments.

The illustration of Henwick Lodge on the edge of a *Map of the Manor of Hallow*, 1747 can have been of interest only to the surveyor rather than the client. The 1755 drawing was made as part of a review of family assets made after Dougharty senior's death and which included the Diglis Pleasures Grounds. The 1747 garden was divided by paths into 6 compartments; the 1755 garden had more than twice as many divisions some identified as kitchen garden and nurseries for trees or plants, and specifying apple, pear and mulberry trees. The Spring Well (? Holy Well) is shown on the terrace close to the Lodge with a conduit house on its south end and a conduit (another candidate for the Holy Well) on the north end on Holywell Hill Lane. Two pyramids are illustrated in the garden, an old-fashioned feature found at other Dougharty sites, certainly on College Green and probably at Hartlebury Castle. The 1747 drawing shows the neighbour, 'Tripleton' (Holywell House) the other side of Holywell Hill lane as having a terraced garden sloping down to the river with pavilions attached to the upper terrace. This house is only roughly indicated in the drawing of 1755 when much more is made of the 2 storeyed Henwick Lodge itself. The latter was designed with large windows on the river front and a gazebo on the roof; a rather Chinese look is probably unintentional.

It is not clear from maps how long the Henwick Lodge gardens survived, but their development from formal to less formal in mid-century is already indicated in Doharty's drawings. General planting of trees or shrubs is all that can be gleaned from the Mainley-Crisp map of 1828 (WAAS 4120/144) or Crisp's printed City map of 1832 (WAAS 3901/2). The latter makes a feature of the fall of the land towards the Severn.

B. S. Smith, "The Dougharty Family, 18th century Mapmakers", *Worcs. Archaeol. Soc., Trans.*, 3rd Series, Vol. 15, 1996.

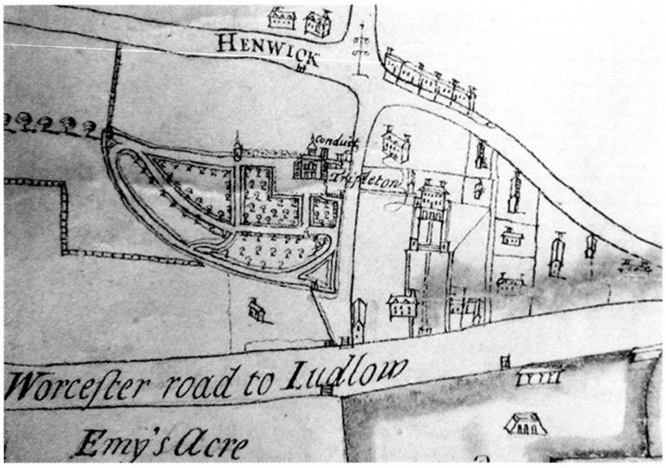

John Doharty junior, Henwick Lodge, from *Map of the Manor of Hallow*, 1747. © WAAS 5303/3.

(P) Worcester, Perdiswell Park

HER Ref: WCM91044 Postcode:WR3 7SN O.S. 25" Map No. 28.16 Date of Map: 1889

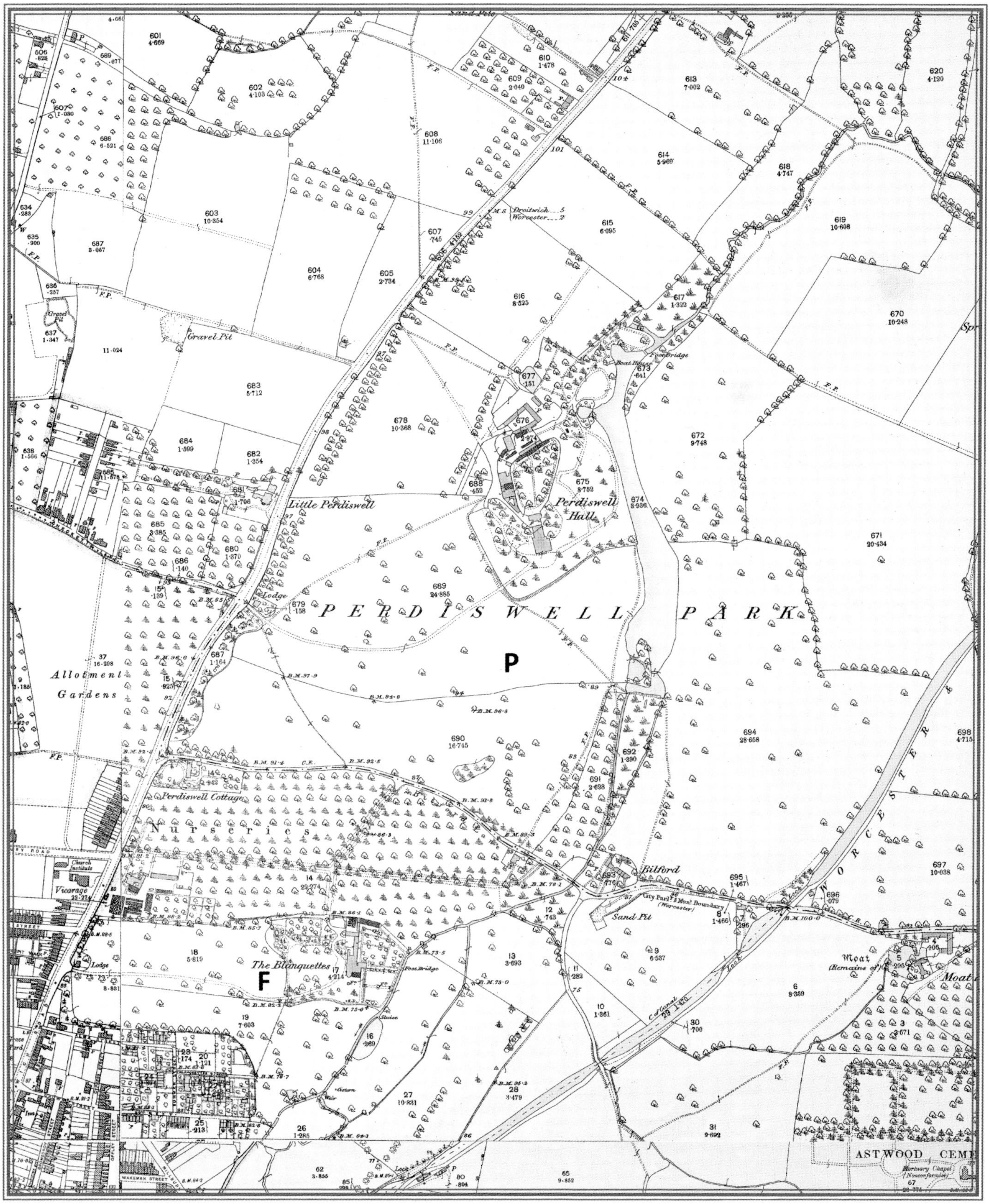

Perdiswell Park

..........continued from previous page

The residence designed by George Byfield in 1787-8 is noticed by Tunnicliff in 1788 and the gate piers decorated with Coade stone reliefs of *Agriculture* and *Navigation* on the Worcester Road are of that date. The latter was the main entrance to the mansion and its park. The *Beauties* in 1810 (p. 164) comment on the "sidescreens, background of luxurious plantations laid out with considerable taste ... though yet in their infancy." Paterson in 1829 (p. 413) is more expansive: "This is an elegant modern edifice composed of free-stone and approached from the road by a gateway of light and pleasing proportions, ornamented with medallions representing Plenty and Commerce by symbolical illustrations of agriculture and navigation. The grounds by which the mansion is surrounded, are laid out in a style of corresponding elegance, profusely embellished with luxuriant plantations, and although a dead flat, have been made to present a pleasing appearance."

The 1883 6 inch OS gives the west boundary of the park as the Worcester-Droitwich Road, the south boundary as Bilford Lane and the Worcester-Birmingham Canal as the east boundary at its southern end. The north-east section of the park had been pulled back closer to the east side of the lake which received the Barbourne Brook and which together formed the principal landscape feature. The 1930 OS shows planting along the Worcester-Droitwich road and on the west side of the fish pond as on the 1813 survey for the first OS one inch.

Some of the features of the park as defined in 1813 and 1930 can in fact be traced back to John Doharty junior's map of 1751 (WAAS 5403/10) including the planting along the Worcester-Droitwich road and the drive from this road to the house which had an avenue and gates. There was also planting west of the barns and pools. Doharty shows other features not retained later such as a walled or fenced forecourt at the end of the drive to the house, with gate piers and urns and an avenue behind the house leading to some pieces of formal water as well as pools. There was an orchard south-east of the house.

Gwilliam describes the mid-19th century situation when the property was let to A. C. Sheriff, M.P., and the grounds were open to the public. "There were several charming walks through the grounds and its beauties were captured by a number of local artists" (p. 137).

The Perdiswell Estate began to be dismembered by a sale in 1876 (WAAS 5240/7) and the mansion was demolished in 1956 after a fire. The large walled garden was invaded by office blocks in the early-21st century; the latter are set partially outside and partially inside the garden and dwarf remaining sections of wall and the attached Stables. There is further large-scale development taking place immediately to the north of this central group of buildings which has replaced the heart of the estate.

The 1930 OS shows the growing sports use of the park grounds, e.g. the old Wigornians's cricket pitch south-west of the Hall. Allotments and a golfing range now occupy the park along the Droitwich Road and leisure activities have been developed along the entrance drive and the Bilford Road.

The 1930 sports field, briefly converted to a park-and-ride car park, is now intended for school use, close to Perdiswell Primary School. East of this is the Leisure Centre with indoor swimming pool and facilities to serve the soccer pitches immediately to the north which are bounded by the Canal. This open area makes up one recognisable section of the original park and today's public park.

The other park-like area is the open landscape east of the mansion which has a heath-like atmosphere and apart from open "common", has some rather hap-hazard modern planting and two lines of conifers set at right angles to each other, perhaps relics of the 2nd World War when the park was used as an airfield.

The shrubberies on the north side of the Hall, now unmaintained, once extended to the north end of the vanished Fish Pond and its Boathouse (OS 1905 and 1930) and now link with a dell around the Barbourne Brook at the point that it vanishes underground to run unremarked from north-east to south-west.

H. W. Gwilliam, *Old Worcester, People and Places,* 1977.
HWGT Newsletter 14, Winter 2000.
A. Brooks & N. Pevsner, *Worcestershire,* 2007 (BoE).
Paterson's Roads, 1829.
W. Tunnicliff, *A Survey of the County of Worcester,* 1788.
Beauties of England and Wales, Vol XV, 1814.

The surviving stable block, 2019. Photo, R. Lockett.

(Q) Worcester, Pitchcroft

HER Ref: WCM96637 Postcode:WR1 3JW O.S. 25" Map No. 33.3 Date of Map: 1904

Pitchcroft

..........continued from previous page

Although Pitchcroft has never been either a public park in the modern sense or an area used historically as a public space such as Sansome Fields, it was regarded in some senses as a common from medieval times. "Although Worcester seems to have had common fields early in its life, their only survival by the sixteenth century was Pitchcroft ... The citizens were mostly interested in Pitchcroft, as pasture for their horses and the stock owned by butchers, supplemented by pasture fields at a greater distance ..." (Dyer, p. 17). In the 18th and into the 19th century, Pitchcroft was advertised through City and County guidebooks as one of the areas for "genteel" promenading.

From 1718, Pitchcroft was occasionally used for horse racing, as it is today. In the early-19th century when the adjoining Pound Fields were being developed, potential buyers were advised that the use of the north end of the racecourse was by agreement. The first permanent grandstand was erected in 1781-2 (Wardle, p. 165). By 1837 there were two race meetings a year, in August and November. These were major social events for which temporary stalls etc. were erected. *The Corporation Properties Survey* of 1794 (surveyed by J. Aird in 1784) (WAAS 9360) shows the grandstand sited on the river bank more or less in its present position with the grounds stretching down to the Bridge, all on land owned by the Dean and Chapter; racing "furniture" consisted of a thatched booth beside the grandstand, a winning (umpire's) chair, and a corporation booth to the south end of the course. The grandstand has been rebuilt several times, most recently in 1975 (Wardle, pp. 165-6).

As today, Pitchcroft has in the past hosted other events such as mustering of the Worcestershire Yeomanry (some troops can be seen drilling in Nash's "North View ... from the Porto Bello" (op. cit.) or in 1824 the fight between Tom Spring and Jack Langan for the All England Bare Knuckle Boxing Championship said to have attracted 40,000 people (Wardle, op. cit.). The Worcester Rowing Club, founded in 1874, is the other resident on the river bank.

A. D. Dyer, *The City of Worcester in the Sixteenth Century,* 1973.
C. & T. Wardle, *The History of Barbourne,* 2007.
C. Pitt, *Pitchcroft: 300 Years of Racing in Worcester,* 2018.
T. R. Nash, *Collections for the History of Worcestershire,* Vol II, 1782.
D. Whitehead, *The Book of Worcester,* 1976.

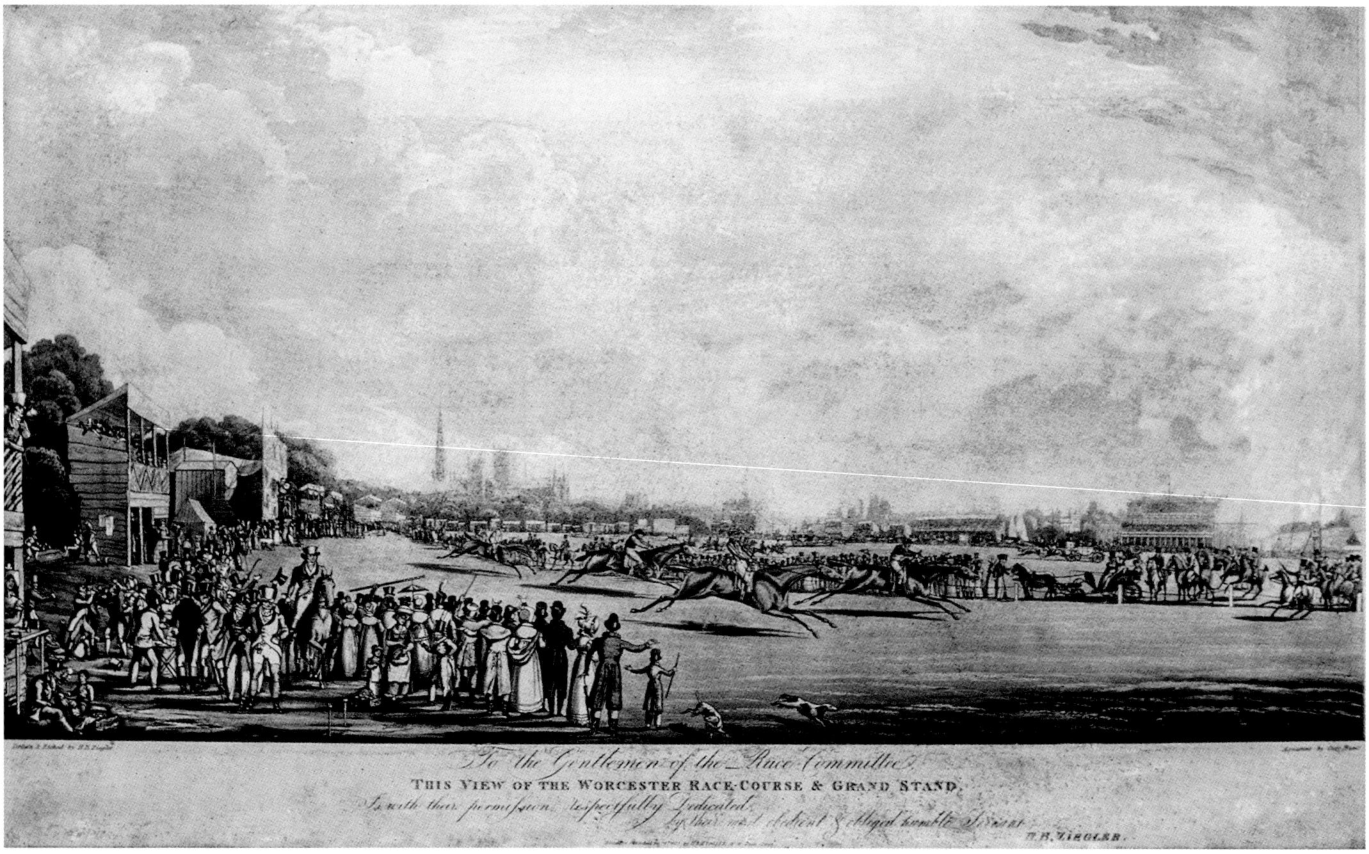

View of Worcester Race Courses & Grandstand. Drawn & Etched by H. M. Zugler. Courtesy of Clive Haynes (Changing Face of Worcester).

(R) Worcester, Pitmaston House

HER Ref: WCM98915 Postcode:WR2 4ZF O.S. 25" Map No. 33.7 Date of Map: 1888

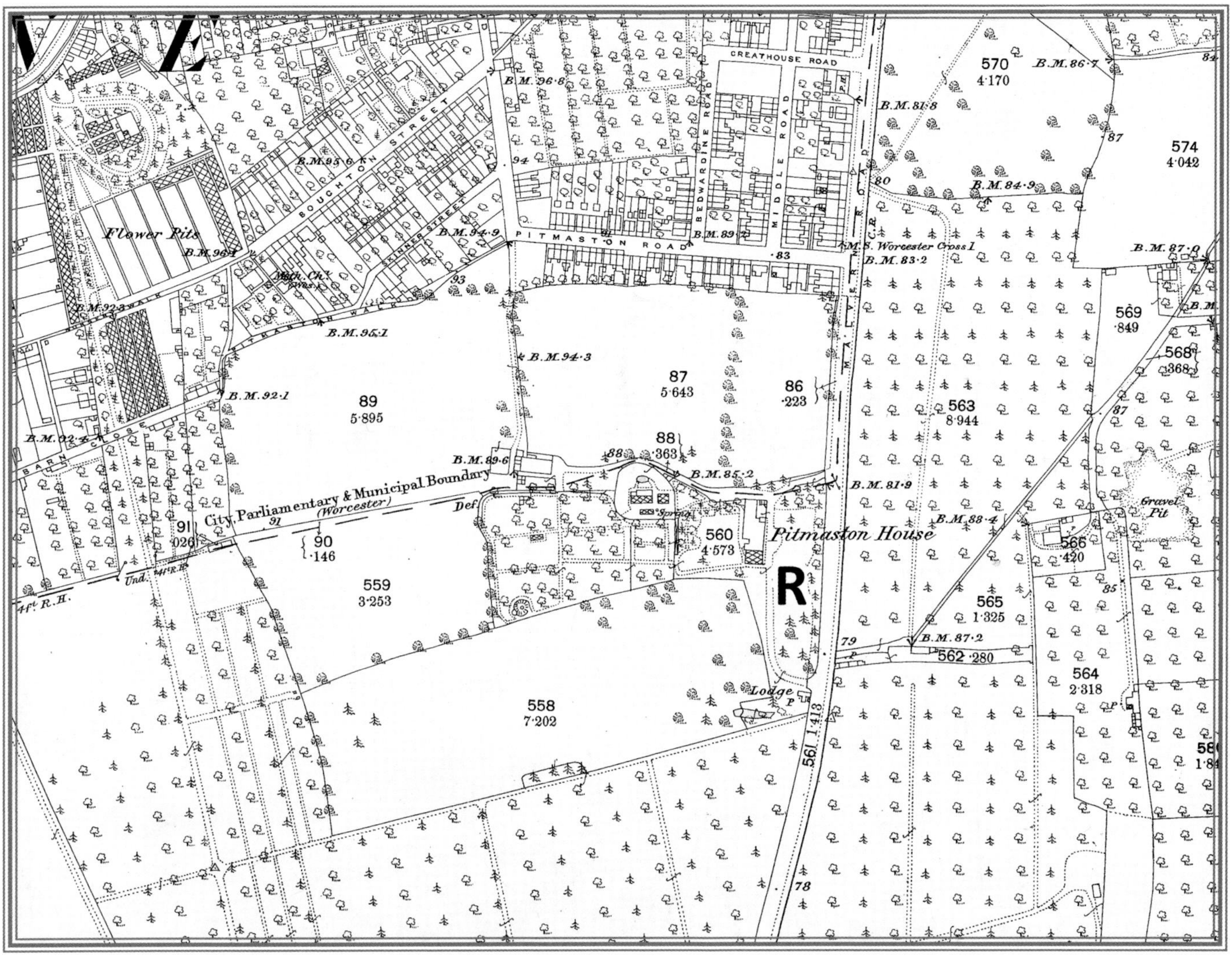

Pitmaston House on the Bromwich Road with ice-house and lodge to its south, Vernon Park on its north side and comfortably set within fields, can be seen with small grounds on the 1930 OS. A tower and the ice-house "were destroyed about 1945" (Gwilliam, p. 189). Not much had changed since the first OS in 1888.

The BoE (p. 775) dates the house to the early-19th century, gothicised in the 1830s and with a large, Gothick, Coade stone conservatory. The house is shown on Charles Crisp's 1832 Worcester City map. The grounds are now largely taken up with the Pitmaston Primary School and Vernon Park. Vernon Park was put up for sale in 37 lots in 1894 (WAAS 438).

Pitmaston is first mapped on the OS one inch in 1828 and, as a residence of John Williams, is noticed by the *Cambrian Traveller* in 1813 and by Greenwood's County map of 1822. Mylechreest (op. cit.) says that Williams moved to Pitmaston House circa 1803 and learned "the deliberate breeding of cultivated plants from Thomas Andrew Knight of Downton Castle in about 1807". His commercial success is marked by his appointment as High Sheriff in 1823. Williams is listed as one of the subscribers to William Dean's *Hortus Croomensis* in 1824 as J. Williams Esq., F. H. S., Sherrif, Pitmarston (sic). He was celebrated for developing new varieties of fruit including the Pitmaston Duchess Pear, Pitmaston Golden Wreath apple and the Pitmaston Champagne Gooseberry. "An interest in climate led to experiments on controlling the environment of the conservatory at Pitmaston House for growing grapes" (Mylechreest op.cit.). The walls of the fruit garden remained complete until the 1950's (Gwilliam, p. 189).

H. W. Gwilliam, *Old Worcester People and Places*, 1977.
M. Mylechreest, "John Williams of Pitmaston, Worcester", *Worcester Civic Society Newsletter*, Summer 2016, 10, Issue 1.
A. Brooks & N. Pevsner, *Worcestershire*, 2007 (BoE).

(S) Worcester, Pleasure Grounds

HER Ref: WCM91116 Postcode: WR1 1NB area Sale Particulars, 1864. © WAAS 372/1.

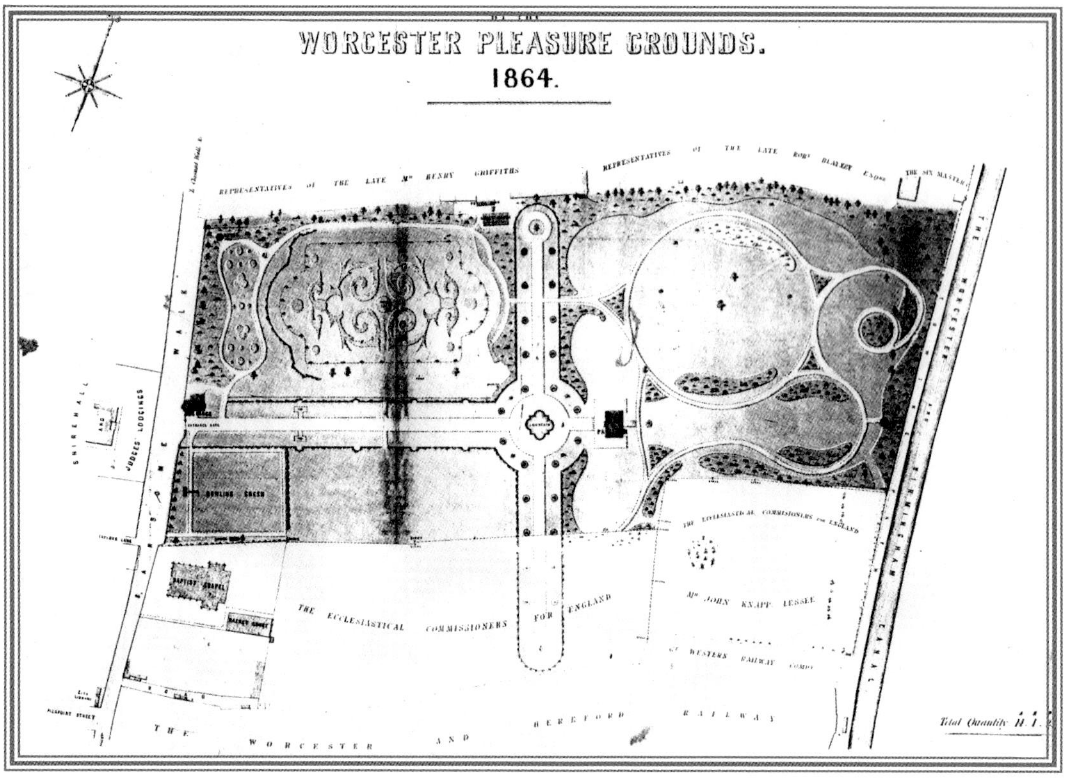

The Worcester Pleasure Grounds occupied part of the site of the Sansome Fields promenades as recorded by street names such as Chestnut Walk. Sansome Fields lost their semi-public status when the estate of Sir Trubshaw Withers (ob, 1804) was auctioned in 1811. Thomas Blayney donated Sansome Walk itself to the City in 1815. The Worcester Public Pleasure Grounds Company was set up in 1857 (Covins op. cit.) and the Arboretum Pleasure Grounds were opened in 1859 with one free day's admission a week (Grundy op. cit.). The lay-out was based on a cross with an elaborate fountain in the centre; one lawn was given over to broderie parterres and another to serpentine walks. The company was bankrupt by 1864 when the grounds were put up for sale (WAAS 372/1) and acquired by the Worcester Engine Company with the intention of developing the site with houses and industry. The 1864 sale particulars show an entrance lodge (surviving, illus. Covins, p. 87), pavilion, dwelling house (lodge), a noble terrace, walks, large central fountain, ornamental glass pavilion, bowling green, archery grounds and lawns "and a tastefully laid out Panelled Garden. The grounds are adorned with specimens of scarce evergreens and shrubs and magnificent horse-chestnut, elm and other forest trees ... laid out by the eminent Landscape Gardener, Mr. Wm. Barrow of Elvaston." The principal entrance gates were moved to the Worcester Royal Infirmary.

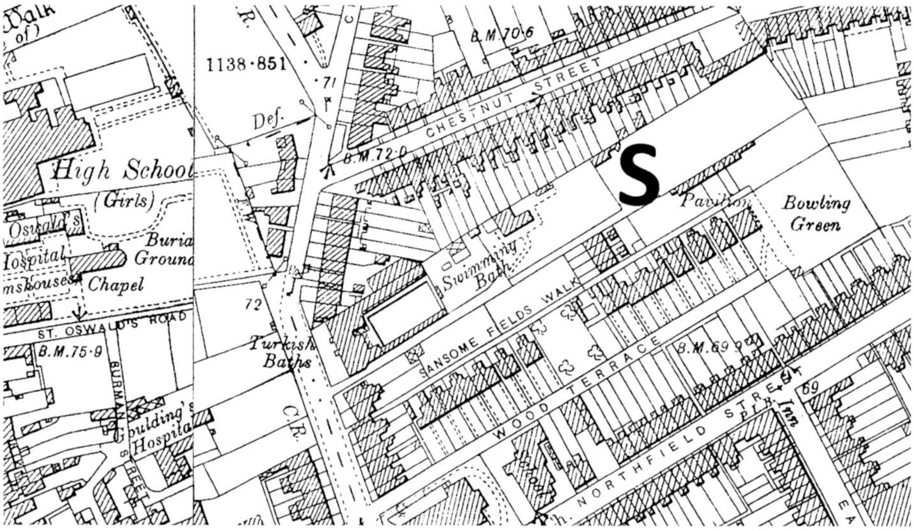

O.S. 25" Map No. 33.3, 33.4 Date of Maps: both 1904

M. Grundy, *Worcester's Memory Lane,* 1987.
F. Covins, *The Arboretum Story,* 1989.

(T) Worcester, Porto Bello Gardens

HER Ref: WCM91088. Postcode:WR2 5PL area. O.S. 25" Map No. 33.3. Date of Map: 1884.

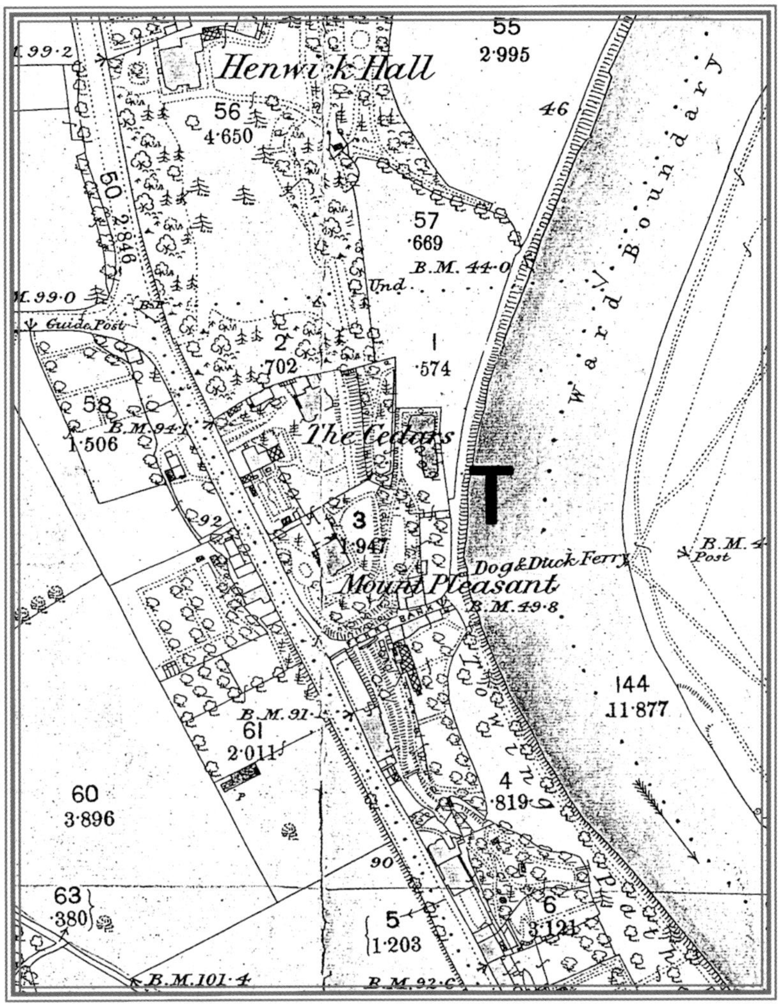

Among 4 views of Worcester illustrating Nash's second volume in 1782 (op. cit.), is one taken "from the Porto Bello Henwick Hill". A gentleman, seated on a gravelled terrace taking tea, contemplates the City across Pitchcroft. Cooke, circa 1800, mentions the "lately established public gardens, which are much frequented during the summer months; from their beautiful situation near the river, they have been called the Porto Bello Gardens" (op. cit., p. 70). Lord Torrington in 1781 had described the same: "opposite are Bird's Gardens at Henwick Hill (a bread and butter manufactory) to which we cross'd the ferry; whence is the best view of the town, and the adjacent country" (Brun Andrews, op. cit.). In 1794, the proprietor advertised Public Breakfasts (Hayes, op. cit.). In 1809, at the start of a 40 year lease, the premises were described as a public house and garden and, despite a puff from Dugdale in 1819 (op. cit.), the gardens were already in decline.

In 1854 the Hallow Parish Charity granted a 99 year lease in return for residential redevelopment which became The Cedars. Gaynor Hayes (op. cit.) has traced the history of the site and its charitable ownership back to 1618, which only came to an end in 1955! The entrance to the Porto Bello was at the south-west corner of the grounds of Henwick Hall as illustrated on a plan of the Hall estate by Samuel Barnett in 1848 (WAAS 385/1). The Porto Bello Gardens extended along the Henwick Road (redeveloped with Nos. 220-224) and across King Stephen's Mount/Mount Pleasant (also redeveloped) to a boundary at Ferry Bank lane. Plans with the 1856 lease by Webb & Buck (WAAS 850 Hallow) suggest that Nash's terrace was half way down the garden on the edge of the slope towards the river.

Leases in 1853-4 (WAAS 850 Hallow) refer to house, garden and ferry. The Ferry House is marked on a map of 1777 by George Young (WAAS 1691/43). The Mainley-Crisp City plan of 1828 (WAAS 4120/144) shows the Porto Bello as partly divided up, with the ferry point at the foot of the lane and the paths on Pitchcroft converging towards it. Much of the site remains undeveloped today.

The North View of the CITY of WORCESTER, *from the Porto Bello Henwick Hill.*

Porto Bello from T. R. Nash, *Collections for the History of Worcestershire*, Vol II, 1782.

G. Hayes, *'The Cedars, a Property with a Past'*, Report to Birmingham University, 1998. un. pub.

G. A. Cooke, *Topographical and Statistical Description of the Co. of Worcester,* circa 1801.

H. W. Gwilliam, *Old Worcester, People and Places,* 1993.

P. Hughes and A. Leech, *The Story of Worcester,* 2011.

T. R. Nash, *Collections for the History of Worcestershire,* 2 vols., 1781-2.

D. Whitehead, *The Book of Worcester,* 1976.

C. Bruyn Andrews (ed.), *The Torrington Diaries: Tour to the West,* 1781, 1954.

J. Dugdale, *The New British Traveller,* 1819.

S. Mainley & C. Crisp, *Plan of the City and Environs of Worcester,* 1828.

(U) Worcester, Rose Hill

HER Ref: WCM98664 Postcode: WR5 1BU O.S. 25" Map No. 33.8 Date of Map: 1904

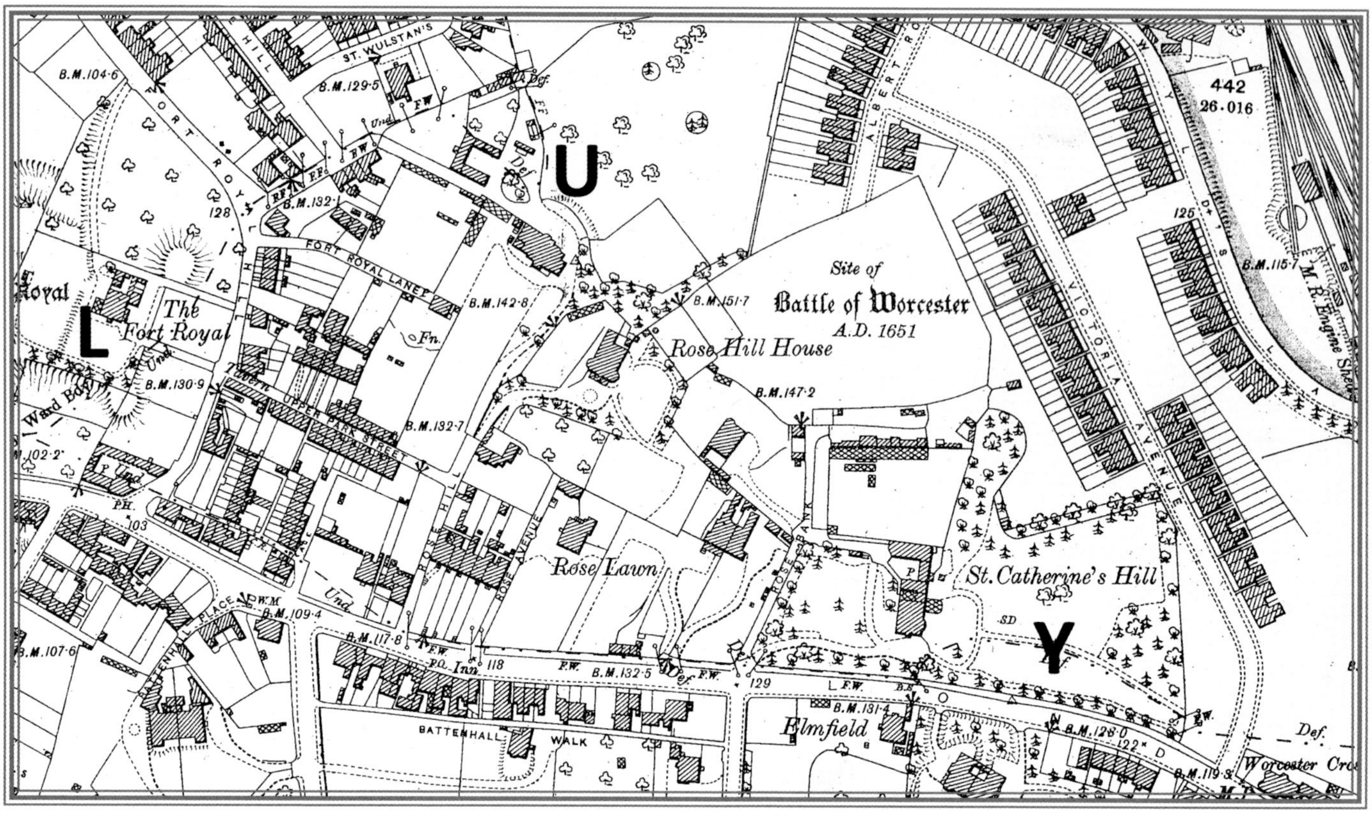

Rose Hill is the adjoining property, immediately west of Rose Hill House. Rose Hill was known as Rose Hill Cottage in 1827 and Rose Hill Villa in 1839 when sold by Geo. Munn, Esq. as "an elegant Italian double-fronted villa erected within a few years" when it was advertised with a number of other buildings such as coach house and stables, cow-house, pig sties ... the latter suggestive of a small farm. The site lying to the east of Fort Royal Hill was composed of fields and orchards mostly in small plots except for a 10 acre field (The Clay Pits) leased in 1839 from Christchurch College, Oxford, which had been granted Commandery lands at the Dissolution of the Monasteries circa 1540 (Napthan, op. cit.). By 1891 this could be sold with the rest of the property and represented a small park with a tennis lawn close to the house. This was called Meadow in 1839 and Pasture in 1891 and today contains the Fort Royal Community Primary School. Other buildings on the north-west side in 1891, such as the Stables and Dog Kennels survive as rebuilt or replaced. The house itself has returned to residential use.

The history of the site is probably characteristic of the buying up of parcels of land to create small, urban villas. This one, more modest than its neighbour, St. Catherine's Hill, probably grew out of the older Rose Hill House which had extensive gardens including a "large plantation of Roses used in medicine" belonging to Richard Birlingham before 1800 (Napthan op. cit.). There is a plan surveyed by J. G. Jones in 1809 showing the lots from which Rose Hill was developed (WAAS 385) beginning with the residence built by John Malpas around 1813 which by an 1827 sale had a developed garden. In a subsequent sale in 1839 the gardens are advertised: "From the south-west front is a raised portico ornamented with iron railing, which opens to a sloping Lawn and Flower Garden, belted by Plantations of Shrubs and Evergreens; a large kitchen garden immediately adjoins, nearly surrounded by lofty walls, clothed with the choicest of fruit trees."

The 1827 plan shows all this and the access from the London Road as beginning with a carriage drive shared with that of Rose Hill House until it separates at two gates to the individual properties. There was a small turning area by the north front with a ha-ha separating the front from the field described above. A small slip of garden with summer-house to the east abutted the boundary of Rose Hill House itself. The "Garden" immediately on the south-west corner of the house seems too small to be "a large and productive kitchen garden immediately adjoins, mainly surrounded by lofty walls, clothed with the choicest of fruit trees". The rest of the garden extended south to Upper Park Street with a small pond towards the bottom of the "Lawn" with "Plantations" either side - all on a small scale. This lay-out remained the skeleton of the garden until the break-up of the property in 1891. An 1860's plan shows the south front garden descending from a terrace

..........continued from previous page

to a lawn, to a parterre and to a lower garden with steps on either side. Much of the garden south of Rose Hill has gone to car parking and residential development.

The 1827 details refer to a "large and very productive GARDEN, walled in, let to a respectable tenant at £10 per annum". The location of the 1827/1839 kitchen gardens close to the house is puzzling since the present Walled Garden (6 Rose Terrace) was not added to the Rose Hill estate until 1879/80 (Napthan) since when it evidently developed into something close in form to that shown in 1891 and that being restored today. (The 1839 Tithe Plan shows the borders of the garden and 3 separate plots within them: two gardens and one orchard). The Walled Garden was acquired by Will and Julia Scott in 1995 who, with some planting advice from Maggie Knowles, have continued to restore this rare, urban survival. Structures surviving from the 1880-1891 period are 2 vineries (one restored) and perhaps the original red Black Madresfield and the white Muscat of Alexandria grapes, a melon pit and the base of an astronomical observatory (Will Scott). The 1891 sale particulars detail: Tool House, Early Vinery, Late Vinery, Stove and Greenhouse, Potting Shed and Boiler House, Soil Shed, Early and Late Peach House many of which had been fitted with the latest technical improvements for heating and ventilation by Boulton & Paul of Norwich. The melon pits are "Green House" on the 1891 plan within the garden and the Stove House and Vinery are situated on the outside of the east wall by the main house.

The 1891 plan shows another kitchen garden opening out of the 10 acre Pasture (and containing the cow sheds), and behind the Stables. This walled garden would not be shown on the earlier sale plans being leasehold at the time but it might date back to gardens belonging to Rose Hill House prior to the development of Rose Hill Villa/ Rose Hill.

M. Napthan, *The Walled Garden, Rose Terrace, Rose Hill, Worcester: Archaeological Programme of Works*, 2008, unpub.

M. Knowles, *19th century Walled Garden to 21st century Herb Garden,* 2008, unpub.

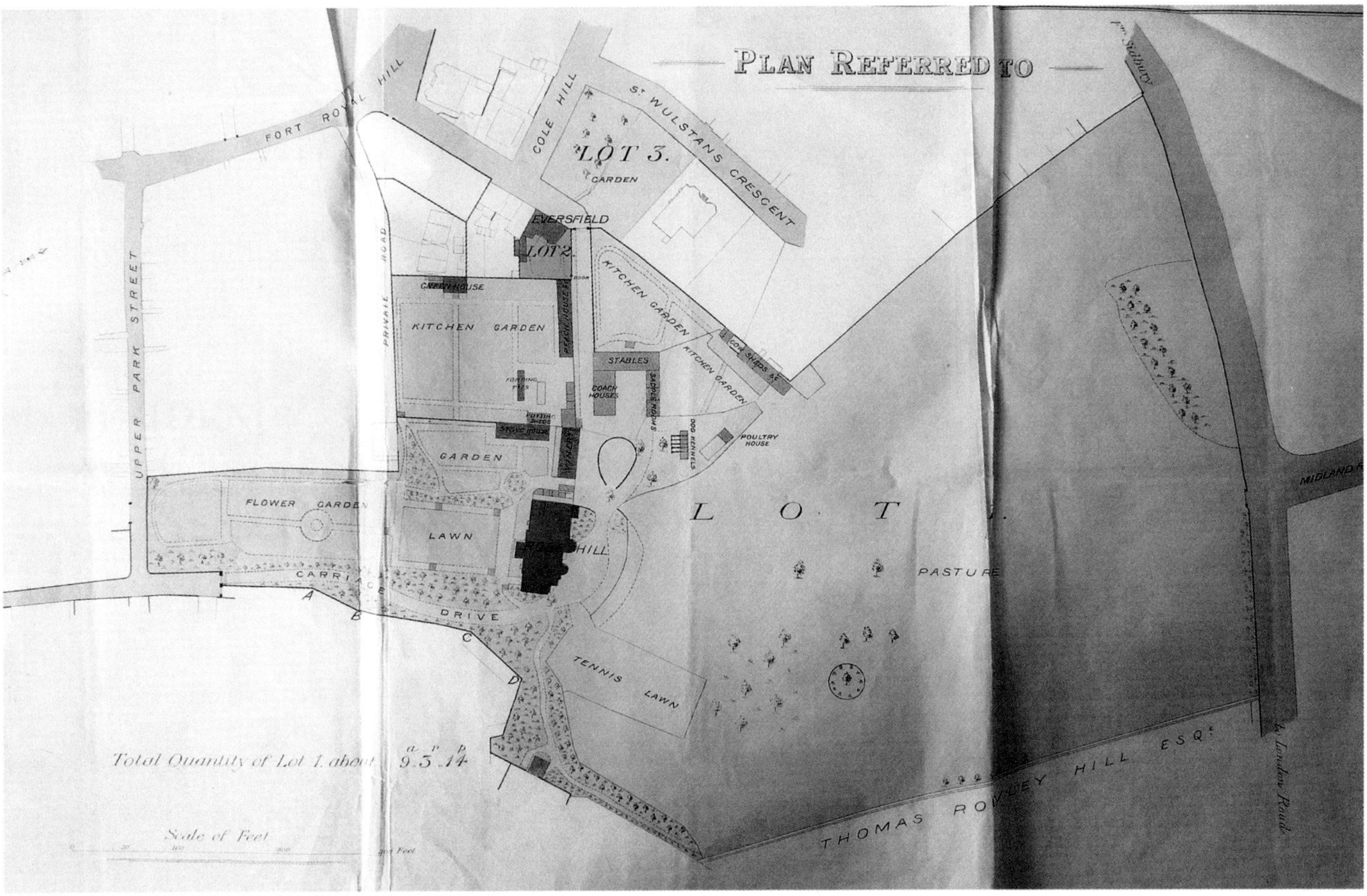

Sale particulars, 1891.

(V) Worcester, Royal Infirmary

HER Ref: WCM96077 Postcode:WR1 3AS area O.S. 25" Map No. 33.3, 33.4 Date of Maps: both 1904

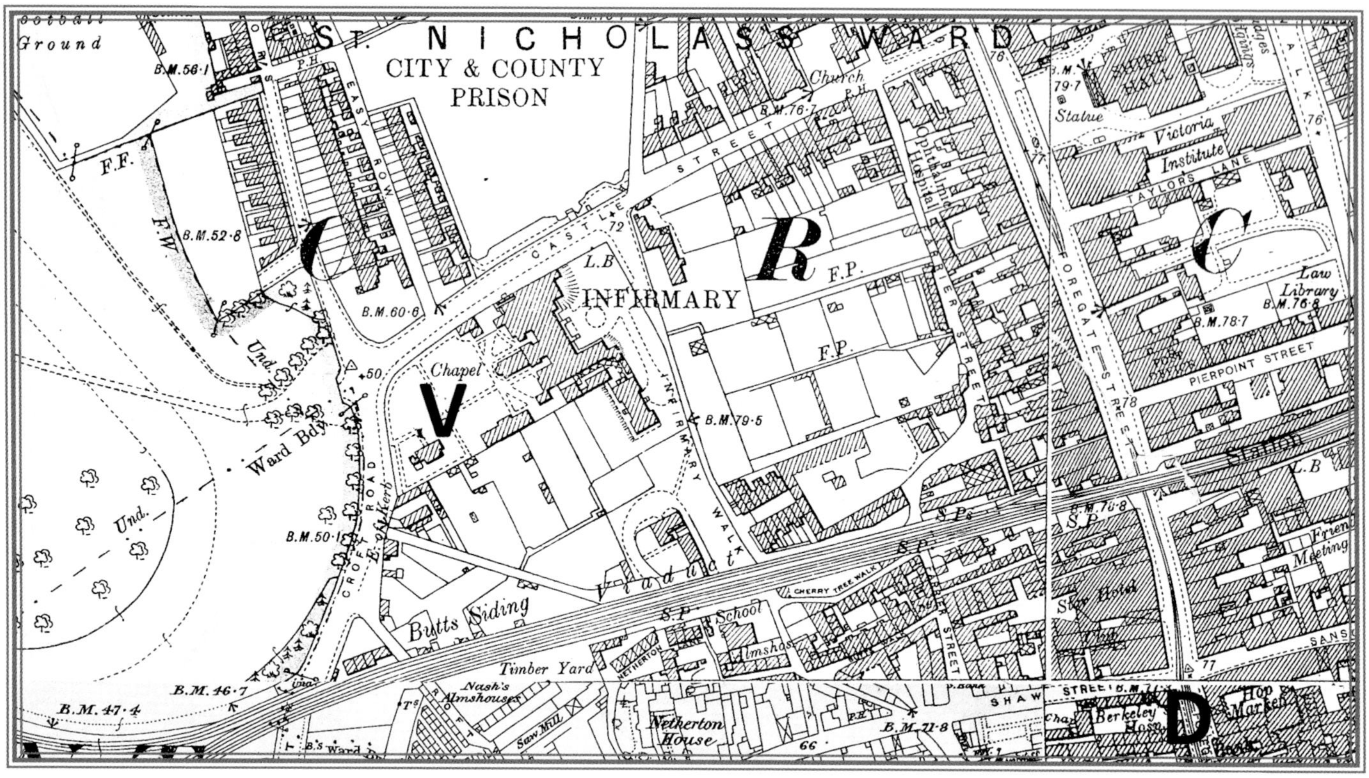

The Royal Infirmary was built by subscription in 1766-70 and designed by Anthony Keck, responsible for several other houses included in the *Survey* for their gardens: Bevere House, Ham Court and Middle Hill. The Infirmary gardens were laid out by Samuel Wheeler in 1775-6 (Whitehead, correspondence) on a green field outside the line of the City Wall on Salt Lane which connected the River with the Tything and Foregate Street. This area is labelled as "The new plantations" on the very small-scale map in Green's *Survey of the City of Worcester* published in 1764, also known as the Artichoke Field. The gardens, laid out geometrically to the west and south of the Infirmary, are shown on George Young's Map of 1779 and on a lesser scale in Vol. 2 of Nash's *History* (1782). A watercolour by E. F. Burney shows plain lawns either side of the gravel path and semi-circle to the stepped entrance to the Infirmary (WAAS 2432). The grounds were surrounded either by low brick walls and iron railings or with high brick walls.

The gardens were bounded on two sides by Salt Lane (Infirmary Road later New Road) and Infirmary Walk and, to the south, the grounds of Walnut House, roughly on the line of the Railway Viaduct built in 1860. Hughes and Leech (p. 149) illustrate a plan of circa 1824 with a detail of the garden on the corner of Salt Lane and New Road laid out with a square of paths and the quarters further divided by trees into 8 compartments.

The gardens can be followed in the Worcester maps of Samuel Mainley of 1822 (WAAS 10776/1),and Mainley & Crisp of 1828 (WAAS 4120/144) and Charles Crsp of 1832 (WAAS 3901/2).

In the 1860's, the Infirmary was extended and gates to Infirmary Walk were acquired from the Worcester Pleasure Grounds, a short-lived commercial venture of the same decade. Hughes and Leech show the grounds apparently full of mature trees by the end of the 19th century (p. 180). The land to the south of the Infirmary gardens, including those of Walnut House, were broken up into small plots in the late-19th and early-20th centuries All of the ground between Castle Street, Infirmary Walk and the Railway Viaduct has or will be redeveloped for the University of Worcester.

P. Hughes & A. Leech, *The Story of Worcester*, 2011.

T. R. Nash, *Collections for the History of Worcestershire*, Vol II, 1782.

S. Mainley & C. Crisp, *Plan of the City and Environs of Worcester*, 1828.

Charles Crisp, *Map of the City and Suburbs of Worcester according to the new Act of Parliament*, 1832.

(W) Worcester, Sansome House & Fields

HER Ref: WCM96654. Postcode: WR1 1NU.

George Young's map from Valentine Green's *The History and Antiquities of the City and Suburbs of Worcester,* Vol. II, 1796.

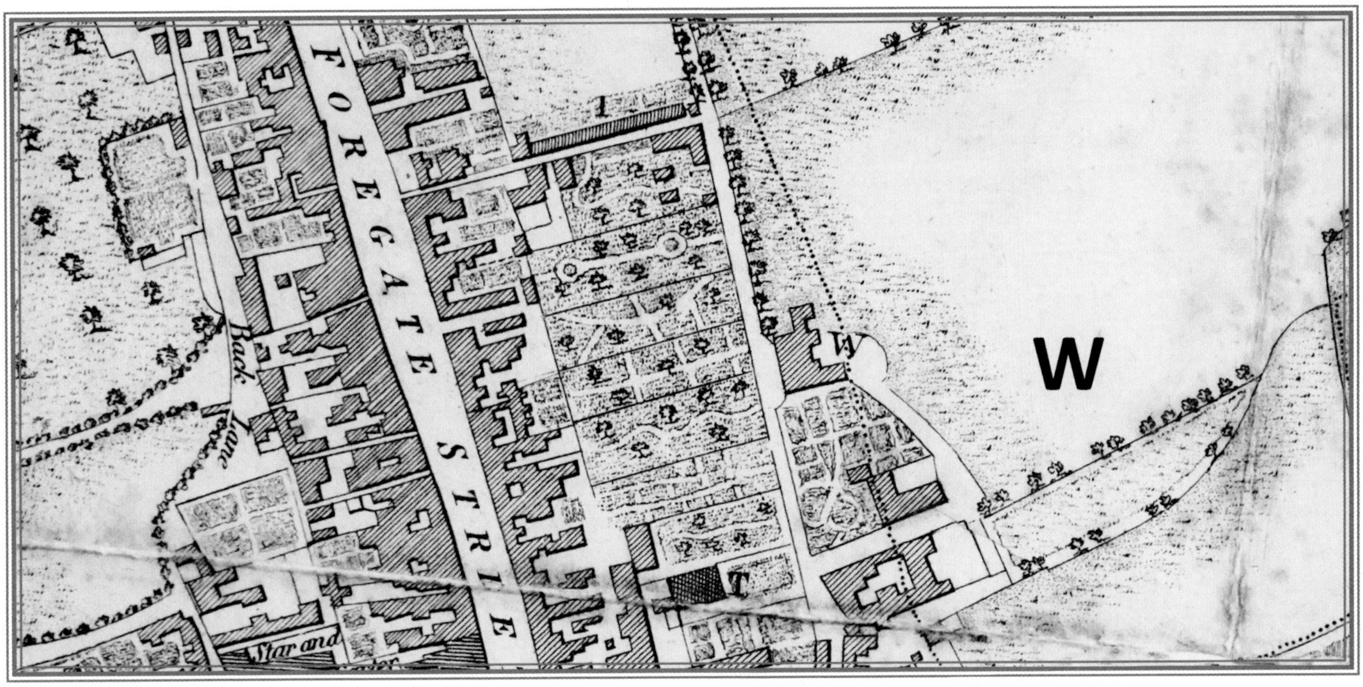

An engraving of Sansome House in Nash's 2nd volume published in 1782 shows a circular lawn and driveway flanked by walls opening directly onto the street. There was a small formal garden on the south side in front of the stables and some ruins (garden feature). This is confirmed in a plan by George Young of 1779 (Hughes & Leech, p. 226) and another surveyed in 1790 published by Valentine Green in 1796 (op. cit.). The amenity of Sansome House as a major residence must have been shattered by the coming of the Railway (1859) and the embankment which buried the garden on the south side. The modern view up Pierpoint Street gives little idea of the status of the house or the importance of this part of the city to the citizens.

Sansome Fields, belonging to Sansome House, on the eastern edge of the City, were used as a public space throughout the 18th century. *Beauties* in 1814: "the principal public walk, or mall, is in Sansom Fields ... Sir C. T. Withers Knt ... who has laid open to the public a very agreeable line of footway ... the walks themselves consist of a gravelly way, shaded on each side by high embowering elms, with foot paths leading to pleasant rambles in the surrounding fields ... as early as 1757 these walks were in vogue."

This long-standing city amenity was threatened by the death of Sir Trubshaw Withers in 1804 and the auctioning of his estate in 1811. The area was still undeveloped circa 1839 (Plan of the Sansome Fields Estate by James Webb, WAAS 5403/20) by which time the house and site had been divided into two. A late-18th century obelisk in the grounds of St. Oswald's Hospital, marks the north end of the Sansome Walk promenade (BoE, p. 756), the avenue footpath which was a continuation of the street.

Set within the area occupied by Sansome Fields were the Worcester Pleasure Grounds or Arboretum (1857) and the 1972 Municipal Baths preceded by an open-air bath of 1854. Most of Sansome Fields, bordered to the east by the Canal, were developed in the 19th and 20th century for housing apart from open space left for school playing fields.

T. R. Nash, *Collections for the History of Worcestershire,* Vol II, 1782.
P. Hughes & A. Leech, *The Story of Worcester,* 2011.
A. Brooks & N. Pevsner, *Worcestershire,* 2007 (BoE).
Beauties of England and Wales, Vol XV, 1814.
V. Green, *History and Antiquities of Worcester,* 1796.

Sansome Fields from T. R. Nash, *Collections for the History of Worcestershire,* Vol II, 1782.

(X) Worcester, South Bank

HER Ref: WCM98479 Postcode:WR5 3YB O.S. 25" Map No. 33.8, 33.12 Date of Maps: both 1904

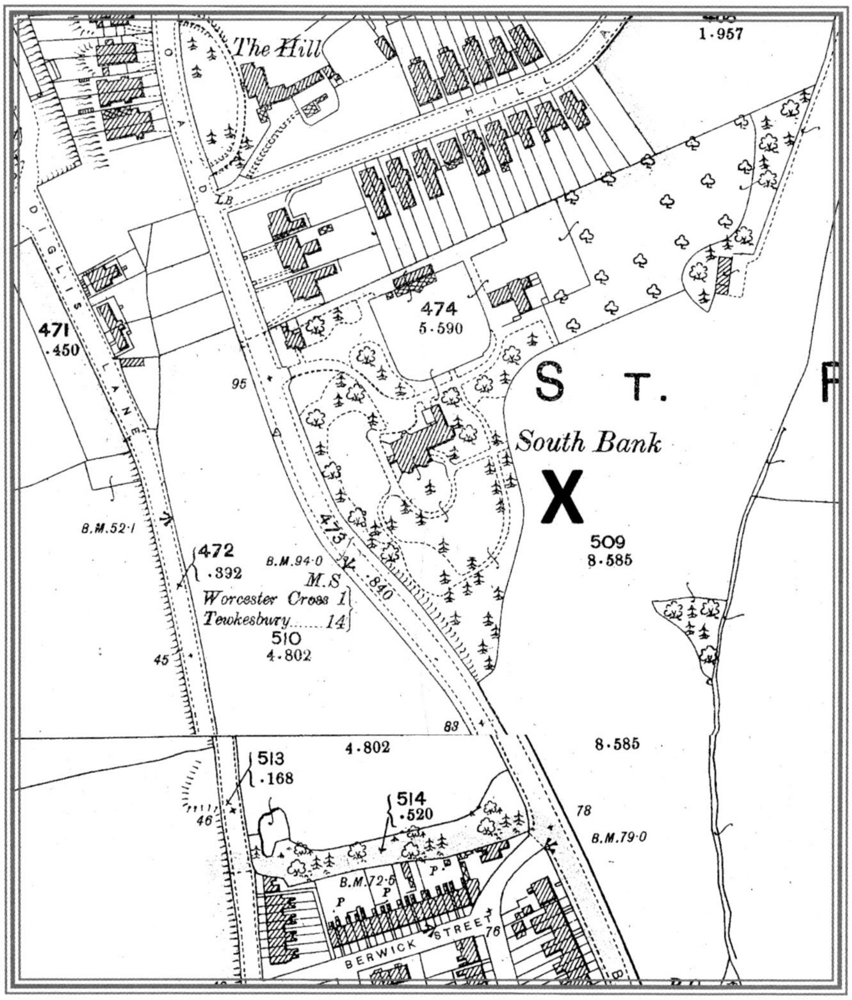

The house of 1866 by Sir George Gilbert Scott was demolished circa 1983 (BoE, p. 773). H. W. Gwilliam says that South Bank was "one of the most expensive houses built in the City at that time." This is included in this *Survey* as a representative of a large Victorian garden set in a city suburb. It was sold circa 1900 with 24 acres of which, house, gardens, pleasure grounds and orchard amounted to 5 acres. "The pleasure grounds are fully matured and luxuriantly timbered with forest and evergreen trees and shrubs of the choicest kinds, and include tennis, croquet and other lawns, summer house, shaded walks, and flower gardens, and there are some exceptionally fine yew and holly hedges. The capital kitchen garden, walled on three sides with range of glass houses, including two vineries, greenhouse, peach house, forcing and potting houses, fruit room etc." (WAAS 4192/1) The kitchen garden is now a car park for hospital use but the garden wall, executed with elaborate brickwork, survives with one gabled, gothic doorway.

A. Brooks & N. Pevsner, *Worcestershire,* 2007 (BoE).

H. W. Gwilliam, *Old Worcester: People and Places,* Vols. 1 & 2, 1977.

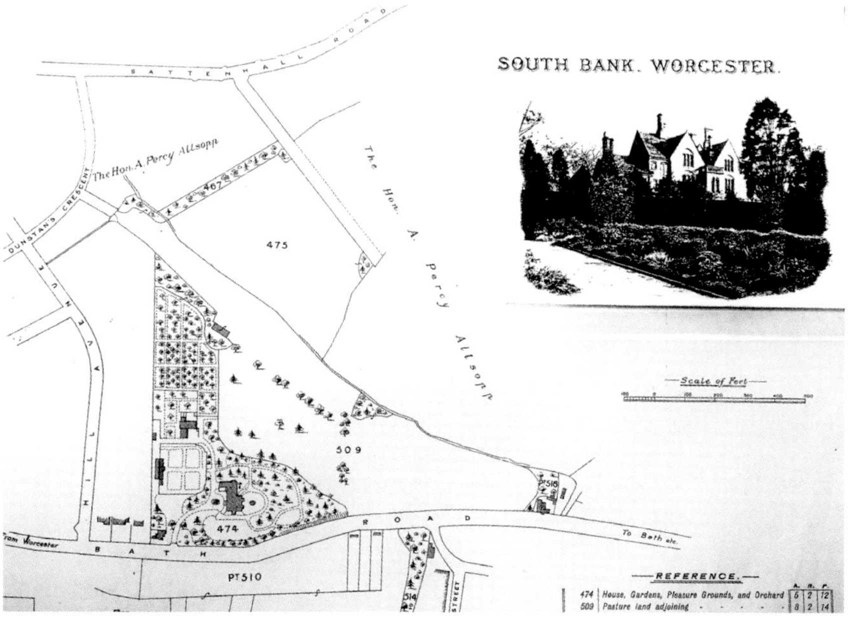

Sale particulars, circa 1900. © WAAS 4192/1.

(Y) Worcester, St. Catherine's Hill

HER Ref: WCM99098 Postcode: WR5 2EA O.S. 25" Map No. 33.8 Date of Map: 1904

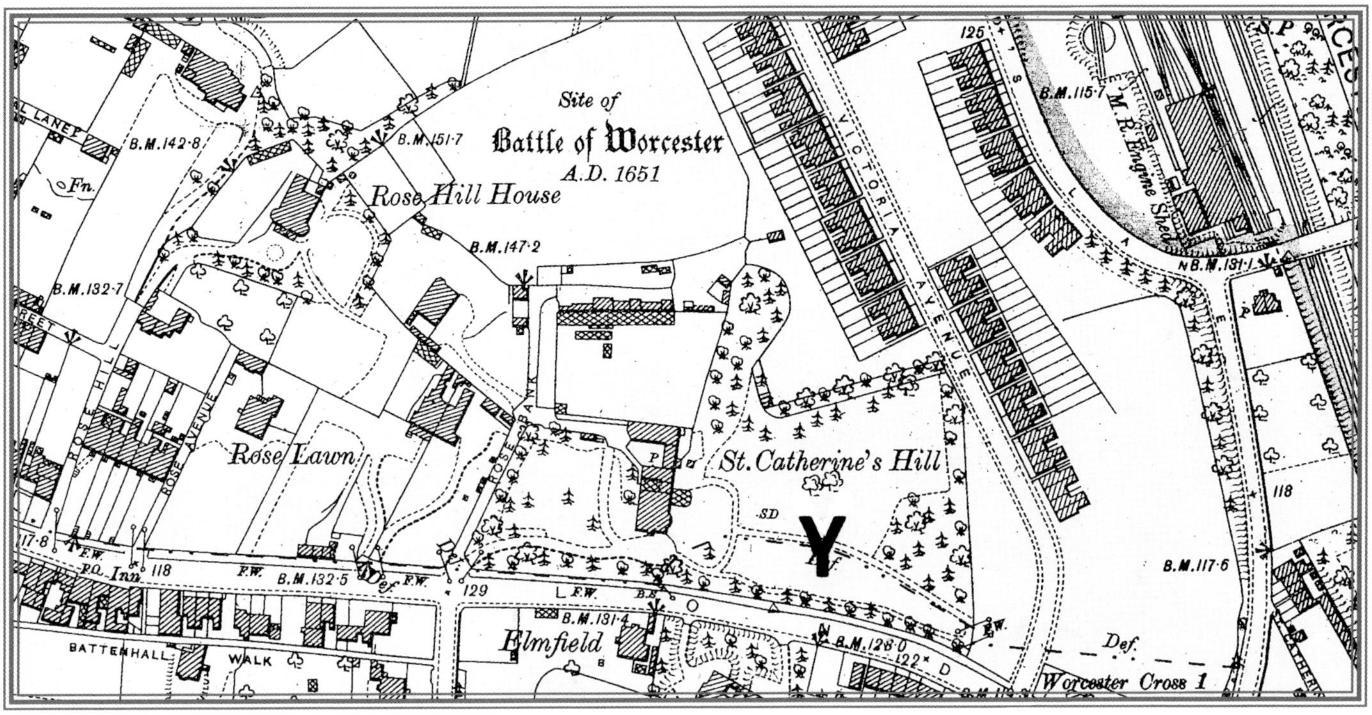

St. Catherine's Hill house occupied a substantial plot off the London Road in Crisp's 1832 map, clearly separated from its neighbour, Rose Hill House. An early-19th century view of the house in the middle distance in the occupation of Mr. Burlingham in 1806, (WAAS 385/1) is illustrated by Hughes & Leech (p. 156). Most of the grounds, if not the park, were still intact in 1905 according to the OS 6 inch map but by then were cut off from Perry Wood by the railway. By 1897, Catherine Vale House, Catherine Villas, Rosedale and Elderslie had been developed within the grounds (WAAS 5240/6). The main house has been demolished but part of its large walled garden survives.

The garden lay-out that went with the Regency house belonging to Thomas Newman (WAAS 385/1) was not much elaborated over the century. There was then already a lawn to the west of the house and a large, walled kitchen garden to the north (1 acre), and planting with walks going east along the London road and away from the house to the north-east, all this on a small scale. There were about 7 acres of meadow to the north and east. There was an orangery in the kitchen garden.

St. Catherine's Hill house is an example of how pleasure grounds for urban villas could be made up: 2.3 acres were freehold (House, Lawn and part of the Plantations) to which a narrow strip of land along the Worcester/Oxford Road "land inclosed from the waste adjoining the Turnpike Road" was leased from Sir John Sebright; 6.3 acres made up of 1.1 acres of Garden and 5.2 acres of Meadow (on part of which the walled garden was set) which was held on a 99 year lease from Christ Church College, Oxford.

The 1897 Sale particulars (WAAS 5240/6) show that later development was minor, principally the addition of glasshouses within the Kitchen Garden and a conservatory attached to the main house, prominent in photographs.

P. Hughes & A. Leech, *The Story of Worcester,* 2011.

Photo from sale particulars, 1897. WAAS 5240/6.

Yewtree House

Parish: Belbroughton

HER Ref: WSM28895.

Grid Ref: SO 922 775. Postcode: DY9 9SN.

O.S. 6" Map No. 9SE.

Date of Map: 1884, with extent of park & gardens shaded as 1905 OS.

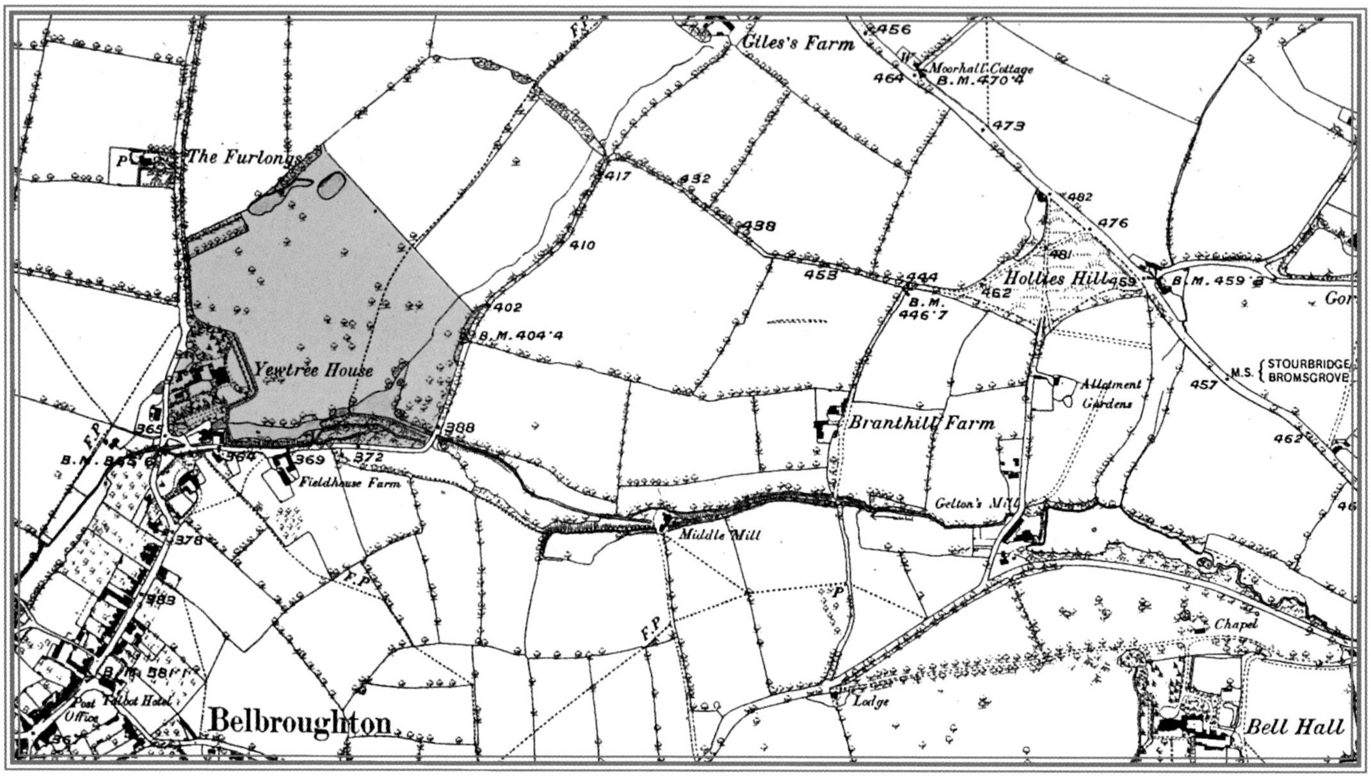

No park is shown with sale particulars in 1824 when the Homestead, Buildings, Yard, Garden etc. amounted to two acres. The Regency house had an early-19th century attached conservatory.

The house is first shown with a park on the 1882 OS 6 inch and again on the 1906 Bartholomew's .

The park landscape is still intact with many veteran trees, watercourse and ponds.

Index of Walled Gardens

During the research for this Survey we made a note of any walled gardens that were still in existence. There are 92 in the list below. Not all have an entry in the Survey. Many are intact and in good order, some are derelict and some barely discernible. However, as long as some of the walls survive, we have included them. There will inevitably be some omissions for which we apologise. If anyone is aware of a walled garden in Worcestershire not on the list, perhaps they might be kind enough to inform the Hereford and Worcester Gardens Trust at www.hwgt.org.uk

Abberley Hall
Areley House/Castle
Astley Hall
Astley Rectory
Barber's Farm
Beaucastle
Bell Hall
Bentley House
Beoley Hall
Birtsmorton Court
Blackmore Park
Blakeshall Hall
Bockleton Court
Bordesley Hall
Bradford House
Bredons Norton Manor House
Bricklehampton Hall
Brockencote Hall
Brookfield Hall
Cattespool
Chamber's Court
Clent Grove
Clent House
Cookhill Priory
Cotheridge Court
Craycombe House
Croome Court
Crown East
Dripshill
Eardiston
Elmley Castle Park
Froxmere Court
Grafton Manor
Great Blakes, Shelsley Beauchamp
Hagley Hall
Ham Court
Hanbury Hall
Hanley Court
Hewell Grange
Hobden Hall
Holt Castle
Hopton Court
Ismere House
Kemerton Court
Kemerton Upper Court
Kent's Green Court
Kyre Park
Kyrewood House
Laughern Hill
Leigh Court
Little Malvern Court
Madresfield Court
Malt House, Wyre Piddle
Nash (The)
Newnham Court
Noak (The)
Norton Park
Ombersley Court
Overbury Court
Parkfield
Pensax Court
Pull Court
Ravenshill Farm
Rhydd (The)
Ribbesford House
Rochford House
Rose Hill, Worcester
Rous Lench Court
Severn Bank
Severn End
Shakenhurst
Shrawley Wood House
Sion Hill House
Sion House
Sodington Hall
South Bank, Worcester
Spetchley Park
Springfield
St. Catherine's Hill, Worcester
Stanford Court
Stone House Cottage
Strensham Court
Syntley Farm
Thorngrove
Wassell Grove
Westwood Park
Wick Episcopi
Winterdyne
Winterfold House
Witley Court
Wolverton Hall
Wood Hall

Index of Parishes